Beginning Visual C#

Karli Watson
Christian Nagel
Jacob Hammer Pedersen
Jon D. Reid
Morgan Skinner
Eric White

WILEY

Wiley Publishing, Inc.

Beginning Visual C#® 2005

Published by
Wiley Publishing, Inc.
10475 Crosspoint Boulevard
Indianapolis, IN 46256
www.wiley.com

Copyright © 2006 by Wiley Publishing, Inc., Indianapolis, Indiana

Published simultaneously in Canada

ISBN-13: 978-0-7645-7847-2
ISBN-10: 0-7645-7847-2

Manufactured in the United States of America

10 9 8 7 6 5 4 3 2 1

1O/RR/RQ/QV/IN

Library of Congress Cataloging-in-Publication Data:

Beginning Visual C# 2005 / Karli Watson ... [et al.].
    p. cm.
  Updated ed. of: Beginning Visual C#. 2003.
  Includes index.
  ISBN-13: 978-0-7645-7847-2 (paper/website)
  ISBN-10: 0-7645-7847-2 (paper/website)
 1. C# (Computer program language) 2. Microsoft .NET Framework. I. Watson, Karli. II. Beginning Visual C#.
 QA76.73.C154B483 2005
 005.13'3--dc22

                            2005010692

Credits

Acquisitions Editor
Katie Mohr

Development Editor
Tom Dinse

Technical Editor
Todd Meister

Production Editor
Angela Smith

Copy Editor
Foxxe Editorial Services

Editorial Manager
Mary Beth Wakefield

Vice President & Executive Group Publisher
Richard Swadley

Vice President and Publisher
Joseph B. Wikert

Project Coordinators
Ryan Steffen
Erin Smith

Graphics and Production Specialists
Andrea Dahl
Denny Hager
Jennifer Heleine
Stephanie Jumper
Barbara Moore
Shelley Norris
Lynsey Osborn
Heather Ryan
Alicia South
Ron Terry
Julie Trippetti

Quality Control Technicians
Laura Albert
Leeann Harney
Carl William Pierce

Proofreading and Indexing
TECHBOOKS Production Services

for donna

—Karli Watson

I'd like to dedicate my portion of this book to my wife, Beth, and our children Nathaniel, Timothy, and Walter. Thanks for your support and encouragement. Also a big thank you to my co-authors and the team at Wrox/Wiley.

—Jon Reid

About the Authors

Karli Watson is the technical director of 3form (www.3form.net), as well as a freelance IT specialist, author, developer, and consultant. For the most part, he immerses himself in .NET (in particular C#) and has written numerous books in the field for several publishers. He specializes in communicating complex ideas in a way that is accessible to anyone with a passion to learn, and spends much of his time playing with new technology to find new things to teach people about.

During those (seemingly few) times where he isn't doing the above, Karli will probably be wishing he was hurtling down a mountain on a snowboard. Or possibly trying to get his novel published. Either way, you'll know him by his brightly colored clothes.

Christian Nagel is a software architect, trainer, and consultant, and an associate of Thinktecture, offering training and coaching based on Microsoft .NET technologies. His achievements in the developer community have earned him a position as Microsoft Regional Director and MVP for Visual C#. He enjoys an excellent reputation as an author of several .NET books, such as *Professional C#, Pro .NET Network Programming* and *C# Web Services*, and he speaks regularly at international industry conferences.

Christian looks back on more than 15 years of experience as a developer and software architect. He started his computing career on PDP 11 and VAX/VMS, covering a variety of languages and platforms. Since 2000 he has been working with .NET and C#, developing and architecting distributed solutions.

http://www.christiannagel.com
http://www.thinktecture.com

Jacob Hammer Pedersen is a systems developer at Fujitsu Service, Denmark. He's been programming the PC since the early 90s using languages such as Pascal, Visual Basic, C/C++, and in later years C#. Jacob is an MCSD who works almost exclusively on the Microsoft platform where his expertise includes .NET, COM, COM+/Enterprise Services, SQL Server, and MS Office development. A Danish citizen, he works and lives in Aarhus, Denmark.

Jon D. Reid is the President and Chief Technology Officer for Savitar Corporation, an independent software vendor and consulting company that develops database tools for the Microsoft.NET environment. He has co-authored many .NET books, including *Pro Visual Studio .NET, Fast Track to C# Programming, ADO.NET Programmer's Reference,* and *Professional SQL Server 2000 XML.* Jon would like to thank his family, co-authors, and the team at Wrox for their support and encouragement.

Morgan Skinner began his computing career at a tender age on a Sinclair ZX80 at school, where he was underwhelmed by some code a teacher had written and so began programming in assembly language. After getting hooked on Z80 (which he believes is far better than those paltry 3 registers on the 6502), he graduated through the school's ZX81s to his own ZX Spectrum.

Since then he's used all sorts of languages and platforms, including VAX Macro Assembler, Pascal, Modula2, Smalltalk, X86 assembly language, PowerBuilder, C/C++, VB, and currently C#. He's been programming in .NET since the PDC release in 2000, and liked it so much, he joined Microsoft in 2001. He now works in Premier Support for Developers and spends most of his time assisting customers with C#.

You can reach Morgan at http://www.morganskinner.com.

About the Authors

Eric White is an independent software consultant with over 20 years experience in building management information systems and accounting systems. When he isn't hunched over a screen programming in C#, he will most likely be found with an ice axe in hand, climbing some mountain.

Contents

Contents

Contents

Contents

Contents

Contents

Contents

Contents

Contents

Contents

Contents

Contents

Contents

Contents

Contents

Contents

Contents

Introduction

C# is a relatively new language that was unveiled to the world when Microsoft released the first version of its .NET Framework. Since then its popularity has rocketed, and it has arguably become the language of choice for both Windows and Web developers who use .NET. Part of the appeal of C# comes from its clear syntax, which derives from C/C++, but simplifies some things that have previously discouraged some programmers. Despite this simplification, C# has retained the power of C++, and there is now no reason not to move into C#. The language is not difficult, and is an excellent one to learn elementary programming techniques with. This ease of learning, combined with the capabilities of the .NET Framework, make C# an excellent way to start your programming career.

The latest release of C#, part of .NET 2.0, builds on the existing successes and adds even more attractive features. Some of these, again, have their roots in C++—at least superficially—but some are entirely new. The latest release of Visual Studio also brings many tweaks and improvements to make your life easier and dramatically increase your productivity.

This book is intended to teach you about all aspects of C# programming, from the language itself, through Windows and Web programming, to making use of data sources, and finally to some advanced techniques such as graphics programming. You'll also learn about the capabilities of Visual Studio 2005 and all the ways that it can aid your application development. The book is written in a friendly, mentor-style fashion, where each chapter builds on previous ones and every effort is made to ease you into advanced techniques painlessly. At no point will technical terms appear from nowhere to discourage you from continuing; every concept is introduced and discussed as required. Technical jargon is kept to a minimum, but where it is necessary, it too will be properly defined and laid out in context.

The authors of this book are all experts in their field, and are all enthusiastic in their passion for both the C# language and the .NET Framework. Nowhere will you find a group of people better qualified to take you under their collective wing and nurture your understanding of C# from first principles to advanced techniques. Along with the fundamental knowledge it provides, this book is packed full of helpful hints, tips, exercises, and fully-fledged example code (available for download at p2p.wrox.com) that you will find yourself using time and again as your career progresses.

We pass this knowledge on without begrudging it, and hope that you will be able to use it to become the best programmer you can be. Good luck, and all the best!

Who This Book Is For

This book is for everyone who wants to learn how to program in C# using the .NET Framework. The early chapters cover the language itself, assuming no prior programming experience. If you have programmed in other languages before, then much of the material in these chapters will be familiar. Many aspects of C# syntax are shared with other languages, and many structures are common to practically all programming languages (such as looping and branching structures). However, even if you are an experienced programmer you will benefit from looking through these chapters to learn the specifics of how these techniques apply to C#.

If you are new to programming, you should start from the beginning. If you are new to .NET but know how to program, you should read Chapter 1 and then skim through the next few chapters before getting on to the application of the C# language. If you know how to program but haven't encountered an object oriented programming language before, you should read the chapters from Chapter 8 onward.

Alternatively, if you already know the C# language you may wish to concentrate on the chapters dealing with .NET 2.0 changes, specifically the chapters on Collections and Generics (Chapters 11 and 12), or skip the first section of the book completely and start with Chapter 14.

The chapters in this book are written with a dual purpose in mind: They can be read sequentially to provide a complete tutorial in the C# language, and they can be dipped into as required as a reference material.

In addition to the core material, each chapter also includes a selection of exercises that you can work through to ensure that you have understood the material taught. The exercises range from simple multiple choice or true/false questions to more involved questions that require you to modify or build applications. The answers to all the exercises are provided online at p2p.wrox.com.

How This Book Is Structured

This book is divided into six sections, as follows:

❑ **Introduction:** which you're reading at the moment.

❑ **The C# Language:** which covers all aspects of the C# language, from the fundamentals to object-oriented techniques.

❑ **Windows Programming:** this section looks at how to write Windows applications in C#, and how to deploy them.

❑ **Web Programming:** this section describes Web application development, Web services, and Web application deployment.

❑ **Data Access:** which looks at using data in your applications, including data stored in files on your hard disk, data stored in XML format, and data in databases.

❑ **Additional Techniques:** this section examines some extra ways of using C# and the .NET Framework, including assemblies, attributes, XML documentation, networking, and graphics programming with GDI+.

The following sections describe the chapters in the five major sections of this book.

The C# Language (Chapters 1–13)

Chapter 1 introduces you to C# and how it fits into the .NET landscape. You'll learn the fundamentals of programming in this environment, and how VS fits in.

Chapter 2 starts you off with writing C# applications in VS. You'll look at the syntax of C# and put the language to use with sample command line and Windows applications. These examples will show you just how quick and easy it can be to get up and running, and along the way you'll be introduced to the VS development environment and the basic windows and tools that you'll be using throughout the book.

Next you'll learn more about the basics of the C# language. You'll learn what variables are and how to manipulate them in **Chapter 3**. You'll enhance the structure of your applications with flow control (looping and branching) in **Chapter 4,** and see some more advanced variable types such as arrays in **Chapter 5**. In **Chapter 6** you'll start to encapsulate your code in the form of functions, which make it much easier to perform repetitive operations and make your code much more readable.

By the start of **Chapter 7** you'll have a handle on the fundamentals of the C# language, and will focus on debugging your applications. This involves looking at outputting trace information as your applications are executed, and at how VS can be used to trap errors and lead you to solutions for them with its powerful debugging environment.

From **Chapter 8** onward you'll learn about Object-Oriented Programming (OOP), starting with a look at what this term means, and an answer to the eternal question "What is an object?" OOP can seem quite difficult at first. The whole of Chapter 8 is devoted to demystifying it and explaining what makes it so great, and you won't actually be dealing with much C# code until the very end of the chapter.

All this changes in **Chapter 9,** when you put theory into practice and start using OOP in your C# applications. This is where the true power of C# lies. You'll start by looking at how to define classes and interfaces, then move on to class members (including fields, properties, and methods) in **Chapter 10**. At the end of that chapter you'll start to assemble a card game application, which will be developed over several chapters, and will help to illustrate OOP.

Once you've leaned how OOP works in C#, you'll move on in **Chapter 11** to look at common OOP scenarios, including dealing with collections of objects, and comparing and converting objects. **Chapter 12** then moves on to look at a new and very useful feature of C# in .NET 2.0: generics, which allows you to create very flexible classes. Finally **Chapter 13** rounds off the discussion of the C# language and OOP with some additional techniques, and notable events, which become very important in, for example, Windows programming.

Windows Programming (Chapters 14–17)

Chapter 14 starts by introducing you to what is meant by Windows programming, and looks at how this is achieved in VS. Again, you'll start with the basics and build up your knowledge over this chapter and in **Chapter 15,** seeing how you can use the wealth of controls supplied by the .NET Framework in your applications. You'll quickly understand how .NET enables you to build Windows applications in a graphical way, and assemble advanced applications with the minimum of effort and time.

Chapter 16 looks at some commonly used features that can add specialized features with ease, such as file management, printing, and so on. **Chapter 17** then discusses deploying your applications, including making installation programs to enable your users to get up and running with your applications in double-quick time.

Web Programming (Chapters 18–21)

This section is structured in a similar way to the Windows programming section. It starts with **Chapter 18** describing the controls that make up the simplest of Web applications, and how you can fit them together and make them perform tasks using ASP.NET. **Chapter 19** builds on this and introduces more advanced techniques, versatile controls, and state management in the context of the Web, as well as conforming to Web standards.

Chapter 20 is an excursion into the wonderful world of Web services, which are set to revolutionize the way people use the Internet. Web services enable you to expose complex data and functionality to Web and windows applications in a platform-independent way. This chapter discusses how to use and create Web services, and the additional tools that .NET provides, including security.

Finally, **Chapter 21** examines the deployment of Web applications and services, in particular the new features of VS that enable you to publish applications to the Web with the click of a button.

Data Access (Chapters 22–25)

Chapter 22 looks at how your applications can save and retrieve data to disk, both as simple text files and as more complex representations of data. You'll also see how to compress data, how to work with legacy data such as comma separated value (CSV) files, and how to monitor and act on file system changes.

In **Chapter 23** you'll learn about what is fast becoming the de-facto standard for data exchange, namely XML. You'll have touched on XML at several times in preceding chapters, but in this chapter you'll lay out the ground rules and see what all the excitement is about. This will be put into practice straight away in **Chapter 24,** where you'll see how to use ADO.NET to interact with databases. ADO.NET includes techniques to deal with XML, and much more.

Chapter 25 will then show you some excellent ways to make use of ADO.NET in your applications via data binding, which is a great way to simplify database access—especially since it requires little effort on your part to provide a user interface to data.

Additional Techniques (Chapters 26–30)

In the last section of the book you'll look at a wide variety of additional C# and .NET subjects. In **Chapter 26** you'll learn more about .NET assemblies, the basic building blocks of all sorts of .NET applications. In **Chapter 27** you'll look at attributes, a powerful way to both include additional information about types in assemblies, and add functionality that would otherwise be difficult to implement.

Chapter 28 deals with XML documentation and how you can document your applications at the source code level. You'll see how to add this information and how to use and extract it. You'll take this to the point where you'll be able to generate expansive MSDN-style documentation from your code.

Next you'll look at networking in **Chapter 29,** and how your applications can communicate with each other and with other services across various types of networks. Finally, **Chapter 30** comes almost as a bit of light relief from many of the involved techniques you'll have seen earlier in the book by covering the subject of graphics programming with GDI+. You'll learn how to manipulate graphics and style your applications, opening the door to a vast array of C# applications and having a bit of fun along the way.

What You Need to Use This Book

The code and descriptions of C# and the .NET Framework in this book apply to .NET 2.0. You don't need anything other than the Framework to understand this aspect of the book, but many of the examples require Visual Studio 2005 (VS). There is also quite a lot of explanation of the VS development environment which may not apply to other tools, such as Visual C# 2005 Express.

Conventions

To help you get the most from the text and keep track of what's happening, we've used a number of conventions throughout the book.

Try It Out

The *Try It Out* is an exercise you should work through, following the text in the book.

1. They usually consist of a set of steps.
2. Each step has a number.
3. Follow the steps through with your copy of the database.

How It Works

After each *Try It Out*, the code you've typed will be explained in detail.

> **Boxes like this one hold important, not-to-be forgotten information that is directly relevant to the surrounding text.**

Tips, hints, tricks, and asides to the current discussion are offset and placed in italics like this.

As for styles in the text:

- ❑ We *highlight* new terms and important words when we introduce them.
- ❑ We show keyboard strokes like this: Ctrl+A.
- ❑ We show file names, URLs, and code within the text like so: `persistence.properties`.
- ❑ We present code in two different ways:

```
In code examples we highlight new and important code with a gray background.
```

```
The gray highlighting is not used for code that's less important in the present
context, or has been shown before.
```

Source Code

As you work through the examples in this book, you may choose either to type in all the code manually or to use the source code files that accompany the book. All of the source code used in this book is available for download at http://www.wrox.com. Once at the site, simply locate the book's title (either by using the Search box or by using one of the title lists) and click the Download Code link on the book's detail page to obtain all the source code for the book.

*Because many books have similar titles, you may find it easiest to search by ISBN; for this book the
ISBN is 0-7645-7847-2.*

Once you download the code, just decompress it with your favorite compression tool. Alternately,
you can go to the main Wrox code download page at `http://www.wrox.com/dynamic/books/`
`download.aspx` to see the code available for this book and all other Wrox books.

Errata

We make every effort to ensure that there are no errors in the text or in the code. However, no one is
perfect, and mistakes do occur. If you find an error in one of our books, like a spelling mistake or faulty
piece of code, we would be very grateful for your feedback. By sending in errata you may save another
reader hours of frustration and at the same time you will be helping us provide even higher quality
information.

To find the errata page for this book, go to `http://www.wrox.com` and locate the title using the Search box
or one of the title lists. Then, on the book details page, click the Book Errata link. On this page you can view
all errata that has been submitted for this book and posted by Wrox editors. A complete book list including
links to each's book's errata is also available at `www.wrox.com/misc-pages/booklist.shtml`.

If you don't spot "your" error on the Book Errata page, go to `www.wrox.com/contact/techsupport`
`.shtml` and complete the form there to send us the error you have found. We'll check the information
and, if appropriate, post a message to the book's errata page and fix the problem in subsequent editions
of the book.

p2p.wrox.com

For author and peer discussion, join the P2P forums at `p2p.wrox.com`. The forums are a Web-based
system for you to post messages relating to Wrox books and related technologies and interact with other
readers and technology users. The forums offer a subscription feature to e-mail you topics of interest of
your choosing when new posts are made to the forums. Wrox authors, editors, other industry experts,
and your fellow readers are present on these forums.

At `http://p2p.wrox.com` you will find a number of different forums that will help you not only as
you read this book, but also as you develop your own applications. To join the forums, just follow these
steps:

1. Go to `p2p.wrox.com` and click the Register link.

2. Read the terms of use and click Agree.

3. Complete the required information to join as well as any optional information you wish to pro-
    vide and click Submit.

4. You will receive an e-mail with information describing how to verify your account and com-
    plete the joining process.

You can read messages in the forums without joining P2P but in order to post your own messages, you must join.

Once you join, you can post new messages and respond to messages other users post. You can read messages at any time on the Web. If you would like to have new messages from a particular forum e-mailed to you, click the Subscribe to this Forum icon by the forum name in the forum listing.

For more information about how to use the Wrox P2P, be sure to read the P2P FAQs for answers to questions about how the forum software works as well as many common questions specific to P2P and Wrox books. To read the FAQs, click the FAQ link on any P2P page.

Part I
The C# Language

Introducing C#

Welcome to the first chapter of the first section of this book. Over the course of this section, you look at the basic knowledge required to get up and running with C#. In this first chapter, you get an overview of C# and the .NET Framework, and you consider what these technologies are, the motivation for using them, and how they relate to each other.

You start with a general discussion of the .NET Framework. This is still a new technology and contains many concepts that are tricky to come to grips with at first (mainly because the Framework introduces a new way of doing things to application development). This means that the discussion will, by necessity, cover many new concepts in a short space of time. However, a quick look at the basics is essential to understand how to program in C#, so this is a necessary evil. Later in the book you will revisit many of the topics covered here in more detail.

After this general discussion, you move on to a simple description of C# itself, including its origins and similarities to C++. Finally, you look at the primary tool used throughout this book: Visual Studio 2005 (VS).

In this chapter, you learn:

- ❑ What C# and the .NET Framework are
- ❑ How the .NET Framework works and what makes it special
- ❑ What you can do with C#
- ❑ What Visual Studio 2005 is and how it fits in with this book

What Is the .NET Framework?

The .NET Framework is a new and revolutionary platform created by Microsoft for developing applications.

The most interesting thing about this statement is how vague I've been — but there are good reasons for this. For a start, note that I didn't say "developing applications on the Windows operating system." Although the Microsoft release of the .NET Framework runs on the Windows operating system, it is fast becoming possible to find alternative versions that will work on others. One example of this is Mono, an open source version of the .NET Framework (including a C# compiler) that will run on several operating systems, including various flavors of Linux and Mac OS. More such projects are in the pipeline and may be available by the time you read this. In addition, you can use the Microsoft .NET Compact Framework (essentially a subset of the full .NET Framework) on personal digital assistant (PDA) class devices and even some smartphones. One of the key motivational forces behind the .NET Framework is its intended use as a means of integrating disparate operating systems.

In addition, the definition of the .NET Framework given above includes no restriction on the type of applications that are possible. This is because there is no restriction — the .NET Framework allows the creation of Windows applications, Web applications, Web services, and pretty much anything else you can think of.

The .NET Framework has been designed so that it can be used from any language. This includes the subject of this book, C#, as well as C++, Visual Basic, JScript, and even older languages such as COBOL. For this to work, .NET-specific versions of these languages have also appeared, and more are being released all the time. Not only do all of these have access to the .NET Framework, but they can also communicate with each other. It is perfectly possible for C# developers to make use of code written by Visual Basic programmers, and vice versa.

All of this provides a hitherto unthinkable level of versatility and is part of what makes using the .NET Framework such an attractive prospect.

What's in the .NET Framework?

The .NET Framework consists primarily of a gigantic library of code that you use from your client languages (such as C#) using object-oriented programming (OOP) techniques. This library is categorized into different modules — you use portions of it depending on the results you want to achieve. For example, one module contains the building blocks for Windows applications, another for network programming, and another for Web development. Some modules are divided into more specific submodules, such as a module for building Web services within the module for Web development.

The intention here is for different operating systems to support some or all of these modules, depending on their characteristics. A PDA, for example, would include support for all the core .NET functionality, but is unlikely to require some of the more esoteric modules.

Part of the .NET Framework library defines some basic *types*. A type is a representation of data, and specifying some of the most fundamental of these (such as "a 32-bit signed integer") facilitates interoperability between languages using the .NET Framework. This is called the *Common Type System (CTS)*.

As well as supplying this library, the Framework also includes the .NET *Common Language Runtime (CLR)*, which is responsible for maintaining the execution of all applications developed using the .NET library.

How Do I Write Applications Using the .NET Framework?

Writing an application using the .NET Framework means writing code (using any of the languages that support the Framework) using the .NET code library. In this book you use VS for your development—VS is a powerful, integrated development environment that supports C# (as well as managed and unmanaged C++, Visual Basic, and some others). The advantage of this environment is the ease with which .NET features can be integrated into your code. The code that you will create will be entirely C# but will use the .NET Framework throughout, and you make use of the additional tools in VS where necessary.

In order for C# code to execute, it must be converted into a language that the target operating system understands, known as *native* code. This conversion is called *compiling* code, an act that is performed by a *compiler*. Under the .NET Framework, however, this is a two-stage process.

MSIL and JIT

When you compile code that uses the .NET Framework library, you don't immediately create operating system–specific native code. Instead, you compile your code into *Microsoft Intermediate Language (MSIL)* code. This code isn't specific to any operating system and isn't specific to C#. Other .NET languages—for example, Visual Basic .NET—also compile to this language as a first stage. This compilation step is carried out by VS when you use it to develop C# applications.

Obviously, to execute an application more work is necessary. This is the job of a *Just-in-Time (JIT)* compiler, which compiles MSIL into native code that is specific to the OS and machine architecture being targeted. Only at this point can the OS execute the application. The *just-in-time* part of the name here reflects the fact that MSIL code is only compiled as and when it is needed.

In the past, it was often necessary to compile your code into several applications, each of which targeted a specific operating system and CPU architecture. Often, this was a form of optimization (to get code to run faster on an AMD chipset, for example), but at times it was critical (for applications to work in both Win9*x* and WinNT/2000 environments, for example). This is now unnecessary, because JIT compilers (as their name suggests) use MSIL code, which is independent of the machine, operating system, and CPU. Several JIT compilers exist, each targeting a different architecture, and the appropriate one will be used to create the native code required.

The beauty of all this is that it requires a lot less work on your part—in fact, you can just forget about system-dependent details and concentrate on the more interesting functionality of your code.

Assemblies

When you compile an application, the MSIL code created is stored in an *assembly*. Assemblies include both executable application files that you can run directly from Windows without the need for any other programs (these have a `.exe` file extension), and libraries for use by other applications (which have a `.dll` extension).

As well as containing MSIL, assemblies also contain *meta* information (that is, information about the information contained in the assembly, also known as *metadata*) and optional *resources* (additional data used by the MSIL, such as sound files and pictures). The meta information allows assemblies to be fully self-descriptive. You need no other information to use an assembly, meaning that you avoid situations such as failing to add required data to the system registry and so on, which was often a problem when developing with other platforms.

This means that deploying applications is often as simple as copying the files into a directory on a remote computer. Since no additional information is required on the target systems, you can just run an executable file from this directory and (assuming the .NET CLR is installed) away you go.

Of course, you won't necessarily want to include everything required to run an application in one place. You might write some code that performs tasks required by multiple applications. In situations like this, it is often useful to place this reusable code in a place accessible to all applications. In the .NET Framework, this is the *Global Assembly Cache (GAC)*. Placing code in this cache is simple — you just place the assembly containing the code in the directory containing this cache.

Managed Code

The role of the CLR doesn't end once you have compiled your code to MSIL, and a JIT compiler has compiled this to native code. Code written using the .NET Framework is *managed* when it is executed (this stage is usually referred to as being at *runtime*). This means that the CLR looks after your applications by managing memory, handling security, allowing cross-language debugging, and so on. By contrast, applications that do not run under the control of the CLR are said to be *unmanaged* and certain languages such as C++ can be used to write such applications that, for example, access low-level functions of the operating system. However, in C# you can write only code that runs in a managed environment. You will make use of the managed features of the CLR and allow .NET itself to handle any interaction with the operating system.

Garbage Collection

One of the most important features of managed code is the concept of *garbage collection*. This is the .NET method of making sure that the memory used by an application is freed up completely when the application is no longer in use. Prior to .NET this has mostly been the responsibility of programmers, and a few simple errors in code could result in large blocks of memory mysteriously disappearing as a result of being allocated to the wrong place in memory. This usually meant a progressive slowdown of your computer followed by a system crash.

.NET garbage collection works by inspecting the memory of your computer every so often and removing anything from it that is no longer needed. There is no set timeframe for this; it might happen thousands of times a second, once every few seconds, or whenever, but you can rest assured that it will happen.

There are some implications for programmers here. Since this work is done for you at an unpredictable time applications have to be designed with this in mind. Code that requires a lot of memory to run should tidy itself up rather than waiting for garbage collection to happen, but this isn't anything like as tricky as it sounds.

Fitting It Together

Before moving on, I'll summarize the steps required to create a .NET application as discussed previously:

1.   Application code is written using a .NET-compatible language such as C#, as shown in Figure 1-1.

Figure 1-1

2. This code is compiled into MSIL, which is stored in an assembly, as shown in Figure 1-2.

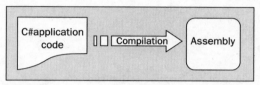

Figure 1-2

3. When this code is executed (either in its own right if it is an executable or when it is used from other code) it must first be compiled into native code using a JIT compiler, as shown in Figure 1-3.

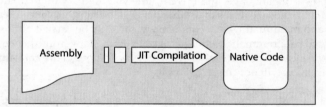

Figure 1-3

4. The native code is executed in the context of the managed CLR, along with any other running applications or processes, as shown in Figure 1-4.

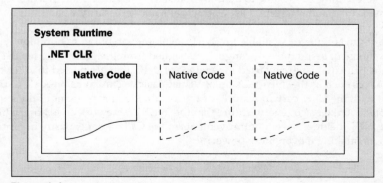

Figure 1-4

Linking

There is one additional point to note concerning the preceding process. The C# code that compiles into MSIL in step 2 needn't be contained in a single file. It is possible to split application code across multiple source code files, which are then compiled together into a single assembly. This process is known as *linking* and is extremely useful. The reason for this is that it is far easier to work with several smaller files than one enormous one. You can separate out logically related code into an individual file, so that it can be worked on independently and then practically forgotten about when completed. This also makes it much easier to locate specific pieces of code when you need them and enables teams of developers to divide up the programming burden into manageable chunks, where individuals can "check out" pieces of code to work on without risking damage to otherwise satisfactory sections or sections that other people are working on.

What Is C#?

C#, as mentioned earlier, is one of the languages that can be used to create applications that will run in the .NET CLR. It is an evolution of the C and C++ languages and has been created by Microsoft specifically to work with the .NET platform. Because it is a recent development, the C# language has been designed with hindsight, taking into account many of the best features from other languages, while clearing up their problems.

Developing applications using C# is simpler than using C++, because the language syntax is simpler. However, C# is a powerful language, and there is little you might want to do in C++ that you can't do in C#. Having said that, those features of C# that parallel the more advanced features of C++, such as directly accessing and manipulating system memory, can only be carried out using code marked as *unsafe*. This advanced programmatic technique is potentially dangerous (hence its name), because it is possible to overwrite system-critical blocks of memory with potentially catastrophic results. For this reason, and others, this book will not cover this topic.

At times, C# code is slightly more verbose than C++. This is a consequence of C# being a *type-safe* language (unlike C++). In layperson's terms, this means that once some data has been assigned to a type, it cannot subsequently transform itself into another unrelated type. Consequently, there are strict rules that must be adhered to when converting between types, which means that you will often need to write more code to carry out the same task in C# than you might write in C++, but you get the benefits that code is more robust and debugging is simpler — .NET can always track what type a piece of data is at any time. In C#, you therefore may not be able to do things such as "take the region of memory 4 bytes into this data and 10 bytes long and interpret it as X," but that's not necessarily a bad thing.

C# is just one of the languages available for .NET development, but in my opinion it is certainly the best. It has the advantage of being the only language designed from the ground up for the .NET Framework and may be the principal language used in versions of .NET that are ported to other operating systems. To keep languages such as the .NET version of Visual Basic as similar as possible to their predecessors yet compliant with the CLR, certain features of the .NET code library are not fully supported. By contrast, C# is able to make use of every feature that the .NET Framework code library has to offer. The latest version of .NET includes several improvements to the C# language, partly in response to requests from developers, making it even more powerful.

What Kind of Applications Can I Write with C#?

The .NET Framework has no restrictions on the types of applications that are possible, as discussed earlier. C# uses the Framework and so also has no restrictions on possible applications. However, here are a few of the more common application types:

❑ **Windows Applications:** These are applications, such as Microsoft Office, which have a familiar Windows look and feel about them. This is made simple by using the Windows Forms module of the .NET Framework, which is a library of *controls* (such as buttons, toolbars, menus, and so on) that you can use to build a Windows user interface (UI).

❑ **Web Applications:** These are Web pages such as might be viewed through any Web browser. The .NET Framework includes a powerful system of generating Web content dynamically, allowing personalization, security, and much more. This system is called ASP.NET (Active Server Pages .NET), and you can use C# to create ASP.NET applications using Web Forms.

❑ **Web Services:** These are a new and exciting way of creating versatile distributed applications. Using Web services you can exchange virtually any data over the Internet, using the same simple syntax regardless of the language used to create a Web service or the system that it resides on.

Any of these types may also require some form of database access, which can be achieved using the ADO.NET (Active Data Objects .NET) section of the .NET Framework. Many other resources can be drawn on, such as tools for creating networking components, outputting graphics, performing complex mathematical tasks, and so on.

C# in This Book

The first section of this book deals with the syntax and usage of the C# language without too much emphasis on the .NET Framework. This is necessary, because you won't be able to use the .NET Framework at all without a firm grounding in C# programming. You start off even simpler, in fact, and leave the more involved topic of object-oriented programming (OOP) until you've covered the basics. These will be taught from first principles, assuming no programming knowledge at all.

Once you have done this, you will be ready to move on to developing the types of application listed in the last section. Section two of this book will look at Windows Forms programming, Section three will look at Web application and Web service programming, Section four will examine data access (for database, file system and XML data), and Section five covers some other .NET topics of interest (such as more about assemblies and graphics programming).

Visual Studio 2005

In this book, you use Visual Studio 2005 (VS) for all of your C# development, from simple command-line applications to the more complex project types considered. VS isn't essential for developing C# applications, but it makes things much easier for you. You can (if you wish to) manipulate C# source code files in a basic text editor, such as the ubiquitous Notepad application, and compile code into assemblies using the command-line compiler that is part of the .NET Framework. However, why do this when you have the full power of VS to help you?

The following is a quick list of some of the features of VS that make it an appealing choice for .NET development:

❑ VS automates the steps required to compile source code but at the same time gives you complete control over any options used should you wish to override them.

❑ The VS text editor is tailored to the languages VS supports (including C#) so that it can intelligently detect errors and suggest code where appropriate as you are typing.

❑ VS includes designers for Windows Forms and Web Forms applications, allowing simple drag-and-drop design of UI elements.

❑ Many of the types of project possible in C# may be created with "boilerplate" code already in place. Instead of starting from scratch, you will often find that various code files are started off for you, reducing the amount of time spent getting started on a project. This is especially true of the new "Starter Kit" project type, which allows you to develop from a fully functional application base. Some starter kits are included with the VS installation, and you can find plenty more online to play with.

❑ VS includes several wizards that automate common tasks, many of which can add appropriate code to existing files without you having to worry about (or even, in some cases, remember) the correct syntax.

❑ VS contains many powerful tools for visualizing and navigating through elements of your projects, whether they are C# source code files or other resources such as bitmap images or sound files.

❑ As well as simply writing applications in VS, it is possible to create deployment projects, making it easy to supply code to clients and for them to install it without much trouble.

❑ VS enables you to use advanced debugging techniques when developing projects, such as the ability to step through code one instruction at a time while keeping an eye on the state of your application.

There is much more than this, but hopefully you have the idea!

Visual Studio 2005 Express Products

In addition to Visual Studio 2005, Microsoft also supplies several simpler development tools known as Visual Studio 2005 Express Products. These are currently (at the time of this writing) in beta versions, but are freely available at http://lab.msdn.microsoft.com/express.

Two of these products, Visual C# 2005 Express and Visual Web Developer 2005 Express, together allow you to create almost any C# application you'd care to mention. They both function as cut-down versions of VS and retain the same look and feel. While they offer many of the same features as VS, there are some notable feature absences, although not so many that they would prevent you from using them to work through this book.

VS Solutions

When you use VS to develop applications, you do so by creating *solutions*. A solution, in VS terms, is more than just an application. Solutions contain *projects*, which might be "Windows Forms projects,"

"Web Form projects," and so on. However, solutions can contain multiple projects, so that you can group together related code in one place, even if it will eventually compile to multiple assemblies in various places on your hard disk.

This is very useful, because it allows you to work on shared code (which might be placed in the GAC) at the same time as applications that use this code. Debugging code is a lot easier when only one development environment is used, because you can step through instructions in multiple code modules.

Summary

In this chapter, you looked at the .NET Framework in general terms and discovered how it makes it easy for you to create powerful and versatile applications. You saw what is necessary to turn code in languages such as C# into working applications and what benefits you gain from using managed code running in the .NET Common Language Runtime.

You also saw what C# actually is and how it relates to the .NET Framework, and you were introduced to the tool that you'll use for C# development — Visual Studio .NET.

In this chapter, you learned:

❑   What the .NET Framework is, why it was created, and what makes it such an attractive environment to program in

❑   What C# is and what makes it an idea tool to program in the .NET Framework

❑   What you need to develop .NET applications effectively, namely a development environment such as Visual Studio 2005

In the next chapter, you get some C# code running using VS, which will give you enough knowledge to sit back and concentrate on the C# language itself, rather than worrying too much about how VS works.

2

Writing a C# Program

Now that you've spent some time learning what C# is and how it fits into the .NET Framework, it's time to get your hands dirty and write some code. You use Visual Studio 2005 (VS) throughout this book, so the first thing to do is to have a look at some of the basics of this development environment. VS is an enormous and complicated product, and can be daunting to first-time users, but using it to create basic applications can be surprisingly simple. As you start to use VS in this chapter, you will see that you don't need to know a huge amount about it in order to start playing with C# code. Later on in the book you will see some of the more complicated operations that VS can perform, but for now a basic working knowledge is all that is required.

Once you've had a look at VS, you put together two simple applications. You don't need to worry too much about the code in these for now, you just prove that things work and run through the application creation procedures that will become second nature before too long.

The first application you create is a simple *console application*. Console applications are those that don't make use of the graphical Windows environment, so you won't have to worry about buttons, menus, interaction with the mouse pointer, and so on. Instead, you will run the application in a command prompt window, and interact with it in a much simpler way.

The second application is a *Windows Forms application*. The look and feel of this will be very familiar to Windows users, and (surprisingly) the application doesn't require much more effort to create. However, the syntax of the code required is more complicated, even though in many cases you don't actually have to worry about details.

You use both types of application over the next two sections of the book, with slightly more emphasis on console applications to start with. The additional flexibility of Windows applications isn't necessary when you are learning the C# language, while the simplicity of console applications allows you to concentrate on learning the syntax and not worry about the look and feel of the application.

In this chapter, you learn:

❑   A basic working knowledge of Visual Studio 2005

❑   How to write a simple console application

❑   How to write a Windows Form application

So, without further ado, it's time to get started!

The Visual Studio .NET Development Environment

When VS is first loaded, it immediately presents you with a host of windows, most of which are empty, along with an array of menu items and toolbar icons. You will be using most of these in the course of this book, and you can rest assured that they will look far more familiar before too long.

If this is the first time you have run VS, you will be presented with a list of preferences intended for users with experience of previous releases of this development environment. The choice you make here affects a number of things, such as the layout of windows, the way that console windows run, and so on. For this reason you should choose Visual C# Developer as shown in Figure 2-1, otherwise you may find that things don't quite work as described in this book. Note that the options available may vary depending on the options you chose when installing VS, but as long as you chose to install C# the highlighted option will be available.

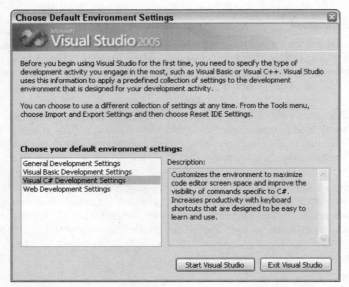

Figure 2-1

If this isn't the first time that you've run VS but you chose a different option the first time, don't panic. In order to reset the settings to Visual C# Developer you simply have to import them. To do this, Click Import and Export Settings... on the Tools menu and select the Reset all settings option as shown in Figure 2-2.

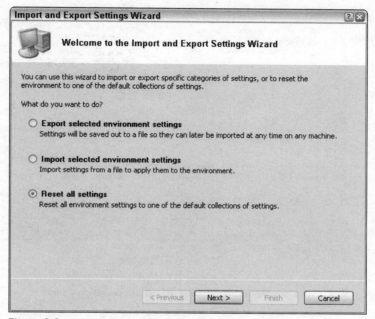

Figure 2-2

Click Next, and choose whether you want to save your existing settings before proceeding. If you have customized things you might want to do this, otherwise select No and click Next again. From the next dialog, select Visual C# Development settings as shown in Figure 2-3. Again, the available options may vary.

Finally, click Finish to apply the settings.

As is evident from the above, the VS environment layout is completely customizable, but again the default is fine for you. With C# developer settings, it is arranged as shown in Figure 2-4.

The main window, which will contain a helpful Start Page by default when VS is started, is the one where all your code will be displayed. This window can contain many documents, each indicated by a tab, so that you can switch between several files with ease by clicking on their filenames. It also has other functions: it can display graphical user interfaces that you are designing for your projects, plain-text files, HTML, and various tools that are built into VS. You will come across all of these in the course of this book.

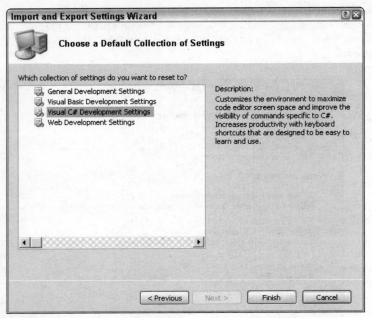

Figure 2-3

Toolbox   Main Window (with Start Page)   Solution Explorer window   Menu and Toolbar

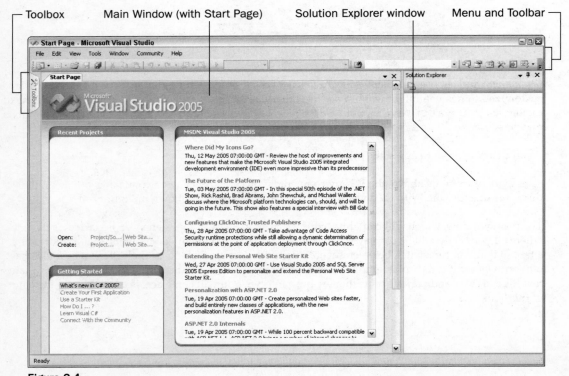

Figure 2-4

Above the main window, you have toolbars and the VS menu. There are several different toolbars that can be placed here, with functionality ranging from saving and loading files to building and running projects to debugging controls. Again, you will be introduced to these as and when you need to use them.

Here are brief descriptions of each of the main features of VS that you will use the most:

❑ The Toolbox toolbar pops up when the mouse moves over it and provides access to, among other things, the user interface building blocks for Windows applications. Another tab, Server Explorer, can also appear here (it is selectable via the View ⇨ Server Explorer menu option) and includes various additional capabilities, such as providing access to data sources, server settings, services, and so on.

❑ The Solution Explorer window displays information about the currently loaded *solution*. A solution is VS terminology for one or more projects along with their configuration. The Solution Explorer window displays various views of the projects in a solution, such as what files they contain and what is contained in those files.

❑ Just below the Solution Explorer window you can display a Properties window, not shown in Figure 2-4. You will see what this looks like shortly, since it only appears when you are working on a project (you can also toggle its display using the View ⇨ Properties Window menu option). This window allows a more detailed view of the contents of a project, allowing you to perform additional configuration of individual elements. For example, you can use this window to change the appearance of a button in a Windows form.

❑ Also not shown in the screenshot is another extremely important window: the Error List window. This window, which you can display using the View ⇨ Error List menu option, displays error, warning, and other information related to projects. This window updates continuously, although some information will appear only when a project is compiled.

This may seem like a lot to take in, but don't worry, it doesn't take long to get used to. You start by building the first of your example projects, which involves many of the VS elements described above.

There are many other windows, both informational and functional, that VS is capable of displaying. Many of these can share screen space with the windows mentioned here, allowing you to switch between them using tabs. You will see many of these windows being used later in the book, and you'll probably discover more yourself when you explore the VS environment in more detail.

Console Applications

You use console applications regularly in this book, particularly to start off with, so the following Try It Out provides a step-by-step guide to the creation of a simple one.

Try It Out	Creating a Simple Console Application

1. Create a new console application project by selecting the File ⇨ New ⇨ Project... menu item, as shown in Figure 2-5.

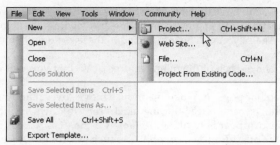

Figure 2-5

2. Select the `Visual C#` node in the `Project Types:` pane of the window that appears, and the `Console Application` project type in the `Templates:` pane. Change the `Location:` text box to `C:\BegVCSharp\Chapter2` (this directory will be created automatically if it doesn't already exist), and leave the default text in the `Name:` text box (`ConsoleApplication1`) and the other settings as they are. This is shown in Figure 2-6.

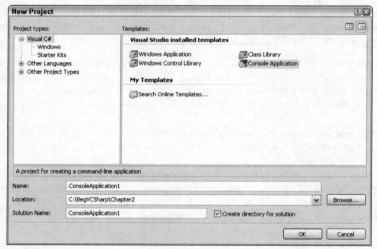

Figure 2-6

3. Click the `OK` button.

4. Once the project is initialized, add the following lines of code to the file displayed in the main window:

```
namespace ConsoleApplication1
{
    class Program
    {
        static void Main(string[] args)
        {
            // Output text to the screen.
            Console.WriteLine("The first app in Beginning C# Programming!");
            Console.ReadKey();
        }
    }
}
```

5.   Select the Debug ⇨ Start menu item. After a few moments you should see the window shown in Figure 2-7.

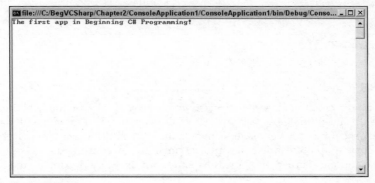

Figure 2-7

6.   Press a key to exit the application (you may need to click on the console window to focus on it first).

Note that the preceding display only appears if the Visual C# Developer settings are applied, as described earlier in this chapter. For example, with Visual Basic Developer settings applied, an empty console window is displayed, and application output appears in a window labeled QuickConsole. In this case, the Console.ReadKey() code also fails, and you will see an error. If you experience this problem, the best solution for working through the examples in this book is to apply the Visual C# Developer settings — that way the results you see will match the results shown here. Should this problem persist then open the Tools ⇨ Options dialog and uncheck the Debugging ⇨ Redirect all output to the Quick Console option as shown in Figure 2-8.

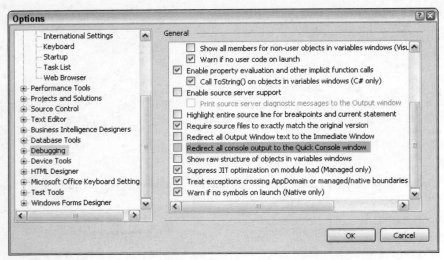

Figure 2-8

How It Works

For now, I won't dissect the code you have used in this project, because the focus here is on how to use VS to get code up and running. As you can see, VS does an awful lot for you and makes the process of compiling and executing code very simple. In fact, there are multiple ways of performing even these simple steps. For example, creating a new project can be achieved using the File@ ⇨ New ⇨ Project... menu item as mentioned earlier, or by pressing Ctrl+Shift+N, or by clicking on the corresponding icon in the toolbar.

Similarly, your code can be compiled and executed in several ways. The process you used above — selecting the Debug ⇨ Start menu item — also has a keyboard shortcut (F5) and a toolbar icon. You can also run code without debugging mode using the Debug ⇨ Start without debugging menu item (also by pressing Ctrl+F5), or compile your project without running it (with debugging on or off) using Build ⇨ Build Solution or F6. Note that executing a project without debugging or building a project can be done using toolbar icons, although these icons don't appear on the toolbar by default. Once you have compiled your code, you can also execute it simply by running the .exe file produced in Windows Explorer, or from the command prompt. To do this, you open a command prompt window, change the directory to C:\BegVCSharp\Chapter2\ConsoleApplication1\bin\Debug\, type **ConsoleApplication1**, and press return.

In future examples, I'll just say "create a new console project" or "execute the code," and you can choose whichever method you wish to perform these steps. Unless otherwise stated, all code should be run with debugging enabled. Also, note that the terms "start," "execute," and "run" are used interchangeably in this book, and that discussions following examples always assume that you have exited the application in the example.

One point to note here is that console applications will terminate as soon as they finish execution, which can mean that you don't get a chance to see the results. To get around this in the preceding example, the code is told to wait for a key press before terminating, using the line:

```
Console.ReadKey();
```

You will see this technique used many times in later examples.

Now that you've created a project, you can take a more detailed look at some of the regions of the development environment.

The Solution Explorer

The first window to look at is the Solution Explorer window in the top right of the screen. This window shares space with another useful window called Class View, which you can display using the View ⇨ Class View menu item. Figure 2-9 shows both of these windows with all nodes expanded (you can toggle between them by clicking on the tabs at the bottom of the window).

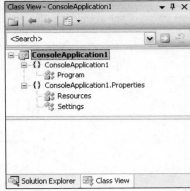

Figure 2-9

This Solution Explorer view shows the files that make up the ConsoleApplication1 project. The file you added code to, Program.cs, is shown along with another code file, AssemblyInfo.cs, and a resource file, Resources.resx.

All C# code files have a .cs file extension.

These other files aren't ones that you have to worry about for the moment. They contain extra information about your project that doesn't concern you yet.

You can use this window to change what code is displayed in the main window by double-clicking on .cs files, right-clicking on them and selecting View Code, or selecting them and clicking on the toolbar button that appears at the top of the window. You can also perform other operations on files here, such as renaming them or deleting them from your project. Other types of files can appear here as well, such as project resources (resources are files used by the project that might not be C# files, such as bitmap images and sound files). Again, you can manipulate them through the same interface.

The References entry contains a list of the .NET libraries you are using in your project. Again, this is something you will look at later; the standard references are fine for you to get started with.

The other view, Class View, presents an alternative view of your project by looking at the structure of the code you have created. You will come back to this later in the book; for now the Solution Explorer display is the display of choice.

As you click on files or other icons in these windows, you may notice that the contents of the Properties window (shown in Figure 2-10) changes.

The Properties Window

This window (which you can display using the View⇨ Properties Window menu option if you haven't already done so) shows additional information about whatever you select in the window above it. For example, the view shown in Figure 2-10 is displayed when the Program.cs file from the project is selected. This window will also display information about other things that might be selected, such as user interface components (as you will see in the "Windows Forms Applications" section of this chapter).

Figure 2-10

Often, changes you make to entries in the Properties window will affect your code directly, adding lines of code or changing what you have in your files. With some projects, you spend as much time manipulating things through this window as making manual code changes.

Next, you will look at the Error List window.

The Error List Window

Currently, the Error List window (View⇨ Error List) isn't showing much of interest at all. This is because there is nothing wrong with the application. However, this is a very useful window indeed. As a test, try removing the semicolon from one of the lines of code you added in the last section. After a moment, you should see a display like the one shown in Figure 2-11.

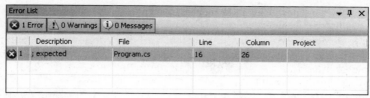

Figure 2-11

Also, the project will no longer compile.

> *In Chapter 3, when you start looking at C# syntax, you will see how semicolons are expected throughout your code — at the end of most lines in fact.*

This window will help you eradicate bugs in your code, because it keeps track of what you have to do in order to compile projects. If you double-click the error shown here, the cursor will jump to the position of the error in your source code (the source file containing the error will be opened if it isn't already open), so you can fix it quickly. You will also see red wavy lines at the positions of errors in the code, so you can quickly scan the source code to see where problems lie.

Note that the error location was specified as a line number. By default, line numbers aren't displayed in the VS text editor, but this is something that is well worth turning on. To do this, you need to tick the relevant check box in the Options dialog, obtained through the Tools ⇨ Options... menu item. The check box is called Line numbers, and is found in the Text Editor ⇨ C# ⇨ General category, as shown in Figure 2-12.

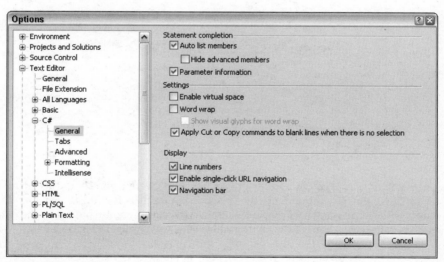

Figure 2-12

There are many useful options that can be found through this dialog, and you will use several of them later in this book.

Windows Forms Applications

It is often easier to demonstrate code by running it as part of a Windows application rather than through a console window or via a command prompt. You can do this using user interface building blocks to piece together a user interface.

For now, the following Try It Out shows you just the basics of doing this, and I'll show you how to get a Windows application up and running, though I won't go into too much detail about what the application is actually doing. Later in the book, you will take a detailed look at Windows applications.

Try It Out   Creating a Simple Windows Application

1. Create a new project of type `Windows Application` in the same location as before (`C:\BegVCSharp\Chapter2`) with the default name `WindowsApplication1`. If the first project is still open, then make sure the `Create new Solution` option is selected in order to start a new solution. These settings are shown in Figure 2-13.

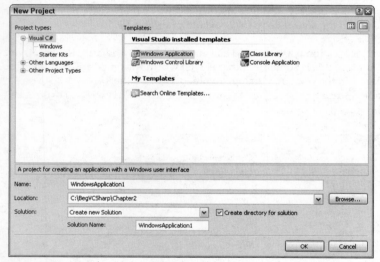

Figure 2-13

2. After you have clicked OK and the project has been created, you should see an empty windows form. Move the mouse pointer to the `Toolbox` bar on the left of the screen, then to the `Button` entry of the `Windows Forms` tab, and double-click the left mouse button on the entry to add a button to the main form of the application (`Form1`), as shown in Figure 2-14.

Figure 2-14

3. Double-click the button that has been added to the form.

4. The C# code in `Form1.cs` should now be displayed. Modify it as follows (only part of the code in the file is shown here for brevity):

```
private void button1_Click(object sender, EventArgs e)
{
    MessageBox.Show("The first Windows app in the book!");
}
```

5. Run the application.

6. Click the button presented to open a message dialog box, as shown in Figure 2-15.

Figure 2-15

7. Exit the application by clicking on the x in the top right, as per standard Windows applications.

How It Works

Again, it is plain that VS has done a lot of work for you and made it simple to create functional Windows applications with little effort. The application you have created behaves just like other windows—you can move it around, resize it, minimize it, and so on. You don't have to write the code to do that—it just works. The same goes for the button you added. Simply by double-clicking it, VS knew that you wanted to write code to execute when a user clicked on the button in the running application. All you had to do was to provide that code, getting full button-clicking functionality for free.

Of course, Windows applications aren't limited to plain forms with buttons. If you have a look at the toolbar where you found the `Button` option, you will see a whole host of user interface building blocks, some of which may be familiar and some not. You will get to use most of these at some point in the book, and you'll find that they are all just as easy to use, saving you a lot of time and effort.

The code for your application, in `Form1.cs`, doesn't look much more complicated than the code in the last section, and the same is true for the code in the other files in the Solution Explorer window. Much of the code generated is hidden from you by default and is concerned with the layout of *controls* on the form, which is why you can view the code in *Design View* in the main window—which is a visual translation of this layout code. A button is an example of a control that you can use, as are the rest of the UI building blocks found in the `Windows Forms` section of the `Toolbox` bar.

You can take a closer look at the button as a control example. Switch back to the Design View of the form using the tab on the main window, and click once on the button to select it. When you do this, the `Properties` window in the bottom right of the screen will show the properties of the button control (controls have properties much like the files you saw in the last example). Ensure the application isn't currently running, then scroll down to the `Text` property, which is currently set to `button1`, and change the value to `Click Me`, as shown in Figure 2-16.

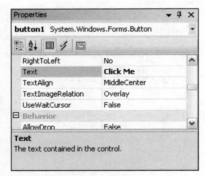

Figure 2-16

The text written on the button in `Form1` should also change to reflect this.

There are many properties for this button, ranging from simple formatting of the color and size to more obscure settings such as data binding settings, which allow you to establish links to databases. As briefly mentioned in the last example, changing properties often results in direct changes to code, and this is no exception. However, if you switch back to the code view of `Form1.cs` you won't see any change in the code.

To see the modified code, you need to look at the hidden file mentioned above. To view this file, you need to click on the Show All Files icon in the Solution Explorer window. This reveals several extra files and folders that you don't need to worry about for now, but more importantly allows you to expand the Form1.cs node, revealing a Form1.Designer.cs node. Double-click on this file to see what's inside.

At a cursory glance, you might not notice anything in this code to reflect the Button property change at all. This is because the sections of C# code that deal with the layout and formatting of controls on a form are hidden from you (after all, you hardly need to look at the code if you have a graphical display of the results).

VS uses a system of *code outlining* to achieve this subterfuge. You can see this in Figure 2-17.

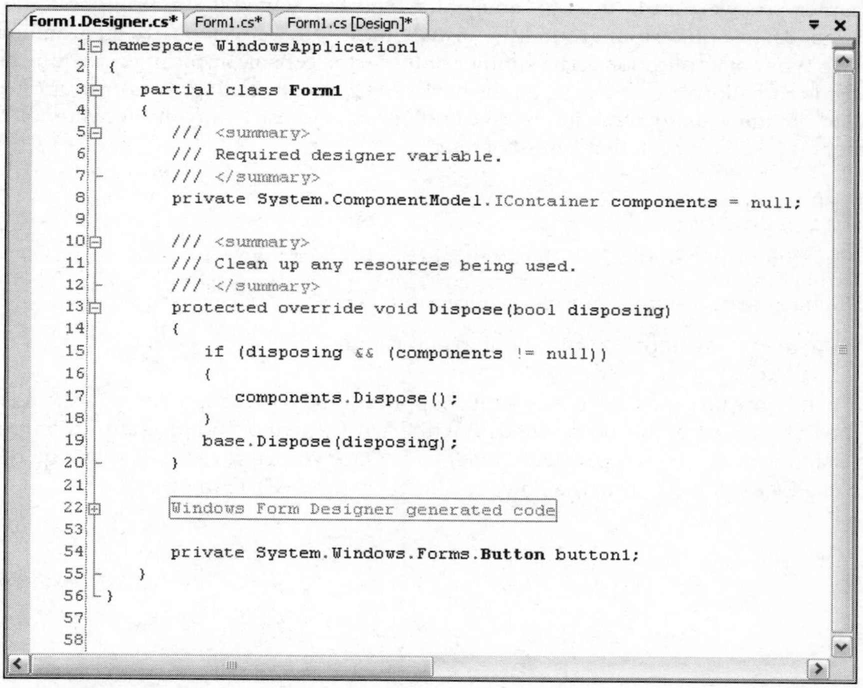

Figure 2-17

Looking down the left-hand side of the code (just next to the line numbers if you've turned them on), you may notice some gray lines and boxes with + and – symbols in them. These boxes are used to expand and contract regions of code. Toward the bottom of the file (line 22 in mine, although this may vary) is a box with a + in it and a box in the main body of the code reading Windows Form Designer generated code. This label basically is saying "here is some code generated by VS that you don't need to know about." You can look at it if you want, however, and see what you have done by changing the button properties. Simply click on the box with the + in it and the code will become visible, and somewhere in there you should see the following line:

```
this.button1.Text = "Click Me";
```

Without worrying too much about the syntax used here, you can see that the text you typed in to the `Properties` window has popped up directly in your code.

This outlining method can be very handy when you are writing code, because you can expand and contract many other regions, not just those that are normally hidden from you. Just as looking at the table of contents of a book can help you by giving you a quick summary of the contents, looking at a series of collapsed regions of code can make it much easier for you to navigate through what can be vast amounts of C# code.

Summary

In this chapter, you were introduced to some of the tools that you will use throughout the rest of this book. You have had a quick tour around the Visual Studio .NET development environment and used it to build two types of applications. The simpler of these, the console application, is quite enough for most of your needs and allows you to focus on the basics of C# programming. Windows applications are more complicated but are visually more impressive and intuitive to use to anyone accustomed to a Windows environment (and let's face it, that's most of us).

In this chapter, you learned:

❑   How the Visual Studio 2005 development environment works

❑   How to create a simple console application

❑   How to get a Windows application up and running

Now that you know how you can create simple applications, you can get down to the real task of learning C#. The next section of this book will deal with basic C# syntax and program structure, before you move on to more advanced object-oriented methods. Once you've covered all that, you can start to look at how to use C# to gain access to the power available in the .NET Framework.

Variables and Expressions

To learn how to use C# effectively, it's important to understand what you're actually doing when you create a computer program. Perhaps the most fundamental description of a computer program is that it is a series of operations that manipulate data. This is true even of the most complicated examples, such as vast, multifeatured Windows applications like the Microsoft Office Suite. Although this is often completely hidden from the users of applications, it is always going on behind the scenes.

To illustrate this further, consider the display unit of your computer. What you see on screen is often so familiar that it is difficult to imagine it as anything other than a "moving picture." In fact, what you see is only a representation of some data, which in its raw form is merely a stream of zeros and ones stashed away somewhere in the memory of your computer. Anything you do on-screen, then, whether it is moving a mouse pointer, clicking on an icon, or typing text into a word processor, will result in the shunting around of data in memory.

Of course, there are less abstract situations that show this just as well. If you use a calculator application, you are supplying data in the form of numbers and performing operations on these numbers in much the same way as you would do with piece of paper and a pencil—although a lot quicker!

If computer programs are fundamentally performing operations on data, then this implies that you need some way of storing that data and some methods of manipulating it. These two functions are provided by *variables* and *expressions*, respectively, and in this chapter you will explore what this means both in general and specific terms.

Before you start with that, though, you should take a look at the basic syntax involved in C# programming, because you need a context within which to learn about and use variables and expressions in the C# language.

In this chapter, you learn about:

- ❑ Basic C# syntax
- ❑ Variables and how to use them
- ❑ Expressions and how to use them

Basic C# Syntax

The look and feel of C# code is similar to that of C++ and Java. At first, this syntax can look quite confusing and is a lot less like written English than some other languages. However, you will find as you immerse yourself in the world of C# programming that the style used is a sensible one, and it is possible to write very readable code without too much trouble.

Unlike the compilers of some other languages, C# compilers take no notice of additional spacing in code, whether made up of spaces, carriage returns, or tab characters (these characters are known collectively as *white space* characters). This means that you have a lot of freedom in the way that you format your code, although conforming to certain rules can help to make things easier to read.

C# code is made up of a series of *statements*, each of which is terminated with a semicolon. Since white space is ignored, you can have multiple statements on one line, but for readability's sake it is usual to add carriage returns after semicolons, so you don't have multiple statements on one line. It is perfectly acceptable (and quite normal), however, to use statements that span several lines of code.

C# is a *block-structured* language, meaning that all statements are part of a *block* of code. These blocks, which are delimited with curly brackets ({ and }), may contain any number of statements, or none at all. Note that the curly bracket characters do not need accompanying semicolons.

So, a simple block of C# code could take the following form:

```
{
    <code line 1, statement 1>;
    <code line 2, statement 2>
       <code line 3, statement 2>;
}
```

Here, the *<code line x, statement y>* sections are not actual pieces of C# code; I've just used this text as a placeholder where C# statements would go. Note that in this case, the second and third lines of code are part of the same statement, because there is no semicolon after the second line.

In this simple section of code, I have also used *indentation* to clarify the C# itself. This isn't some random invention of mine, it is standard practice, and in fact VS will automatically do this for you by default. In general, each block of code has its own level of indentation, meaning how far to the right it is. Blocks of code may be *nested* inside each other (that is, blocks may contain other blocks), in which case nested blocks will be indented further:

```
{
    <code line 1>;
    {
       <code line 2>;
       <code line 3>;
    }
    <code line 4>;
}
```

Also, lines of code that are continuations of previous lines are usually indented further as well, as in the third line of code in the first example above.

If you look in the VS Options dialog, accessible via Tools ⇨ Options, you can find the rules that VS uses for formatting your code. There are a whole lot of these, in subcategories of the Text Editor ⇨ C# ⇨ Formatting node. Most of the settings here reflect parts of C# that I haven't covered yet, but it can be worth returning to these settings later should you wish to tweak the settings to sort your personal style better. In this book, all code snippets are shown as they would be formatted by the default settings for clarity.

Remember, this kind of style is by no means mandatory. If you don't use it, however, you will quickly find that things can get very confusing as you move through this book!

Another thing you will often see in C# code is *comments*. A comment is not strictly speaking C# code at all, but happily cohabits with it. Comments do exactly what it says on the tin: they allow you to add descriptive text to your code — in plain English (or French, German, Outer Mongolian, and so on) — that will be ignored by the compiler. When you start dealing with lengthy sections of code, it can be useful to add reminders about exactly what you are doing, such as "this line of code asks the user for a number" or "this section of code was written by Bob." C# has two ways of doing this. You can either place markers at the beginning and end of a comment, or you can use a marker that means "everything on the rest of this line is a comment." This latter method is an exception to the rule mentioned above about C# compilers ignoring carriage returns, but it is a special case.

To mark out comments using the first method, you use /* characters at the start of the comment and */ characters at the end. These may occur on a single line, or on different lines, in which case all lines in between are part of the comment. The only thing you can't type in the body of a comment is */, because this is interpreted as the end marker. So, the following are OK:

```
/* This is a comment */

/* And so...

            ... is this! */
```

But the following will cause problems:

```
/* Comments often end with "*/" characters */
```

Here, the end of the comment (the characters after "*/") will be interpreted as C# code, and errors will occur.

The other commenting approach involves starting a comment with //. Next, you can write whatever you like — as long as you keep to one line! The following is OK:

```
// This is a different sort of comment.
```

But the following will fail, because the second line will be interpreted as C# code:

```
// So is this,
   but this bit isn't.
```

This sort of commenting is useful to document statements, because both can be placed on a single line:

```
<A statement>;          // Explanation of statement
```

Previously, I said that there were two ways of commenting C# code. However, there is a third type of comment in C# — although strictly speaking this is a development of the `//` syntax. You can use single-line comments that start with three `/` symbols instead of two, like this:

```
/// A special comment
```

Under normal circumstances, they are ignored by the compiler — just like other comments, but you can configure VS to extract the text after these comments and create a specially formatted text file when a project is compiled, which you can then use to create documentation. This is covered in detail in Chapter 28.

A *very* important point to note about C# code is that it is *case-sensitive*. Unlike some other languages, you must enter code using exactly the right case, because simply using an uppercase letter instead of a lower-case one will prevent a project from compiling.

This is difficult to illustrate without learning a bit more about the C# language, but take a look at this line of code, which is used in the first example in Chapter 2:

```
Console.WriteLine("The first app in Beginning C# Programming!");
```

This code is understood by the C# compiler, as the casing of the `Console.WriteLine()` command is correct. However, none of the following lines of code will work:

```
console.WriteLine("The first app in Beginning C# Programming!");
CONSOLE.WRITELINE("The first app in Beginning C# Programming!");
Console.Writeline("The first app in Beginning C# Programming!");
```

Here, the casing used is wrong, so the C# compiler won't know what you are trying to do.

Luckily, as you soon discover, VS is very helpful when it comes to entering code, and most of the time it knows (as much as a program can know) what you are trying to do. As you type, it suggests commands that you might like to use, and it tries as best it can to correct casing problems.

Basic C# Console Application Structure

Let's take a closer look at the console application example from Chapter 2 (`ConsoleApplication1`), and break down the structure a bit. The code was:

```
using System;
using System.Collections.Generic;
using System.Text;

namespace ConsoleApplication1
{
    class Program
    {
        static void Main(string[] args)
        {
```

```
        // Output text to the screen.
        Console.WriteLine("The first app in Beginning C# Programming!");
        Console.ReadKey();
    }
  }
}
```

You can immediately see that all the syntactic elements discussed in the last section are present here. There are semicolons, curly braces, and comments, along with appropriate indentation.

The most important section of code as far as you're concerned at the moment is the following:

```
static void Main(string[] args)
{
    // Output text to the screen.
    Console.WriteLine("The first app in Beginning C# Programming!");
    Console.ReadKey();
}
```

This is the code that is executed when you run your console application, or to be more precise, the code block enclosed in curly braces is what is executed. The comment line doesn't do anything, as mentioned earlier; it's just there for clarity. The other two code lines output some text to the console window and wait for a response, respectively, though the exact mechanisms of this shouldn't concern you for now.

At this point, it's worth noting how to achieve the code outlining functionality that was seen in the last chapter, albeit for a Windows application, since it is such a useful feature. You can do this with the `#region` and `#endregion` keywords, which define the start and end of a region of code that can be expanded and collapsed. For example, you could modify the generated code for `ConsoleApplication1` as follows:

```
#region Using directives
```

```
using System;
using System.Collections.Generic;
using System.Text;
```

```
#endregion
```

This would allow you to collapse these lines of code into a single line, and expand it again later should you want to look at the details. The `using` statements contained here, and the `namespace` statement just underneath, will be explained at the end of this chapter.

> Note that any keyword that starts with a # is actually a preprocessor directive and not, strictly speaking, a C# keyword. Other than the two described here, #region and #endregion, these can be quite complicated, and have quite specialized uses. For that reason this is one subject you might like to investigate yourself once you have worked through this book.

For now, you shouldn't worry about the other code in the example, because the purpose of these first few chapters is to explain basic C# syntax, so the exact method of how the application execution gets to the point where `Console.WriteLine()` is called is of no concern. Later on, the significance of this additional code will be made clear.

Variables

As discussed in the introduction to this chapter, variables are concerned with the storage of data. Essentially, you can think of variables in computer memory as boxes sitting on a shelf. You can put things in boxes and take them out again, or you can just look inside a box to see if anything is there. The same goes for variables; you place data in them and can take it out or look at it, as required.

Although all data in a computer is effectively the same thing (a series of zeros and ones), variables come in different flavors, known as *types*. Again using the box analogy, you can imagine that your boxes come in different shapes and sizes, and some things will only fit in certain boxes. The reasoning behind this type system is that different types of data may require different methods of manipulation, and by restricting variables to individual types you can avoid getting mixed up. It wouldn't, for example, make much sense to treat the series of zeros and ones that make up a digital picture as an audio file.

To use variables, you have to *declare* them. This means that you have to assign them a *name* and a *type*. Once you have declared variables you can use them as storage units for the type of data that you declared them to hold.

The C# syntax for declaring variables simply involves specifying the type and variable name as follows:

```
<type> <name>;
```

If you try to use a variable that hasn't been declared, then your code won't compile, but in this case the compiler will tell you exactly what the problem was, so this isn't really a disastrous error. In addition, trying to use a variable without assigning it a value will also cause an error, but again, the compiler will detect this.

So, what are the types that you can use?

Well, in fact there are an almost infinite number of types that you can use. The reason for this is that you can define your own types to hold whatever convoluted data you like.

Having said this, there are certain types of data that just about everyone will want to use at some point or another, such as a variable that stores a number. Therefore, there are a number of simple, predefined types that you should be aware of.

Simple Types

Simple types are those types such as numbers and Boolean (true or false) values that make up the fundamental building blocks for your applications, and for other, more complex types. Most of the simple types available are numeric, which at first glance seems a bit strange—surely, you only need one type to store a number?

The reason for the plethora of numeric types is down to the mechanics of storing numbers as a series of zeros and ones in the memory of a computer. For integer values, you simply take a number of *bits* (individual digits that can be zero or one) and represent your number in binary format. A variable storing N bits will allow you to represent any number between 0 and $(2^N - 1)$. Any numbers above this value will be too big to fit into this variable.

As an example, let's say you have a variable that can store 2 bits. The mapping between integers and the bits representing those integers is, therefore, as follows:

```
0 = 00
1 = 01
2 = 10
3 = 11
```

If you want to be able to store more numbers, you need more bits (3 bits will let you store the numbers from 0 to 7, for example).

The inevitable conclusion of this argument is that you would need an infinite number of bits to be able to store every imaginable number, which isn't going to fit in your trusty PC. Even if there were a quantity of bits you could use for every number, it surely wouldn't be efficient to use all these bits for a variable that, for example, was only required to store the numbers between 0 and 10 (because storage would be wasted). Four bits would do the job fine here, allowing you to store many more values in this range in the same space of memory.

Instead, you have a number of different integer types that can be used to store various ranges of numbers, and take up differing amounts of memory (up to 64 bits). The list of these is shown in the following table.

> Note that each of these types makes use of one of the standard types defined in the .NET Framework. As discussed in Chapter 1, this use of standard types is what allows interoperability between languages. The names you use for these types in C# are aliases for the types defined in the Framework. The table lists the names of these types as they are referred to in the .NET Framework library.

Type	Alias For	Allowed Values
sbyte	System.SByte	Integer between –128 and 127.
byte	System.Byte	Integer between 0 and 255.
short	System.Int16	Integer between –32768 and 32767.
ushort	System.UInt16	Integer between 0 and 65535.
int	System.Int32	Integer between –2147483648 and 2147483647.
uint	System.UInt32	Integer between 0 and 4294967295.
long	System.Int64	Integer between –9223372036854775808 and 9223372036854775807.
ulong	System.UInt64	Integer between 0 and 18446744073709551615.

The us before some variable names are shorthand for *unsigned*, meaning that you can't store negative numbers in variables of those types, as can be seen in the Allowed Values column of the table.

Of course, as well as integers you also need to store *floating-point* values, which are those that aren't whole numbers. There are three floating-point variable types that you can use: float, double, and decimal. The first two of these store floating points in the form $+/- m \times 2e$, where the allowed values for m and e differ for each type. decimal uses the alternative form +/− m×10e. These three types are shown in the following table, along with their allowed values of m and e, and these limits in real numeric terms:

Type	Alias For	Minm	Maxm	Mine	Maxe	Approx. Min Value	Approx. Max Value
float	System.Single	0	224	-149	104	1.5×10^{-45}	3.4×10^{38}
double	System.Double	0	253	-1075	970	5.0×10^{-324}	1.7×10^{308}
decimal	System.Decimal	0	296	-26	0	1.0×10^{-28}	7.9×10^{28}

In addition to numeric types, there are three other simple types available, shown in the next table.

Type	Alias For	Allowed Values
char	System.Char	Single Unicode character, stored as an integer between 0 and 65535
bool	System.Boolean	Boolean value, true or false
string	System.String	A sequence of characters

Note that there is no upper limit on the amount of characters making up a string, because it can use varying amounts of memory.

The Boolean type bool is one of the most commonly used variable types in C#, and indeed similar types are equally prolific in code in other languages. Having a variable that can be either true or false has important ramifications when it comes to the flow of logic in an application. As a simple example, consider how many questions there are that can be answered with true or false (or yes and no). Performing comparisons between variable values or validating input are just two of the programmatic uses of Boolean variables that you will examine very soon.

Now that you've seen these types, let's have a quick example of declaring and using them. In the following Try It Out you use some simple code that declares two variables, assigns them values, and then outputs these values.

Try It Out   Using Simple Type Variables

1. Create a new console application called Ch03Ex01 in the directory C:\BegVCSharp\Chapter3.

2. Add the following code to Program.cs:

```
static void Main(string[] args)
{
    int myInteger;
    string myString;
    myInteger = 17;
    myString = "\"myInteger\" is";
    Console.WriteLine("{0} {1}.", myString, myInteger);
    Console.ReadKey();
}
```

3. Execute the code. The result is shown in Figure 3-1.

Figure 3-1

How It Works

The code you have added does three things:

❑   It declares two variables.

❑   It assigns values to those two variables.

❑   It outputs the values of the two variables to the console.

Variable declaration occurs in the following code:

```
int myInteger;
string myString;
```

The first line declares a variable of type `int` with a name of `myInteger`, and the second line declares a variable of type `string` called `myString`.

> *Note that variable naming is restricted and you can't use just any sequence of characters. You look at this in the following section on naming variables.*

The next two lines of code assign values:

```
myInteger = 17;
myString = "\"myInteger\" is";
```

Here, you assign two fixed values (known as *literal* values in code) to your variables using the = *assignment operator* (the *Expressions* section of this chapter will cover more on operators). You assign the integer value 17 to `myInteger`, and the string `"myInteger"` (including the quotes) to `myString`. When you assign string literal values in this way, note that double quotation marks are required to enclose the string. Because of this, there are certain characters that may cause problems if they are included in the string itself, such as the double quotation characters, and you must *escape* some characters by substituting a sequence of characters (an *escape sequence*) that represents the character you want to use. In this example, you use the sequence \" to escape a double quotation mark:

```
myString = "\"myInteger\" is";
```

If you didn't use these escape sequences and tried coding this as

```
myString = ""myInteger" is";
```

you would get a compiler error.

37

Note that assigning string literals is another situation in which you must be careful with line breaks — the C# compiler will reject string literals that span more than one line. If you want to add a line break, you can use the escape sequence for a carriage return in your string, which is \n. For example, the following assignment

```
myString = "This string has a\nline break.";
```

would be displayed on two lines in the console view as follows:

```
This string has a
line break.
```

All escape sequences consist of the backslash symbol followed by one of a small set of characters (you look at the full set a little later). Because this symbol is used for this purpose, there is also an escape sequence for the backslash symbol itself, which is simply two consecutive backslashes, \\.

Getting back to the code, there is one more new line that you haven't looked at:

```
Console.WriteLine("{0} {1}.", myString, myInteger);
```

This looks similar to the simple method of writing out text to the console that you saw in the first example, but now you are specifying your variables. Now, I don't want to get too far ahead here, so I'm not going to go into too much detail about this line of code at this point. Suffice to say that it is the technique you will be using in the first part of this book to output text to the console window. Within the brackets you have two things:

❑   A string

❑   A list of variables whose values you want to insert into the output string, separated by commas

The string you are outputting, "{0} {1}.", doesn't seem to contain much useful text. As you have seen, however, this is not what you actually see when you run the code. The reason for this is that the string is actually a template into which you insert the contents of your variables. Each set of curly brackets in the string is a placeholder that will contain the contents of one of the variables in the list. Each placeholder (or format string) is represented as an integer enclosed in curly brackets. The integers start at 0 and are incremented by 1, and the total number of placeholders should match the number of variables specified in the comma-separated list following the string. When the text is output to the console, each placeholder is replaced by the corresponding value for each variable. In the example you just saw, the {0} is replaced with the actual value of the first variable, myString, and {1} is replaced with the contents of myInteger.

This method of outputting text to the console is what you will use to display output from your code in the examples that follow.

Finally, the code has the line seen in the earlier example for waiting for user input before terminating:

```
Console.ReadKey();
```

Again, I don't want to dissect this code at this point, but you will see it quite a lot in subsequent examples. All you need to know for now is that it pauses code execution until you press a key.

Variable Naming

As mentioned in the last section, you can't just choose any sequence of characters as a variable name. This isn't as worrying as it might sound at first, however, because you're still left with a very flexible naming system.

The basic variable naming rules are:

❑ The first character of a variable name must be either a letter, an underscore character (_), or the *at* symbol (@).

❑ Subsequent characters may be letters, underscore characters, or numbers.

In addition, there are certain keywords that have a specialized meaning to the C# compiler, such as the using and namespace keywords you saw earlier. If you should use one of these by mistake, the compiler will complain, and you'll soon know you've done something wrong, so don't worry about this too much.

For example, the following variable names are fine:

```
myBigVar
VAR1
_test
```

These aren't, however:

```
99BottlesOfBeer
namespace
It's-All-Over
```

And remember, C# is case-sensitive, so you have to be careful not to forget the exact case used when you declare your variables. References to them made later in the program with even so much as a single letter in the wrong case will prevent compilation.

A further consequence of this is that you can have multiple variables whose names differ only in case, for example the following are all separate names:

```
myVariable
MyVariable
MYVARIABLE
```

Naming Conventions

Variable names are something you will use *a lot*. Because of this, it's worth spending a bit of time discussing the sort of names that you should use. Before you get started, though, it is worth bearing in mind that this is controversial ground. Over the years, different systems have come and gone, and some developers will fight tooth and nail to justify their personal system.

Until recently the most popular system was what is known as *Hungarian notation*. This system involves placing a lowercase prefix on all variable names that identifies the type. For example, if a variable were of type int then you might place an i (or n) in front of it, for example iAge. Using this system, it is easy to see at a glance what types different variables are.

More modern languages, however, such as C# make this system tricky to implement. So, for the types you've seen so far you could probably come up with one or two letter prefixes signifying each type. However, since you can create your own types, and there are many hundreds of these more complex types in the basic .NET Framework, this quickly becomes unworkable. With several people working on a project, it would be easy for different people to come up with different and confusing prefixes, with potentially disastrous consequences.

Developers have now realized that it is far better to name variables appropriately for their purpose. If any doubt arises, it is easy enough to work out what the type of a variable is. In VS, you just have to hover the mouse pointer over a variable name and a pop-up box will tell you what the type is soon enough.

There are currently two naming conventions in use in the .NET Framework namespaces, known as *PascalCase* and *camelCase*. The casing used in the names is indicative of their usage. They both apply to names that are made up of multiple words and specify that each word in a name should be in lowercase except for its first letter, which should be uppercase. In camelCasing, there is an additional rule: that the first word should start with a lowercase letter.

The following are camelCase variable names:

```
age
firstName
timeOfDeath
```

Then the following are PascalCase:

```
Age
LastName
WinterOfDiscontent
```

For your simple variables, you should stick to camelCase, and you should use PascalCase for certain more advanced naming, which is the Microsoft recommendation.

Finally, it is worth noting that many past naming systems involved frequent use of the underscore character, usually as a separator between words in variable names, such as yet_another_variable. This usage is now discouraged (one thing I'm happy about — I always thought it looked ugly!).

Literal Values

In the previous Try It Out, you saw two examples of literal values: integer and string. The other variable types also have associated literal values, as shown in the following table. Many of these involve *suffixes*, where you add a sequence of characters to the end of the literal value to specify the type desired. Some literals have multiple types, determined at compile time by the compiler based on their context, as shown in the table.

Type(s)	Category	Suffix	Example/Allowed Values
`bool`	Boolean	None	`true` or `false`
`int, uint, long, ulong`	Integer	None	`100`
`uint, ulong`	Integer	u or U	`100U`
`long, ulong`	Integer	l or L	`100L`
`ulong`	Integer	ul, uL, Ul, UL, lu, lU, Lu, or LU	`100UL`
`float`	Real	f or F	1.5F
`double`	Real	None, d or D	1.5
`decimal`	Real	m or M	1.5M
`char`	Character	None	`'a'`, or escape sequence
`string`	String	None	`"a...a"`, may include escape sequences

String Literals

Earlier in this chapter, you saw a few of the escape sequences that you can use in string literals. It is worth presenting a full table of these for reference purposes.

Escape Sequence	Character Produced	Unicode Value of Character
`\'`	Single quotation mark	0x0027
`\"`	Double quotation mark	0x0022
`\\`	Backslash	0x005C
`\0`	Null	0x0000
`\a`	Alert (causes a beep)	0x0007
`\b`	Backspace	0x0008
`\f`	Form feed	0x000C
`\n`	New line	0x000A
`\r`	Carriage return	0x000D
`\t`	Horizontal tab	0x0009
`\v`	Vertical tab	0x000B

The Unicode value column of the preceding table shows the hexadecimal values of the characters as they are found in the Unicode character set.

As well as the preceding, you can specify any Unicode character using a Unicode escape sequence. These consist of the standard \ character followed by a u and a four-digit hexadecimal value (for example, the four digits after the x in the preceding table).

This means that the following strings are equivalent:

```
"Karli\'s string."
"Karli\u0027s string."
```

Obviously, you have more versatility using Unicode escape sequences.

You can also specify strings *verbatim*. This means that all characters contained between two double quotation marks are included in the string, including end-of-line characters and characters that would otherwise need escaping. The only exception to this is the escape sequence for the double quotation mark character, which must be specified in order to avoid ending the string. To do this, you place the @ character before the string:

```
@"Verbatim string literal."
```

This string could just as easily be specified in the normal way, but the following requires this method:

```
@"A short list:
item 1
item 2"
```

Verbatim strings are particularly useful in filenames, since these use plenty of backslash characters. Using normal strings, you'd have to use double backslashes all the way along the string, for example:

```
"C:\\Temp\\MyDir\\MyFile.doc"
```

With verbatim string literals you can make this more readable. The following verbatim string is equivalent to the preceding one:

```
@"C:\Temp\MyDir\MyFile.doc"
```

Note that, as you will see later in the book, strings are reference types, unlike the other types you've seen in this chapter, which are value types. One consequence of this is that strings can also be assigned the value null, which means that the string variable doesn't reference a string.

Variable Declaration and Assignment

As a quick recap, recall that you declare variables simply using their type and name, for example:

```
int age;
```

You then assign values to variables using the = assignment operator:

```
age = 25;
```

Remember that variables must be initialized before you use them. The preceding assignment could be used as an initialization.

There are a couple of other things you can do here that you are likely to see in C# code. The first is declaring multiple variables of the same type at the same time, which you can do by separating their names with commas after the type, for example:

```
int xSize, ySize;
```

Here, xSize and ySize are both declared as integer types.

The second technique you are likely to see is assigning values to variables at the same time as declaring them, which basically means combining two lines of code:

```
int age = 25;
```

You can use both these techniques together:

```
int xSize = 4, ySize = 5;
```

Here, both xSize and ySize are assigned different values.

Note that the following

```
int xSize, ySize = 5;
```

will result in only ySize being initialized — xSize is just declared, and it still needs to be initialized before it's used.

Expressions

Now that you've seen how to declare and initialize variables, it's time to look at manipulating them. C# contains a number of *operators* for this purpose, including the = assignment operator you've used already. By combining operators with variables and literal values (together referred to as *operands* when used with operators), you can create *expressions*, which are the basic building blocks of computation.

The operators available range from the simple to the highly complex, some of which you might never encounter outside of mathematical applications. The simple ones include all the basic mathematical operations, such as the + operator to add two operands, and the complex ones include manipulations of variable content via the binary representation of this content. There are also logical operators specifically for dealing with Boolean values, and assignment operators such as =.

In this chapter, you concentrate on the mathematical and assignment operators, leaving the logical ones for the next chapter, where you examine Boolean logic in the context of controlling program flow.

Operators can be roughly classified into three categories:

- *Unary* operators, which act on single operands
- *Binary* operators, which act on two operands
- *Ternary* operators, which act on three operands

Most operators fall into the binary category, with a few unary ones, and a single ternary one called the *conditional* operator (the conditional operator is a logical one, that is it returns a Boolean value; this is discussed in Chapter 4).

Let's start by looking at the mathematical operators, which span both unary and binary categories.

Mathematical Operators

There are five simple mathematical operators, two of which have binary and unary forms. In the next table, I've listed each of these operators, along with a quick example of its use and the results when it's used with simple numeric types (integer and floating point).

Operator	Category	Example Expression	Result
+	Binary	var1 = var2 + var3;	Var1 is assigned the value that is the sum of var2 and var3.
-	Binary	var1 = var2 - var3;	Var1 is assigned the value that is the value of var3 subtracted from the value of var2.
*	Binary	var1 = var2 * var3;	Var1 is assigned the value that is the product of var2 and var3.
/	Binary	var1 = var2 / var3;	Var1 is assigned the value that is the result of dividing var2 by var3.
%	Binary	var1 = var2 % var3;	Var1 is assigned the value that is the remainder when var2 is divided by var3.
+	Unary	var1 = +var2;	Var1 is assigned the value of var2.
-	Unary	var1 = -var2;	Var1 is assigned the value of var2 multiplied by –1.

The + (unary) operator is slightly odd, since it has no effect on the result. It doesn't force values to be positive as you might think—if var2 is -1 then +var is also -1. However, it is a universally recognized operator, and as such is included. The most useful fact about this operator is where you might customize its action, as you will see later in this book when you look at operator overloading.

I've shown examples using simple numeric types, since the result can be unclear when using the other simple types. What would you expect if you add two Boolean values together, for example? In this case, nothing, because the compiler will complain if you try to use + (or any of the other mathematical operators) with bool variables. Adding char variables is also slightly confusing. Remember, char variables are actually stored as numbers, so adding two `char` variables together will also give you a number (of type `int`, to be precise). This is an example of *implicit conversion*, and I'll have a lot more to say about this subject (and *explicit conversion*) shortly, because it also applies to cases where `var1`, `var2`, and `var3` are of mixed types.

Having said all this, the binary + operator *does* make sense when used with string type variables. In this case, the table entry should read as shown in the following table.

Operator	Category	Example Expression	Result
+	Binary	`var1 = var2 + var3;`	`var1` is assigned the value that is the concatenation of the two strings stored in `var2` and `var3`.

None of the other mathematical operators, however, will work with strings.

The other two operators you should look at here are the increment and decrement operators, both of which are unary operators that can be used in two ways: either immediately before or immediately after the operand. The results obtained in simple expressions are shown in the next table.

Operator	Category	Example Expression	Result
++	Unary	`var1 = ++var2;`	`var1` is assigned the value of `var2` + 1. `var2` is incremented by 1.
--	Unary	`var1 = --var2;`	`var1` is assigned the value of `var2` – 1. `var2` is decremented by 1.
++	Unary	`var1 = var2++;`	`var1` is assigned the value of `var2`. `var2` is incremented by 1.
--	Unary	`var1 = var2--;`	`var1` is assigned the value of `var2`. `var2` is decremented by 1.

The key factor here is that these operators always result in a change to the value stored in their operand:

❑   ++ always results in its operand being incremented by one.

❑   -- always results in its operand being decremented by one.

The difference between the results stored in `var1` are a consequence of the fact that the placement of the operator determines when it takes effect. Placing one of these operators before its operand means that the operand is affected before any other computation takes place. Placing it after the operand means that the operand is affected after all other computation of the expression is completed.

This merits another example! Consider this code:

```
int var1, var2 = 5, var3 = 6;
var1 = var2++ * --var3;
```

Chapter 3

The question is what value will be assigned to `var1`? Before the expression is evaluated, the `--` operator preceding `var3` will take effect, changing its value from 6 to 5. You can ignore the `++` operator that follows `var2`, as it won't take effect until after the calculation is completed, so `var1` will be the product of 5 and 5, or 25.

These simple unary operators come in very handy in a surprising amount of situations. They are really just a shorthand for expressions such as:

```
var1 = var1 + 1;
```

This sort of expression has many uses, however, particularly where *looping* is concerned, as you will see in the next chapter.

In the following Try It Out, you look at an example of how to use the mathematical operators, and it introduces a couple of other useful concepts as well. The code will prompt you to type in a string and two numbers and then demonstrate the results of performing some calculations.

Try It Out   Manipulating Variables with Mathematical Operators

1. Create a new console application called `Ch03Ex02` in the directory `C:\BegVCSharp\Chapter3`.

2. Add the following code to `Program.cs`:

```
static void Main(string[] args)
{
    double firstNumber, secondNumber;
    string userName;
    Console.WriteLine("Enter your name:");
    userName = Console.ReadLine();
    Console.WriteLine("Welcome {0}!", userName);
    Console.WriteLine("Now give me a number:");
    firstNumber = Convert.ToDouble(Console.ReadLine());
    Console.WriteLine("Now give me another number:");
    secondNumber = Convert.ToDouble(Console.ReadLine());
    Console.WriteLine("The sum of {0} and {1} is {2}.", firstNumber,
            secondNumber, firstNumber + secondNumber);
    Console.WriteLine("The result of subtracting {0} from {1} is {2}.",
            secondNumber, firstNumber, firstNumber - secondNumber);
    Console.WriteLine("The product of {0} and {1} is {2}.", firstNumber,
            secondNumber, firstNumber * secondNumber);
    Console.WriteLine("The result of dividing {0} by {1} is {2}.",
            firstNumber, secondNumber, firstNumber / secondNumber);
    Console.WriteLine("The remainder after dividing {0} by {1} is {2}.",
            firstNumber, secondNumber, firstNumber % secondNumber);
    Console.ReadKey();
}
```

3. Execute the code. The display shown in Figure 3-2 appears.

Figure 3-2

4. Enter your name and press enter, as shown in Figure 3-3.

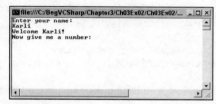

Figure 3-3

5. Enter a number, press enter, then another number, then enter again, as shown in Figure 3-4.

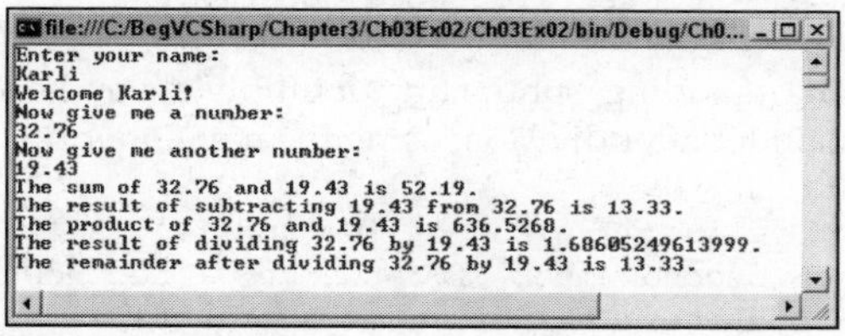

Figure 3-4

How It Works

As well as demonstrating the mathematical operators, this code introduces two important concepts, which you will come across many times in your worked examples:

❑ User input

❑ Type conversion

User input uses a similar syntax to the `Console.WriteLine()` command you've already seen — you use `Console.ReadLine()`. This command prompts the user for input, which is stored in a `string` variable:

```
string userName;
Console.WriteLine("Enter your name:");
userName = Console.ReadLine();
Console.WriteLine("Welcome {0}!", userName);
```

This code writes the contents of the assigned variable, `userName`, straight to the screen.

You also read in two numbers in this example. This is slightly more involved, because the `Console.ReadLine()` command generates a string, and you want a number. This introduces the topic of *type conversion*. You will look at this in more detail in Chapter 5, but let's have a look at the code used in this example first.

First, you declare the variables you want to store the number input in:

```
double firstNumber, secondNumber;
```

Next, you supply a prompt and use the command `Convert.ToDouble()` on a string obtained by `Console.ReadLine()` to convert the string into a `double` type. You assign this number to the `firstNumber` variable you have declared:

```
Console.WriteLine("Now give me a number:");
firstNumber = Convert.ToDouble(Console.ReadLine());
```

This syntax is remarkably simple, and you may not be surprised to learn that many other conversions can be performed in a similar way.

The remainder of the code obtains a second number in the same way:

```
Console.WriteLine("Now give me another number:");
secondNumber = Convert.ToDouble(Console.ReadLine());
```

Next, you output the results of adding, subtracting, multiplying, and dividing the two numbers, in addition to displaying the remainder after division, using the remainder (%) operator:

```
Console.WriteLine("The sum of {0} and {1} is {2}.", firstNumber,
        secondNumber, firstNumber + secondNumber);
Console.WriteLine("The result of subtracting {0} from {1} is {2}.",
        secondNumber, firstNumber, firstNumber - secondNumber);
Console.WriteLine("The product of {0} and {1} is {2}.", firstNumber,
        secondNumber, firstNumber * secondNumber);
Console.WriteLine("The result of dividing {0} by {1} is {2}.",
        firstNumber, secondNumber, firstNumber / secondNumber);
Console.WriteLine("The remainder after dividing {0} by {1} is {2}.",
        firstNumber, secondNumber, firstNumber % secondNumber);
```

Note that you are supplying the expressions, `firstNumber + secondNumber` and so on, as a parameter to the `Console.WriteLine()` statement, without going via an intermediate variable:

```
Console.WriteLine("The sum of {0} and {1} is {2}.", firstNumber,
        secondNumber, firstNumber + secondNumber);
```

This kind of syntax can make your code very readable, and cut down on the amount of lines of code you need to write.

Assignment Operators

Up till now, you've been using the simple = assignment operator, and it may come as a surprise that any other assignment operators exist at all. There are more, however, and the biggest surprise is probably that they're quite useful!

All of the assignment operators other than = work in a similar way. As with = they all result in a value being assigned to the variable on their left side based on the operands and operators on their right side.

As before, let's look at the operators and their explanations in tabular form in the next table.

Operator	Category	Example Expression	Result
=	Binary	var1 = var2;	var1 is assigned the value of var2.
+=	Binary	var1 += var2;	var1 is assigned the value that is the sum of var1 and var2.
-=	Binary	var1 -= var2;	var1 is assigned the value that is the value of var2 subtracted from the value of var1.
*=	Binary	var1 *= var2;	var1 is assigned the value that is the product of var1 and var2.
/=	Binary	var1 /= var2;	var1 is assigned the value that is the result of dividing var1 by var2.
%=	Binary	var1 %= var2;	var1 is assigned the value that is the remainder when var1 is divided by var2.

As you can see, the additional operators result in var1 being included in the calculation so, code like

```
var1 += var2;
```

gives exactly the same result as:

```
var1 = var1 + var2;
```

Note that the += operator can also be used with strings, just like +.

Using these operators, especially when employing long variable names, can make code much easier to read.

Operator Precedence

When an expression is evaluated, each operator is processed in sequence. However, this doesn't necessarily mean evaluating these operators from left to right.

As a trivial example, consider the following:

```
var1 = var2 + var3;
```

Here, the + operator acts before the = operator.

There are other situations where operator precedence isn't so obvious, for example:

```
var1 = var2 + var3 * var4;
```

Here, the * operator acts first, followed by the + operator, and finally the = operator. This is the standard mathematical order of doing things and gives the same result as you would expect from working out the equivalent algebraic calculation on paper.

Like such calculations, you can gain control over operator precedence by using parentheses, for example:

```
var1 = (var2 + var3) * var4;
```

Here, the content of the parentheses is evaluated first, meaning that the + operator acts before the * operator.

Of the operators you've encountered so far, the order of precedence is as shown in the following table, where operators of equal precedence (such as * and /) are evaluated from left to right.

Precedence	Operators
Highest	++, -- (used as prefixes); +, - (unary)
	*, /, %
	+, -
	=, *=, /=, %=, +=, -=
Lowest	++, -- (used as suffixes)

Note that parentheses can be used to override this precedence order, as described previously.

Namespaces

Before moving on, it's worth spending some time on one more important subject — *namespaces*. These are the .NET way of providing containers for application code, such that code and its contents may be uniquely identified. Namespaces are also used as a means of categorizing items in the .NET Framework. Most of these items are type definitions, such as the simple types detailed in this chapter (System.Int32 and so on).

C# code, by default, is contained in the *global namespace*. This means that items contained in this code are accessible from other code in the global namespace simply by referring to them by name. You can use the namespace keyword, however, to explicitly define the namespace for a block of code enclosed in curly brackets. Names in such a namespace must be *qualified* if they are to be used from code outside of this namespace.

A qualified name is one that contains all of its hierarchical information. In basic terms, this means that if you have code in one namespace that needs to use a name defined in a different namespace, you must include a reference to this namespace. Qualified names use period characters (.) between namespace levels.

For example:

```
namespace LevelOne
{
    // code in LevelOne namespace

    // name "NameOne" defined
}

// code in global namespace
```

This code defines one namespace, LevelOne, and a name in this namespace, NameOne (note that I haven't shown any actual code here in order to keep the discussion general; instead, I've placed a comment where this definition would go). Code written inside the LevelOne namespace can simply refer to this name using NameOne — no classification is necessary. Code in the global namespace, however, must refer to this name using the classified name LevelOne.NameOne.

Within a namespace, you can define nested namespaces, also using the namespace keyword. Nested namespaces are referred to via their hierarchy, again using periods to classify each level of the hierarchy. This is best illustrated with an example. Consider the following namespaces:

```
namespace LevelOne
{
    // code in LevelOne namespace

    namespace LevelTwo
    {
        // code in LevelOne.LevelTwo namespace

        // name "NameTwo" defined
    }
}

// code in global namespace
```

Here, NameTwo must be referred to as LevelOne.LevelTwo.NameTwo from the global namespace, LevelTwo.NameTwo from the LevelOne namespace, and NameTwo from the LevelOne.LevelTwo namespace.

The important point to note here is that names are uniquely defined by their namespace. You could define the name NameThree in the LevelOne and LevelTwo namespaces:

```
namespace LevelOne
{
    // name "NameThree" defined

    namespace LevelTwo
    {
        // name "NameThree" defined
    }
}
```

This defines two separate names, `LevelOne.NameThree` and `LevelOne.LevelTwo.NameThree`, which can be used independently of each other.

Once namespaces are set up, you can use the `using` statement to simplify access to the names they contain. In effect, the `using` statement says "OK, I'll be needing names from this namespace, so don't bother asking me to classify them every time." For example, in the following code you are saying that code in the `LevelOne` namespace should have access to names in the `LevelOne.LevelTwo` namespace without classification:

```
namespace LevelOne
{
   using LevelTwo;

   namespace LevelTwo
   {
      // name "NameTwo" defined
   }
}
```

Code in the `LevelOne` namespace can now refer to `LevelTwo.NameTwo` by simply using `NameTwo`.

There are times, as with the `NameThree` example above, when this can lead to problems with clashes between identical names in different namespaces (if you use such a name then your code won't compile — the compiler will let you know that there is an ambiguity). In cases such as these, you can provide an *alias* for a namespace as part of the `using` statement:

```
namespace LevelOne
{
   using LT = LevelTwo;

   // name "NameThree" defined

   namespace LevelTwo
   {
      // name "NameThree" defined
   }
}
```

Here, code in the `LevelOne` namespace can refer to `LevelOne.NameThree` as `NameThree` and `LevelOne.LevelTwo.NameThree` as `LT.NameThree`.

`using` statements apply to the namespace they are contained in, and any nested namespaces that might also be contained in this namespace. In the preceding code, the global namespace can't use `LT.NameThree`. However, if this `using` statement were declared as follows:

```
using LT = LevelOne.LevelTwo;

namespace LevelOne
{
   // name "NameThree" defined

   namespace LevelTwo
```

```
    {
        // name "NameThree" defined
    }
}
```

then code in the global namespace and the LevelOne namespace can use LT.NameThree.

There is one more important point to note here. The using statement doesn't in itself give you access to names in another namespace. Unless the code in a namespace is in some way linked to your project, by being defined in a source file in the project or being defined in some other code linked to the project, you won't have access to the names contained. Also, if code containing a namespace is linked to your project, you have access to the names contained in that code, regardless of whether you use using. using simply makes it easier for you to access these names and can shorten otherwise lengthy code to make it more readable.

Going back to the code in ConsoleApplication1 you saw at the start of this chapter, you see the following lines that apply to namespaces:

```
#region Using directives

using System;
using System.Collections.Generic;
using System.Text;

#endregion

namespace ConsoleApplication1
{
    ...
}
```

The three lines in the Using directives region use using to declare that the System, System .Collections.Generic, and System.Text namespaces will be used in this C# code and should be accessible from all namespaces in this file without classification. The System namespace is the root namespace for .NET Framework application and contains all the basic functionality you need for console applications. The other two namespaces are very often used in console applications, so they are there just in case.

Finally, a namespace is declared for the application code itself, ConsoleApplication1.

Summary

In this chapter, you covered a fair amount of ground on the way to creating usable (if basic) C# applications. You've looked at the basic C# syntax and analyzed the basic console application code that VS generates for you when you create a console application project.

The major part of this chapter concerned the use of variables. You have seen what variables are, how you create them, how you assign values in them, and how you manipulate them and the values that they contain. Along the way, you've also looked at some basic user interaction, by showing how you can output text to a console application and read user input back in. This involved some very basic type conversion, a complex subject that is covered in more depth in Chapter 5.

You have also seen how you can assemble operators and operands into expressions and looked at the way these are executed, and the order in which this takes place.

Finally, you looked at namespaces, which will become more and more important as the book progresses. By introducing this topic in a fairly abstract way here, the groundwork is completed for later discussions.

In this chapter, you learned:

- How basic C# syntax works
- What Visual Studio does when you create a console application project
- How to understand and use variables
- How to understand and use expressions
- What a namespace is

So far, all of your programming has taken the form of line-by-line execution. In the next chapter, you see how to make your code more efficient by controlling the flow of execution using looping techniques and conditional branching.

Exercises

1. In the following code, how would you refer to the name great from code in the namespace fabulous?

```
namespace fabulous
{
   // code in fabulous namespace
}

namespace super
{
   namespace smashing
   {
      // great name defined
   }
}
```

2. Which of the following is not a legal variable name?

- myVariableIsGood
- 99Flake
- _floor
- time2GetJiggyWidIt
- wrox.com

3. Is the string `"supercalifragilisticexpialidocious"` too big to fit in a `string` variable? Why?

4. By considering operator precedence, list the steps involved in the computation of the following expression:

```
resultVar += var1 * var2 + var3 % var4 / var5;
```

5. Write a console application that obtains four `int` values from the user and displays the product. Hint: you may recall that the `Convert.ToDouble()` command was used to covert the input from the console to a `double`; the equivalent command to convert from a `string` to an `int` is `Convert.ToInt32()`.

Flow Control

All of the C# code you've seen so far has had one thing in common. In each case, program execution has proceeded from one line to the next in top-to-bottom order, missing nothing. If all applications worked like this then you would be very limited in what you could do.

In this chapter, you look at two methods of controlling program flow, that is, the order of execution of lines of C# code. These two methods are:

❑ *Branching*, where you execute code conditionally, depending on the outcome of an evaluation, such as "only execute this code if `myVal` is less than 10."

❑ *Looping*, or repeatedly executing the same statements (for a certain number of times or until a test condition has been reached).

Both of these techniques involve the use of *Boolean logic*. In the last chapter you saw the `bool` type, but didn't actually do much with it. In this chapter you use it a lot, and so the chapter will start by discussing what is meant by Boolean logic so that you can use it in flow control scenarios.

In this chapter, you learn:

❑ What Boolean logic is and how to use it.

❑ How to control the execution of your code.

Boolean Logic

The `bool` type introduced in the last chapter can hold one of only two values, `true` or `false`. This type is often used to record the result of some operation, so that you can act on this result. In particular, `bool` types are used to store the result of a *comparison*.

> *As an historical aside, it is worth remembering (and respecting) the English mathematician George Boole, whose work in the mid-nineteenth-century forms the basis of Boolean logic.*

As an example, consider the situation (as mentioned in the introduction to this chapter) that you want to execute code based on whether a variable, `myVal`, is less than 10. To do this, you need some indication of whether the statement "`myVal` is less than 10" is true or false, that is, you need to know the Boolean result of a comparison.

Boolean comparisons require the use of Boolean *comparison* operators (also known as *relational* operators), which are shown in the following table. In all cases here `var1` is a `bool` type variable, while the types of `var2` and `var3` may vary.

Operator	Category	Example Expression	Result
==	Binary	`var1 = var2 == var3;`	`var1` is assigned the value `true` if `var2` is equal to `var3`, or `false` otherwise.
!=	Binary	`var1 = var2 != var3;`	`var1` is assigned the value `true` if `var2` is not equal to `var3`, or `false` otherwise.
<	Binary	`var1 = var2 < var3;`	`var1` is assigned the value `true` if `var2` is less than `var3`, or `false` otherwise.
>	Binary	`var1 = var2 > var3;`	`var1` is assigned the value `true` if `var2` is greater than `var3`, or `false` otherwise.
<=	Binary	`var1 = var2 <= var3;`	`var1` is assigned the value `true` if `var2` is less than or equal to `var3`, or `false` otherwise.
>=	Binary	`var1 = var2 >= var3;`	`var1` is assigned the value true if `var2` is greater than or equal to `var3`, or false otherwise.

You might use operators such as these on numeric values in code such as:

```
bool isLessThan10;
isLessThan10 = myVal < 10;
```

This code will result in `isLessThan10` being assigned the value `true` if `myVal` stores a value less than 10, or `false` otherwise.

You can also use these comparison operators on other types, such as strings:

```
bool isKarli;
isKarli = myString == "Karli";
```

Here, `isKarli` will only be true if `myString` stores the string `"Karli"`.

You can also focus on Boolean values:

```
bool isTrue;
isTrue = myBool == true;
```

although here you are limited to the use of `==` and `!=` operators.

Note that a common code error occurs if you unintentionally assume that because val1 < val2 is false, then val1 > val2 is true. If val1 == val2 then both these statements will be false. I'm mentioning this here because it's a mistake I've made in the past!

There are some other Boolean operators that are intended specifically for working with Boolean values, shown in the following table.

Operator	Category	Example Expression	Result
!	Unary	var1 = ! var2;	var1 is assigned the value true if var2 is false, or false if var2 is true. (Logical NOT.)
&	Binary	var1 = var2 & var3;	var1 is assigned the value true if var2 and var3 are both true, or false otherwise. (Logical AND.)
|	Binary	var1 = var2 | var3;	var1 is assigned the value true if either var2 or var3 (or both) are true, or false otherwise. (Logical OR.)
^	Binary	var1 = var2 ^ var3;	var1 is assigned the value true if either var2 or var3, but not both, are true, or false otherwise. (Logical XOR, or exclusive OR.)

So, the last code snippet above could also be expressed as:

```
bool isTrue;
isTrue = myBool & true;
```

The & and | operators also have two similar operators, known as *conditional Boolean* operators, shown in the next table.

Operator	Category	Example Expression	Result
&&	Binary	var1 = var2 && var3;	var1 is assigned the value true if var2 and var3 are both true, or false otherwise. (Logical AND.)
||	Binary	var1 = var2 || var3;	var1 is assigned the value true if either var2 or var3 (or both) are true, or false otherwise. (Logical OR.)

The result of these operators is exactly the same as & and |, but there is an important difference in the way this result is obtained, which can result in better performance. Both of these look at the value of their first operand (var2 in the preceding table) and based on the value of this operand may not need to process the second operator (var3 above) at all.

If the value of the first operand of the `&&` operator is `false`, then there is no need to consider the value of the second operand, because the result will be `false` regardless. Similarly, the `||` operator will return `true` if its first operand is `true`, regardless of the value of the second operand.

This isn't the case for the `&` and `|` operators you saw earlier. With these, both operands will always be evaluated.

Because of this conditional evaluation of operands, you will see a small performance increase if you use `&&` and `||` instead of `&` and `|`. This will be particularly apparent in applications that use these operators a lot. As a rule of thumb, *always* use `&&` and `||` where possible.

Note that these operators really come into their own in more complicated situations, where computation of the second operand is only possible with certain values of the first operand, for example:

```
var1 = (var2 != 0) && (var3 / var2 > 2);
```

Here, if `var2` is zero then dividing `var3` by `var2` will result in either a "division by zero" error or `var1` being defined as infinite (the latter is possible, and detectable, with some types such as `float`).

Bitwise Operators

In the light of the discussion in the last section, you may be asking why the `&` and `|` operators exist at all. The reason is that these operators may be used to perform operations on numeric values. In fact, they operate on the series of bits stored in a variable rather than the value of the variable.

Let's consider these in turn, starting with `&`. Each bit in the first operand is compared with the bit in the same position in the second operand, resulting in the bit in the same position in the resultant value being assigned a value as shown in the following table.

Operand 1 Bit	Operand 2 Bit	& Result Bit
1	1	1
1	0	0
0	1	0
0	0	0

`|` is similar, but the result bits are different, as shown in the next table.

Operand 1 Bit	Operand 2 Bit	| Result Bit
1	1	1
1	0	1
0	1	1
0	0	0

For example, consider the operation shown in the following code:

```
int result, op1, op2;
op1 = 4;
op2 = 5;
result = op1 & op2;
```

Here, you must consider the binary representations of op1 and op2, which are 100 and 101, respectively. The result is obtained by comparing the binary digits in equivalent positions in these two representations as follows:

❑ The leftmost bit of result is 1 if the leftmost bit of op1 and op2 are both 1, or 0 otherwise.

❑ The next bit of result is 1 if the next bit of op1 and op2 are both 1, or 0 otherwise.

❑ Continue for all remaining bits.

In this example, the leftmost bits of op1 and op2 are both 1, so the leftmost bit of result will be 1, too. The next bits are both 0, and the third bits are 1 and 0, respectively, so the second and third bits of result will be 0. The final value of result in binary representation is, therefore, 100, so result is assigned the value 4. This is shown graphically in the following table.

	1	0	0			4
&	1	0	1		&	5
	1	0	0			4

The same process occurs if you use the | operator, except that in this case each result bit is 1 if either of the operand bits in the same position is 1. This is shown in the next table.

	1	0	0			4
|	1	0	1		|	5
	1	0	1			5

You can also use the ∆^ operator in the same way, where each result bit is 1 if one or other of the operand bits in the same position is one, but not both, as shown in the following table.

Operand 1 Bit	Operand 2 Bit	^ Result Bit
1	1	0
1	0	1
0	1	1
0	0	0

C# also allows the use of a unary bitwise operator (~), which acts on its operand by inverting each of its bits, such that the result is a variable having values of 1 for each bit in the operand that is 0, and vice versa: This is shown in the following table.

Operand Bit	~ Result Bit
1	0
0	1

Note that the way integer numbers are stored in .NET, known as Two's Complement, means that using the ~ unary operator can give results that look a little odd. If you remember that, for example, an int *type is a 32-bit number, then knowing that the ~ operator acts on all 32 of those bits can help you to see what is going on. For example, the number 5 in its full binary representation is:*

```
00000000000000000000000000000101
```

The number −5 is:

```
11111111111111111111111111111011
```

In actual fact, by the Two's Complement system (−x) is defined as (~x + 1). This may seem odd, but this system is very useful when it comes to adding numbers together. For example, adding 10 and −5 (that is, subtracting 5 from 10) looks like this in binary format:

```
   00000000000000000000000000001010
+  11111111111111111111111111111011
= 100000000000000000000000000000101
```

By simply ignoring the 1 on the far left, you are left with the binary representation for 5. So, while results such as ~1 = −2 may look odd, the reason is that the underlying structures force this result.

The bitwise operations you've seen in this section are quite useful in certain situations, because they allow a simple method of making use of individual variable bits to store information. Consider a simple representation of a color using 3 bits to specify red, green, and blue content. You can set these bits independently to change the 3 bits to 1 of the configurations shown in the next table.

Bits	Decimal Representation	Meaning
000	0	black
100	4	red
010	2	green
001	1	blue
101	5	magenta
110	6	yellow
011	3	cyan
111	7	white

Let's say you store these values in a variable of type `int`. Starting from a black color, that is, an `int` variable with the value of 0, you can perform operations like:

```
int myColor = 0;
bool containsRed;
myColor = myColor | 2;          // Add green bit, myColor now stores 010
myColor = myColor | 4;          // Add red bit, myColor now stores 110
containsRed = (myColor & 4) == 4; // Check value of red bit
```

The final line of code assigns a value of `true` to `containsRed`, as the red bit of `myColor` is 1.

This technique can be quite useful for making efficient use of information, particularly because the operations involved can be used to check the values of multiple bits simultaneously (32 in the case of `int` values). However, there are better ways of storing extra information in single variables, making use of the advanced variable types discussed in the next chapter.

In addition to these four bitwise operators, there are two others that I'd like to look at in this section. These are shown in the following table.

Operator	Category	Example Expression	Result
>>	Binary	var1 = var2 >> var3;	var1 is assigned the value obtained when the binary content of var2 is shifted var3 bits to the right.
<<	Binary	var1 = var2 << var3;	var1 is assigned the value obtained when the binary content of var2 is shifted var3 bits to the left.

These operators, commonly called *bitwise shift operators*, are best illustrated with a quick example:

```
int var1, var2 = 10, var3 = 2;
var1 = var2 << var3;
```

Here, `var1` is assigned the value 40. This can be explained by considering that the binary representation of 10 is 1010, which shifted to the left by two places is 101000 — the binary representation of 40. In effect, what you have done is carried out a multiplication operation. Each bit shifted to the left multiplies the value by 2, so two bit-shifts to the left results in multiplication by 4. Conversely, each bit shifted to the right has the effect of dividing the operand by 2 with any integer remainder being lost:

```
int var1, var2 = 10;
var1 = var2 >> 1;
```

In this example, `var1` contains the value 5, whereas the following code gives a value of 2:

```
int var1, var2 = 10;
var1 = var2 >> 2;
```

You are unlikely to use these operators in most code, but it is worth being aware of their existence. Their primary use is in highly optimized code, where the overhead of other mathematical operations just won't do. For this reason, they are often used in, for example, device drivers or system code.

Boolean Assignment Operators

The last operators to look at in this section are those that combine some of the operators you've seen above with assignment, much like the mathematical assignment operators in the last chapter (+=, *=, and so on). These are shown in the following table.

Operator	Category	Example Expression	Result
&=	Binary	var1 &= var2;	var1 is assigned the value that is the result of var1 & var2.
|=	Binary	var1 |= var2;	var1 is assigned the value that is the result of var1 | var2.
^=	Binary	var1 ^= var2;	var1 is assigned the value that is the result of var1 ^ var2.

These work with both Boolean and numeric values in the same way as &, |, and ^.

Note that &= and |= use & and |, not && and ||, and get the overhead associated with these simpler operators.

The bitwise shift operators also have assignment operators as shown in the next table.

Operator	Category	Example Expression	Result
>>=	Unary	var1 >>= var2;	var1 is assigned the value obtained when the binary content of var1 is shifted var2 bits to the right.
<<=	Unary	var1 <<= var2;	var1 is assigned the value obtained when the binary content of var1 is shifted var2 bits to the left.

Now it's time for an example. The Try It Out that follows lets you type in an integer, and then the code performs various Boolean evaluations using that integer.

Try It Out   Using the Boolean and Bitwise Operators

1. Create a new console application called Ch04Ex01 in the directory C:\BegVCSharp\Chapter4.
2. Add the following code to Program.cs:

```
static void Main(string[] args)
{
```

```
        Console.WriteLine("Enter an integer:");
        int myInt = Convert.ToInt32 (Console.ReadLine());
        Console.WriteLine("Integer less than 10? {0}", myInt < 10);
        Console.WriteLine("Integer between 0 and 5? {0}",
                          (0 <= myInt) && (myInt <= 5));
        Console.WriteLine("Bitwise AND of Integer and 10 = {0}", myInt & 10);
        Console.ReadKey();
    }
```

3. Execute the application and enter an integer when prompted. The result is shown in Figure 4-1.

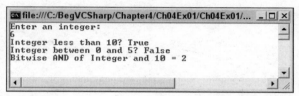

Figure 4-1

How It Works

The first two lines of code prompt for and accept an integer value using techniques you've already seen:

```
        Console.WriteLine("Enter an integer:");
        int myInt = Convert.ToInt32(Console.ReadLine());
```

You use `Convert.ToInt32()` to obtain an integer from the string input, which is simply another conversion command in the same family as the `Convert.ToDouble()` command you used previously.

The remaining three lines of code perform various operations on the number obtained and display results. You work through this code assuming that the user enters 6, as shown in the screenshot.

The first output is the result of the operation `myInt < 10`. If `myInt` is 6, which is less than 10, then the result will be `true`, which is what you see displayed. Values of `myInt` of 10 or above will result in `false`.

The second output is a more involved calculation: `(0 <= myInt) && (myInt <= 5)`. This involves two comparison operations, to see whether `myInt` is greater than or equal to 0 and less than or equal to 5, and a Boolean AND operation on the results obtained. With a value of 6 `(0 <= myInt)` returns `true`, and `(myInt <= 5)` returns `false`. The end result is then `(true) && (false)`, which is `false` as you can see from the display.

Finally, you perform a bitwise AND on the value of `myInt`. The other operand is 10, which has the binary representation 1010. If `myInt` is 6, which has the binary representation 110, then the result of this operation is 10, or 2 in decimal, as shown in the following table.

	0	1	1	0		6
&	1	0	1	0	&	10
	0	0	1	0		2

Operator Precedence Updated

Now that you have a few more operators to consider, the operator precedence table from the last chapter should be updated to include them. The new order is shown in the following table.

Precedence	Operators
Highest	++, -- (used as prefixes); (), +, - (unary), !, ~
	*, /, %
	+, -
	<<, >>
	<, >, <=, >=
	==, !=
	&
	^
	|
	&&
	||
	=, *=, /=, %=, +=, -=, <<=, >>=, &=, ^=, |=
Lowest	++, -- (used as suffixes)

This adds quite a few more levels, but explicitly defines how expressions such as the following will be evaluated:

```
var1 = var2 <= 4 && var2 >= 2;
```

where the && operator is processed after the <= and >= operators.

One point to note here is that it doesn't hurt to add parentheses to make expressions such as this one clearer. The compiler knows what order to process operators in, but we humans are prone to forget such things (and you might want to change the order). Writing the above expression as:

```
var1 = (var2 <= 4) && (var2 >= 2);
```

solves this problem by being explicit about the order of computation.

The goto Statement

C# allows you to label lines of code and then jump straight to them using the goto statement. This has its benefits and problems. The main benefit is that it is a very simple way of controlling what code is executed when. The main problem is that excessive use of this technique can result in difficult to understand *spaghetti* code.

The goto statement is used as follows:

```
goto <labelName>;
```

and labels are defined in the following way:

```
<labelName>:
```

For example, consider the following:

```
int myInteger = 5;
goto myLabel;
myInteger += 10;
myLabel:
Console.WriteLine("myInteger = {0}", myInteger);
```

Execution proceeds as follows:

❑   myInteger is declared as an int type and assigned the value 5.

❑   The goto statement interrupts normal execution and transfers control to the line marked myLabel:.

❑   The value of myInteger is written to the console.

The line of code highlighted below is *never* executed:

```
int myInteger = 5;
goto myLabel;
myInteger += 10;
myLabel:
Console.WriteLine("myInteger = {0}", myInteger);
```

In fact, if you try this out in an application, you will see that this is noted in the error list window as a warning when you try to compile the code, labeled "Unreachable code detected" along with location details.

goto statements have their uses, but they can make things very confusing indeed.

As an example of some spaghetti code arising from the use of goto, consider the following:

```
start:
int myInteger = 5;
goto addVal;
writeResult:
Console.WriteLine("myInteger = {0}", myInteger);
goto start;
addVal:
myInteger += 10;
goto writeResult;
```

This is perfectly valid code, but very difficult to read! You might like to try this out for yourself and see what happens. Before doing that, though, try and work out what this code will do by looking at it, so you can give yourself a pat on the back if you're right.

You come back to this statement a little later, because it has implications for use with some of the other structures in this chapter (although, to be honest, I don't advocate its use).

Branching

Branching is the act of controlling which line of code should be executed next. The line to jump to is controlled by some kind of conditional statement. This conditional statement will be based on a comparison between a test value and one or more possible values using Boolean logic.

In this section, you will look at the three branching techniques available in C#:

❑   The ternary operator

❑   The if statement

❑   The switch statement

The Ternary Operator

The simplest way of performing a comparison is to use the *ternary* (or *conditional*) operator mentioned in the last chapter. You've already seen unary operators that work on one operand, and binary operators that work on two operands, so it may come as no surprise that this operator works on three operands. The syntax is as follows:

```
<test> ? <resultIfTrue> : <resultIfFalse>
```

Here, *<test>* is evaluated to obtain a Boolean value, and the result of the operator is either *<resultIfTrue>* or *<resultIfFalse>* based on this value.

You might use this as follows:

```
string resultString = (myInteger < 10) ? "Less than 10"
                                        : "Greater than or equal to 10";
```

Here, the result of the ternary operator is one of two strings, both of which may be assigned to resultString. The choice of which string to assign is made by comparing the value of myInteger to 10, where a value of less than 10 results in the first string being assigned, and a value of greater than or equal to 10 the second string. For example, if myInteger is 4 then resultString will be assigned the string Less than 10.

This operator is fine for simple assignments such as this, but isn't really suitable for executing larger amounts of code based on a comparison. A much better way of doing this is to use the if statement.

The if Statement

The if statement is a far more versatile and useful way of making decisions. Unlike ?: statements, if statements don't have a result (so you can't use them in assignments); instead you use the statement to conditionally execute other statements.

The simplest use of an if statement is as follows:

```
if (<test>)
   <code executed if <test> is true>;
```

Where *<test>* is evaluated (it *must* evaluate to a Boolean value for the code to compile) and the line of code that follows the statement is executed if *<test>* evaluates to true. After this code is executed, or if it isn't executed due to *<test>* evaluating to false, program execution resumes at the next line of code.

You can also specify additional code using the else statement in combination with an if statement. This statement will be executed if *<test>* evaluate to false:

```
if (<test>)
   <code executed if <test> is true>;

else
   <code executed if <test> is false>;
```

Both sections of code can span multiple lines using blocks in braces:

```
if (<test>)
{
   <code executed if <test> is true>;
}
else
{
   <code executed if <test> is false>;
}
```

As a quick example, you could rewrite the code from the last section that used the ternary operator:

```
string resultString = (myInteger < 10) ? "Less than 10"
                                        : "Greater than or equal to 10";
```

Since the result of the if statement cannot be assigned to a variable, you have to assign a value to the variable in a separate step:

```
string resultString;
if (myInteger < 10)
   resultString = "Less than 10";
else
   resultString = "Greater than or equal to 10";
```

Code such as this, although more verbose, is far easier to read and understand than the equivalent ternary form, and allows far more flexibility.

Using the if Statement

1. Create a new console application called `Ch04Ex02` in the directory `C:\BegVCSharp\Chapter4`.

2. Add the following code to `Program.cs`:

```
static void Main(string[] args)
{
    string comparison;
    Console.WriteLine("Enter a number:");
    double var1 = Convert.ToDouble(Console.ReadLine());
    Console.WriteLine("Enter another number:");
    double var2 = Convert.ToDouble(Console.ReadLine());
    if (var1 < var2)
        comparison = "less than";
    else
    {
        if (var1 == var2)
            comparison = "equal to";
        else
            comparison = "greater than";
    }
    Console.WriteLine("The first number is {0} the second number.",
                        comparison);
    Console.ReadKey();
}
```

3. Execute the code, and enter two numbers at the prompts, as shown in Figure 4-2.

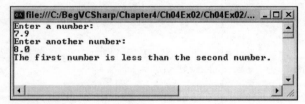

Figure 4-2

How It Works

The first section of code is familiar and simply obtains two `double` values from user input:

```
string comparison;
Console.WriteLine("Enter a number:");
double var1 = Convert.ToDouble(Console.ReadLine());
Console.WriteLine("Enter another number:");
double var2 = Convert.ToDouble(Console.ReadLine());
```

Next, you assign a string to the `string` variable `comparison` based on the values obtained for `var1` and `var2`. First, you check to see if `var1` is less than `var2`:

```
if (var1 < var2)
    comparison = "less than";
```

If this isn't the case, then `var1` is either greater than or equal to `var2`. In the `else` section of the first comparison, you need to nest a second comparison:

```
else
{
    if (var1 == var2)
        comparison = "equal to";
```

The `else` section of this second comparison will only be reached if `var1` is greater than `var2`:

```
else
        comparison = "greater than";
}
```

Finally, you write the value of comparison to the console:

```
Console.WriteLine("The first number is {0} the second number.",
                    comparison);
```

The nesting you have used here is just one way of doing things. You could equally have written:

```
if (var1 < var2)
    comparison = "less than";
if (var1 == var2)
    comparison = "equal to";
if (var1 > var2)
     comparison = "greater than";
```

The disadvantage with this method is that you are performing three comparisons regardless of the values of `var1` and `var2`. With the first method, you only perform one comparison if `var1 < var2` is `true` and two comparisons otherwise (you also perform the `var1 == var2` comparison), resulting in fewer lines of code being executed. The difference in performance here will be slight, but would be significant in applications where speed of execution is crucial.

Checking More Conditions Using if Statements

In the preceding example, you checked for three conditions involving the value of `var1`. This covered all possible values for this variable. At other times, you might want to check for specific values, say if `var1` is equal to 1, 2, 3, or 4, and so on. Using code such as that above can result in annoyingly nested code, for example:

```
if (var1 == 1)
{
    // Do something.
}
else
{
    if (var1 == 2)
    {
```

```
            // Do something else.
        }
        else
        {
            if (var1 == 3 || var1 == 4)
            {
                // Do something else.
            }
            else
            {
                // Do something else.
            }
        }
    }
```

Note that it is a common mistake to write conditions such as the third condition as if (var1 == 3 || 4). Here, owing to operator precedence, the == operator is processed first, leaving the || operator to oper-ate on a Boolean and a numeric operand. This will cause an error.

In these situations, it can be worth using a slightly different indentation scheme and contracting the block of code for the else blocks (that is, using a single line of code after the else blocks rather than a block of code). When you do this, you end up with a structure involving else if statements:

```
if (var1 == 1)
{
    // Do something.
}
else if (var1 == 2)
{
    // Do something else.
}
else if (var1 == 3 || var1 == 4)
{
    // Do something else.
}
else
{
    // Do something else.
}
```

These else if statements are really two separate statements, and the code is functionally identical to the above code. However, this code is much easier to read.

When making multiple comparisons such as this, it can be worth considering the switch statement as an alternative branching structure.

The switch Statement

The switch statement is very similar to the if statement in that it executes code conditionally based on the value of a test. However, switch allows you to test for multiple values of a test variable in one go, rather than just a single condition. This test is limited to discrete values, rather than clauses such as "greater than X," so its use is slightly different, but it can be a powerful technique.

The basic structure of a `switch` statement is:

```
switch (<testVar>)
{
   case <comparisonVal1>:
      <code to execute if <testVar> == <comparisonVal1> >
      break;
   case <comparisonVal2>:
      <code to execute if <testVar> == <comparisonVal2> >
      break;
   ...
   case <comparisonValN>:
      <code to execute if <testVar> == <comparisonValN> >
      break;
   default:
      <code to execute if <testVar> != comparisonVals>
      break;
}
```

The value in `<testVar>` is compared to each of the `<comparisonValX>` values (specified with `case` statements), and if there is a match, then the code supplied for this match is executed. If there is no match, then the code in the `default` section is executed if this block exists.

On completion of the code in each section, you have an additional command, `break`. It is illegal for the flow of execution to reach a second `case` statement after processing one `case` block.

> Note that this behavior is one area where C# differs from C++, where the processing of case statements is allowed to run from one to another.

The `break` statement here simply terminates the `switch` statement, and processing continues on the statement following the structure.

There are alternative methods of preventing flow from one case statement to the next in C# code. You can use the `return` statement, which results in termination of the current function rather than just the `switch` structure (see Chapter 6 for more details about this), or a `goto` statement. `goto` statements (as detailed earlier) work here, since `case` statements in effect define labels in C# code. For example:

```
switch (<testVar>)
{
   case <comparisonVal1>:
      <code to execute if <testVar> == <comparisonVal1> >

      goto case <comparisonVal2>;
   case <comparisonVal2>:
      <code to execute if <testVar> == <comparisonVal2> >
      break;
   ...
```

There is one exception to the rule that the processing of one `case` statement can't run freely into the next. If you place multiple `case` statements together (*stack* them) before a single block of code, you are in effect checking for multiple conditions at once. If any of these conditions is met the code is executed, for example:

```
switch (<testVar>)
{

    case <comparisonVal1>:
    case <comparisonVal2>:

        <code to execute if <testVar> == <comparisonVal1> or
                            <testVar> == <comparisonVal2> >
        break;
    ...
```

Note that these conditions also apply to the `default` statement. There is no rule saying that this statement must be the last in the list of comparisons, and you can stack it with case statements if you wish. Adding a break point with `break`, `goto`, or `return` ensures that a valid execution path exists through the structure in all cases.

Each of the `<comparisonValX>` comparisons must be a constant value. One way of doing this is to provide literal values, for example:

```
switch (myInteger)
{
    case 1:
        <code to execute if myInteger == 1 >
        break;
    case -1:
        <code to execute if myInteger == -1 >
        break;
    default:
        <code to execute if myInteger != comparisons>
        break;
}
```

Another way is to use *constant variables*. Constant variables (also known as just "constants," avoiding the oxymoron) are just like any other variable, except for one key factor: the value they contain *never* changes. Once you assign a value to a constant variable, that is the value it will have for the duration of code execution. Constant variables can come in handy here, because it is often easier to read code where the actual values being compared are hidden from you at the time of comparison.

You declare constant variables using the `const` keyword in addition to the variable type, and you *must* assign them values at this time, for example:

```
const int intTwo = 2;
```

This code is perfectly valid, but if you try

```
const int intTwo;
intTwo = 2;
```

you will get an error and won't be able to compile your code. This also happens if you try to change the value of a constant variable through any other means after initial assignment.

In the following Try It Out, you use a `switch` statement to write different strings to the console, depending on the value you enter for a test string.

Try It Out   Using the switch Statement

1. Create a new console application called `Ch04Ex03` in the directory `C:\BegVCSharp\Chapter4`.

2. Add the following code to `Program.cs`:

```
static void Main(string[] args)
{
    const string myName = "karli";
    const string sexyName = "angelina";
    const string sillyName = "ploppy";
    string name;
    Console.WriteLine("What is your name?");
    name = Console.ReadLine();
    switch (name.ToLower())
    {
        case myName:
            Console.WriteLine("You have the same name as me!");
            break;
        case sexyName:
            Console.WriteLine("My, what a sexy name you have!");
            break;
        case sillyName:
            Console.WriteLine("That's a very silly name.");
            break;
    }
    Console.WriteLine("Hello {0}!", name);
    Console.ReadKey();
}
```

3. Execute the code and enter a name. The result is shown in Figure 4-3.

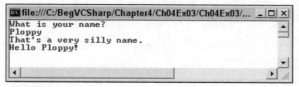

Figure 4-3

How It Works

The code sets up three constant strings, accepts a string from the user, and then writes out text to the console based on the string entered. In this case the strings are names.

When you compare the name entered (in the variable `name`) to your constant values, you first force it into lowercase with `name.ToLower()`. This is a standard command that will work with all string variables, and it comes in handy when you're not sure what has been entered by the user. Using this technique the strings `Karli`, `kArLi`, `karli`, and so on will all match the test string `karli`.

The `switch` statement itself attempts to match the string entered with the constant values you have defined and writes out a personalized message, if successful, to greet the user. If no match is made, you simply greet the user.

`switch` statements have no limit on the amount of `case:` sections they contain, so you could extend this code to cover every name you can think of should you wish . . . but it might take a while!

Looping

Looping is when statements are executed repeatedly. This technique can come in very handy, because it means that you can repeat operations as many times as you want (thousands, even millions, of times) without having to write the same code each time.

As a simple example, consider the following code for calculating the amount of money in a bank account after 10 years, assuming that interest is paid each year and no other money flows into or out of the account:

```
double balance = 1000;
double interestRate = 1.05; // 5% interest/year
balance *= interestRate;
balance *= interestRate;
balance *= interestRate;
balance *= interestRate;
balance *= interestRate;
balance *= interestRate;
balance *= interestRate;
balance *= interestRate;
balance *= interestRate;
balance *= interestRate;
```

Writing the same code out 10 times seems a bit wasteful, and what if you wanted to change the duration from 10 years to some other value? You'd have to manually copy the line of code the required amount of times, which would be a bit of a pain!

Luckily, you don't have to do this. Instead, you can just have a loop that executes the instruction you want the required number of times.

Another important type of loop is one where you loop until a certain condition is fulfilled. These loops are slightly simpler than the situation detailed above (although no less useful), so they're a good starting point.

do Loops

`do` loops operate in the following way. The code you have marked out for looping is executed, then a Boolean test is performed, and the code executes again if this test evaluates to `true`, and so on. When the test evaluates to `false` the loop exits.

The structure of a do loop is as follows:

```
do
{
    <code to be looped>
} while (<Test>);
```

where <Test> evaluates to a Boolean value.

The semicolon after the while statement is required, and it's a common error to leave this out.

For example, you could use this to write out the numbers from 1 to 10 in a column:

```
int i = 1;
do
{
    Console.WriteLine("{0}", i++);
} while (i <= 10);
```

Here, you use the suffix version of the ++ operator to increment the value of i after it is written to the screen, so you need to check for i <= 10 in order to include 10 in the numbers written to the console.

The following Try It Out uses this for a slightly modified version of the code in the introduction to this section, where you calculated the balance in an account after 10 years. Here, you will use a loop to calculate how many years it will take to get a specified amount of money in your account based on a starting amount and an interest rate.

Try It Out   Using do Loops

1. Create a new console application called Ch04Ex04 in the directory C:\BegVCSharp\Chapter4.

2. Add the following code to Program.cs:

```
static void Main(string[] args)
{
    double balance, interestRate, targetBalance;
    Console.WriteLine("What is your current balance?");
    balance = Convert.ToDouble(Console.ReadLine());
    Console.WriteLine("What is your current annual interest rate (in %)?");
    interestRate = 1 + Convert.ToDouble(Console.ReadLine()) / 100.0;
    Console.WriteLine("What balance would you like to have?");
    targetBalance = Convert.ToDouble(Console.ReadLine());

    int totalYears = 0;
    do
    {
        balance *= interestRate;
        ++totalYears;
    }
    while (balance < targetBalance);
    Console.WriteLine("In {0} year{1} you'll have a balance of {2}.",
                totalYears, totalYears == 1 ? "" : "s", balance);
    Console.ReadKey();
}
```

3. Execute the code and enter some values. The result is shown in Figure 4-4.

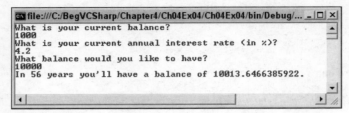

Figure 4-4

How It Works

This code simply repeats the simple annual calculation of balance with a fixed interest rate as many times as is necessary for the balance to satisfy the terminating condition. You keep a count of how many years have been accounted for by incrementing a counter variable with each loop cycle:

```
int totalYears = 0;
do
{
    balance *= interestRate;
    ++totalYears;
}
while (balance < targetBalance);
```

You can then use this counter variable as part of the result output:

```
Console.WriteLine("In {0} year{1} you'll have a balance of {2}.",
                  totalYears, totalYears == 1 ? "" : "s", balance);
```

Note that this is perhaps the most common usage of the ?: (ternary) operator — to conditionally format text with the minimum of code. Here, you output an "s" after "year" if totalYears isn't equal to 1.

Unfortunately, this code isn't perfect. Consider the situation in which the target balance is less than the current balance. The output will be along the lines of that shown in Figure 4-5.

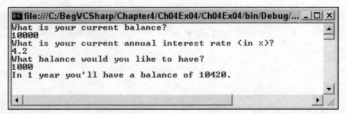

Figure 4-5

`do` loops *always* execute at least once. Sometimes, as in this situation, this isn't ideal. Of course, you could add an `if` statement:

```
        int totalYears = 0;
        if (balance < targetBalance)
        {
            do
            {
                balance *= interestRate;
                ++totalYears;
            }
            while (balance < targetBalance);
        }
        Console.WriteLine("In {0} year{1} you'll have a balance of {2}.",
                          totalYears, totalYears == 1 ? "" : "s", balance);
```

But this does seem as if you're adding unnecessary complexity. A far better solution is to use a `while` loop.

while Loops

`while` loops are very similar to `do` loops, but have one important difference. The Boolean test in a `while` loop takes place at the start of the loop cycle, not the end. If the test evaluates to `false`, then the loop cycle is *never* executed. Instead, program execution jumps straight to the code following the loop.

`while` loops are specified in the following way:

```
while (<Test>)
{
    <code to be looped>
}
```

and can be used in almost the same way as `do` loops, for example:

```
int i = 1;
while (i <= 10)
{
    Console.WriteLine("{0}", i++);
}
```

This code gives the same result as the `do` loop you saw earlier; it outputs the numbers 1 to 10 in a column.

The following Try It Out demonstrates how you can modify the last example to use a `while` loop.

Try It Out   Using while Loops

1. Create a new console application called `Ch04Ex05` in the directory `C:\BegVCSharp\Chapter4`.

2. Modify the code as follows (use the code from `Ch04Ex04` as a starting point, and remember to delete the `while` statement at the end of the original `do` loop):

```
static void Main(string[] args)
{
    double balance, interestRate, targetBalance;
    Console.WriteLine("What is your current balance?");
```

```
balance = Convert.ToDouble(Console.ReadLine());
Console.WriteLine("What is your current annual interest rate (in %)?");
interestRate = 1 + Convert.ToDouble(Console.ReadLine()) / 100.0;
Console.WriteLine("What balance would you like to have?");
targetBalance = Convert.ToDouble(Console.ReadLine());

int totalYears = 0;
while (balance < targetBalance)
{
    balance *= interestRate;
    ++totalYears;
}
Console.WriteLine("In {0} year{1} you'll have a balance of {2}.",
                totalYears, totalYears == 1 ? "" : "s", balance);
Console.ReadKey();
}
```

3. Execute the code again, but this time use a target balance that is less than the starting balance, as shown in Figure 4-6.

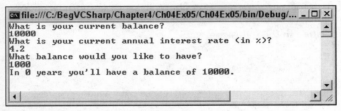

Figure 4-6

How It Works

This simple change from a `do` loop to a `while` loop has solved the problem in the last example. By moving the Boolean test to the start you provide for the circumstance where no looping is required, and you can jump straight to the result.

There are, of course, other alternatives in this situation. For example, you could check the user input to ensure that the target balance is greater than the starting balance. In situations like this, you can place the user input section in a loop as follows:

```
Console.WriteLine("What balance would you like to have?");
do
{
    targetBalance = Convert.ToDouble(Console.ReadLine());
    if (targetBalance <= balance)
        Console.WriteLine("You must enter an amount greater than " +
                "your current balance!\nPlease enter another value.");
}
while (targetBalance <= balance);
```

This will reject values that don't make sense, so you get output as shown in Figure 4-7.

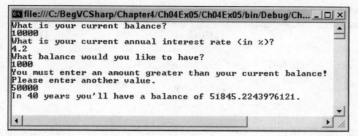

Figure 4-7

This *validation* of user input is an important topic when it comes to application design, and you see many examples of it over the course of this book.

for Loops

The last type of loop you look at in this chapter is the `for` loop. This type of loop is one that executes a set number of times and maintains its own counter. To define a `for` loop you need the following information:

- ❏ A starting value to initialize the counter variable
- ❏ A condition for continuing the loop, involving the counter variable
- ❏ An operation to perform on the counter variable at the end of each loop cycle

For example, if you want a loop with a counter that increments from 1 to 10 in steps of one, then the starting value is 1, the condition is that the counter is less than or equal to 10, and the operation to perform at the end of each cycle is to add one to the counter.

This information must be placed into the structure of a `for` loop as follows:

```
for (<initialization>; <condition>; <operation>)
{
   <code to loop>
}
```

This works in exactly the same way as the following `while` loop:

```
<initialization>
while (<condition>)
{
   <code to loop>
   <operation>
}
```

But the format of the `for` loop makes the code easier to read, because the syntax involves the complete specification of the loop in one place, rather than divide it over several statements in different areas of the code.

Earlier, you used `do` and `while` loops to write out the numbers from 1 to 10. The code that follows shows what is required for you to do this using a `for` loop:

```
int i;
for (i = 1; i <= 10; ++i)
{
   Console.WriteLine("{0}", i);
}
```

The counter variable, an integer called `i`, starts with a value of 1 and is incremented by 1 at the end of each cycle. During each cycle the value of `i` is written to the console.

Note that when code resumes after the loop `i` has a value of 11. This is because at the end of the cycle where `i` is equal to 10, `i` is incremented to 11. This happens before the condition that `i <= 10` is processed, at which point the loop ends.

As with `while` loops, `for` loops only execute if the condition evaluates to `true` before the first cycle, so the code in the loop doesn't necessarily run at all.

As a final note, you can declare the counter variable as part of the `for` statement, rewriting the preceding code as:

```
for (int i = 1; i <= 10; ++i)
{
   Console.WriteLine("{0}", i);
}
```

If you do this, though, the variable `i` won't be accessible from code outside this loop (see the section on variable scope in Chapter 6).

The next Try It Out uses `for` loops. Since you have used loops quite a bit now, I'll make this example a bit more interesting: it will display a Mandelbrot set (using plain-text characters, so it won't look that spectacular!).

Try It Out   Using for Loops

1. Create a new console application called `Ch04Ex06` in the directory `C:\BegVCSharp\Chapter4`.

2. Add the following code to `Program.cs`:

```
static void Main(string[] args)
{
    double realCoord, imagCoord;
    double realTemp, imagTemp, realTemp2, arg;
    int iterations;
    for (imagCoord = 1.2; imagCoord >= -1.2; imagCoord -= 0.05)
    {
        for (realCoord = -0.6; realCoord <= 1.77; realCoord += 0.03)
        {
            iterations = 0;
            realTemp = realCoord;
            imagTemp = imagCoord;
            arg = (realCoord * realCoord) + (imagCoord * imagCoord);
            while ((arg < 4) && (iterations < 40))
```

```
         {
             realTemp2 = (realTemp * realTemp) - (imagTemp * imagTemp)
                 - realCoord;
             imagTemp = (2 * realTemp * imagTemp) - imagCoord;
             realTemp = realTemp2;
             arg = (realTemp * realTemp) + (imagTemp * imagTemp);
             iterations += 1;
         }
         switch (iterations % 4)
         {
             case 0:
                 Console.Write(".");
                 break;
             case 1:
                 Console.Write("o");
                 break;
             case 2:
                 Console.Write("O");
                 break;
             case 3:
                 Console.Write("@");
                 break;
         }
     }
     Console.Write("\n");
 }
 Console.ReadKey();
}
```

3. Execute the code. The result is shown in Figure 4-8.

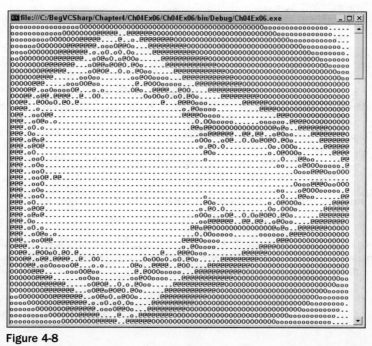

Figure 4-8

How It Works

Now, I don't want to go into too much detail about how to calculate Mandelbrot sets, but I will go through the basics to explain why you need the loops that you have used in this code. Feel free to skim through the following two paragraphs if the mathematics doesn't interest you, because it's an understanding of the code that is important here.

Each position in a Mandelbrot image corresponds to an imaginary number of the form $N = x + y*i$, where the real part is x, the imaginary part is y, and i is the square root of -1. The x and y coordinates of the position in the image correspond to the x and y parts of the imaginary number.

For each position on the image you look at the argument of N, which is the square root of $x*x + y*y$. If this value is greater than or equal to 2, you say that the position corresponding to this number has a value of 0. If the argument of N is less than 2, you change N to a value of $N*N - N$ (giving you $N = (x*x-y*y-x) + (2*x*y-y)*i$), and check the argument of this new value of N again. If this value is greater than or equal to 2, you say that the position corresponding to this number has a value of 1. This process continues until you either assign a value to the position on the image or perform more than a certain number of iterations.

Based on the values assigned to each point in the image you would, in a graphical environment, place a pixel of a certain color on the screen. However, because you are using a text display you simply place characters on screen instead.

Now, back to the code, and the loops contained in it.

You start by declaring the variables you will need for your calculation:

```
double realCoord, imagCoord;
double realTemp, imagTemp, realTemp2, arg;
int iterations;
```

Here, `realCoord` and `imagCoord` are the real and imaginary parts of N, and the other `double` variables are for temporary information during computation. `iterations` records how many iterations it takes before the argument of N (`arg`) is 2 or greater.

Next, you start two `for` loops to cycle through coordinates covering the whole of the image (using slightly more complex syntax for modifying your counters than `++` or `--`, a common and powerful technique):

```
for (imagCoord = 1.2; imagCoord >= -1.2; imagCoord -= 0.05)
{
    for (realCoord = -0.6; realCoord <= 1.77; realCoord += 0.03)
    {
```

I've chosen appropriate limits to show the main section of the Mandelbrot set. Feel free to play around with these if you want to try "zooming in" on the image.

Within these two loops you have code that pertains to a single point in the Mandelbrot set, giving you a value for N to play with. This is where you perform your calculation of iteration required, giving you a value to plot for the current point.

First, you initialize some variables:

```
iterations = 0;
realTemp = realCoord;
imagTemp = imagCoord;
arg = (realCoord * realCoord) + (imagCoord * imagCoord);
```

Next, you have a `while` loop to perform your iterating. You use a `while` loop rather than a `do` loop, in case the initial value of N has an argument greater than 2 already, in which case `iterations = 0` is the answer you are looking for and no further calculations are necessary.

Note that I'm not quite calculating the argument fully here, I'm just getting the value of x*x + y*y and checking to see if that value is less than 4. This simplifies the calculation, because you know that 2 is the square root of 4 and don't have to calculate any square roots yourself:

```
while ((arg < 4) && (iterations < 40))
{
    realTemp2 = (realTemp * realTemp) - (imagTemp * imagTemp)
               - realCoord;
    imagTemp = (2 * realTemp * imagTemp) - imagCoord;
    realTemp = realTemp2;
    arg = (realTemp * realTemp) + (imagTemp * imagTemp);
    iterations += 1;
}
```

The maximum number of iterations of this loop, which calculates values as detailed above, is 40.

Once you have a value for the current point stored in `iterations`, you use a `switch` statement to choose a character to output. You just use four different characters here, instead of the 40 possible values, and use the modulus operator (%) so that values of 0, 4, 8, and so on give one character; values of 1, 5, 9, and so on give another character; and so forth:

```
switch (iterations % 4)
{
    case 0:
        Console.Write(".");
        break;
    case 1:
        Console.Write("o");
        break;
    case 2:
        Console.Write("O");
        break;
    case 3:
        Console.Write("@");
        break;
}
```

Note that you use `Console.Write()` here rather than `Console.WriteLine()`, because you don't want to start a new line every time you output a character.

At the end of one of the innermost `for` loops, you do want to end a line, so you simply output an end-of-line character using the escape sequence you saw earlier:

```
        }
        Console.Write("\n");
    }
```

This results in each row being separated from the next and lining up appropriately.

The final result of this application, though not spectacular, is fairly impressive, and certainly shows how useful looping and branching can be.

Interrupting Loops

There are times when you want finer-grained control over the processing of looping code. C# provides four commands that help you here, three of which you've seen before in other situations:

❑   `break`: Causes the loop to end immediately

❑   `continue`: Causes the current loop cycle to end immediately (execution continues with the next loop cycle)

❑   `goto`: Allows jumping out of a loop to a labeled position (not recommended if you want your code to be easy to read and understand)

❑   `return`: Jumps out of the loop and its containing function (see Chapter 6)

The `break` command simply exits the loop, and execution continues at the first line of code after the loop, for example:

```
int i = 1;
while (i <= 10)
{
    if (i == 6)
        break;
    Console.WriteLine("{0}", i++);
}
```

This code will write out the numbers from 1 to 5, because the `break` command causes the loop to exit when i reaches 6.

`continue` only stops the current cycle, not the whole loop, for example:

```
int i;
for (i = 1; i <= 10; i++)
{
    if ((i % 2) == 0)
        continue;
    Console.WriteLine(i);
}
```

In the preceding example, whenever the remainder of i divided by 2 is zero, the `continue` statement stops the execution of the current cycle, and so only the numbers 1,3,5,7,9 are displayed.

The third method of interrupting a loop is to use `goto` as you saw earlier, for example:

```
int i = 1;
while (i <= 10)
{
    if (i == 6)
        goto exitPoint;
    Console.WriteLine("{0}", i++);
}
Console.WriteLine("This code will never be reached.");
exitPoint:
Console.WriteLine("This code is run when the loop is exited using goto.");
```

Note that exiting a loop with `goto` is legal (if slightly messy), but it is illegal to use `goto` to jump into a loop from outside.

Infinite Loops

It is possible, through both coding errors or design, to define loops that never end, so-called *infinite* loops. As a very simple example, consider the following:

```
while (true)
{
    // code in loop
}
```

This situation can be useful at times, and you can always exit such loops using code such as `break` statements or manually by using the Windows Task Manager.

However, when this occurs by accident it can be annoying. Consider the following loop, which is similar to the `for` loop in the last section:

```
int i = 1;
while (i <= 10)
{
    if ((i % 2) == 0)
        continue;
    Console.WriteLine("{0}", i++);
}
```

Here, i isn't incremented until the last line of code in the loop, which occurs after the `continue` statement. If this `continue` statement is reached (which it will be when i is 2), the next loop cycle will be using the same value of i, continuing the loop, testing the same value of i, continuing the loop, and so on. This will cause the application to freeze. Note that it's still possible to quit the frozen application in the normal way, so you won't have to reboot your computer if this happens.

Summary

In this chapter, you have developed your programming knowledge by considering various structures that you can use in your code. The proper use of these structures is essential when you start making more complex applications, and you will see them time and again throughout this book.

First, you spent some time looking at Boolean logic, with a bit of bitwise logic thrown in for good measure. Looking back on this after working through the rest of the chapter confirms the initial assumption that this topic is very important when it comes to implementing branching and looping code in your programs. It is essential to become very familiar with the operators and techniques detailed in this section.

Branching enables you to conditionally execute code, which, when combined with looping, allows you to create convoluted structures in your C# code. When you have loops inside loops inside `if` structures inside loops, you start to see why code indentation is so useful! If you shift all your code to the left of the screen, it instantly becomes difficult to parse by eye, and even more difficult to debug. It is well worth making sure you've got the hang of indentation at this stage — you'll appreciate it later on! VS does a lot of this for you, but it's a good idea to indent code as you type it anyway.

In this chapter, you learned:

❑ How to use Boolean logic

❑ Techniques for structuring your code

In the next chapter, you look at variables in more depth.

Exercises

1. If you have two integers stored in variables var1 and var2, what Boolean test can you perform to see if one or the other (but not both) is greater than 10?

2. Write an application that includes the logic from Exercise 1, obtains two numbers from the user, and displays them, but rejects any input where both numbers are greater than 10 and asks for two new numbers.

3. What is wrong with the following code?

```
int i;
for (i = 1; i <= 10; i++)
{
   if ((i % 2) = 0)
      continue;
   Console.WriteLine(i);
}
```

4. Modify the Mandelbrot set application to request image limits from the user and display the chosen section of the image. The current code outputs as many characters as will fit on a single line of a console application; consider making every image chosen fit in the same amount of space to maximize the viewable area.

More about Variables

Now that you've seen a bit more of the C# language, it's time to go back and tackle some of the more involved topics concerning variables.

The first topic you look at in this chapter is *type conversion*, where you convert values from one type into another. You've already seen a bit of this, but you look at it formally here. A grasp of this topic gives you a greater understanding of what happens when you mix types in expressions (intentionally or unintentionally) and tighter control over the way that data is manipulated. This helps you to streamline your code and avoid nasty surprises.

Once you've covered this, you will look at a few more types of variable that you can use:

❑ **Enumerations:** Variable types that have a user-defined discrete set of possible values that can be used in a human-readable way

❑ **Structs:** Composite variable types made up of a user-defined set of other variable types

❑ **Arrays:** Types that hold multiple variables of one type, allowing index access to the individual values

These are slightly more complex than the simple types you've been using up to now, but they can make your life much easier.

Once you've covered these topics, you look at another useful subject concerning strings — basic string manipulation.

Type Conversion

Earlier in this book you saw that all data, regardless of type, is simply a sequence of bits, that is, a sequence of zeros and ones. The meaning of the variable comes through the way in which this data is interpreted. The simplest example of this is the char type. This type represents a character in the Unicode character set using a number. In fact, this number is stored in exactly the same way as a ushort — both of them store a number between 0 and 65535.

However, in general, you will find that the different types of variables use varying schemes to represent data. This implies that even if it is possible to place the sequence of bits from one variable into a variable of a different type (perhaps they use the same amount of storage, or perhaps the target type has enough storage space to include all the source bits), the results might not be what you expect!

Instead of this one-to-one mapping of bits from one variable into another, you need to use *type conversion* on the data.

Type conversion takes two forms:

❑ **Implicit conversion:** Where conversion from type *A* to type *B* is possible in all circumstances, and the rules for performing the conversion are simple enough for you to trust in the compiler.

❑ **Explicit conversion:** Where conversion from type *A* to type *B* is only possible in certain circumstances or where the rules for conversion are complicated enough to merit additional processing of some kind.

Implicit Conversions

Implicit conversion requires no work on your part and no additional code. Consider the code shown here:

```
var1 = var2;
```

This assignment may involve an implicit conversion if the type of `var2` can be implicitly converted into the type of `var1`, but it could just as easily involve two variables with the same type, and no implicit conversion is necessary.

Here's an example:

The values of `ushort` and `char` are effectively interchangeable, because both store a number between 0 and 65535. You can convert values between these types implicitly, as illustrated by the following code:

```
ushort destinationVar;
char sourceVar = 'a';
destinationVar = sourceVar;
Console.WriteLine("sourceVar val: {0}", sourceVar);
Console.WriteLine("destinationVar val: {0}", destinationVar);
```

Here, the value stored in `sourceVar` is placed in `destinationVar`. When you output the variables with the two `Console.WriteLine()` commands, you get the following output:

```
sourceVar val: a
destinationVar val: 97
```

Even though the two variables store the same information, they are interpreted in different ways using their type.

There are many implicit conversions of simple types; `bool` and `string` have no implicit conversions, but the numeric types have a few. For reference, the following table shows the numeric conversions that the compiler can perform implicitly (remember that `chars` are stored as numbers, so `char` counts as a numeric type):

Type	Can Safely Be Converted To
Byte	short, ushort, int, uint, long, ulong, float, double, decimal
Sbyte	short, int, long, float, double, decimal
Short	int, long, float, double, decimal
Ushort	int, uint, long, ulong, float, double, decimal
Int	long, float, double, decimal
Uint	long, ulong, float, double, decimal
Long	float, double, decimal
Ulong	float, double, decimal
Float	double
Char	ushort, int, uint, long, ulong, float, double, decimal

Don't worry — you don't need to learn this table by heart, because it's actually quite easy to work out which conversions the compiler can do implicitly. Back in Chapter 3, you saw a table showing the range of possible values for every simple numeric type. The implicit conversion rule for these types is this: any type *A* whose range of possible values completely fits inside the range of possible values of type *B* can be implicitly converted into that type.

The reasoning for this is simple. If you try to fit a value into a variable, but that value is outside the range of values the variable can take, there will be a problem. For example, a `short` type variable is capable of storing values up to 32767, and the maximum value allowed into a `byte` is 255, so there could be problems if you try to convert a `short` value into a `byte` value. If the `short` holds a value between 256 and 32767, it simply won't fit into a byte.

However, if you *know* that the value in your `short` type variable is less than 255, then surely you should be able to convert the value, right?

The simple answer is that, of course, you can. The slightly more complex answer is that, of course, you can, but you must use an *explicit* conversion. Performing an explicit conversion is a bit like saying "OK, I know you've warned me about doing this, but I'll take responsibility for what happens."

Explicit Conversions

As their name suggests, explicit conversions occur when you explicitly ask the compiler to convert a value from one data type to another. Because of this, they require extra code, and the format of this code may vary, depending on the exact conversion method. Before you look at any of this explicit conversion code, you should look at what happens if you *don't* add any.

For example, the following modification to the code from the last section attempts to convert a short value into a byte:

```
byte destinationVar;
short sourceVar = 7;
destinationVar = sourceVar;
Console.WriteLine("sourceVar val: {0}", sourceVar);
Console.WriteLine("destinationVar val: {0}", destinationVar);
```

If you attempt to compile this code, you will receive the following error:

```
Cannot implicitly convert type 'short' to 'byte'. An explicit conversion exists
(are you missing a cast?)
```

Luckily for you, the C# compiler can detect missing explicit conversions!

To get this code to compile, you need to add the code to perform an explicit conversion. The easiest way to do this in this context is to *cast* the short variable into a byte (as suggested by the error string shown above). Casting basically means forcing data from one type into another and involves the following simple syntax:

```
(destinationType)sourceVar
```

This will convert the value in sourceVar into destinationType.

Note that this is only possible in some situations. Types that bear little or no relation to each other are likely not to have casting conversions defined.

You can, therefore, modify your example using this syntax to force the conversion from a short to a byte

```
byte destinationVar;
short sourceVar = 7;
destinationVar = (byte)sourceVar;
Console.WriteLine("sourceVar val: {0}", sourceVar);
Console.WriteLine("destinationVar val: {0}", destinationVar);
```

resulting in the following output:

```
sourceVar val: 7
destinationVar val: 7
```

So, what happens when you try to force a value into a variable into which it won't fit? Modifying your code as follows illustrates this:

```
byte destinationVar;
short sourceVar = 281;
destinationVar = (byte)sourceVar;
Console.WriteLine("sourceVar val: {0}", sourceVar);
Console.WriteLine("destinationVar val: {0}", destinationVar);
```

This results in:

```
sourceVar val: 281
destinationVar val: 25
```

What happened? Well, if you look at the binary representations of these two numbers, along with the maximum value that can be stored in a byte, which is 255

```
281 = 100011001
 25 = 000011001
255 = 011111111
```

you can see that the leftmost bit of the source data has been lost. This immediately raises a question: how can you tell when this happens? Obviously, there will be times when you will need to explicitly cast one type into another, and it would be nice to know if any data has been lost along the way. If you didn't detect this, it could cause serious errors, for example in an accounting application or an application determining the trajectory of a rocket to the moon.

One way of doing this is simply to check the value of the source variable and compare it with the known limits of the destination variable. You also have another technique available, which is to force the system to pay special attention to the conversion at runtime. Attempting to fit a value into a variable when that value is too big for the type of that variable results in an *overflow*, and this is the situation you want to check for.

Two keywords exist for setting what is called the *overflow checking context* for an expression: checked and unchecked. You use these in the following way:

```
checked(expression)
unchecked(expression)
```

You can force overflow checking in the last example:

```
byte destinationVar;
short sourceVar = 281;
destinationVar = checked((byte)sourceVar);
Console.WriteLine("sourceVar val: {0}", sourceVar);
Console.WriteLine("destinationVar val: {0}", destinationVar);
```

When this code is executed, it will crash with the error message shown in Figure 5-1 (I've compiled this in a project called OverflowCheck).

However, if you replace checked with unchecked in this code, you will get the result you saw earlier, and no error will occur. This is identical to the default behavior you saw earlier.

As well as these two keywords, you can configure your application to behave as if every expression of this type includes the checked keyword, unless that expression explicitly uses the unchecked keyword (in other words, you can change the default setting for overflow checking). To do this, you modify the properties for your project in VS by right-clicking on the project in the Solution Explorer window and selecting the Properties option. Click on Build on the left side of the window, and this will bring up the Build settings, as shown in Figure 5-2.

Figure 5-1

Figure 5-2

The property you want to change is one of the `Advanced` settings, so you click the `Advanced` button. In the dialog that appears, check the `Check for arithmetic overflow/underflow` option, as shown in Figure 5-3. By default, this setting is disabled, but enabling it gives the `checked` behavior detailed previously.

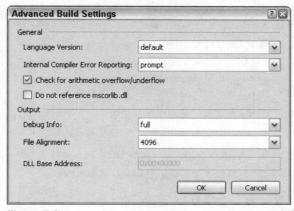

Figure 5-3

Explicit Conversions Using the Convert Commands

The type of explicit conversion you have been using in many of the Try It Out examples in this book is a bit different from those you have seen so far in this chapter. You have been converting string values into numbers using commands such as `Convert.ToDouble()`, which is obviously something that won't work for every possible string.

If, for example, you try to convert a string like `Number` into a double value using `Convert.ToDouble()`, you will see the dialog shown in Figure 5-4 when you execute the code.

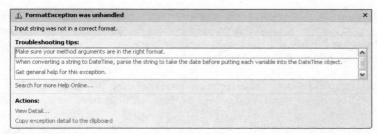

Figure 5-4

As you can see, the operation fails. For this type of conversion to work, the string supplied *must* be a valid representation of a number, and that number must be one that won't cause an overflow. A valid representation of a number is one that contains an optional sign (that is, plus or minus), zero or more digits, an optional period followed by one or more digits, and an optional "e" or "E" followed by an optional sign and one or more digits and *nothing else except spaces* (before or after this sequence). Using all of these optional extras, you can recognize strings as complex as -1.2451e-24 as being a number.

There are many such explicit conversions that you can specify in this way, as the following table shows:

Command	Result
Convert.ToBoolean(val)	val converted to bool.
Convert.ToByte(val)	val converted to byte.
Convert.ToChar(val)	val converted to char.
Convert.ToDecimal(val)	val converted to decimal.
Convert.ToDouble(val)	val converted to double.
Convert.ToInt16(val)	val converted to short.
Convert.ToInt32(val)	val converted to int.
Convert.ToInt64(val)	val converted to long.
Convert.ToSByte(val)	val converted to sbyte.
Convert.ToSingle(val)	val converted to float.
Convert.ToString(val)	val converted to string.
Convert.ToUInt16(val)	val converted to ushort.
Convert.ToUInt32(val)	val converted to uint.
Convert.ToUInt64(val)	val converted to ulong.

Here val can be most types of variable (if it's a type that can't be handled by these commands, the compiler will tell you).

Unfortunately, as the table shows, the names of these conversions are slightly different from the C# type names; for example, to convert to an int you use Convert.ToInt32(). This is so because these commands come from the .NET Framework System namespace, rather than being native C#. This allows them to be used from other .NET-compatible languages besides C#.

The important thing to note about these conversions is that they are *always* overflow-checked, and the checked and unchecked keywords and project property settings have no effect.

The next Try It Out is an example that covers many of the conversion types from this section. It declares and initializes a number of variables of different types, then converts between them implicitly and explicitly.

Try It Out   Type Conversions in Practice

1. Create a new console application called Ch05Ex01 in the directory C:\BegVCSharp\Chapter5.
2. Add the following code to Program.cs:

```csharp
static void Main(string[] args)
{
    short   shortResult, shortVal = 4;
    int     integerVal = 67;
    long    longResult;
    float   floatVal = 10.5F;
    double doubleResult, doubleVal = 99.999;
    string stringResult, stringVal = "17";
    bool    boolVal = true;

    Console.WriteLine("Variable Conversion Examples\n");

    doubleResult = floatVal * shortVal;
    Console.WriteLine("Implicit, -> double: {0} * {1} -> {2}", floatVal,
        shortVal, doubleResult);

    shortResult = (short)floatVal;
    Console.WriteLine("Explicit, -> short:  {0} -> {1}", floatVal,
        shortResult);

    stringResult = Convert.ToString(boolVal) +
        Convert.ToString(doubleVal);
    Console.WriteLine("Explicit, -> string: \"{0}\" + \"{1}\" -> {2}",
        boolVal, doubleVal, stringResult);

    longResult = integerVal + Convert.ToInt64(stringVal);
    Console.WriteLine("Mixed,     -> long:  {0} + {1} -> {2}",
        integerVal, stringVal, longResult);
    Console.ReadKey();
}
```

3. Execute the code. The result is shown in Figure 5-5.

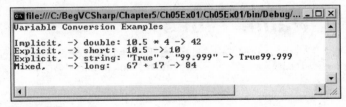

Figure 5-5

How It Works

This example contains all of the conversion types you've seen so far, both in simple assignments as in the short code examples in the preceding discussion and in expressions. You need to consider both cases, because the processing of *every* nonunary operator may result in type conversions, not just assignment operators. For example:

```csharp
shortVal * floatVal
```

Here, you are multiplying a `short` value by a `float` value. In situations such as this, where no explicit conversion is specified, implicit conversion will be used if possible. In this example, the only implicit conversion that makes sense is to convert the `short` into a `float` (as converting a `float` into a `short` requires explicit conversion), so this is the one that will be used.

However, you can override this behavior should you wish, using:

```
shortVal * (short)floatVal
```

This doesn't mean that a `short` will be returned from this operation. Since the result of multiplying two `short` values is quite likely to exceed 32767 (the maximum value a `short` can hold), this operation actually returns an `int`.

Explicit conversions performed using this casting syntax take the same operator precedence as other unary operators (such as ++ used as a prefix), that is, the highest level of precedence.

When you have statements involving mixed types, conversions occur as each operator is processed, according to the operator precedence. This means that "intermediate" conversions may occur, for example:

```
doubleResult = floatVal + (shortVal * floatVal);
```

The first operator to be processed here is *, which, as discussed previously, will result in `shortVal` being converted to a `float`. Next, you process the + operator, which won't require any conversion, because it acts on two `float` values (`floatVal` and the `float` type result of `shortVal * floatVal`). Finally, the `float` result of this calculation is converted into a `double` when the = operator is processed.

This conversion process can seem complex at first glance, but as long as you break expressions down into parts by taking the operator precedence order into account, you should be able to work things out.

Complex Variable Types

So far you've looked at all the simple variable types that C# has to offer. There are three slightly more complex (but very useful) sorts of variable that you will look at here:

❑ Enumerations

❑ Structures

❑ Arrays

Enumerations

Each of the types you've seen so far (with the exception of `string`) has a clearly defined set of allowed values. Admittedly, this set is so large in types such as `double` that it can practically be considered a continuum, but it *is* a fixed set nevertheless. The simplest example of this is the `bool` type, which can only take one of two values: `true` or `false`.

There are many other situations in which you might want to have a variable that can take one of a fixed set of results. For example, you might want to have an `orientation` type that can store one of the values `north`, `south`, `east`, or `west`.

In situations like this, *enumerations* can be very useful. Enumerations do exactly what you want in this `orientation` type: they allow the definition of a type that can take one of a finite set of values that you supply.

What you need to do, then, is create your own enumeration type called `orientation` that can take one of the four possible values shown above.

Note that there is an additional step involved here — you don't just declare a variable of a given type, you declare and detail a user-defined type and then you declare a variable of this new type.

Defining Enumerations

Enumerations can be defined using the `enum` keyword as follows:

```
enum typeName
{
    value1,
    value2,
    value3,
    ...
    valueN
}
```

Next, you can declare variables of this new type with

```
typeName varName;
```

and assign values using:

```
varName = typeName.value;
```

Enumerations have an *underlying type* used for storage. Each of the values that an enumeration type can take is stored as a value of this underlying type, which by default is `int`. You can specify a different underlying type by adding the type to the enumeration declaration:

```
enum typeName : underlyingType
{
    value1,
    value2,
    value3,
    ...
    valueN
}
```

Enumerations can have underlying types of `byte`, `sbyte`, `short`, `ushort`, `int`, `uint`, `long`, and `ulong`.

By default, each value is assigned a corresponding underlying type value automatically according to the order in which it is defined, starting from zero. This means that `value1` will get the value 0, `value2` will get 1, `value3` will get 2, and so on. You can override this assignment by using the = operator and specifying actual values for each enumeration value:

```
enum typeName : underlyingType
{
    value1 = actualVal1,
    value2 = actualVal2,
    value3 = actualVal3,
    ...
    valueN = actualValN
}
```

In addition, you can specify identical values for multiple enumeration values by using one value as the underlying value of another:

```
enum typeName : underlyingType
{
    value1 = actualVal1,
    value2 = value1,
    value3,
    ...
    valueN = actualValN
}
```

Any values left unassigned will be given an underlying value automatically, where the values used are in a sequence starting from 1 greater than the last explicitly declared one. In the preceding code, for example, `value3` will get the value `value1 + 1`.

Note that this can cause problems, with values specified after a definition such as `value2 = value1` being identical to other values. For example, in the following code `value4` will have the same value as `value2`:

```
enum typeName : underlyingType
{
    value1 = actualVal1,
    value2,
    value3 = value1,
    value4,
    ...
    valueN = actualValN
}
```

Of course, if this is the behavior you want then this code is fine.

Note also that assigning values in a circular fashion will cause an error, for example:

```
enum typeName : underlyingType
{
    value1 = value2,
    value2 = value1
}
```

The following Try It Out is an example of all of this. The code defines an enumeration called `orientation` and then demonstrates its use.

Try It Out   Using an Enumeration

1.   Create a new console application called `Ch05Ex02` in the directory `C:\BegVCSharp\Chapter5`.

2.   Add the following code to `Program.cs`:

```
namespace Ch05Ex02
{
    enum orientation : byte
    {
        north = 1,
        south = 2,
        east  = 3,
        west  = 4
    }

    class Program
    {
        static void Main(string[] args)
        {
            orientation myDirection = orientation.north;
            Console.WriteLine("myDirection = {0}", myDirection);
            Console.ReadKey();
        }
    }
}
```

3.   Execute the application. You should see the output shown in Figure 5-6.

Figure 5-6

4.   Quit the application and modify the code as follows:

```
            byte directionByte;
            string directionString;
            orientation myDirection = orientation.north;
            Console.WriteLine("myDirection = {0}", myDirection);
            directionByte = (byte)myDirection;
            directionString = Convert.ToString(myDirection);
            Console.WriteLine("byte equivalent = {0}", directionByte);
            Console.WriteLine("string equivalent = {0}", directionString);
            Console.ReadKey();
```

5.   Execute the application again. The output is shown in Figure 5-7.

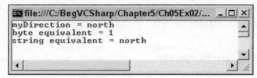

Figure 5-7

How It Works

This code defines and uses an enumeration type called `orientation`. The first thing to notice is that the type definition code is placed in your namespace, `Ch05Ex02`, but not in the same place as the rest of your code. This is because definitions are not executed as such; that is, at runtime you don't step through the code in a definition as you do the lines of code in your application. Application execution starts in the place you're used to and has access to your new type because it belongs to the same namespace.

The first iteration of the example demonstrates the basic method of creating a variable of your new type, assigning it a value and outputting it to the screen.

Next, you modified your code to show the conversion of enumeration values into other types. Note that you *must* use explicit conversions here. Even though the underlying type of `orientation` is `byte`, you still have to use the `(byte)` cast to convert the value of `myDirection` into a `byte` type:

```
directionByte = (byte)myDirection;
```

The same explicit casting is necessary in the other direction too; if you want to convert a `byte` into an `orientation`. For example, you could use the following code to convert a `byte` variable called `myByte` into an orientation and assign this value to `myDirection`:

```
myDirection = (orientation)myByte;
```

Of course, care must be taken here because not all permissible values of `byte` type variables map to defined `orientation` values. The `orientation` type can store other byte values, so you won't get an error straight away, but this may break logic later in the application.

To get the string value of an enumeration value you can use `Convert.ToString()`:

```
directionString = Convert.ToString(myDirection);
```

Using a `(string)` cast won't work, because the processing required is more complicated than just placing the data stored in the enumeration variable into a `string` variable.

Alternatively, you can use the `ToString()` command of the variable itself. The following code gives you the same result as using `Convert.ToString()`:

```
directionString = myDirection.ToString();
```

Converting a `string` to an enumeration value is also possible, except that here the syntax required is slightly more complex. A special command exists for this sort of conversion, `Enum.Parse()`, which is used in the following way:

```
(enumerationType)Enum.Parse(typeof(enumerationType), enumerationValueString);
```

This uses another operator, `typeof`, which obtains the type of its operand. You could use this for your `orientation` type as follows:

```
string myString = "north";
orientation myDirection = (orientation)Enum.Parse(typeof(orientation),
                                                  myString);
```

Of course, not all string values will map to an `orientation` value! If you pass in a value that doesn't map to one of your enumeration values, you will get an error. Like everything else in C#, these values are case-sensitive, so you still get an error if your string agrees with a value in everything but case (for example, if `myString` is set to `North` rather than `north`).

Structs

The next sort of variable that you will look at is the *struct* (short for structure). Structs are just that — data structures are composed of several pieces of data, possibly of different types. They allow you to define your own types of variables based on this structure. For example, suppose that you want to store the route to a location from a starting point, where the route consists of a direction and a distance in miles. For simplicity you can assume that the direction is one of the compass points (such that it can be represented using the `orientation` enumeration from the last section) and that distance in miles can be represented as a `double` type.

Now, you could use two separate variables for this using code you've seen already:

```
orientation myDirection;
double      myDistance;
```

There is nothing wrong with using two variables like this, but it is far simpler (especially where multiple routes are required) to store this information in one place.

Defining Structs

Structs are defined using the `struct` keyword as follows:

```
struct <typeName>
{
    <memberDeclarations>
}
```

The `<memberDeclarations>` section contains declarations of variables (called the *data members* of the struct) in almost the same format as usual. Each member declaration takes the form:

```
<accessibility> <type> <name>;
```

To allow the code that calls the struct to access the struct's data members, you use the keyword `public` for `<accessibility>`. For example:

```
struct route
{
    public orientation direction;
    public double      distance;
}
```

Once you have a struct type defined, you use it by defining variables of the new type

```
route myRoute;
```

and have access to the data members of this composite variable via the period character:

```
myRoute.direction = orientation.north;
myRoute.distance = 2.5;
```

This is illustrated in the following Try It Out, where the `orientation` enumeration from the last Try It Out is used with the `route` struct shown previously. This struct is then manipulated in code to give you a feel for how structs work.

Try It Out   **Using a Struct**

1.   Create a new console application called Ch05Ex03 in the directory C:\BegVCSharp\Chapter5.

2.   Add the following code to Program.cs:

```
namespace Ch05Ex03
{
    enum orientation : byte
    {
        north = 1,
        south = 2,
        east  = 3,
        west  = 4
    }
    struct route
    {
        public orientation direction;
        public double      distance;
    }

    class Program
    {
        static void Main(string[] args)
        {
            route myRoute;
            int myDirection = -1;
            double myDistance;
            Console.WriteLine("1) North\n2) South\n3) East\n4) West");
            do
            {
                Console.WriteLine("Select a direction:");
                myDirection = Convert.ToInt32(Console.ReadLine());
            }
```

```
        while ((myDirection < 1) || (myDirection > 4));
        Console.WriteLine("Input a distance:");
        myDistance = Convert.ToDouble(Console.ReadLine());
        myRoute.direction = (orientation)myDirection;
        myRoute.distance = myDistance;
        Console.WriteLine("myRoute specifies a direction of {0} and a " +
            "distance of {1}", myRoute.direction, myRoute.distance);
        Console.ReadKey();
    }
  }
}
```

3. Execute the code, select a direction, and then enter a distance. The result is shown in Figure 5-8.

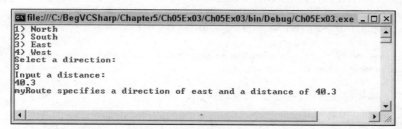

Figure 5-8

How It Works

Structs, like enumerations, are declared outside of the main body of the code. You declare your `route` struct just inside the namespace declaration, along with the `orientation` enumeration that it uses:

```
enum orientation : byte
{
   north = 1,
   south = 2,
   east  = 3,
   west  = 4
}
struct route
{
   public orientation direction;
   public double      distance;
}
```

The main body of the code follows a similar structure to some of the example code you've already seen, requesting input from the user and displaying it. You perform some simple validation of user input by placing the direction selection in a do loop, rejecting any input that isn't an integer between 1 and 4 (with values chosen such that they map onto the enumeration members for easy assignment).

The interesting point to note is that when you refer to the members of route they are treated in exactly the same way as variables of the same type as the member would be. The assignment is as follows:

```
myRoute.direction = (orientation)myDirection;
myRoute.distance = myDistance;
```

You could simply take the input value directly into `myRoute.distance` with no ill effects as follows:

```
myRoute.distance = Convert.ToDouble(Console.ReadLine());
```

The extra step allows for more validation, although none is performed in this code.

Any access to members of a structure is treated in the same way. Expressions of the form `structVar.memberVar` can be said to evaluate to a variable of the type of `memberVar`.

Arrays

All the types you've seen so far have one thing in common: each of them stores a single value (or a single set of values in the case of structs). Sometimes, in situations where you want to store a lot of data, this isn't very convenient. Sometimes, you want to store several values of the same type at the same time, without having to use a different variable for each value.

For example, you might want to perform some processing that involves the names of all of your friends. You could use simple string variables such as:

```
string friendName1 = "Robert Barwell";
string friendName2 = "Mike Parry";
string friendName3 = "Jeremy Beacock";
```

But this looks like it will need a lot of effort, especially because you need to write different code to process each variable. You couldn't, for example, iterate through this list of strings in a loop.

The alternative is to use an *array*. Arrays are indexed lists of variables stored in a single array type variable. For example, you might have an array that stores the three names shown above, called `friendNames`. You can access individual members of this array by specifying their index in square brackets, as shown here:

```
friendNames[<index>]
```

This index is simply an integer, starting with 0 for the first entry, using 1 for the second, and so on. This means that you can go through the entries using a loop, for example:

```
int i;
for (i = 0; i < 3; i++)
{
    Console.WriteLine("Name with index of {0}: {1}", i, friendNames[i]);
}
```

Arrays have a single *base type*, that is, individual entries in an array are all of the same type. This `friendNames` array has a base type of `string`, as it is intended for storing `string` variables.

Array entries are often referred to as *elements*.

Declaring Arrays

Arrays are declared in the following way:

```
<baseType>[] <name>;
```

Here, `<baseType>` may be any variable type, including the enumeration and struct types you've seen in this chapter.

Arrays must be initialized before you have access to them. You can't just access or assign values to the array elements like this:

```
int[] myIntArray;
myIntArray[10] = 5;
```

Arrays can be initialized in two ways. You can either specify the complete contents of the array in a literal form, or you can specify the size of the array and use the `new` keyword to initialize all array elements.

Specifying an array using literal values simply involves providing a comma-separated list of element values enclosed in curly braces, for example:

```
int[] myIntArray = {5, 9, 10, 2, 99};
```

Here `myIntArray` has five elements, each with an assigned integer value.

The other method requires the following syntax:

```
int[] myIntArray = new int[5];
```

Here, you use the `new` keyword to explicitly initialize the array and a constant value to define the size. This method results in all the array members being assigned a default value, which is 0 for numeric types. You can also use nonconstant variables for this initialization, for example:

```
int[] myIntArray = new int[arraySize];
```

You can also combine these two methods of initialization if you wish:

```
int[] myIntArray = new int[5] {5, 9, 10, 2, 99};
```

With this method the sizes *must* match. You can't, for example, write:

```
int[] myIntArray = new int[10] {5, 9, 10, 2, 99};
```

Here, the array is defined as having 10 members, but only 5 are defined, so compilation will fail. A side effect of this is that if you define the size using a variable that variable must be a constant, for example:

```
const int arraySize = 5;
int[] myIntArray = new int[arraySize] {5, 9, 10, 2, 99};
```

If you omit the `const` keyword, this code will fail.

As with other variable types, there is no need to initialize an array on the same line that you declare it. The following is perfectly legal:

```
int[] myIntArray;
myIntArray = new int[5];
```

You've done enough to look at an example, so it's time to try out some code. In the following Try It Out you create and use an array of strings, using the example from the introduction to this section.

Try It Out   Using an Array

1. Create a new console application called Ch05Ex04 in the directory C:\BegVCSharp\Chapter5.

2. Add the following code to Program.cs:

```
static void Main(string[] args)
{
    string[] friendNames = {"Robert Barwell", "Mike Parry",
                            "Jeremy Beacock"};
    int i;
    Console.WriteLine("Here are {0} of my friends:",
                        friendNames.Length);
    for (i = 0; i < friendNames.Length; i++)
    {
        Console.WriteLine(friendNames[i]);
    }
    Console.ReadKey();
}
```

3. Execute the code. The result is shown in Figure 5-9.

Figure 5-9

How It Works

This code sets up a string array with three values and lists them in the console in a for loop. Note that you have access to the number of elements in the array using friendNames.Length:

```
Console.WriteLine("Here are {0} of my friends:", friendNames.Length);
```

This is a handy way to get the size of an array.

Outputting values in a for loop is easy to get wrong. For example, try changing < to <= as follows:

```
for (i = 0; i <= friendNames.Length; i++)
{
    Console.WriteLine(friendNames[i]);
}
```

Compiling this results in the dialog shown in Figure 5-10 popping up.

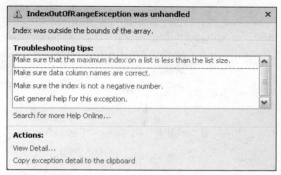

Figure 5-10

Here, you have attempted to access `friendNames[3]`. Remember, array indices start from 0, so the last element is `friendNames[2]`. If you attempt to access elements outside of the array size, the code will fail.

It just so happens that there is a more resilient method of accessing all the members of an array, using `foreach` loops.

foreach Loops

A `foreach` loop allows you to address each element in an array using this simple syntax:

```
foreach (<baseType> <name> in <array>)
{
   // can use <name> for each element
}
```

This loop will cycle through each element, placing each one in the variable <name> in turn, without danger of accessing illegal elements. You don't have to worry about how many elements there are in the array, and you can be sure that you'll get to use each one in the loop. Using this approach, you can modify the code in the last example as follows:

```
static void Main(string[] args)
{
    string[] friendNames = {"Robert Barwell", "Mike Parry",
                            "Jeremy Beacock"};
    Console.WriteLine("Here are {0} of my friends:",
                    friendNames.Length);
    foreach (string friendName in friendNames)
    {
        Console.WriteLine(friendName);
    }
    Console.ReadKey();
}
```

The output of this code will be exactly the same that of the previous Try It Out.

The main difference between using this method and a standard `for` loop is that `foreach` gives you *read-only* access to the array contents, so you can't change the values of any of the elements. You couldn't, for example, do the following:

```
foreach (string friendName in friendNames)
{
    friendName = "Rupert the bear";
}
```

If you try this, compilation will fail. If you use a simple `for` loop, however, you can assign values to array elements.

Multidimensional Arrays

From the title of this section, you would be forgiven for thinking that you are about to discover some low-budget science fiction addition to the C# language. In actual fact, a multidimensional array is simply one that uses multiple indices to access its elements.

For example, consider the situation in which you want to plot the height of a hill against the position measured. You might specify a position using two coordinates, x and y. You want to use these two coordinates as indices, such that an array called `hillHeight` would store the height at each pair of coordinates. This involves using multidimensional arrays.

A two-dimensional array such as this is declared as follows:

```
<baseType>[,] <name>;
```

Arrays of more dimensions simply require more commas; for example:

```
<baseType>[,,,] <name>;
```

This would declare a four-dimensional array.

Assigning values also uses a similar syntax, with commas separating sizes. To declare and initialize the two-dimensional array `hillHeight`, discussed previously, with a base type of `double`, an x size of 3, and a y size of 4 requires the following:

```
double[,] hillHeight = new double[3,4];
```

Alternatively, you can use literal values for initial assignment. Here, you use nested blocks of curly braces, separated by commas, for example:

```
double[,] hillHeight = {{1, 2, 3, 4}, {2, 3, 4, 5}, {3, 4, 5, 6}};
```

This array has the same dimensional sizes as the previous one, but has values explicitly defined.

To access individual elements of a multidimensional array, you simply specify the indices separated by commas; for example:

```
hillHeight[2,1]
```

You can then manipulate this element just as you can other elements.

This expression will access the second element of the third nested array as defined previously (the value will be 4). Remember that you start counting from 0 and that the first number is the nested array. In other words, the first number specifies the pair of curly braces, and the second number specifies the element within that pair of braces. You can represent this array visually, as shown in Figure 5-11.

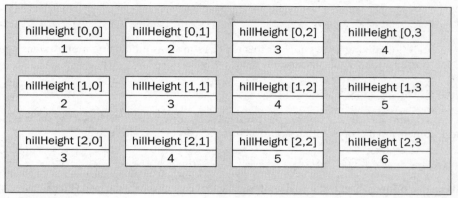

Figure 5-11

The `foreach` loop allows you access to all elements in a multidimensional way just as with single-dimensional arrays, for example:

```
double[,] hillHeight = {{1, 2, 3, 4}, {2, 3, 4, 5}, {3, 4, 5, 6}};
foreach (double height in hillHeight)
{
    Console.WriteLine("{0}", height);
}
```

The order in which the elements are output is the same as the order used to assign literal values

```
hillHeight[0,0]
hillHeight[0,1]
hillHeight[0,2]
hillHeight[0,3]
hillHeight[1,0]
hillHeight[1,1]
hillHeight[1,2]
```

and so on.

Arrays of Arrays

Multidimensional arrays, as discussed in the last section, are said to be *rectangular*. This is so because each "row" is the same size. Using the last example, you can have a y coordinate of 0 to 3 for any of the possible x coordinates.

111

It is also possible to have *jagged* arrays, where "rows" may be different sizes. To do this, you need to have an array where each element is another array. You could also have arrays of arrays of arrays if you want, or even more complex situations. However, note that all this is only possible if the arrays have the same base type.

The syntax for declaring arrays of arrays involves specifying multiple sets of square brackets in the declaration of the array, for example:

```
int[][] jaggedIntArray;
```

Unfortunately, initializing arrays such as this isn't as simple as initializing multidimensional arrays. You can't, for example, follow this declaration with:

```
jaggedIntArray = new int[3][4];
```

Even if you could do this, it wouldn't be that useful, because you can achieve the same effect with simple multidimensional arrays with less effort. You also can't use code such as:

```
jaggedIntArray = {{1, 2, 3}, {1}, {1, 2}};
```

You have two options. You can initialize the array that contains other arrays (I'll call these subarrays for clarity) and then initialize the subarrays in turn

```
jaggedIntArray = new int[2][];
jaggedIntArray[0] = new int[3];
jaggedIntArray[1] = new int[4];
```

or you can use a modified form of the preceding literal assignment:

```
jaggedIntArray = new int[3][] {new int[] {1, 2, 3}, new int[] {1},
                              new int[] {1, 2}};
```

This can be simplified if the array is initialized on the same line as it is declared, as follows:

```
int[][] jaggedIntArray = {new int[] {1, 2, 3}, new int[] {1}, new int[] {1, 2}};
```

You can use `foreach` loops with jagged arrays, but you often need to nest these to get to the actual data. For example, say you have the following jagged array that contains 10 arrays, each of which contains an array of integers that are divisors of an integer between 1 and 10:

```
int[][] divisors1To10 = {new int[] {1},
                         new int[] {1, 2},
                         new int[] {1, 3},
                         new int[] {1, 2, 4},
                         new int[] {1, 5},
                         new int[] {1, 2, 3, 6},
                         new int[] {1, 7},
                         new int[] {1, 2, 4, 8},
                         new int[] {1, 3, 9},
                         new int[] {1, 2, 5, 10}};
```

The following code will fail:

```
foreach (int divisor in divisors1To10)
{
    Console.WriteLine(divisor);
}
```

This is because the array `divisors1To10` contains `int[]` elements, not `int` elements. Instead, you have to loop through every subarray as well as through the array itself:

```
foreach (int[] divisorsOfInt in divisors1To10)
{
    foreach(int divisor in divisorsOfInt)
    {
        Console.WriteLine(divisor);
    }
}
```

As you can see, the syntax for using jagged arrays can quickly become complex! In most cases, it is easier to use rectangular arrays or a simpler storage method. However, there may well be situations in which you are forced to use this method, and a working knowledge can't hurt!

String Manipulation

Your use of strings so far has consisted of writing strings to the console, reading strings from the console, and concatenating strings using the + operator. In the course of programming more interesting applications, you will soon discover that the manipulation of strings is something that you end up doing *a lot*. Because of this, it is worth spending a few pages looking at some of the more common string manipulation techniques available in C#.

To start with, it is well worth noting that a `string` type variable can be treated as a read-only array of `char` variables. This means that you can access individual characters using syntax like:

```
string myString = "A string";
char myChar = myString[1];
```

However, you can't assign individual characters in this way.

To get a `char` array that you can write to, you can use the following code. This uses the `ToCharArray()` command of the array variable

```
string myString = "A string";
char[] myChars = myString.ToCharArray();
```

and then you can manipulate the `char` array in the standard way.

You can also use strings in `foreach` loops, for example:

```
foreach (char character in myString)
{
   Console.WriteLine("{0}", character);
}
```

As with arrays, you can also get the number of elements using `myString.Length`. This gives you the number of characters in the string, for example:

```
string myString = Console.ReadLine();
Console.WriteLine("You typed {0} characters.", myString.Length);
```

Other basic string manipulation techniques use commands with a format similar to this `<string>.ToCharArray()` command. Two simple, but useful, ones are `<string>.ToLower()` and `<string>.ToUpper()`. These enable strings to be converted into lower- and uppercase, respectively. To see why this is useful, consider the situation in which you want to check for a specific response from a user, for example the string `yes`. If you convert the string entered by the user into lowercase, then you can also check for the strings `YES`, `Yes`, `yeS`, and so on — you saw an example of this in the previous chapter if you recall:

```
string userResponse = Console.ReadLine();
if (userResponse.ToLower() == "yes")
{
   // Act on response.
}
```

Note that this command, like the others in this section, doesn't actually change the string to which it is applied. Instead, combining this command with a string results in a new string being created, which you can compare to another string (as shown above) or assign to another variable. This other variable may be the same one that is being operated on, for example:

```
userResponse = userResponse.ToLower();
```

This is an important point to remember, because just writing

```
userResponse.ToLower();
```

doesn't actually achieve very much!

There are other things you can do to ease the interpretation of user input. What if the user accidentally put an extra space at the beginning or end of their input? In this case, the preceding code won't work. You need to trim the string entered, which you can do using the `<string>.Trim()` command:

```
string userResponse = Console.ReadLine();
userResponse = userResponse.Trim();
if (userResponse.ToLower() == "yes")
{
   // Act on response.
}
```

Using this, you will also be able detect strings like:

```
"  YES"
"Yes "
```

You can also use these commands to remove any other characters, by specifying them in a `char` array, for example:

```
char[] trimChars = {' ', 'e', 's'};
string userResponse = Console.ReadLine();
userResponse = userResponse.ToLower();
userResponse = userResponse.Trim(trimChars);
if (userResponse == "y")
{
    // Act on response.
}
```

This gets rid of any occurrences of spaces, the letter "e," and the letter "s" from the beginning or end of your string. Providing that there isn't any other character in the string, this will result in the detection of strings such as

```
"Yeeeees"
"  y"
```

and so on.

You can also use the `<string>.TrimStart()` and `<string>.TrimEnd()` commands, which will trim spaces from the beginning and end of a string, respectively. These can also have `char` arrays specified.

There are two other string commands that you can use to manipulate the spacing of strings: `<string>.PadLeft()` and `<string>.PadRight()`. These allow you to add spaces to the left or right of a string to force it to the desired length. You use these as follows:

```
<string>.PadX(<desiredLength>);
```

For example:

```
myString = "Aligned";
myString = myString.PadLeft(10);
```

This would result in three spaces being added to the left of the word `Aligned` in `myString`. These methods can be useful for aligning strings in columns, which is particularly useful for placing number strings below others.

As with the trimming commands, you can also use these commands in a second way, by supplying the character to pad the string with. This involves a single `char`, not an array of `chars` as with trimming. For example:

```
myString = "Aligned";
myString = myString.PadLeft(10, '-');
```

This would add three dashes to the start of myString.

There are many more of these string manipulation commands, many of which are only useful in very specific situations. I'll discuss these as and when you use them in the forthcoming chapters. Before moving on, though, it is worth looking at one of the features of VS that you may have noticed over the course of the last few chapters, and especially this one. In the following Try It Out, you examine auto-completion in VS, where the IDE tries to help you out by suggesting what code you might like to insert.

Try It Out   Statement Auto-completion in VS

1. Create a new console application called Ch05Ex05 in the directory C:\BegVCSharp\Chapter5.

2. Type the following code to Program.cs, exactly as written, noting windows that pop up as you do so.

    ```csharp
    static void Main(string[] args)
    {
        string myString = "This is a test.";
        char[] separator = {' '};
        string[] myWords;
        myWords = myString.
    }
    ```

3. As you type the final period, note that the window shown in Figure 5-12 pops up.

Figure 5-12

4. Without moving the cursor, type "s". The pop-up window changes, and a yellow tooltip pop-up appears, as shown in Figure 5-13.

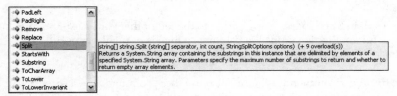

Figure 5-13

5. Type the following characters: (separator);. The code should look as follows, and the pop-up windows should disappear:

```
       static void Main(string[] args)
       {
           string myString = "This is a test.";
           char[] separator = {' '};
           string[] myWords;
           myWords = myString.Split(separator);
       }
```

6. Add the following code, noting the windows as they pop up:

```
       static void Main(string[] args)
       {
           string myString = "This is a test.";
           char[] separator = {' '};
           string[] myWords;
           myWords = myString.Split(separator);
           foreach (string word in myWords)
           {
               Console.WriteLine("{0}", word);
           }
           Console.ReadKey();
       }
```

7. Execute the code. The result is shown in Figure 5-14.

Figure 5-14

How It Works

There are two main points to note in this code. The first is the new string command you have used, and the second is the use of the auto-completion function in VS. You will tackle these one at a time.

The command you have used, `<string>.Split()`, converts a `string` into a `string` array by splitting it at the points specified. These points take the form of a `char` array, which in this case is simply populated by a single element, the space character:

```
       char[] separator = {' '};
```

The following code obtains the substrings you get when the string is split at each space, that is, you get an array of individual words:

```
       string[] myWords;
       myWords = myString.Split(separator);
```

Next, you loop through the words in this array using `foreach` and write each one to the console:

```
foreach (string word in myWords)
{
    Console.WriteLine("{0}", word);
}
```

Note that each word obtained will have no spaces, neither embedded in the word nor at either end. The separators are removed when you use `Split()`.

Next, on to the auto-completion. VS is a very intelligent package, and works out a lot of information about your code as you type it in. Even as you type the first character on a new line VS tries to help you, by suggesting that you might want to type a keyword, a variable name, a type name, and so on. Only three letters into the preceding code (`str`), VS has guessed that you want to type `string`. Even more useful is when you type variable names. In long pieces of code, you often forget the names of variables you want to use. Since VS pops up a list of these as you type, you can work along just fine without having to refer to earlier code.

By the time you type the period after `myString`, it knows that `myString` is a string, detects that you want to specify a string command, and presents the available options. At this point, you can stop typing, should you wish to, and select the command you want using the up and down arrow keys. As you move through what is available, VS tells you what the currently selected command means and what the syntax for using it is.

When you start typing more characters VS moves the selected command to the top of the commands you might mean automatically. Once it shows the command you want, you can simply carry on typing as if you'd typed the whole name, so typing " (" takes you straight to the point where you specify the additional information that some commands require — and VS even tells you the format this extra information must be in, presenting options for those commands that accept varying amounts of information.

This feature of VS (also known as IntelliSense) can come in very handy, and allows you to find out information about strange types with ease. You may find it interesting to look at all the commands that the `string` type exposes and experiment — nothing you do is going to break the computer, so play away!

Summary

In this chapter, you've spent some time expanding your current knowledge of variables and filling in some of the blanks from earlier on. Perhaps the most important topic covered in this chapter is type conversion, because this is one that will come back and haunt you throughout this book. Getting a sound grasp of the concepts involved now will make things a lot easier later!

You've also seen a few more variable types that you can use to help you to store data in a more developer-friendly way. You've seen how enumerations can make your code much more readable with easily discernable values, how structs can be used to combine multiple related data elements in one place, and how you can group similar data together in arrays. You see all of these types used many times throughout the rest of this book.

Finally, you looked at string manipulation, discussing some of the basic techniques and principles involved. There are many individual string commands available here, and you only examined a few, but you also saw how you can look at the available commands in VS. Using this technique, you can have some fun trying things out. At least one of the examples below can be solved using one or more string commands you haven't seen yet, but I'm not telling you which!

In this chapter, you extended your knowledge of variables to cover:

❑ Type conversions

❑ Enumerations

❑ Structs

❑ Arrays

❑ String manipulation

Exercises

1. Which of the following conversions can't be performed implicitly:

   ❑ int to short

   ❑ short to int

   ❑ bool to string

   ❑ byte to float

2. Give the code for a `color` enumeration based on the `short` type containing the colors of the rainbow plus black and white. Can this enumeration be based on the `byte` type?

3. Modify the Mandelbrot set generator example from the last chapter to use the following struct for complex numbers:

```
struct imagNum
{
    public double real, imag;
}
```

4. Will the following code compile? If not, why not?

```
string[] blab = new string[5]
string[5] = 5th string.
```

5. Write a console application that accepts a string from the user and outputs a string with the characters in reverse order.

6. Write a console application that accepts a string and replaces all occurrences of the string `no` with `yes`.

7. Write a console application that places double quotation marks around each word in a string.

Functions

All the code you have seen so far has taken the form of a single block, perhaps with some looping to repeat lines of code and branching to execute statements conditionally. If you've needed to perform an operation on your data, then this has meant placing the code required right where you want it to work.

This kind of code structure is limited. You will often find that some tasks, for example finding the highest value in an array, may need to be performed at several points in a program. You can just place identical (or near identical) sections of code in your application whenever necessary, but this has its own problems. Changing even one minor detail concerning a common task (to correct a code error, for example) may require changes to multiple sections of code, which may be spread throughout the application. Missing one of these could have dramatic consequences and cause the whole application to fail. In addition, the application could get very lengthy.

The solution to this problem is to use *functions*. Functions in C# are a means of providing blocks of code that can be executed at any point in an application.

> Functions of the specific type examined in this chapter are known as methods. However, this term has a very specific meaning in .NET programming that will only become clear later in this book, so for now this term will not be used.

For example, you could have a function that calculates the maximum value in an array. You can use this function from any point in your code, and use the same lines of code in each case. Since you only need to supply this code once, any changes you make to it will affect this calculation wherever it is used. This function can be thought of as containing *reusable* code.

Functions also have the advantage of making your code more readable, as you can use them to group related code together. If you do this, then your application body itself can be made very short, as the inner workings of the code are separated out. This is similar to the way in which you can collapse regions of code together in VS using the outline view, and it gives a more logical structure to your application.

Functions can also be used to create *multipurpose* code, allowing them to perform the same operations on varying data. You can supply a function with information to work with in the form of *parameters*, and you can obtain results from functions in the form of *return values*. In the preceding example, you could supply an array to search as a parameter and obtain the maximum value in the array as a return value. This means that you can use the same function to work with a different array each time. The parameters and return value of a function collectively define the *signature* of a function.

In this chapter, you:

❑ Look at how to define and use simple functions that don't accept or return any data.

❑ Look at the way you can transfer data to and from functions.

❑ Learn about the issue of *variable scope*. This concerns the way that data in a C# application is localized to specific regions of code, an issue that becomes especially important when you are separating your code into multiple functions.

❑ Take an in-depth look at an important function in C# applications: `Main()`. You see how you can use the built-in behavior of this function to make use of *command-line arguments*, which enable you to transfer information into applications when you run them.

❑ See an additional feature of the struct types that you saw in the last chapter, the fact that you can supply functions as members of struct types.

The chapter will end with two more advanced topics: *function overloading* and *delegates*.

❑ Function overloading is a technique that allows you to provide multiple functions with the same name, but different signatures.

❑ A delegate is a variable type that allows you to use functions indirectly. The same delegate can be used to call any function that matches a specific signature, giving you the ability to choose between several functions at runtime.

Defining and Using Functions

In this section, you see how you can add functions to your applications and then use (*call*) them from your code. You start with the basics, looking at simple functions that don't exchange any data with code that calls them, and then move on to look at more advanced function usage.

The following Try It Out will get things moving.

Try It Out   Defining and Using a Basic Function

1. Create a new console application called `Ch06Ex01` in the directory `C:\BegVCSharp\Chapter6`.

2. Add the following code to `Program.cs`:

```
class Program
{
    static void Write()
    {
        Console.WriteLine("Text output from function.");
    }

    static void Main(string[] args)
```

```
        {
            Write();
            Console.ReadKey();
        }
    }
```

3. Execute the code. The result is shown in Figure 6-1.

Figure 6-1

How It Works

The following four lines of your code define a function called `Write()`:

```
static void Write()
{
    Console.WriteLine("Text output from function.");
}
```

The code contained here simply outputs some text to the console window. However, this behavior isn't that important at the moment, because the focus here is on the mechanisms behind function definition and use.

The function definition here consists of the following:

❑   Two keywords, `static` and `void`

❑   A function name followed by parentheses, `Write()`

❑   A block of code to execute enclosed in curly braces

Function names are usually written in PascalCasing.

The code that defines the `Write()` function looks very similar to some of the other code in your application:

```
static void Main(string[] args)
{
    ...
}
```

This is so because all the code you have written so far (apart from type definitions) has been part of a function. This function, `Main()`, is (as suggested by the comment in the auto-generated code) the *entry point* function for a console application. When a C# application is executed, the entry point function it contains is called, and when this function is completed the application terminates. All C# executable code must have an entry point.

The only difference between the `Main()` function and your `Write()` function (apart from the lines of code they contain) is that there is some code inside the parentheses after the function name `Main`. This is how you specify parameters, which you see in more detail shortly.

As mentioned earlier, both `Main()` and `Write()` are defined using `static` and `void` keywords. The `static` keyword relates to object-oriented concepts, which you come back to later in the book. For now, you only need to remember that all the functions you use in your applications in this section of the book *must* use this keyword.

`void`, in contrast, is much simpler to explain. This keyword is to indicate the function does not return a value. Later on in this chapter, you see what you need to write when a function has a return value.

Moving on, the code that calls your function is:

```
Write();
```

You simply type the name of the function followed by empty parentheses. When program execution reaches this point the code in the `Write()` function will run.

Note that the parentheses used, both in the function definition and where the function is called, are mandatory. Try removing them if you like — the code won't compile.

Return Values

The simplest way of exchanging data with a function is to make use of a return value. Functions that have return values *evaluate* to that value, in exactly the same way as variables evaluate to the value they contain when you use them in expressions. Just like variables, return values have a type.

For example, you might have a function called `GetString()` whose return value is a string. You could use this in code, such as:

```
string myString;
myString = GetString();
```

Alternatively, you might have a function called `GetVal()` that returns a `double` value, which you could use in a mathematical expression:

```
double myVal;
double multiplier = 5.3;
myVal = GetVal() * multiplier;
```

When a function returns a value, you have to modify your function in two ways:

❑ Specify the type of the return value in the function declaration instead of using the `void` keyword

❑ Use the `return` keyword to end the function execution and transfer the return value to the calling code

In code terms, this looks like the following in a console application function of the type you've been looking at:

```
static <returnType> <functionName>()
{
    ...
    return <returnValue>;
}
```

The only limitation here is that `<returnValue>` must be a value that is either of type `<returnType>` or can be implicitly converted to that type. However, `<returnType>` can be any type you want, including the more complicated types you've seen.

This might be as simple as:

```
static double GetVal()
{
    return 3.2;
}
```

However, return values are usually the result of some processing carried out by the function; the above could be achieved just as easily by using a `const` variable.

When the `return` statement is reached, program execution returns to the calling code immediately. No lines of code after this statement will be executed. However, this doesn't mean that `return` statements can only be placed on the last line of a function body. You can use `return` earlier in the code, perhaps after performing some branching logic. Placing `return` in a `for` loop, an `if` block, or any other structure causes the structure to terminate immediately and the function to terminate. For example:

```
static double GetVal()
{

    double checkVal;
    // CheckVal assigned a value through some logic.
    if (checkVal < 5)
        return 4.7;

    return 3.2;
}
```

Here one of two values may be returned, depending on the value of `checkVal`.

The only restriction here is that a return statement must be processed before reaching the closing } of the function. The following is illegal:

```
static double GetVal()
{
    double checkVal;
    // CheckVal assigned a value through some logic.
    if (checkVal < 5)
        return 4.7;
}
```

If `checkVal` is >= 5, then no `return` statement is met, which isn't allowed. All processing paths must reach a `return` statement. In most cases, the compiler will detect this and give you the error "not all code paths return a value."

As a final note, `return` can be used in functions declared using the `void` keyword (that don't have a return value). If you do so, then the function will simply terminate. When you use return in this way, it is an error to provide a return value in between the `return` keyword and the semicolon that follows.

Parameters

When a function is to accept parameters, you must specify the following:

❑ A list of the parameters accepted by a function in its definition, along with the types of those parameters

❑ A matching list of parameters in each function call

This involves the following code:

```
static <returnType> <functionName>(<paramType> <paramName>, ...)
{
    ...
    return <returnValue>;
}
```

Where you can have any number of parameters, each with a type and a name. The parameters are separated using commas. Each of these parameters is accessible from code within the function as a variable.

For example, a simple function might take two `double` parameters and return their product:

```
static double Product(double param1, double param2)
{
    return param1 * param2;
}
```

The following Try It Out provides a more complex example.

Try It Out   Exchanging Data with a Function

1. Create a new console application called `Ch06Ex02` in the directory `C:\BegVCSharp\Chapter6`.

2. Add the following code to `Program.cs`:

```
class Program
{
    static int MaxValue(int[] intArray)
    {
        int maxVal = intArray[0];
        for (int i = 1; i < intArray.Length; i++)
        {
            if (intArray[i] > maxVal)
                maxVal = intArray[i];
        }
        return maxVal;
    }
```

```
static void Main(string[] args)
{
    int[] myArray = {1, 8, 3, 6, 2, 5, 9, 3, 0, 2};
    int maxVal = MaxValue(myArray);
    Console.WriteLine("The maximum value in myArray is {0}", maxVal);
    Console.ReadKey();
}
}
```

3.   Execute the code. The result is shown in Figure 6-2.

Figure 6-2

How It Works

This code contains a function that does what the example function discussed in the introduction to this chapter hoped to do. It accepts an array of integers as a parameter and returns the highest number in the array. The function definition is as follows:

```
static int MaxValue(int[] intArray)
{
    int maxVal = intArray[0];
    for (int i = 1; i < intArray.Length; i++)
    {
        if (intArray[i] > maxVal)
            maxVal = intArray[i];
    }
    return maxVal;
}
```

The function, MaxValue(), has a single parameter defined, an int array called intArray. It also has a return type of int. The calculation of the maximum value is simple. A local integer variable called maxVal is initialized to the first value in the array, and then this value is compared with each of the subsequent elements in the array. If an element contains a higher value than maxVal, then this value replaces the current value of maxVal. When the loop finishes, maxVal contains the highest value in the array, and is returned using the return statement.

The code in Main() declares and initializes a simple integer array to use with the MaxValue() function:

```
int[] myArray = {1, 8, 3, 6, 2, 5, 9, 3, 0, 2};
```

The call to MaxValue() is used to assign a value to the int variable maxVal:

```
int maxVal = MaxValue(myArray);
```

Next, you write this value to the screen using Console.WriteLine():

```
Console.WriteLine("The maximum value in myArray is {0}", maxVal);
```

Parameter Matching

When you call a function, you must match the parameters as specified in the function definition exactly. This means matching the parameter types, the number of parameters, and the order of the parameters. This means, for example, that the following function

```
static void MyFunction(string myString, double myDouble)
{
    ...
}
```

can't be called using:

```
MyFunction (2.6, "Hello");
```

Here, you are attempting to pass a `double` value as the first parameter and a `string` value as the second parameter, which is not the order in which the parameters are defined in the function definition.

You also can't use:

```
MyFunction("Hello");
```

Here, you are only passing a single `string` parameter, where two parameters are required.

Attempting to use either of the two preceding function calls will result in a compiler error, because the compiler forces you to match the signatures of the functions you use.

Going back to the example, this means that `MaxValue()` can only be used to obtain the maximum `int` in an array of `int` values. If you replace the code in `Main()` with the following code

```
static void Main(string[] args)
{
    double[] myArray = {1.3, 8.9, 3.3, 6.5, 2.7, 5.3};
    double maxVal = MaxValue(myArray);
    Console.WriteLine("The maximum value in myArray is {0}", maxVal);
    Console.ReadKey();
}
```

then the code won't compile, because the parameter type is wrong.

Later on in this chapter, in the "Overloading Functions" section, you see a useful technique for getting round this problem.

Parameter Arrays

C# allows you to specify one (and only one) special parameter for a function. This parameter, which must be the last parameter in the function definition, is known as a *parameter array*. Parameter arrays allow you to call functions using a variable amount of parameters and are defined using the `params` keyword.

Parameter arrays can be a useful way to simplify your code, because you don't have to pass arrays from your calling code. Instead, you pass several parameters of the same type that are placed in an array that you can use from within your function.

The following code is required to define a function that uses a parameter array:

```
static <returnType> <functionName>(<p1Type> <p1Name>, ... ,
                                   params <type>[] <name>)
{
   ...
   return <returnValue>;
}
```

You can call this function using code like:

```
<functionName>(<p1>, ... , <val1>, <val2>, ...)
```

Here `<val1>`, `<val2>`, and so on are values of type `<type>`, which are used to initialize the `<name>` array. The number of parameters that you can specify here is almost limitless; the only restriction is that they are all of type `<type>`. You can even specify no parameters at all.

This final point makes parameter arrays particularly useful for specifying additional information for functions to use in their processing. For example, say that you have a function called `GetWord()` that takes a `string` value as its first parameter and returns the first word in the string:

```
string firstWord = GetWord("This is a sentence.");
```

Here `firstWord` will be assigned the string `This`.

You might add a `params` parameter to `GetWord()`, allowing you to optionally select an alternative word to return by its index:

```
string firstWord = GetWord("This is a sentence.", 2);
```

Assuming that you start counting at 1 for the first word, this would result in `firstWord` being assigned the string `is`.

You might also add the capability to limit the amount of characters returned in a third parameter, also accessible through the `params` parameter:

```
string firstWord = GetWord("This is a sentence.", 4, 3);
```

Here `firstWord` would be assigned the string `sen`.

Here's a full example. In the following Try It Out you define and use a function with a `params` type parameter.

Exchanging Data with a Function Part 2

1. Create a new console application called `Ch06Ex03` in the directory `C:\BegVCSharp\Chapter6`.

2. Add the following code to `Program.cs`:

```
class Program
{
    static int SumVals(params int[] vals)
    {
        int sum = 0;
        foreach (int val in vals)
        {
            sum += val;
        }
        return sum;
    }

    static void Main(string[] args)
    {
        int sum = SumVals(1, 5, 2, 9, 8);
        Console.WriteLine("Summed Values = {0}", sum);
        Console.ReadKey();
    }
}
```

3. Execute the code. The result is shown in Figure 6-3.

Figure 6-3

How It Works

In this example, the function `SumVals()` is defined using the `params` keyword to accept any number of `int` parameters (and no others):

```
static int SumVals(params int[] vals)
{
    ...
}
```

The code in this function simply iterates through the value in the `vals` array and adds the values together, returning the result.

In `Main()`, you call this function with five integer parameters:

```
int sum = SumVals (1, 5, 2, 9, 8);
```

However, you could just as easily have called this function with none, one, two, or a hundred integer parameters — there is no limit to the amount you can specify.

Reference and Value Parameters

All the functions defined so far in this chapter have had *value* parameters. What I mean by this is that when you have used parameters you have passed a value into a variable used by the function. Any changes made to this variable in the function have *no effect* on the parameter specified in the function call. For example, consider a function that doubles and displays the value of a passed parameter:

```
static void ShowDouble(int val)
{
    val *= 2;
    Console.WriteLine("val doubled = {0}", val);
}
```

Here, the parameter, val, is doubled in this function. If you call it in the following way:

```
int myNumber = 5;
Console.WriteLine("myNumber = {0}", myNumber);
ShowDouble(myNumber);
Console.WriteLine("myNumber = {0}", myNumber);
```

The text output to the console is as follows:

```
myNumber = 5
val doubled = 10
myNumber = 5
```

Calling showDouble() with myNumber as a parameter doesn't affect the value of myNumber in Main(), even though the parameter it is assigned to, val, is doubled.

This is all very well, but if you *want* the value of myNumber to change you have a problem. You could use a function that returns a new value for myNumber, for example:

```
static int DoubleNum(int val)
{
    val *= 2;
    return val;
}
```

You could call this function using:

```
int myNumber = 5;
Console.WriteLine("myNumber = {0}", myNumber);
myNumber = DoubleNum(myNumber);
Console.WriteLine("myNumber = {0}", myNumber);
```

But this code is hardly intuitive and won't cope with changing the values of multiple variables used as parameters (as functions have only one return value).

Instead, you want to pass the parameter by *reference*. This means that the function will work with exactly the same variable as the one used in the function call, not just a variable that has the same value. Any changes made to this variable will, therefore, be reflected in the value of the variable used as a parameter. To do this, you simply have to use the ref keyword to specify the parameter:

```
static void ShowDouble(ref int val)
{
   val *= 2;
   Console.WriteLine("val doubled = {0}", val);
}
```

And again in the function call (this is mandatory, as the fact that the parameter is a `ref` parameter is part of the function signature):

```
int myNumber = 5;
Console.WriteLine("myNumber = {0}", myNumber);
ShowDouble(ref myNumber);
Console.WriteLine("myNumber = {0}", myNumber);
```

The text output to the console is now:

```
myNumber = 5
val doubled = 10
myNumber = 10
```

This time `myNumber` has been modified by `ShowDouble()`.

There are two limitations on the variable used as a `ref` parameter. First, the function *may* result in a change to the value of a reference parameter, so you must use a *nonconstant* variable in the function call. The following is therefore illegal:

```
const int myNumber = 5;
Console.WriteLine("myNumber = {0}", myNumber);
ShowDouble(ref myNumber);
Console.WriteLine("myNumber = {0}", myNumber);
```

Second, you must use an initialized variable. C# doesn't allow you to assume that a `ref` parameter will be initialized in the function that uses it. The following code is also illegal:

```
int myNumber;
ShowDouble(ref myNumber);
Console.WriteLine("myNumber = {0}", myNumber);
```

Out Parameters

In addition to passing values by reference, you can also specify that a given parameter is an *out* parameter by using the `out` keyword, which is used in the same way as the `ref` keyword (as a modifier to the parameter in the function definition and in the function call). In effect, this gives you almost exactly the same behavior as a reference parameter in that the value of the parameter at the end of the function execution is returned to the variable used in the function call. However, there are important differences:

❑ Whereas it is illegal to use an unassigned variable as a `ref` parameter, you can use an unassigned variable as an `out` parameter.

❑ In addition, an `out` parameter must be treated as an unassigned value by the function that uses it.

This means that while it is permissible for calling code to use an assigned variable as an `out` parameter, the value stored in this variable will be lost when the function executes.

As an example, consider an extension to the `MaxValue()` function you saw earlier, which returns the maximum value of an array. You modify the function slightly so that you obtain the index of the element with the maximum value within the array. To keep things simple, you obtain just the index of the first occurrence of this value when there are multiple elements with the maximum value. To do this, you add an out parameter by modifying the function as follows:

```
static int MaxValue(int[] intArray, out int maxIndex)
{
    int maxVal = intArray[0];
    maxIndex = 0;
    for (int i = 1; i < intArray.Length; i++)
    {
        if (intArray[i] > maxVal)
        {
            maxVal = intArray[i];
            maxIndex = i;
        }
    }
    return maxVal;
}
```

You might use this function as follows:

```
int[] myArray = {1, 8, 3, 6, 2, 5, 9, 3, 0, 2};
int maxIndex;
Console.WriteLine("The maximum value in myArray is {0}",
                MaxValue(myArray, out maxIndex));
Console.WriteLine("The first occurrence of this value is at element {0}",
                maxIndex + 1);
```

This results in:

```
The maximum value in myArray is 9
The first occurrence of this value is at element 7
```

An important point to note here is that you must use the `out` keyword in the function call, just as with the `ref` keyword.

Note that I've added one to the value of maxIndex returned here when it is displayed on screen. This is to translate the index to a more readable form, so that the first element in the array is referred to element 1 rather than element 0.

Variable Scope

Throughout the last section, you may have been wondering why exchanging data with functions is necessary. The reason is that variables in C# are only accessible from localized regions of code. A given variable is said to have a *scope* from where it is accessible.

Variable scope is an important subject and one best introduced with an example. The following Try It Out illustrates a situation in which a variable is defined in one scope, and an attempt to use it is made in a different scope.

Try It Out   Defining and Using a Basic Function

1.   Make the following changes to Ch06Ex01 in Program.cs:

```
class Program
{
   static void Write()
   {
      Console.WriteLine("myString = {0}", myString);
   }

   static void Main(string[] args)
   {
      string myString = "String defined in Main()";
      Write();
      Console.ReadKey();
   }
}
```

2.   Compile the code, and note the error and warning that appear in the task list:

```
The name 'myString' does not exist in the current context
The variable 'myString' is assigned but its value is never used
```

How It Works

So, what went wrong? Well, the variable myString defined in the main body of your application (the Main() function) isn't accessible from the Write() function.

The reason for this inaccessibility is that variables have a scope within which they are valid. This scope encompasses the code block that they are defined in and any directly nested code blocks. The blocks of code in functions are separate from the blocks of code from which they are called. Inside Write() the name myString is undefined, and the myString variable defined in Main() is *out of scope* — it can only be used from within Main().

In fact, you can have a completely separate variable in Write() called myString. Try modifying the code as follows:

```
class Program
{
   static void Write()
   {
      string myString = "String defined in Write()";
      Console.WriteLine("Now in Write()");
      Console.WriteLine("myString = {0}", myString);
   }

   static void Main(string[] args)
   {
```

```
        string myString = "String defined in Main()";
        Write();
        Console.WriteLine("\nNow in Main()");
        Console.WriteLine("myString = {0}", myString);
        Console.ReadKey();
    }
}
```

This code does compile, and it results in the output shown in Figure 6-4.

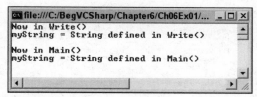

Figure 6-4

The operations performed by this code are:

- ❏ `Main()` defines and initializes a string variable called `myString`.

- ❏ `Main()` transfers control to `Write()`.

- ❏ `Write()` defines and initializes a string variable called `myString`, which is a different variable to the `myString` defined in `Main()`.

- ❏ `Write()` outputs a string to the console containing the value of `myString` as defined in `Write()`.

- ❏ `Write()` transfers control back to `Main()`.

- ❏ `Main()` outputs a string to the console containing the value of `myString` as defined in `Main()`.

Variables whose scope covers a single function in this way are known as *local* variables. It is also possible to have *global* variables, whose scope covers multiple functions. Modify the code as follows:

```
class Program
{
    static string myString;

    static void Write()
    {
        string myString = "String defined in Write()";
        Console.WriteLine("Now in Write()");
        Console.WriteLine("Local myString = {0}", myString);
        Console.WriteLine("Global myString = {0}", Program.myString);
    }

    static void Main(string[] args)
    {
        string myString = "String defined in Main()";
```

```
        Program.myString = "Global string";
        Write();
        Console.WriteLine("\nNow in Main()");
        Console.WriteLine("Local myString = {0}", myString);
        Console.WriteLine("Global myString = {0}", Program.myString);
        Console.ReadKey();
    }
}
```

The result is now as shown in Figure 6-5.

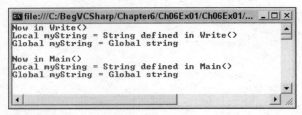

Figure 6-5

Here, you have added another variable called myString, this time further up the hierarchy of names in the code. This variable is defined as follows:

```
        static string myString;
```

Note that again you require the static keyword here. Again, I'm not going to say any more about this at this point other than that in this type of console application, you *must* use either the static or const keyword for global variables of this form. If you want to modify the value of the global variable, you need to use static, because const prohibits the value of the variable changing.

To differentiate between this variable and the local variables in Main() and Write() with the same names, you have to classify the variable name using a fully qualified name, as introduced in Chapter 3. Here, you refer to the global version as Program.myString. Note that this is only necessary when you have global and local variables with the same name, if there was no local myString variable, you could simply use myString to refer to the global variable, rather than Program.myString. When you have a local variable with the same name as a global variable, the global variable is said to be *hidden*.

The value of the global variable is set in Main() with

```
        Program.myString = "Global string";
```

and accessed in Write() with:

```
        Console.WriteLine("Global myString = {0}", Program.myString);
```

Now, you may be wondering why you shouldn't just use this technique to exchange data with functions, rather than the parameter passing you saw earlier; there are indeed situations in which this is the preferable way to exchange data, but there are just as many (if not more) where it isn't. The choice of whether to use global variables depends on the intended use of the function in question. The problem with using global variables is that they are generally unsuitable for "general-purpose" functions, which are capable of working with whatever data you supply, not just data in a specific global variable. You look at this in more depth a little later.

Variable Scope in Other Structures

Before moving on, it is worth noting that one of the points made in the last section has consequences above and beyond variable scope between functions. I stated that the scope of variables encompasses the code block that they are defined in and any directly nested code blocks. This also applies to other code blocks, such as those in branching and looping structures. Consider the following code:

```
int i;
for (i = 0; i < 10; i++)
{
    string text = "Line " + Convert.ToString(i);
    Console.WriteLine("{0}", text);
}
Console.WriteLine("Last text output in loop: {0}", text);
```

Here, the string variable `text` is local to the `for` loop. This code won't compile, because the call to `Console.WriteLine()` that occurs outside of this loop attempts to use the variable `text`, which is out of scope outside of the loop. Try modifying the code as follows:

```
int i;
string text;
for (i = 0; i < 10; i++)
{
    text = "Line " + Convert.ToString(i);
    Console.WriteLine("{0}", text);
}
Console.WriteLine("Last text output in loop: {0}", text);
```

This code will also fail. The reason for this is that variables must be declared and be initialized before use, and `text` is only initialized in the `for` loop. The value assigned to text is lost when the loop block is exited. However, you can also make the following change:

```
int i;
string text = "";
for (i = 0; i < 10; i++)
{
    text = "Line " + Convert.ToString(i);
    Console.WriteLine("{0}", text);
}
Console.WriteLine("Last text output in loop: {0}", text);
```

This time `text` is initialized outside of the loop, and you have access to its value. The result of this simple code is shown in Figure 6-6.

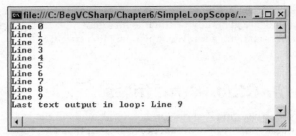

Figure 6-6

Here, the last value assigned to `text` in the loop is accessible from outside the loop.

As you can see, this topic requires a bit of work to come to grips with. It is not immediately obvious why, in the light of the earlier example, `text` doesn't retain the empty string it is assigned before the loop in the code after the loop.

The explanation for this behavior concerns the memory allocation for the `text` variable, and indeed any variable. Simply declaring a simple variable type doesn't result in very much happening. It is only when values are assigned to the variable that values are allocated a place in memory to be stored. When this allocation takes place inside a loop, the value is essentially defined as a local value and goes out of scope outside of the loop.

Even though the variable itself isn't localized to the loop, the value it contains is. However, assigning a value outside of the loop ensures that the value is local to the main code, and it is still in scope inside the loop. This means that the variable doesn't go out of scope before the main code block is exited, so you have access to its value outside of the loop.

Luckily for you, the C# compiler will detect variable scope problems, and responding to the error messages it generates certainly helps you to understand the topic of variable scope.

As a final note, you should be aware of *best practice*. In general, it is worth declaring and initializing all variables before any code blocks that use them. An exception to this is when you declare looping variables as part of a loop block, for example:

```
for (int i = 0; i < 10; i++)
{
    ...
}
```

Here `i` is localized to the looping code block, but this is fine, because you will rarely require access to this counter from external code.

Parameters and Return Values versus Global Data

In this section, you take a closer look at exchanging data with functions via global data and via parameters and return values. To recap, consider the following code:

```
class Program
{
    static void ShowDouble(ref int val)
    {
        val *= 2;
        Console.WriteLine("val doubled = {0}", val);
    }

    static void Main(string[] args)
    {
        int val = 5;
        Console.WriteLine("val = {0}", val);
        ShowDouble(ref val);
        Console.WriteLine("val = {0}", val);
    }
}
```

Note that this code is slightly different from the code you saw earlier in this chapter, when you used the variable name myNumber *in* Main(). *This illustrates the fact that local variables can have identical names and yet not interfere with each other. It also means that the two code samples shown here are more similar, allowing you to focus more on the specific differences without worrying about variable names.*

And compare it with this code:

```
class Program
{
    static int val;

    static void ShowDouble()
    {
        val *= 2;
        Console.WriteLine("val doubled = {0}", val);
    }

    static void Main(string[] args)
    {
        val = 5;
        Console.WriteLine("val = {0}", val);
        ShowDouble();
        Console.WriteLine("val = {0}", val);
    }
}
```

The results of both of these showDouble() functions are identical.

Now, there are no hard and fast rules for using one method rather than another, and both techniques are perfectly valid. However, there are some guidelines you might like to consider.

To start with, as mentioned when this topic was first introduced, the ShowDouble() version that uses the global value will only ever use the global variable val. To use this version, you *must* use this global variable. This limits the versatility of the function slightly and means that you must continuously copy the global variable value into other variables if you intend to store the results. In addition, global data might be modified by code elsewhere in your application, which could cause unpredicted results (values might change without you realizing this until it's too late).

However, this loss of versatility can often be a bonus. There are times when you only ever want to use a function for one purpose, and using a global data store reduces the possibility that you will make an error in a function call, perhaps passing it the wrong variable.

Of course, it could also be argued that this simplicity actually makes your code more difficult to understand. Explicitly specifying parameters allows you to see at a glance what is changing. If you see a call that reads `myFunction(val1, out val2)`, you instantly know that `val1` and `val2` are the important variables to consider and that `val2` will be assigned a new value when the function is completed. Conversely, if this function took no parameters, you would be unable to make any assumptions as to what data it manipulated.

Finally, it should be remembered that using global data isn't always possible. Later on in this book, you will see code written in different files and/or belonging to different namespaces communicating with each other via functions. In cases such as this, the code is often separated to such a degree that there is no obvious choice for a global storage location.

So, to summarize, feel free to use either technique to exchange data. I would, in general, urge you to use parameters rather than global data, but there are certainly cases where global data might be more suitable, and it certainly isn't an error to use this technique.

The Main() Function

Now that you've covered most of the simple techniques used in the creation and use of functions, it's time to go back and take a closer look at the `Main()` function.

Earlier, you saw that `Main()` is the entry point for a C# application and that the execution of this function encompasses the execution of the application. That is to say that when execution is initiated, the `Main()` function executes, and when the `Main()` function finishes, execution ends. You also saw that this function has a parameter, `string[] args`, but I haven't explained what this parameter represents yet. In this section, you see what this parameter is and how you use it.

Note that there are four possible signatures that you can use for the `Main()` *function:*

- ❑   `static void Main()`
- ❑   `static void Main(string[] args)`
- ❑   `static int Main()`
- ❑   `static int Main(string[] args)`

You can, if you wish, omit the `args` *argument discussed here. The reason you've used the version with this argument up till now is that it is the version that is generated automatically for you when you create a console application in VS.*

The third and fourth versions shown above return an int *value, which can be used to signify how the application terminates, often used as an indication of an error (although this is by no means mandatory). In general, returning a value of 0 reflects normal termination (that is, the application has completed and can terminate safely).*

The args parameter of Main() is a method for accepting information from outside the application, specified at runtime. This information takes the form of *command-line parameters*.

You may well have come across command-line parameters already. When you execute an application from the command line, you are often able to specify information directly, such as a file to load on application execution. As an example, consider the Notepad application in Windows. You can run this application simply by typing **Notepad** in a command prompt window or in the window that appears when you select the Run option from the Windows Start Menu. You can also type something like **Notepad "myfile.txt"** in these locations. The result of this is that Notepad will load the file myfile.txt when it runs or offer to create this file if it doesn't already exist. Here, "myfile.txt" is a command-line argument. You can write console applications that work in much the same way by making use of the args parameter.

When a console application is executed, any command-line parameters that are specified are placed in this args array. You can then use these parameters in your application as required.

Here's an example of this in action. In the following Try It Out, you'll be able to specify any number of command-line arguments, each of which will be output to the console.

Try It Out   Command-Line Arguments

1. Create a new console application called Ch06Ex04 in the directory C:\BegVCSharp\Chapter6.

2. Add the following code to Program.cs:

```
class Program
{
    static void Main(string[] args)
    {
        Console.WriteLine("{0} command line arguments were specified:",
                          args.Length);
        foreach (string arg in args)
            Console.WriteLine(arg);
        Console.ReadKey();
    }
}
```

3. Open up the property pages for the project (right-click on the Ch06Ex04 project name in the Solution Explorer window and select Properties).

4. Select the Debug page and add whatever command-line arguments you want to the Command line arguments setting. An example is shown in Figure 6-7.

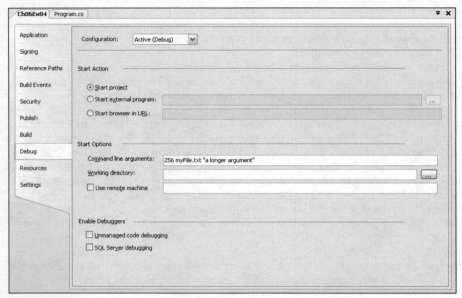

Figure 6-7

5. Run the application. The output is shown in Figure 6-8.

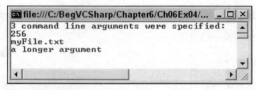

Figure 6-8

How It Works

The code used here is very simple:

```
Console.WriteLine("{0} command line arguments were specified:",
                  args.Length);
foreach (string arg in args)
   Console.WriteLine(arg);
```

You're just using the `args` parameter as you would any other string array. You're not doing anything fancy with the arguments, you're just writing whatever is specified to the screen.

In this example, you supplied the arguments via the project properties in VS. This is a handy way of using the same command-line arguments whenever you run the application from VS, rather than having to type them at a command-line prompt every time. The same result could be obtained by opening a command prompt window in the same directory as the project output (`C:\BegCSharp\Chapter6\Ch06Ex04\bin\Debug`) and typing the following:

```
Ch06Ex04 256 myFile.txt "a longer argument"
```

Note that each argument is separated from the next by spaces. If you want to supply an argument that includes spaces, you can enclose it in double quotation marks, which will prevent it from being interpreted as multiple arguments.

Struct Functions

In the last chapter you looked at struct types for storing multiple data elements in one place. Structs are actually capable of a lot more than this. One important extra capability they offer is the ability to contain functions as well as data. This is something that may seem a little strange at first, but it is in fact very useful indeed.

As a simple example, consider the following struct:

```
struct customerName
{
    public string firstName, lastName;
}
```

If you have variables of type `customerName`, and you want to output a full name to the console, you are forced to build the name from its component parts. You might use the following syntax for a `customerName` variable called `myCustomer`, for example:

```
customerName myCustomer;
myCustomer.firstName = "John";
myCustomer.lastName = "Franklin";
Console.WriteLine("{0} {1}", myCustomer.firstName, myCustomer.lastName);
```

By adding functions to structs, you can simplify this by centralizing the processing of common tasks such as this. You can add a suitable function to the struct type as follows:

```
struct customerName
{
    public string firstName, lastName;

    public string Name ()
    {
        return firstName + " " + lastName;
    }
}
```

This looks much like any other function you've looked at in this chapter, except that you haven't used the `static` modifier. The reasons for this will become clear later in the book, for now it is enough to know that this keyword isn't required for struct functions. You can use this function as follows:

```
customerName myCustomer;
myCustomer.firstName = "John";
myCustomer.lastName = "Franklin";
Console.WriteLine(myCustomer.Name());
```

This syntax is much simpler, and much easier to understand, than the earlier one.

An important point to note here is that the `Name()` function has direct access to the `firstName` and `lastName` struct members. Within the `customerName` struct, they can be thought of as global.

Overloading Functions

Earlier in this chapter, you saw how you must match the signature of a function when you call it. This implied that you would need to have separate functions to operate on different types of variable. Function overloading provides you with the ability to create multiple functions with the same name, but each working with different parameter types.

For example, earlier you used the following code, which contained a function called `MaxValue()`:

```
class Program
{
    static int MaxValue(int[] intArray)
    {
        int maxVal = intArray[0];
        for (int i = 1; i < intArray.Length; i++)
        {
            if (intArray[i] > maxVal)
                maxVal = intArray[i];
        }
        return maxVal;
    }

    static void Main(string[] args)
    {
        int[] myArray = {1, 8, 3, 6, 2, 5, 9, 3, 0, 2};
        int maxVal = MaxValue(myArray);
        Console.WriteLine("The maximum value in myArray is {0}", maxVal);
        Console.ReadKey();
    }
}
```

This function can only be used with arrays of `int` values. Now, you could provide different named functions for different parameter types, perhaps renaming the above function as `IntArrayMaxValue()` and adding functions such as `DoubleArrayMaxValue()` to work with other types. Alternatively, you could just add the following function to your code:

```
...
        static double MaxValue(double[] doubleArray)
        {
            double maxVal = doubleArray[0];
            for (int i = 1; i < doubleArray.Length; i++)
            {
                if (doubleArray[i] > maxVal)
                    maxVal = doubleArray[i];
            }
            return maxVal;
        }
...
```

The difference here is that you are using `double` values. The function name, `MaxValue()`, is the same, but (crucially) its *signature* is different. It would be an error to define two functions with the same name and signature, but since these two functions have different signatures, this is fine.

Now, you have two versions of `MaxValue()`, which accept `int` and `double` arrays, and return an `int` or `double` maximum, respectively.

The beauty of this type of code is that you don't have to explicitly specify which of these two functions you wish to use. You simply provide an array parameter, and the correct function will be executed depending on the type of the parameter used.

At this point, it is worth noting another feature of the IntelliSense feature in VS. If you have the two functions shown above in an application and then proceed to type the name of the function in (for example) `Main()`, VS will show you the available overloads for the function. If you type the following:

```
        double result = MaxValue(
```

VS gives you information about both versions of `MaxValue()`, which you can scroll between using the up and down arrow keys, as shown in Figure 6-9.

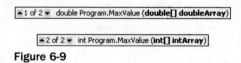

Figure 6-9

All aspects of the function signature are included when overloading functions. You might, for example, have two different functions that take parameters by value and by reference, respectively:

```
static void ShowDouble(ref int val)
{
    ...
}
```

```
static void ShowDouble(int val)
{
    ...
}
```

The choice as to which of these versions to use is based purely on whether the function call contains the `ref` keyword. The following would call the reference version

```
ShowDouble(ref val);
```

and the following would call the value version:

```
ShowDouble(val);
```

Alternatively, you could have functions that differ in the number of parameters they require, and so on.

Delegates

A *delegate* is a type that enables you to store references to functions. Although this sounds quite involved, the mechanism is surprisingly simple. The most important purpose of delegates won't become clear until later in this book when you look at events and event handling, but you can get a fair amount of mileage by looking at delegates here. When you come to use them later on, they'll look familiar, which will make some more complicated topics a lot easier to comprehend.

Delegates are declared much like functions, but with no function body and using the `delegate` keyword. The delegate declaration specifies a function signature consisting of a return type and the parameter list. After defining a delegate, you can declare a variable with the type of that delegate. You can then initialize this variable as a reference to any function that has the same signature as that delegate. Once you have done this, you can call that function by using the delegate variable as if it were a function.

When you have a variable that refers to a function, you can also perform other operations that would be impossible by any other means. For example, you can pass a delegate variable to a function as a parameter, then that function can use the delegate to call whatever function it refers to, without having knowledge as to what function will be called until runtime.

The following Try It Out gives an example of using a delegate to access one of two functions.

Try It Out   **Using a Delegate to Call a Function**

1. Create a new console application called Ch06Ex05 in the directory C:\BegVCSharp\Chapter6.

2. Add the following code to Program.cs:

```
class Program
{
    delegate double ProcessDelegate(double param1, double param2);

    static double Multiply(double param1, double param2)
    {
        return param1 * param2;
    }

    static double Divide(double param1, double param2)
    {
        return param1 / param2;
```

```
        }

        static void Main(string[] args)
        {
            ProcessDelegate process;
            Console.WriteLine("Enter 2 numbers separated with a comma:");
            string input = Console.ReadLine();
            int commaPos = input.IndexOf(',');
            double param1 = Convert.ToDouble(input.Substring(0, commaPos));
            double param2 = Convert.ToDouble(input.Substring(commaPos + 1,
                                                input.Length - commaPos - 1));
            Console.WriteLine("Enter M to multiply or D to divide:");
            input = Console.ReadLine();
            if (input == "M")
                process = new ProcessDelegate(Multiply);
            else
                process = new ProcessDelegate(Divide);
            Console.WriteLine("Result: {0}", process(param1, param2));
            Console.ReadKey();
        }
    }
```

3.   Execute the code. The result is shown in Figure 6-10.

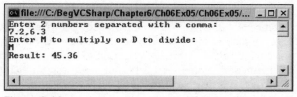

Figure 6-10

How It Works

This code defines a delegate (`ProcessDelegate`) whose signature matches that of the two functions (`Multiply()` and `Divide()`). The delegate definition is:

```
delegate double ProcessDelegate(double param1, double param2);
```

The `delegate` keyword specifies that the definition is for a delegate, rather than a function (the definition appears in the same place as a function definition might). Next, you have a signature that specifies a `double` return value and two `double` parameters. The actual names used are arbitrary, so you can call the delegate type and parameter name whatever you like. Here, you've used a delegate name of `ProcessDelegate` and double parameters called `param1` and `param2`.

The code in `Main()` starts by declaring a variable using the new delegate type:

```
static void Main(string[] args)
{
    ProcessDelegate process;
```

Next, you have some fairly standard C# code that requests two numbers separated by a comma and places these numbers in two `double` variables:

```
Console.WriteLine("Enter 2 numbers separated with a comma:");
string input = Console.ReadLine();
int commaPos = input.IndexOf(',');
double param1 = Convert.ToDouble(input.Substring(0, commaPos));
double param2 = Convert.ToDouble(input.Substring(commaPos + 1,
                                    input.Length - commaPos - 1));
```

Note that, for demonstration purposes, I've included no user input validation here. If this were "real" code, you'd spend much more time ensuring that you got valid values in the local param1 and param2 variables.

Next, you ask the user whether to multiply or divide these numbers:

```
Console.WriteLine("Enter M to multiply or D to divide:");
input = Console.ReadLine();
```

Based on the user's choice you initialize the `process` delegate variable:

```
if (input == "M")
    process = new ProcessDelegate(Multiply);
else
    process = new ProcessDelegate(Divide);
```

To assign a function reference to a delegate variable, you use slightly odd looking syntax. Much like assigning array values, you must use the `new` keyword to create a new delegate. After this keyword, you specify the delegate type and supply a parameter referring to the function you want to use, namely the `Multiply()` or `Divide()` function. Note that this parameter doesn't match the parameters of the delegate type or the target function, it is a syntax unique to delegate assignment. The parameter is simply the name of the function to use, without any parentheses.

Finally, you call the chosen function using the delegate. The same syntax works here, regardless of which function the delegate refers to:

```
Console.WriteLine("Result: {0}", process(param1, param2));
Console.ReadKey();
    }
```

Here, you treat the delegate variable just as if it were a function name. Unlike a function, however, you can also perform additional operations on this variable, such as passing it to a function via a parameter. A simple example of such a function is:

```
static void ExecuteFunction(ProcessDelegate process)
{
    process(2.2, 3.3);
}
```

This means that you can control the behavior of functions by passing them function delegates, much like choosing a "snap-in" to use. For example, you might have a function that sorts a string array alphabetically. There are several methods of sorting lists with varying performance, depending on the characteristics of the list being sorted. By using delegates, you can specify the method to use by passing a sorting algorithm function delegate to a sorting function.

There are many such uses for delegates, but, as mentioned earlier, their most prolific use is in *event handling*. You come to this subject in Chapter 12.

Summary

In this chapter, you've seen a fairly complete overview of the use of functions in C# code. Much of the additional features that functions offer (delegates in particular) are more abstract, and you need to understand them only in the light of object-oriented programming, which is a subject that you will encounter in Chapter 8.

This chapter covered:

❑   Defining and using functions in console applications

❑   Exchanging data with functions via return values and parameters

❑   Passing parameter arrays to functions

❑   Passing values by reference or by value

❑   Specifying parameters for additional return values

❑   The concept of variable scope, where variables can be hidden from sections of code where they aren't required

❑   Details of the `Main()` function, including command-line parameter usage

❑   Using functions in struct types

❑   Function overloading, where you can supply different parameters to the same function to get additional functionality

❑   Delegates and how to dynamically select functions for execution at runtime

A knowledge of how to use functions is central to all of the programming you are likely to be doing in the future. In later chapters, particularly when you learn about OOP (from Chapter 8 onwards), you will learn a more formal structure for functions and how they apply to classes. From then on, you will find that the ability to abstract code into reusable blocks is possibly the most useful aspect of C# programming.

Exercises

1.   The following two functions have errors. What are they?

```
static bool Write()
{
   Console.WriteLine("Text output from function.");
}
```

```
static void myFunction(string label, params int[] args, bool showLabel)
{
   if (showLabel)
      Console.WriteLine(label);
   foreach (int i in args)
      Console.WriteLine("{0}", i);
}
```

2. Write an application that uses two command-line arguments to place values into a string and an integer variable, respectively. Then display these values.

3. Create a delegate and use it to impersonate the `Console.ReadLine()` function when asking for user input.

4. Modify the following struct to include a function that returns the total price of an order:

```
struct order
{
   public string itemName;
   public int    unitCount;
   public double unitCost;
}
```

5. Add another function to the `order` struct that returns a formatted string as follows, where italic entries enclosed in angle brackets are replaced by appropriate values:

Order Information: <unit count> <item name> items at $<unit cost> each, total cost $<total cost>

Debugging and
Error Handling

So far in this book, you have covered all the basics of simple programming in C#. Before you move on to look at object-oriented programming in the next section of the book, it's time to look at debugging and error handling in C# code.

Errors in code are something that will always be with you. No matter how good a programmer is, there will always be problems that slip through, and part of being a good programmer is realizing that this is the case and being prepared to deal with it. Of course, these may be minor problems that don't affect the execution of an application, perhaps a spelling mistake on a button or the like. They may also be glaring errors that cause applications to fail completely (usually known as *fatal* errors). Fatal errors include simple errors in code that will prevent compilation (*syntax* errors), but may be more involved and only occur at runtime. Alternatively, errors may be subtler. Perhaps your application will fail to add a record to a database if a requested field is missing or adds a record with the wrong data in other restricted circumstances. Errors such as these, where application logic is in some way flawed, are known as *semantic* errors (also known as *logic* errors).

Often, the first that you might hear about the more subtle errors will be when a user of your application complains that something isn't working properly. This leaves you with the task of tracing through your code to try to find out what *is* happening and how you can change your code so that it does what it was intended to do.

In situations like this, you will find that the debugging capabilities of VS are a fantastic help. In the first part of this chapter, you look at some of the techniques available and apply them to some common problems.

In addition to this, you will also look at the *error-handling* techniques available in C#. These enable you to take precautions in cases where errors are likely, and write code that is resilient enough to cope with errors that might otherwise be fatal. These techniques are part of the C# language rather than a debugging feature of VS, but VS does provide some tools to help you here too.

In this chapter you look at:

❑ The debugging methods available in Visual Studio

❑ The error-handling techniques available in C#

Debugging in Visual Studio

When programs are run in debug mode, there is more going on than simply the code you have written being executed. Debug builds maintain *symbolic information* about your application, so that VS is capable of knowing exactly what is happening as each line of code is executed. Symbolic information means keeping track of, for example, the names of variables used in uncompiled code, so that they can be matched up to the values that exist in the compiled machine code application, which won't contain such human-readable information. This information is contained in .pdb files, which you may have seen appearing in Debug directories on your computer. This enables you to perform many useful operations, which include:

❑ Outputting debugging information to VS

❑ Looking at (and editing) the values of variables in scope during application execution

❑ Pausing and restarting program execution

❑ Automatically halting execution at certain points in the code

❑ Stepping through program execution a line at a time

❑ Monitoring changes in variable content during application execution

❑ Modifying variable content at runtime

❑ Performing test calls of functions

In this section, you take a look at these techniques and how you can use them to identify and fix those areas of code that do not work as expected, a process more commonly known as debugging.

I divide the techniques into two sections by the way they are used. In general, debugging is performed either by interrupting program execution or by making notes for later analysis. In VS terms, an application is either running or is in *Break mode*, that is, normal execution is halted. You'll look at the *Nonbreak mode* (runtime or normal) techniques first.

Debugging in Nonbreak (Normal) Mode

One of the commands you've been using throughout this book is the Console.WriteLine() function that outputs text to the console. When you are developing applications, this function can come in handy for getting extra feedback on operations, for example:

```
Console.WriteLine("MyFunc() Function about to be called.");
MyFunc ("Do something.");
Console.WriteLine("MyFunc() Function execution completed.");
```

This code snippet shows how you can give extra information concerning a function called `MyFunc()`.

Doing this is all very well but can make your console output a bit cluttered. As an alternative, you can output text to a separate location — the `Output` window in VS.

Back in Chapter 2, you saw the Error List window, and I mentioned that other windows could also be displayed in the same place. One of these windows, the `Output` window, can be very useful when it comes to debugging. To display this window, select `View` ⇨ `Output` from the VS menu. With this window, you can see information relating to the compilation and execution of code, including errors encountered during compilation and so forth. You can also use this window to display custom diagnostic information by writing to it directly. This window is shown in Figure 7-1.

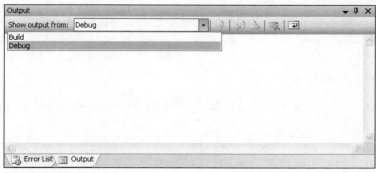

Figure 7-1

Note that this window has two modes that can be selected using the drop-down box it contains. You can toggle between `Build` and `Debug` modes. These modes show you compilation and runtime information, respectively. When I refer to "writing to the `Output` window" in this section, I actually mean "writing to the `Debug` mode view of the `Output` window."

Alternatively, you might want to create a *logging* file, which would have information appended to it when your application is executed. The techniques for doing this are much the same as those for writing text to the `Output` window, although the process requires an understanding of how to access the file system from C# applications. For now, leave this functionality on the back burner, because there is plenty you can do without getting bogged down by file access techniques.

Outputting Debugging Information

Writing text to the `Output` window at runtime is very simple. You simply need to replace calls to `Console.WriteLine()` with the required call to write text where you want it. There are two commands you can use to do this:

❑　`Debug.WriteLine()`

❑　`Trace.WriteLine()`

These commands function in almost exactly the same way — with one key difference. The first of these two commands only works in debug builds; the latter will work for release builds as well. In fact, the `Debug.WriteLine()` command won't even be compiled into a release build; it'll just disappear, which certainly has its advantages (the compiled code will be smaller in size for a start). You can, in effect, have two versions of your application created from a single source file. The debug version displays all kinds of extra diagnostic information, whereas the release version won't have this overhead, and won't display messages to users that might otherwise be annoying!

Note that these functions don't work exactly like `Console.WriteLine()`. They only work with a single string parameter for the message to output, rather than letting us insert variable values using `{X}` syntax. This means that you must use the + operator to insert variable values in strings. However, you can (optionally) supply a second string parameter, which is used to display a *category* for the output text. This allows you to see at a glance what output messages are displayed in the `Output` window, which is useful for times when similar messages are output from different places in the application.

The general output of these functions is:

```
<category>: <message>
```

For example, the following statement, which has `"MyFunc"` as the optional category parameter

```
Debug.WriteLine("Added 1 to i", "MyFunc");
```

would result in:

```
MyFunc: Added 1 to i
```

In the following Try It Out, you see an example of outputting debugging information in this way.

Try It Out   Writing Text to the Output Window

1. Create a new console application called `Ch07Ex01` in the directory `C:\BegVCSharp\Chapter7`.

2. Modify the code as follows:

```
using System;
using System.Collections.Generic;
using System.Text;
using System.Diagnostics;

namespace Ch07Ex01
{
    class Program
    {
        static void Main(string[] args)
        {
            int[] testArray = {4, 7, 4, 2, 7, 3, 7, 8, 3, 9, 1, 9};
            int[] maxValIndices;
            int maxVal = Maxima(testArray, out maxValIndices);
            Console.WriteLine("Maximum value {0} found at element indices:",
                              maxVal);
            foreach (int index in maxValIndices)
```

```
        {
            Console.WriteLine(index);
        }
        Console.ReadKey();
    }
```

```
    static int Maxima(int[] integers, out int[] indices)
    {
        Debug.WriteLine("Maximum value search started.");
        indices = new int[1];
        int maxVal = integers[0];
        indices[0] = 0;
        int count = 1;
        Debug.WriteLine("Maximum value initialized to " + maxVal +
                    ", at element index 0.");
        for (int i = 1; i < integers.Length; i++)
        {
            Debug.WriteLine("Now looking at element at index " + i + ".");
            if (integers[i] > maxVal)
            {
                maxVal = integers[i];
                count = 1;
                indices = new int[1];
                indices[0] = i;
                Debug.WriteLine("New maximum found. New value is " + maxVal +
                            ", at element index " + i + ".");
            }
            else
            {
                if (integers[i] == maxVal)
                {
                    count++;
                    int[] oldIndices = indices;
                    indices = new int[count];
                    oldIndices.CopyTo(indices, 0);
                    indices[count - 1] = i;
                    Debug.WriteLine("Duplicate maximum found at element index " +
                                i + ".");
                }
            }
        }
        Trace.WriteLine("Maximum value " + maxVal + " found, with " + count +
                    " occurrences.");
        Debug.WriteLine("Maximum value search completed.");
        return maxVal;
    }
}
```

3. Execute the code in debug mode. The result is shown in Figure 7-2.

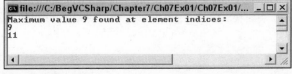

Figure 7-2

4. Terminate the application, and look at the contents of the Output window (in Debug mode). This is shown (truncated) below.

. . .

```
Maximum value search started.
Maximum value initialized to 4, at element index 0.
Now looking at element at index 1.
New maximum found. New value is 7, at element index 1.
Now looking at element at index 2.
Now looking at element at index 3.
Now looking at element at index 4.
Duplicate maximum found at element index 4.
Now looking at element at index 5.
Now looking at element at index 6.
Duplicate maximum found at element index 6.
Now looking at element at index 7.
New maximum found. New value is 8, at element index 7.
Now looking at element at index 8.
Now looking at element at index 9.
New maximum found. New value is 9, at element index 9.
Now looking at element at index 10.
Now looking at element at index 11.
Duplicate maximum found at element index 11.
Maximum value 9 found, with 2 occurrences.
Maximum value search completed.
The program '[1084] Ch07Ex01.vshost.exe: Managed' has exited with code -1073741510
(0xc000013a).
```

5. Change to Release mode using the drop-down menu on the Standard toolbar, as shown in Figure 7-3.

Figure 7-3

6. Run the program again, this time in Release mode, and take another look at the Output window when execution terminates (ignore the warning dialog that pops up when you execute the application, just click OK to dismiss it). The output (again truncated) is shown below.

. . .
```
Maximum value 9 found, with 2 occurrences.
The program '[4720] Ch07Ex01.vshost.exe: Managed' has exited with code -1073741510
(0xc000013a).
```

How It Works

This application is an expanded version of one that you saw in Chapter 6, using a function to calculate the maximum value in an integer array. This version also returns an array of the indices where maximum values are found in an array, so that the calling code can manipulate these elements.

To start with, note that an additional `using` directive appears at the start of the code:

```
using System.Diagnostics;
```

This simplifies access to the functions discussed prior to this example, as they are contained in the `System.Diagnostics` namespace. Without this `using` directive, code such as

```
Debug.WriteLine("Bananas");
```

would need further qualification, and would need to be rewritten as:

```
System.Diagnostics.Debug.WriteLine("Bananas");
```

The `using` directive keeps your code simple and reduces verbosity.

The code in `Main()` simply initializes a test array of integers called `testArray`; it also declares another integer array called `maxValIndices` to store the index output of `Maxima()` (the function that performs the calculation), then calls this function. Once the function returns, the code simply outputs the results.

`Maxima()` is slightly more complicated, but doesn't use much code that you haven't already seen. The search through the array is performed in a similar way to the `MaxVal()` function in the last chapter, except that a record is kept of the indices of maximum values.

Perhaps the key point to note in the code (other than those lines that output debugging information) is the function used to keep track of the indices. Rather than returning an array that would be large enough to store every index in the source array (needing the same dimensions as the source array), `Maxima()` returns an array just large enough to hold the indices found. It does this by continually recreating arrays of different sizes as the search progresses. This is necessary because arrays can't be resized once they are created.

To start with, the search is initialized by assuming that the first element in the source array (called `integers` locally) is the maximum value and that there is only one maximum value in the array. Values can, therefore, be set for `maxVal` (the return value of the function and the maximum value found) and `indices`, the `out` parameter array that stores the indices of the maximum values found. `maxVal` is assigned the value of the first element in `integers`, and `indices` is assigned a single value, simply 0, which is the index of the first element in the array. You also store the number of maximum values found in a variable called `count`, which allows you to keep track of the `indices` array.

The main body of the function is a loop that cycles through the values in the `integers` array, omitting the first one because this has already been processed. Each value is compared to the current value of `maxVal` and ignored if `maxVal` is greater. If the currently inspected array value is greater than `maxVal`, then `maxVal` and `indices` are changed to reflect this. If the value is equal to `maxVal`, then `count` is incremented and a new array is substituted for `indices`. This new array is one element bigger than the old `indices` array, containing the new index found.

The code for this last piece of functionality is:

```
if (integers[i] == maxVal)
{
    count++;
```

```
        int[] oldIndices = indices;
        indices = new int[count];
        oldIndices.CopyTo(indices, 0);
        indices[count - 1] = i;
        Debug.WriteLine("Duplicate maximum found at element index " +
                        i + ".");
}
```

Note that this works by *backing up* the old `indices` array into `oldIndices`, an integer array local to this `if` code block. Note also that the values in `oldIndices` are copied into the new `indices` array using the `<array>.CopyTo()` function. This function simply takes a target array and an index to use for the first element to copy to and pastes all values into the target array.

Throughout the code, various pieces of text are output using the `Debug.WriteLine()` and `Trace.WriteLine()` functions. The end result of this when run in debug mode is a complete record of the steps taken in the loop that give you the result. In release mode, you see just the end result of the calculation, because no `Debug.WriteLine()` functions work.

In addition to these `WriteLine()` functions, there are a few more you should be aware of. To start with, there are equivalents to `Console.Write()`:

❑ `Debug.Write()`
❑ `Trace.Write()`

Both these functions use the same syntax as the `WriteLine()` functions (one or two parameters, with a message and an optional category), but differ in that they don't add end-of-line characters.

There are also the following commands:

❑ `Debug.WriteLineIf()`
❑ `Trace.WriteLineIf()`
❑ `Debug.WriteIf()`
❑ `Trace.WriteIf()`

Each of these has the same parameters as the non-`If` counterparts, with the addition of an extra, mandatory parameter that precedes them in the parameter list. This parameter takes a Boolean value (or an expression that evaluates to a Boolean value) and will result in the function only writing text if this value evaluates to `true`. You can use these functions to conditionally output text to the `Output` window.

For example, you might require only debugging information to be output in certain situations, so you can have a great many `Debug.WriteLineIf()` statements in your code that all depend on a certain condition being met. If this condition doesn't occur, then they won't be displayed, which will stop the `Output` window from getting cluttered up with superfluous information.

Tracepoints

An alternative to writing information to the `Output` window is to use *tracepoints*. These are a feature of VS rather than C#, but serve the same function as using `Debug.WriteLine()`. Essentially, they are a way to output debugging information without modifying your code.

To illustrate tracepoints, you can use them to replace the debugging commands in the previous example. In the downloadable code for this chapter I've done this in `Ch07Ex01TracePoints`. The process for adding a tracepoint is as follows:

1. Position the cursor at the line where you wish the tracepoint to be inserted. Note that the tracepoint will be processed *before* this line of code is executed.

2. Right-click the line of code and select `Breakpoint ⇨ Insert Tracepoint`.

3. Type the string to be output in the `Print a message:` text box in the `When Breakpoint is Hit` dialog that appears. If you wish to output variable values, enclose the variable name in curly braces.

4. Click `OK`.

5. A red diamond appears to the left of the line of code containing a tracepoint, and the line of code itself is shown with red highlighting.

As is implied by the title of the dialog for adding tracepoints, and the menu selections required for them, tracepoints are a form of breakpoints (and can cause application execution to pause, just like a breakpoint, if desired). You look at breakpoints, which typically serve a more advanced debugging purpose, a little later in the chapter.

Figure 7-4 shows the breakpoint required for line 36 of `Ch07Ex01TracePoints`, where line numbering applies to the code after the existing `Debug.WriteLine()` statements have been removed.

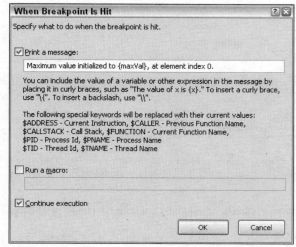

Figure 7-4

As shown in the text in this dialog, tracepoints allow you to insert other useful information concerning the location and context of the tracepoint. You should experiment with these values, particularly `$FUNCTION` and `$CALLER`, to see what additional information you can glean.

You can also see that it is possible for the tracepoint to execute a macro, although this is an advanced feature that I won't be covering here.

There is another window you can use to quickly see the tracepoints in an application. To display this window, select Debug ➪ Windows ➪ Breakpoints from the VS menu. This is a general window for displaying breakpoints (where tracepoints, as noted earlier, are a form of breakpoint). You can customize the display to show more tracepoint-specific information by adding the When Hit column from the Columns drop down in this window. Figure 7-5 shows the display with this column configured and all the tracepoints added to Ch07Ex01TracePoints.

Figure 7-5

Executing this application in debug mode will give exactly the same result as before.

You can remove or temporarily disable tracepoints either by right-clicking on them in the code window or via the Breakpoints window. In the Breakpoints window, the check box to the left of the tracepoint shows whether the tracepoint is enabled; disabled tracepoints are unchecked and are displayed in the code window as diamond outlines rather than solid diamonds.

Diagnostics Output versus Tracepoints

Now that you have seen two methods of outputting essentially the same information, it is worth examining the pros and cons of each.

The first thing to notice is that tracepoints have no equivalent to the `Trace` commands, that is, there is no way to output information in a Release build using tracepoints. This is due to the way that tracepoints are included in your applications, or rather the fact that they aren't. Tracepoints are handled by Visual Studio, and as such do not exist in the compiled version of your application. You will see tracepoints doing something only when your application is running in the VS debugger.

The chief disadvantage of tracepoints is also their major advantage, which is that they are stored in VS. This makes them quick and easy to add to your applications as and when you need to, but also all too easy to delete. Deleting a tracepoint is as simple as clicking on the red diamond indicating its position, which can be annoying if you are outputting a complicated string of information.

One bonus of tracepoints, though, is the additional information that can be easily added, such as `$FUNCTION`, as noted in the previous section. While this information is available to code written using `Debug` and `Trace` commands, it is trickier to obtain.

So, to sum up, it is probably best to use these two methods of outputting debug information as follows:

❑ **Diagnostics output:** Use when debug output is something you always want to output from an application, particularly where the string you wish to output is complex, involving several variables or a lot of information. In addition, `Trace` commands are often the only option should you wish output during execution of an application built in Release mode.

❑ **Tracepoints:** Use when debugging an application to quickly output important information that may help you to resolve semantic errors.

Debugging in Break Mode

The rest of the debugging techniques you look at in this chapter work in Break mode. This mode can be entered in several ways, all of which result in the program pausing in some way. The first thing you look at in this section is how you go about this, and then you look at what you can achieve once Break mode is entered.

Entering Break Mode

The simplest way of entering Break mode is to hit the pause button in VS while an application is running. This pause button is found on the `Debug` toolbar, which you should add to the toolbars that appear by default in VS. To do this, right-click in the toolbar area and select the `Debug` toolbar, as shown in Figure 7-6.

Figure 7-6

The toolbar that appears is shown in Figure 7-7.

Start

Figure 7-7

The first four buttons on this toolbar allow manual control of breaking. In Figure 7-7, three of these are grayed out, because they won't work with a program that isn't currently executing. The one that is enabled, Start, is identical to the button that exists on the standard toolbar. In the following sections, you look at the rest of the buttons when needed.

When an application is running, the toolbar changes to look like Figure 7-8.

Stop

Pause | Restart

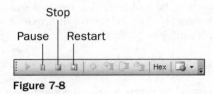

Figure 7-8

Now, the three buttons that were grayed out before are enabled, and let you:

❑ Pause the application and enter Break mode

❑ Stop the application completely (this doesn't enter Break mode, it just quits)

❑ Restart the application

Pausing the application is perhaps the simplest way of entering Break mode, but it doesn't give you fine-grained control over exactly where to stop. You are likely to stop in a natural pause in the application, perhaps where you request user input. You might also be able to enter Break mode during a lengthy operation, or a long loop, but the exact point you stop at is likely to be fairly random.

In general, it is far better to use *breakpoints*.

Breakpoints

A breakpoint is a marker in your source code that triggers automatic entry into Break mode. Breakpoints may be configured to:

❑ Enter Break mode immediately when the breakpoint is reached.

❑ Enter Break mode when the breakpoint is reached if a Boolean expression evaluates to true.

❑ Enter Break mode once the breakpoint is reached a set number of times.

❑ Enter Break mode once the breakpoint is reached and a variable value has changed since the last time the breakpoint was reached.

❑ Output text to the debug window or execute a macro (see the section on tracepoints earlier in the chapter).

Note that these features are available only in debug builds. If you compile a release build then all breakpoints will be ignored.

There are several ways of adding breakpoints. To add simple breakpoints that break when a line is reached, you simply left-click on the gray area to the left of the line of code, right-click on the line, and select Breakpoint ⇨ Insert Breakpoint; select Debug ⇨ Toggle Breakpoint from the VS menu; or press F9. Figure 7-9 shows the *right-clicking on a line* option.

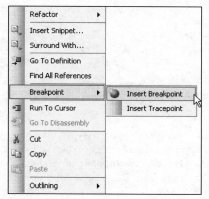

Figure 7-9

The breakpoint will appear as a red circle next to the line of code and a highlight on the line of code, as shown in Figure 7-10.

```
14    static void Main(string[] args)
15    {
16        int[] testArray = {
17            4, 7, 4, 2, 7, 3, 7, 8, 3, 9, 1, 9
18        };
19        int[] maxValIndices;
20        int maxVal = Maxima(testArray, out maxValIndices);
21        Console.WriteLine("Maximum value {0} found at element indices:",
22                        maxVal);
23        foreach (int index in maxValIndices)
24        {
25            Console.WriteLine(index);
26        }
27        Console.ReadKey();
28    }
```

Figure 7-10

You can also see information about the breakpoints in a file using the Breakpoints window (you saw how to enable this window earlier, in the section on tracepoints).

You can use the Breakpoints window to disable breakpoints (by removing the tick to the left of a description; a disabled breakpoint shows up as an unfilled red circle), delete breakpoints, and edit the properties of breakpoints.

The columns shown in this window, `Condition` and `Hit Count`, are only two of the available ones, but they are the most useful. You can edit these by right-clicking on a breakpoint (in code or in this window) and selecting the `Condition...` or `Hit Count...` menu option.

Selecting `Condition...` pops up the dialog shown in Figure 7-11.

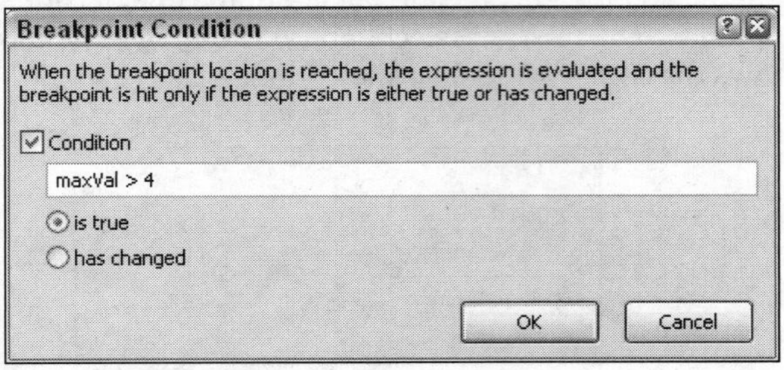

Figure 7-11

Here, you can type any Boolean expression, which may involve any variables that are in scope at the breakpoint. Figure 7-11 shows a breakpoint that will trigger when it is reached and the value of `maxVal` is greater than 4. You can also check to see if this expression has changed and only trigger the breakpoint then (you might trigger it if `maxVal` had changed from 2 to 6 between breakpoint encounters, for example).

Selecting `Hit Count...` pops up the dialog shown in Figure 7-12.

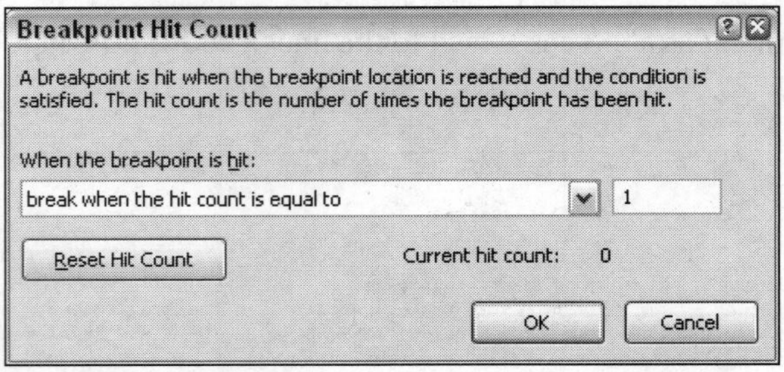

Figure 7-12

Here, you can specify how many times a breakpoint needs to be hit before it is triggered. The drop-down list offers the following options:

❑   Break always

❑   Break when the hit count is equal to

❑   Break when the hit count is a multiple of

❑   Break when the hit count is greater than or equal to

The option chosen, combined with the value entered in the text box next to the list, determines the behavior of the breakpoint.

This hit count is useful in long loops, when you might want to break after, say, the first 5000 cycles. It would be a pain to break and restart 5000 times if you couldn't do this!

Note that a breakpoint with additional properties set, such as a condition or hit count, is displayed slightly differently. Instead of a simple red circle, a configured breakpoint consists of a red circle containing a white plus symbol. This can be useful, since it allows you to see at a glance which breakpoints will always cause Break mode to be entered and which will only do so in certain circumstances.

Other Ways of Entering Break Mode

There are two additional ways to get into Break mode. One is to choose to enter it when an *unhandled exception* is thrown. This subject is covered later in this chapter, when you look at error handling. The other way is to break when an *assertion* is generated.

Assertions are instructions that can interrupt application execution with a user-defined message. They are often used in the development of an application as a means to test that things are going smoothly. For example, you might, at some point in your application, require a given variable to have a value less than 10. You can use an assertion to check that this is true and interrupt the program if this isn't the case. When the assertion occurs, you have the option to Abort, which will terminate the application; Retry, causing Break mode to be entered; or Ignore, and the application will continue as normal.

As with the debug output functions you saw earlier, there are two versions of the assertion function:

❑   Debug.Assert()

❑   Trace.Assert()

Again, the debug version will only be compiled into debug builds.

These functions take three parameters. The first is a Boolean value, where a value of false will cause the assertion to trigger. The second and third are two string parameters to write information both to a pop-up dialog and the Output window. The preceding example would need a function call such as:

```
Debug.Assert(myVar < 10, "myVar is 10 or greater.",
             "Assertion occurred in Main().");
```

Assertions are often useful in the early stages of user adoption of an application. You can distribute release builds of your application containing Trace.Assert() functions to keep tabs on things. Should an assertion be triggered, the user will be informed, and they can pass this information on to you .You'll then be able to work out what has gone wrong even if you don't know *how* it went wrong.

You might, for example, provide a brief description of the error in the first string with instructions as to what to do next as the second string:

```
Trace.Assert(myVar < 10, "Variable out of bounds.",
             "Please contact vendor with the error code KCW001.");
```

Should this assertion occur, the user will see the dialog shown in Figure 7-13.

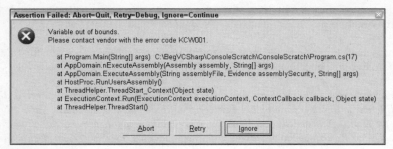

Figure 7-13

Admittedly this isn't the most user-friendly dialog in the world, since it contains much information that could confuse users, but should they send you a screenshot of the error, it would enable you to track down the problem quickly.

The next topics to cover concern what you can actually do once application execution is halted, and you find yourself in Break mode. In general, you will be entering Break mode in order to track down an error in your code (or just to reassure yourself that things are working properly). Once you are in Break mode, there are various techniques that you can draw on, all of which enable you to analyze your code and the exact state of your application at the point in its execution where it is paused.

Monitoring Variable Content

Monitoring variable content is just one example of an area where VS helps you a great deal by making things simple. The easiest way of checking the value of a variable is to hover the mouse over its name in the source code while in Break mode. A yellow tooltip showing information about the variable will appear, including the current value of the variable.

You can also highlight whole expressions to get information about their results in the same way. For more complex values, such as arrays, you can even expand values in the tooltip to see individual element entries.

Now, you may have noticed that when you run an application through VS, the layout of the various windows in the environment changes. By default, the following changes are likely to occur at runtime (this behavior may vary slightly depending on your installation, but the general points here will hold true):

❑   The `Properties` window disappears, along with some other windows, including probably the Solution Explorer window.

❑   The `Error List` window is replaced with two new windows across the bottom of the window.

❑   Several new tabs appear in the new window.

The new screen layout can be seen in Figure 7-14. This may not match your display exactly, and some of the tabs and windows may not look exactly the same. However, the functionality of these windows as discussed later will be the same for you, and this display is completely customizable via the `View` and `Debug` ⇨ `Windows` menus (during Break mode), as well as by dragging windows around the screen to reposition them.

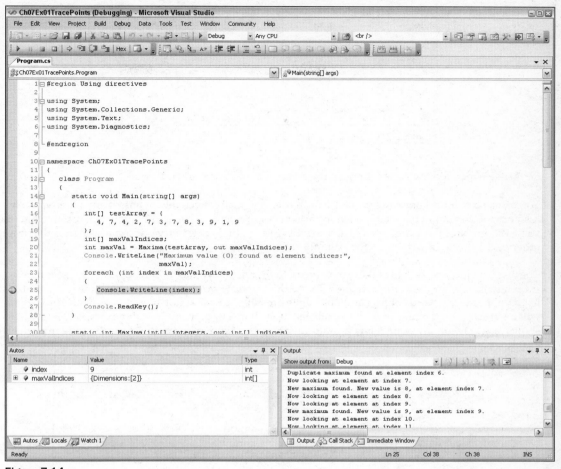

Figure 7-14

The new window that appears in the bottom left is a particularly useful one for debugging. It allows you to keep tabs on the values of variables in your application when in Break mode. The tabs that can be displayed here include:

❑ `Autos`: Variables in use in the current and previous statements (*Ctrl+D, A*)

❑ `Locals`: All variables in scope (*Ctrl+D, L*)

❑ `Watch` *N*: Customizable variable and expression display (where *N* is 1 to 4, found on `Debug` ➪ `Windows` ➪ `Watch`)

All these tabs work in more or less the same way, with various additional features depending on their specific function. In general, each tab will contain a list of variables, with information on the variables' name, value, and type. More complex variables, such as arrays, may be further interrogated using the + and – tree expansion/contraction symbols to the left of their names, allowing a tree view of their content. For example, Figure 7-15 shows the `Locals` tab obtained by placing a breakpoint in the code for the earlier example, as shown in Figure 7-14.

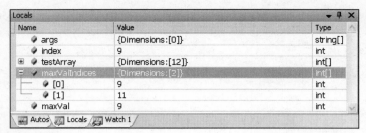

Figure 7-15

Here, I've expanded the view for one of the array variables, `maxValIndices`.

You can also edit the content of variables from this view. This effectively bypasses any other variable assignment that might have happened in earlier code. To do this, you simply type a new value into the `Value` column for the variable you want to edit. You might do this to try out some scenarios that might otherwise require code changes, for example.

The `Watch` windows, of which there may be up to four, allow you to monitor specific variables or expressions involving specific variables. To use this window, you simply type the name of a variable or expression into the `Name` column and observe the results. Note that not all variables in an application will be in scope all the time and will be labeled as such in a `Watch` window. For example, Figure 7-16 shows a `Watch` window with a few sample variables and expressions in it. Again, the code from the last example is used here, although this time the breakpoint is in the execution of the `Maxima()` function (on line 55 in fact).

Watch 1		▾ ⌷ ✕
Name	Value	Type
maxVal * count	18	int
indices[1]	11	int
testArray	The name 'testArray' does not exist in the current context ⟳	

Autos | Locals | Watch 1

Figure 7-16

The `testArray` array is local to `Main()`, so you don't see a value here. Instead, you get a message informing you that the variable isn't in scope.

You can also add variables to a `Watch` window by dragging them from the source code into the window.

One nice feature about the various displays of variables accessible in this window is that they show you variables that have changed between breakpoints. Any new value is shown in red rather than black, making it easy to see whether a value has changed.

As mentioned earlier, to add more watch windows, in Break mode you can use the `Debug` ⇨ `Windows` ⇨ `Watch` ⇨ `Watch N` menu options to toggle the four possible windows on or off. Each window may contain an individual set of watches on variables and expressions, so you can group related variables together for easy access.

As well as these watch windows, there is also a `QuickWatch` window that can give you detailed information about a variable in the source code quickly. To use this, you simply right-click on the variable you want to interrogate and select the `QuickWatch` menu option. In most cases, though, it is just as easy to use the standard `Watch` windows.

An important point to note about watches is that they are maintained between application executions. If you terminate an application then rerun it you don't have to add watches again—VS will remember what you were looking at the last time.

Stepping through Code

So far, you've seen how to discover what is going on in your applications at the point where Break mode is entered. Next, you will look at how you can use VS to *step through* code while remaining in Break mode, allowing you to see exactly the results of the code being executed. This is an extremely valuable technique for those of us who can't think as fast as computers can.

When Break mode is entered, a cursor appears to the left of the code view (which may initially appear inside the red circle of a breakpoint if a breakpoint has been used to enter Break mode), by the line of code that is about to be executed, as shown in Figure 7-17.

```
14      static void Main(string[] args)
15      {
16          int[] testArray = {
17              4, 7, 4, 2, 7, 3, 7, 8, 3, 9, 1, 9
18          };
19          int[] maxValIndices;
20          int maxVal = Maxima(testArray, out maxValIndices);
21          Console.WriteLine("Maximum value (0) found at element indices:",
22                            maxVal);
23          foreach (int index in maxValIndices)
24          {
25              Console.WriteLine(index);
26          }
27          Console.ReadKey();
28      }
```

Figure 7-17

This shows you what point execution has reached when Break mode is entered. At this point, you can choose to have execution proceed on a line-by-line basis. To do this, you use some more of the `Debug` toolbar buttons you saw earlier. These buttons are shown in Figure 7-18.

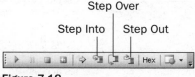

Figure 7-18

The sixth, seventh, and eighth icons control program flow in Break mode. In order, they are:

❑ `Step Into`: Execute and move to the next statement to execute

❑ `Step Over`: As above, but won't enter nested blocks of code, including functions

❑ `Step Out`: Run to end of code block and resume Break mode at the statement that follows

If you want to look at every single operation carried out by the application, then you can use Step Into to follow the instructions sequentially. This includes moving inside functions, such as Maxima() in the preceding example. Clicking on this icon when the cursor reaches line 20, the call to Maxima(), will result in the cursor moving to the first line inside the Maxima() function. Alternatively, clicking on Step Over when you reach line 20, will move the cursor straight to line 21, without having to go through the code in Maxima() (although this code is still executed). If you do step into a function that you aren't interested in you can hit Step Out to return to the code that called the function.

As you step through code, the values of variables are likely to change. By keeping an eye on the monitoring windows discussed in the last section, you can see this happening with ease.

In code that has semantic errors, this technique is perhaps the most useful one at your disposal. You can step through code right up to the point where you expect problems to occur, and the errors will be generated as if you were running the program normally. Along the way, you can keep an eye on data and see just what is going wrong. Later on in this chapter, you will use this technique to find out what is happening in an example application.

There are a few more windows left to cover: Command Window, Immediate, and Call Stack.

Immediate and Command Windows

The Command and Immediate windows (found on the View ➪ Other Windows menu) allow you to execute commands while an application is running. The Command window allows you to perform VS operations manually (such as menu and toolbar operations), and the Immediate window allows you to execute additional code in addition to the source code lines being executed and to evaluate expressions.

These windows are intrinsically linked (in fact, earlier versions of VS treated them as the same thing). You can even switch between them by entering commands: immed to move from the Command window to the Immediate window and >cmd to move back.

This section concentrates on the Immediate window, because the Command window is only really useful for complex operations.

The simplest use of this window is simply to evaluate expressions, a bit like a *one shot* use of the Watch windows. To do this, you simply type an expression and press return. The information requested will then be displayed. An example is shown in Figure 7-19.

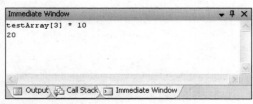

Figure 7-19

You can also change variable content here, as demonstrated in Figure 20.

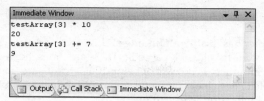

Figure 7-20

In most cases, you can get the effects you want more easily using the variable monitoring windows you saw earlier, but this technique can still be handy for tweaking values and is good for testing expressions where you are unlikely to be interested in the results at a later date.

The Call Stack Window

The final window you look at here shows you the way in which the current location was reached. In simple terms, this means showing the current function along with the function that called it, the function that called that, and so on (that is, a list of nested function calls). The exact points where calls are made are also recorded.

In the earlier example, entering Break mode when in Maxima(), or moving into this function using code stepping, reveals the information shown in Figure 7-21.

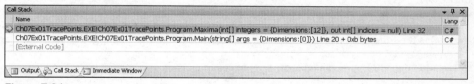

Figure 7-21

If you double-click an entry, you'll be taken to the appropriate location, allowing you to track the way code execution has reached the current point.

This window is particularly useful when errors are first detected, because they allow you to see what has happened immediately before the error. Where errors occur in commonly used functions, this will help you to see the source of the error.

> *Note that sometimes this window will show some very confusing information. Sometimes, for example, errors occur outside of your applications due to using external functions in the wrong way. At times like this, there could be a long list of entries in this window, but only one or two look familiar. You can see external references (should you ever need to) by right-clicking on the window and selecting* Show External Code.

Error Handling

The first part of this chapter has dealt with finding and correcting errors during application development so that they won't occur in release level code. There are times, however, when you know that errors are likely to occur and there is no way of being 100 percent sure that they won't. In these situations, it may be preferable to anticipate problems and write code that is robust enough to deal with these errors gracefully, without interrupting execution.

Error handling is the name for all techniques of this nature, and here you look at exceptions and how you can deal with them.

Exceptions

An exception is an error generated either in your code or in a function called by your code that occurs at runtime. The definition of *error* here is more vague than it has been up until now, because exceptions may be generated manually in functions and so on. For example, you might generate an exception in a function if one of its string parameters doesn't start with the letter *a*. This isn't strictly speaking an error outside of the context of this function, although it is treated as one by the code that calls the function.

You've come across exceptions a few times already in this book. Perhaps the simplest example is attempting to address an array element that is out of range, for example:

```
int[] myArray = {1, 2, 3, 4};
int myElem = myArray[4];
```

This generates the following exception message and then terminates the application:

```
Index was outside the bounds of the array.
```

You've seen some examples of the window that is displayed already. The window has a line connecting it to the offending code and includes links to reference topics in the VS help files as well as a View Detail... *link that enables you to find out more about the exception that occurred.*

Exceptions are defined in namespaces, and most have names that make it clear what they are intended for. In this example, the exception generated is called System.IndexOutOfRangeException, which makes sense because you have supplied an index that is not in the range of indices permissible in myArray.

This message only appears and the application only terminates when the exception is *unhandled*. So, what exactly do you have to do to *handle* an exception?

try . . . catch . . . finally

The C# language includes syntax for *Structured Exception Handling (SEH)*. Keywords exist to mark code out as being able to handle exceptions, along with instructions as to what to do if an exception occurs. The three keywords you use for this are try, catch, and finally. Each of these has an associated code block and must be used in consecutive lines of code. The basic structure is as follows:

```
try
{
    ...
}
catch (<exceptionType> e)
{
    ...
}
finally
{
    ...
}
```

It is also possible, however, to have a `try` block and a `finally` block with no `catch` block, or a `try` block with multiple `catch` blocks. If one or more `catch` blocks exist, then the `finally` block is optional, else it is mandatory.

The usage of the blocks is as follows:

❑ `try`: Contains code that might throw exceptions (*throw* is the C# way of saying *generate* or *cause* when talking about exceptions).

❑ `catch`: Contains code to execute when exceptions are thrown. `catch` blocks may be set to respond only to specific exception types (such as `System.IndexOutOfRangeException`) using `<exceptionType>`, hence the ability to provide multiple `catch` blocks. It is also possible to omit this parameter entirely, to get a *general* `catch` block that will respond to all exceptions.

❑ `finally`: Contains code that is always executed, either after the `try` block if no exception occurs, after a `catch` block if an exception is handled, or just before an unhandled exception terminates the application (the fact that this block is processed at this time is the reason for its existence; otherwise, you might just as well place code after the block).

The sequence of events that occurs after an exception occurs in code in a `try` block is:

❑ The `try` block terminates at the point where the exception occurred.

❑ If a `catch` block exists, then a check is made to see if the block matches the type of exception that has been thrown. If no `catch` block exists, then the `finally` block (which must be present if there are no `catch` blocks) executes.

❑ If a `catch` block exists, but there is no match, then a check is made for other `catch` blocks.

❑ If a `catch` block matches the exception type, the code it contains executes, and then the `finally` block executes if it is present.

❑ If no `catch` blocks match the exception type, then the `finally` block of code executes if it is present.

Here's an example to demonstrate handling exceptions. This Try It Out throws and handles exceptions in several ways, so that you can work through the code to see how things work.

Try It Out   **Exception Handling**

1.   Create a new console application called Ch07Ex02 in the directory C:\BegVCSharp\Chapter7.

2.   Modify the code as follows (the line number comments shown here will help you to match up your code to the discussion afterwards, and are duplicated in the downloadable code for this chapter for your convenience):

```csharp
class Program
{
    static string[] eTypes = {"none", "simple", "index", "nested index"};

    static void Main(string[] args)
    {
        foreach (string eType in eTypes)
        {
            try
            {
                Console.WriteLine("Main() try block reached.");          // Line 23
                Console.WriteLine("ThrowException(\"{0}\") called.", eType);
                                                                         // Line 24
                ThrowException(eType);
                Console.WriteLine("Main() try block continues.");        // Line 26
            }
            catch (System.IndexOutOfRangeException e)                    // Line 28
            {
                Console.WriteLine("Main() System.IndexOutOfRangeException catch"
                            + " block reached. Message:\n\"{0}\"",
                            e.Message);
            }
            catch                                                        // Line 34
            {
                Console.WriteLine("Main() general catch block reached.");
            }
            finally
            {
                Console.WriteLine("Main() finally block reached.");
            }
            Console.WriteLine();
        }
        Console.ReadKey();
    }

    static void ThrowException(string exceptionType)
    {
                                                                        // Line 49
        Console.WriteLine("ThrowException(\"{0}\") reached.", exceptionType);
        switch (exceptionType)
        {
            case "none" :
                Console.WriteLine("Not throwing an exception.");
                break;                                                  // Line 54
            case "simple" :
                Console.WriteLine("Throwing System.Exception.");
```

```
            throw (new System.Exception());                        // Line 57
        case "index" :
            Console.WriteLine("Throwing System.IndexOutOfRangeException.");
            eTypes[4] = "error";                                   // Line 60
            break;
        case "nested index" :
            try                                                    // Line 63
            {
                Console.WriteLine("ThrowException(\"nested index\") " +
                                "try block reached.");
                Console.WriteLine("ThrowException(\"index\") called.");
                ThrowException("index");                           // Line 68
            }
            catch                                                  // Line 70
            {
                Console.WriteLine("ThrowException(\"nested index\") general"
                                + " catch block reached.");
            }
            finally
            {
                Console.WriteLine("ThrowException(\"nested index\") finally"
                                + " block reached.");
            }
            break;
        }
    }
}
```

3. Run the application. The result is shown in Figure 7-22.

Figure 7-22

How It Works

This application has a `try` block in `Main()` that calls a function called `ThrowException()`. This function may throw exceptions, depending on the parameter it is called with:

❑   `ThrowException("none")`: Doesn't throw an exception

❑   `ThrowException("simple")`: Generates a general exception

❑   `ThrowException("index")`: Generates a `System.IndexOutOfRangeException` exception

❑   `ThrowException("nested index")`: Contains its own `try` block, which contains code that calls `ThrowException("index")` to generate a `System.IndexOutOfRangeException` exception

Each of these `string` parameters is held in the global `eTypes` array, which is iterated through in the `Main()` function to call `ThrowException()` once with each possible parameter. During this iteration, various messages are written to the console to indicate what is happening.

This code gives you an excellent opportunity to use the code-stepping techniques you saw earlier in this chapter. By working your way through the code a line at a time, you can see exactly how code execution progresses.

Add a new breakpoint (with the default properties) to line 23 of the code, which reads:

```
Console.WriteLine("Main() try block reached.");
```

Note that I'll refer to code by line numbers as they appear in the downloadable version of this code. If you have line numbers turned off, remember that you can turn them back on through the Tools ⇨ Options... menu item and the Text Editor ⇨ C# ⇨ General option section. Comments are included in the code shown above so that you can follow the text without having the file open in front of you.

Run the application in debug mode.

Almost immediately, the program will enter Break mode, with the cursor on line 23. If you select the `Locals` tab in the variable monitoring window, you should see that `eType` is currently `"none"`. Use the `Step Into` button to process lines 23 and 24, and check that the first line of text has been written to the console. Next, use the `Step Into` button to step into the `ThrowException()` function on line 25.

Once in the `ThrowException()` function (on line 49), the `Locals` window changes. `eType` and `args` are no longer in scope (they are local to `Main()`); instead, you see the local `exceptionType` argument, which is of course `"none"`. Keep pressing `Step Into` and you'll reach the `switch` statement that checks the value of `exceptionType` and execute the code that writes out the string `Not throwing an exception` to the screen. When you execute the `break` statement (on line 54), you exit the function and resume processing in `Main()` at line 26. Because no exception was thrown the `try` block continues.

Next, processing continues with the `finally` block. Click `Step Into` a few more times to complete the finally `block` and the first cycle of the `foreach` loop. The next time you reach line 25, `ThrowException()` is called using a different parameter, `simple`.

Continue using `Step Into` through `ThrowException()`, and you'll eventually reach line 57:

```
throw (new System.Exception());
```

Here you use the C# `throw` keyword to generate an exception. This keyword simply needs to be provided with a new-initialized exception as a parameter, and it will throw that exception. Here, you are using another exception from the `System` namespace, `System.Exception`.

Note that no break; statement is necessary in this case: block – throw is enough to end execution of the block.

When you process this statement with `Step Into`, you find yourself at the general `catch` block starting on line 34. There was no match with the earlier `catch` block starting on line 28, so this one is processed instead. Stepping through this code takes you through this block, through the `finally` block, and back into another loop cycle that calls `ThrowException()` with a new parameter on line 25. This time the parameter is `"index"`.

This time, `ThrowException()` generates an exception on line 60:

```
eTypes[4] = "error";
```

The `eTypes` array is global, so you have access to it here. However, here you are attempting to access the fifth element in the array (remember counting starts at 0), which generates a `System.IndexOutOfRangeException` exception.

This time there is a matched `catch` block in `Main()`, and stepping into the code takes you to this block, starting at line 28.

The `Console.WriteLine()` call in this block writes out the message stored in the exception using `e.Message` (you have access to the exception through the parameter of the `catch` block). Again, stepping through takes you through the `finally` block (but not the second `catch` block, as the exception is already handled) and back into the loop cycle, again calling `ThrowException()` on line 25.

When you reach the `switch` structure in `ThrowException()`, this time you enter a new `try` block, starting on line 63. When you reach line 68, you perform a nested call to `ThrowException()`, this time with the parameter `"index"`. If you like, use the `Step Over` button to skip the lines of code that are executed here, because you've been through them already. As before, this call generates a `System.IndexOutOfRangeException` exception. However, this time the exception is handled in the nested `try . . . catch . . . finally` structure, the one in `ThrowException()`. This structure has no explicit match for this type of exception, so the general `catch` block (starting on line 70) deals with it.

As with the earlier exception handling, you now step through this `catch` block and the associated `finally` block, and reach the end of the function call. However, there is one crucial difference. Although an exception has been thrown, it has also been handled — by the code in `ThrowException()`. This means that there is no exception left to handle in `Main()`, so you go straight to the `finally` block, and after that the application terminates.

Listing and Configuring Exceptions

The .NET Framework contains a whole host of exception types, and you are free to throw and handle any of these in your own code, or even throw them from your code so that they may be caught in more complex applications. VS supplies a dialog for examining and editing the available exceptions, which can be called up with the Debug ➪ Exceptions... menu item (or by pressing Ctrl+D, E). This dialog is shown in Figure 7-23.

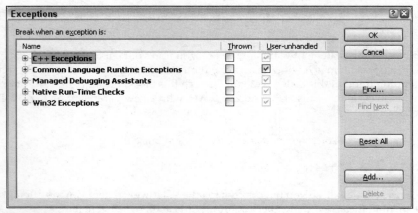

Figure 7-23

Exceptions are listed by category and .NET library namespace. You can see the exceptions in the System namespace by expanding the Common Language Runtime Exceptions tab, and then the System tab. This list includes the System.IndexOutOfRangeException exception you used above.

Each exception may be configured using the check boxes shown. You can use the first option, (break when) Thrown, to cause a break into the debugger even for exceptions that are handled. The second option allows you to ignore unhandled exceptions, and suffer the consequences. In most cases, this will result in Break mode being entered in any case, so you are likely only to need to do this in exceptional circumstances.

In most cases, the default settings here are fine.

Notes on Exception Handling

Note that you must always supply catch blocks for more specific exceptions before more general catching. If you get this the wrong way round the application will fail to compile.

Note also that you can throw exceptions from within catch blocks, either in the ways used in the last example or simply by using the expression:

```
throw;
```

This expression results in the exception handled by the catch block being rethrown.

If you throw an exception in this way, it will not be handled by the current `try . . . catch . . . finally` block, but by parent code (although the `finally` block in the nested structure will still execute).

For example, if you changed the `try . . . catch . . . finally` block in `ThrowException()` as follows

```
try
{
    Console.WriteLine("ThrowException(\"nested index\") " +
                        "try block reached.");
    Console.WriteLine("ThrowException(\"index\") called.");
    ThrowException("index");
}
catch
{
    Console.WriteLine("ThrowException(\"nested index\") general"
        + " catch block reached.");
    throw;
}
finally
{
    Console.WriteLine("ThrowException(\"nested index\") finally"
        + " block reached.");
}
```

then execution would proceed first to the `finally` block shown here, then with the matching `catch` block in `Main()`. The resulting console output changes, as shown in Figure 7-24.

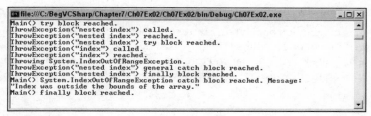

Figure 7-24

In this screenshot, you see extra lines of output from the `Main()` function, as the `System.IndexOutOfRangeException` is caught in this function.

Summary

This chapter has concentrated on techniques that you can use to debug your applications. There are a variety of techniques available here, most of which are available for whatever type of project you are creating, not just console applications.

Chapter 7

In this chapter, you learned to:

❏   Use `Debug.WriteLine()` and `Trace.WriteLine()` to write text to the Output window

❏   Use tracepoints to write text to the Output window

❏   Enter and use Break mode, including how to use the versatile breakpoints

❏   Use debugging information windows in VS

❏   Step through code

❏   Handle exceptions using `try . . . catch . . . finally`

You have now covered everything that you need to produce simple console applications, along with the methods of debugging them. In the next section of this book, you will look at the powerful technique of object-oriented programming.

Exercises

1.   "Using `Trace.WriteLine()` is preferable to using `Debug.WriteLine()` as the `Debug` version only works in debug builds." Do you agree with this statement? Why?

2.   Provide code for a simple application containing a loop that generates an error after 5000 cycles. Use a breakpoint to enter Break mode just before the error is caused on the 5000th cycle (note: a simple way to generate an error is to attempt to access a nonexistent array element, such as `myArray[1000]` in an array with a hundred elements).

3.   "`finally` code blocks only execute if a `catch` block isn't executed." True or false?

4.   Given the enumeration data type `orientation` defined below, write an application that uses Structured Exception Handling (SEH) to cast a `byte` type variable into an `orientation` type variable in a safe way. Note that you can force exceptions to be thrown using the `checked` keyword, an example of which is shown below. This code should be used in your application:

```
enum orientation : byte
{
    north = 1,
    south = 2,
    east  = 3,
    west  = 4
}
myDirection = checked((orientation)myByte);
```

Introduction to Object-Oriented Programming

At this point in the book, you've covered all the basics of C# syntax and programming, and have seen how to debug your applications. Already, you can assemble usable console applications. However, to get access to the real power of the C# language and the .NET Framework, you need to make use of *object-oriented programming* (*OOP*) techniques. In actual fact, as you will soon see, you've been using these techniques already, although, to keep things simple, I haven't focused on this when presenting the code examples.

In this chapter, you will steer away from code temporarily and focus instead on the principles behind OOP. This will soon lead you back into the C# language, because it has a symbiotic relationship with OOP. All of the concepts introduced in this chapter will be returned to in later chapters, with illustrative code — so don't panic if you don't grasp everything in the first read-through of this material.

To start with, you'll look at the basics of OOP, which will include answering that most fundamental of questions "What is an *object*?" You will quickly find that there is a lot of terminology related to OOP that can be quite confusing at first, and there will be plenty of explanation of the language used. You will also see that using OOP requires you to look at programming in a different way.

As well as discussing the general principles of OOP, this chapter will also take a look at one area where a thorough understanding of OOP is essential: in Windows Forms applications. This type of application (which makes use of the Windows environment with features such as menus, buttons, and so on) provides plenty of scope for description, and you will be able to illustrate OOP points effectively in the Windows Forms environment.

In this chapter you learn:

- ❏ What object-oriented programming is
- ❏ OOP techniques
- ❏ How Windows Forms applications rely on OOP

Note that OOP as presented in this chapter is really .NET OOP and that some of the techniques presented here don't apply to other OOP environments. When programming in C#, you use .NET-specific OOP, so it makes good sense to concentrate on these aspects.

What Is Object-Oriented Programming?

Object-oriented programming is a relatively new approach to creating computer applications that seeks to address many of the problems with so-called *traditional* programming techniques. The type of programming you have seen so far is known as *functional* (or *procedural*) programming, often resulting in so-called *monolithic* applications, meaning that all functionality is contained in a few modules of code (often just one). With OOP techniques, you often use many more modules of code, each offering specific functionality, and each module may be isolated or even completely independent of others. This *modular* method of programming gives you much more versatility and provides more opportunity for code reuse.

To illustrate this further, imagine that a high-performance application on your computer is a top-of-the-range racing car. If written with traditional programming techniques this sports car is basically a single unit. If you want to improve this car, you have to replace the whole unit by sending it back to the manufacturer and getting their expert mechanics to upgrade it, or by buying a new one. If OOP techniques are used, then you can simply buy a new engine from the manufacturer and follow their instructions to replace it yourself, rather than taking a hacksaw to the bodywork.

In a more traditional application the flow of execution is often simple and linear. Applications are loaded into memory, start executing at point *A*, end at point *B*, and are then unloaded from memory. Along the way various other entities might be used, such as files on storage media, or the capabilities of a video card, but the main body of the processing goes on in one place. The code along the way is generally concerned with manipulating data through various mathematical and logical means. The methods of manipulation are usually quite simple, using basic types such as integers and Boolean values to build up more complex representations of data.

With OOP things are rarely so linear. Although the same results are achieved, the way of getting there is often very different. OOP techniques are firmly rooted in the structure and meaning of data, and the interaction between that data and other data. This usually means putting more effort into the design stages of a project, but it has the benefit of extensibility. Once an agreement is made as to the representation of a specific type of data, that agreement can be worked into later versions of an application, and even entirely new applications. The fact that such an agreement exists can reduce development time dramatically. This explains how the racing car example works. The agreement here is how the code for the "engine" is structured, such that new code (for a new engine) can be substituted with ease, rather than requiring a trip back to the manufacturer.

As well as providing an agreed-on approach to data representation, OOP programming often simplifies things by providing an agreement on the structure and usage of more abstract entities. For example, an agreement can be made not just on the format of data that should be used to send output to a device such as a printer but also on the methods of data exchange with that device. This would include what instructions it understands and so on. Going back to the racing car example, the agreement would include how the engine connects to the fuel tank, how it passes drive power to the wheels of the car, and so on.

As the name of the technology suggests, this is achieved using *objects*. So, what is an object?

What Is an Object?

An *object* is a building block of an OOP application. This building block encapsulates part of the application, which may be a process, a chunk of data, or some more abstract entity.

In the simplest sense, an object may be very similar to a struct type such as those you saw earlier in the book, containing members of variable and function types. The variables contained make up the data stored in the object, and the functions contained give access to the functionality of the object. Slightly more complex objects might not maintain any data; instead, they can represent a process by containing only functions. For example, an object representing a printer might be used, which would have functions enabling control over a printer (allowing you to print a document, print a test page, and so on).

Objects in C# are created from types, just like the variables you've seen already. The type of an object is known by a special name in OOP, its *class*. You can use class definitions to *instantiate* objects, which means to create a real, named *instance* of a class. The phrases *instance of a class* and *object* mean the same thing here; be sure to note at this point that *class* and *object* mean fundamentally different things.

> *The terms class and object are often confused, and it is important to get the distinction right from the beginning. It may help you to visualize these terms using the earlier racing car example. In this example, a class might be thought of as the template for the car, or perhaps the plans used to build the car. The car itself is an instance of those plans, so it could be referred to as an object.*

In this chapter, you picture classes and objects using *Universal Modeling Language (UML)* syntax. UML is a language designed for modeling applications, from the objects that build them up, to the operations they perform, and to the use cases that are expected. Here, you use only the basics of this language, which will be explained as you go along. I won't be going into the more complex aspects because UML is a specialized subject that has whole books devoted to it.

> *The diagrams in this chapter have been created using Microsoft Visio, which ships with the Enterprise Architect edition of VS. There is also a class viewer in VS that is a powerful tool in its own right. You look at that in Chapter 9.*

Figure 8-1 shows a UML representation of your printer class, called `Printer`.

Figure 8-1

The class name is shown in the top section of this box (you learn about the bottom two sections a little later).

Figure 8-2 shows a UML representation of an instance of this Printer class called myPrinter.

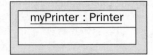

Figure 8-2

Here, the instance name is shown first in the top section, followed by the name of its class. These two names are separated by a colon.

Properties and Fields

Properties and fields provide access to the data contained in an object. This object data is what differentiates separate objects, because it is possible for different objects of the same class to have different values stored in properties and fields.

At this point it is worth introducing another term — the various pieces of data contained in an object together make up the *state* of that object.

Imagine an object class that represents a cup of coffee, called CupOfCoffee. When you instantiate this class (that is, you create an object of this class), you must provide it with a state for it to be meaningful. Here, you might use properties and fields to enable code using this object to set the type of coffee used, whether the coffee contains milk or sugar, whether the coffee is instant, and so on. A given coffee cup object would then have a given state, such as "Columbian filter coffee with milk and two sugars."

Both fields and properties are typed, so you can store information in them as string variables, as int variables, and so on. However, properties differ from fields in that they don't provide *direct* access to data. Objects are capable of shielding users from the nitty-gritty details of their data, which needn't be represented on a 1-to-1 basis in the properties that exist. If you used a field for the number of sugars in a CupOfCoffee instance then users could place whatever value they liked in the field, limited only by the limits of the type used to store this information. If, for example, you used an int to store this data then users could use any value between –2147483648 and 2147483647, as you saw in Chapter 3. Obviously, not all values here make sense, particularly the negative ones — and some of the large positive amounts might require an inordinately large cup. However, if you used a property for this information, then you could limit this value to, say, a number between 0 and 2.

In general, it is better to provide properties rather than fields for state access, because you have more control over what goes on. This choice doesn't affect code that uses object instances, because the syntax for using properties and fields is the same.

Read/write access to properties may also be clearly defined by an object. Certain properties may be read-only, allowing you to see what they are but not change them (at least not directly). This is often a useful technique for reading several pieces of state simultaneously. You might have a read-only property of the CupOfCoffee class called Description, returning a string representing the state of an instance of this class (such as the string given earlier) when requested. You might be able to assemble the same data by interrogating several properties, but a property such as this one may save you time and effort. You might also have write-only properties operating in a similar way.

As well as this read/write access for properties, it is also possible to specify a different sort of access permission for both fields and properties, known as *accessibility*. Accessibility determines what code can access these members, that is, whether they are available to all code (*public*), are available only to code within the class (*private*), or use a more complex scheme (this is covered in more detail later on in the chapter, when it becomes pertinent). One very common practice is to make fields private and provide access to them via public properties. This means that code within the class can have direct access to the data stored in the field, while the `public` property shields external users from this data and prevents them from placing invalid content here. Public members are said to be *exposed* by the class.

One way of visualizing this is to equate it with variable scope. Private fields and properties, for example, can be thought of as local to the object that possesses them, whereas the scope of public fields and properties also encompasses code external to the object.

In the UML representation of a class, you use the second section to display properties and fields, as shown in Figure 8-3.

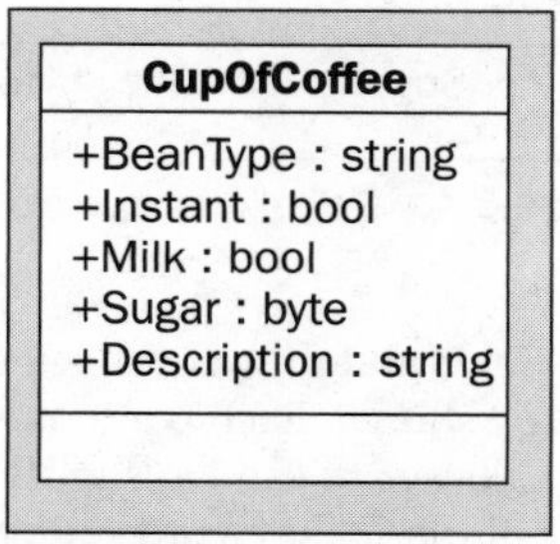

```
┌─────────────────────────┐
│      CupOfCoffee         │
├─────────────────────────┤
│ +BeanType : string       │
│ +Instant : bool          │
│ +Milk : bool             │
│ +Sugar : byte            │
│ +Description : string     │
├─────────────────────────┤
│                         │
└─────────────────────────┘
```

Figure 8-3

This is a representation of the `CupOfCoffee` class, with five members (properties or fields, because no distinction is made in UML) defined as discussed earlier. Each of the entries contains the following information:

❑ Accessibility: A + symbol is used for a public member, a - symbol is used for a private member. In general, though, I won't show private members in the diagrams in this chapter, because this information is internal to the class. No information is provided as to read/write access.

❑ The member name.

❑ The type of the member.

A colon is used to separate the member names and types.

Methods

Method is the term used to refer to functions exposed by objects. These may be called in the same way as any other function and may use return values and parameters in the same way — you looked at functions in detail in Chapter 6.

Methods are used to give access to the functionality of objects. Like fields and properties, they can be public or private, restricting access to external code as necessary. They will often make use of an objects' state to affect their operation, and have access to private members such as private fields if required. For example, the `CupOfCoffee` class might define a method called `AddSugar()`, which would provide a more readable syntax for incrementing the sugar property than setting the corresponding `Sugar` property.

In UML, class boxes show methods in the third section, as shown in Figure 8-4.

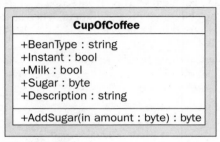

Figure 8-4

The syntax here is similar to that for fields and properties, except that the type shown at the end is the return type and method parameters are shown. Each parameter is displayed in UML with one of the following identifiers: `in`, `out`, or `inout`. These are used to signify the direction of data flow, where `out` and `inout` roughly correspond to the use of the C# keywords `out` and `ref` described in Chapter 6. `in` roughly corresponds to the default C# behavior, where neither the `out` nor `ref` keyword is used.

Everything's an Object

At this point it's time for me to come clean — you have been using objects, properties, and methods throughout this book. In fact, everything in C# and the .NET Framework is an object! The `Main()` function in a console application is a method of a class. Every variable type you've looked at is a class. Every command you have used has been a property or a method, such as `<String>.Length`, `<String>.ToUpper()`, and so on. The period character here separates the object instance's name from the property or method's name.

Objects really are everywhere, and the syntax to use them is often very simple. It has certainly been simple enough for you to concentrate on some of the more fundamental aspects of C# up until now.

From here on in, you start to look at objects in more detail. Bear in mind that the concepts introduced here have far-reaching consequences — applying even to that simple little `int` variable you've been happily playing around with.

The Lifecycle of an Object

Every object has a clearly defined lifecycle. Apart from the normal state of "being in use," this lifecycle includes two important stages:

❑ **Construction:** When an object is first instantiated it needs to be initialized. This initialization is known as construction and is carried out by a *constructor* function.

❑ **Destruction:** When an object is destroyed, there will often be some clean up tasks to perform, such as freeing up memory. This is the job of a *destructor* function.

Constructors

Basic initialization of an object is automatic. For example, you don't have to worry about finding the memory to fit a new object into. However, there are times where you will want to perform additional tasks during an object's initialization stage, such as initializing the data stored by an object. A constructor function is what you use to do this.

All objects have a *default constructor*, which is a parameterless method with the same name as the class itself. In addition, a class definition might include several constructor methods with parameters, known as *nondefault constructors*. These enable code that instantiates an object to do so in many ways, perhaps providing initial values for data stored in the object.

In C#, constructors are called using the `new` keyword. For example, you could instantiate a `CupOfCoffee` object using its default constructor in the following way:

```
CupOfCoffee myCup = new CupOfCoffee();
```

Objects may also be instantiated using nondefault constructors. For example, the `CupOfCoffee` class might have a nondefault constructor that uses a parameter to set the bean type at instantiation:

```
CupOfCoffee myCup = new CupOfCoffee("Blue Mountain");
```

Constructors, like fields, properties, and methods, may be public or private. Code external to a class can't instantiate an object using a private constructor; it must use a public constructor. In this way, you can, for example, force users of your classes to use a nondefault constructor (by making the default constructor private).

Some classes have no public constructors, meaning that it is impossible for external code to instantiate them. However, this doesn't make them completely useless, as you will see shortly.

Destructors

Destructors are used by the .NET Framework to clean up after objects. In general, you don't have to provide code for a destructor method; instead, the default operation works for you. However, you can provide specific instructions if anything important needs to be done before the object instance is deleted.

When a variable goes out of scope, for example, it may not be accessible from your code, but it may still exist somewhere in your computer's memory. It is only when the .NET runtime performs its garbage collection clean up that the instance is completely destroyed.

This means that you shouldn't rely on the destructor to free up resources that are used by an object instance, as this may be a long time after the object is of no further use to you. If the resources in use are critical this can cause problems. However, there is a solution to this — as you see in the "Disposable Objects" section later in this chapter.

Static and Instance Class Members

As well as having members such as properties, methods, and fields that are specific to object instances, it is also possible to have *static* (also known as *shared*, particularly to our Visual Basic brethren) members, which may be methods, properties, or fields. Static members are shared between instances of a class, so they can be thought of as global for objects of a given class. Static properties and fields allow you access to data that is independent of any object instances, and static methods allow you to execute commands related to the class type but not specific to object instances. When using static members, in fact, you don't even need to instantiate an object.

For example, the `Console.WriteLine()` and `Convert.ToString()` methods you have been using are static. At no point do you need to instantiate the `Console` or `Convert` classes (indeed, if you try it you'll find that you can't, as the constructors of these classes aren't publicly accessible, as discussed earlier).

There are many situations such as these where static properties and methods can be used to good effect. For example, you might use a static property to keep track of how many instances of a class have been created.

In UML syntax, static members of classes are shown underlined, as shown in Figure 8-5.

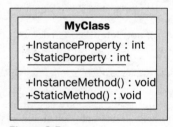

Figure 8-5

Static Classes

Often, you will want to use classes that only contain static members and cannot be used to instantiate objects (such as `Console`). A shorthand way of doing this, rather than making the constructors of the class private, is to use a *static class*. A static class can only contain static members and needs no constructor definition, since by implication it can never be instantiated.

OOP Techniques

Now that you've covered the basics and know what objects are and how they work, you should spend some time looking at some of the other features of objects. In this section, you look at:

❑ Interfaces

❑ Inheritance

❑ Polymorphism

❑ Relationships between objects

❑ Operator overloading

❑ Events

❑ Reference versus value types

Interfaces

An interface is a collection of public methods and properties that are grouped together to encapsulate specific functionality. Once an interface has been defined, you can implement it in a class. This means that the class will then support all of the properties and members specified by the interface.

Note that interfaces cannot exist on their own. You can't "instantiate an interface" as you can a class. In addition, interfaces cannot contain any code that implements its members; it just defines the members themselves. The implementation must come from classes that implement the interface.

In the earlier coffee example, you might group together many of the more general-purpose properties and methods into an interface, such as `AddSugar()`, `Milk`, `Sugar`, and `Instant`. You could call this interface something like `IHotDrink` (interface names are normally prefixed with a capital `I`). You could use this interface on other objects, perhaps those of a `CupOfTea` class. You could therefore treat these objects in a similar way, and they may still have their own individual properties (`BeanType` for `CupOfCoffee` and `LeafType` for `CupOfTea`, for example).

Interfaces implemented on objects in UML are shown using a *lollipop* syntax. In Figure 8-6, I've split the members of `IHotDrink` into a separate box using classlike syntax (unfortunately, the current version of Visio doesn't allow interfaces to possess fields or properties).

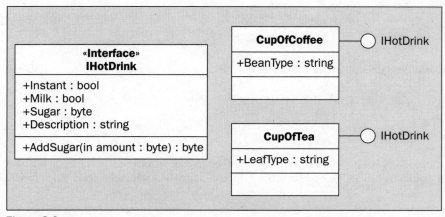

Figure 8-6

A class can support multiple interfaces, and multiple classes can support the same interface. The concept of an interface, therefore, makes life easier for users and other developers. For example, you might have some code that uses an object with a certain interface. Provided that you don't use other properties and methods of this object, it is possible to replace one object with another (code using the IHotDrink interface shown earlier could work with both CupOfCoffee and CupOfTea instances, for example). In addition, the developer of the object itself could supply you with an updated version of an object, and as long as it supports an interface that is already in use it becomes easy to use this new version in your code.

Once an interface is published, that is, it has been made available to other developers or end users, it is good practice not to change it. One way of thinking about this is to imagine the interface as a contract between class creators and class consumers. You are effectively saying "every class that supports Interface X will support these methods and properties." If the interface changed at a later date, perhaps due to an upgrade of the underlying code, this could cause consumers of that interface to run incorrectly, or even fail completely. Instead, you should create a new interface that extends the old one, perhaps including a version number such as IHotDrink2. This has become the standard way of doing things, and you are likely to come across numbered interfaces frequently.

Disposable Objects

One interface of particular interest is IDisposable. An object that supports the IDisposable interface must implement the Dispose() method, that is, they must provide code for this method. This method can be called when an object is no longer needed (just before it goes out of scope, for example) and should be used to free up any critical resources that might otherwise linger until the destructor method is called on garbage collection. This gives you more control over the resources used by your objects.

C# allows you to use a structure that makes excellent use of this method. The using keyword allows you to initialize an object that uses critical resources in a code block, where Dispose() is automatically called at the end of this code block. The usage is:

```
<ClassName> <VariableName> = new <ClassName>();

...

Using (<VariableName>)
{
   ...
}
```

Alternatively, you an instantiate the object <VariableName> as part of the using statement:

```
using (<ClassName> <VariableName> = new <ClassName>())
{
   ...
}
```

In both cases, the variable <VariableName> will be usable within the using code block and will be disposed of automatically at the end (that is, Dispose() is called when the code block finishes executing).

Inheritance

Inheritance is one of the most important features of OOP. Any class may *inherit* from another, which means that it will have all the members that the class it inherits from has. In OOP terminology, the class being inherited (also known as *derived*) from is the *parent* class (also known as the *base* class). Note that classes in C# may descend only from a single base class directly, although of course that base class may have a base class of its own, and so on.

Inheritance allows you to extend or create more specific classes from a single, more generic base class. For example, consider a class that represents a farm animal (as used by ace octogenarian developer Old MacDonald in his livestock application). This class might be called `Animal` and possesses methods such as `EatFood()` or `Breed()`. You could create a derived class called `Cow`, which would support all of these methods, but might also supply its own, such as `Moo()` and `SupplyMilk()`. You could also create another derived class, `Chicken`, with `Cluck()`, and `LayEgg()` methods.

In UML you indicate inheritance using arrows, as shown in Figure 8-7.

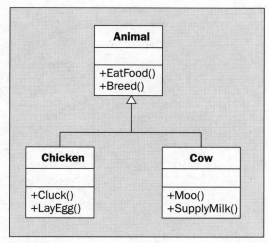

Figure 8-7

In Figure 8-7 I've omitted the member return types for clarity.

When using inheritance from a base class, the question of member accessibility becomes an important one. Private members of the base class will not be accessible from a derived class, but public members will. However, public members are accessible to both the derived class and external code. This means that if you could use only these two levels of accessibility, you couldn't have a member that was accessible by the base class and the derived class but not external code.

To get around this, there is a third type of accessibility, *protected*, where only derived classes have access to a member. As far as external code is aware, this is identical to a private member — it doesn't have access in either case.

As well as defining the protection level of a member, you can also define an inheritance behavior for it. Members of a base class may be *virtual*, which means that the member can be *overridden* by the class that inherits it. What this means is that the derived class *may* provide an alternative implementation for the member. This alternative implementation doesn't delete the original code, which is still accessible from within the class, but it does shield it from external code. If no alternative is supplied, the external code has access to the base class implementation of the member.

> *Note that virtual members cannot be private, as this would cause a paradox — it is impossible to say that a member can be overridden by a derived class at the same time you say that it is inaccessible from the derived class.*

In the animals example, you could make `EatFood()` virtual and provide a new implementation for it on any derived class — for example just on the `Cow` class, as shown in Figure 8-8.

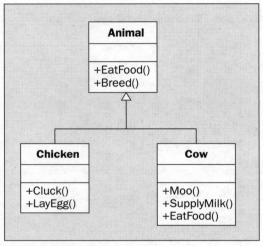

Figure 8-8

Here I've displayed the `EatFood()` method on the `Animal` and `Cow` classes to signify that they have their own implementations.

Base classes may also be defined as *abstract* classes. An abstract class can't be instantiated directly; to use it you need to inherit from it. Abstract classes may have abstract members, which have no implementation in the base class, so an implementation *must* be supplied in the derived class.

If `Animal` were an abstract class, then the UML would look as shown in Figure 8-9.

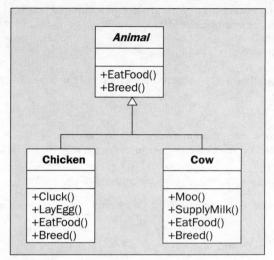

Figure 8-9

Abstract classes are shown with their name in italics (or sometimes with a dashed line for their box).

In Figure 8-9 both `EatFood()` and `Breed()` are shown in the derived classes `Chicken` and `Cow`, implying that these methods are either abstract (and, therefore, must be overridden in derived classes) or virtual (and, in this case, have been overridden in `Chicken` and `Cow`). It is of course possible for abstract base classes to provide implementation of members, which is in fact very common. The fact that you can't instantiate an abstract class doesn't mean that you can't encapsulate functionality in an abstract class.

Finally, a class may be *sealed*. A sealed class may not be used as a base class, so no derived classes are possible.

In C#, there is a common base class for all objects called `object` (which is an alias for the `System.Object` class in the .NET Framework). You take a closer look at this class in Chapter 9.

Interfaces, described earlier in this chapter, may also inherit from other interfaces. Unlike classes, interfaces may inherit from multiple base interfaces (in the same way that classes can support multiple interfaces).

Polymorphism

One consequence of inheritance is that classes deriving from a base class have an overlap in the methods and properties that they expose. Because of this, it is often possible to treat objects instantiated from classes with a base type in common using identical syntax. For example, if a base class called `Animal` has a method called `EatFood()`, then the syntax for calling this method from the derived classes `Cow` and `Chicken` will be similar:

```
Cow myCow = new Cow();
Chicken myChicken = new Chicken();
myCow.EatFood();
myChicken.EatFood();
```

Polymorphism takes this a step further. You can assign a variable that is of the base type to a variable of one of the derived types, for example:

```
Animal myAnimal = myCow;
```

No casting is required for this. You can then call methods of the base class through this variable:

```
myAnimal.EatFood();
```

This will result in the implementation of EatFood() in the derived class being called. Note that you can't call methods defined on the derived class in the same way. The following code won't work:

```
myAnimal.Moo();
```

However, you can cast a base type variable into a derived class variable and call the method of the derived class that way:

```
Cow myNewCow = (Cow)myAnimal;
myNewCow.Moo();
```

This casting will cause an exception to be raised if the type of the original variable was anything other than Cow or a class derived from Cow. There are ways of telling what type an object is, but I'll leave that until the next chapter.

Polymorphism is an extremely useful technique for performing tasks on different objects descending from a single class with the minimum of code.

Note that it isn't just classes sharing the same parent class that can make use of polymorphism. It is also possible to treat, say, a child and a grandchild class in the same way, as long as there is a common class in their inheritance hierarchy.

As a further note here, remember that in C# all classes derive from the base class object at the root of their inheritance hierarchy. It is, therefore, possible to treat *all* objects as instances of the class object. This is how Console.WriteLine() is able to process an almost infinite number of parameter combinations when building up strings. Every parameter after the first is treated as an object instance, allowing output from any object to be written to the screen. To do this, the method ToString() (a member of object) is called. You can override this method to provide an implementation suitable for your class, or simply use the default, which returns the class name (qualified according to any namespaces it is in).

Interface Polymorphism

Earlier, you were introduced to the concept of interfaces for grouping together related methods and properties. Although you cannot instantiate interfaces in the same way as objects, it is possible to have a variable of an interface type. You can then use this variable to get access to methods and properties exposed by this interface on objects that support it.

For example, say that instead of an Animal base class being used to supply the EatFood() method, you place this EatFood() method on an interface called IConsume. The Cow and Chicken classes could both support this interface; the only difference being that they are forced to provide an implementation for EatFood() (as interfaces contain no implementation). You can then access this method using code such as:

```
Cow myCow = new Cow();
Chicken myChicken = new Chicken();
IConsume consumeInterface;
consumeInterface = myCow;
consumeInterface.EatFood();
consumeInterface = myChicken;
consumeInterface.EatFood();
```

This provides a simple way for multiple objects to be called in the same way, and doesn't rely on a common base class. In this code, calling consumeInterface.EatFood() results in the EatFood() method of the Cow or Chicken class being called, depending on which instance has been assigned to the interface type variable.

It is worth mentioning here that derived classes inherit the interfaces supported by their base classes. In the preceding example, it may either be the case that it is Animal that supports IConsume or that both Cow and Chicken support IConsume. Always remember — classes that have a base class in common do not necessarily have interfaces in common, and vice versa.

Relationships between Objects

Inheritance is a simple relationship between objects that results in a base class being completely exposed by a derived class, where the derived class may also have some access to the inner workings of its base class (through protected members). There are other situations in which relationships between objects become important.

In this section you take a brief look at:

❑ **Containment:** Where one class contains another. This is similar to inheritance but allows the containing class to control access to the members of the contained class and even perform additional processing before using members of a contained class.

❑ **Collections:** Where one class acts as a container for multiple instances of another class. This is similar to having arrays of objects, but collections have additional functionality, including indexing, sorting, resizing, and more.

Containment

Containment is simple to achieve by using a member field to hold an object instance. This member field might be public, in which case users of the container object will have access to its exposed methods and properties much as with inheritance. However, you won't have access to the internals of the class via the derived class as you would with inheritance.

Alternatively, you can make the contained member object a private member. If you do this, none of its members will be accessible directly by users, even if they are public. Instead, you can provide access to these members using members of the containing class. This means that you have complete control over which members of the contained class to expose, if any, and you can also perform additional processing in the containing class members before accessing the contained class members.

For example, a Cow class might contain an Udder class with the public method Milk(). The Cow object could call this method as required, perhaps as part of its SupplyMilk() method, but these details will not be apparent (or important) to users of the Cow object.

Contained classes may be visualized in UML using an association line. For simple containment, you label the ends of the lines with 1s, showing a one-to-one relationship (one Cow instance will contain one Udder instance). You can also show the contained Udder class instance as a private field of the Cow class for clarity. This is illustrated in Figure 8-10.

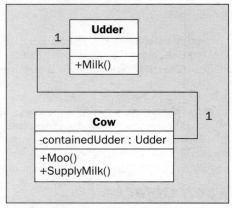

Figure 8-10

Collections

Back in Chapter 5, you saw how you can use arrays to store multiple variables of the same type. This also works for objects (remember, the variable types you have been using are really objects, so this is no real surprise). For example:

```
Animal[] animals = new Animal[5];
```

A collection is basically an array with bells and whistles. Collections are implemented as classes in much the same way as other objects. They are often named in the plural form of the objects they store, for example a class called Animals might contain a collection of Animal objects.

The main difference from arrays is that collections usually implement additional functionality, such as Add() and Remove() methods to add and remove items to and from the collection. There is also usually an Item property that returns an object based on its index. More often than not this property is implemented in such a way as to allow more sophisticated access. For example, it would be possible to design Animals so that a given Animal object could be accessed by its name.

In UML you can visualize this as shown in Figure 8-11.

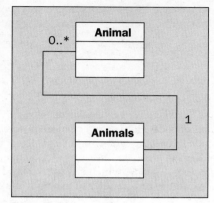

Figure 8-11

I've left off the members in Figure 8-11, because it's the relationship that is being illustrated. The numbers on the ends of the connecting lines show that one `Animals` object will contain zero or more `Animal` objects.

You take a more detailed look at collections in Chapter 11.

Operator Overloading

Earlier in the book, you saw how operators can be used to manipulate simple variable types. There are times when it is logical to use operators with objects instantiated from your own classes. This is possible because classes can contain instructions as to how operators should be treated.

For example, you might add a new property to the `Animal` class called `Weight`. You could then compare animal weights using:

```
if (cowA.Weight > cowB.Weight)
{
    ...
}
```

Using operator overloading, you can provide logic that used the `Weight` property implicitly in your code, so that you can write code such as:

```
if (cowA > cowB)
{
    ...
}
```

Here, the greater than operator (>) has been *overloaded*. An overloaded operator is one for which you have written the code to perform the operation involved — this code is added to the class definition of one of the classes that it operates on. In the preceding example, you are using two `Cow` objects, so the operator overload definition is contained in the `Cow` class. You can also overload operators to work with different classes in the same way, where one (or both) of the class definitions contains the code to achieve this.

Note that you can only overload existing C# operators in this way; you can't create new ones. However, you can provide implementations for both unary and binary usages of operators such as +.

You see how to do this in C# in Chapter 13.

Events

Objects may raise (and consume) *events* as part of their processing. Events are important occurrences that you can act on in other parts of code, similar to (but more powerful than) exceptions. You might, for example, want some specific code to execute when an `Animal` object is added to an `Animals` collection, where that code isn't part of either the `Animals` class or the code that calls the `Add()` method. To do this, you need to add an *event handler* to your code, which is a special kind of function that is called when the event occurs. You also need to configure this handler to listen for the event you are interested in.

Using events, you can create *event-driven* applications, which are far more prolific than you might think at this stage. As an example, it is worth bearing in mind that Windows-based applications are entirely dependent on events. Every button click or scrollbar drag you perform is achieved through event handling, where the events are triggered by the mouse or keyboard.

Later in this chapter you see how this works in Windows applications, and there will be a more in-depth discussion of events in Chapter 13.

Reference versus Value Types

Data in C# is stored in a variable in one of two ways, depending on the type of the variable. This type will fall into one of two categories; it is either a *reference* type or a *value* type. The difference is as follows:

❑   Value types store themselves and their content in one place in memory.

❑   Reference types hold a reference to somewhere else in memory (called the heap) where content is stored.

In fact, you don't have to worry about this too much when using C#. So far, you've used `string` variables (which are reference types) and other simple variables (most of which are value types, such as `int`) in pretty much the same way.

One key difference between value and reference types is that value types always contain a value, whereas reference types can be `null`, reflecting the fact that they contain no value. It is, however, possible to create a value type that behaves like a reference type in this respect (that is, it can be `null`) by the use of *nullable types*, which are a form of *generic*. This is an advanced topic that you will examine in Chapter 12.

The only simple types that are reference types are `string` and `object`, although arrays are implicitly reference types as well. Every class you create will be a reference type, which is why I'm making this point now.

Structs

There is an important point to note. The key difference between struct types and classes is that struct types are value types.

The fact that struct types and classes are similar may have occurred to you, particularly when you saw in Chapter 6 how you can use functions in struct types. You see more details about this in Chapter 9.

OOP in Windows Applications

In Chapter 2, you saw how to create a simple Windows application in C#. Windows applications are heavily dependent on OOP techniques, and in this section you take a look at this to illustrate some of the points made in this chapter. To do this, in the following Try It Out you work through a simple example.

Try It Out   **Objects in Action**

1.   Create a new Windows application in the directory `C:\BegVCSharp\Chapter8` called `Ch08Ex01`.

2.   Add a new `Button` control using the Toolbox, and position it in the center of `Form1`, as shown in Figure 8-12.

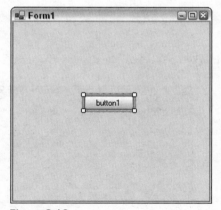

Figure 8-12

3.   Double-click on the button to add code for a mouse click. Modify the code that appears as follows:

```
private void button1_Click(object sender, System.EventArgs e)
{
    ((Button)sender).Text = "Clicked!";
    Button newButton = new Button();
    newButton.Text = "New Button!";
    newButton.Click += new EventHandler(newButton_Click);
    Controls.Add(newButton);
```

```
    }

    private void newButton_Click(object sender, System.EventArgs e)
    {
        ((Button)sender).Text = "Clicked!!";
    }
}
```

4. Run the application. The form is shown in Figure 8-13.

Figure 8-13

5. Click on the button marked `button1`. The display changes, as shown in Figure 8-14.

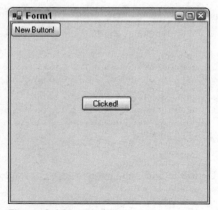

Figure 8-14

6. Click on the button marked `New Button!`. The display changes, as shown in Figure 8-15.

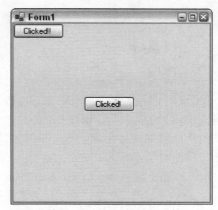

Figure 8-15

How It Works

By adding just a few lines of code you've created a Windows application that does something, while at the same time illustrating some OOP techniques in C#. The phrase "Everything's an object" is even more true when it comes to Windows applications. From the form that runs to the controls on the form, you need to make use of OOP techniques all the time. Throughout this example's description, I've highlighted some of the concepts that you've looked at earlier in this chapter to show how everything fits together.

The first thing you did in your application was to add a new button to the Form1 form. This button is an *object*, called Button. Next, by double-clicking the button, you added an *event handler* to listen for the Click *event* that the Button object generates. This event handler is added into the code for the Form object that encapsulates your application, as a *private method*:

```
private void button1_Click(object sender, System.EventArgs e)
{
}
```

This code uses the C# keyword private as a qualifier. Don't worry too much about this for now; in the next chapter, you look at the C# code required for the OOP techniques you've seen in this chapter.

The first line of code you added changes the text on the button that is clicked. This makes use of *polymorphism* as seen earlier in this chapter. The Button object representing the button that you click is sent to the event handler as an object parameter, which you cast into a Button type (this is possible because the Button object *inherits* from System.Object, which is the .NET class that object is an alias for). You then change the Text *property* of the object to change the text displayed:

```
((Button)sender).Text = "Clicked!";
```

Next, you create a new Button object with the new keyword (note that namespaces are set up in this project to enable this simple syntax, otherwise you'd need to use the fully qualified name of this object, System.Windows.Forms.Button):

```
Button newButton = new Button();
newButton.Text = "New Button!";
```

Elsewhere in the code a new *event handler* is added, which you use to respond to the `Click` event generated by the new button:

```
private void newButton_Click(object sender, System.EventArgs e)
{
    ((Button)sender).Text = "Clicked!!";
}
```

You then register this event handler as a listener for the `Click` event, using some *overloaded operator* syntax. Along the way, you create a new `EventHandler` object using a *nondefault constructor*, with the name of the new event handler function:

```
newButton.Click += new EventHandler(newButton_Click);
```

Finally, you make use of the `Controls` property. This property is an object that is a collection of all the controls on your form, and you use its `Add()` method to add your new button to the form:

```
Controls.Add(newButton);
```

The `Controls` property illustrates that properties need not necessarily be simple types such as strings or integers but can be any kind of object.

This short example has used almost all the techniques introduced in this chapter. As you can see, OOP programming needn't be complicated—it just requires a different point of view to get right.

Summary

This chapter has presented you with a full description of object-oriented techniques. You have gone through this in the context of C# programming, but this has mainly been illustrative. The vast majority of this chapter is relevant to OOP in any language.

You started by covering the basics, such as what is meant by the term *object* and how an object is an *instance* of a *class*. Next, you saw how objects can have various *members*, such as *fields*, *properties*, and *methods*. These members can have restricted accessibility, and you looked at what is meant by *public* and *private* members. Later on, you saw that members can also be *protected*, as well as being *virtual* and *abstract* (where abstract methods are only permissible for abstract classes). You also looked at the difference between *static* (*shared*) and *instance* members, and saw why you might want to use *static classes*.

Next, you took a quick look at the lifecycle of an object, including how *constructors* are used in object creation and *destructors* are used in object deletion. Later on, after examining groups of members in *interfaces*, you looked at more advanced object destruction with *disposable* objects supporting the `IDisposable` interface.

Most of the remainder of the chapter covered the features of OOP, many of which you'll be seeing in more depth in the chapters that follow. You looked at *inheritance*, where classes *inherit* from *base classes*; two versions of *polymorphism*, through base classes and shared interfaces; and how objects can be used to contain one or more other objects (through *containment* and *collections*). Finally, you saw how *operator overloading* can be used to simplify the syntax of object usage and how objects often raise *events*.

The last part of this chapter demonstrated much of the theory in this chapter, using a Windows application as an example.

In this chapter you learned:

❑   What object-oriented programming is

❑   The key terms and features of OOP

❑   How to create, use, and delete an object

❑   How to use OOP in a Windows application

In the next chapter, you look at defining classes using C#.

Exercises

1.   Which of the following are real levels of accessibility in OOP?

❑   Friend

❑   Public

❑   Secure

❑   Private

❑   Protected

❑   Loose

❑   Wildcard

2.   "You must call the destructor of an object manually, or it will waste memory." True or false?

3.   Do you need to create an object in order to call a static method of its class?

4.   Draw a UML diagram similar to the ones shown in this chapter for the following classes and interface:

❑   An abstract class called `HotDrink` that has the methods `Drink()`, `AddMilk()`, and `AddSugar()`, and the properties `Milk`, and `Sugar`.

❑   An interface called `ICup` that has the methods `Refill()` and `Wash()`, and the properties `Color` and `Volume`.

❑   A class called `CupOfCoffee` that derives from `HotDrink`, supports the `ICup` interface, and has the additional property `BeanType`.

❑   A class called `CupOfTea` that derives from `HotDrink`, supports the `ICup` interface, and has the additional property `LeafType`.

5.   Write some code for a function that will accept either of the two cup objects in the preceding example as a parameter. The function should call the `AddMilk()`, `Drink()`, and `Wash()` methods for any cup object it is passed.

Defining Classes

In Chapter 8, you looked at the features of object-oriented programming (OOP). In this chapter, you put theory into practice and look at defining classes in C#.

I won't go so far as to define class members in this chapter but will concentrate on the class definitions themselves for now. This may sound a little limiting, but don't worry, there's plenty here to get your teeth into!

To start, you look at the basic class definition syntax, the keywords you can use to determine class accessibility and so on, and the way in which you can specify inheritance. You also look at interface definitions, because they are similar to class definitions in many ways.

The rest of the chapter covers various topics that apply when defining classes in C#, including:

❑ The System.Object class

❑ Helpful tools provided by Visual Studio 2005 (VS)

❑ Class libraries

❑ A comparison between interfaces and abstract classes

❑ Struct types

❑ Copying objects

So, to start with, here are the basics.

Class Definitions in C#

C# uses the class keyword to define classes. The basic structure required is:

```
class MyClass
{
    // Class members.
}
```

This code defines a class called `MyClass`. Once you have defined a class you are free to instantiate it anywhere else in your project that has access to the definition. By default, classes are declared as *internal*, meaning that only code in the current project will have access to them. You can specify this explicitly using the `internal` access modifier keyword as follows (although you don't have to):

```
internal class MyClass
{
    // Class members.
}
```

Alternatively, you can specify that the class is public and should also be accessible to code in other projects. To do this, you use the `public` keyword:

```
public class MyClass
{
    // Class members.
}
```

Note that classes declared in their own right in this way cannot be private or protected. However, it is possible to use these modifiers for declaring classes as class members, which you look at in the next chapter.

In addition to these two access modifier keywords, you can also specify that the class is either *abstract* (cannot be instantiated, only inherited, and can have abstract members) or *sealed* (cannot be inherited). To do this, you use one of the two mutually exclusive keywords `abstract` or `sealed`. An abstract class must, therefore, be declared in the following way:

```
public abstract class MyClass
{
    // Class members, may be abstract.
}
```

Here `MyClass` is a public abstract class, while internal abstract classes are also possible.

Sealed classes are declared as follows:

```
public sealed class MyClass
{
    // Class members.
}
```

As with abstract classes, sealed classes may be public or internal.

Inheritance can also be specified in the class definition. To do this, you simply put a colon after the class name, followed by the base class name. For example:

```
public class MyClass : MyBase
{
    // Class members.
}
```

Note that *only one* base class is permitted in C# class definitions and that if you inherit from an abstract class you *must* implement all the abstract members inherited (unless the derived class is also abstract).

The compiler will not allow a derived class to be more accessible than its base class. This means that an internal class *can* inherit from a public base, but a public class *can't* inherit from an internal base. This means that the following code is legal:

```
public class MyBase
{
    // Class members.
}
```

```
internal class MyClass : MyBase
{
    // Class members.
}
```

But the following code won't compile:

```
internal class MyBase
{
    // Class members.
}
```

```
public class MyClass : MyBase
{
    // Class members.
}
```

If no base class is used, then the class will inherit only from the base class `System.Object` (which has the alias `object` in C#). Ultimately, *all* classes have `System.Object` at the root of their inheritance hierarchy. You take a closer look at this fundamental class a little later.

As well as specifying base classes in this way, you can also specify interfaces supported after the colon character. If a base class is specified, it must be the first thing after the colon, with interfaces specified afterward. If there is no base class specified, you specify the interfaces straight after the colon. Commas must be used to separate the base class name (if there is one) and the interface names from one another.

For example, you could add an interface to `MyClass` as follows:

```
public class MyClass : IMyInterface
{
    // Class members.
}
```

All interface members *must* be implemented in any class that supports the interface, although you can provide an "empty" implementation (with no functional code) if you don't want to do anything with a given interface member, and you can implement interface members as abstract in abstract classes.

The following declaration is invalid, because the base class `MyBase` isn't the first entry in the inheritance list:

```
public class MyClass : IMyInterface, MyBase
{
    // Class members.
}
```

The correct way to specify a base class and an interface is as follows:

```
public class MyClass : MyBase, IMyInterface
{
    // Class members.
}
```

And remember that multiple interfaces are possible, so the following is also valid:

```
public class MyClass : MyBase, IMyInterface, IMySecondInterface
{
    // Class members.
}
```

As a quick recap, the following table shows the allowed access modifier combinations for class definitions.

Modifier	Meaning
none or `internal`	Class accessible only from within the current project
`public`	Class accessible from anywhere
`abstract` or `internal abstract`	Class accessible only from within the current project, cannot be instantiated, only derived from
`public abstract`	Class accessible from anywhere, cannot be instantiated, only derived from
`sealed` or `internal sealed`	Class accessible only from within the current project, cannot be derived from, only instantiated
`public sealed`	Class accessible from anywhere, cannot be derived from, only instantiated

Interface Definitions

Interfaces are declared in a similar way to classes, but using the `interface` keyword rather than `class`. For example:

```
interface IMyInterface
{
    // Interface members.
}
```

The access modifier keywords `public` and `internal` are used in the same way, so to make an interface publicly accessible you must use the `public` keyword:

```
public interface IMyInterface
{
    // Interface members.
}
```

The keywords `abstract` and `sealed` are not allowed in interfaces because neither modifier makes sense in the context of interfaces (they contain no implementation, so they can't be instantiated directly, and they must be inheritable to be useful).

Interface inheritance is also specified in a similar way to class inheritance. The main difference here is that multiple base interfaces can be used, for example:

```
public interface IMyInterface : IMyBaseInterface, IMyBaseInterface2
{
    // Interface members.
}
```

Interfaces are not classes, and thus do not inherit from `System.Object`. However, the members of `System.Object` are available via an interface type variable, purely for convenience.

Also, as already discussed, it is impossible to instantiate an interface in the same way as a class. The following Try It Out provides an example of some class definitions, along with some code that uses them.

Try It Out   Defining Classes

1. Create a new console application called `Ch09Ex01` in the directory `C:\BegVCSharp\Chapter9`.

2. Modify the code in `Program.cs` as follows:

```
namespace Ch09Ex01
{
    public abstract class MyBase
    {
    }

    internal class MyClass : MyBase
    {
    }

    public interface IMyBaseInterface
    {
    }

    internal interface IMyBaseInterface2
    {
    }

    internal interface IMyInterface : IMyBaseInterface, IMyBaseInterface2
    {
```

```
      }

      internal sealed class MyComplexClass : MyClass, IMyInterface
      {
      }

   class Program
   {
      static void Main(string[] args)
      {
         MyComplexClass myObj = new MyComplexClass();
         Console.WriteLine(myObj.ToString());
         Console.ReadKey();
      }
   }
}
```

3.   Execute the project. The output is shown in Figure 9-1.

Figure 9-1

How It Works

This project defines classes and interfaces in the inheritance hierarchy shown in Figure 9-2.

I've included `Program` here because it is a class defined in the same way as the other classes, even though it isn't part of the main class hierarchy. The `Main()` method possessed by this class is the entry point for your application as discussed earlier in the book.

`MyBase` and `IMyBaseInterface` are public definitions, so they are available from other projects. The other classes and interfaces are internal and are only available in this project.

The code in `Main()` calls the `ToString()` method of `myObj`, an instance of `MyComplexClass`:

```
         MyComplexClass myObj = new MyComplexClass();
         Console.WriteLine(myObj.ToString());
```

This is one of the methods inherited from `System.Object` (not shown in the diagram because I've omitted the members of this class for clarity) and simply returns the class name of the object as a string, qualified by any relevant namespaces.

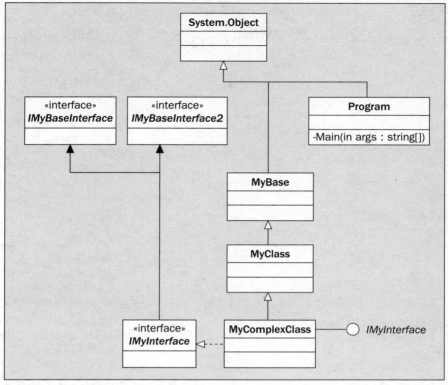

Figure 9-2

System.Object

Since all classes inherit from `System.Object`, all classes will have access to the protected and public members of this class. This means that it is well worth taking a look at what is available there. `System.Object` contains the methods shown in the following table.

Method	Return Type	Virtual	Static	Description
Object()	N/A	No	No	Constructor for the `System.Object` type. Automatically called by constructors of derived types.
~Object() (also known as Finalize() — see next section)	N/A	No	No	Destructor for the `System.Object` type. Automatically called by destructors of derived types, cannot be called manually.

Table continued on following page

Method	Return Type	Virtual	Static	Description
Equals(object)	bool	Yes	No	Compares the object for which this method is called with another object and returns true if they are equal. The default implementation checks to see if the object parameter *refers* to the same object (because objects are reference types). This method can be overridden if you wish to compare objects in a different way, for example if they hold equivalent data.
Equals(object, object)	bool	No	Yes	This method compares the two objects passed to it and checks to see if they are equal This check is performed using the Equals(object) method. Note that if both objects are null references this method returns true.
ReferenceEquals (object, object)	bool	No	Yes	This method compares the two objects passed to it and checks to see if they are references to the same instance.
ToString()	string	Yes	No	Returns a string corresponding to the object instance. By default, this is the qualified name of the class type (see earlier example), but this can be overridden to provide an implementation appropriate to the class type.
MemberwiseClone()	object	No	No	Copies the object by creating a new object instance and copying members. Note that this member copying will *not* result in new instances of these members. Any reference type members of the new object will refer to the same objects as the original class. This method is protected and so can only be used from within the class or from derived classes.

Method	Return Type	Virtual	Static	Description
GetType()	System.Type	No	No	Returns the type of the object in the form of a System.Type object.
GetHashCode()	int	Yes	No	Used as a *hash function* for objects where this is required. A hash function is one that returns a value identifying the object state in some compressed form.

These methods are the basic ones that must be supported by object types in the .NET Framework, although you might never use some of them (or use them only in special circumstances, such as GetHashCode()).

GetType() is a useful method when you are using polymorphism, because it allows you to perform different operations with objects depending on their type, rather than the same operation for all objects as is often the case. For example, if you have a function that accepts an object type parameter (meaning that you can pass it just about anything), you might perform additional tasks if certain objects are encountered. Using a combination of GetType() and typeof() (a C# operator that converts a class name into a System.Type object) you can perform comparisons such as:

```
if (myObj.GetType() == typeof(MyComplexClass))
{
    // myObj is an instance of the class MyComplexClass.
}
```

The System.Type object returned is capable of a lot more than this, but I won't cover this here. This topic is covered in more detail in Chapter 27.

It can also be very useful to override the ToString() method, particularly in situations where the contents of an object can be easily represented with a single human-readable string.

You see these System.Object methods repeatedly over the coming chapters, so I'll end this discussion for now and go into more detail as necessary.

Constructors and Destructors

When you define a class in C#, there is often no need to define associated constructors and destructors, because the base class System.Object provides a default implementation for you. However, you can provide your own if required, enabling you to initialize and clean up after your objects, respectively.

A simple constructor can be added to a class using the following syntax:

```
class MyClass
{
    public MyClass()
    {
        // Constructor code.
    }
}
```

This constructor has the same name as the class that contains it, has no parameters (making it the default constructor for the class), and is public so that objects of the class may be instantiated using this constructor (check back to the discussion in the last chapter for more information on this).

You can also use a private default constructor, meaning that object instances of this class cannot be created using this constructor (see the discussion in the last chapter):

```
class MyClass
{
    private MyClass()
    {
        // Constructor code.
    }
}
```

Finally, you can add nondefault constructors to your class in a similar way, simply by providing parameters. For example:

```
class MyClass
{
    public MyClass()
    {
        // Default constructor code.
    }

    public MyClass(int myint)
    {
        // Nondefault constructor code (uses myInt).
    }
}
```

There is no limit to the number of constructors you can supply (apart from running out of memory or distinct sets of parameters of course, so maybe "almost limitless" is more appropriate).

Destructors are declared using a slightly different syntax. The destructors used in .NET (and supplied by the System.Object class) is called Finalize(), but this isn't the name you use to declare a destructor. Instead of overriding Finalize() you use the following:

```
class MyClass
{
    ~MyClass()
    {
        // Destructor body.
    }
}
```

Thus the destructor of a class is declared by the class name (like the constructor is), with the ~ prefix. The code in the destructor will be executed when garbage collection occurs, allowing you to free resources. After this destructor is called, implicit calls to the destructors of base classes also occur, including a call to `Finalize()` in the `System.Object` root class. This technique allows the .NET Framework to ensure that this occurs, because overriding `Finalize()` would mean that base class calls would need to be explicitly performed, which is potentially dangerous (you see how to call base class methods in the next chapter).

Constructor Execution Sequence

If you perform multiple tasks in the constructors of a class, it can be handy to have this code in one place, which has the same benefits as splitting code into functions, as you saw in Chapter 6. You could do this using a method (see Chapter 10), but C# provides a nice alternative. Any constructor can be configured to call any other constructor before it executes its own code.

Before looking at this, though, you need to take a closer look at what happens by default when you instantiate a class instance. Apart from facilitating the centralization of initialization code as noted above, this is also worth knowing about in its own right. It is often the case during development that objects don't behave quite as you expect them to owing to errors during constructor calling — usually due to a base class somewhere in the inheritance hierarchy of your class that you are not instantiating correctly, or where information is not being properly supplied to base class constructors. Understanding what happens when during this phase of the lifecycle of an object can make it much easier to solve this sort of problem.

In order for a derived class to be instantiated its base class must be instantiated. In order for this base class to be instantiated the base class of this base class must be instantiated, and so on all the way back to `System.Object`. The result of this is that whatever constructor you use to instantiate a class, `System.Object.Object()` is always called first.

If you use a nondefault constructor of a class, then the default behavior is to use a constructor on the base class that matches the signature of this constructor. If none is found, then the default constructor for the base class is used (which will always happen for the ultimate root `System.Object`, because this class has no nondefault constructors). Here's a quick example of this to illustrate the sequence of events. Consider the following object hierarchy:

```
public class MyBaseClass
{
    public MyBaseClass()
    {
    }

    public MyBaseClass(int i)
    {
    }
}

public class MyDerivedClass : MyBaseClass
{
    public MyDerivedClass()
    {
```

```
    }

    public MyDerivedClass(int i)
    {
    }

    public MyDerivedClass(int i, int j)
    {
    }
}
```

You could instantiate MyDerivedClass in the following way:

```
MyDerivedClass myObj = new MyDerivedClass();
```

In this case, the following sequence of events will occur:

❑   The System.Object.Object() constructor will execute.

❑   The MyBaseClass.MyBaseClass() constructor will execute.

❑   The MyDerivedClass.MyDerivedClass() constructor will execute.

Alternatively, you could use the following:

```
MyDerivedClass myObj = new MyDerivedClass(4);
```

Here, the sequence will be:

❑   The System.Object.Object() constructor will execute.

❑   The MyBaseClass.MyBaseClass(int i) constructor will execute.

❑   The MyDerivedClass.MyDerivedClass(int i) constructor will execute.

Finally, you could use the following:

```
MyDerivedClass myObj = new MyDerivedClass(4, 8);
```

This results in the following sequence:

❑   The System.Object.Object() constructor will execute.

❑   The MyBaseClass.MyBaseClass() constructor will execute.

❑   The MyDerivedClass.MyDerivedClass(int i, int j) constructor will execute.

This system works fine and ensures that any inherited members are accessible to constructors in your derived classes. However, there are times when a little more control over the events that take place is required, or just desirable. For example, in the last instantiation example, you might want to have the following sequence:

❑   The `System.Object.Object()` constructor will execute.

❑   The `MyBaseClass.MyBaseClass(int i)` constructor will execute.

❑   The `MyDerivedClass.MyDerivedClass(int i, int j)` constructor will execute.

Using this you could place the code that uses the `int i` parameter in `MyBaseClass(int i)`, meaning that the `MyDerivedClass(int i, int j)` constructor would have less work to do — it would only need to process the `int j` parameter. (This assumes that the `int i` parameter has an identical meaning in both cases, which might not always be the case, but in practice with this kind of arrangement it usually is.) C# allows you to specify this kind of behavior should you wish.

To do this, you simply specify the base class constructor to use in the definition of the constructor in your derived class as follows:

```
public class MyDerivedClass : MyBaseClass
{
    ...

    public MyDerivedClass(int i, int j) : base(i)
    {
    }
}
```

The `base` keyword directs the .NET instantiation process to use the base class constructor matching the signature specified. Here, you are using a single `int` parameter, so `MyBaseClass(int i)` will be used. Doing this means that `MyBaseClass()` will not be called, giving you the sequence of events listed prior to this example — exactly what you wanted here.

You can also use this keyword to specify literal values for base class constructors, perhaps using the default constructor of `MyDerivedClass` to call a nondefault constructor of `MyBaseClass`:

```
public class MyDerivedClass : MyBaseClass
{
    public MyDerivedClass() : base(5)
    {
    }
    ...
}
```

This gives you the following sequence:

❑   The `System.Object.Object()` constructor will execute.

❑   The `MyBaseClass.MyBaseClass(int i)` constructor will execute.

❑   The `MyDerivedClass.MyDerivedClass()` constructor will execute.

As well as this `base` keyword, there is one more keyword that you can use here: `this`. This keyword instructs the .NET instantiation process to use a nondefault constructor on the *current* class before the specified constructor is called. For example:

```
public class MyDerivedClass : MyBaseClass
{
    public MyDerivedClass() : this(5, 6)
    {
    }

    ...

    public MyDerivedClass(int i, int j) : base(i)
    {
    }
}
```

Here, you will have the following sequence:

❑   The `System.Object.Object()` constructor will execute.

❑   The `MyBaseClass.MyBaseClass(int i)` constructor will execute.

❑   The `MyDerivedClass.MyDerivedClass(int i, int j)` constructor will execute.

❑   The `MyDerivedClass.MyDerivedClass()` constructor will execute.

The only limitation to all this is that you can only specify a single constructor using the `this` or `base` keywords. However, as demonstrated in the last example, this isn't much of a limitation, because you can still construct fairly sophisticated execution sequences.

You see this technique in action a little later in the book.

OOP Tools in Visual Studio 2005

Since OOP is such a fundamental subject in the .NET Framework, there are several tools provided by VS to aid development of OOP applications. In this section, you look at some of these.

The Class View Window

Back in Chapter 2, you saw that the `Solution Explorer` window shares space with a window called `Class View`. This window shows you the class hierarchy of your application and enables you to see at a glance the characteristics of the classes you use. For the example project in the previous Try It Out, the view is as shown in Figure 9-3.

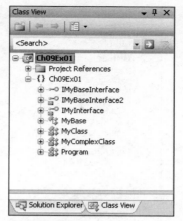

Figure 9-3

This window is divided into two halves, where the bottom half shows members of types. To see this in action with this example project, and to see what else is possible with the `Class View` window, you need to show some items that are currently hidden. To do this, you need to tick the items in the `Class View Grouping` drop-down at the top of the `Class View` window, as shown in Figure 9-4.

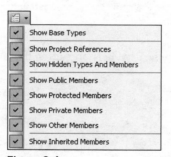

Figure 9-4

Now, you can see members and additional information, as shown in Figure 9-5.

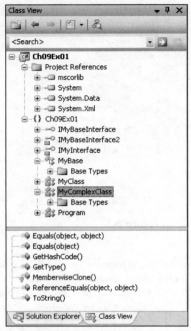

Figure 9-5

There are many symbols that may be used here, including those shown in the following table.

Icon	Meaning
	Project
{ }	Namespace
	Class
	Interface
	Method
	Property
	Field
	Struct
	Enumeration
	Enumeration item
	Event

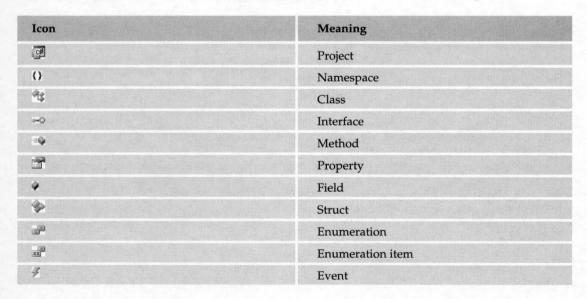

Note that some of these are used for type definitions other than classes, such as enumerations and struct types.

Some of the entries may have other symbols placed below them signifying their access level (no symbol appears for public entries). These symbols are shown in the next table.

Icon	Meaning
⬙	Private
⬙	Protected
⬙	Internal

No symbols are used to denote abstract, sealed, or virtual entries.

As well as being able to look at this information here, you can also get access to the relevant code for many of these items. Double-clicking on an item, or right-clicking and selecting Go To Definition, takes you straight to the code in your project that defines the item, if it is available. If the code isn't available, such as code in an inaccessible base type like System.Object, you will instead have the option of selecting Browse Definition, and selecting that will take you to the Object Browser view (which you look at in the next section).

One other section that appears in Figure 9-5 is Project References. This enables you to see what assemblies are referenced by your projects, which in this case includes the core .NET types in mscorlib and system, data access types in system.data, and XML manipulation types in system.xml. The references here can also be expanded, showing you the namespaces and types contained within these assemblies.

There is also a function available from the Class View that enable you to find occurrences of types and members in your code. These are available by right-clicking on an item and selecting Find All References. Either choice gives you a list of search results in the Find Symbol Results window, which appears at the bottom of the screen, as a tabbed window in the Error List display area. You can also rename items using the Class View. If you do this, you're given the option to rename references to the item wherever they occur in your code. This means that you've got no excuse for spelling mistakes in class names because you can change them as often as you like!

The Object Browser

The Object Browser is an expanded version of the Class View window, allowing you to view other classes available to your project, and even completely external classes. It is entered either automatically (for example in the situation noted in the last section) or manually via View ⇨ Other Windows ⇨ Object Browser. The view appears in the main window, and you can browse it in the same way as the Class View window.

This window shows the same information as Class View but also shows you more of the .NET types. When an item is selected, you also get information about it in a third window, as shown in Figure 9-6.

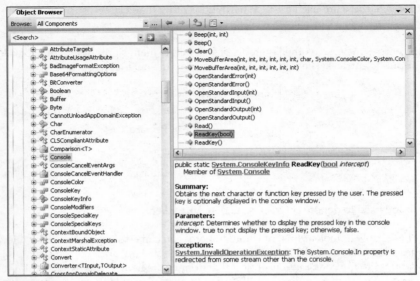

Figure 9-6

In Figure 9-6 the `ReadKey(bool intercept)` method of the `Console` class has been selected. (`Console` is found in the `System` namespace in the `mscorlib` assembly.) The information window in the bottom right shows you the method signature, the class the method belongs to, a summary of the method function, and details about the `intercept` parameter. This information can be very useful when you are exploring the .NET types, or if you are just refreshing your memory about what a particular class can do.

In addition, you can make use of this information window in types that you create. Try making the following change to the code in `Ch09Ex01`:

```
/// <summary>
/// This class contains my program!
/// </summary>
class Program
{
    static void Main(string[] args)
    {
        MyComplexClass myObj = new MyComplexClass();
        Console.WriteLine(myObj.ToString());
        Console.ReadKey();
    }
}
```

If you then return to the object browser, you'll see that the change is reflected in the information window. This is an example of XML documentation, which you look at in Chapter 28.

If you made the code change shown above manually, you noticed that simply typing the three slashes `///` causes VS to add most of the rest of the typing for you. It automatically analyzes the code to which you are applying XML documentation and builds the basic XML documentation — more evidence, should you need any, that VS is a great tool to work with!

Adding Classes

VS contains tools that can speed up some common tasks, and some of these are applicable to OOP. One of these tools allows you to add new classes to your project with the minimum of typing.

This tool is accessible through the Project ⇨ Add New Item... menu item or by right-clicking on your project in the Solution Explorer window and selecting the appropriate item. Either way, a dialog appears, allowing you to choose the type of item to add. To add a class, you select the Class entry in the Templates: window, provide a filename for the file that will contain the class, then click Add. The class created will be named according to the filename chosen. (See Figure 9-7.)

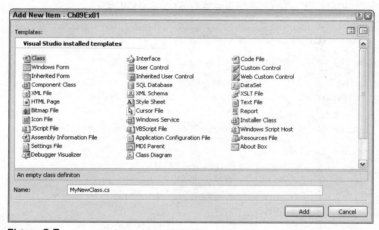

Figure 9-7

In the Try It Out earlier in this chapter, you added class definitions manually to your Program.cs file. It is often the case that keeping classes in separate files makes it easier to keep track of your classes.

Entering the information in the dialog above when the Ch09Ex01 project is open results in the following code being generated in MyNewClass.cs:

```csharp
using System;
using System.Collections.Generic;
using System.Text;

namespace Ch09Ex01
{
    public class MyNewClass
    {
        public MyNewClass()
        {

        }
    }
}
```

This class, `MyNewClass`, is defined in the same namespace as your entry point class, `Program`, so you can use it from code just as if it were defined in the same file.

As you can see from the code, the class that is generated for you contains a default constructor.

Class Diagrams

One powerful feature of VS that you haven't looked at yet is the ability to generate class diagrams from code and to use class diagrams to modify projects. The class diagram editor in VS enables you to generate UML-like diagrams of your code with ease. To see this in action, in the following Try It Out you generate a class diagram for the `Ch09Ex01` project you created earlier.

Try It Out   Generating a Class Diagram

1. Open the `Ch09Ex01` project created earlier in this chapter.

2. In the `Solution Explorer` window, select `Program.cs` and click the `View Class Diagram` button in the `Solution Explorer` toolbar, as shown in Figure 9-8.

Figure 9-8

3. A class diagram appears, called `ClassDiagram1.cd`.

4. Click on the `IMyInterface` lollipop and, using the `Properties` window, change its `Position` property to `Right`.

5. Right-click on `MyBase` and select `Show Base Type` from the context menu that appears.

6. Move the objects in the drawing around by dragging them to give a more pleasing layout. After these steps the diagram should look a little like Figure 9-9.

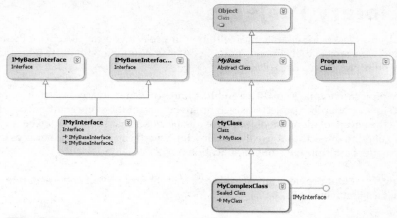

Figure 9-9

How It Works

With very little effort, you have created a class diagram not unlike the UML diagram presented way back in Figure 9-2. The following features are evident:

- ❏ Classes are shown as blue boxes, including their name and type.
- ❏ Interfaces are shown as green boxes, including their name and type.
- ❏ Inheritance is shown with arrows with white heads and (in some cases) text inside class boxes.
- ❏ Classes implementing interfaces have lollipops.
- ❏ Abstract classes are shown with a dotted outline and italicized name.
- ❏ Sealed classes are shown with a thick black outline.

Clicking on an object shows you additional information in a Class Details window at the bottom of the screen. Here, you can see (and modify) class members. You can also modify class details in the `Properties` window.

> *In the next chapter, you take a more in depth look at adding members to classes using the class diagram.*

From the Toolbox bar, you can add new items to the diagram, such as classes, interfaces, enums, and so on, and define relationships between objects in the diagram. If you do this, the code for the new items is automatically generated for you.

Using this editor, it is possible to design whole families of types graphically, without ever having to use the code editor. Obviously, when it comes to actually adding the functionality you will have to do things by hand, but this can be a great way to get started.

You come back to this view in later chapters and learn more about what it can do for you, including using the `Object Test Bench` to test your classes before using them in your code. For now, though, I'll leave you to explore things on your own.

Class Library Projects

As well as placing classes in separate files within your project, you can also place them in completely separate projects. A project that contains nothing but classes (along with other relevant type definitions, but no entry point) is called a *class library*.

Class library projects compile into .dll assemblies, and you can gain access to their contents by adding references to them from other projects (which might be part of the same solution, but don't have to be). This extends the encapsulation that objects provide, because class libraries may be revised and updated without touching the projects that use them, allowing you to easily upgrade services provided by classes (which might affect multiple consumer applications).

The following Try It Out provides an example of a class library project and a separate project that makes use of the classes that it contains.

Try It Out   Using a Class Library

1. Create a new project of type `Class Library` called `Ch09ClassLib` in the directory `C:\BegVCSharp\Chapter9`, as shown in Figure 9-10.

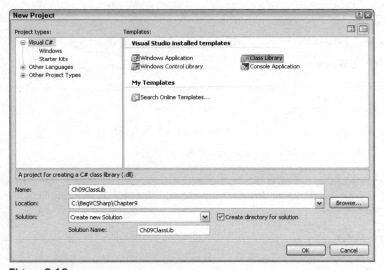

Figure 9-10

2. Rename the file `Class1.cs` as `MyExternalClass.cs` (you can do this by right-clicking on the file in the `Solution Explorer` window and selecting `Rename`). Click `Yes` on the dialog that appears.

3. Note that the code in `MyExternalClass.cs` automatically changes to reflect this class name change:

```
public class MyExternalClass
{
}
```

4. Add a new class to the project, using the filename `MyInternalClass.cs`.

5. Modify the code to make the class `MyInternalClass` internal:

```
internal class MyInternalClass
{
}
```

6. Compile the project (note that this project has no entry point, so you can't run it as normal— instead you can build it by selecting the `Build ⇨ Build Solution` menu option).

7. Create a new console application project called `Ch09Ex02` in the directory `C:\BegVCSharp\Chapter9`.

8. Select the `Project ⇨ Add Reference...` menu item, or select the same option after right-clicking on `References` in the `Solution Explorer` window.

9. Click on the `Browse` tab, navigate to `C:\BegVCSharp\Chapter9\Ch09ClassLib\bin\Debug\`, and double-click on `Ch09ClassLib.dll`.

10. When the operation completes, check that a reference has been added in the `Solution Explorer` window, as shown in Figure 9-11.

Figure 9-11

11. Open the `Object Browser` window and examine the new reference to see what objects it contains, as shown in Figure 9-12.

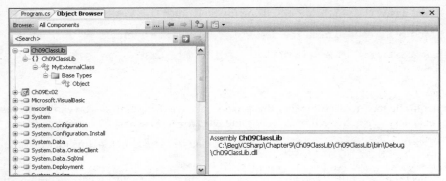

Figure 9-12

12. Modify the code in `Program.cs` as follows:

```
using System;
using System.Collections.Generic;
using System.Text;
using Ch09ClassLib;

namespace Ch09Ex02
{
   class Program
   {
      static void Main(string[] args)
      {
         MyExternalClass myObj = new MyExternalClass();
         Console.WriteLine(myObj.ToString());
         Console.ReadKey();
      }
   }
}
```

13. Run the application. The result is shown in Figure 9-13.

Figure 9-13

How It Works

In this example you have created two projects, one class library project and one console application project. The class library project, `Ch09ClassLib`, contains two classes: `MyExternalClass`—which is publicly accessible—and `MyInternalClass`—which is internally accessible. The console application, `Ch09Ex02`, contains simple code that makes use of the class library project.

To use the classes in Ch09ClassLib, you added a reference to Ch09ClassLib.dll to the console application. For the purposes of this example, you simply pointed at the output file for the class library, although it would have been just as easy to copy this file to a location local to Ch09Ex02, allowing you to continue development of the class library without affecting the console application. To replace the old version of the assembly with the new one, you simply copy the newly generated DLL file over the old one.

After adding the reference you took a look at the available classes using the object browser. Since one of the two classes (MyInternalClass) is internal, you can't see it in this display—it isn't accessible to external projects. However, the other class (MyExternalClass) is accessible, and this is the one you use in the console application.

You could replace the code in the console application with code attempting to use the internal class as follows:

```
static void Main(string[] args)
{
    MyInternalClass myObj = new MyInternalClass();
    Console.WriteLine(myObj.ToString());
    Console.ReadKey();
}
```

If you attempt to compile this code, you will receive the following compilation error:

```
'Ch09ClassLib.MyInternalClass' is inaccessible due to its protection level
```

This technique of making use of classes in external assemblies is key to programming with C# and the .NET Framework. It is in fact exactly what you are doing when you make use of any of the classes in the .NET Framework, because they are treated in the same way.

Interfaces versus Abstract Classes

In this chapter you've seen how you can create both interfaces and abstract classes (without members for now—you get to them in the next chapter). The two types are similar in a number of ways, and it is worth taking a look at this to see how to determine when you would want to use one technique or the other.

First, the similarities: both abstract classes and interfaces may contain members that can be inherited by a derived class. Neither interfaces nor abstract classes may be directly instantiated, but you can declare variables of these types. If you do so, you can use polymorphism to assign objects that inherit from these types to variables of these types. In both cases, you can then use the members of these types through these variables, although you don't have direct access to the other members of the derived object.

And now, the differences: derived classes may only inherit from a single base class, which means that only a single abstract class may be inherited directly (although it is possible for a chain of inheritance to include multiple abstract classes). Conversely, classes may use as many interfaces as they wish. However, this doesn't make a massive difference—similar results can be achieved in either case. It's just that the interface way of doing things is slightly different.

Abstract classes may possess both abstract members (these have no code body and *must* be implemented in the derived class unless the derived class is itself abstract) and nonabstract members (these possess a code body, and can be virtual so that they *may* be overridden in the derived class). Interface members, on the other hand, must *all* be implemented on the class that uses the interface — they do not possess code bodies. Also, interface members are by definition public (because they are intended for external use), but members of abstract classes may also be private (as long as they aren't abstract), protected, internal, or protected internal (where protected internal members are accessible only from code within the application or from a derived class). In addition, interfaces can't contain fields, constructors, destructors, static members, or constants.

> *This indicates that the two types are intended for different purposes. Abstract classes are intended for use as the base class for families of objects that share certain central characteristics, such as a common purpose and structure. Interfaces are intended for use by classes that might differ on a far more fundamental level, but can still do some of the same things.*

As an example, consider a family of objects representing trains. The base class, `Train`, contains the core definition of a train, such as wheel gauge and engine type (which could be steam, diesel, and so on). However, this class is abstract, because there is no such thing as a "generic" train. To create an "actual" train you need to add characteristics specific to that train. To do this you derive classes such as `PassengerTrain`, `FreightTrain`, and `424DoubleBogey`, as shown in Figure 9-14.

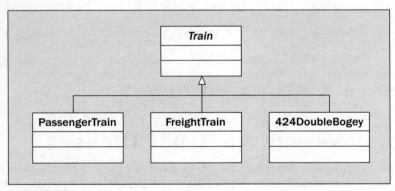

Figure 9-14

A family of car objects might be defined in the same way, with an abstract base class of `Car` and derived classes such as `Compact`, `SUV`, and `PickUp`. `Car` and `Train` might even derive from a common base class, such as `Vehicle`. This is shown in Figure 9-15.

Now, some of the classes further down the hierarchy may share characteristics because of their purpose, not just because of what they are derived from. For example, `PassengerTrain`, `Compact`, `SUV`, and `Pickup` are all capable of carrying passengers, so they might possess an `IPassengerCarrier` interface. `FreightTrain` and `PickUp` can carry heavy loads, so they might both have an `IHeavyLoadCarrier` interface as well. This is illustrated in Figure 9-16.

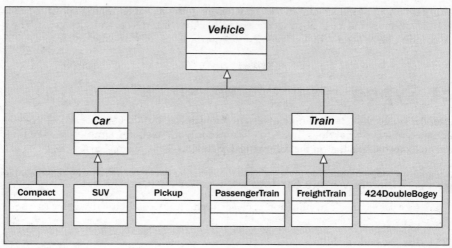

Figure 9-15

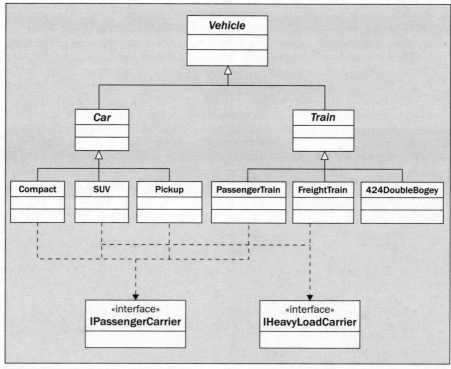

Figure 9-16

By breaking down an object system in this way before going about assigning specifics, you can clearly see which situations should use abstract classes rather than interfaces, and vice versa. The result of this example couldn't have been achieved using only interfaces or only abstract inheritance.

Struct Types

In Chapter 8, I noted that structs and classes are very similar, but that structs are value types and classes are reference types. So, what does this actually mean to you? Well, the simplest way of looking at this is to look at an example like that in the following Try It Out.

Try It Out   **Classes versus Structs**

1.   Create a new console application project called Ch09Ex03 in the directory C:\BegVCSharp\ Chapter9.

2.   Modify the code as follows:

```
namespace Ch09Ex03
{
    class MyClass
    {
        public int val;
    }

    struct myStruct
    {
        public int val;
    }

    class Program
    {
        static void Main(string[] args)
        {
            MyClass objectA = new MyClass();
            MyClass objectB = objectA;
            objectA.val = 10;
            objectB.val = 20;
            myStruct structA = new myStruct();
            myStruct structB = structA;
            structA.val = 30;
            structB.val = 40;
            Console.WriteLine("objectA.val = {0}", objectA.val);
            Console.WriteLine("objectB.val = {0}", objectB.val);
            Console.WriteLine("structA.val = {0}", structA.val);
            Console.WriteLine("structB.val = {0}", structB.val);
            Console.ReadKey();
        }
    }
}
```

3.   Run the application. The output is shown in Figure 9-17.

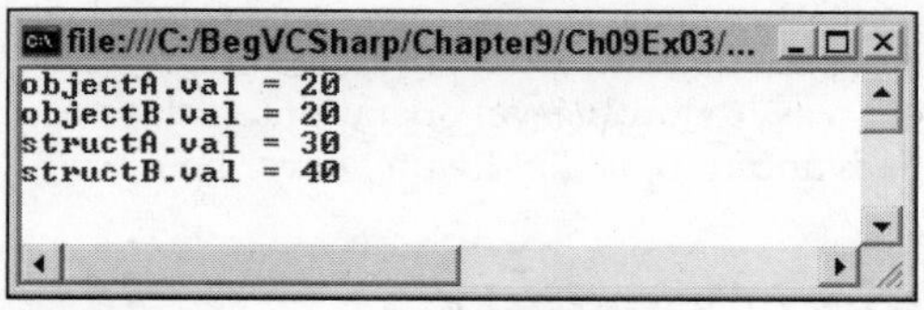

Figure 9-17

How It Works

This application contains two type definitions, one for a struct called `myStruct`, which has a single public `int` field called `val`, and one for a class called `MyClass` that contains an identical field (you look at class members such as fields in the next chapter, for now it's enough just to point out that the syntax is the same here). Next, you perform the same operations on instances of both of these types:

❑   Declare a variable of the type.

❑   Create a new instance of the type in this variable.

❑   Declare a second variable of the type.

❑   Assign the first variable to the second variable.

❑   Assign a value to the `val` field in the instance in the first variable.

❑   Assign a value to the `val` field in the instance in the second variable.

❑   Display the values of the `val` fields for both variables.

Although you are performing the same operations on variables of both types, the outcome is different. When you display the values of the `val` field, you find that both `object` types have the same value, while the struct types have different values.

So, what has happened?

Objects are *reference* types. When you assign an object to a variable you are actually assigning that variable with a *pointer* to the object it refers to. A pointer, in real code terms, is an address in memory. In this case the address is the point in memory where the object is found. When you assign the first object reference to the second variable of type `MyClass` with the following line, you are actually copying this address.

```
MyClass objectB = objectA;
```

This means that both variables contain pointers to the *same object*.

Structs are *value* types. Instead of the variable holding a pointer to the struct, the variable contains the struct itself. When you assign the first struct to the second variable of type `myStruct` with the following line, you are actually copying all the information from one struct to the other.

```
myStruct structB = structA;
```

You have seen behavior like this earlier in this book for simple variable types such as `int`. The end result is that the two struct type variables contain *different* structs.

This whole technique of using pointers is hidden from us in managed C# code, making your code much simpler. It is possible to get access to lower-level operations such as pointer manipulation in C# using unsafe code, but that is an advanced topic that I won't cover here.

Shallow versus Deep Copying

Copying objects from one variable to another by value instead of by reference (that is, copying them in the same way as structs) can be quite complex. Because a single object may contain references to many other objects, such as field members and so on, there may be an awful lot of processing involved. Simply copying each member from one object to another might not work, because some of these members might be reference types in their own right.

The .NET Framework takes this into account. Simple object copying by members is achievable through the method `MemberwiseClone()`, inherited from `System.Object`. This is a protected method, but it would be easy to define a public method on an object that called this method. The copying supplied by this method is known as *shallow* copying, in that it doesn't take reference type members into account. This means that reference members in the new object will refer to the same objects as the equivalent members in the source object, which isn't ideal in many cases. If you want to create new instances of the members in question, copying the values across rather than the references, then you need to perform a *deep* copy.

There is an interface you can implement that allows you to do this in a standard way: `ICloneable`. If you use this interface, you must implement the single method it contains, `Clone()`. This method returns a value of type `System.Object`. You can use whatever processing you wish to obtain this object, by implementing the method body however you choose. This means that you can implement a deep copy if you wish to (although the exact behavior isn't mandatory, so you could perform a shallow copy if you wanted to).

You take a closer look at this in Chapter 11.

Summary

In this chapter, you've seen how you can define classes and interfaces in C#, which has put the theory from the last chapter into a more concrete form. You've seen the C# syntax required for basic declarations as well as the accessibility keywords you can use, the way in which you can inherit from interfaces and other classes, how to define abstract and sealed classes to control this inheritance, and how to define constructors and destructors.

You took a look at `System.Object`, which is the root base class of *any* class that you define. This class supplies several methods, some of which are `virtual`, so you can override their implementation. This class also allows you to treat any object instance as an instance of this type, enabling polymorphism with any object.

You also took a look at some of the tools supplied by VS for OOP development, including the `Class View` window, the `Object Browser` window, and a quick way to add new classes to a project. As an extension of this multifile concept, you also saw how you can create assemblies that you can't execute, but that contain class definitions that you can use in other projects.

Next you drilled down into abstract classes and interfaces, looking at the similarities and differences between them and the situations where you might use one or the other.

Finally, I resumed the discussion of reference and value types, looking at structs (the value type equivalent of objects) in slightly more detail. This led to a discussion on shallow and deep copying of objects, a subject you return to later on in the book.

In this chapter you learned:

❑ How to define classes and interfaces in C#

❑ The basic syntax for C# declarations

❑ How inheritance works

❑ How to define constructors and destructors

❑ How to use `System.Object`

❑ How to use a selection of VS tools for OOP development

❑ How to use abstract classes and interfaces

❑ More about reference and value types

In the next chapter you look at defining class members, such as properties and methods, which will allow you to take OOP in C# to the level required to create real applications.

Exercises

1. What is wrong with the following code?

```
public sealed class MyClass
{
    // Class members.
}

public class myDerivedClass : MyClass
{
    // Class members.
}
```

2. How would you define a noncreatable class?

3. Why are noncreatable classes still useful? How do you make use of their capabilities?

4. Write code in a class library project called Vehicles that implements the Vehicle family of objects discussed earlier in this chapter, in the section on interfaces versus abstract classes. There are nine objects and two interfaces that require implementation.

5. Create a console application project, Traffic, which references Vehicles.dll (created in question 4). Include a function called AddPassenger() that accepts any object with the IPassengerCarrier interface. To prove that the code works, call this function using instances of each object that supports the interface, calling the ToString() method inherited from System.Object on each one and writing the result to the screen.

Defining Class Members

In this chapter, I continue the discussion of class definitions in C# by looking at how you define field, property, and method class members.

You start by looking at the code required for each of these types, and also look at how to generate the structure of this code using VS wizards. You also see how you can modify members quickly by editing their properties.

When you've covered the basics of member definition you'll take a look at some more advanced techniques involving members: hiding base class members, calling overridden base class members, nested type definitions, and partial class definitions.

Finally, you put theory into practice and create a class library that you can build on and use in later chapters.

In this chapter, you:

- ❑ Learn about field, property, and method class members
- ❑ Create a class library

Member Definitions

Within a class definition, you provide definitions for all members of the class, including fields, methods, and properties. All members have their own accessibility level, defined in all cases by one of the following keywords:

- ❑ `public`: Member is accessible from any code
- ❑ `private`: Member is accessible only from code that is part of the class (the default if no keyword is used)
- ❑ `internal`: Member is accessible only from code within the project (assembly) where it is defined
- ❑ `protected`: Member accessible only from code that is part of either the class or a derived class

The last two of these can be combined, so `protected internal` members are also possible. These are only accessible from code-derived classes within the project (more accurately, the assembly — you will cover assemblies in Chapter 26).

Fields, methods, and properties can also be declared using the keyword `static`, which means that they will be static members owned by the class rather than by object instances, as discussed in Chapter 8.

Defining Fields

Fields are defined using standard variable declaration format (with optional initialization), along with the modifiers discussed previously. For example:

```
class MyClass
{
    public int MyInt;
}
```

> *Public fields in the .NET Framework are named using PascalCasing rather than camelCasing, and I'll use this casing methodology here. This is why the field in this example is called* `MyInt` *instead of* `myInt`*. This is only a suggested casing scheme, but it makes a lot of sense. There is no recommendation for private fields, which are usually named using camelCasing.*

Fields can also use the keyword `readonly`, meaning that the field may be assigned a value only during constructor execution or by initial assignment. For example:

```
class MyClass
{
    public readonly int MyInt = 17;
}
```

As noted in the introduction to this chapter, fields may be declared as static using the `static` keyword, for example:

```
class MyClass
{
    public static int MyInt;
}
```

Static fields may be accessed via the class that defines them (`MyClass.MyInt` in the preceding example), not through object instances of that class.

In addition, you can use the keyword `const` to create a constant value. `const` members are static by definition, so there is no need to use the `static` modifier (indeed, it is an error to do so).

Defining Methods

Methods use standard function format, along with accessibility and optional `static` modifiers. For example:

```
class MyClass
{
    public string GetString()
    {
        return "Here is a string.";
    }
}
```

Public methods in the .NET framework, like fields, are named using PascalCasing rather than camelCasing.

Note that if you use the `static` keyword this method will only be accessible through the class, not the object instance.

You can also use the following keywords with method definitions:

❑   `virtual`: Method may be overridden

❑   `abstract`: Method must be overridden in nonabstract derived classes (only permitted in abstract classes)

❑   `override`: Method overrides a base class method (must be used if a method is being overridden)

❑   `extern`: Method definition is found elsewhere

The following code shows an example of a method override:

```
public class MyBaseClass
{
    public virtual void DoSomething()
    {
        // Base implementation.
    }
}

public class MyDerivedClass : MyBaseClass
{
    public override void DoSomething()
    {
        // Derived class implementation, overrides base implementation.
    }
}
```

If `override` is used, then `sealed` may also be used to specify that no further modifications can be made to this method in derived classes, that is, this method can't be overridden by derived classes. For example:

```
public class MyDerivedClass : MyBaseClass
{
    public override sealed void DoSomething()
    {
        // Derived class implementation, overrides base implementation.
    }
}
```

Using `extern` allows you to provide the implementation of a method externally to the project. This is an advanced topic, and I won't go into any more detail here.

Defining Properties

Properties are defined in a similar way to fields, but there's more to them. Properties, as already discussed, are more involved than fields in that they can perform additional processing before modifying state — and, indeed, might not modify state at all. They achieve this by possessing two function-like blocks, one for getting the value of the property and one for setting the value of the property.

These blocks, also known as *accessors*, defined using `get` and `set` keywords, respectively, may be used to control the access level of the property. It is possible to omit one or the other of these blocks to create read-only or write-only properties (where omitting the `get` block gives you write-only access, and omitting the `set` block gives you read-only access). Of course, this only applies to external code, because code elsewhere within the class will have access to the same data that these code blocks have. You can also include accessibility modifiers on accessors, for example making a `get` block that is public while the `set` block is protected. You must include at least one of these blocks to obtain a valid property (and, let's face it, a property you can neither read nor change wouldn't be that useful).

The basic structure of a property consists of the standard access modifying keyword (`public`, `private`, and so on), followed by a type name, the property name, and one or both of the `get` and `set` blocks that contain the property processing, for example:

```
public int MyIntProp
{
   get
   {
      // Property get code.
   }
   set
   {
      // Property set code.
   }
}
```

> *Public properties in the .NET Framework are also named using PascalCasing rather than camelCasing, and as with fields and methods, I'll use this casing here.*

The first line of the definition is the bit that is very similar to a field definition. The difference is that there is no semicolon at the end of the line; instead, you have a code block containing nested `get` and `set` blocks.

`get` blocks must have a return value of the type of the property. Simple properties are often associated with a single private field controlling access to that field, in which case the `get` block may return the value of that field directly, for example:

```
// Field used by property.
private int myInt;

// Property.
```

```
public int MyIntProp
{
    get
    {
        return myInt;
    }
    set
    {
        // Property set code.
    }
}
```

Note that code external to the class *cannot* access this myInt field directly due to its accessibility level (it's private). Instead external code *must* use the property to get access to the field.

The set function assigns a value to the field in a similar way. Here, you can use the keyword value to refer to the value received from the user of the property:

```
// Field used by property.
private int myInt;

// Property.
public int MyIntProp
{
    get
    {
        return myInt;
    }
    set
    {
        myInt = value;
    }
}
```

value equates to a value of the same type as the property, so if the property uses the same type as the field, you never have to worry about casting in situations like this.

This simple property does little more than shield direct access to the myInt field. The real power of properties comes when you exert a little more control over the proceedings. For example, you might implement your set block using:

```
set
{
    if (value >= 0 && value <= 10)
        myInt = value;
}
```

Here, you only modify `myInt` if the value assigned to the property is between 0 and 10. In situations like this, you have an important design choice to make: what should you do if an invalid value is used? You have four options:

- ❏ Do nothing (as in the preceding code).
- ❏ Assign a default value to the field.
- ❏ Continue as if nothing had gone wrong but log the event for future analysis.
- ❏ Throw an exception.

In general, the last two options are the preferable ones. The choice between these two options depends on how the class will be used, and how much control should be assigned to the users of the class. Exception throwing gives users a fair amount of control and lets them know what is going on so that they can respond appropriately. You can use a standard `System` exception for this, for example:

```
set
{
    if (value >= 0 && value <= 10)
        myInt = value;
    else
        throw (new ArgumentOutOfRangeException("MyIntProp", value,
                "MyIntProp must be assigned a value between 0 and 10."));
}
```

This can be handled using `try . . . catch . . . finally` logic in the code that uses the property, as you saw in Chapter 7.

Logging data, perhaps to a text file, can be useful in (for example) production code where problems really shouldn't occur. They allow developers to check up on performance and perhaps debug existing code if necessary.

Properties can use the `virtual`, `override`, and `abstract` keywords just like methods, something that isn't possible with fields.

Finally, as mentioned earlier, accessors can have their own accessibility, for example:

```
// Field used by property.
private int myInt;

// Property.
public int MyIntProp
{
    get
    {
        return myInt;
    }
    protected set
    {
        myInt = value;
    }
}
```

Here, only code within the class or derived classes can use the set accessor.

The accessibilities that are permitted for accessors depend on the accessibility of the property, and it is forbidden to make an accessor more accessible than the property it belongs to. This means that a private property cannot contain any accessibility modifiers for its accessors, while public properties can use all modifiers on their accessors.

In the following Try It Out, you experiment with defining and using fields, methods, and properties.

Try It Out   Using Fields, Methods, and Properties

1. Create a new console application project called `Ch10Ex01` in the directory `C:\BegVCSharp\Chapter10`.

2. Add a new class called `MyClass`, using the VS shortcut, which will cause the new class to be defined in a new file called `MyClass.cs`.

3. Modify the code in `MyClass.cs` as follows:

```csharp
public class MyClass
{
    public readonly string Name;
    private int intVal;

    public int Val
    {
        get
        {
            return intVal;
        }
        set
        {
            if (value >= 0 && value <= 10)
                intVal = value;
            else
                throw (new ArgumentOutOfRangeException("Val", value,
                    "Val must be assigned a value between 0 and 10."));
        }
    }
    public override string ToString()
    {
        return "Name: " + Name + "\nVal: " + Val;
    }

    private MyClass() : this("Default Name")
    {
    }

    public MyClass(string newName)
    {
        Name = newName;
        intVal = 0;
    }
}
```

4. Modify the code in `Program.cs` as follows:

```csharp
static void Main(string[] args)
{
    Console.WriteLine("Creating object myObj...");
    MyClass myObj = new MyClass("My Object");
    Console.WriteLine("myObj created.");
    for (int i = -1; i <= 0; i++)
    {
        try
        {
            Console.WriteLine("\nAttempting to assign {0} to myObj.Val...",
                              i);
            myObj.Val = i;
            Console.WriteLine("Value {0} assigned to myObj.Val.", myObj.Val);
        }
        catch (Exception e)
        {
            Console.WriteLine("Exception {0} thrown.", e.GetType().FullName);
            Console.WriteLine("Message:\n\"{0}\"", e.Message);
        }
    }
    Console.WriteLine("\nOutputting myObj.ToString()...");
    Console.WriteLine(myObj.ToString());
    Console.WriteLine("myObj.ToString() Output.");
    Console.ReadKey();
}
```

5. Run the application. The result is shown in Figure 10-1.

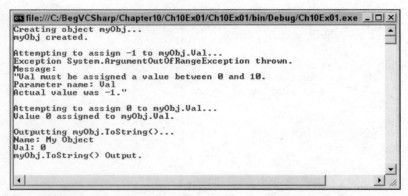

Figure 10-1

How It Works

The code in `Main()` creates and uses an instance of the `MyClass` class defined in `MyClass.cs`. Instantiating this class must be performed using a nondefault constructor, because the default constructor of `MyClass` is private:

```csharp
private MyClass() : this("Default Name")
{
}
```

Note that I've used this("Default Name") to ensure that Name gets a value if this constructor ever gets called, which is possible if this class is used to derive a new class. This is necessary because not assigning a value to the Name field could be a source of errors later.

The nondefault constructor used assigns values to the readonly field Name (you can only do this by assignment in the field declaration or in a constructor) and the private field intVal.

Next, Main() attempts two assignments to the Val property of myObj (the instance of MyClass). A for loop is used to assign the values -1 and 0 in two cycles, and a try . . . catch structure is used to check for any exception thrown. When -1 is assigned to the property an exception of type System .ArgumentOutOfRangeException is thrown, and code in the catch block outputs information about the exception to the console window. In the next loop cycle, the value 0 is successfully assigned to the Val property, and through that property to the private intVal field.

Finally, you use the overridden ToString() method to output a formatted string representing the contents of the object:

```
public override string ToString()
{
    return "Name: " + Name + "\nVal: " + Val;
}
```

This method must be declared using the override keyword, because it is overriding the virtual ToString() method of the base System.Object class. The code here uses the property Val directly rather than the private field intVal. There is no reason why you shouldn't use properties from within classes in this way, although there may be a small performance hit (so small that you are unlikely to notice it). Of course, using the property also gives you the validation inherent in property use, which may be beneficial for code within the class as well.

Adding Members from a Class Diagram

In the last chapter, you saw how you can use the class diagram to explore the classes in a project. I also mentioned that the class diagram could be used to add members, and this is what you will look at in this section.

All the tools for adding and editing members are shown in the Class Details window in the Class Diagram View. To see this in action, create a class diagram for the MyClass class created in Ch10Ex01. You can see the existing members by expanding the view of the class in the class designer (by clicking on the icon that looks like two downward pointing chevrons). The resultant view is shown in Figure 10-2.

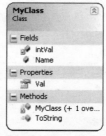

Figure 10-2

In the `Class Details` window, you can see the information shown in Figure 10-3 when the class is selected.

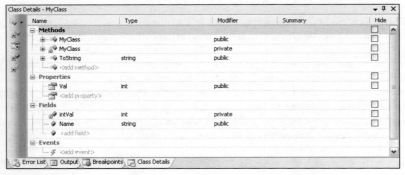

Figure 10-3

This shows all the currently defined members for the class and has spaces for you to add new members simply by typing in the relevant spaces. In the next sections, you look at adding methods, properties, and fields using this window.

Adding Methods

Simply typing in the box labeled <add method> results in a method being added to your class. Once you have named a method, you can use the Tab key to navigate to subsequent settings, starting with the return type of the method, and moving on to the accessibility of the method, summary information (which translates to XML documentation, which you look at in Chapter 28), and whether to hide the method in the class diagram.

Once you have added a method, you can expand the entry and add parameters in the same way. For parameters, you also have the option to use the modifiers `out`, `ref`, and `params`. An example of a new method is shown in Figure 10-4.

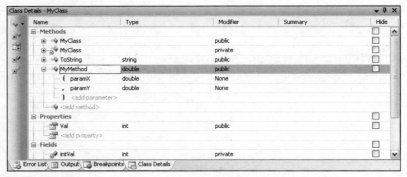

Figure 10-4

With this new method, the following code is added to your class:

```
public double MyMethod(double paramX, double paramY)
{
    throw new System.NotImplementedException();
}
```

Additional configuration of a method can be done in the Properties window, shown in Figure 10-5.

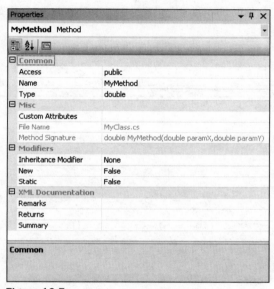

Figure 10-5

Here you can, among other things, make the method static.

Obviously, this technique can't provide the method implementation for you, but it does provide the basic structure, and certainly cuts down on typing errors!

Adding Properties

Adding properties is achieved in much the same way. Figure 10-6 shows a new property added using the Class Details window.

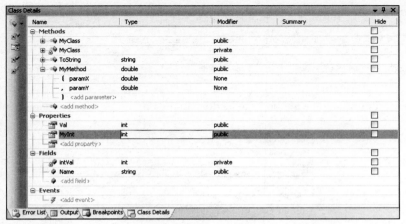

Figure 10-6

This adds a property as shown here:

```
public int MyInt
{
    get
    {
        throw new System.NotImplementedException();
    }
    set
    {
    }
}
```

Note that you are left to provide the complete implementation yourself, which includes matching up the property with a field for simple properties, removing an accessor if you want the property to be read- or write-only, or applying accessibility modifiers to accessors. However, the basic structure is provided for you.

Adding Fields

Adding fields is just as simple. You just have to type the name of the field, choose a type and access modifier, and away you go.

Refactoring Members

One tool that comes in handy when adding properties is the ability to generate a property from a field. This is an example of *refactoring*, which in general simply means modifying your code using a tool rather than by hand. This can be accomplished using a class diagram by right-clicking on a member or simply by right-clicking on a member in code view.

For example, if the MyClass class contained the following field:

```
public string myString;
```

You could right-click on the field and select `Refactor ⇨ Encapsulate Field. . . .` This would bring up the dialog shown in Figure 10-7.

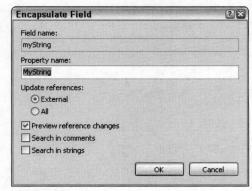

Figure 10-7

Accepting the default options modifies the code for `MyClass` as follows:

```
private string myString;
public string MyString
{
   get
   {
      return myString;
   }

   set
   {
      myString = value;
   }
}
```

The `myString` field has had its accessibility changed to `private`, and a public property called `MyString` has been created and automatically linked to `myString`.

Believe me—cutting down on the time required to monotonously create properties for fields is a big plus!

Additional Class Member Topics

Now that you've covered the basics of member definition, it's time to look at some more advanced member topics. In this section, you look at:

❑   Hiding base class methods

❑   Calling overridden or hidden base class methods

❑   Nested type definitions

Hiding Base Class Methods

When you inherit a (nonabstract) member from a base class, you also inherit an implementation. If the inherited member is virtual, you can override this implementation with the `override` keyword. Regardless of whether the inherited member is virtual, you can, if you want to, *hide* the implementation. This is useful when, for example, a public inherited member doesn't work quite as you want it to.

You can do this simply by using code such as:

```
public class MyBaseClass
{
   public void DoSomething()
   {
      // Base implementation.
   }
}
public class MyDerivedClass : MyBaseClass
{
   public void DoSomething()
   {
      // Derived class implementation, hides base implementation.
   }
}
```

Although this code works fine, it will generate a warning that you are hiding a base class member. This gives you the chance to correct things if you have accidentally hidden a member that you actually want to use. If you really do want to hide the member, you can say explicitly that this is what you want to do using the `new` keyword:

```
public class MyDerivedClass : MyBaseClass
{
   new public void DoSomething()
   {
      // Derived class implementation, hides base implementation.
   }
}
```

This will work in exactly the same way, but won't show a warning.

At this point, it is worth pointing out the difference between hiding and overriding base class members. Consider the following code:

```
public class MyBaseClass
{
   public virtual void DoSomething()
   {
      Console.WriteLine("Base imp");
   }
}

public class MyDerivedClass : MyBaseClass
{
   public override void DoSomething()
```

```
    {
        Console.WriteLine("Derived imp");
    }
}
```

Here, the overriding method replaces the implementation in the base class, such that the following code will use the new version, even though it does so through the base class type (using polymorphism):

```
MyDerivedClass myObj = new MyDerivedClass();
MyBaseClass myBaseObj;
myBaseObj = myObj;
myBaseObj.DoSomething();
```

This gives the output:

```
Derived imp
```

Alternatively, you could hide the base class method instead, using:

```
public class MyBaseClass
{
    public virtual void DoSomething()
    {
        Console.WriteLine("Base imp");
    }
}

public class MyDerivedClass : MyBaseClass
{
    new public void DoSomething()
    {
        Console.WriteLine("Derived imp");
    }
}
```

The base class method needn't be virtual for this to work, but the effect is exactly the same and the preceding code only requires changes to one line of code. The result, for a virtual or nonvirtual base class method, is the following:

```
Base imp
```

Although the base implementation is hidden, you still have access to it through the base class.

Calling Overridden or Hidden Base Class Methods

Whether you override or hide a member, you still have access to the base class member from the derived class. There are many situations in which this can be useful, for example:

❑   When you want to hide an inherited public member from users of a derived class but still want access to its functionality from within the class.

❑   When you want to add to the implementation of an inherited virtual member rather than simply replacing it with a new overridden implementation.

To achieve this, you can use the base keyword, which refers to the implementation of the base class that is contained within a derived class (in a similar way to its use in controlling constructors, as you saw in the last chapter), for example:

```
public class MyBaseClass
{
   public virtual void DoSomething()
   {
      // Base implementation.
   }
}

public class MyDerivedClass : MyBaseClass
{
   public override void DoSomething()
   {
      // Derived class implementation, extends base class implementation.
      base.DoSomething();
      // More derived class implementation.
   }
}
```

This code executes the version of DoSomething() contained in MyBaseClass, the base class of MyDerivedClass, from within the version of DoSomething() contained in MyDerivedClass.

As base works using object instances it is an error to use it from within a static member.

The this Keyword

As well as using base in the last chapter you also used the this keyword. As with base, this can also be used from within class members, and, like base, this keyword refers to an object instance. The object instance referred to by this is the current object instance (which means that you can't use this keyword in static members, because static members are not part of an object instance).

The most useful function of the this keyword is the ability to pass a reference to the current object instance to a method, for example:

```
public void doSomething()
{
   MyTargetClass myObj = new MyTargetClass();
   myObj.DoSomethingWith(this);
}
```

Here, the MyTargetClass that is instantiated has a method called DoSomethingWith(), which takes a single parameter of a type compatible with the class that contains the preceding method. This parameter type might be of this class type, a class type that is inherited by this class, an interface implemented by the class, or (of course) System.Object.

Nested Type Definitions

As well as defining types such as classes in namespaces, you can also define them inside other classes. If you do this, then you can use the full range of accessibility modifiers for the definition, rather than just `public` and `internal`, and you may also use the `new` keyword to hide a type definition inherited from a base class.

For example, the following code defining `MyClass` also defines a nested class called `myNestedClass`:

```
public class MyClass
{
    public class myNestedClass
    {
        public int nestedClassField;
    }
}
```

If you want to instantiate `myNestedClass` from outside `MyClass`, you must qualify the name, for example:

```
MyClass.myNestedClass myObj = new MyClass.myNestedClass();
```

However, you may not be able to do this at all if the nested class is declared as `private` or another accessibility level that is incompatible with the code at the point at which this instantiation is performed.

The main reason for the existence of this feature is to define classes that are private to the containing class, so that no other code in the namespace has access to them.

Interface Implementation

Before moving on, it's worth taking a closer look at how you go about defining and implementing interfaces. In the last chapter, you saw that interfaces are defined in a similar way to classes, using code such as:

```
interface IMyInterface
{
    // Interface members.
}
```

Interface members are defined like class members except for a few important differences:

- ❑ No access modifiers (`public`, `private`, `protected`, or `internal`) are allowed — all interface members are implicitly public.

- ❑ Interface members can't contain code bodies.

- ❑ Interfaces can't define field members.

- ❑ Interface members can't be defined using the keywords `static`, `virtual`, `abstract`, or `sealed`.

- ❑ Type definition members are forbidden.

You can, however, define members using the `new` keyword if you wish to hide members inherited from base interfaces. For example:

```
interface IMyBaseInterface
{
   void DoSomething();
}

interface IMyDerivedInterface : IMyBaseInterface
{
   new void DoSomething();
}
```

This works in exactly the same way as hiding inherited class members.

Properties defined in interfaces define either or both of the access blocks, `get` and `set`, which are permitted for the property. For example:

```
interface IMyInterface
{
   int MyInt
   {
      get;
      set;
   }
}
```

Here, the `int` property `MyInt` has both `get` and `set` accessors. Either of these may be omitted for a property with more restricted access.

Note, though, that interfaces do not specify how the property should be stored. Interfaces cannot specify fields, for example, which might be used to store property data.

Finally, interfaces, like classes, may be defined as members of classes (but not as members of other interfaces, since interfaces cannot contain type definitions).

Implementing Interfaces in Classes

A class that implements an interface *must* contain implementations for all members of that interface, which must match the signatures specified (including matching the specified `get` and `set` blocks), and must be public. For example:

```
public interface IMyInterface
{
   void DoSomething();
   void DoSomethingElse();
}

public class MyClass : IMyInterface
{
   public void DoSomething()
   {
```

```
    }

    public void DoSomethingElse()
    {
    }
}
```

It is also possible to implement interface members using the keywords `virtual` or `abstract`, but not `static` or `const`. Interface members may also be implemented on base classes, for example:

```
public interface IMyInterface
{
    void DoSomething();
    void DoSomethingElse();
}
public class MyBaseClass
{
    public void DoSomething()
    {
    }
}

public class MyDerivedClass : MyBaseClass, IMyInterface
{
    public void DoSomethingElse()
    {
    }
}
```

Inheriting from a base class that implements a given interface means that the interface is implicitly supported by the derived class, for example:

```
public interface IMyInterface
{
    void DoSomething();
    void DoSomethingElse();
}

public class MyBaseClass : IMyInterface
{
    public virtual void DoSomething()
    {
    }

    public virtual void DoSomethingElse()
    {
    }
}

public class MyDerivedClass : MyBaseClass
{
    public override void DoSomething()
    {
    }
}
```

As shown in the preceding example, it is useful to define implementations in base classes as virtual, so that derived classes can replace the implementation rather than hiding it. If you were to hide a base class member using the `new` keyword rather than overriding it in this way, then the method `IMyInterface.DoSomething()` would always refer to the base class version, even if the derived class were being accessed via this interface.

Explicit Interface Member Implementation

Interface members can also be implemented *explicitly* by a class. If you do this, then the member can only be accessed through the interface, not through the class. *Implicit* members, which are what you used in the code in the last section, can be accessed either way.

For example, if the class `MyClass` implemented the `DoSomething()` method of `IMyInterface` implicitly, as in the preceding example, then the following code would be valid:

```
MyClass myObj = new MyClass();
myObj.DoSomething();
```

as would be:

```
MyClass myObj = new MyClass();
IMyInterface myInt = myObj;
myInt.DoSomething();
```

Alternatively, if `MyDerivedClass` implements `DoSomething()` explicitly, then only the latter technique is permitted. The code for doing this is:

```
public class MyClass : IMyInterface
{
   void IMyInterface.DoSomething()
   {
   }

   public void DoSomethingElse()
   {
   }
}
```

Here `DoSomething()` is implemented explicitly and `DoSomethingElse()` implicitly. Only the latter is accessible directly through an object instance of `MyClass`.

Adding Property Accessors with Nonpublic Accessibility

I said earlier that if you implement an interface with a property, then you must implement matching `get`/`set` accessors. This isn't strictly true — it is possible to add a `get` block to a property in class where the interface defining that property only contains a `set` block, and vice versa. However, this is only possible if you add the accessor with an accessibility modifier that is more restrictive than the accessibility modifier on the accessor defined in the interface. Since the accessor defined by the interface is, by definition, public, this means that you can only add nonpublic accessors. For example:

```
public interface IMyInterface
{
   int MyIntProperty
```

```
        {
            get;
        }
    }

public class MyBaseClass : IMyInterface
{
    protected int myInt;

    public int MyIntProperty
    {
        get
        {
            return myInt;
        }
        protected set
        {
            myInt = value;
        }
    }
}
```

Partial Class Definitions

When you create classes with a lot of members of one type or another, things can get quite confusing, and code files can get very long. One thing that can help here, that you've looked at in earlier chapters, is to use code outlining. By defining regions in code, you can collapse and expand sections to make things easier to read. For example, you might have a class defined as follows:

```
public class MyClass
{
    #region Fields
    private int myInt;
    #endregion

    #region Constructor
    public MyClass()
    {
        myInt = 99;
    }
    #endregion

    #region Properties
    public int MyInt
    {
        get
        {
            return myInt;
        }

        set
        {
            myInt = value;
```

```
        }
    }
    #endregion

    #region Methods
    public void DoSomething()
    {
        // Do something...
    }
    #endregion
}
```

Here, you can expand and contract fields, properties, the constructor, and methods for the class, allowing you to focus just on what you are interested in.

It is even possible to nest regions in this way, so some regions are only visible when the region that contains them is expanded.

However, even using this technique, things can still get out of hand. One alternative is to use *partial class definitions*. Put simply, you use partial class definitions to split the definition of a class across multiple files. You could, for example, put the fields, properties, and constructor in one file and the methods in another.

To do this, you just need to use the `partial` keyword with the class in each file that contains part of the definition, as follows:

```
public partial class MyClass
{
    ...
}
```

If you use partial class definitions, then this keyword must appear in this position in every file containing part of the definition.

Partial classes are used to great effect in Windows applications to hide the code relating to the layout of forms from you. You've already seen this in fact, back in Chapter 2. A Windows form, in a class called `Form1` say, has code stored in both `Form1.cs` and `Form1.Designer.cs`. This enables you to concentrate on the functionality of your forms, without having to worry about your code being cluttered with information that doesn't really interest you.

One final note about partial classes: Interfaces applied to one partial class part apply to the whole class. This means that the following definitions are equivalent:

```
public partial class MyClass : IMyInteface1
{
    ...
}

public partial class MyClass : IMyInteface2
{
    ...
}
```

and:

```
public class MyClass : IMyInteface1, IMyInteface2
{
    ...
}
```

This also applies to attributes, which you look at in Chapter 27.

Example Application

To illustrate some of the techniques you've been using so far, you'll develop a class module that you'll be able to build on and make use of in subsequent chapters. This class module will contain two classes:

❑ Card: Represents a standard playing card, with a suit of club, diamond, heart, or spade, and a rank that lies between ace and king

❑ Deck: Represents a full deck of 52 cards, with access to cards by position in the deck and the ability to shuffle the deck

You'll also develop a simple client to make sure that things are working, but you won't use the deck in a full card game application — yet!

Planning the Application

The class library for this application, Ch10CardLib, will contain your classes. Before you get down to any code, though, you should plan the required structure and functionality of your classes.

The Card Class

The Card class is basically a container for two read-only fields: suit and rank. The reason for making the fields read-only is that it doesn't make sense to have a "blank" card, and cards shouldn't be able to change once they have been created. To facilitate this, you'll make the default constructor private, and provide an alternative constructor that builds a card from a supplied suit and rank.

Other than this, the Card class will override the ToString() method of System.Object, so that you can easily obtain a human-readable string representing the card. To make things a little simpler, you'll provide enumerations for the two fields suit and rank.

The Card class is shown in Figure 10-8.

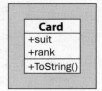

Figure 10-8

The Deck Class

The Deck class will maintain 52 Card objects. You'll just use a simple array type for this. This array won't be directly accessible, because access to the Card objects will be achieved through a GetCard() method, which will return the Card object with the given index.

This class should also expose a Shuffle() method to rearrange the cards in the array. The Deck class is shown in Figure 10-9.

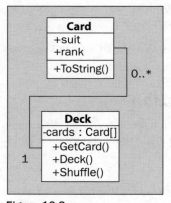

Figure 10-9

Writing the Class Library

For the purposes of this example, I'll assume that you are familiar enough with VS to move away from the standard Try It Out way of doing things, so I won't list the steps explicitly. The important thing here is to look at and discuss the code, not to see how to enter it into VS, which is done with the same steps you've seen in many Try It Outs. Having said that, I will include some pointers to make sure that you don't run into any problems along the way.

Both your classes and your enumerations will be contained in a class library project called Ch10CardLib. This project will contain four .cs files, Card.cs that contains the Card class definition, Deck.cs that contains the Deck class definition, and Suit.cs and Rank.cs files containing enumerations.

To illustrate the power of the class diagram you saw earlier, you can put together a lot of this code using this tool. To get started here you need to do the following:

1. Create a new class library project called `Ch10CardLib` in the directory `C:\BegVCSharp\Chapter10`.

2. Remove `Class1.cs` from the project.

3. Open the class diagram for the project using the `Solution Explorer` window (you must have the project selected, rather than the solution, for the class diagram icon to appear).

The class diagram should be blank to start with, since the project contains no classes.

If you can see the Resources and Settings classes in this view, they can be hidden by right-clicking on them and selecting `Remove from Diagram`.

Adding the Suit and Rank Enumerations

Using the Toolbox, you can add an enumeration by dragging an Enum from the Toolbox into the diagram, then filling in the dialog that appears. For example, for the `Suit` enumeration fill out the dialog as shown in Figure 10-10.

Figure 10-10

Next, you can add the members of the enumeration using the `Class Details` window. The values required are shown in Figure 10-11.

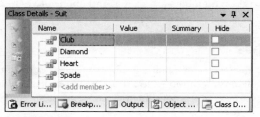

Figure 10-11

The values required for the `Rank` enumeration are shown in Figure 10-12.

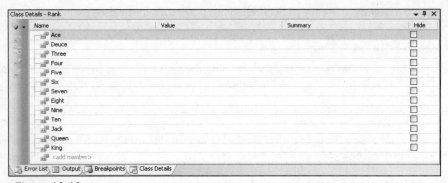

Figure 10-12

Note the value entry for the first member, Ace. This is so that the underlying storage of the enum matches the rank of the card, such that Six is stored as 6, for example.

Once you have done this for both Suit and Rank the diagram should look as shown in Figure 10-13.

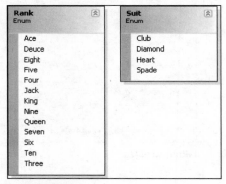

Figure 10-13

Unfortunately, the enumeration members are shown alphabetically here, but you can see from the code in Rank.cs and Suit.cs that the actual orders match the entries in the Class Details window.

Adding the Card Class

In this section, you'll add the Card class, using a mix of the class designer and code editor. Adding a class is much like adding an enumeration — you drag the appropriate entry from the Toolbox into the diagram. In this case, you drag a Class into the diagram, and name the new class Card.

To add the fields rank and suit, which will be `public` and `readonly`, you use the `Class Details` window to add the fields, then the Properties window to set the `Constant Kind` of the field to `readonly`. You also need to add two constructors, one a default constructor (private), and one that takes two parameters, `newSuit` and `newRank`, of types `Suit` and `Rank`, respectively (public). Finally, you need to override `ToString()`, which requires a modification of the `Inheritance Modifier` in the `Properties` window, which needs to be set to `override`.

Figure 10-14 shows the Class Details window and the `Card` class with all information entered.

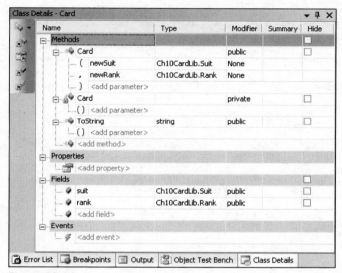

Figure 10-14

Next, you need to modify the code for the class in `Card.cs` as follows:

```
public class Card
{
    public readonly Suit suit;
    public readonly Rank rank;

    public Card(Suit newSuit, Rank newRank)
    {
        suit = newSuit;
        rank = newRank;
    }

    private Card()
    {

    }

    public override string ToString()
    {
        return "The " + rank + " of " + suit + "s";
    }
}
```

The overridden `ToString()` method writes the string representation of the enumeration value stored to the returned string, and the nondefault constructor initializes the values of the `suit` and `rank` fields.

Adding the Deck Class

The `Deck` class needs the following members defined using the class diagram:

❑   A private field called `cards`, of type `Card[]`.

❑   A public default constructor.

❑   A public method called `GetCard()`, which takes one `int` parameter called `cardNum` and returns an object of type `Card`.

❑   A public method called `Shuffle()` which takes no parameters and returns `void`.

When these are added, the Class Details for the `Deck` class will look as they do in Figure 10-15.

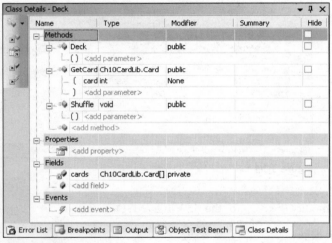

Figure 10-15

To make things clearer in the diagram, you can show the relationships between the members and types you have added. Right-click on each of the following in turn, and select Show as Association from the menu:

❑   cards in Deck

❑   suit in Card

❑   rank in Card

When you have finished, the diagram should look like Figure 10-16.

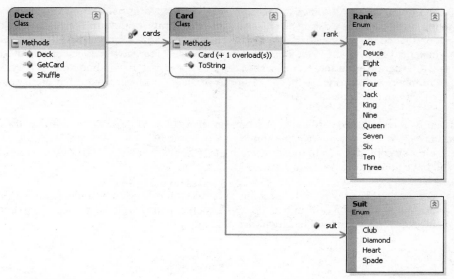

Figure 10-16

Next, you need to modify the code in Deck.cs. First, you'll do the constructor, which simply creates and assigns 52 cards in the cards field. You'll iterate through all combinations of the two enumerations, using each to create a card. This results in cards initially containing an ordered list of cards:

```
public Deck()
{
    cards = new Card[52];
    for (int suitVal = 0; suitVal < 4; suitVal++)
    {
        for (int rankVal = 1; rankVal < 14; rankVal++)
        {
            cards[suitVal * 13 + rankVal -1] = new Card((Suit)suitVal,
                                                (Rank)rankVal);
        }
    }
}
```

Next, you implement the GetCard() method, which either returns the Card object with the requested index or throws an exception in the same way you saw earlier:

```
public Card GetCard(int cardNum)
{
    if (cardNum >= 0 && cardNum <= 51)
        return cards[cardNum];
    else
        throw (new System.ArgumentOutOfRangeException("cardNum", cardNum,
                "Value must be between 0 and 51."));
}
```

Finally, you implement the `Shuffle()` method. This method works by creating a temporary card array and copying cards from the existing `cards` array into this array at random. The main body of this function is a loop that counts from 0 to 51. On each cycle, you generate a random number between 0 and 51, using an instance of the `System.Random` class from the .NET Framework. Once instantiated, an object of this class will generate a random number between `0` and `X`, using the method `Next(X)`. When you have a random number, you simply use that as the index of the `Card` object in your temporary array in which to copy a card from the `cards` array.

To keep a record of assigned cards, you also have an array of `bool` variables and assign these to `true` as each card is copied. When you are generating random numbers, you check against this array to see if you have already copied a card to the location in the temporary array specified by the random number, and if you have you simply generate another.

This isn't the most efficient way of doing things, because many random numbers may be generated before a vacant slot to copy a card into is found. However, it works, it's very simple, and because C# code executes so quickly you will hardly notice a delay.

The code is:

```
public void Shuffle()
{
    Card[] newDeck = new Card[52];
    bool[] assigned = new bool[52];
    Random sourceGen = new Random();
    for (int i = 0; i < 52; i++)
    {
        int destCard = 0;
        bool foundCard = false;
        while (foundCard == false)
        {
            destCard = sourceGen.Next(52);
            if (assigned[destCard] == false)
                foundCard = true;
        }
        assigned[destCard] = true;
        newDeck[destCard] = cards[i];
    }
    newDeck.CopyTo(cards, 0);
}
```

The last line of this method uses the `CopyTo()` method of the `System.Array` class (used whenever you create an array) to copy each of the cards in `newDeck` back into `cards`. This means that you are using the same set of `Card` objects in the same `cards` object rather than creating any new instances. If you had instead used `cards = newDeck`, then you would be replacing the object instance referred to by cards with another. This could cause problems if code elsewhere was retaining a reference to the original `cards` instance — which wouldn't be shuffled!

That completes the class library code.

A Client Application for the Class Library

To keep things simple here, you can add a client console application to the solution containing the class library. To do this, you simply need to ensure that the `Add to Solution` option is selected when you create the project, which I'll call `Ch10CardClient`.

To use the class library you have created from this new console application project, you simply need to add a reference to your `Ch10CardLib` class library project. Once the console project has been created, you can do this though the `Projects` tab of the `Add Reference` dialog, as shown in Figure 10-17.

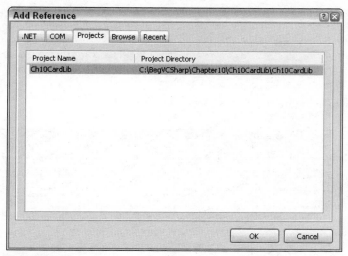

Figure 10-17

Select the project, then click `OK`, and the reference is added.

Because this new project was the second one to be created, you also need to specify that it is the startup project for the solution, meaning that it is the one that will be executed when you press the run button. To do this, you simply right-click on the project name in the `Solution Explorer` window and select the `Set as StartUp Project` menu option.

Next, you need to add the code that uses your new classes. This doesn't require anything particularly special, so the following code will do:

```
using System;
using System.Collections.Generic;
using System.Text;
using Ch10CardLib;

namespace Ch10CardClient
{
    class Class1
    {
```

```
        static void Main(string[] args)
        {
            Deck myDeck = new Deck();
            myDeck.Shuffle();
            for (int i = 0; i < 52; i++)
            {
                Card tempCard = myDeck.GetCard(i);
                Console.Write(tempCard.ToString());
                if (i != 51)
                    Console.Write(", ");
                else
                    Console.WriteLine();
            }
            Console.ReadKey();
        }
    }
}
```

The result is shown in Figure 10-18.

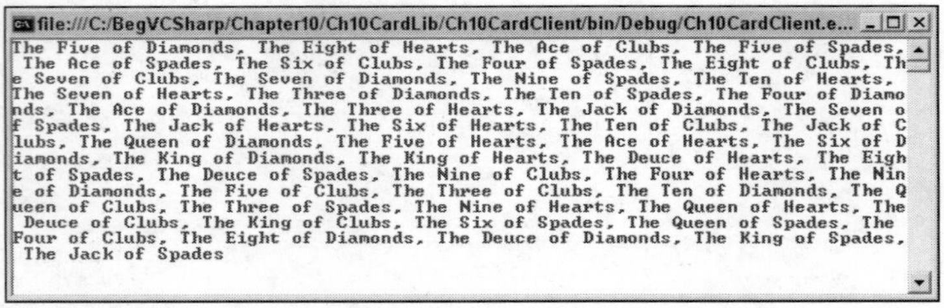

Figure 10-18

This is a random arrangement of the 52 playing cards in the deck.

You'll continue to develop and use this class library in later chapters.

Summary

In this chapter, I have completed the discussion of how to define basic classes. There's plenty still to cover, but the techniques covered so far enable you to create quite complicated applications already.

You looked at how to define fields, methods, and properties, covering the various access levels and modifier keywords as you went along. To cap this off, you looked at the VS tools that can be used to get the outline of a class together in double-quick time.

Once you covered these basic subjects, you looked in greater detail at inheritance behavior, by seeing how you can hide unwanted inherited members with the new keyword and extend base class members rather than replacing their implementation, using the base keyword. You also looked at nested class definitions.

After this, you took a more detailed look at interface definition and implementation, including the concepts of explicit and implicit implementation.

Finally, you developed and used a simple class library representing a deck of playing cards, making use of the handy class diagram tool to make things easier. You'll make further use of this library in later chapters.

In this chapter, you:

❑   Learned how to define fields, methods, and properties.

❑   Discovered the tools available in VS for creating the outline of a class.

❑   Learned more about inheritance behavior.

❑   Learned about interface definition and implementation.

❑   Created and deployed a simple class library.

In the next chapter, you look at collections, which are a type of class that you will use time and time again in your development.

Exercises

1.   Write code that defines a base class, `MyClass`, with the virtual method `GetString()`. This method should return the string stored in the protected field `myString`, accessible through the write-only public property `ContainedString`.

2.   Derive a class, `MyDerivedClass`, from `MyClass`. Override the `GetString()` method to return the string from the base class, using the base implementation of the method, but add the text `"(output from derived class)"` to the returned string.

3.   Write a class called `MyCopyableClass` that is capable of returning a copy of itself using the method `GetCopy()`. This method should use the `MemberwiseClone()` method inherited from `System.Object`. Add a simple property to the class, and write client code that uses the class to check that everything is working.

4.   Write a console client for the `Ch10CardLib` library that draws five cards at a time from a shuffled `Deck` object. If all five cards are the same suit, then the client should display the card names on screen along with the text `Flush!`; otherwise, it should quit after 50 cards with the text `No flush`.

Collections, Comparisons, and Conversions

You've covered all the basic OOP techniques in C# now, but there are some more advanced techniques that are worth becoming familiar with. In this chapter, you look at the following:

❑ **Collections:** Collections enable you to maintain groups of objects. Unlike arrays, which you've used in earlier chapters, collections can include more advanced functionality, such as controlling access to the objects they contain, searching and sorting, and so on. You'll see how to use and create collection classes, and also learn about some powerful techniques for getting the most out of them.

❑ **Comparisons:** Often when dealing with objects, you will want to make comparisons between them. This is especially important in collections, since it is how sorting is achieved. You'll look at how to compare objects in a number of ways, including operator overloading and using the `IComparable` and `IComparer` interface to sort collections.

❑ **Conversions:** In earlier chapters, you've seen how to cast objects from one type into another. In this chapter, you round things off by looking at how type conversions can be customized to suit your needs.

Collections

In Chapter 5, you saw how you can use arrays to create variable types that contain a number of objects or values. Arrays, however, have their limitations. The biggest of these is that once they have been created, they have a fixed size, so you can't add new items to the end of an existing array without creating a new one. This often means that the syntax used to manipulate arrays can become overly complicated. OOP techniques allow you to create classes that perform much of this manipulation internally, thus simplifying the code that uses lists of items or arrays.

Arrays in C# are implemented as instances of the `System.Array` class and are just one type of what are known as *collection* classes. Collection classes in general are used for maintaining lists of objects and may expose more functionality than simple arrays. Much of this functionality comes through implementing interfaces from the System.Collections namespace, thus standardizing collection syntax. This namespace also contains some other interesting things, such as classes that implement these interfaces in ways other than System.Array.

As the collection functionality (including basic functions such as accessing collection items using [index] syntax) is available through interfaces you aren't limited to using basic collection classes such as System.Array. Instead, you can create your own customized collection classes. These can be made more specific to the objects you wish to enumerate (that is, the objects you want to maintain collections of). One advantage of doing this, as you will see, is that custom collection classes can be *strongly typed*. This means that when you extract items from the collection you don't need to cast them into the correct type. Another advantage is the capability to expose specialized methods. For example, you may provide a quick way to obtain subsets of items, such as all Card items of a particular suit.

There are a number of interfaces in the System.Collections namespace that provide basic collection functionality:

❑   IEnumerable: Provides the capability to loop through items in a collection.

❑   ICollection: Provides the ability to obtain the number of items in a collection and to copy items into a simple array type (inherits from IEnumerable).

❑   IList: Provides a list of items for a collection along with the capabilities for accessing these items, and some other basic capabilities related to lists of items (inherits from IEnumerable and ICollection).

❑   IDictionary: Similar to IList, but provides a list of items accessible via a key value rather than an index (inherits from IEnumerable and ICollection).

The System.Array class implements IList, ICollection, and IEnumerable, but doesn't support some of the more advanced features of IList, and represents a list of items with a fixed size.

Using Collections

One of the classes in the Systems.Collections namespace, System.Collections.ArrayList, also implements IList, ICollection, and IEnumerable, but does so in a more sophisticated way than System.Array. Whereas arrays are fixed in size (you can't add or remove elements), this class may be used to represent a variable length list of items. To give you more of a feel for what is possible with such a highly advanced collection, the following Try It Out provides an example that uses this class, as well as a simple array.

Try It Out	Arrays versus More Advanced Collections

1.   Create a new console application called Ch11Ex01 in the directory C:\BegVCSharp\ Chapter11.

2.   Add three new classes, Animal, Cow, and Chicken to the project by right-clicking on the project in the Solution Explorer window and selecting Add ⇨ Class for each.

3. Modify the code in `Animal.cs` as follows:

```
namespace Ch11Ex01
{
    public abstract class Animal
    {
        protected string name;

        public string Name
        {
            get
            {
                return name;
            }
            set
            {
                name = value;
            }
        }

        public Animal()
        {
            name = "The animal with no name";
        }

        public Animal(string newName)
        {
            name = newName;
        }

        public void Feed()
        {
            Console.WriteLine("{0} has been fed.", name);
        }
    }
}
```

4. Modify the code in `Cow.cs` as follows:

```
namespace Ch11Ex01
{
    public class Cow : Animal
    {
        public void Milk()
        {
            Console.WriteLine("{0} has been milked.", name);
        }

        public Cow(string newName) : base(newName)
        {
        }
    }
}
```

5. Modify the code in `Chicken.cs` as follows:

```
namespace Ch11Ex01
{
    public class Chicken : Animal
    {
        public void LayEgg()
        {
            Console.WriteLine("{0} has laid an egg.", name);
        }

        public Chicken(string newName) : base(newName)
        {
        }
    }
}
```

6. Modify the code in `Program.cs` as follows:

```
using System;
using System.Collections;
using System.Collections.Generic;
using System.Text;

namespace Ch11Ex01

{
    class Program
    {
        static void Main(string[] args)
        {
            Console.WriteLine("Create an Array type collection of Animal " +
                              "objects and use it:");

            Animal[] animalArray = new Animal[2];
            Cow myCow1 = new Cow("Deirdre");
            animalArray[0] = myCow1;
            animalArray[1] = new Chicken("Ken");

            foreach (Animal myAnimal in animalArray)
            {
                Console.WriteLine("New {0} object added to Array collection, " +
                                  "Name = {1}", myAnimal.ToString(), myAnimal.Name);
            }

            Console.WriteLine("Array collection contains {0} objects.",
                              animalArray.Length);
            animalArray[0].Feed();
            ((Chicken)animalArray[1]).LayEgg();
            Console.WriteLine();

            Console.WriteLine("Create an ArrayList type collection of Animal " +
                              "objects and use it:");
            ArrayList animalArrayList = new ArrayList();
            Cow myCow2 = new Cow("Hayley");
```

```
    animalArrayList.Add(myCow2);
    animalArrayList.Add(new Chicken("Roy"));

    foreach (Animal myAnimal in animalArrayList)
    {
        Console.WriteLine("New {0} object added to ArrayList collection," +
                        " Name = {1}", myAnimal.ToString(), myAnimal.Name);
    }
    Console.WriteLine("ArrayList collection contains {0} objects.",
        animalArrayList.Count);
    ((Animal)animalArrayList[0]).Feed();
    ((Chicken)animalArrayList[1]).LayEgg();
    Console.WriteLine();

    Console.WriteLine("Additional manipulation of ArrayList:");
    animalArrayList.RemoveAt(0);
    ((Animal)animalArrayList[0]).Feed();
    animalArrayList.AddRange(animalArray);
    ((Chicken)animalArrayList[2]).LayEgg();
    Console.WriteLine("The animal called {0} is at index {1}.",
                    myCow1.Name, animalArrayList.IndexOf(myCow1));
    myCow1.Name = "Janice";
    Console.WriteLine("The animal is now called {0}.",
                    ((Animal)animalArrayList[1]).Name);
    Console.ReadKey();
    }
  }
}
```

7.   Run the application. The result is shown in Figure 11-1.

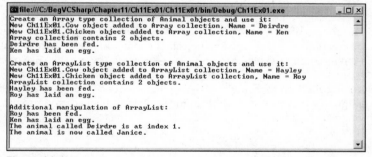

Figure 11-1

How It Works

This example creates two collections of objects, the first using the `System.Array` class (that is, a simple array), and the second using the `System.Collections.ArrayList` class. Both collections are of `Animal` objects, which are defined in `Animal.cs`. The `Animal` class is abstract, so it can't be instantiated, although you can (through polymorphism, discussed in Chapter 8) have items in your collection that are instances of the `Cow` and `Chicken` classes, which are derived from `Animal`.

Once created in the `Main()` method in `Class1.cs`, these arrays are manipulated to show their characteristics and capabilities. Several of the operations performed apply to both `Array` and `ArrayList` collections, although their syntax differs slightly. There are some, however, that are only possible using the more advanced `ArrayList` type.

I'll cover the similar operations first, comparing the code and results for both types of collection.

First, collection creation. With simple arrays you must initialize the array with a fixed size in order to use it. You do this to an array called `animalArray` using the standard syntax you saw in Chapter 5:

```
Animal[] animalArray = new Animal[2];
```

`ArrayList` collections, on the other hand, don't need a size to be initialized, so you can create your list (called `animalArrayList`) simply by using:

```
ArrayList animalArrayList = new ArrayList();
```

There are two other constructors you can use with this class. The first copies the contents of an existing collection to the new instance by specifying the existing collection as a parameter; the other sets the *capacity* of the collection, also via a parameter. This capacity, specified as an `int` value, sets the initial number of items that can be contained in the collection. This is not an absolute capacity, however, because it will be doubled automatically if the number of items in the collection ever exceeds this value.

With arrays of reference types (such as the `Animal` and `Animal`-derived objects), simply initializing the array with a size doesn't initialize the items it contains. In order to use a given entry, that entry needs to be initialized, which means that you need to assign initialized objects to the items:

```
Cow myCow1 = new Cow("Deirdre");
animalArray[0] = myCow1;
animalArray[1] = new Chicken("Ken");
```

This code does this in two ways: once by assignment using an existing `Cow` object, and once by assignment through the creation of a new `Chicken` object. The main difference here is that the former method leaves you with a reference to the object in the array—a fact that you make use of later in the code.

With the `ArrayList` collection there are no existing items, not even `null`-referenced ones. This means that you can't assign new instances to indices in the same way. Instead, you use the `Add()` method of the `ArrayList` object to add new items:

```
Cow myCow2 = new Cow("Hayley");
animalArrayList.Add(myCow2);
animalArrayList.Add(new Chicken("Roy"));
```

Apart from the slightly different syntax, you can add new or existing objects to the collection in the same way.

Once you have added items in this way, you can overwrite them using syntax identical to that for arrays, for example:

```
animalArrayList[0] = new Cow("Alma");
```

You won't do this in this example though.

In Chapter 5, you saw how the `foreach` structure can be used to iterate through an array. This is possible as the `System.Array` class implements the `IEnumerable` interface, and the only method on this interface, `GetEnumerator()`, allows you to loop through items in the collection. You'll look at this in more depth a little later in the chapter. In your code, you write out information about each `Animal` object in the array:

```
foreach (Animal myAnimal in animalArray)
{
    Console.WriteLine("New {0} object added to Array collection, " +
                      "Name = {1}", myAnimal.ToString(), myAnimal.Name);
}
```

The `ArrayList` object you use also supports the `IEnumerable` interface and can also be used with `foreach`. In this case, the syntax is identical:

```
foreach (Animal myAnimal in animalArrayList)
{
    Console.WriteLine("New {0} object added to ArrayList collection, " +
                      "Name = {1}", myAnimal.ToString(), myAnimal.Name);
}
```

Next, you use the `Length` property of the array to output to the screen the number of items in the array:

```
Console.WriteLine("Array collection contains {0} objects.",
                  animalArray.Length);
```

You can achieve the same thing with the `ArrayList` collection, except that you use the `Count` property that is part of the `ICollection` interface:

```
Console.WriteLine("ArrayList collection contains {0} objects.",
                  animalArrayList.Count);
```

Collections — whether simple arrays or more complex collections — wouldn't be much use unless they provided access to the items that belong to them. Simple arrays are strongly typed — that is, they allow direct access to the type of the items they contain. This means that you can call the methods of the item directly:

```
animalArray[0].Feed();
```

The type of the array is the abstract type `Animal`; therefore, you can't call methods supplied by derived classes directly. Instead you must use casting:

```
((Chicken)animalArray[1]).LayEgg();
```

The `ArrayList` collection is a collection of `System.Object` objects (you have assigned `Animal` objects via polymorphism). This means that you must use casting for all items:

```
((Animal)animalArrayList[0]).Feed();
((Chicken)animalArrayList[1]).LayEgg();
```

The remainder of the code looks at some of the capabilities of the `ArrayList` collection that go beyond those of the `Array` collection.

First, you can remove items using the `Remove()` and `RemoveAt()` methods, part of the `IList` interface implementation in the `ArrayList` class. These remove items from an array based on an item reference or index, respectively. In this example, you use the latter method to remove the first item added to the list, the `Cow` object with a `Name` property of `Hayley`:

```
animalArrayList.RemoveAt(0);
```

Alternatively, you could use

```
animalArrayList.Remove(myCow2);
```

because you already have a local reference to this object — you added an existing reference to the array via `Add()`, rather than creating a new object.

Either way, the only item left in the collection is the `Chicken` object, which you access in the following way:

```
((Animal)animalArrayList[0]).Feed();
```

Any modifications to the items in the `ArrayList` object resulting in N items being left in the array will be executed in such a way as to maintain indices from 0 to N-1. For example, removing the item with the index 0 results in all other items being shifted one place in the array, so you access the `Chicken` object with the index 0, not 1. There is no longer an item with an index of 1 (because you only had two items in the first place), so an exception would be thrown if you tried the following:

```
((Animal)animalArrayList[1]).Feed();
```

`ArrayList` collections allow you to add several items at once with the `AddRange()` method. This method accepts any object with the `ICollection` interface, which includes the `animalArray` array you created earlier in the code:

```
animalArrayList.AddRange(animalArray);
```

To check that this works, you can attempt to access the third item in the collection, which will be the second item in `animalArray`:

```
((Chicken)animalArrayList[2]).LayEgg();
```

The `AddRange()` method isn't part of any of the interfaces exposed by `ArrayList`. This method is specific to the `ArrayList` class and demonstrates the fact that you can exhibit customized behavior in your collection classes, above and beyond what is required by the interfaces you have looked at. This class exposes other interesting methods too, such as `InsertRange()`, for inserting an array of objects at any point in the list, and methods for tasks such as sorting and reordering the array.

Finally, you make use of the fact that you can have multiple references to the same object. Using the `IndexOf()` method (part of the `IList` interface), you can see not only that `myCow1` (an object originally added to `animalArray`) is now part of the `animalArrayList` collection but also what its index is:

```
Console.WriteLine("The animal called {0} is at index {1}.",
                  myCow1.Name, animalArrayList.IndexOf(myCow1));
```

As an extension of this, the next two lines of code rename the object via the object reference and display the new name via the collection reference:

```
myCow1.Name = "Janice";
Console.WriteLine("The animal is now called {0}.",
                  ((Animal)animalArrayList[1]).Name);
```

Defining Collections

Now that you've seen what is possible using more advanced collection classes, it's time to look at how you can create your own strongly typed collection. One way of doing this is to implement the required methods manually, but this can be quite time-consuming, and in some cases quite complex. Alternatively, you can derive your collection from a class, such as `System.Collections.CollectionBase`, an abstract class that supplies much of the implementation of a collection for you. I strongly recommend this option.

The `CollectionBase` class exposes the interfaces `IEnumerable`, `ICollection`, and `IList` but only provides some of the required implementation, notably the `Clear()` and `RemoveAt()` methods of `IList`, and the `Count` property of `ICollection`. You need to implement everything else yourself if you want the functionality provided.

To facilitate this, `CollectionBase` provides two protected properties that give access to the stored objects themselves. You can use `List`, which gives you access to the items through an `IList` interface, and `InnerList`, which is the `ArrayList` object used to store items.

For example, the basics of a collection class to store `Animal` objects could be defined as follows (you'll see a fuller implementation shortly):

```
public class Animals : CollectionBase
{
   public void Add(Animal newAnimal)
   {
      List.Add(newAnimal);
   }

   public void Remove(Animal oldAnimal)
   {
      List.Remove(oldAnimal);
   }

   public Animals()
   {
   }
}
```

Here, `Add()` and `Remove()` have been implemented as strongly typed methods that use the standard `Add()` method of the `IList` interface used to access the items. The methods exposed will now only work with `Animal` classes or classes derived from `Animal`, unlike the `ArrayList` implementations you saw earlier, which work with any object.

The `CollectionBase` class allows you to use the `foreach` syntax with your derived collections. You can, for example, use code, such as:

```
Console.WriteLine("Using custom collection class Animals:");
Animals animalCollection = new Animals();
animalCollection.Add(new Cow("Sarah"));
foreach (Animal myAnimal in animalCollection)
{
    Console.WriteLine("New {0} object added to custom collection, " +
                    "Name = {1}", myAnimal.ToString(), myAnimal.Name);
}
```

You can't however, do the following:

```
animalCollection[0].Feed();
```

In order to access items via their indices in this way, you need to use an indexer.

Indexers

An *indexer* is a special kind of property that you can add to a class to provide array-like access. In fact, you can provide more complex access via an indexer, because you can define and use complex parameter types with the square bracket syntax as you wish. Implementing a simple numeric index for items, however, is the most common usage.

You can add an indexer to the `Animals` collection of `Animal` objects as follows:

```
public class Animals : CollectionBase
{
    ...
    public Animal this[int animalIndex]
    {
        get
        {
            return (Animal)List[animalIndex];
        }
        set
        {
            List[animalIndex] = value;
        }
    }
}
```

The `this` keyword is used along with parameters in square brackets, but otherwise this looks much like any other property. This syntax is logical, because you'll access the indexer using the name of the object followed by the index parameter(s) in square brackets (for example, `MyAnimals[0]`).

This code uses an indexer on the List property (that is, on the IList interface that gives you access to the ArrayList in CollectionBase that stores your items):

```
return (Animal)List[animalIndex];
```

Explicit casting *is* necessary here, as the IList.List property returns a System.Object object.

The important thing to note here is that you define a type for this indexer. This is the type that will be obtained when accessing an item using this indexer. This means that you can write code such as:

```
animalCollection[0].Feed();
```

rather than:

```
((Animal)animalCollection[0]).Feed();
```

This is another handy feature of strongly typed custom collections. In the following Try It Out, you expand the last example properly to put this into action.

Try It Out   Implementing an Animals Collection

1. Create a new console application called Ch11Ex02 in the directory C:\BegVCSharp\ Chapter11.

2. Right-click on the project name in the Solution Explorer window, and select the Add ⇨ Existing Item... option.

3. Select the Animal.cs, Cow.cs, and Chicken.cs files from the C:\BegVCSharp\Chapter11\ Ch11Ex01\Ch11Ex01 directory, and click Add.

4. Modify the namespace declaration in the three files you have added as follows:

```
namespace Ch11Ex02
```

5. Add a new class called Animals.

6. Modify the code in Animals.cs as follows:

```
using System;
using System.Collections;
using System.Collections.Generic;
using System.Text;

namespace Ch11Ex02
{
    public class Animals : CollectionBase
    {
        public void Add(Animal newAnimal)
        {
            List.Add(newAnimal);
```

```
        }

        public void Remove(Animal newAnimal)
        {
            List.Remove(newAnimal);
        }

        public Animals()
        {
        }

        public Animal this[int animalIndex]
        {
            get
            {
                return (Animal)List[animalIndex];
            }
            set
            {
                List[animalIndex] = value;
            }
        }
    }
}
```

7. Modify Program.cs as follows:

```
static void Main(string[] args)
{
    Animals animalCollection = new Animals();
    animalCollection.Add(new Cow("Jack"));
    animalCollection.Add(new Chicken("Vera"));
    foreach (Animal myAnimal in animalCollection)
    {
        myAnimal.Feed();
    }
    Console.ReadKey();
}
```

8. Execute the application. The result is shown in Figure 11-2.

Figure 11-2

How It Works

This example uses code detailed in the last section to implement a strongly typed collection of Animal objects in a class called Animals. The code in Main() simply instantiates an Animals object called animalCollection, adds two items (an instance each of Cow and Chicken), and uses a foreach loop to call the Feed() method that both these objects inherit from their base class Animal.

Adding a Cards Collection to CardLib

In the last chapter, you created a class library project called Ch10CardLib that contained a Card class representing a playing card, and a Deck class representing a deck of cards — that is, a collection of Card classes. This collection was implemented as a simple array.

In this chapter, you'll add a new class to this library, which you'll rename Ch11CardLib. This new class, Cards, will be a custom collection of Card objects, giving you all the benefits described earlier in this chapter. You may find it easier to create a new class library called Ch11CardLib in the C:\BegVCSharp\ Chapter11 directory, and from Project ⇨ Add Existing Item..., select the Card.cs, Deck.cs, Suit.cs, and Rank.cs files from the C:\BegVCSharp\Chapter10\ Ch10CardLib\Ch10CardLib directory and add them to your project. As with the previous version of this project, introduced in Chapter 10, I'll present these changes without resorting to the standard Try It Out format. Should you wish to jump straight to the code feel free to open the version of this project included in the download-able code for this chapter.

> Don't forget that when copying the source files from Ch10CardLib to Ch11CardLib, you must change the namespace declarations to refer to Ch11CardLib. This also applies to the Ch10CardClient console application that you will use for testing.

> The downloadable code for this chapter includes a project that contains all the code you need for the various expansions to Ch11CardLib. The code is divided into regions, and you can uncomment the section you want to experiment with.

The code for your new class, in Cards.cs, is as follows (where code that is modified from that generated by the wizard is highlighted):

```csharp
using System;
using System.Collections;
using System.Collections.Generic;
using System.Text;

namespace Ch11CardLib
{
    public class Cards : CollectionBase
    {
        public void Add(Card newCard)
        {
            List.Add(newCard);
        }

        public void Remove(Card oldCard)
        {
            List.Remove(oldCard);
        }

        public Cards()
        {
        }

        public Card this[int cardIndex]
        {
            get
```

```
        {
            return (Card)List[cardIndex];
        }
        set
        {
            List[cardIndex] = value;
        }
    }

    // Utility method for copying card instances into another Cards
    // instance - used in Deck.Shuffle(). This implementation assumes that
    // source and target collections are the same size.
    public void CopyTo(Cards targetCards)
    {
        for (int index = 0; index < this.Count; index++)
        {
            targetCards[index] = this[index];
        }
    }

    // Check to see if the Cards collection contains a particular card.
    // This calls the Contains method of the ArrayList for the collection,
    // which you access through the InnerList property.
    public bool Contains(Card card)
    {
        return InnerList.Contains(card);
    }
    }
}
```

Next, you need to modify Deck.cs to make use of this new collection, rather than an array:

```
using System;

namespace Ch11CardLib
{
    public class Deck
    {
    private Cards cards = new Cards();

        public Deck()
        {
            // Line of code removed here
            for (int suitVal = 0; suitVal < 4; suitVal++)
            {
                for (int rankVal = 1; rankVal < 14; rankVal++)
                {
                    cards.Add(new Card((Suit)suitVal, (Rank)rankVal));
                }
            }
        }

        public Card GetCard(int cardNum)
        {
```

```
        if (cardNum >= 0 && cardNum <= 51)
            return cards[cardNum];
        else
            throw (new System.ArgumentOutOfRangeException("cardNum", cardNum,
                "Value must be between 0 and 51."));
    }

    public void Shuffle()
    {
        Cards newDeck = new Cards();
        bool[] assigned = new bool[52];
        Random sourceGen = new Random();
        for (int i = 0; i < 52; i++)
        {
            int sourceCard = 0;
            bool foundCard = false;
            while (foundCard == false)
            {
                sourceCard = sourceGen.Next(52);
                if (assigned[sourceCard] == false)
                    foundCard = true;
            }
            assigned[sourceCard] = true;
            newDeck.Add(cards[sourceCard]);
        }
        newDeck.CopyTo(cards);
    }
  }
}
```

There aren't that many changes necessary here. Most of those involve changing the shuffling logic to allow for the fact that cards are added to the beginning of the new `Cards` collection `newDeck` from a random index in cards, rather than to a random index in `newDeck` from a sequential position in `cards`.

The client console application for the `Ch10CardLib` solution, `Ch10CardClient`, may be used with this new library with the same result as before, as the method signatures of `Deck` are unchanged. Clients of this class library can now make use of the `Cards` collection class, however, rather than relying on arrays of `Card` objects, for example in defining hands of cards in a card game application.

Keyed Collections and IDictionary

Instead of the `IList` interface, it is also possible for collections to implement the similar `IDictionary` interface, which allows items to be indexed via a key value (such as a string name) rather than by an index.

This is also achieved by using an indexer, although this time the indexer parameter used is a key associated with a stored item, rather than an `int` index, which can make the collection a lot more user-friendly.

As with indexed collections, there is a base class that you can use to simplify implementation of the `IDictionary` interface: `DictionaryBase`. This class also implements `IEnumerable` and `ICollection`, providing the basic collection manipulation capabilities that are the same for any collection.

DictionaryBase, like CollectionBase, implements some (but not all) of the members obtained through its supported interfaces. Like CollectionBase, the Clear() and Count members are implemented, although RemoveAt() isn't. This is so because RemoveAt() is a method on the IList interface and doesn't appear on the IDictionary interface. IDictionary does, however, have a Remove() method, which is one of the methods you should implement in a custom collection class based on DictionaryBase.

The following code shows an alternative version of the Animals class from the last section, this time derived from DictionaryBase. Implementations are included for Add(), Remove(), and a key-accessed indexer:

```
public class Animals : DictionaryBase
{
    public void Add(string newID, Animal newAnimal)
    {
        Dictionary.Add(newID, newAnimal);
    }

    public void Remove(string animalID)
    {
        Dictionary.Remove(animalID);
    }

    public Animals()
    {
    }

    public Animal this[string animalID]
    {
        get
        {
            return (Animal)Dictionary[animalID];
        }
        set
        {
            Dictionary[animalID] = value;
        }
    }
}
```

The differences in these members are:

❑ Add(): Takes two parameters, a key and a value, to store together. The dictionary collection has a member called Dictionary inherited from DictionaryBase, which is an IDictionary interface. This interface has its own Add() method, which takes two object parameters. Your implementation takes a string value as a key and an Animal object as the data to store alongside this key.

❑ Remove(): Takes a key parameter rather than an object reference. The item with the key value specified is removed.

❑ Indexer: Uses a string key value rather than an index, which is used to access the stored item via the Dictionary inherited member. Again, casting is necessary here.

One other difference between collections based on `DictionaryBase` and collections based on `CollectionBase` is that `foreach` works slightly differently. The collection from the last section allowed you to extract `Animal` objects directly from the collection. Using `foreach` with the `DictionaryBase` derived class gives you `DictionaryEntry` structs, another type defined in the `System.Collections` namespace. To get to the `Animal` objects themselves you must use the `Value` member of this struct, or you can use the `Key` member of the struct to get the associated key. To get code equivalent to the earlier

```
foreach (Animal myAnimal in animalCollection)
{
    Console.WriteLine("New {0} object added to custom collection, " +
                    "Name = {1}", myAnimal.ToString(), myAnimal.Name);
}
```

you need the following:

```
foreach (DictionaryEntry myEntry in animalCollection)
{
    Console.WriteLine("New {0} object added to custom collection, " +
                    "Name = {1}", myEntry.Value.ToString(),
                    ((Animal)myEntry.Value).Name);
}
```

It is possible to override this behavior so that you can get at `Animal` objects directly through `foreach`. There are a number of ways of doing this, the simplest being to implement an iterator. You'll see what iterators are, and how they can solve this problem, in the next section.

Iterators

Earlier in this chapter, you saw that the `IEnumerable` interface is responsible for allowing you to use `foreach` loops. Often, you will find it a great benefit to use your classes in `foreach` loops and not just collection classes such as those examined in previous sections of this chapter.

However, overriding this behavior, or providing your own custom implementation of it, is not necessarily a simple thing to do. To illustrate this, it's time to put on your best gloves and get under the hood of `foreach` loops. What actually happens in a `foreach` loop iterating through a collection called `collectionObject` is:

1. `collectionObject.GetEnumerator()` is called, which returns an `IEnumerator` reference. This method is available through implementation of the `IEnumerable` interface, although this is optional.

2. The `MoveNext()` method of the returned `IEnumerator` interface is called.

3. If `MoveNext()` returns `true` then the `Current` property of the `IEnumerator` interface is used to get a reference to an object, which is used in the `foreach` loop.

4. The preceding two steps repeat until `MoveNext()` returns `false`, at which point the loop terminates.

So, to allow this to happen in your classes, you have to override several methods, keep track of indices, maintain the `Current` property, and so on. This can be a lot of work to achieve very little.

A simpler alternative is to use an iterator. Effectively, using iterators will generate a lot of the code for you behind the scenes and hook it all up correctly. And the syntax for using iterators is much easier to come to grips with.

A good definition of an iterator is that it is a block of code that supplies all the values to be used in a `foreach` block in sequence. Typically, this block of code will be a method, although it is also possible to use property accessors and other blocks of code as iterators. However, to keep things simple here you'll just look at methods.

Whatever the block of code is, its return type is restricted. Perhaps contrary to expectations, this return type isn't the same as the type of object being enumerated. For example, in a class that represents a collection of `Animal` objects, the return type of the iterator block can't be `Animal`. Two possible return types are the interface types mentioned earlier, `IEnumerable` or `IEnumerator`. You use these types:

❑ If you want to iterate over a class, use a method called `GetEnumerator()` with a return type of `IEnumerator`.

❑ If you want to iterate over a class member, such as a method, use `IEnumerable`.

Within an iterator block you select the values to be used in the `foreach` loop using the `yield` keyword. The syntax for doing this is:

```
yield return value;
```

That information is all you need to build a very simple example, as follows:

```
public static IEnumerable SimpleList()
{
    yield return "string 1";
    yield return "string 2";
    yield return "string 3";
}

public static void Main(string[] args)
{
    foreach (string item in SimpleList())
        Console.WriteLine(item);

    Console.ReadKey();
}
```

Here, the static method `SimpleList()` is the iterator block. It is a method, so you use a return type of `IEnumerable`. `SimpleList()` uses the `yield` keyword to supply three values to the `foreach` block that uses it, each of which is written to the screen. The result is shown in Figure 11-3.

Figure 11-3

Obviously, this iterator isn't a particularly useful one, but it does enable you to see things in action and to see how simple the implementation can be. Looking at the code, you might be wondering how the code knows to return `string` type items. In fact, it doesn't; it returns `object` type values. Since, as you know, `object` is the base class for all types this means that you can return anything from the `yield` statements.

However, the compiler is intelligent enough so that you can interpret the returned values as whatever type you want in the context of the `foreach` loop. Here, the code asks for `string` type values, so that is what the values you get to work with are. Should you change one of the `yield` lines so that it returns, say, an integer, you'll get a bad cast exception in the `foreach` loop.

There's one more thing to note about iterators. It is possible to interrupt the return of information to the `foreach` loop using the following statement:

```
yield break;
```

When this statement is encountered in an iterator, the iterator processing terminates immediately, as does the `foreach` loop using it.

Now it's time for a more complicated — and useful! — example. In this Try It Out, you'll implement an iterator that obtains prime numbers.

Try It Out   Implementing an Iterator

1. Create a new console application called `Ch11Ex03` in the directory `C:\BegVCSharp\Chapter11`.

2. Add a new class called `Primes`, and modify the code as follows:

```
using System;
using System.Collections;
using System.Collections.Generic;
using System.Text;

namespace Ch11Ex03
{
    public class Primes
    {
        private long min;
        private long max;

        public Primes() : this(2, 100)
        {
        }

        public Primes(long minimum, long maximum)
        {
            if (min < 2)
            {
                min = 2;
            }
            min = minimum;
            max = maximum;
```

```
        }

        public IEnumerator GetEnumerator()
        {
            for (long possiblePrime = min; possiblePrime <= max; possiblePrime++)
            {
                bool isPrime = true;
                for (long possibleFactor = 2; possibleFactor <=
                    (long)Math.Floor(Math.Sqrt(possiblePrime)); possibleFactor++)
                {
                    long remainderAfterDivision = possiblePrime % possibleFactor;
                    if (remainderAfterDivision == 0)
                    {
                        isPrime = false;
                        break;
                    }
                }
                if (isPrime)
                {
                    yield return possiblePrime;
                }
            }
        }
    }
}
```

3. Modify the code in `Program.cs` as follows:

```
static void Main(string[] args)
{
    Primes primesFrom2To1000 = new Primes(2, 1000);
    foreach (long i in primesFrom2To1000)
        Console.Write("{0} ", i);

    Console.ReadKey();
}
```

4. Execute the application. The result is shown in Figure 11-4.

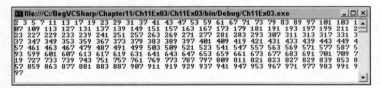

Figure 11-4

How It Works

This example consists of a class that enables you to enumerate over a collection of prime numbers between an upper and lower limit. The class that encapsulates the prime numbers makes use of an iterator to provide this functionality.

The code for `Primes` starts off with the basics, with two fields to hold the maximum and minimum values to search between, and constructors to set these values. Note that the minimum value is restricted — it can't be less than 2. This makes sense, because 2 is the lowest prime number there is. The interesting code is all in the `GetEnumerator()` method. The method signature fulfils the rules for an iterator block in that it returns an `IEnumerator` type:

```
public IEnumerator GetEnumerator()
{
```

To extract prime numbers between limits, you need to test each number in turn, so you start with a `for` loop:

```
for (long possiblePrime = min; possiblePrime <= max; possiblePrime++)
{
```

Since you don't know whether a number is prime or not, you assume that it is to start off with and then check to see if it isn't. Checking to see if it isn't means checking to see if any number between 2 and the square root of the number to be tested is a factor. If this turns out to be true then the number isn't prime, so you move on to the next one. If the number is indeed prime, you pass it to the `foreach` loop using `yield`.

```
bool isPrime = true;
for (long possibleFactor = 2; possibleFactor <=
    (long)Math.Floor(Math.Sqrt(possiblePrime)); possibleFactor++)
{
    long remainderAfterDivision = possiblePrime % possibleFactor;
    if (remainderAfterDivision == 0)
    {
        isPrime = false;
        break;
    }
}
if (isPrime)
{
    yield return possiblePrime;
}
}
}
```

An interesting fact reveals itself through this code if you set the minimum and maximum limits to very big numbers. When you execute the application, you'll notice that the results appear one at a time, with pauses in between, rather than in one go. This is evidence that the iterator code returns results one at a time, despite the fact that there is no obvious place where the code terminates between `yield` calls. Behind the scenes, calling `yield` does interrupt the code, which resumes when another value is requested, that is, when the `foreach` loop using the iterator begins a new cycle.

Iterators and Collections

Earlier you received a promise — that you'd see how iterators can be used to iterate over the objects stored in a dictionary-type collection without having to deal with `DictionaryItem` objects. You saw the following collection class, `Animals`:

```
public class Animals : DictionaryBase
{
   public void Add(string newID, Animal newAnimal)
   {
      Dictionary.Add(newID, newAnimal);
   }

   public void Remove(string animalID)
   {
      Dictionary.Remove(animalID);
   }

   public Animals()
   {
   }

   public Animal this[string animalID]
   {
      get
      {
         return (Animal)Dictionary[animalID];
      }
      set
      {
         Dictionary[animalID] = value;
      }
   }
}
```

You can add the following simple iterator to this code to get the desired behavior:

```
public new IEnumerator GetEnumerator()
{
   foreach (object animal in Dictionary.Values)
      yield return (Animal)animal;
}
```

Now, you can use code as follows to iterate through the Animal objects in the collection:

```
foreach (Animal myAnimal in animalCollection)
{
   Console.WriteLine("New {0} object added to custom collection, " +
                     "Name = {1}", myAnimal.ToString(), myAnimal.Name);
}
```

Deep Copying

In Chapter 9, you saw how you can perform shallow copying with the System.Object
.MemberwiseClone() protected method, using a method like the GetCopy() one shown here:

```
public class Cloner
{
   public int Val;

   public Cloner(int newVal)
   {
      Val = newVal;
   }

   public object GetCopy()
   {
      return MemberwiseClone();
   }
}
```

Suppose that you have fields that are reference types rather than value types (for example, objects):

```
public class Content
{
   public int Val;
}

public class Cloner
{
   public Content MyContent = new Content();

   public Cloner(int newVal)
   {
      MyContent.Val = newVal;
   }
   public object GetCopy()
   {
      return MemberwiseClone();
   }
}
```

In this case, the shallow copy obtained though GetCopy() will have a field that refers to the same object as the original object.

The following code demonstrates this using this class:

```
Cloner mySource = new Cloner(5);
Cloner myTarget = (Cloner)mySource.GetCopy();
Console.WriteLine("myTarget.MyContent.Val = {0}", myTarget.MyContent.Val);
mySource.MyContent.Val = 2;
Console.WriteLine("myTarget.MyContent.Val = {0}", myTarget.MyContent.Val);
```

The fourth line, which assigns a value to mySource.MyContent.Val, the Val public field of the MyContent public field of the original object, also changes the value of myTarget.MyContent.Val. This is because mySource.MyContent refers to the same object instance as myTarget.MyContent. The output of the preceding code is:

```
myTarget.MyContent.Val = 5
myTarget.MyContent.Val = 2
```

To get round this, you need to perform a deep copy. You could just modify the `GetCopy()` method used previously to do this, but it is preferable to use the standard .NET Framework way of doing things. To do this, you implement the `ICloneable` interface, which has the single method `Clone()`. This method takes no parameters and returns an `object` type result, giving it a signature identical to the `GetCopy()` method used earlier.

Modifying the preceding classes, you might use the following deep copy code:

```
public class Content
{
    public int Val;
}
```

```
public class Cloner : ICloneable
{
    public Content MyContent = new Content();

    public Cloner(int newVal)
    {
        MyContent.Val = newVal;
    }

    public object Clone()
    {
        Cloner clonedCloner = new Cloner(MyContent.Val);
        return clonedCloner;
    }
}
```

Here, you create a new `Cloner` object using the `Val` field of the `Content` object contained in the original `Cloner` object (`MyContent`). This field is a value type, so no deeper copying is necessary.

Using code similar to that shown above to test the shallow copy, but using `Clone()` instead of `GetCopy()`, gives you the following result:

```
myTarget.MyContent.Val = 5
myTarget.MyContent.Val = 5
```

This time, the contained objects are independent.

Note that there are times where calls to `Clone()` will be made recursively, in more complex object systems. For example, if the `MyContent` field of the `Cloner` class also required deep copying, you might need the following:

```
public class Cloner : ICloneable
{
    public Content MyContent = new Content();

    ...
```

```
    public object Clone()
    {
        Cloner clonedCloner = new Cloner();
        clonedCloner.MyContent = MyContent.Clone();
        return clonedCloner;
    }
}
```

You're calling the default constructor here to simplify the syntax of creating a new `Cloner` object. For this code to work, you would also need to implement `ICloneable` on the `Content` class.

Adding Deep Copying to CardLib

You can put this into practice by implementing the capability to copy `Card`, `Cards`, and `Deck` objects using the `ICloneable` interface. This might be useful in some card games, where you might not necessarily want two decks with references to the same set of `Card` objects, although you might conceivably want to set up one deck to have the same card order as another.

Implementing cloning functionality for the `Card` class in `Ch11CardLib` is simple, because shallow copying is sufficient (`Card` only contains value-type data, in the form of fields). You just need to make the following changes to the class definition:

```
public class Card : ICloneable
{
    public object Clone()
    {
        return MemberwiseClone();
    }
```

Note that this implementation of `ICloneable` is just a shallow copy. There is no rule determining what should happen in the `Clone()` method, and this is sufficient for your purposes.

Next, you need to implement `ICloneable` on the `Cards` collection class. This is slightly more complicated because it involves cloning every `Card` object in the original collection—so you need to make a deep copy:

```
public class Cards : CollectionBase, ICloneable
{
    public object Clone()
    {
        Cards newCards = new Cards();
        foreach (Card sourceCard in List)
        {
            newCards.Add(sourceCard.Clone() as Card);
        }
        return newCards;
    }
```

Finally, you need to implement ICloneable on the Deck class. There is a slight problem here: the Deck class has no way of modifying the cards it contains, short of shuffling them. There is no way, for example, to modify a Deck instance to have a given card order. To get around this, you define a new private constructor for the Deck class that allows a specific Cards collection to be passed in when the Deck object is instantiated. The code to implement cloning in this class is:

```csharp
public class Deck : ICloneable
{
    public object Clone()
    {
        Deck newDeck = new Deck(cards.Clone() as Cards);
        return newDeck;
    }

    private Deck(Cards newCards)
    {
        cards = newCards;
    }
}
```

Again, you can test this out with some simple client code (as before, this code should be placed within the Main() method of a client project to test this out):

```csharp
Deck deck1 = new Deck();
Deck deck2 = (Deck)deck1.Clone();
Console.WriteLine("The first card in the original deck is: {0}",
                  deck1.GetCard(0));
Console.WriteLine("The first card in the cloned deck is: {0}",
                  deck2.GetCard(0));
deck1.Shuffle();
Console.WriteLine("Original deck shuffled.");
Console.WriteLine("The first card in the original deck is: {0}",
                  deck1.GetCard(0));
Console.WriteLine("The first card in the cloned deck is: {0}",
                  deck2.GetCard(0));
Console.ReadKey();
```

The output will be something like the screenshot shown in Figure 11-5.

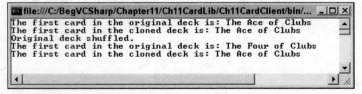

Figure 11-5

Comparisons

In this section, you will look at two types of comparisons between objects:

❏   Type comparisons

❏   Value comparisons

Type comparisons, that is, determining what an object is, or what it inherits from, are important in all areas of C# programming. Often when you pass an object to a method, say, what happens next depends on what type the object is. You've seen this in passing at various points in this and earlier chapters, but here you will see some more useful techniques.

Value comparisons are also something you've seen a lot of, at least with simple types. When it comes to comparing values of objects things get a little more complicated. You have to define what is meant by a comparison for a start, and what operators such as > mean in the context of your classes. This is especially important in collections, where you might want to sort objects according to some condition, perhaps alphabetically or perhaps according to some more complicated algorithm.

Type Comparison

When you are comparing objects you will often need to know their type, which may enable you to determine whether a value comparison is possible. Back in Chapter 9 you saw the GetType() method, which all classes inherit from System.Object, and how this method can be used in combination with the typeof() operator to determine (and take action depending on) object types:

```
if (myObj.GetType() == typeof(MyComplexClass))
{
    // myObj is an instance of the class MyComplexClass.
}
```

You've also seen the way that the default implementation of ToString(), also inherited from System.Object, will get you a string representation of the type of an object. You can compare these strings too, although this is a bit of a messy way of doing things.

In this section, you're going to look at a handy shorthand way of doing things: the is operator. This allows for much more readable code and also, as you will see, has the advantage of examining base classes.

Before looking at the is operator, though, you need to be aware of something that often happens behind the scenes when dealing with value types (as opposed to reference types): boxing and unboxing.

Boxing and Unboxing

In Chapter 8, you saw the difference between reference and value types, which was illustrated in Chapter 9 by comparing structs (which are value types) with classes (which are reference types). *Boxing* is the act of converting a value type into the System.Object type or to an interface type that is implemented by the value type. *Unboxing* is the opposite conversion.

For example, suppose that you have the following struct type:

```
struct MyStruct
{
    public int Val;
}
```

You can box a struct of this type by placing it into an `object`-type variable:

```
MyStruct valType1 = new MyStruct();
valType1.Val = 5;
object refType = valType1;
```

Here, you create a new variable (`valType1`) of type `MyStruct`, assign a value to the `Val` member of this struct, then box it into an `object`-type variable (`refType`).

The object created by boxing a variable in this way contains a reference to a copy of the value-type variable, not a reference to the original value-type variable. You can verify this by modifying the contents of the original struct, then unboxing the struct contained in the object into a new variable and examining its contents:

```
valType1.Val = 6;
MyStruct valType2 = (MyStruct)refType;
Console.WriteLine("valType2.Val = {0}", valType2.Val);
```

This code gives you the following output:

```
valType2.Val = 5
```

When you assign a reference type to an object, however, you get a different behavior. You can illustrate this by changing `MyStruct` into a class (ignoring the fact that the name of this class isn't appropriate any more):

```
class MyStruct
{
    public int Val;
}
```

With no changes to the client code shown above (again ignoring the misnamed variables), you get the following output:

```
valType2.Val = 6
```

You can also box value types into interface types, so long as they implement that interface. For example, suppose the `MyStruct` type implements the `IMyInterface` interface as follows:

```
interface IMyInterface
{
}
```

```
struct MyStruct : IMyInterface
```

```
    {
        public int Val;
    }
```

You can then box the struct into an `IMyInterface` type as follows:

```
    MyStruct valType1 = new MyStruct();
    IMyInterface refType = valType1;
```

and you can unbox it using the normal casting syntax:

```
    MyStruct ValType2 = (MyStruct)refType;
```

As you can see from these examples, boxing is performed without your intervention (that is, you don't have to write any code to make this possible). Unboxing a value requires an explicit conversion, however, and requires you to make a cast (boxing is implicit and doesn't have this requirement).

You might be wondering why you would actually want to do this. There are actually two very good reasons why boxing is extremely useful. First, it allows you to use value types in collections (such as `ArrayList`), where the items are of type `object`. Second, it's the internal mechanism that allows you to call `object` methods on value types, such as `int`s and structs.

As a final note, it is worth remarking that unboxing is necessary before access to the value type contents is possible.

The is Operator

Despite its name, the `is` operator isn't a way to tell if an object *is* a certain type. Instead, the `is` operator allows you to check whether an object either is or *can be converted into* a given type. If this is the case, then the operator evaluates to `true`.

In the earlier examples you saw a `Cow` and a `Chicken` class, both of which inherit from `Animal`. Using the `is` operator to compare objects with the `Animal` type will return `true` for objects of all three of these types, not just `Animal`. This is something you'd have a great deal of difficulty achieving with the `GetType()` method and `typeof()` operator seen previously.

The `is` operator has the syntax:

```
    <operand> is <type>
```

The possible results of this expression are:

❑ If `<type>` is a class type, then the result is `true` if `<operand>` is of that type, if it inherits from that type or if it can be boxed into that type.

❑ If `<type>` is an interface type, then the result is `true` if `<operand>` is of that type or if it is a type that implements the interface.

❑ If `<type>` is a value type then the result is `true` if `<operand>` is of that type or if it is a type that can be unboxed into that type.

The Try It Out that follows provides a few examples to see how this works in practice.

Try It Out   Using the is Operator

1. Create a new console application called `Ch11Ex04` in the directory `C:\BegVCSharp\Chapter11`.

2. Modify the code in `Program.cs` as follows:

```csharp
namespace Ch11Ex04
{
    class Checker
    {
        public void Check(object param1)
        {
            if (param1 is ClassA)
                Console.WriteLine("Variable can be converted to ClassA.");
            else
                Console.WriteLine("Variable can't be converted to ClassA.");
            if (param1 is IMyInterface)
                Console.WriteLine("Variable can be converted to IMyInterface.");
            else
                Console.WriteLine("Variable can't be converted to IMyInterface.");

            if (param1 is MyStruct)
                Console.WriteLine("Variable can be converted to MyStruct.");
            else
                Console.WriteLine("Variable can't be converted to MyStruct.");
        }
    }

    interface IMyInterface
    {
    }

    class ClassA : IMyInterface
    {
    }

    class ClassB : IMyInterface
    {
    }

    class ClassC
    {
    }

    class ClassD : ClassA
    {
    }

    struct MyStruct : IMyInterface
    {
    }
```

```
class Program
{
    static void Main(string[] args)
    {
        Checker check = new Checker();
        ClassA try1 = new ClassA();
        ClassB try2 = new ClassB();
        ClassC try3 = new ClassC();
        ClassD try4 = new ClassD();
        MyStruct try5 = new MyStruct();
        object try6 = try5;
        Console.WriteLine("Analyzing ClassA type variable:");
        check.Check(try1);

        Console.WriteLine("\nAnalyzing ClassB type variable:");
        check.Check(try2);
        Console.WriteLine("\nAnalyzing ClassC type variable:");
        check.Check(try3);
        Console.WriteLine("\nAnalyzing ClassD type variable:");
        check.Check(try4);
        Console.WriteLine("\nAnalyzing MyStruct type variable:");
        check.Check(try5);
        Console.WriteLine("\nAnalyzing boxed MyStruct type variable:");
        check.Check(try6);
        Console.ReadKey();
    }
}
```

3. Execute the code. The result is shown in Figure 11-6.

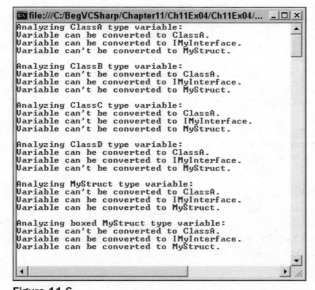

Figure 11-6

How It Works

This example illustrates the various results possible when using the `is` operator. Three classes, an interface, and a structure are defined and used as parameters to a method of a class that uses the `is` operator to see if they can be converted into the `ClassA` type, the interface type, and the struct type.

Only `ClassA` and `ClassD` (which inherits from `ClassA`) types are compatible with `ClassA`. Types that don't inherit from a class are not compatible with that class.

The `ClassA`, `ClassB`, and `MyStruct` types all implement `IMyInterface`, so these are all compatible with the `IMyInterface` type. `ClassD` inherits from `ClassA`, so that it too is compatible. Therefore, only `ClassC` is incompatible.

Finally, only variables of type `MyStruct` itself and boxed variables of that type are compatible with `MyStruct`, because you can't convert reference types to value types (except, of course, that you can unbox previously boxed variables).

Value Comparison

Consider two `Person` objects representing people, each with an integer `Age` property. You might want to compare them to see which person is older. You can simply use the following code:

```
if (person1.Age > person2.Age)
{
    ...
}
```

This works fine, but there are alternatives. You might prefer to use syntax such as:

```
if (person1 > person2)
{
    ...
}
```

This is possible using operator overloading, which you'll look at in this section. This is a powerful technique, but should be used judiciously. In the preceding code, it is not immediately obvious that ages are being compared — it could be height, weight, IQ, or just general "greatness."

Another option is to use the `IComparable` and `IComparer` interface, which allow you to define how objects will be compared to each other in a standard way. This way of doing things is supported by the various collection classes in the .NET Framework, making it an excellent way to sort objects in a collection.

Operator Overloading

Operator overloading enables you to use standard operators, such as +, >, and so on, with classes that you design. This is called overloading, because you are supplying your own implementations for these operators when used with specific parameter types, in much the same way that you overload methods by supplying different parameters for methods with the same name.

Operator overloading is useful as you can perform whatever processing you want in the implementation of the operator overload, which might not be as simple as, say, + meaning "add these two operands together." In a little while, you'll see a good example of this in a further upgrade of the `CardLib` library. You'll provide implementations for comparison operators that compare two cards to see which would beat the other in a trick (one round of card game play). Because a trick in many card games depends on the suits of the cards involved, this isn't as straightforward as comparing the numbers on the cards. If the second card laid down is a different suit from the first, then the first card will win regardless of its rank. You can implement this by considering the order of the two operands. You can also take a trump suit into account, where trumps beat other suits, even if that isn't the first suit laid down. This means that calculating that `card1 > card2` is `true` (that is, `card1` will beat `card2`, if `card1` is laid down first), doesn't necessarily imply that `card2 > card1` is `false`. If neither `card1` nor `card2` are trumps and they belong to different suits, then both these comparisons will be `true`.

To start with, though, here's a look at the basic syntax for operator overloading.

Operators may be overloaded by adding operator type members (which must be `static`) to a class. Some operators have multiple uses (such as -, which has unary and binary capabilities); therefore, you also specify how many operands you are dealing with and what the types of these operands are. In general, you will have operands that are the same type as the class where the operator is defined, although it is possible to define operators that work on mixed types, as you will see shortly.

As an example, consider the simple type `AddClass1`, defined as follows:

```
public class AddClass1
{
    public int val;
}
```

This is just a wrapper around an `int` value but will serve to illustrate the principles.

With this class, code such as the following, will fail to compile:

```
AddClass1 op1 = new AddClass1();
op1.val = 5;
AddClass1 op2 = new AddClass1();
op2.val = 5;
AddClass1 op3 = op1 + op2;
```

The error you get informs you that the + operator cannot be applied to operands of the `AddClass1` type. This is so because you haven't defined an operation to perform yet.

Code such as the following, will work, although it won't give you the result you might want:

```
AddClass1 op1 = new AddClass1();
op1.val = 5;
AddClass1 op2 = new AddClass1();
op2.val = 5;
bool op3 = op1 == op2;
```

Here, op1 and op2 are compared using the == binary operator to see if they refer to the same object, and *not* to verify whether their values are equal. op3 will be `false` in the preceding code, even though op1.val and op2.val are identical.

To overload the + operator, you use the following code:

```
public class AddClass1
{
    public int val;

    public static AddClass1 operator +(AddClass1 op1, AddClass1 op2)
    {
        AddClass1 returnVal = new AddClass1();
        returnVal.val = op1.val + op2.val;
        return returnVal;
    }
}
```

As you can see, operator overloads look much like standard `static` method declarations, except that they use the keyword `operator` and the operator itself rather than a method name.

You can now successfully use the + operator with this class, as in the previous example:

```
AddClass1 op3 = op1 + op2;
```

Overloading all binary operators fits the same pattern. Unary operators look similar but only have one parameter:

```
public class AddClass1
{
    public int val;

    public static AddClass1 operator +(AddClass1 op1, AddClass1 op2)
    {
        AddClass1 returnVal = new AddClass1();
        returnVal.val = op1.val + op2.val;
        return returnVal;
    }

    public static AddClass1 operator -(AddClass1 op1)
    {
        AddClass1 returnVal = new AddClass1();
        returnVal.val = -op1.val;
        return returnVal;
    }
}
```

Both these operators work on operands of the same type as the class and have return values that are also of that type. Consider, however, the following class definitions:

```
public class AddClass1
{
    public int val;

    public static AddClass3 operator +(AddClass1 op1, AddClass2 op2)
    {
        AddClass3 returnVal = new AddClass3();
        returnVal.val = op1.val + op2.val;
        return returnVal;
    }
}

public class AddClass2
{
    public int val;
}

public class AddClass3
{
    public int val;
}
```

This will allow the following code:

```
AddClass1 op1 = new AddClass1();
op1.val = 5;
AddClass2 op2 = new AddClass2();
op2.val = 5;
AddClass3 op3 = op1 + op2;
```

When appropriate, you can mix types in this way. Note, however, that if you added the same operator to AddClass2, the preceding code would fail, because it would be ambiguous as to which operator to use. You should, therefore, take care not to add operators with the same signature to more than one class.

Also, note that if you mix types, the operands *must* be supplied in the same order as the parameters to the operator overload. If you attempt to use your overloaded operator with the operands in the wrong order, the operation will fail. So, you can't use the operator like this:

```
AddClass3 op3 = op2 + op1;
```

unless, of course, you supply another overload with the parameters reversed:

```
public static AddClass3 operator +(AddClass2 op1, AddClass1 op2)
{
    AddClass3 returnVal = new AddClass3();
    returnVal.val = op1.val + op2.val;
    return returnVal;
}
```

The following operators can be overloaded:

- ❑ **Unary operators:** +, -, !, ~, ++, --, true, false
- ❑ **Binary operators:** +, -, *, /, %, &, |, ^, <<, >>
- ❑ **Comparison operators:** ==, !=, <, >, <=, >=

If you overload the true *and* false *operators, then you can use classes in Boolean expressions, such as* if (op1) {}.

You can't overload assignment operators, such as +=, but these operators use their simple counterparts, such as +, so you don't have to worry about that. Overloading + means that += will function as expected. The = operator is included in this — it makes little sense to overload this operator, since it has such a fundamental usage. This operator, however, is related to the user-defined conversion operators, which you'll look at in the next section.

You also can't overload && and ||, but these operators use the & and | operators to perform their calculations, so overloading these is enough.

Some operators, such as < and >, must be overloaded in pairs. That is to say, you can't overload < unless you also overload >. In many cases, you can simply call other operators from these to reduce the code required (and the errors that might occur), for example:

```
public class AddClass1
{
    public int val;

    public static bool operator >=(AddClass1 op1, AddClass1 op2)
    {
        return (op1.val >= op2.val);
    }

    public static bool operator <(AddClass1 op1, AddClass1 op2)
    {
        return !(op1 >= op2);
    }

    // Also need implementations for <= and > operators.
}
```

In more complex operator definitions, this can save on lines of code, and it also means that you have less code to change should you wish to change the implementation of these operators.

The same applies to == and !=, but with these operators it is often worth overriding Object.Equals() and Object.GetHashCode(), because both of these functions may also be used to compare objects. By overriding these methods, you ensure that whatever technique users of the class use, they get the same result. This isn't essential, but is worth adding for completeness. It requires the following nonstatic override methods:

```
public class AddClass1
{
```

```
    public int val;

    public static bool operator ==(AddClass1 op1, AddClass1 op2)
    {
        return (op1.val == op2.val);
    }

    public static bool operator !=(AddClass1 op1, AddClass1 op2)
    {
        return !(op1 == op2);
    }

    public override bool Equals(object op1)
    {
        return val == ((AddClass1)op1).val;
    }

    public override int GetHashCode()
    {
        return val;
    }
}
```

GetHashCode() is used to obtain a unique int value for an object instance based on its state. Here, using val is fine, because it is also an int value.

Note that Equals() uses an object type parameter. You need to use this signature or you will be overloading this method rather than overriding it, and the default implementation will still be accessible to users of the class. This means that you must use casting to get the result you require. It is often worth checking object type using the is operator discussed earlier in this chapter in code such as this:

```
    public override bool Equals(object op1)
    {
        if (op1 is AddClass1)
        {
            return val == ((AddClass1)op1).val;
        }
        else
        {
            throw new ArgumentException(
                "Cannot compare AddClass1 objects with objects of type "
                + op1.GetType().ToString());
        }
    }
```

In this code, an exception is thrown if the operand passed to Equals is of the wrong type or cannot be converted into the correct type.

Of course, this behavior may not be what you want. You may want to be able to compare objects of one type with objects of another type, in which case more branching would be necessary. Alternatively, you may want to restrict comparisons to those where both objects are of exactly the same type, which would require the following change to the first `if` statement:

```
if (op1.GetType() == typeof(AddClass1))
```

Next, you see how you can make use of operator overloads in `CardLib`.

Adding Operator Overloads to CardLib

Now, you'll upgrade your `Ch11CardLib` project again, adding operator overloading to the card class. First, though, you'll add the extra fields to the `Card` class that allow for trump suits and a choice to place Aces high. You make these static, since when they are set, they apply to all `Card` objects:

```
public class Card
{
    // Flag for trump usage. If true, trumps are valued higher
    // than cards of other suits.
    public static bool useTrumps = false;

    // Trump suit to use if useTrumps is true.
    public static Suit trump = Suit.Club;

    // Flag that determines whether aces are higher than kings or lower
    // than deuces.
    public static bool isAceHigh = true;
```

One point to note here is that these rules apply to all `Card` objects in every `Deck` in an application. It is not possible to have two decks of cards with cards contained in each that obey different rules. This is fine for this class library, however, as you can safely assume that if a single application wants to use separate rules, then it could maintain these itself, perhaps setting the static members of `Card` whenever decks are switched.

Since you have done this, it is worth adding a few more constructors to the `Deck` class, in order to initialize decks with different characteristics:

```
public Deck()
{
    for (int suitVal = 0; suitVal < 4; suitVal++)
    {
        for (int rankVal = 1; rankVal < 14; rankVal++)
        {
            cards.Add(new Card((Suit)suitVal, (Rank)rankVal));
        }
    }
}

// Nondefault constructor. Allows aces to be set high.
public Deck(bool isAceHigh) : this()
{
    Card.isAceHigh = isAceHigh;
}
```

```
   // Nondefault constructor. Allows a trump suit to be used.
   public Deck(bool useTrumps, Suit trump) : this()
   {
      Card.useTrumps = useTrumps;
      Card.trump = trump;
   }
```

```
   // Nondefault constructor. Allows aces to be set high and a trump suit
   // to be used.
   public Deck(bool isAceHigh, bool useTrumps, Suit trump) : this()
   {
      Card.isAceHigh = isAceHigh;
      Card.useTrumps = useTrumps;
      Card.trump = trump;
   }
```

Each of these constructors is defined using the : this() syntax you saw in Chapter 9, so that in all cases, the default constructor is called before the nondefault one, initializing the deck.

Next, you add your operator overloads (and suggested overrides) to the Card class:

```
   public Card(Suit newSuit, Rank newRank)
   {
      suit = newSuit;
      rank = newRank;
   }
```

```
   public static bool operator ==(Card card1, Card card2)
   {
      return (card1.suit == card2.suit) && (card1.rank == card2.rank);
   }
```

```
   public static bool operator !=(Card card1, Card card2)
   {
      return !(card1 == card2);
   }
```

```
   public override bool Equals(object card)
   {
      return this == (Card)card;
   }
   public override int GetHashCode()
   {
      return 13*(int)rank + (int)suit;
   }
```

```
   public static bool operator >(Card card1, Card card2)
   {
      if (card1.suit == card2.suit)
      {
         if (isAceHigh)
         {
            if (card1.rank == Rank.Ace)
            {
```

```
                if (card2.rank == Rank.Ace)
                    return false;
                else
                    return true;
            }
            else
            {
                if (card2.rank == Rank.Ace)
                    return false;
                else
                    return (card1.rank > card2.rank);
            }
        }
        else
        {
            return (card1.rank > card2.rank);
        }
    }
    else
    {
        if (useTrumps && (card2.suit == Card.trump))
            return false;
        else
            return true;
    }
}
```

```
public static bool operator <(Card card1, Card card2)
{
    return !(card1 >= card2);
}
```

```
public static bool operator >=(Card card1, Card card2)
{
    if (card1.suit == card2.suit)
    {
        if (isAceHigh)
        {
            if (card1.rank == Rank.Ace)
            {
                return true;
            }
            else
            {
                if (card2.rank == Rank.Ace)
                    return false;
                else
                    return (card1.rank >= card2.rank);
            }
        }
        else
        {
            return (card1.rank >= card2.rank);
```

```
            }
        }
        else
        {
            if (useTrumps && (card2.suit == Card.trump))
                return false;
            else
                return true;
        }
    }
```

```
    public static bool operator <=(Card card1, Card card2)
    {
        return !(card1 > card2);
    }
```

There's not much to note about this code, except perhaps the slightly lengthy code for the > and >= overloaded operators. If you step through the code for >, you can see how it works and why these steps are necessary.

You are comparing two cards, card1 and card2, where card1 is assumed to be the first one laid down on the table. As discussed earlier, this becomes important when you are using trump cards, because a trump will beat a nontrump, even if the nontrump has a higher rank. Of course, if the suits of the two cards are identical then whether the suit is the trump suit or not is irrelevant, so this is the first comparison you make:

```
    public static bool operator >(Card card1, Card card2)
    {
        if (card1.suit == card2.suit)
        {
```

If the static isAceHigh flag is true, then you can't compare the cards' ranks directly via their value in the Rank enumeration, because the rank of ace has a value of 1 in this enumeration, which is less than that of all other ranks. Instead, you need the following steps:

❑   If the first card is an ace, you check to see if the second card is also an ace. If it is, then the first card won't beat the second. If the second card isn't an ace, then the first card will win:

```
            if (isAceHigh)
            {
                if (card1.rank == Rank.Ace)
                {
                    if (card2.rank == Rank.Ace)
                        return false;
                    else
                        return true;
                }
```

❑ If the first card isn't an ace you also need to check to see if the second one is. If it is, then the second card wins; otherwise, you can compare the rank values because you know that aces aren't an issue:

```
else
{
    if (card2.rank == Rank.Ace)
        return false;
    else
        return (card1.rank > card2.rank);
}
}
```

❑ Alternatively, if aces aren't high, you can just compare the rank values:

```
else
{
    return (card1.rank > card2.rank);
}
```

The remainder of the code concerns the case where the suits of card1 and card2 are different. Here, the static useTrumps flag is important. If this flag is true and card2 is of the trump suit, then you can say definitively that card1 isn't a trump (because the two cards have different suits), and trumps always win, so card2 is the higher card:

```
else
{
    if (useTrumps && (card2.suit == Card.trump))
        return false;
```

If card2 isn't a trump (or useTrumps is false), then card1 wins, because it was the first card laid down:

```
    else
        return true;
    }
}
```

Only one other operator (>=) uses code similar to this, and the other operators are very simple, so there's no need to go into any more detail about them.

The following simple client code tests these operators (place it in the Main() function of a client project to test it, like the client code you saw earlier in the earlier CardLib examples):

```
Card.isAceHigh = true;
Console.WriteLine("Aces are high.");
Card.useTrumps = true;
Card.trump = Suit.Club;
Console.WriteLine("Clubs are trumps.");

Card card1, card2, card3, card4, card5;
card1 = new Card(Suit.Club, Rank.Five);
card2 = new Card(Suit.Club, Rank.Five);
card3 = new Card(Suit.Club, Rank.Ace);
```

```
card4 = new Card(Suit.Heart, Rank.Ten);
card5 = new Card(Suit.Diamond, Rank.Ace);
Console.WriteLine("{0} == {1} ? {2}",
    card1.ToString(), card2.ToString(), card1 == card2);
Console.WriteLine("{0} != {1} ? {2}",
    card1.ToString(), card3.ToString(), card1 != card3);
Console.WriteLine("{0}.Equals({1}) ? {2}",
    card1.ToString(), card4.ToString(), card1.Equals(card4));
Console.WriteLine("Card.Equals({0}, {1}) ? {2}",
    card3.ToString(), card4.ToString(), Card.Equals(card3, card4));
Console.WriteLine("{0} > {1} ? {2}",
    card1.ToString(), card2.ToString(), card1 > card2);
Console.WriteLine("{0} <= {1} ? {2}",
    card1.ToString(), card3.ToString(), card1 <= card3);
Console.WriteLine("{0} > {1} ? {2}",
    card1.ToString(), card4.ToString(), card1 > card4);
Console.WriteLine("{0} > {1} ? {2}",
    card4.ToString(), card1.ToString(), card4 > card1);
Console.WriteLine("{0} > {1} ? {2}",
    card5.ToString(), card4.ToString(), card5 > card4);
Console.WriteLine("{0} > {1} ? {2}",
    card4.ToString(), card5.ToString(), card4 > card5);
Console.ReadKey();
```

The results are as shown in Figure 11-7.

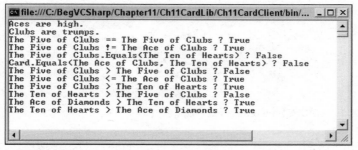

Figure 11-7

In each case, the operators are applied taking the specified rules into account. This is particularly apparent in the last four lines of output, demonstrating how trump cards always beat nontrumps.

The IComparable and IComparer Interfaces

The IComparable and IComparer interfaces are the standard way to compare objects in the .NET Framework. The difference between the interfaces is as follows:

❑ IComparable is implemented in the class of the object to be compared and allows comparisons between that object and another object.

❑ IComparer is implemented in a separate class, which will allow comparisons between any two objects.

Typically, you will give a class default comparison code using `IComparable`, and nondefault comparisons using other classes.

`IComparable` exposes the single method `CompareTo()`. This method accepts an object, so you could, for example, implement it in such a way as to enable you to pass a `Person` object to it and tell you if that person is older or younger than the current person. In fact, this method returns an `int`, so you could get it to tell you how much older or younger the second person was using code such as:

```
if (person1.CompareTo(person2) == 0)
{
    Console.WriteLine("Same age");
}
else if (person1.CompareTo(person2) > 0)
{
    Console.WriteLine("person 1 is Older");
}
else
{
    Console.WriteLine("person1 is Younger");
}
```

`IComparer` exposes the single method `Compare()`. This method accepts two objects and returns an integer result just like `CompareTo()`. With an object supporting `IComparer`, you could use code like:

```
if (personComparer.Compare(person1, person2) == 0)
{
    Console.WriteLine("Same age");
}
else if (personComparer.Compare(person1, person2) > 0)
{
    Console.WriteLine("person 1 is Older");
}
else
{
    Console.WriteLine("person1 is Younger");
}
```

In both cases, the parameters supplied to the methods are of the type `System.Object`. This means that you can compare one object to another object of any other type, so you'll usually have to perform some type comparison before returning a result and maybe even throw exceptions if the wrong types are used.

The .NET Framework includes a default implementation of the `IComparer` interface on a class called `Comparer`, found in the `System.Collections` namespace. This class is capable of performing culture-specific comparisons between simple types, as well as any type which supports the `IComparable` interface. You can use it, for example, with the following code:

```
string firstString = "First String";
string secondString = "Second String";
Console.WriteLine("Comparing '{0}' and '{1}', result: {2}",
    firstString, secondString,
    Comparer.Default.Compare(firstString, secondString));
```

```
int firstNumber = 35;
int secondNumber = 23;
Console.WriteLine("Comparing '{0}' and '{1}', result: {2}",
    firstNumber, secondNumber,
    Comparer.Default.Compare(firstNumber, secondNumber));
```

Here, you use the `Comparer.Default` static member to obtain an instance of the `Comparer` class, then use the `Compare()` method to compare first two strings, then two integers. The result is as follows:

```
Comparing 'First String' and 'Second String', result: -1
Comparing '35' and '23', result: 1
```

Since F comes before S in the alphabet it is deemed "less than" S, so the result of the first comparison is -1. Similarly, 35 is greater than 23, hence the result of 1. Note that the results here give you no idea of the magnitude of the difference.

When using `Comparer`, you must use types that can be compared. Attempting to compare `firstString` with `firstNumber`, for example, will generate an exception.

There are a few more points to note about the behavior of this class:

❑ Objects passed to `Comparer.Compare()` are checked to see if they support `IComparable`. If they do, then that implementation is used.

❑ `null` values are allowed, and interpreted as being "less than" any other object.

❑ Strings are processed according to the current culture. To process strings according to a different culture (or language) the `Comparer` class must be instantiated using its constructor, which allows you to pass a `System.Globalization.CultureInfo` object specifying the culture to use.

❑ Strings are processed in a case-sensitive way. To process them in a non-case-sensitive way you need to use the `CaseInsensitiveComparer` class, which otherwise works in exactly the same way.

You see the default `Comparer` class, and some nondefault comparisons, in the next section.

Sorting Collections Using the IComparable and IComparer Interfaces

Many collection classes allow sorting, either by default comparisons between objects or by custom methods. `ArrayList` is one example, containing the method `Sort()`. This method can be used with no parameters, in which case default comparisons are used, or it can be passed an `IComparer` interface to use to compare pairs of objects.

When you have an `ArrayList` filled with simple types, such as integers or strings, the default comparer is fine. For your own classes, you must either implement `IComparable` in your class definition or create a separate class supporting `IComparer` to use for comparisons.

Note that some classes in the `System.Collection` namespace, including `CollectionBase`, don't expose a method for sorting. If you want to sort a collection you have derived from this class, you'll have to put a bit more work in and sort the internal `List` collection yourself.

In the following Try It Out, you'll see how to use a default and a nondefault comparer to sort a list.

Try It Out   Sorting a List

1. Create a new console application called Ch11Ex05 in the directory C:\BegVCSharp\Chapter11.

2. Add a new class called Person, and modify the code as follows:

```
namespace Ch11Ex05
{
    class Person : IComparable
    {
        public string Name;
        public int Age;

        public Person(string name, int age)
        {
            Name = name;
            Age = age;
        }

        public int CompareTo(object obj)
        {
            if (obj is Person)
            {
                Person otherPerson = obj as Person;
                return this.Age - otherPerson.Age;
            }
            else
            {
                throw new ArgumentException(
                    "Object to compare to is not a Person object.");
            }
        }
    }
}
```

3. Add a new class called PersonComparerName, and modify the code as follows:

```
using System;
using System.Collections;
using System.Collections.Generic;
using System.Text;

namespace Ch11Ex05
{
    public class PersonComparerName : IComparer
    {
        public static IComparer Default = new PersonComparerName();

        public int Compare(object x, object y)
        {
            if (x is Person && y is Person)
            {
```

```
            return Comparer.Default.Compare(
                ((Person)x).Name, ((Person)y).Name);
        }
        else
        {
            throw new ArgumentException(
                "One or both objects to compare are not Person objects.");
        }
    }
}
}
```

4. Modify the code in `Program.cs` as follows:

```
using System;
using System.Collections;
using System.Collections.Generic;
using System.Text;

namespace Ch11Ex05
{
    class Program
    {
        static void Main(string[] args)
        {
            ArrayList list = new ArrayList();
            list.Add(new Person("Jim", 30));
            list.Add(new Person("Bob", 25));
            list.Add(new Person("Bert", 27));
            list.Add(new Person("Ernie", 22));

            Console.WriteLine("Unsorted people:");
            for (int i = 0; i < list.Count; i++)
            {
                Console.WriteLine("{0} ({1})",
                    (list[i] as Person).Name, (list[i] as Person).Age);
            }
            Console.WriteLine();

            Console.WriteLine(
                "People sorted with default comparer (by age):");
            list.Sort();
            for (int i = 0; i < list.Count; i++)
            {
                Console.WriteLine("{0} ({1})",
                    (list[i] as Person).Name, (list[i] as Person).Age);
            }
            Console.WriteLine();

            Console.WriteLine(
                "People sorted with nondefault comparer (by name):");
            list.Sort(PersonComparerName.Default);
            for (int i = 0; i < list.Count; i++)
            {
                Console.WriteLine("{0} ({1})",
```

```
                         (list[i] as Person).Name, (list[i] as Person).Age);
            }

            Console.ReadKey();
        }
    }
}
```

5. Execute the code. The result is shown in Figure 11-8.

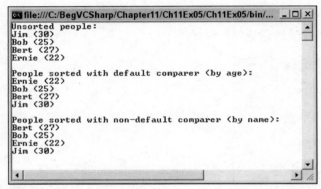

Figure 11-8

How It Works

In this example, an `ArrayList` containing `Person` objects is sorted in two different ways. By calling the `ArrayList.Sort()` method with no parameters, the default comparison is used, which is the `CompareTo()` method in the `Person` class (since this class implements `IComparable`):

```
public int CompareTo(object obj)
{
    if (obj is Person)
    {
        Person otherPerson = obj as Person;
        return this.Age - otherPerson.Age;
    }
    else
    {
        throw new ArgumentException(
            "Object to compare to is not a Person object.");
    }
}
```

This method first checks to see if its argument can be compared to a `Person` object, that is, that the object can be converted into a `Person` object. If there is a problem then an exception is thrown. Otherwise, the `Age` properties of the two `Person` objects are compared.

Next, a nondefault comparison sort is performed, using the `PersonComparerName` class, which implements `IComparer`. This class has a `public static` field for ease of use:

```
public static IComparer Default = new PersonComparerName();
```

This enables you to get an instance using `PersonComparerName.Default`, just like the `Comparer` class you saw earlier. The `CompareTo()` method of this class is:

```
public int Compare(object x, object y)
{
    if (x is Person && y is Person)
    {
        return Comparer.Default.Compare(
            ((Person)x).Name, ((Person)y).Name);
    }
    else
    {
        throw new ArgumentException(
            "One or both objects to compare are not Person objects.");
    }
}
```

Again, arguments are first checked to see if they are `Person` objects, and if they aren't then an exception is thrown. If they are then the default `Comparer` object is used to compare the two string `Name` fields of the `Person` objects.

Conversions

Throughout the book so far, you have used casting whenever you have needed to convert one type into another. However, this isn't the only way to do things. In the same way that an `int` can be converted into a `long` or a `double` implicitly as part of a calculation, it is possible to define how classes you have created may be converted into other classes (either implicitly or explicitly). To do this, you can overload conversion operators, in much the same way as other operators were overloaded earlier in this chapter. You'll look at this in the first part of this section.

Also in this section, you'll see another useful operator, the `as` operator, which in general is preferable to casting when using reference types.

Overloading Conversion Operators

As well as overloading mathematical operators, as shown earlier, you can define both implicit and explicit conversions between types. This is necessary if you want to convert between types that aren't related, if there is no inheritance relationship between them and no shared interfaces, for example.

Say that you define an implicit conversion between `ConvClass1` and `ConvClass2`. This means that you can write code such as:

```
ConvClass1 op1 = new ConvClass1();
ConvClass2 op2 = op1;
```

Alternatively, you can define an explicit conversion, called in the following code:

```
ConvClass1 op1 = new ConvClass1();
ConvClass2 op2 = (ConvClass2)op1;
```

As an example, consider the following code:

```
public class ConvClass1
{
   public int val;

   public static implicit operator ConvClass2(ConvClass1 op1)
   {
      ConvClass2 returnVal = new ConvClass2();
      returnVal.val = op1.val;
      return returnVal;
   }
}

public class ConvClass2
{
   public double val;

   public static explicit operator ConvClass1(ConvClass2 op1)
   {
      ConvClass1 returnVal = new ConvClass1();
      checked {returnVal.val = (int)op1.val;};
      return returnVal;
   }
}
```

Here, `ConvClass1` contains an `int` value and `ConvClass2` contains a `double` value. Since `int` values may be converted into `double` values implicitly, you can define an implicit conversion between `ConvClass1` and `ConvClass2`. The reverse is not true, however, and you should define the conversion operator between `ConvClass2` and `ConvClass1` as explicit.

In the code, you specify this using the `implicit` and `explicit` keywords as shown.

With these classes the following code is fine:

```
ConvClass1 op1 = new ConvClass1();
op1.val = 3;
ConvClass2 op2 = op1;
```

A conversion in the other direction, however, requires the following explicit casting conversion:

```
ConvClass2 op1 = new ConvClass2();
op1.val = 3e15;
ConvClass1 op2 = (ConvClass1)op1;
```

Note that as you have used the `checked` keyword in your explicit conversion, you will get an exception in the preceding code, since the `val` property of `op1` is too large to fit into the `val` property of `op2`.

The as Operator

The as operator converts a type into a specified reference type, using the following syntax:

```
<operand> as <type>
```

This is only possible in certain circumstances:

❑ If <operand> is of type <type>

❑ If <operand> can be implicitly converted to type <type>

❑ If <operand> can be boxed into type <type>

If no conversion from <operand> to <type> is possible, then the result of the expression will be null.

Note that conversion from a base class to a derived class is possible using an explicit conversion, but it won't always work. Consider the two classes ClassA and ClassD from an earlier example, where ClassD inherits from ClassA:

```
class ClassA : IMyInterface
{
}

class ClassD : ClassA
{
}
```

The following code uses the as operator to convert from a ClassA instance stored in obj1 into the ClassD type:

```
ClassA obj1 = new ClassA();
ClassD obj2 = obj1 as ClassD;
```

This will result in obj2 being null.

However, it is possible to store ClassD instances in ClassA-type variables using polymorphism. The following code illustrates this, and uses the as operator to convert from a ClassA-type variable containing a ClassD-type instance into the ClassD type:

```
ClassD obj1 = new ClassD();
ClassA obj2 = obj1;
ClassD obj3 = obj2 as ClassD;
```

This time the result is that obj3 ends up containing a reference to the same object as obj1, not null.

This functionality makes the as operator very useful, because the following code using simple casting results in an exception being thrown:

```
ClassA obj1 = new ClassA();
ClassD obj2 = (ClassD)obj1;
```

The `as` equivalent of this code results in a `null` value being assigned to `obj2` — no exception is thrown. This means that code such as the following (using two of the classes developed earlier in this chapter, `Animal` and a class derived from `Animal` called `Cow`) is very common in C# applications:

```
public void MilkCow(Animal myAnimal)
{
    Cow myCow = myAnimal as Cow;
    if (myCow != null)
    {
        myCow.Milk();
    }
    else
    {
        Console.WriteLine("{0} isn't a cow, and so can't be milked.",
            myAnimal.Name);
    }
}
```

This is much simpler than checking for exceptions!

Summary

In this chapter, you have covered many of the techniques that you can use to make your OOP applications far more powerful — and more interesting. Although these techniques take a little effort to accomplish, they can make your classes much easier to work with and, therefore, simplify the task of writing the rest of the code.

Each of the topics covered has many uses. You're likely to come across collections of one form or another in almost any application, and creating strongly typed collections can make your life much easier if you need to work with a group of objects of the same type. You also saw how you can add indexers and iterators to get easy access to objects within the collection.

Comparisons and conversions are another area that will crop up time and again. You saw how various comparisons can be performed, as well as some of the underlying functionality with boxing and unboxing. You also saw how to overload operators for both comparisons and conversions, and how to link things together with list sorting.

In this chapter, you looked at:

- ❏ Collections
    - ❏ Using collections
    - ❏ Indexers
    - ❏ Iterators

- Comparisons
  - Type comparison
  - Value comparison
- Conversions

In the next chapter, you'll be looking at something entirely new — generics. They allow you to create classes that automatically customize themselves to work with dynamically chosen types. This is especially useful when it comes to collections, and you'll see how much of the code in this chapter can be simplified dramatically using generic collections.

Exercises

1. Create a collection class called `People` that is a collection of the `Person` class shown below. The items in the collection should be accessible via a string indexer that is the name of the person, identical to the `Person.Name` property:

```
public class Person
{
    private string name;
    private int age;

    public string Name
    {
        get
        {
            return name;
        }
        set
        {
            name = value;
        }
    }

    public int Age
    {
        get
        {
            return age;
        }
        set
        {
            age = value;
        }
    }
}
```

2. Extend the Person class from the preceding exercise so that the >, <, >=, and <= operators are overloaded, and compare the Age properties of Person instances.

3. Add a GetOldest() method to the People class that returns an array of Person objects with the greatest Age property (1 or more objects, as multiple items may have the same value for this property), using the overloaded operators defined above.

4. Implement the ICloneable interface on the People class to provide deep copying capability.

5. Add an iterator to the People class that enables you to get the ages of all members in a foreach loop as follows:

```
foreach (int age in myPeople.Ages)
{
    // Display ages.
}
```

Generics

One of the (admittedly few) criticisms leveled against the first version of C# was its lack of support for *generics*. Generics in C++ (known as *templates* in that language) had long been regarded as an excellent way of doing things, allowing a single type definition to spawn a multitude of specialized types at compile time and thus saving an awful lot of time and effort. For whatever reason, generics didn't quite make it into the first release of C#, and the language suffered because of it. Perhaps this was so because generics are often seen as being quite difficult to come to grips with, or maybe it was decided that they weren't necessary. Thankfully though, with C# version 2.0 generics have come to join the party. And no, they aren't really that difficult to use, although they do require a slightly different way of looking at things. The end result of your efforts, though, will be richly rewarded!

In this chapter, you:

- ❑ Look at what a generic is. You learn about generics in fairly abstract terms at first, since learning the concepts behind generics is crucial to being able to use them effectively.

- ❑ See some of the generic types in the .NET Framework in action. This will help you to understand more about their functionality and power, as well as the new syntax required in your code.

- ❑ Define your own generic types. This will include generic classes, interfaces, methods, and delegates. You also see additional techniques for further customizing generic types: the `default` keyword and type constraints.

What Is a Generic?

To best illustrate what a generic is, and why they are so useful, recall the collection classes from the last chapter. You saw how basic collections could be contained in classes such as `ArrayList`, but that such collections suffered from being untyped, so you needed to cast `object` items into whatever type of objects you had actually stored in the collection. Since anything that inherits from `System.Object` (that is, practically anything) can be stored in an `ArrayList`, you needed to be careful. Assuming that certain types were all that was contained in the collection could lead to exceptions being thrown, and code logic to break down. You saw techniques that can help you to deal with this, including the code required to check the type of an object. However, you discovered that a much better solution is to use a strongly typed collection class to start off with. By deriving from `CollectionBase` and proving your own methods for adding, removing, and otherwise accessing members of the collection, you saw how it was possible to restrict collection members to those derived from a certain base type or supporting a certain interface.

And this is where you run up against a problem. Every time you create a new class that needs to be held in a collection, you must do one of the following:

❑ Use a collection class you've already made that can contain items of the new type.

❑ Create a new collection class that can hold items of the new type, implementing all the required methods.

Typically, with a new type you'll need extra functionality, so more often that not you'll need a new collection class anyway. So, making collection classes may take up a fair amount of your time!

Generic classes, on the other hand, make things a lot simpler. A generic class is one that is built around whatever type, or types, you supply during instantiation, enabling you to strongly type an object with hardly any effort at all. In the context of collections, creating a "collection of type T objects" is as simple as saying it out loud—and achievable in a single line of code. Instead of code such as

```
CollectionClass col = new CollectionClass();
col.Add(new ItemClass());
```

you can use:

```
CollectionClass<ItemClass> col = new CollectionClass<ItemClass>();
col.Add(new ItemClass());
```

The angle bracket syntax is the way you pass variable types to generic types. In the preceding code, read `CollectionClass<ItemClass>` as `CollectionClass` of `ItemClass`. You will, of course, examine this syntax in more detail later in the chapter.

There's more to the subject of generics that just collections, but they are particularly suited to this area, as you will see later in the chapter when you look at the `System.Collections.Generic` namespace. By creating a generic class, you can generate methods that have a signature that can be strongly typed to any type you wish, even catering for the fact that a type may be a value or reference type, and deal with individual cases as they occur. You can even allow only a subset of types to be used, by restricting the types used to instantiate a generic class to those that support a given interface or are derived from a certain type. And you're not restricted to generic classes—you can create generic interfaces, generic methods (which can be defined on nongeneric classes), even generic delegates.

All this adds a great deal of flexibility to your code, and judicious use of generics can cut hours off development time.

One question you may be asking is how this is all possible. Usually, when you create a class it is compiled into a type that you can then use in your code. You might think that when you create a generic class it would have to be compiled into a plethora of types, so that you could instantiate it. Fortunately, this is not the case — and given the infinite amount of classes possible in .NET that's just as well. Behind the scenes, the .NET runtime allows generic classes to be dynamically generated as and when you need them. A given generic class *A* of *B* won't even exist until you ask for it by instantiating it.

> *For those of you who are familiar with C++, or are just interested, this is one difference between C++ templates and C# generic classes. In C++ the compiler would detect where you had used a specific type of template, for example* A *of* B*, and compile the code necessary to create this type. In C# everything happens at runtime.*

To summarize, generics enable you to create flexible types that process objects of one or more specific type, where these types are determined when you instantiate or otherwise use the generic. Now it's time to see them in action.

Using Generics

Before you look at how to create your own generics, it's worth looking at those that are supplied by the .NET Framework. These include the types in the `System.Collections.Generic` namespace, a namespace that you've seen several times in your code since it is included by default in console applications. You haven't as yet used any of the types in this namespace, but that's about to change. In this section, you'll look at the types in this namespace and how you can use them to create strongly typed collections and improve the functionality of your existing collections.

First, though, you'll look at another, simpler generic type which gets round a minor issue with value types: *nullable types*.

Nullable Types

In earlier chapters, you saw that one of the ways value types (most of the basic types like `int` and `double` as well as all structs) differ from reference types (`string` and any class) is that they must contain a value. They can exist in an unassigned state, just after they are declared and before a value is assigned, but you can't make use of this in any way. Conversely, reference types may be `null`.

There are times, and they crop up more often than you think, when it is useful to have a value type that can be `null`. Generics give you a way to do this using the `System.Nullable<T>` type. For example:

```
System.Nullable<int> nullableInt;
```

This code declares a variable called `nullableInt`, which can have any value that an `int` variable can, plus the value `null`. This allows you to write code such as:

```
nullableInt = null;
```

If `nullableInt` were an `int` type variable, then the preceding code wouldn't compile.

The preceding assignment is equivalent to:

```
nullableInt = new System.Nullable<int>();
```

As with any other variable, you can't just use it before some kind of initialization, whether to `null` (through either syntax shown above) or by assigning a value.

You can test nullable types to see if they are `null` just like you test reference types:

```
if (nullableInt == null)
{
    ...
}
```

Alternatively, you can use the `HasValue` property:

```
if (nullableInt.HasValue)
{
    ...
}
```

This wouldn't work for reference types, even one with a `HasValue` property of its own, since having a `null` valued reference type variable means that no object exists through which to access this property, and an exception would be thrown.

You can also look at the value of a reference type using the `Value` property. If `HasValue` is `true`, then you are guaranteed a non-`null` value for `Value`, but if `HasValue` is `false`, that is, `null` has been assigned to the variable, then accessing `Value` will result in an exception of type `System.InvalidOperationException`.

One point to note about nullable types is that they are so useful that they have resulted in a modification of C# syntax. Rather than using the syntax shown above to declare a nullable type variable, you can instead use the following:

```
int? nullableInt;
```

`int?` is simply a shorthand for `System.Nullable<int>`, but is much more readable. In subsequent sections you'll use this syntax.

Operators and Nullable Types

With simple types, such as `int`, you can use operators such as `+`, `-`, and so on to work with values. With nullable type equivalents, there is no difference: the values contained in nullable types are implicitly converted to the required type and the appropriate operators are used. This also applies to structs with operators that you have supplied. For example:

```
int? op1 = 5;
int? result = op1 * 2;
```

Note that here the `result` variable is also of type `int?`. The following code will not compile:

```
int? op1 = 5;
int result = op1 * 2;
```

In order to get this to work you must perform an explicit conversion:

```
int? op1 = 5;
int result = (int)op1 * 2;
```

This will work fine as long as `op1` has a value — if it is `null`, then you will get an exception of type `System.InvalidOperationException`.

This leads you straight on to the next question, what happens when one or both values in an operator evaluation are `null`, such as `op1` in the preceding code? The answer is that for all simple nullable types other than `bool?` the result of the operation will be `null`, which you can interpret as "unable to compute." For structs you can define your own operators to deal with this situation (as you will see later in the chapter), and for `bool?` there are operators defined for `&` and `|` that may result in non-`null` return values. These are shown in the following table.

op1	op2	op1 & op2	op1 | op2
true	true	true	true
true	false	false	true
true	null	null	true
false	true	false	true
false	false	false	false
false	null	false	null
null	true	null	true
null	false	false	null
null	null	null	**null**

The results of these operators are as you would expect — if there is enough information to work out the answer of the computation without needing to know the value of one of the operands then it doesn't matter if that operand is `null`.

The ?? Operator

To further reduce the amount of code you need to deal with nullable types, and to make it easier to deal with variables that can be `null`, you can use the `??` operator. This operator enables you to supply default values to use if a nullable type is `null` and is used as follows:

```
int? op1 = null;
int result = op1 * 2 ?? 5;
```

Since in this example `op1` is `null`, `op1 * 2` will also be `null`. However, the `??` operator detects this and assigns the value 5 to `result`. A very important point to note here is that no explicit conversion is required to put the result in the `int` type variable `result`. The `??` operator handles this conversion for you. You can, however, pass the result of a `??` evaluation into an `int?` with no problems:

```
int? result = op1 * 2 ?? 5;
```

Chapter 12

This makes the `??` operator a versatile one to use when dealing with nullable variables and a handy way to supply defaults without using a block of code in an `if` structure.

In the following Try It Out, you'll experiment with a nullable `Vector` type.

Try It Out   Nullable Types

1. Create a new console application project called `Ch12Ex01` in the directory `C:\BegVCSharp\Chapter12`.

2. Add a new class called `Vector` using the VS shortcut, in the file `Vector.cs`.

3. Modify the code in `Vector.cs` as follows:

```csharp
public class Vector
{
    public double? R = null;
    public double? Theta = null;

    public double? ThetaRadians
    {
        get
        {
            // Convert degrees to radians.
            return (Theta * Math.PI / 180.0);
        }
    }

    public Vector(double? r, double? theta)
    {
        // Normalize.
        if (r < 0)
        {
            r = -r;
            theta += 180;
        }
        theta = theta % 360;

        // Assign fields.
        R = r;
        Theta = theta;
    }

    public static Vector operator +(Vector op1, Vector op2)
    {
        try
        {
            // Get (x, y) coordinates for new vector.
            double newX = op1.R.Value * Math.Sin(op1.ThetaRadians.Value)
                + op2.R.Value * Math.Sin(op2.ThetaRadians.Value);
            double newY = op1.R.Value * Math.Cos(op1.ThetaRadians.Value)
                + op2.R.Value * Math.Cos(op2.ThetaRadians.Value);

            // Convert to (r, theta).
```

330

```
            double newR = Math.Sqrt(newX * newX + newY * newY);
            double newTheta = Math.Atan2(newX, newY) * 180.0 / Math.PI;

            // Return result.
            return new Vector(newR, newTheta);
        }
        catch
        {
            // Return "null" vector.
            return new Vector(null, null);
        }
    }

    public static Vector operator -(Vector op1)
    {
        return new Vector(-op1.R, op1.Theta);
    }

    public static Vector operator -(Vector op1, Vector op2)
    {
        return op1 + (-op2);
    }

    public override string ToString()
    {
        // Get string representation of coordinates.
        string rString = R.HasValue ? R.ToString() : "null";
        string thetaString = Theta.HasValue ? Theta.ToString() : "null";

        // Return (r, theta) string.
        return string.Format("({0}, {1})", rString, thetaString);
    }
}
```

4.   Modify the code in `Program.cs` as follows:

```
class Program
{
    public static void Main(string[] args)
    {
        Vector v1 = GetVector("vector1");
        Vector v2 = GetVector("vector1");
        Console.WriteLine("{0} + {1} = {2}", v1, v2, v1 + v2);
        Console.WriteLine("{0} - {1} = {2}", v1, v2, v1 - v2);
        Console.ReadKey();
    }

    public static Vector GetVector(string name)
    {
        Console.WriteLine("Input {0} magnitude:", name);
        double? r = GetNullableDouble();
        Console.WriteLine("Input {0} angle (in degrees):", name);
        double? theta = GetNullableDouble();
        return new Vector(r, theta);
```

```
    }

    public static double? GetNullableDouble()
    {
        double? result;
        string userInput = Console.ReadLine();
        try
        {
            result = double.Parse(userInput);
        }
        catch
        {
            result = null;
        }
        return result;
    }
}
```

5. Execute the application and enter values for two vectors. Sample output is shown in Figure 12-1.

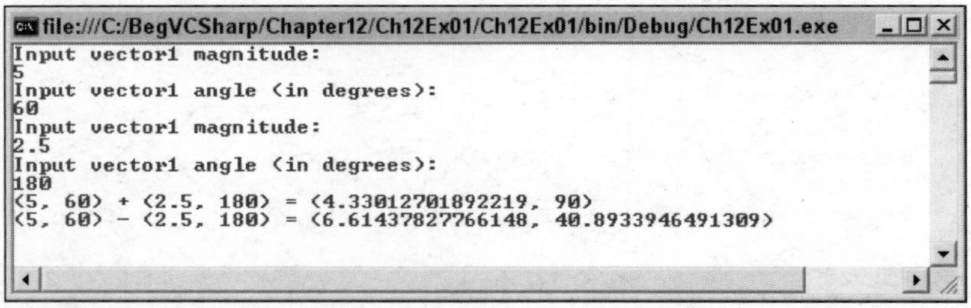

Figure 12-1

6. Execute the application again, but this time skip at least one of the four values. Sample output is shown in Figure 12-2.

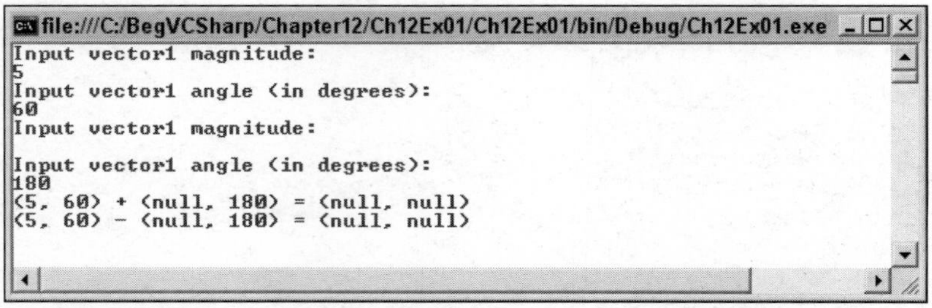

Figure 12-2

How It Works

In this example, you have created a class called `Vector` that represents a vector with polar coordinates (that is, with a magnitude and an angle), as shown in Figure 12-3.

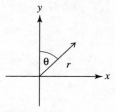

Figure 12-3

The coordinates *r* and _ are represented in code by the public fields `R` and `Theta`, where `Theta` is expressed in degrees. `ThetaRad` is supplied to obtain the value of `Theta` in radians — necessary because the `Math` class uses radians in its static methods. Both `R` and `Theta` are of type `double?`, so they can be null.

```
public class Vector
{
    public double? R = null;
    public double? Theta = null;

    public double? ThetaRadians
    {
        get
        {
            // Convert degrees to radians.
            return (Theta * Math.PI / 180.0);
        }
    }
}
```

The constructor for `Vector` normalizes the initial values of `R` and `Theta` then assigns the public fields.

```
public Vector(double? r, double? theta)
{
    // Normalize.
    if (r < 0)
    {
        r = -r;
        theta += 180;
    }
    theta = theta % 360;

    // Assign fields.
    R = r;
    Theta = theta;
}
```

The main functionality of the Vector class is to add and subtract vectors using operator overloading, which requires some fairly basic trigonometry, which I won't go into here. The important thing about the code is that if an exception is thrown when obtaining the Value property of R or ThetaRadians, that is, if either are null, a "null" vector is returned.

```
public static Vector operator +(Vector op1, Vector op2)
{
    try
    {
        // Get (x, y) coordinates for new vector.
        ...
    }
    catch
    {
        // Return "null" vector.
        return new Vector(null, null);
    }
}
```

If either of the coordinates making up a vector are null, the vector is invalid, which is signified here by a Vector class with null values for both R and Theta.

The rest of the code in the Vector class overrides the other operators required to extend the addition functionality to subtraction and overrides ToString() to obtain a string representation of a Vector object.

The code in Program.cs tests the Vector class by enabling the user to initialize two vectors, then adds and subtracts them to and from one another. Should the user omit a value, it will be interpreted as null, and the rules mentioned previously apply.

The System.Collections.Generics Namespace

In practically every application you've seen so far in this book you have seen the following namespaces:

```
using System;
using System.Collections.Generic;
using System.Text;
```

The System namespace contains most of the basic types used in .NET applications. The System.Text namespace includes types relating to string processing and encoding, but what about System.Collections.Generic, and why is it included by default in console applications?

The answer is that this namespace contains generic types for dealing with collections and is likely to be used so often that it is configured with a using statement ready for you to use without qualification.

As promised earlier in the chapter, you'll now look at these types, and I can guarantee that they will make your life easier. They make it possible for you to create strongly typed collection classes with hardly any effort. The following table describes the types you look at in this section. You see more of these types later in this chapter.

Type	Description
List<T>	Collection of type T objects
Dictionary<K, V>	Collection if items of type V, associated with keys of type K

You also see various interfaces and delegates used with these classes.

List<T>

Rather than deriving a class from CollectionBase and implementing the required methods as you did in the last chapter, it can be quicker and easier simply to use this generic collection type. One added bonus here is that many of the methods you'd normally have to implement (such as Add()) are implemented for you.

Creating a collection of type T objects requires the following code:

```
List<T> myCollection = new List<T>();
```

And that's it. No defining classes, implementing methods, or anything else. You can also set a starting list of items in the collection by passing a List<T> object to the constructor.

An object instantiated using this syntax will support the methods and properties shown in the following table (where the type supplied to the List<T> generic is T).

Member	Description
int Count	Property giving the number of items in the collection.
void Add(T item)	Adds item to the collection.
void AddRange(IEnumerable<T>)	Adds multiple items to the collection.
IList<T> AsReadOnly()	Returns a read-only interface to the collection.
int Capacity	Gets or sets the number of items that the collection can contain.
void Clear()	Removes all items from the collection.
bool Contains(T item)	Determines if item is contained in the collection.
void CopyTo(T[] array, int index)	Copies the items in the collection into the array array, starting from index index in the array.
IEnumerator<T> GetEnumerator()	Obtains an IEnumerator<T> instance for iteration through the collection. Note that the interface returned is strongly typed to T, so no casting will be required in foreach loops.
int IndexOf(T item)	Obtains the index of item, or –1 if the item is not contained in the collection.

Table continued on following page

Member	Description
`void Insert(int index, T item)`	Inserts `item` into the collection at the specified index.
`bool Remove(T item)`	Removes the first occurrence of `item` from the collection and returns `true`. If `item` is not contained in the collection, returns `false`.
`void RemoveAt(int index)`	Removes the item at index `index` from the collection.

`List<T>` also has an `Item` property, allowing arraylike access such as:

```
T itemAtIndex2 = myCollectionOfT[2];
```

There are also several other methods that this class supports, but the above is plenty to get you started.

In the following Try It Out, you'll see how to use `Collection<T>` in practice.

Try It Out   Using Collection<T>

1. Create a new console application called `Ch12Ex02` in the directory `C:\BegVCSharp\Chapter12`.

2. Right-click on the project name in the `Solution Explorer` window, and select the `Add ⇨ Add Existing Item...` option.

3. Select the `Animal.cs`, `Cow.cs`, and `Chicken.cs` files from the `C:\BegVCSharp\Chapter11\Ch11Ex01\Ch11Ex01` directory, and click `Add`.

4. Modify the namespace declaration in the three files you have added as follows:

```
namespace Ch12Ex02
```

5. Modify `Program.cs` as follows:

```
static void Main(string[] args)
{
    List<Animal> animalCollection = new List<Animal>();
    animalCollection.Add(new Cow("Jack"));
    animalCollection.Add(new Chicken("Vera"));
    foreach (Animal myAnimal in animalCollection)
    {
        myAnimal.Feed();
    }
    Console.ReadKey();
}
```

6. Execute the application. The result is exactly the same as for `Ch11Ex02` in the last chapter.

How It Works

There are only two differences between this example and Ch11Ex02. The first is that this line of code

```
Animals animalCollection = new Animals();
```

has been replaced with:

```
List<Animal> animalCollection = new List<Animal>();
```

The second, and more crucial, difference is that there is *no longer an Animals collection class in the project.* All that hard work you did earlier to create this class has been achieved in a single line of code, using a generic collection class.

An alternate way of getting the same result is to leave the code in Program.cs because it was in the last chapter, and use the following definition of Animals:

```
public class Animals : List<Animal>
{
}
```

Doing this has the advantage that the code in Program.cs is slightly easier to read, plus you can add additional members to the Animals class as you see fit.

You may, of course, be wondering why you'd ever want to derive classes from CollectionBase, which is a good question. In fact, I can't think of many situations where you would. It's certainly a good thing to know how things work internally, since List<T> works in much the same way, but really CollectionBase is there for backward compatibility. The only situation I can think of in which you might want to use CollectionBase is when you want much more control over the members exposed to users of the class. If you wanted a collection class with an internal access modifier on its Add() method, for example, then using CollectionBase might be the best option.

You can also pass an initial capacity to use to the constructor of List<T> (as an int), or an initial list of items using an IEnumerable<T> interface. Classes supporting this interface include List<T>.

Sorting and Searching Generic Lists

Sorting a generic list is much the same as sorting any other list. In the last chapter, you saw how you can use the IComparer and IComparable interfaces to compare two objects and, thus, sort a list of that type of object. The only difference here is that you can use the generic interfaces IComparer<T> and IComparable<T>, which expose slightly different, type-specific methods. The following table explains these differences.

Generic Method	Nongeneric Method	Difference

`int IComparable<T>.CompareTo(`
`  T otherObj)`
	`int IComparable.`
	`CompareTo(`
	`    object otherObj)`
		Strongly typed in generic version

`bool IComparable<T>.Equals(` `  T otherObj)`	N/A	Doesn't exist on nongeneric interface — can use inherited `object.Equals()` instead

`int IComparer<T>.Compare(`
`  T objectA,`
`  T object B)`
	`int IComparer.Compare(`
	`    object objectA,`
	`    object object B)`
		Strongly typed in generic version

`bool IComparer<T>.Equals(`
`  T objectA,`
`  T object B)`
	N/A	Doesn't exist on nongeneric interface — can use inherited `object.Equals()` instead

`int IComparer<T>.GetHashCode(` `  T objectA)`	N/A	Doesn't exist on nongeneric interface — can use inherited `object.GetHashCode()` instead

So, to sort a `List<T>` you can supply an `IComparable<T>` interface on the type to be sorted, or supply an `IComparer<T>` interface. Alternatively, you can supply a *generic delegate* as a sorting method. From the point of view of seeing how things are done, this is far more interesting, since implementing the interfaces shown above is really no more effort than implementing their nongeneric cousins.

In general terms, all you need to sort a list is a method that compares two objects of type `T`, and for searching all you need is a method that checks an object of type `T` to see if it meets certain criteria. It is a simple matter to define such methods, and to aid you there are two generic delegates that you can use:

❏   `Comparison<T>`: A delegate type for a method used for sorting, with the signature:

```
int method(T objectA, T objectB)
```

❏   `Predicate<T>`: A delegate type for a method used for searching, with the signature:

```
bool method(T targetObject)
```

You can define any number of such methods, and use them to "snap-in" to the searching and sorting methods of `List<T>`. The following Try It Out illustrates this.

Try It Out   **Sorting and Searching List<T>**

1. Create a new console application called `Ch12Ex03` in the directory `C:\BegVCSharp\Chapter12`.

2. Right-click on the project name in the `Solution Explorer` window, and select the `Add` ⇨ `Add Existing Item...` option.

3. Select the `Vector.cs` file from the `C:\BegVCSharp\Chapter12\Ch12Ex01\Ch12Ex01` directory, and click `Add`.

4. Modify the namespace declaration in the file you have added as follows:

```
namespace Ch12Ex03
```

5. Add a new class called `Vectors`.

6. Modify `Vectors.cs` as follows:

```csharp
public class Vectors : List<Vector>
{
    public Vectors()
    {
    }

    public Vectors(IEnumerable<Vector> initialItems)
    {
        foreach (Vector vector in initialItems)
        {
            Add(vector);
        }
    }

    public string Sum()
    {
        StringBuilder sb = new StringBuilder();
        Vector currentPoint = new Vector(0.0, 0.0);
        sb.Append("origin");
        foreach (Vector vector in this)
        {
            sb.AppendFormat(" + {0}", vector);
            currentPoint += vector;
        }
        sb.AppendFormat(" = {0}", currentPoint);
        return sb.ToString();
    }
}
```

7. Add a new class called `VectorDelegates`.

8. Modify `VectorDelegates.cs` as follows:

```csharp
public static class VectorDelegates
{
    public static int Compare(Vector x, Vector y)
    {
        if (x.R > y.R)
```

```
        {
            return 1;
        }
        else if (x.R < y.R)
        {
            return -1;
        }
        return 0;
    }

    public static bool TopRightQuadrant(Vector target)
    {
        if (target.Theta >= 0.0 && target.Theta <= 90.0)
        {
            return true;
        }
        else
        {
            return false;
        }
    }
}
```

9.   Modify `Program.cs` as follows:

```
static void Main(string[] args)
{
    Vectors route = new Vectors();
    route.Add(new Vector(2.0, 90.0));
    route.Add(new Vector(1.0, 180.0));
    route.Add(new Vector(0.5, 45.0));
    route.Add(new Vector(2.5, 315.0));

    Console.WriteLine(route.Sum());

    Comparison<Vector> sorter = new Comparison<Vector>(VectorDelegates.Compare);
    route.Sort(sorter);
    Console.WriteLine(route.Sum());

    Predicate<Vector> searcher =
        new Predicate<Vector>(VectorDelegates.TopRightQuadrant);
    Vectors topRightQuadrantRoute = new Vectors(route.FindAll(searcher));
    Console.WriteLine(topRightQuadrantRoute.Sum());

    Console.ReadKey();
}
```

10.   Execute the application. The result is shown in Figure 12-4.

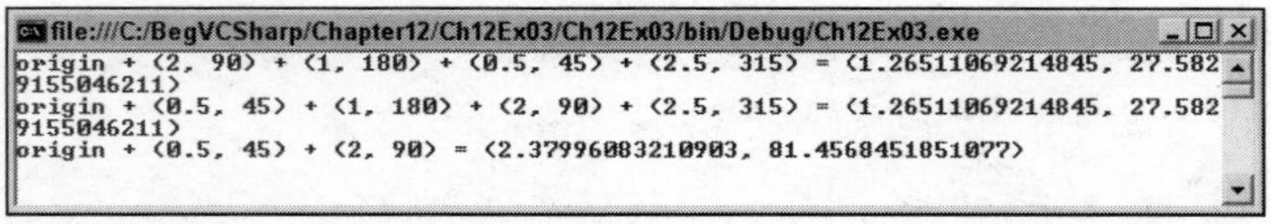

```
file:///C:/BegVCSharp/Chapter12/Ch12Ex03/Ch12Ex03/bin/Debug/Ch12Ex03.exe
origin + (2, 90) + (1, 180) + (0.5, 45) + (2.5, 315) = (1.26511069214845, 27.582
9155046211)
origin + (0.5, 45) + (1, 180) + (2, 90) + (2.5, 315) = (1.26511069214845, 27.582
9155046211)
origin + (0.5, 45) + (2, 90) = (2.37996083210903, 81.4568451851077)
```

Figure 12-4

How It Works

In this example, you have created a collection class, `Vectors`, for the `Vector` class created in `Ch12Ex01`. You could just use a variable of type `List<Vector>`, but since you want additional functionality you use a new class, `Vectors`, and derive from `List<Vector>`, allowing you to add whatever additional members you want.

One member, `Sum()`, returns a string listing each vector in turn along with the result of summing them all together (using the overloaded + operator from the original `Vector` class). Since each vector can be thought of as being a direction and a distance, this effectively constitutes a route with an endpoint.

```
public string Sum()
{
    StringBuilder sb = new StringBuilder();
    Vector currentPoint = new Vector(0.0, 0.0);
    sb.Append("origin");
    foreach (Vector vector in this)
    {
        sb.AppendFormat(" + {0}", vector);
        currentPoint += vector;
    }
    sb.AppendFormat(" = {0}", currentPoint);
    return sb.ToString();
}
```

This method uses the handy `StringBuilder` class, found in the `System.Text` namespace, to build the response string. This class has members such as `Append()` and `AppendFormat()` (used here), which make it easy to assemble a string — and the performance is better than concatenating individual strings. You use the `ToString()` method of this class to obtain the resultant string.

You also create two methods to be used as delegates, as static members of `VectorDelegates`. `Compare()` is used for comparison (sorting) and `TopRightQuadrant()` for searching. You'll look at these as you look through the code in `Program.cs`.

The code in `Main()` starts with the initialization of a `Vectors` collection, to which are added several `Vector` objects:

```
Vectors route = new Vectors();
route.Add(new Vector(2.0, 90.0));
route.Add(new Vector(1.0, 180.0));
route.Add(new Vector(0.5, 45.0));
route.Add(new Vector(2.5, 315.0));
```

The `Vectors.Sum()` method is used to write out the items in the collection as noted earlier, this time in their initial order:

```
Console.WriteLine(route.Sum());
```

Next, you create the first of your delegates, `sorter`. This delegate is of type `Comparison<Vector>` and, therefore, can be assigned a method with the signature:

```
int method(Vector objectA, Vector objectB)
```

This matched `VectorDelegates.Compare()`, which is the method you assign to the delegate:

```
Comparison<Vector> sorter = new Comparison<Vector>(VectorDelegates.Compare);
```

`Compare()` compares the magnitudes of two vectors as follows:

```
public static int Compare(Vector x, Vector y)
{
    if (x.R > y.R)
    {
        return 1;
    }
    else if (x.R < y.R)
    {
        return -1;
    }
    return 0;
}
```

This allows you to order the vectors by magnitude:

```
route.Sort(sorter);
Console.WriteLine(route.Sum());
```

The output of the application gives the result you'd expect — the result of the summation is the same, since the endpoint of following the "vector route" is the same whatever order you carry out the individual steps in.

Next, you obtain a subset of the vectors in the collection by searching. This uses `VectorDelegates.TopRightQuadrant()`:

```
public static bool TopRightQuadrant(Vector target)
{
    if (target.Theta >= 0.0 && target.Theta <= 90.0)
    {
        return true;
    }
    else
    {
        return false;
    }
}
```

This method returns `true` if its `Vector` argument has a value of `Theta` between 0 and 90 degrees — that is, it points up and/or right in a diagram of the sort you saw earlier.

In main, you use this method via a delegate of type `Predicate<Vector>` as follows:

```
Predicate<Vector> searcher =
    new Predicate<Vector>(VectorDelegates.TopRightQuadrant);
Vectors topRightQuadrantRoute = new Vectors(route.FindAll(searcher));
Console.WriteLine(topRightQuadrantRoute.Sum());
```

This requires the constructor defined in `Vectors`:

```
public Vectors(IEnumerable<Vector> initialItems)
{
    foreach (Vector vector in initialItems)
    {
        Add(vector);
    }
}
```

Here, you initialize a new `Vectors` collection using an interface of `IEnumerable<Vector>`, necessary since `List<Vector>.FindAll()` returns a `List<Vector>` instance, not a `Vectors` instance.

The result of the searching is that only a subset of `Vector` objects is returned, so (again as you'd expect) the result of the summation is different.

Dictionary<K, V>

This type allows you to define a collection of key-value pairs. Unlike the other generic collection types you've looked at in this chapter, this class requires two types to be instantiated, the types for both the key and value that represent each item in the collection.

Once a `Dictionary<K, V>` object is instantiated, you can perform much the same operations on it as you can on a class that inherits from `DictionaryBase`, but with type-safe methods and properties already in place. You can, for example, add key-value pairs using a strongly typed `Add()` method:

```
Dictionary<string, int> things = new Dictionary<string, int>();
things.Add("Green Things", 29);
things.Add("Blue Things", 94);
things.Add("Yellow Things", 34);
things.Add("Red Things", 52);
things.Add("Brown Things", 27);
```

You can iterate through keys and values in the collection using the `Keys` and `Values` properties:

```
foreach (string key in things.Keys)
{
    Console.WriteLine(key);
}

foreach (int value in things.Values)
{
    Console.WriteLine(value);
}
```

And you can iterate through items in the collection by obtaining each as a `KeyValuePair<K, V>` instance, much as with the `DictionaryEntry` objects you saw in the last chapter:

```
foreach (KeyValuePair<string, int> thing in things)
{
    Console.WriteLine("{0} = {1}", thing.Key, thing.Value);
}
```

One thing to note about `Dictionary<K, V>` is that the key for each item must be unique. Attempting to add an item with an identical key to one already added will cause an `ArgumentException` exception to be thrown. Because of this, `Dictionary<K, V>` allows you to pass an `IComparer<K>` interface to its constructor. This may be necessary if you use your own classes as keys and they don't support an `IComparable` or `IComparable<K>` interface, or should you want to compare objects using a nondefault process. For example, in the example shown above you could use a case-insensitive method to compare string keys:

```
Dictionary<string, int> things =
    new Dictionary<string, int>(StringComparer.CurrentCultureIgnoreCase);
```

Now, you'll get an exception if you use keys such as:

```
things.Add("Green Things", 29);
things.Add("Green things", 94);
```

You can also pass an initial capacity (with an `int`) or set of items (with an `IDictionary<K,V>` interface) to the constructor.

Modifying CardLib to Use a Generic Collection Class

One simple modification you can make to the `CardLib` project you've been building up over recent chapters is to modify the `Cards` collection class to use a generic collection class, thus saving many lines of code. The required modification to the class definition for `Cards` is:

```
public class Cards : List<Card>, ICloneable
{
    ...
}
```

You can also remove all the methods of `Cards` apart from `Clone()`, which is required for `ICloneable`, and `CopyTo()`, since the version of `CopyTo()` supplied by `List<Card>` works with an array of `Card` objects, not a `Cards` collection.

Rather than showing the code here for what is a very simple modification, the updated version of `CardLib`, called `Ch12CardLib`, is included in the downloadable code for this chapter, along with the client code from the last chapter.

Defining Generics

You've now seen enough about generics to be ready to create your own. You've seen plenty of code involving generic types and have had plenty of practice using generic syntax. In this section, you'll look at defining:

❑   Generic classes

❑   Generic interfaces

❑   Generic methods

❑   Generic delegates

You'll also see some more advanced techniques for dealing with the issues that come up when defining generic types along the way, namely:

- ❏ The `default` keyword
- ❏ Constraining types
- ❏ Inheriting from generic classes
- ❏ Generic operators

Defining Generic Classes

To create a generic class, all you need to do is to include the angle bracket syntax in the class definition:

```
class MyGenericClass<T>
{
    ...
}
```

Here `T` can be any identifier you like, following the usual C# naming rules, such as not starting with a number and so on.

A generic class can have any number of types in its definition, separated by commas, for example:

```
class MyGenericClass<T1, T2, T3>
{
    ...
}
```

Once these types are defined, you can use them in the class definition just like any other type. You can use them as types for member variables, return types for members such as properties or methods, and parameter types for method arguments. For example:

```
class MyGenericClass<T1, T2, T3>
{
    private T1 innerT1Object;

    public MyGenericClass(T1 item)
    {
        innerT1Object = item;
    }

    public T1 InnerT1Object
    {
        get
        {
            return innerT1Object;
        }
    }
}
```

Here, an object of type T1 can be passed to the constructor, and read-only access is permitted to this object via the property InnerT1Object.

An important point to note is that you can make practically no assumptions as to what the types supplied to the class are. The following code, for example, will not compile:

```
class MyGenericClass<T1, T2, T3>
{
    private T1 innerT1Object;

    public MyGenericClass()
    {
        innerT1Object = new T1();
    }

    public T1 InnerT1Object
    {
        get
        {
            return innerT1Object;
        }
    }
}
```

Since you don't know what T1 is, you can't use any of its constructors — it might not even have any, or have no publicly accessible default constructor at any rate. Without more complicated code involving the techniques you'll see later in this section, you can pretty much make only the following assumption about T1:

❑   You can treat it as a type that either inherits from, or can be boxed into, System.Object.

Obviously, this means that you can't really do very much interesting with instances of this type, or any of the other types supplied to the generic class MyGenericClass. Without using *reflection*, which is an advanced technique used to examine types at runtime, and which you won't be looking at in this chapter, you're limited pretty much to code as complicated as:

```
public string GetAllTypesAsString()
{
    return "T1 = " + typeof(T1).ToString()
        + ", T2 = " + typeof(T2).ToString()
        + ", T3 = " + typeof(T3).ToString();
}
```

There is a bit more that you can do, particularly in terms of collections, since dealing with groups of objects is a pretty simple process and doesn't need any assumptions about the object types — which is one good reason why the generic collection classes you've seen earlier in this chapter exist.

Another limitation that you need to be aware of is that using the operators == and != are only permitted when comparing a value of a type supplied to a generic type to null. That is, the following code works fine:

```
public bool Compare(T1 op1, T1 op2)
{
    if (op1 != null && op2 != null)
    {
        return true;
    }
    else
    {
        return false;
    }
}
```

Here, if `T1` is a value type, then it is always assumed to be non-`null`, so in the above code `Compare` will always return `true`.

However, attempting to compare the two arguments `op1` and `op2` fails to compile:

```
public bool Compare(T1 op1, T1 op2)
{
    if (op1 == op2)
    {
        return true;
    }
    else
    {
        return false;
    }
}
```

The reason for this is that this code assumes that T1 supports the == operator.

What all this boils down to is that to do anything really interesting with generics you need to know a bit more about the types used in the class.

The default Keyword

One of the most basic things you might want to find out about types used to create generic class instances is whether they are reference or value types. Without knowing this you can't even assign null values with code such as:

```
public MyGenericClass()
{
    innerT1Object = null;
}
```

Should `T1` be a value type then `innerT1Object` can't have the value `null`, so this code won't compile.

Luckily, this problem has been thought out and has resulted in a new use for the `default` keyword (which you've seen being used in `switch` structures earlier in the book). This is used as follows:

```
public MyGenericClass()
{
    innerT1Object = default(T1);
}
```

The result of this is that `innerT1Object` is assigned a value of `null` if it is a reference type, or a default value if it is a value type. This default value is 0 for numeric types, while structs have each of their members initialized to 0 or `null` in the same way.

The `default` keyword gets you some way to be able to do a little more with the types you are forced to use, but to get further you need to constrain the types that are supplied.

Constraining Types

The types you have used with generic classes up till now are known as *unbounded* types, since no restrictions are placed on what they can be. By *constraining* types, it is possible to restrict the types that can be used to instantiate a generic class. There are a number of ways of doing this. For example, it is possible to restrict a type to one that inherits from a certain type. To refer back to the `Animal`, `Cow`, and `Chicken` classes you used earlier, it would be possible to restrict a type to one that was or inherited from `Animal`, so this code would be fine:

```
MyGenericClass<Cow> = new MyGenericClass<Cow>();
```

whereas the following would fail to compile:

```
MyGenericClass<string> = new MyGenericClass<string>();
```

In your class definitions, this is achieved using the `where` keyword:

```
class MyGenericClass<T> where T : constraint
{
    ...
}
```

Here, `constraint` defines what the constraint is.

You can supply a number of constraints in this way by separating them by commas:

```
class MyGenericClass<T> where T : constraint1, constraint2
{
    ...
}
```

And you can define constraints on any or all of the types required by the generic class using multiple `where` statements:

```
class MyGenericClass<T1, T2> where T1 : constraint1 where T2 : constraint2
{
    ...
}
```

Any constraints must appear after the inheritance specifiers:

```
class MyGenericClass<T1, T2> : MyBaseClass, IMyInterface
    where T1 : constraint1 where T2 : constraint2
{
    ...
}
```

The available constraints are shown in the following table:

Constraint	Definition	Example Usage
struct	Type must be a value type.	In a class that requires value types to function, for example where a member variable of type T being 0 means something
class	Type must be a reference type.	In a class that requires reference types to function, for example where a member variable of type T being null means something
base class	Type must be, or inherit from, base class.	In a class that requires certain baseline functionality inherited from base class in order to function
interface	Type must be, or implement, interface.	In a class that requires certain baseline functionality exposed by interface in order to function
new()	Type must have a public, parameterless constructor.	In a class where you need to be able to instantiate variables of type T, perhaps in a constructor

If new() is used as a constraint it must be the last constraint specified for a type.

It is possible to use one type parameter as a constraint on another as follows:

```
class MyGenericClass<T1, T2> where T2 : T1
{
    ...
}
```

Here T2 must be the same type as T1 or inherit from T1. This is known as a *naked type constraint*, meaning that one generic type parameter is used as a constraint on another.

Circular type constraints are forbidden, for example:

```
class MyGenericClass<T1, T2> where T2 : T1 where T1 : T2
{
    ...
}
```

This code will not compile.

In the following Try It Out you'll define and use a generic class that uses the Animal family of classes you've seen in earlier chapters.

Try It Out   Defining a Generic Class

1. Create a new console application called Ch12Ex04 in the directory C:\BegVCSharp\
    Chapter12.

2. Right-click on the project name in the Solution Explorer window, and select the Add ⇨ Add
    Existing Item... option.

3. Select the Animal.cs, Cow.cs, and Chicken.cs files from the C:\BegVCSharp\Chapter12\
    Ch12Ex02\Ch12Ex02 directory, and click Add.

4. Modify the namespace declaration in the file you have added as follows:

```
namespace Ch12Ex04
```

5. Modify Animal.cs as follows:

```
public abstract class Animal
{
    ...

    public abstract void MakeANoise();
}
```

6. Modify Chicken.cs as follows:

```
public class Chicken : Animal
{
    ...

    public override void MakeANoise()
    {
        Console.WriteLine("{0} says 'cluck!'", name);
    }
}
```

7. Modify Cow.cs as follows:

```
public class Cow : Animal
{
    ...

    public override void MakeANoise()
    {
        Console.WriteLine("{0} says 'moo!'", name);
    }
}
```

8. Add a new class called SuperCow.cs as follows:

```
public class SuperCow : Cow
{
    public void Fly()
    {
        Console.WriteLine("{0} is flying!", name);
```

```
      }

      public SuperCow(string newName) : base(newName)
      {
      }

      public override void MakeANoise()
      {
         Console.WriteLine("{0} says 'here I come to save the day!'", name);
      }
   }
```

9. Add a new class called `Farm.cs` as follows:

```
using System;
using System.Collections;
using System.Collections.Generic;
using System.Text;

namespace Ch12Ex04
{
   public class Farm<T> : IEnumerable<T>
      where T : Animal
   {
      private List<T> animals = new List<T>();

      public List<T> Animals
      {
         get
         {
            return animals;
         }
      }

      public IEnumerator<T> GetEnumerator()
      {
         return animals.GetEnumerator();
      }

      IEnumerator IEnumerable.GetEnumerator()
      {
         return animals.GetEnumerator();
      }

      public void MakeNoises()
      {
         foreach (T animal in animals)
         {
            animal.MakeANoise();
         }
```

```
        }

        public void FeedTheAnimals()
        {
            foreach (T animal in animals)
            {
                animal.Feed();
            }
        }

        public Farm<Cow> GetCows()
        {
            Farm<Cow> cowFarm = new Farm<Cow>();
            foreach (T animal in animals)
            {
                if (animal is Cow)
                {
                    cowFarm.Animals.Add(animal as Cow);
                }
            }
            return cowFarm;
        }
    }
}
```

10. Modify `Program.cs` as follows:

```
    static void Main(string[] args)
    {
        Farm<Animal> farm = new Farm<Animal>();
        farm.Animals.Add(new Cow("Jack"));
        farm.Animals.Add(new Chicken("Vera"));
        farm.Animals.Add(new Chicken("Sally"));
        farm.Animals.Add(new SuperCow("Kevin"));
        farm.MakeNoises();

        Farm<Cow> dairyFarm = farm.GetCows();
        dairyFarm.FeedTheAnimals();

        foreach (Cow cow in dairyFarm)
        {
            if (cow is SuperCow)
            {
                (cow as SuperCow).Fly();
            }
        }
        Console.ReadKey();
    }
```

11. Execute the application. The result is shown in Figure 12-5.

Figure 12-5

How It Works

In this example, you have created a generic class called `Farm<T>`, which rather than inheriting from a generic list class, exposes a generic list class as a public property. The type of this list is determined by the type parameter `T` that is passed to `Farm<T>` and is constrained to be or inherit from `Animal`:

```
public class Farm<T> : IEnumerable<T>
   where T : Animal
{
   private List<T> animals = new List<T>();

   public List<T> Animals
   {
      get
      {
         return animals;
      }
   }
}
```

`Farm<T>` also implements `IEnumerable<T>`, where `T` is passed into this generic interface and is therefore also constrained in the same way. You implement this interface to make it possible to iterate through the items contained in `Farm<T>` without needing to explicitly iterate over `Farm<T>.Animals`. This is simple to achieve, you simply return the enumerator exposed by `Animals`, which is a `List<T>` class that also implements `IEnumerable<T>`:

```
public IEnumerator<T> GetEnumerator()
{
   return animals.GetEnumerator();
}
```

Since `IEnumerable<T>` inherits from `IEnumerable` we also need to implement `IEnumerable.GetEnumerator()`:

```
IEnumerator IEnumerable.GetEnumerator()
{
   return animals.GetEnumerator();
}
```

Next, `Farm<T>` includes two methods that make use of methods of the abstract `Animal` class:

```
public void MakeNoises()
{
    foreach (T animal in animals)
    {
        animal.MakeANoise();
    }
}

public void FeedTheAnimals()
{
    foreach (T animal in animals)
    {
        animal.Feed();
    }
}
```

Because `T` is constrained to `Animal` this code compiles fine — you are guaranteed to have access to these methods whatever `T` actually is.

The next method, `GetCows()`, is more interesting. This method simply extracts all the items in the collection that are of type `Cow` (or inherit from `Cow`, such as the new `SuperCow` class):

```
public Farm<Cow> GetCows()
{
    Farm<Cow> cowFarm = new Farm<Cow>();
    foreach (T animal in animals)
    {
        if (animal is Cow)
        {
            cowFarm.Animals.Add(animal as Cow);
        }
    }
    return cowFarm;
}
```

What is interesting here is that this method seems a bit wasteful. Should you want other methods of the same sort, such as `GetChickens()` and so on, you'd need to implement them explicitly too. In a system with many more types you'd need many more methods. A far better solution here would be to use a *generic method* here, which you'll implement a little later in the chapter.

The client code in `Program.cs` simply tests the various methods of `Farm` and doesn't really contain much you haven't already seen, so there's no need to examine this code in any more depth — despite the flying cow.

Inheriting from Generic Classes

The `Farm<T>` class in the preceding example, as well as several other classes you've seen in this chapter, inherit from a generic type. In the case of `Farm<T>` this type was an interface; `IEnumerable<T>`. Here the constraint on `T` supplied by `Farm<T>` resulted in an additional constraint on `T` used in `IEnumerable<T>`.

This can be a useful technique for constraining otherwise unbounded types. However, there are some rules that need to be followed.

First, you can't "unconstrain" types that are constrained in a type you are inheriting from. What this means is that a type T that is used in a type you are inheriting from must be constrained at least as much as it is in that type. For example, the following code is fine:

```
class SuperFarm<T> : Farm<T>
     where T : SuperCow
{
}
```

This works as T is constrained to `Animal` in `Farm<T>`, and constraining it to `SuperCow` is constraining T to a subset of these values. However, this won't compile:

```
class SuperFarm<T> : Farm<T>
     where T : struct
{
}
```

Here, you can say definitively that the type T supplied to `SuperFarm<T>` cannot be converted into a T usable by `Farm<T>`, so the code won't compile. Even situations where the constraint is a superset have the same problem:

```
class SuperFarm<T> : Farm<T>
     where T : class
{
}
```

Even though types such as `Animal` would be allowed by `SuperFarm<T>`, other types that satisfy the class constraint won't be allowed in `Farm<T>`. Again, compilation will fail.

This rule applies to all the types of constraints you looked at earlier in this chapter.

Another important thing is that if you inherit from a generic type you must supply all the required type information, either in the form of other generic type parameters, as shown above, or explicitly. This also applies to nongeneric classes that inherit from generic types as you've seen elsewhere, for example:

```
public class Cards : List<Card>, ICloneable
{
}
```

This is fine, but attempting the following will fail:

```
public class Cards : List<T>, ICloneable
{
}
```

Here, no information is supplied for T, so no compilation is possible.

Note that if you supply a parameter to a generic type, as in `List<Card>` *above, you can refer to the type as closed. Similarly, inheriting from* `List<T>` *is inheriting from an open generic type.*

Generic Operators

Operator overrides are implemented in C# just like other methods and can be implemented in generic classes.

For example, you could define the following implicit conversion operator in Farm<T>:

```
public static implicit operator List<Animal>(Farm<T> farm)
{
   List<Animal> result = new List<Animal>();
   foreach (T animal in farm)
   {
       result.Add(animal);
   }
   return result;
}
```

This allows the Animal objects in a Farm<T> to be accessed directly as a List<Animal> should you require it. This comes in handy if you want to add two Farm<T> instances together, for example with the following operators:

```
public static Farm<T> operator +(Farm<T> farm1, List<T> farm2)
{
   Farm<T> result = new Farm<T>();
   foreach (T animal in farm1)
   {
       result.Animals.Add(animal);
   }
   foreach (T animal in farm2)
   {
       if (!result.Animals.Contains(animal))
       {
           result.Animals.Add(animal);
       }
   }
   return result;
}
```

```
public static Farm<T> operator +(List<T> farm1, Farm<T> farm2)
{
   return farm2 + farm1;
}
```

You could then add instances of Farm<Animal> and Farm<Cow> as follows:

```
Farm<Animal> newFarm = farm + dairyFarm;
```

In this code dairyFarm (an instance of Farm<Cow>) is implicitly converted into List<Animal>, which is usable by the overloaded + operator in Farm<T>.

You might think that this could be achieved using simply:

```
public static Farm<T> operator +(Farm<T> farm1, Farm<T> farm2)
{
    Farm<T> result = new Farm<T>();
    foreach (T animal in farm1)
    {
        result.Animals.Add(animal);
    }
    foreach (T animal in farm2)
    {
        if (!result.Animals.Contains(animal))
        {
            result.Animals.Add(animal);
        }
    }
    return result;
}
```

However, since `Farm<Cow>` cannot be converted into `Farm<Animal>`, the summation will fail. To take this a step further, you could solve this using the following conversion operator:

```
public static implicit operator Farm<Animal>(Farm<T> farm)
{
    Farm <Animal> result = new Farm <Animal>();
    foreach (T animal in farm)
    {
        result.Animals.Add(animal);
    }
    return result;
}
```

With this operator, instances of `Farm<T>`, such as `Farm<Cow>` can be converted into instances of `Farm<Animal>`, solving the problem. So, you can use either of the methods shown above, although the latter is preferable for its simplicity. Both are included in the example code for this chapter.

Generic Structs

You have seen in earlier chapters that structs are essentially the same as classes, barring some minor differences and the fact that a struct is a value type, not a reference type. As this is the case, *generic structs* can be created in the same way as generic classes, for example:

```
public struct MyStruct<T1, T2>
{
    public T1 item1;
    public T2 item2;
}
```

Defining Generic Interfaces

You've now seen several generic interfaces in use, namely those in the `Systems.Collections.Generic` namespace such as `IEnumerable<T>` used in the last example.

Defining a generic interface involves the same techniques as defining a generic class, for example:

```
interface MyFarmingInterface<T>
    where T : Animal
{
    bool AttemptToBreed(T animal1, T animal2);

    T OldestInHerd
    {
        get;
    }
}
```

Here, the generic parameter `T` is used as the type of the two arguments of `AttemptToBreed()` and the type of the `OldestInHerd` property.

The same inheritance rules apply as for classes. If you inherit from a base generic interface, you must obey the rules such as keeping the constraints of the base interface generic type parameters.

Defining Generic Methods

In the last Try It Out you saw a method called GetCows(), and in the discussion for the example you read that it is possible to make a more general form of this method using a generic method. In this section you'll see how this is possible. A generic method is one where the return and/or parameter types are determined by a generic type parameter or parameters. For example:

```
public T GetDefault<T>()
{
    return default(T);
}
```

This trivial example uses the default keyword you looked at earlier in the chapter to return a default value for a type `T`.

This method is called as follows:

```
int myDefaultInt = GetDefault<T>();
```

The type parameter `T` is provided at the time the method is called.

Note that this `T` is quite separate from the types used to supply generic type parameters to classes. In fact, generic methods can be implemented by nongeneric classes:

```
public class Defaulter
{
    public T GetDefault<T>()
    {
```

```
        return default(T);
    }
}
```

If the class is generic, though, you must use different identifiers for generic method types. The following code won't compile:

```
public class Defaulter<T>
{
    public T GetDefault<T>()
    {
        return default(T);
    }
}
```

The T used by either the method or class must be renamed.

Constraints can be used by generic method parameters in the same way as for classes, and in this case you can make use of any class type parameters, for example:

```
public class Defaulter<T1>
{
    public T2 GetDefault<T2>()
        where T2 : T1
    {
        return default(T2);
    }
}
```

Here, the type T2 supplied to the method must be the same as, or inherit from, T1 supplied to the class. This is a common way to constrain generic methods.

In the Farm<T> class shown earlier, you could include the following method (included, but commented out, in the downloadable code for Ch12Ex04):

```
public Farm<U> GetSpecies<U>() where U : T
{
    Farm<U> speciesFarm = new Farm<U>();
    foreach (T animal in animals)
    {
        if (animal is U)
        {
            speciesFarm.Animals.Add(animal as U);
        }
    }
    return speciesFarm;
}
```

This can replace GetCows() and any other methods of the same type. The generic type parameter used here, U, is constrained by T, which is in turn constrained by the Farm<T> class to Animal. This allows you to treat instances of T as instances of Animal, should you wish to.

In the client code for `Ch12Ex04`, in `Program.cs`, using this new method requires one modification:

```
Farm<Cow> dairyFarm = farm.GetSpecies<Cow>();
```

You could equally write

```
Farm<Chicken> dairyFarm = farm.GetSpecies<Chicken>();
```

or any other class that inherits from `Animal`.

An important point to note here is that having generic type parameters on a method changes the signature of the method. This means that you can have several overloads of a method differing only in generic type parameters, for example:

```
public void ProcessT<T>(T op1)
{
    ...
}
```

```
public void ProcessT<T, U>(T op1)
{
    ...
}
```

Which of these methods to use is determined by the amount of generic type parameters specified when the method is called.

Defining Generic Delegates

The last generic type you have to look at is the *generic delegate*. You saw these in action earlier in the chapter when you saw how to sort and search generic lists. You used the `Comparison<T>` and `Predicate<T>` delegates, respectively, for this.

In Chapter 7, you saw how to define delegates using the signature of a method, the delegate keyword, and a name for the delegate, for example:

```
public delegate int MyDelegate(int op1, int op2);
```

To define a generic delegate, you simply need to declare and use one or more generic type parameters, for example:

```
public delegate T1 MyDelegate<T1, T2>(T2 op1, T2 op2) where T1 : T2;
```

As you can see, constraints can be applied here too, where the same rules apply to constraints used here.

You'll see a lot more about delegates in the next chapter and how you can use them in a common C# programming technique—*events*.

Summary

In this chapter, you:

- ❑ Examined how to use generic types in C#.

- ❑ Looked at how to use structs, including how to create nullable types, and how to use the classes in the `System.Collecitons.Generic` namespace.

- ❑ Saw how to create your own generic types, including classes, interfaces, methods, and delegates.

Generics, as you saw, are an extremely powerful new technique in C#. You can use them to create classes that fill a number of purposes at the same time and are able to be used in a variety of situations. And even if you don't have cause to create your own generic types, you're almost guaranteed to use the generic collection classes time and again.

In the next chapter, I'll finish the discussion of the basic C# language by tying up a few loose ends and looking at events.

Exercises

1. Which of the following can be generic?

   a. classes

   b. methods

   c. properties

   d. operator overloads

   e. structs

   f. enumerations

2. Extend the `Vector` class in `Ch12Ex01` such that the * operator returns the dot product of two vectors.

   The dot product of two vectors is defined as the product of their magnitudes multiplied by the cosine of the angle between them.

3. What is wrong with the following code? Fix it.

```
public class Instantiator<T>
{
   public T instance;

   public Instantiator()
   {
      instance = new T();
   }
}
```

4. What is wrong with the following code? Fix it.

```
public class StringGetter<T>
{
   public string GetString<T>(T item)
   {
      return item.ToString();
   }
}
```

5. Create a generic class called `ShortCollection<T>` that implements `IList<T>` and consists of a collection of items with a maximum size. This maximum size should be an integer that can be supplied to the constructor of `ShortCollection<T>`, or defaults to 10. The constructor should also be able to take an initial list of items via a `List<T>` parameter. The class should function exactly like `Collection<T>`, but throw an exception of type `IndexOutOfRangeException` if an attempt is made to add too many items to the collection, or if the `List<T>` passed to the constructor contains too many items.

Additional OOP Techniques

In this chapter, you round off your discussion on the C# language by looking at a few bits and pieces that haven't quite fitted in elsewhere. This isn't to say that these techniques aren't useful — just that they haven't fallen under any of the headings you've worked through so far.

Specifically, you will look at:

- ❑ The :: operator and the global namespace qualifier
- ❑ Custom exceptions and exception recommendations
- ❑ Events
- ❑ Anonymous methods

You also make some final modifications to the `CardLib` code that you've been building up throughout the last few chapters, and even use `CardLib` to create a card game.

The :: Operator and the Global Namespace Qualifier

The :: operator provides an alternative way to access types in namespaces, where namespace aliases are given priority over the usual type qualification. To see what this means, consider the following code:

```
using MyNamespaceAlias = MyRootNamespace.MyNestedNamespace;

namespace MyRootNamespace
{
    namespace MyNamespaceAlias
    {
        public class MyClass
        {
        }
```

```
    }

    namespace MyNestedNamespace
    {
        public class MyClass
        {
        }
    }
}
```

Code in `MyRootNamespace` can access `MyRootNamespace.MyNamespaceAlias.MyClass` as follows:

```
MyNamespaceAlias.MyClass
```

That is to say that `MyRootNamespace.MyNamespaceAlias` has hidden the alias defined by the using statement, which refers to `MyRootNamespace.MyNestedAlias`. You can still access this namespace, and the class contained within, but you require different syntax:

```
MyRootNamespace.MyNamespaceAlias.MyClass
MyNestedNamespace.MyClass
```

Alternatively, you can use the `::` operator:

```
MyNamespaceAlias::MyClass
```

Using this operator forces the compiler to use the alias defined by the using statement, and therefore the code refers to `MyRootNamespace.MyNestedAlias.MyClass`.

You can also use the keyword `global` with the `::` operator, which is essentially an alias to the top-level, root namespace. This can be useful to make it clearer which namespace you are referring to, for example:

```
global::System.Collections.Generic.List<int>
```

This is definitely the class you expect it to be, the generic `List<T>` collection class. It definitely isn't the class defined with the following code:

```
namespace MyRootNamespace
{
    namespace System
    {
        namespace Collections
        {
            namespace Generic
            {
                class List<T>
                {
                }
            }
        }
    }
}
```

Of course, you should avoid giving your namespaces names that already exist as .NET namespaces, although this problem may arise in large projects, particularly if you are working as part of a large team. Using the :: operator and the `global` keyword may be the only way you can get access to the types you want.

Custom Exceptions

Earlier in the book, in Chapter 7, you looked at exceptions and how you can use `try . . . catch . . . finally` blocks to act on them. You also saw several standard .NET exceptions, including the base class for exceptions `System.Exception`. Sometimes, it can be useful to derive your own exception classes from this base class and use them in your applications, instead of using the standard exceptions. This allows you to be more specific about the information you send to whatever code catches the exception and allows catching code to be more specific about which exceptions it handles. You might, for example, add a new property to your exception class that permits access to some underlying information, making it possible for the receiver of the exception to make the required changes, or just giving more information as to the exception cause.

Once you have defined an exception class you can add it to the list of exceptions recognized by VS using the Debug ⇨ Exceptions... dialog's Add button, then defining exception-specific behavior as you saw in Chapter 7.

Adding Custom Exceptions to CardLib

The use of custom exceptions is, once again, best illustrated by upgrading the CardLib project. The `Deck.GetCard()` method currently throws a standard .NET exception if an attempt is made to access a card with an index less than 0 or greater than 51, but you'll modify this to use a custom exception.

First, you need to create a new class library project called Ch13CardLib and copy the classes from Ch12CardLib as before, changing the namespace to Ch13CardLib as applicable. Next, you define the exception. You do this with a new class defined in a new class file called CardOutOfRangeException.cs, which you can add to the Ch13CardLib project with Project ⇨ Add New Item:

```
public class CardOutOfRangeException : Exception
{
   private Cards deckContents;

   public Cards DeckContents
   {
      get
      {
         return deckContents;
      }
   }

   public CardOutOfRangeException(Cards sourceDeckContents) :
         base("There are only 52 cards in the deck.")
   {
      deckContents = sourceDeckContents;
   }
}
```

An instance of the `Cards` class is required for the constructor of this class. It allows access to this `Cards` object through a `DeckContents` property and supplies a suitable error message to the base `Exception` constructor, so that it is available through the `Message` property of the class.

Next, you add code to throw this exception to `Deck.cs` (replacing the old standard exception):

```
public Card GetCard(int cardNum)
{
    if (cardNum >= 0 && cardNum <= 51)
        return cards[cardNum];
    else
        throw new CardOutOfRangeException(cards.Clone() as Cards);
}
```

The `DeckContents` property is initialized with a deep copy of the current contents of the `Deck` object, in the form of a `Cards` object. This means that you see what the contents were at the point where the exception was thrown, so subsequent modification to the deck contents won't "lose" this information.

To test this, you can use the following client code (in `Ch13CardClient` in the downloadable code for this chapter):

```
Deck deck1 = new Deck();
try
{
    Card myCard = deck1.GetCard(60);
}
catch (CardOutOfRangeException e)
{
    Console.WriteLine(e.Message);
    Console.WriteLine(e.DeckContents[0]);
}
```

This code gives the output shown in Figure 13-1.

Figure 13-1

Here, the catching code has written the exception `Message` property to the screen. You also displayed the first card in the `Cards` object obtained through `DeckContents`, just to prove that you can access the `Cards` collection through your custom exception object.

Events

In this section, you'll look at one of the most frequently used OOP techniques in .NET: *events*.

You'll start, as usual, with the basics — looking at what events actually are. After this, you'll move on to see some simple events in action and look at what you can do with them. Once this is described, you'll move on to look at how you can create and use events of your own.

At the end of this chapter you'll polish off your `CardLib` class library by adding an event. In addition, and since this is the last port of call before hitting some more advanced topics, you'll have a bit of fun. You'll create a card game application that uses this class library.

To start with, then, here's a look at what events are.

What Is an Event?

Events are similar to exceptions in that they are *raised* (thrown) by objects, and you can supply code that acts on them. However, there are several important differences. The most important of these is that there is no equivalent to the `try . . . catch` structure for handling events. Instead, you must *subscribe* to them. Subscribing to an event means supplying code that will be executed when an event is raised, in the form of an *event handler*.

An event can have many handlers subscribed to it, which will all be called when the event is raised. This may include event handlers that are part of the class of the object that raises the event, but event handlers are just as likely to be found in other classes.

Event handlers themselves are simply functions. The only restriction on an event handler function is that it must match the signature (return type and parameters) required by the event. This signature is part of the definition of an event and is specified by a *delegate*.

> *The fact that delegates are used in events is what makes delegates such useful things. This is the reason I devoted some time to them back in Chapter 6, and you may wish to reread that section to refresh your memory as to what delegates are and how you use them.*

The sequence of processing goes something like this.

First, an application creates an object that can raise an event. As an example, say that the application is an instant messaging application, and that the object it creates represents a connection to a remote user. This connection object might raise an event, say, when a message arrives through the connection from the remote user. This is shown in Figure 13-2.

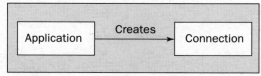

Figure 13-2

Next, the application subscribes to the event. Your instant messaging application would do this by defining a function that could be used with the delegate type specified by the event and passing a reference to this function to the event. This event handler function might be a method on another object, for example an object representing a display device to display instant messages on when they arrive. This is shown in Figure 13-3.

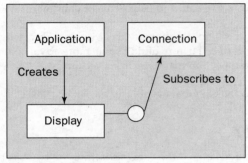

Figure 13-3

When the event is raised, the subscriber is notified. When an instant message arrives through the connection object, the event handler method on the display device object is called. As you are using a standard method, the object that raises the event may pass any relevant information via parameters, making events very versatile. In the example case, one parameter might be the text of the instant message, which the event handler could display on the display device object. This is shown in Figure 13-4.

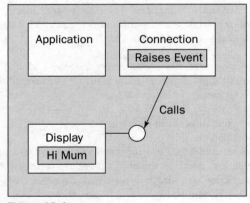

Figure 13-4

Using Events

In this section, you'll look at the code required for handling events, then move on to look at how you can define and use your own events.

Handling Events

As I have discussed, to handle an event you need to subscribe to the event by providing an event handler function whose signature matches that of the delegate specified for use with the event. Here's an example that uses a simple timer object to raise events, which will result in a handler function being called.

Try It Out   **Handling Events**

1. Create a new console application called `Ch13Ex01` in the directory `C:\BegVCSharp\Chapter13`.

2. Modify the code in `Program.cs` as follows:

```csharp
using System;
using System.Collections.Generic;
using System.Text;
using System.Timers;

namespace Ch13Ex01
{
    class Program
    {
        static int counter = 0;

        static string displayString =
                        "This string will appear one letter at a time. ";

        static void Main(string[] args)
        {
            Timer myTimer = new Timer(100);
            myTimer.Elapsed += new ElapsedEventHandler(WriteChar);
            myTimer.Start();
            Console.ReadKey();
        }

        static void WriteChar(object source, ElapsedEventArgs e)
        {
            Console.Write(displayString[counter++ % displayString.Length]);
        }
    }
}
```

3. Run the application (once running, pressing a key will terminate the application). The result, after a short period, is shown in Figure 13-5.

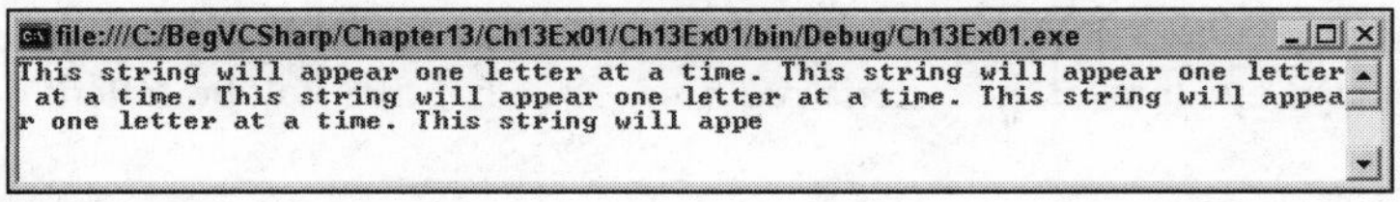

Figure 13-5

How It Works

The object you are using to raise events is an instance of the `System.Timers.Timer` class. This object is initialized with a time period (in milliseconds). When the `Timer` object is started using its `Start()` method a stream of events will be raised, spaced out in time according to the specified time period. `Main()` initializes a `Timer` object with a timer period of 100 milliseconds, so it will raise events 10 times a second when started:

```
static void Main(string[] args)
{
    Timer myTimer = new Timer(100);
```

The `Timer` object possesses an event called `Elapsed`, and the event handler signature required by this event is that of the `System.Timers.ElapsedEventHandler` delegate type, which is one of the standard delegates defined in the .NET Framework. This delegate is used for functions that match the following signature:

```
void functionName(object source, ElapsedEventArgs e);
```

The `Timer` object sends a reference to itself in the first parameter and an instance of an `ElapsedEventArgs` object in its second parameter. It is safe to ignore these parameters for now, but you'll take a look at them a little later.

In your code you have a method that matches this signature:

```
static void WriteChar(object source, ElapsedEventArgs e)
{
    Console.Write(displayString[counter++ % displayString.Length]);
}
```

This method uses the two static fields of `Class1`, `counter` and `displayString`, to display a single character. Every time the method is called the character displayed is different.

The next task is to hook this handler up to the event — to subscribe to it. To do this, you use the `+=` operator to add a handler to the event in the form of a new delegate instance initialized with your event handler method:

```
static void Main(string[] args)
{
    Timer myTimer = new Timer(100);
    myTimer.Elapsed += new ElapsedEventHandler(WriteChar);
```

This command (which uses slightly strange looking syntax, specific to delegates) adds a handler to the list that will be called when the `Elapsed` event is raised. You can add as many handlers as you like to this list, as long as they all meet the criteria required. Each handler will be called in turn when the event is raised.

All that is left for `Main()` is to start the timer running:

```
    myTimer.Start();
```

Since you don't want the application terminating before you have handled any events, you then put the `Main()` function on hold. The simplest way of doing this is to request user input, since this command won't finish processing until the user has pressed a key.

```
Console.ReadKey();
```

Although processing in `Main()` effectively ceases here, processing in the `Timer` object continues. When it raises events it calls the `WriteChar()` method, which runs concurrently with the `Console.ReadLine()` statement.

Defining Events

Next, you'll look at defining and using your own events. In the following Try It Out, you implement an example version of the instant messaging case set out in the introduction to events in this chapter and create a `Connection` object that raises events that are handled by a `Display` object.

Try It Out   Defining Events

1. Create a new console application called `Ch13Ex02` in the directory `C:\BegVCSharp\Chapter13`.

2. Add a new class, `Connection`, stored in `Connection.cs`:

```csharp
using System;
using System.Collections.Generic;
using System.Text;
using System.Timers;

namespace Ch13Ex02
{
    public delegate void MessageHandler(string messageText);

    public class Connection
    {
        public event MessageHandler MessageArrived;

        private Timer pollTimer;

        public Connection()
        {
            pollTimer = new Timer(100);
            pollTimer.Elapsed += new ElapsedEventHandler(CheckForMessage);
        }

        public void Connect()
        {
            pollTimer.Start();
        }

        public void Disconnect()
        {
            pollTimer.Stop();
```

```
        }

        private static Random random = new Random();

        private void CheckForMessage(object source, ElapsedEventArgs e)
        {
            Console.WriteLine("Checking for new messages.");
            if ((random.Next(9) == 0) && (MessageArrived != null))
            {
                MessageArrived("Hello Mum!");
            }
        }
    }
}
```

3.   Add a new class, Display, stored in Display.cs:

```
namespace Ch13Ex02
{
    public class Display
    {
        public void DisplayMessage(string message)
        {
            Console.WriteLine("Message arrived: {0}", message);
        }
    }
}
```

4.   Modify the code in Program.cs as follows:

```
static void Main(string[] args)
{
    Connection myConnection = new Connection();
    Display myDisplay = new Display();
    myConnection.MessageArrived +=
            new MessageHandler (myDisplay.DisplayMessage);
    myConnection.Connect();
    Console.ReadKey();
}
```

5.   Run the application. The result, after a short period, is shown in Figure 13-6.

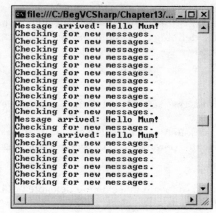

Figure 13-6

How It Works

The class that does most of the work in this application is the Connection class. Instances of this class make use of a Timer object much like the one you saw in the first example of this chapter, initializing it in the class constructor and giving access to its state (enabled or disabled) via Connect() and Disconnect():

```
public class Connection
{
    private Timer pollTimer;

    public Connection()
    {
        pollTimer = new Timer(100);
        pollTimer.Elapsed += new ElapsedEventHandler(CheckForMessage);
    }

    public void Connect()
    {
        pollTimer.Start();
    }
    public void Disconnect()
    {
        pollTimer.Stop();
    }

    ...
}
```

Also in the constructor, you register an event handler for the Elapsed event in the same way as you did in the first example. The handler method, CheckForMessage(), will raise an event on average once every 10 times it is called. Before you look at the code for this, though, it would be useful to look at the event definition itself.

However, before you define an event you must define a delegate type to use with the event—that is, a delegate type that specifies the signature that an event handling method must conform to. You do this using standard delegate syntax, defining it as public inside the Ch13Ex02 namespace in order to make the type available to external code:

```
namespace Ch13Ex02
{
    public delegate void MessageHandler(string messageText);
```

This delegate type, called MessageHandler here, is a signature for a void function that has a single string parameter. You can use this parameter to pass an instant message received by the Connection object to the Display object.

Once a delegate has been defined (or a suitable existing delegate has been located), you can define the event itself, as a member of the Connection class:

```
    public class Connection
    {
        public event MessageHandler MessageArrived;
```

You simply name the event (here you have used the name MessageArrived) and declare it using the event keyword and the delegate type to use (the MessageHandler delegate type defined earlier).

Once you have declared an event in this way, you can raise it simply by calling it by its name as if it were a method with the signature specified by the delegate. For example, you could raise this event using:

```
    MessageArrived("This is a message.");
```

If the delegate had been defined without any parameters you could use simply:

```
    MessageArrived();
```

Alternatively, you could have defined more parameters, which would have required more code to raise the event.

The CheckForMessage() method looks like this:

```
        private static Random random = new Random();

        private void CheckForMessage(object source, ElapsedEventArgs e)
        {
            Console.WriteLine("Checking for new messages.");
            if ((random.Next(9) == 0) && (MessageArrived != null))
            {
                MessageArrived("Hello Mum!");
            }
        }
```

You use an instance of the Random class that you have seen in earlier chapters to generate a random number between 0 and 9, and raise an event if the number generated is 0, which should happen 10 percent of the time. This simulates polling the connection to see if a message has arrived, which won't be the case every time you check. To separate the timer from the instance of Connection, you use a private static instance of the Random class.

Note that you supply additional logic. You only raise an event if the expression `MessageArrived !=
null` evaluates to `true`. This expression, which again uses the delegate syntax in a slightly unusual way,
means: "Does the event have any subscribers?" If there are no subscribers, `MessageArrived` evaluates
to `null`, and there is no point in raising the event.

The class that will subscribe to the event is called `Display` and contains the single method,
`DisplayMessage()`, defined as follows:

```
public class Display
{
   public void DisplayMessage(string message)
   {
      Console.WriteLine("Message arrived: {0}", message);
   }
}
```

This method matches the delegate type method signature (and is public, which is a requirement of event
handlers in classes other than the class that generates the event), so you can use it to respond to the
`MessageArrived` event.

All that is left now is for the code in `Main()` to initialize instances of the `Connection` and `Display`
classes, hook them up, and start things going. The code required here is similar to that from the first
example:

```
static void Main(string[] args)
{
   Connection myConnection = new Connection();
   Display myDisplay = new Display();
   myConnection.MessageArrived +=
            new MessageHandler(myDisplay.DisplayMessage);
   myConnection.Connect();
   Console.ReadKey();
}
```

Again, you call `Console.ReadKey()` to pause the processing of `Main()` once you have started things
moving with the `Connect()` method of the `Connection` object.

Multipurpose Event Handlers

The signature you saw earlier, for the `Timer.Elapsed` event, contained two parameters that are of a
type often seen in event handlers. These parameters are:

- ❑   `object source`: A reference to the object that raised the event
- ❑   `ElapsedEventArgs e`: Parameters sent by the event

The reason that the `object` type parameter is used in this event, and indeed in many other events, is
that you will often want to use a single event handler for several identical events generated by different
objects and still tell which object generated the event.

To explain and illustrate this, I'll extend the last example a little.

Try It Out   Using a Multipurpose Event Handler

1. Create a new console application called `Ch13Ex03` in the directory `C:\BegVCSharp\Chapter13`.

2. Copy the code across for `Program.cs`, `Connection.cs`, and `Display.cs` from `Ch13Ex02`, making sure that you change the namespaces in each file from `Ch13Ex02` to `Ch13Ex03`.

3. Add a new class, `MessageArrivedEventArgs`, stored in `MessageArrivedEventArgs.cs`:

```csharp
namespace Ch13Ex03
{
    public class MessageArrivedEventArgs : EventArgs
    {
        private string message;

        public string Message
        {
            get
            {
                return message;
            }
        }

        public MessageArrivedEventArgs()
        {
            message = "No message sent.";
        }

        public MessageArrivedEventArgs(string newMessage)
        {
            message = newMessage;
        }
    }
}
```

4. Modify `Connection.cs` as follows:

```csharp
namespace Ch13Ex03
{
    public delegate void MessageHandler(Connection source,
                                        MessageArrivedEventArgs e);

    public class Connection
    {
        public event MessageHandler MessageArrived;

        private string name;

        public string Name
        {
            get
            {
```

```
            return name;
        }
        set
        {
            name = value;
        }
    }

    ...

    private void CheckForMessage(object source, EventArgs e)
    {
        Console.WriteLine("Checking for new messages.");
        if ((random.Next(9) == 0) && (MessageArrived != null))
        {
            MessageArrived(this, new MessageArrivedEventArgs("Hello Mum!"));
        }
    }

    ...

    }
}
```

5. Modify `Display.cs` as follows:

```
    public void DisplayMessage(Connection source, MessageArrivedEventArgs e)
    {
        Console.WriteLine("Message arrived from: {0}", source.Name);
        Console.WriteLine("Message Text: {0}", e.Message);
    }
```

6. Modify `Program.cs` as follows:

```
    static void Main(string[] args)
    {
        Connection myConnection1 = new Connection();
        myConnection1.Name = "First connection.";
        Connection myConnection2 = new Connection();
        myConnection2.Name = "Second connection.";
        Display myDisplay = new Display();
        myConnection1.MessageArrived +=
                    new MessageHandler(myDisplay.DisplayMessage);
        myConnection2.MessageArrived +=
                    new MessageHandler(myDisplay.DisplayMessage);
        myConnection1.Connect();
        myConnection2.Connect();
        Console.ReadKey();
    }
```

7. Run the application. The result, after a short period, is shown in Figure 13-7.

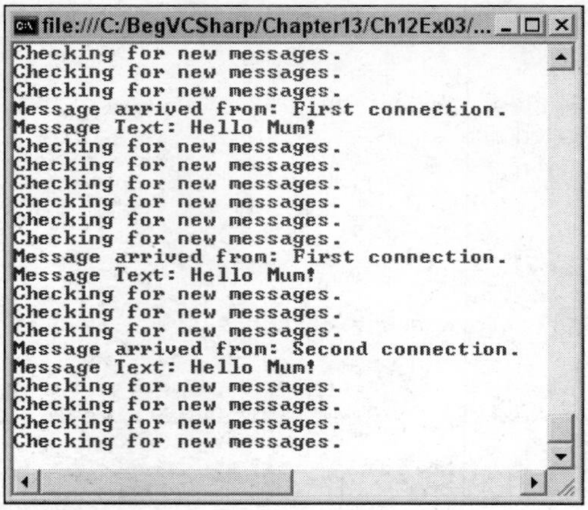

Figure 13-7

How It Works

By sending a reference to the object that raises an event as one of the event handler parameters you can customize the response of the handler to individual objects. The reference gives you access to the source object, including its properties.

By sending parameters that are contained in a class that inherits from `System.EventArgs` (as `ElapsedEventArgs` does), you can supply whatever additional information necessary as parameters (such as the `Message` parameter on the `MessageArrivedEventArgs` class).

In addition, these parameters will benefit from polymorphism. You could define a handler for the `MessageArrived` event such as

```
public void DisplayMessage(object source, EventArgs e)
{
    Console.WriteLine("Message arrived from: {0}",
                      ((Connection)source).Name);
    Console.WriteLine("Message Text: {0}",
                      ((MessageArrivedEventArgs)e).Message);
}
```

and modify the delegate definition in `Connection.cs` as follows:

```
public delegate void MessageHandler(object source, EventArgs e);
```

The application will execute exactly as it did before, but you have made the `DisplayMessage()` function more versatile (in theory at least — more implementation would be needed to make this production quality). This same handler could work with other events, such as the `Timer.Elapsed`, although you'd have to modify the internals of the handler a bit more such that the parameters sent when this event is raised are handled properly (casting them to `Connection` and `MessageArrivedEventArgs` objects in this way will cause an exception; you should use the `as` operator instead and check for `null` values).

Return Values and Event Handlers

All the event handlers you've seen so far have had a return type of void. It is possible to provide a return type for an event, but this can lead to problems. This is because a given event may result in several event handlers being called. If all of these handlers return a value, this leaves you in some doubt as to which value was actually returned.

The system deals with this by only allowing you access to the last value returned by an event handler. This will be the value returned by the last event handler to subscribe to an event.

Perhaps this functionality might be of use in some situations, although I can't think of one off the top of my head. I'd recommend using void type event handlers, as well as avoiding out type parameters.

Anonymous Methods

One more new capability in C# 2.0 is the ability to use *anonymous methods* as delegates. An anonymous method is one that doesn't actually exist as a method in the traditional sense, that is, it isn't a method on any particular class. Instead, an anonymous method is created purely for use as a target for a delegate.

To create a delegate that targets an anonymous method, you need the following code:

```
delegate(parameters)
{
    // Anonymous method code.
};
```

Here, parameters is a list of parameters matching the delegate type you are instantiating, as used by the anonymous method code, for example:

```
delegate(Connection source, MessageArrivedEventArgs e)
{
    // Anonymous method code matching MessageHandler event in Ch13Ex03.
};
```

So, you could use this code to completely bypass the Display, DisplayMessage() method in Ch13Ex03:

```
        myConnection1.MessageArrived +=
            delegate(Connection source, MessageArrivedEventArgs e)
        {
            Console.WriteLine("Message arrived from: {0}", source.Name);
            Console.WriteLine("Message Text: {0}", e.Message);
        };
```

An interesting point to note concerning anonymous methods is that they are effectively local to the code block that contains them, and they have access to local variables in this scope. If you use such a variable it becomes an *outer* variable. Outer variables are not disposed of when they go out of scope like other local variables are; instead, they live on until the anonymous methods that use them are destroyed. This may be some time later than you expect and is definitely something to be careful about!

Expanding and Using CardLib

Now that you've had a look at defining and using events, you can use them to Ch13CardLib. The event you'll add to your library will be generated when the last Card object in a Deck object is obtained using GetCard and will be called LastCardDrawn. This event will allow subscribers to reshuffle the deck automatically, cutting down on the processing necessary by a client. The delegate defined for this event (LastCardDrawnHandler) needs to supply a reference to the Deck object such that the Shuffle() method will be accessible from wherever the handler is. Add the following code to Deck.cs:

```
namespace Ch13CardLib
{
    public delegate void LastCardDrawnHandler(Deck currentDeck);
```

The code to define the event and raise it is simply:

```
    public event LastCardDrawnHandler LastCardDrawn;

    public Card GetCard(int cardNum)
    {
        if (cardNum >= 0 && cardNum <= 51)
        {
            if ((cardNum == 51) && (LastCardDrawn != null))
                LastCardDrawn(this);
            return cards[cardNum];
        }
        else
            throw new CardOutOfRangeException((Cards)cards.Clone());
    }
```

This is all the code required to add the event to the Deck class definition. Now you just need to use it.

A Card Game Client for CardLib

After spending all this time developing the CardLib library, it would be a shame not to use it. Before finishing this section on OOP in C# and the .NET Framework, it's time to have a little fun and write the basics of a card game application that uses the familiar playing card classes.

As in previous chapters, you'll add a client console application to the Ch13CardLib solution, add a reference to the Ch13CardLib project, and make it the startup project. This application will be called Ch13CardClient.

To start with, you'll create a new class called Player in a new file in Ch13CardClient, Player.cs. This class will contain a private Cards field called hand, a private string field called name, and two read-only properties: Name and PlayHand. These properties simply expose the private fields. Note that even though the PlayHand property is read-only, you will have write access to the reference to the hand field returned, allowing you to modify the cards in the player's hand.

You'll also hide the default constructor by making it private, and supply a public nondefault constructor that accepts an initial value for the Name property of Player instances.

Finally, you'll provide a `bool` type method called `HasWon()`. This will return `true` if all the cards in the player's hand are of the same suit (a simple winning condition, but that doesn't matter too much).

The code for `Player.cs` is as follows:

```csharp
using System;
using System.Collections.Generic;
using System.Text;
using Ch13CardLib;

namespace Ch13CardClient
{
    public class Player
    {
        private Cards hand;
        private string name;
        public string Name
        {
            get
            {
                return name;
            }
        }

        public Cards PlayHand
        {
            get
            {
                return hand;
            }
        }

        private Player()
        {
        }

        public Player(string newName)
        {
            name = newName;
            hand = new Cards();
        }

        public bool HasWon()
        {
            bool won = true;
            Suit match = hand[0].suit;
            for (int i = 1; i < hand.Count; i++)
            {
                won &= hand[i].suit == match;
            }
            return won;
        }
    }
}
```

Next, you define a class that will handle the card game itself, called `Game`. This class is found in the file `Game.cs` of the `Ch13CardClient` project.

This class has four private member fields:

- ❑ `playDeck`: A `Deck` type variable containing the deck of cards to use
- ❑ `currentCard`: An `int` value used as a pointer to the next card in the deck to draw
- ❑ `players`: An array of `Player` objects representing the players of the game
- ❑ `discardedCards`: A `Cards` collection for the cards that have been discarded by players but not shuffled back into the deck

The default constructor for the class initializes and shuffles the `Deck` stored in `playDeck`, sets the `currentCard` pointer variable to 0 (the first card in `playDeck`), and wires up an event handler called `Reshuffle()` to the `playDeck.LastCardDrawn` event. This handler simply shuffles the deck, initializes the `discardedCards` collection, and resets `currentCard` to 0, ready to read cards from the new deck.

The `Game` class also contains two utility methods, `SetPlayers()` for setting the players for the game (as an array of `Player` objects) and `DealHands()` for dealing hands to the players (7 cards each). The number of players allowed is restricted from 2 to 7 in order to make sure that there are enough cards to go around.

Finally, there is a `PlayGame()` method that contains the game logic itself. You'll come back to this function shortly, after you've looked at the code in `Program.cs`. The rest of the code in `Game.cs` is as follows:

```
using System;
using System.Collections.Generic;
using System.Text;
using Ch13CardLib;

namespace Ch13CardClient
{
    public class Game
    {
        private int currentCard;
        private Deck playDeck;
        private Player[] players;
        private Cards discardedCards;

        public Game()
        {
            currentCard = 0;
            playDeck = new Deck(true);
            playDeck.LastCardDrawn += new LastCardDrawnHandler(Reshuffle);
            playDeck.Shuffle();
            discardedCards = new Cards();
        }

        private void Reshuffle(Deck currentDeck)
        {
```

```
            Console.WriteLine("Discarded cards reshuffled into deck.");
            currentDeck.Shuffle();
            discardedCards.Clear();
            currentCard = 0;
        }

        public void SetPlayers(Player[] newPlayers)
        {
            if (newPlayers.Length > 7)
                throw new ArgumentException("A maximum of 7 players may play this" +
                                            " game.");

            if (newPlayers.Length < 2)
                throw new ArgumentException("A minimum of 2 players may play this" +
                                            " game.");

            players = newPlayers;
        }

        private void DealHands()
        {
            for (int p = 0; p < players.Length; p++)
            {
                for (int c = 0; c < 7; c++)
                {
                    players[p].PlayHand.Add(playDeck.GetCard(currentCard++));
                }
            }
        }

        public int PlayGame()
        {
            // Code to follow.
        }
    }
}
```

Program.cs contains the Main() function, which will initialize and run the game. This function performs the following steps:

- ❑ An introduction is displayed.

- ❑ The user is prompted for a number of players between 2 and 7.

- ❑ An array of Player objects is set up accordingly.

- ❑ Each player is prompted for a name, used to initialize one Player object in the array.

- ❑ A Game object is created, and players assigned using the SetPlayers() method.

- ❑ The game is started using the PlayGame() method.

- ❑ The int return value of PlayGame() is used to display a winning message (the value returned is the index of the winning player in the array of Player objects).

The code for this (commented for clarity) is shown here:

```
static void Main(string[] args)
{
   // Display introduction.
   Console.WriteLine("KarliCards: a new and exciting card game.");
   Console.WriteLine("To win you must have 7 cards of the same suit in" +
                     " your hand.");
   Console.WriteLine();

   // Prompt for number of players.
   bool inputOK = false;
   int choice = -1;
   do
   {
      Console.WriteLine("How many players (2-7)?");
      string input = Console.ReadLine();
      try
      {
         // Attempt to convert input into a valid number of players.
         choice = Convert.ToInt32(input);
         if ((choice >= 2) && (choice <= 7))
            inputOK = true;
      }
      catch
      {
         // Ignore failed conversions, just continue prompting.
      }
   } while (inputOK == false);

   // Initialize array of Player objects.
   Player[] players = new Player[choice];

   // Get player names.
   for (int p = 0; p < players.Length; p++)
   {
      Console.WriteLine("Player {0}, enter your name:", p + 1);
      string playerName = Console.ReadLine();
      players[p] = new Player(playerName);
   }

   // Start game.
   Game newGame = new Game();
   newGame.SetPlayers(players);
   int whoWon = newGame.PlayGame();

   // Display winning player.
   Console.WriteLine("{0} has won the game!", players[whoWon].Name);
}
```

Next, you come to PlayGame(), the main body of the application. Now, I'm not going to go into a huge amount of detail about this method, but I have filled it with comments to make it a bit more comprehensible. In actual fact, none of the code is that complicated, there's just quite a bit of it.

Play proceeds with each player viewing cards and an upturned card on the table. They may either pick up this card or draw a new one from the deck. After drawing a card each player must discard one, replacing the card on the table with another one if it has been picked up, or placing the discarded card on top of the one on the table (also adding the discarded card to the `discardedCards` collection).

One key point to bear in mind when digesting this code is the way in which the `Card` objects are manipulated. The reason that these objects are defined as reference types rather than as value types (using a struct) should now become clear. A given `Card` object may appear to exist in several places at once, because references can be held by the `Deck` object, the `hand` fields of the `Player` objects, the `discardedCards` collection, and the `playCard` object (the card currently on the table). This makes it easy to keep track of the cards and is used in particular in the code that draws a new card from the deck. The card is only accepted if it isn't in any player's hand or in the `discardedCards` collection.

The code is:

```
public int PlayGame()
{
    // Only play if players exist.
    if (players == null)
        return -1;

    // Deal initial hands.
    DealHands();

    // Initialize game vars, including an initial card to place on the
    // table: playCard.
    bool GameWon = false;
    int currentPlayer;
    Card playCard = playDeck.GetCard(currentCard++);
    discardedCards.Add(playCard);

    // Main game loop, continues until GameWon == true.
    do
    {
        // Loop through players in each game round.
        for (currentPlayer = 0; currentPlayer < players.Length;
            currentPlayer++)
        {
            // Write out current player, player hand, and the card on the
            // table.
            Console.WriteLine("{0}'s turn.", players[currentPlayer].Name);
            Console.WriteLine("Current hand:");
            foreach (Card card in players[currentPlayer].PlayHand)
            {
                Console.WriteLine(card);
            }
            Console.WriteLine("Card in play: {0}", playCard);

            // Prompt player to pick up card on table or draw a new one.
            bool inputOK = false;
            do
            {
                Console.WriteLine("Press T to take card in play or D to " +
```

```
                                       "draw:");
        string input = Console.ReadLine();
        if (input.ToLower() == "t")
        {
            // Add card from table to player hand.
            Console.WriteLine("Drawn: {0}", playCard);
            // Remove from discarded cards if possible (if deck
            // is reshuffled it won't be there any more)
            if (discardedCards.Contains(playCard))
            {
                discardedCards.Remove(playCard);
            }
            players[currentPlayer].PlayHand.Add(playCard);
            inputOK = true;
        }
        if (input.ToLower() == "d")
        {
            // Add new card from deck to player hand.
            Card newCard;
            // Only add card if it isn't already in a player hand
            // or in the discard pile
            bool cardIsAvailable;
            do
            {
                newCard = playDeck.GetCard(currentCard++);
                // Check if card is in discard pile
                cardIsAvailable = !discardedCards.Contains(newCard);
                if (cardIsAvailable)
                {
                    // Loop through all player hands to see if newCard is
                    // already in a hand.
                    foreach (Player testPlayer in players)
                    {
                        if (testPlayer.PlayHand.Contains(newCard))
                        {
                            cardIsAvailable = false;
                            break;
                        }
                    }
                }
            } while (!cardIsAvailable);
            // Add the card found to player hand.
            Console.WriteLine("Drawn: {0}", newCard);
            players[currentPlayer].PlayHand.Add(newCard);
            inputOK = true;
        }
    } while (inputOK == false);

    // Display new hand with cards numbered.
    Console.WriteLine("New hand:");
    for (int i = 0; i < players[currentPlayer].PlayHand.Count; i++)
    {
        Console.WriteLine("{0}: {1}", i + 1,
                          players[currentPlayer].PlayHand[i]);
```

```
        }

        // Prompt player for a card to discard.
        inputOK = false;
        int choice = -1;
        do
        {
            Console.WriteLine("Choose card to discard:");
            string input = Console.ReadLine();
            try
            {
                // Attempt to convert input into a valid card number.
                choice = Convert.ToInt32(input);
                if ((choice > 0) && (choice <= 8))
                    inputOK = true;
            }
            catch
            {
                // Ignore failed conversions, just continue prompting.
            }
        } while (inputOK == false);

        // Place reference to removed card in playCard (place the card
        // on the table), then remove card from player hand and add
        // to discarded card pile.
        playCard = players[currentPlayer].PlayHand[choice - 1];
        players[currentPlayer].PlayHand.RemoveAt(choice - 1);
        discardedCards.Add(playCard);
        Console.WriteLine("Discarding: {0}", playCard);

        // Space out text for players
        Console.WriteLine();

        // Check to see if player has won the game, and exit the player
        // loop if so.
        GameWon = players[currentPlayer].HasWon();
        if (GameWon == true)
            break;
    }
} while (GameWon == false);

// End game, noting the winning player.
return currentPlayer;
}
```

Have fun playing the game—and make sure that you spend some time going through it in detail. One thing to try is to put a breakpoint in the Reshuffle() method and play the game with seven players. If you keep drawing cards and discarding the cards drawn it won't take long for reshuffles to occur, as with seven players there are only three cards spare. This way, you can prove to yourself that things are working properly by noting the three cards when they reappear.

Summary

In this chapter, you saw the final batch of techniques required to complete your knowledge of the C# language. You looked at:

- ❏ The qualification of type names in namespaces (in more detail than you saw in earlier chapters).

- ❏ How to use the :: operator and global keyword to ensure references to types are references to the types you want.

- ❏ How to implement your own exception objects and pass more detailed information to the exception handler.

- ❏ Using a custom exception in the code for CardLib—the card game library you've been developing in the last few chapters.

- ❏ The important topic of events and event handling. Although quite subtle, and initially difficult to get your head around, the code involved is quite simple—and you'll certainly be using event handlers a lot in the rest of the book.

- ❏ Some simple illustrative examples of events and how to handle them.

You also made one final addition to the CardLib library. Once complete, you used this library to create a simple card game application. This application should serve as a demonstration of pretty much all the techniques you've looked at in the first part of this book.

With this chapter, you have completed not only a complete description of OOP as applied to C# programming but also a complete description of the C# language. From this point on, you will be applying this knowledge to more complex scenarios, such as creating Windows and Web applications, as well as making more use of the .NET Framework.

Exercises

1. Show the code for an event handler that uses the general-purpose (object sender, EventArgs e) syntax that will accept either the Timer.Elapsed event or the Connection .MessageArrived event from the code earlier in this chapter. The handler should output a string specifying which type of event has been received, along with the Message property of the MessageArrivedEventArgs parameter or the SignalTime property of the ElapsedEventArgs parameter, depending on which event occurs.

2. Modify the card game example to check for the more interesting winning condition of the popular card game rummy. This means that a player wins the game if their hand contains two "sets" of cards, one of which consists of three cards and one of which consists of four cards. A set is defined as either a sequence of cards of the same suit (such as 3H, 4H, 5H, 6H) or several cards of the same rank (such as 2H, 2D, 2S).

Part II
Windows Programming

Chapter 14: Basic Windows Programming

Chapter 15: Advanced Windows Form Features

Chapter 16: Using Common Dialogs

Chapter 17: Deploying Windows Applications

Basic Windows Programming

In recent years, Visual Basic has won great acclaim for granting programmers the tools for creating highly detailed user interfaces via an intuitive form designer, along with an easy-to-learn programming language that together produced probably the best environment out there for Rapid Application Development. One of the advantages offered by Rapid Application Development (RAD) tool such as Visual Basic is that it provided access to a number of prefabricated controls that could be used to quickly build the user interface for an application.

At the heart of the development of most Visual Basic Windows applications is the form designer. You create a user interface by dragging and dropping controls from a Toolbox to your form, placing them where you want them to be when you run the program, double-clicking the control adds a handler for that control. The controls provided by Microsoft along with further custom controls that could be bought at reasonable prices have supplied programmers with an unprecedented pool of reusable, thoroughly tested code that is no more than a mouse click away. Such application development is now available to C# developers through Visual Studio.

In this chapter, you work with Windows Forms, and use some of the many controls that ship with Visual Studio. These controls cover a wide range of functionality, and through the design capabilities of Visual Studio, developing user interfaces and handling user interaction is very straightforward — and fun! Presenting all of the controls present in Visual Studio is impossible within the scope of this book, so in this chapter you look at some of the most commonly used controls, ranging from labels and text boxes to list views and tab controls.

In this chapter you learn about:

❑   The Windows Forms designer

❑   Controls for displaying information to the user, such as the `Label` and `LinkLabel` controls

❑   Controls for triggering events, such as the `Button` control

❑   Controls that allow you to have the user of you application enter text, such as the `TextBox` control

❑ Controls that allow you to inform the user of the current state of the application and allow the user to change that state, such as the `RadioButton` and `CheckButton` controls

❑ Controls that allow you to display lists of information, such as the `ListBox` and `ListView` controls

❑ Controls that allow you to group other controls together, such as the `TabControl` and `Groupbox`

Controls

You may not notice it, but when you work with Windows Forms, you are working with the `System.Windows.Forms` namespace. This namespace is included in the `using` directives in one of the files that holds the `Form` class. Most controls in .NET derive from the `System.Windows.Forms.Control` class. This class defines the basic functionality of the controls, which is why many properties and events in the controls you'll see are identical. Many of these classes are themselves base classes for other controls, as is the case with the `Label` and `TextBoxBase` classes in Figure 14-1.

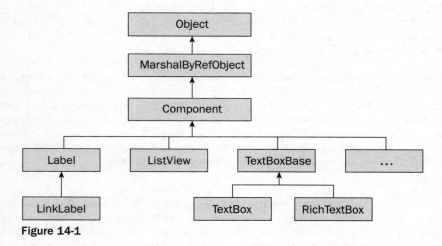

Figure 14-1

Some controls, called custom or user controls, derive from another class: `System.Windows.Forms.UserControl`. *This class is itself derived from the* `Control` *class and provides the functionality you need to create controls. Chapter 11 covers this class. Incidentally, controls used for designing Web user interfaces derive from yet another class,* `System.Web.UI.Control`.

Properties

All controls have a number of properties that are used to manipulate the behavior of the control. The base class of most controls, `System.Windows.Forms.Control`, has a number of properties that other controls either inherit directly or override to provide some kind of custom behavior.

The following table shows some of the most common properties of the `Control` class. These properties will be present in most of the controls you visit in this chapter, and they will, therefore, not be explained in detail again unless their behavior changes for the control in question. Note that this table is not meant to be exhaustive; if you want to see all of the properties in the class, please refer to the .NET Framework SDK documentation.

Name	Description
Anchor	Using this property, you can specify how the control behaves when its container is resized. See below for a detailed explanation of this property.
BackColor	The background color of a control.
Bottom	By setting this property, you specify the distance from the top of the window to the bottom of the control. This is not the same as specifying the height of the control.
Dock	This allows you to make a control dock to the edges of a window. See below for a more detailed explanation of this property.
Enabled	Setting `Enabled` to `true` usually means that the control can receive input from the user. Setting `Enabled` to `false` usually means that it cannot.
ForeColor	The foreground color of the control.
Height	The distance from the top to the bottom of the control.
Left	The left edge of the control relative to the left edge of the window.
Name	The name of the control. This name can be used to reference the control in code.
Parent	The parent of the control.
Right	The right edge of the control relative to the left edge of the window.
TabIndex	The number the control has in the tab order of its container.
TabStop	Specifies whether the control can be accessed by the Tab key.
Tag	This value is usually not used by the control itself and is there for you to store information about the control on the control itself. When this property is assigned a value through the Windows Form designer, you can only assign a string to it.
Text	This holds the text that is associated with this control.
Top	The top edge of the control relative to the top of the window.
Visible	Specifies whether or not the control is visible at runtime.
Width	The width of the control.

If you have experience with Visual Basic, you may notice that in .NET, the Text *property is used to set the text that is displayed, rather than a* Caption *property. You will find that all intrinsic .NET controls use the name* Text *to describe the main text for a control. Before .NET,* Caption *and* Text *were used interchangeably between different controls.*

Anchoring, Docking, and Snapping Controls

With Visual Studio 2005 the form designer default has been changed from using a gridlike surface on which you could lay out your controls to a clean surface that uses snap-lines to position the controls. You can change between the two design styles by choosing Options on the Tools menu. Select the Windows Forms Designer node in the tree to the left and set the Layout Mode. What is best is very much a question of personal preference, but in the following Try It Out, you are going to use the default.

Try It Out   **Using Snap-Lines**

Follow these steps to try and work with snap-lines in the Windows Forms designer:

1. Create a new Windows Forms Application, and name it SnapLines.

2. Drag a single button control from the Toolbox to the middle of the form.

3. Drag the button toward the upper-left corner of the form. Notice that when you are close to the edge of the form, lines appear from the left and top of the form and the controls snap into position. You can move the control beyond the snap-lines or leave it in position. Figure 14-2 shows the snap-lines that are displayed by Visual Studio when the button is moved to the top-left corner.

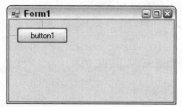

Figure 14-2

4. Move the button back to the center of the form and drag another button from the Toolbox onto the form. Move it under the existing button and notice that snap-lines appear as you move the button below the existing button. These snap-lines are there to allow you to line up the controls so that they are positioned directly above or exactly at the same height as another. If you move the new button up toward the existing button, you will see another snap-line that lets you position the buttons with a preset space between them. Figure 14-3 shows the two buttons as they are being moved close to each other.

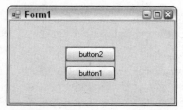

Figure 14-3

5. Resize `button1` to make it wider than the other button. Then resize `button2` as well and notice that when `button2` is the same width as `button1` a snap-line appears to let you set the width of the controls to the same value.

6. Now, add a `TextBox` to the form below the buttons and change the `Text` property of it to Hello World!

7. Add a `Label` to the form. Move the `Label` to the left of the `TextBox`. Notice that as you move the control you get the two snap-lines that let you snap to the top and bottom of the `TextBox` but between them you will see a third snap-line. This snap-line, which is shown in Figure 14-4, allows you to place the `Label` on the form so that the text of the `TextBox` and the `Label` will be at the same height.

Figure 14-4

This concludes the snap-line introduction.

Anchor and Dock Properties

These two properties are especially useful when you are designing your form. Ensuring that a window doesn't become a mess to look at if the user decides to resize the window is far from trivial, and previously numerous lines of code had to be written to achieve this. Many programs solve the problem by simply disallowing the window from being resized, which is clearly the easiest way around the problem, but not always the best. The `Anchor` and `Dock` properties that have been introduced with .NET let you solve this problem without writing a single line of code.

The `Anchor` property is used to specify how the control behaves when a user resizes the window. You can specify that the control should resize itself, anchoring itself in proportion to its own edges, or stay the same size, anchoring its position relative to the window's edges.

The `Dock` property is used to specify that a control should dock to an edge of its container. If a user resizes the window, the control will continue to be docked to the edge of the window. If, for instance, you specify that a control should dock with the bottom of its container, the control will resize and/or move itself to always occupy the bottom part of the window, no matter how the window is resized.

See the `TextBox` example later in this chapter for the exact use of the `Anchor` property.

Events

In Chapter 13, you saw what events are and how to use them. This section covers particular kinds of events, specifically the events generated by Windows Forms controls. These events are usually associated with the actions of the user. For example, when the user clicks or presses a button, that button generates an event in which it says what just happened to it. Handling the event is the means by which the programmer can provide some functionality for that button.

The `Control` class defines a number of events that are common to the controls you use in this chapter. The following table describes a number of these events. Once again, this is just a selection of the most common events; if you need to see the entire list, please refer to the .NET Framework SDK documentation.

Name	Description
Click	Occurs when a control is clicked. In some cases, this event will also occur when a user presses the Enter key.
DoubleClick	Occurs when a control is double-clicked. Handling the `Click` event on some controls, such as the `Button` control, will mean that the `DoubleClick` event can never be called.
DragDrop	Occurs when a drag-and-drop operation is completed — in other words, when an object has been dragged over the control, and the user releases the mouse button.
DragEnter	Occurs when an object being dragged enters the bounds of the control.
DragLeave	Occurs when an object being dragged leaves the bounds of the control.
DragOver	Occurs when an object has been dragged over the control.
KeyDown	Occurs when a key is pressed while the control has focus. This event always occurs before `KeyPress` and `KeyUp`.
KeyPress	Occurs when a key is pressed while a control has focus. This event always occurs after `KeyDown` and before `KeyUp`. The difference between `KeyDown` and `KeyPress` is that `KeyDown` passes the keyboard code of the key that has been pressed, while `KeyPress` passes the corresponding `char` value for the key.
KeyUp	Occurs when a key is released while a control has focus. This event always occurs after `KeyDown` and `KeyPress`.
GotFocus	Occurs when a control receives focus. Do not use this event to perform validation of controls. Use `Validating` and `Validated` instead.
LostFocus	Occurs when a control loses focus. Do not use this event to perform validation of controls. Use `Validating` and `Validated` instead.
MouseDown	Occurs when the mouse pointer is over a control and a mouse button is pressed. This is not the same as a `Click` event because `MouseDown` occurs as soon as the button is pressed and *before* it is released.
MouseMove	Occurs continually as the mouse travels over the control.

Name	Description
MouseUp	Occurs when the mouse pointer is over a control and a mouse button is released.
Paint	Occurs when the control is drawn.
Validated	This event is fired when a control with the CausesValidation property set to true is about to receive focus. It fires after the Validating event finishes and indicates that validation is complete.
Validating	Fires when a control with the CausesValidation property set to true is about to receive focus. Note that the control which is to be validated is the control which is losing focus, not the one that is receiving it.

You will see many of these events in the examples in the rest of the chapter. All the examples will follow the same format, where you first create the form's visual appearance, choosing and positioning controls, and so on, before moving on to adding the event handlers — this is where the main work of the examples takes place.

There are three basic ways of going about handling a particular event. The first is to double-click a control. You will be taken to the event handler for the control's default event — this event is different for different controls. If that's the event you want, then you're fine. If you want a different event from the default, there are two possible ways of proceeding.

One way is to use the Events list in the Properties window, which is displayed when you click the lightning bolt button as shown in Figure 14-5.

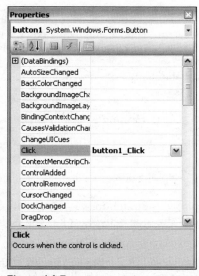

Figure 14-5

The grayed event is the control's default event. To add a handler for a particular event, double-click on that event in the Events list, and the code to subscribe the control to the event will be generated, along with the method signature to handle the event. Alternatively, you can type a name for the method to handle the particular event next to that event in the Events list, and when you press the Enter key, the event handler will be generated with your chosen name.

Another option is to add the code to subscribe to the event yourself — you do this often in this and the next chapter by adding the code to the form's constructor after the `InitializeComponent()` call. Of course, you still have to add the method signature to handle the event, and this method has the drawback that you need to know the exact method signature for that event.

Note that each of these two options requires two steps — subscription to the event and the correct signature for the method handler. If you double-click a control and try to handle another event by editing the method signature of the default event for the event that you actually want handled, you will fail — you also need to alter the event subscription code in `InitializeComponent()`, and so this *cheating* method is not really a quick way to handle particular events.

You are now ready to start looking at the controls themselves, and you start with one that you've undoubtedly used countless times when working with Windows applications: the `Button` control.

The Button Control

When you think of a button, you are probably thinking of a rectangular button that can be clicked to perform some task. However, the .NET Framework provides a class derived from `Control` — `System.Windows.Forms.ButtonBase` — that implements the basic functionality needed in button controls, so any programmer can derive from this class and create his or her custom button controls.

The `System.Windows.Forms` namespace provides three controls that derive from `ButtonBase` — `Button`, `CheckBox`, and `RadioButton`. This section focuses on the `Button` control (which is the standard, well-known rectangular button), and I'll cover the other two later in this chapter.

The `Button` control exists on just about any Windows dialog you can think of. A button is primarily used to perform three kinds of tasks:

❑   To close a dialog with a state (for example, `OK` and `Cancel` buttons)

❑   To perform an action on data entered on a dialog (for example clicking `Search` after entering some search criteria)

❑   To open another dialog or application (for example, `Help` buttons)

Working with the button control is very straightforward. It usually consists of adding the control to your form and double-clicking it to add the code to the `Click` event, which will probably be enough for most applications you work on.

Let's look at some of the commonly used properties and events of the control. This will give you an idea what can be done with it. After that, you create a small example that demonstrates some of the basic properties and events of a button.

Button Properties

The following table lists the most commonly used properties of the Button class, even if technically they are defined in the ButtonBase base class. Only the most commonly used properties are explained here. Please refer to the .NET Framework SDK documentation for a complete listing.

Name	Description
FlatStyle	The style of the button can be changed with this property. If you set the style to Popup, the button will appear flat until the user moves the mouse pointer over it. When that happens, the button pops up to a 3-D look.
Enabled	I'll mention this here even though it is derived from Control, because it's a very important property for a button. Setting the Enabled property to false means that the button becomes grayed out and nothing happens when you click it.
Image	Allows you to specify an image (bitmap, icon, and so on) that will be displayed on the button.
ImageAlign	With this property, you can set where the image on the button appears.

Button Events

By far the most used event of a button is the Click event. This event happens whenever a user clicks the button, which means pressing the left mouse button and releasing it while the pointer is over the button. This means that if you left-click the button and then draw the mouse away from the button before releasing it, the Click event will not be raised. Also, the Click event is raised when the button has focus and the user presses the Enter key. If you have a button on a form, you should always handle this event.

In the following Try It Out, you create a dialog with three buttons. Two of the buttons will change the language used from English to Danish and back. (Feel free to use whatever language you prefer.) The last button closes the dialog.

Try It Out ButtonTest

Follow these steps to create a small Windows application that uses three buttons to change the text in the caption of the dialog:

1. Create a new Windows application called ButtonTest in the directory C:\BegVCSharp\ Chapter14.

2. Pin the Toolbox down by clicking the pin icon next to the x in the top-right corner of the window, and double-click the Button control three times. Then move the buttons and resize the form as shown in Figure 14-6.

3. Right-click a button and select Properties. Then change the name of each button as indicated in the picture above by selecting the (Name) edit field in the Properties window and typing the relevant text.

Figure 14-6

4. Change the `Text` property of each button to be the same as the name, but omit the `button` pre-fix for the `Text` property value.

5. You want to display a flag in front of the text to make it clear what you are talking about. Select the `English` button and find the `Image` property. Click (. . .) to the right of it to bring up a dia-log where you can add images to the resource file of the form. Click the Import button and browse to the icons. The icons you want to display are included in the project ButtonTest you can download from the Wrox homepage. Select the icon `flguk.ico` and `flgDen.ico`.

6. Select FLGUK and click OK. Then select `buttonDanish`, click the (. . .) on the Image property and choose FLGDK before clicking OK.

7. You notice at this point that the button text and icon are placed on top of each other, so you need to change the alignment of the icon. For both the English and Danish buttons, change the `ImageAlign` property to `MiddleLeft`.

8. At this point, you may want to adjust the width of the buttons so that the text doesn't start right where the images end. Do this by selecting each of the buttons and pulling the notch on the right edge of the button.

9. Finally, click on the form and change the `Text` property to `Do you speak English?`

That's it for the user interface of your dialog. You should now have something that looks like Figure 14-7.

Figure 14-7

Now you are ready to add the event handlers to the dialog. Double-click the `English` button. This will take you directly to the event handler for the control's default event — the `Click` event is the default event for the button and so that is the handler created.

Adding the Event Handlers

Double-click the English `button` and add the following code to the event handler:

```
private void buttonEnglish_Click(object sender, EventArgs e)
{
    this.Text = "Do you speak English?";
}
```

When Visual Studio creates a method to handle such an event, the method name is a concatenation of the name of the control, followed by an underscore and the name of the event that is handled.

For the Click event, the first parameter, object sender, will hold the control that was clicked. In this example, this will always be the control indicated by the name of the method, but in other cases many controls may use the same method to handle an event, and in those cases you can find out exactly which control is calling by checking this value. The text box example later in this chapter demonstrates how to use a single method for multiple controls. The other parameter, System.EventArgs e, holds information about what actually happened. In this case, you won't need any of that information.

Return to the design view and double-click the Danish button, and you will be taken to the event handler for that button. Here is the code:

```
private void buttonDanish_Click(object sender, EventArgs e)
{
   this.Text = "Taler du dansk?";
}
```

This method is identical to btnEnglish_Click, except that the text is in Danish. Finally, you add the event handler for the OK button in the same way as you've done twice now. The code is a little different though:

```
private void buttonOK_Click(object sender, EventArgs e)
{
   Application.Exit();
}
```

With this you exit the application and, with it, this first example. Compile it, run it and press a few of the buttons. You will get output similar to what is displayed in Figure 14-8.

Figure 14-8

The Label and LinkLabel Controls

The Label control is probably the most used control of them all. Look at any Windows application and you see a Label on just about every dialog you find. The Label is a simple control with one purpose only — to display text on the form.

The .NET Framework includes two label controls that present themselves in two distinct ways:

❑   Label, the standard Windows label

❑   LinkLabel, a label similar to the standard one (and derived from it), but that presents itself as an Internet link (a hyperlink)

Figure 14-9 shows one of each type of Label has been dragged to a form to illustrate the difference in appearance between the two.

Figure 14-9

And that's it for most uses of the Label control. Usually, you need to add no event handling code for a standard Label, although it does support events like all controls. In the case of the LinkLabel, however, some extra code is needed to allow users clicking it to go to the target of the LinkLabel.

You can set a surprising number of properties for the Label control. Most of these are derived from Control, but some are new. The following table lists the most common properties. Unless stated otherwise, the properties are common to both the Label and LinkLabel controls.

Name	Description
BorderStyle	Allows you to specify the style of the border around the Label. The default is no border.
FlatStyle	Determines how the control is displayed. Setting this property to Popup will make the control appear flat until the user moves the mouse pointer over the control. At that time, the control will appear raised.
Image	This property allows you to specify a single image (bitmap, icon, and so on) to be displayed in the label.
ImageAlign	Where in the Label the image is shown.
LinkArea	(LinkLabel only) The range in the text that should be displayed as a link.
LinkColor	(LinkLabel only) The color of the link.
Links	(LinkLabel only) It is possible for a LinkLabel to contain more than one link. This property allows you to find the link you want. The control keeps track of the links displayed in the text. Not available at design time.
LinkVisited	(LinkLabel only) Setting this to true means that the link is displayed in a different color if it has been clicked.
TextAlign	Where in the control the text is shown.
VisitedLinkColor	(LinkLabel only) The color of the LinkLabel after the user has clicked it.

The TextBox Control

Text boxes should be used when you want users to enter text that you have no knowledge of at design time (for example, the user's name). The primary function of a text box is for users to enter text, but any characters can be entered, and it is quite possible to force users to enter numeric values only.

The .NET Framework comes with two basic controls to take text input from users: `TextBox` and `RichTextBox`. Both controls are derived from a base class called `TextBoxBase` which itself is derived from `Control`.

`TextBoxBase` provides the base functionality for text manipulation in a text box, such as selecting text, cutting to and pasting from the Clipboard, and a wide range of events. Right now you will not focus so much on what is derived from where, but instead look at the simpler of the two controls first — `TextBox`. You build one example that demonstrates the `TextBox` properties and build on that to demonstrate the `RichTextBox` control later.

TextBox Properties

As was the case with the controls earlier in this chapter, there are simply too many properties to describe them all, and so this listing includes only the most common ones.

Name	Description
CausesValidation	When a control with this property set to `true` is about to receive focus, two events are fired: `Validating` and `Validated`. You can handle these events in order to validate data in the control that is losing focus. This may cause the control never to receive focus. The related events are discussed below.
CharacterCasing	A value indicating if the `TextBox` changes the case of the text entered. The possible values are `Lower`: All text entered is converted lowercase. `Normal`: No changes are made to the text. `Upper`: All text entered is converted to uppercase.
MaxLength	A value that specifies the maximum length in characters of any text, entered into the `TextBox`. Set this value to zero if the maximum limit is limited only by available memory.
Multiline	Indicates if this is a multiline control, which means that it is able to show multiple lines of text. When `Multiline` property is set to `true`, you'll usually want to set `WordWrap` to `true` as well.
PasswordChar	Specifies if a password character should replace the actual characters entered into a single-line `TextBox`. If the `Multiline` property is `true`, then this has no effect.
ReadOnly	A Boolean indicating if the text is read-only.
ScrollBars	Specifies if a multiline `TextBox` should display scrollbars.
SelectedText	The text that is selected in the `TextBox`.

Table continued on following page

Name	Description
SelectionLength	The number of characters selected in the text. If this value is set to be larger than the total number of characters in the text, it is reset by the control to be the total number of characters minus the value of SelectionStart.
SelectionStart	The start of the selected text in a TextBox.
WordWrap	Specifies if a multiline TextBox should automatically wrap words if a line exceeds the width of the control.

TextBox Events

Careful validation of the text in the TextBox controls on a form can make the difference between happy users and angry ones.

You have probably experienced how annoying it is when a dialog only validates its contents when you click OK. This approach to validating the data usually results in a message box being displayed informing you that the data in "TextBox number three" is incorrect. You can then continue to click OK until all the data is correct. Clearly, this is not a good approach to validating data, so what can you do instead?

The answer lies in handling the validation events a TextBox control provides. If you want to make sure that invalid characters are not entered in the text box or only values within a certain range are allowed, then you will want to indicate to the user of the control whether the value entered is valid.

The TextBox control provides these events (all of which are inherited from Control).

Name	Description
Enter Leave Validating Validated	These four events occur in the order in which they are listed here. They are known as *focus events* and are fired whenever a control's focus changes, with two exceptions. Validating and Validated are only fired if the control that receives focus has the CausesValidation property set to true. The reason why it's the receiving control that fires the event is that there are times where you do not want to validate the control, even if focus changes. An example of this is when a user clicks a Help button.
KeyDown KeyPress KeyUp	These three events are known as *key events*. They allow you to monitor and change what is entered into your controls. KeyDown and KeyUp receive the key code corresponding to the key that was pressed. This allows you to determine if special keys such as *Shift* or *Control* and *F1* were pressed. KeyPress, on the other hand, receives the character corresponding to a keyboard key. This means that the value for the letter *a* is not the same as the letter *A*. It is useful if you want to exclude a range of characters, for example, only allowing numeric values to be entered.
TextChanged	This event occurs whenever the text in the TextBox is changed, no matter what the change.

In the following Try It Out, you create a dialog on which you can enter your name, address, occupation, and age. The purpose of this example is to give you a good grounding in manipulating properties and using events, not to create something that is incredibly useful.

TextBoxTest

You build the user interface first.

1. Create a new Windows application called `TextBoxTest` in the directory `C:\BegVCSharp\Chapter14`.

2. Create the form shown below by dragging some `Label`, `TextBox`, and `Button` controls onto the design surface. Before you can resize the two `TextBox` controls `txtAddress` and `txtOutput` as shown you must set their `Multiline` property to `true`. Do this by right-clicking the controls and select `Properties`.

3. Name the controls as indicated in Figure 14-10.

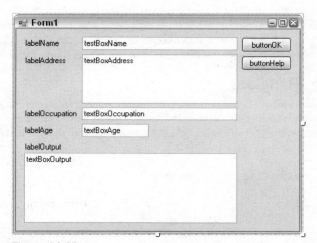

Figure 14-10

4. Set the `Text` property of each `TextBox` to an empty string, which means that they will contain nothing when the application is first run.

5. Set the `Text` property of all the other controls to the same as the name of the control, except for the prefixes that indicate the type of the control (that is, `Button`, `TextBox`, and `Label`). Set the `Text` property of the form to `TextBoxTest`.

6. Set the `Scrollbars` property of the two controls `txtOutput` and `txtAddress` to `Vertical`.

7. Set the `ReadOnly` property of the `txtOutput` control to `true`.

8. Set the `CausesValidation` property of the `btnHelp` `Button` to `false`. Remember from the discussion of the `Validating` and `Validated` events that setting this to `false` will allow users to click this `button` without having to be concerned about entering invalid data.

9. When you have sized the form to fit snugly around the controls, it is time to anchor the controls so that they behave properly when the form is resized. Let's set the Anchor property for each type of control in one go — first, select all the TextBox controls except textBoxOutput by holding down the Ctrl key while you select each TextBox in turn. Once you've selected them all, set the Anchor property to Top, Left, Right from the Properties window, and the Anchor property for each of the selected TextBox controls will be set as well. Select just the textBoxOutput control and set the Anchor property to Top, Bottom, Left, Right. Now set the Anchor property for both Button controls to Top, Right.

   The reason txtOutput is anchored rather than docked to the bottom of the form is that you want the output text area to be resized as you pull the form. If you had docked the control to the bottom of the form, it would be moved to stay at the bottom, but it would not be resized.

10. One final thing should be set. On the form, find the Size and MinimumSize properties. Your form has little meaning if it is sized to something smaller than it is now; therefore, you should set the MinimumSize property to the same as the Size property.

How It Works

The job of setting up the visual part of the form is now complete. If you run it nothing happens when you click the buttons or enter text, but if you maximize or pull in the dialog, the controls behave exactly as you want them to in a proper user interface, staying put and resizing to fill the whole of the dialog.

Adding the Event Handlers

From the design view, double-click the buttonOK button. Repeat this with the other button. As you saw in the button example earlier in this chapter, this causes event handlers for the Click event of the buttons to be created. When the OK button is clicked, you want to transfer the text in the input text boxes to the read-only output box.

Here is the code for the two Click event handlers:

```
private void buttonOK_Click(object sender, EventArgs e)
{
    // No testing for invalid values are made, as that should
    // not be necessary

    string output;

    // Concatenate the text values of the four TextBoxes.
    output = "Name: " + this.textBoxName.Text + "\r\n";
    output += "Address: " + this.textBoxAddress.Text + "\r\n";
    output += "Occupation: " + this.textBoxOccupation.Text + "\r\n";
    output += "Age: " + this.textBoxAge.Text;

    // Insert the new text.
    this.textBoxOutput.Text = output;
}

private void buttonHelp_Click(object sender, EventArgs e)
{
```

```
        // Write a short description of each TextBox in the Output TextBox.
        string output;

        output = "Name = Your name\r\n";
        output += "Address = Your address\r\n";
        output += "Occupation = Only allowed value is 'Programmer'\r\n";
        output += "Age = Your age";

        // Insert the new text.
        this.textBoxOutput.Text = output;
    }
```

In both functions, the Text property of each TextBox is used. The Text property of the textBoxAge control is used to get the value entered as the age of the person and the same property on the textBoxOutput control is used to display the concatenated text.

You insert the information the user has entered without bothering to check if it is correct. This means that you must do the checking elsewhere. In this example, there are a number of criteria to enforce to ensure that the values are correct:

❏   The name of the user cannot be empty.

❏   The age of the user must be a number greater than or equal to zero.

❏   The occupation of the user must be "Programmer" or be left empty.

❏   The address of the user cannot be empty.

From this, you can see that the check that must be done for two of the text boxes (textBoxName and textBoxAddress) is the same. You also see that you should prevent users from entering anything invalid into the Age box, and finally you must check if the user claims to be a programmer.

To prevent users from clicking OK before anything is entered, start by setting the OK button's Enabled property to false—this time you do it in the constructor of your form rather than from the Properties window. If you do set properties in the constructor, make sure not to set them until after the generated code in InitializeComponent() has been called.

```
        public Form1()
        {
            InitializeComponent();
            this.buttonOK.Enabled = false;
        }
```

Now, you create the handler for the two text boxes that must be checked to see if they are empty. You do this by subscribing to the Validating event of the text boxes. You inform the control that the event should be handled by a method named txtBoxEmpty_Validating(), so that's a single event-handling method for two different controls.

You also need a way to know the state of your controls. For this purpose, use the Tag property of the TextBox control. Recall from the discussion of this property earlier in the chapter that only strings can be assigned to the Tag property from the forms designer. However, as you are setting the Tag value from code, you can do pretty much what you want with it, since the Tag property takes an object, and it is more appropriate to enter a Boolean value here.

To the constructor add the following statements:

```
      this.buttonOK.Enabled = false;
```

```
// Tag values for testing if the data is valid
      this.textBoxAddress.Tag = false;
      this.textBoxAge.Tag = false;
      this.textBoxName.Tag = false;
      this.textBoxOccupation.Tag = false;

// Subscriptions to events
      this.textBoxName.Validating += new
System.ComponentModel.CancelEventHandler(this.textBoxEmpty_Validating);
      this.textBoxAddress.Validating += new
            System.ComponentModel.CancelEventHandler(this.textBoxEmpty_
Validating);
```

Unlike the button event handler you've seen previously, the event handler for the `Validating` event is a specialized version of the standard handler `System.EventHandler`. The reason that this event needs a special handler is that should the validation fail, there must be a way to prevent any further processing. If you were to cancel further processing, that would effectively mean that it would be impossible to leave a text box until the data entered is valid.

The `Validating` and `Validated` events combined with the `CausesValidation` property fix a nasty problem that occurred when using the `GotFocus` and `LostFocus` events to perform validation of controls in earlier versions of Visual Studio. The problem occurred when the `GotFocus` and `LostFocus` events were continually fired because validation code was attempting to shift the focus between controls, which created an infinite loop.

Add the event handler as follows:

```
private void textBoxEmpty_Validating (object sender,
                                System.ComponentModel.CancelEventArgs e)
{
    // We know the sender is a TextBox, so we cast the sender object to that.
    TextBox tb = (TextBox)sender;

    // If the text is empty we set the background color of the
    // Textbox to red to indicate a problem. We use the tag value
    // of the control to indicate if the control contains valid
    // information.
    if (tb.Text.Length == 0)
    {
        tb.BackColor = Color.Red;
        tb.Tag = false;

        // In this case we do not want to cancel further processing,
        // but if we had wanted to do this, we would have added this line:
        // e.Cancel = true;
    }
    else
    {
        tb.BackColor = System.Drawing.SystemColors.Window;
```

```
            tb.Tag = true;
        }

        // Finally, we call ValidateOK which will set the value of
        // the OK button.
        ValidateOK();
    }
```

Because more than one text box is using this method to handle the event, you cannot be sure which is calling the function. You do know, however, that the effect of calling the method should be the same no matter who is calling, so you can simply cast the `sender` parameter to a `TextBox` and work on that:

```
    TextBox tb = (TextBox)sender;
```

If the length of the text in the text box is zero, set the background color to red and the `Tag` to `false`. If it is not, set the background color to the standard Windows color for a window.

> You should always use the colors found in the `System.Drawing.SystemColors` enumeration when you want to set a standard color in a control. If you simply set the color to white, your application will look strange if the user has changed the default color settings.

I'll postpone the description of the `ValidateOK()` function until the end of this example.

Keeping with the `Validating` event, the next handler you'll add is for the `Occupation` text box. The procedure is exactly the same as for the two previous handlers, but the validation code is different because occupation must be Programmer or an empty string to be valid. You, therefore, add a new line to the constructor.

```
        this.textBoxOccupation.Validating += new
        System.ComponentModel.CancelEventHandler(this.textBoxOccupation_Validating);
```

And then the handler itself:

```
    private void textBoxOccupation_Validating(object sender,
                                      System.ComponentModel.CancelEventArgs e)
    {
        // Cast the sender object to a textbox.
        TextBox tb = (TextBox)sender;

        // Check if the values are correct.
        if (tb.Text.CompareTo("Programmer") == 0 || tb.Text.Length == 0)
        {
            tb.Tag = true;
            tb.BackColor = System.Drawing.SystemColors.Window;
        }
        else
        {
            tb.Tag = false;
            tb.BackColor = Color.Red;
        }

        // Set the state of the OK button.
        ValidateOK();
    }
```

Your second to last challenge is the Age text box. You don't want users to type anything but positive numbers (including 0 to make the test simpler). To achieve this, you use the KeyPress event to remove any unwanted characters before they are shown in the text box. You'll also limit the number of characters that can be entered into the control to three.

First, set the MaxLength of the textBoxAge control to 3. Then subscribe to the KeyPress event by double-clicking the KeyPress event in the Events list of the Properties window. The KeyPress event handler is specialized as well. The System.Windows.Forms.KeyPressEventHandler is supplied because the event needs information about the key that was pressed.

Add the following code to the event handler itself:

```
private void textBoxAge_KeyPress(object sender, KeyPressEventArgs e)
{
    if ((e.KeyChar < 48 || e.KeyChar > 57) && e.KeyChar != 8)
        e.Handled = true; // Remove the character
}
```

The ASCII values for the characters between 0 and 9 lie between 48 and 57, so you make sure that the character is within this range. You make one exception though. The ASCII value 8 is the Backspace key, and for editing reasons, you allow this to slip through.

Setting the Handled property of KeyPressEventArgs to true tells the control that it shouldn't do anything else with the character, and so if the key pressed isn't a digit or a backspace, it is not shown.

As it is now, the control is not marked as invalid or valid. This is because you need another check to see if anything was entered at all. This is a simple thing as you've already written the method to perform this check, and you simply subscribe to the Validating event for the Age control as well by adding this line to the constructor:

```
this.textBoxAge.Validating += new
        System.ComponentModel.CancelEventHandler(this.textBoxEmpty_Validating);
```

One last case must be handled for all the controls. If the user has entered valid text in all the text boxes and then changes something, making the text invalid, the OK button remains enabled. So, you have to handle one last event handler for all of the text boxes: the Change event, which will disable the OK button should any text field contain invalid data.

The TextChanged event is fired whenever the text in the control changes. You subscribe to the event by adding the following lines to the constructor:

```
    this.textBoxName.TextChanged += new
System.EventHandler(this.textBox_TextChanged);
    this.textBoxAddress.TextChanged += new
            System.EventHandler(this.textBox_TextChanged);
    this.textBoxAge.TextChanged += new
System.EventHandler(this.textBox_TextChanged);
    this.textBoxOccupation.TextChanged += new
                            System.EventHandler(this.textBox_TextChanged);
```

The TextChanged event uses the standard event handler you know from the Click event. Finally, add the event itself.

```
private void textBox_TextChanged(object sender, System.EventArgs e)
{
  // Cast the sender object to a Textbox
  TextBox tb = (TextBox)sender;

  // Test if the data is valid and set the tag and background
  // color accordingly.
  if (tb.Text.Length == 0 && tb != textBoxOccupation)
  {


    tb.Tag = false;
    tb.BackColor = Color.Red;
  }
  else if (tb == textBoxOccupation &&
          (tb.Text.Length != 0 && tb.Text.CompareTo("Programmer") != 0))
  {
    // Don't set the color here, as it will color change while the user
    // is typing.
    tb.Tag = false;
  }
  else
  {
    tb.Tag = true;
    tb.BackColor = SystemColors.Window;
  }

  // Call ValidateOK to set the OK button.
  ValidateOK();
}
```

This time, you must find out exactly which control is calling the event handler, because you don't want the background color of the Occupation text box to change to red when the user starts typing. You do this by checking the Name property of the text box that was passed to you in the sender parameter.

Only one thing remains: the ValidateOK method that enables or disables the OK button.

```
private void ValidateOK()
{
  // Set the OK button to enabled if all the Tags are true.
  this.buttonOK.Enabled = ((bool)(this.textBoxAddress.Tag) &&
                          (bool)(this.textBoxAge.Tag) &&
                          (bool)(this.textBoxName.Tag) &&
                          (bool)(this.textBoxOccupation.Tag));
}
```

The method simply sets the value of the Enabled property of the OK button to true if all of the Tag properties are true. You need to cast the value of the Tag properties to a Boolean because it is stored as an object type.

If you test the program now, you should see something like what is shown in Figure 14-11.

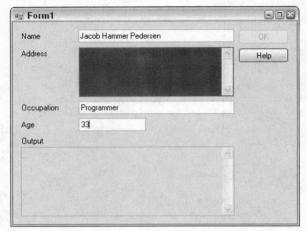

Figure 14-11

Notice that you can click the `Help` button while in a text box with invalid data without the background color changing to red.

The example you just completed is quite long compared to the others you will see in this chapter — this is because you build on this example rather than starting from scratch with each example.

Remember that you can download the source code for all the examples in this book from http://www .wrox.com.

The RadioButton and CheckBox Controls

As mentioned earlier, the `RadioButton` and `CheckBox` controls share their base class with the `Button` control, although their appearance and use differs substantially from the button.

Radio buttons traditionally display themselves as a label with a dot to the left of it, which can be either selected or not. You should use the radio buttons when you want to give the user a choice between several mutually exclusive options, for example, if you want to ask for the user's gender.

To group radio boxes together so they create one logical unit you must use a `GroupBox` control. When you first place a `GroupBox` onto a form and then place the `RadioButton` controls you need within the borders of the `GroupBox`, the `RadioButton` controls will know to change their state to reflect that only one option within the *group box* can be selected. If you do not place the controls within a `GroupBox`, only one `RadioButton` on the *form* can be selected at any given time.

A `CheckBox` control traditionally displays itself as a label with, to the left, a small box with a check mark. You should use a check box when you want to allow users to choose one or more options. An example is a questionnaire asking which operating systems the user has tried (for example, Windows 2000, Windows XP, Linux, and so on).

You'll look at the important properties and events of these two controls, starting with the `RadioButton`, and then move on to a quick example of their use.

RadioButton Properties

Because the `RadioButton` control derives from `ButtonBase` and because you've already seen this in the example that used the button earlier, there are only a few properties to describe (shown in the following table). As always, should you need a complete list, please refer to the .NET Framework SDK documentation.

Name	Description
Appearance	A `RadioButton` can be displayed either as a label with a circular check to the left, middle, or right of it, or as a standard button. When it is displayed as a button, the control will appear depressed when selected and not depressed otherwise.
AutoCheck	When this property is `true`, a black point is displayed when the user clicks the radio button. When it is `false` the radio button must be manually checked in code from the `Click` event handler.
CheckAlign	By using this property, you can change the alignment of the check box portion of the radio button. The default is `ContentAlignment.MiddleLeft`.
Checked	This property indicates the status of the control. It is `true` if the control is displaying a black point or not, and `false` otherwise.

RadioButton Events

You will commonly only use one event when working with `RadioButton` controls, but as always there are many others that can be subscribed to. Only two are covered in this chapter (in the following table), and the only reason that the second event is mentioned is that there is a subtle difference between the two that should be noted.

Name	Description
CheckedChanged	This event is sent when the check of the `RadioButton` changes.
Click	This event is sent every time the `RadioButton` is clicked. This is not the same as the `CheckedChange` event, because clicking a `RadioButton` two or more times in succession only changes the `Checked` property once— and only if it wasn't checked already. Moreover, if the `AutoCheck` property of the button being clicked is `false`, the button will not be checked at all, and again only the `Click` event will be sent.

CheckBox Properties

As you would imagine, the properties and events of this control are very similar to those of the `RadioButton`, but the following table shows two new ones.

Name	Description
CheckState	Unlike the RadioButton, a CheckBox can have three states: Checked, Indeterminate, and Unchecked. When the state of the check box is Indeterminate, the control check next to the label is usually grayed, indicating that the current value of the check is not valid, for some reason cannot be determined (for example if the check indicates the read-only state of files, and two are selected, of which one is read-only and the other is not), or has no meaning under the current circumstances.
ThreeState	When this property is false, the user will not be able to change the CheckState state to Indeterminate. You can, however, still change the CheckState property to Indeterminate from code.

CheckBox Events

You will normally use only one or two events on this control. Note that, even though the CheckChanged event exists on both the RadioButton and the CheckBox controls, the effects of the events differ. The following table shows the CheckBox events.

Name	Description
CheckedChanged	Occurs whenever the Checked property of the check box changes. Note that in a CheckBox where the ThreeState property is true, it is possible to click the check box without changing the Checked property. This happens when the check box changes from checked to indeterminate state.
CheckStateChanged	Occurs whenever the CheckedState property changes. As Checked and Unchecked are both possible values of the CheckedState property, this event will be sent whenever the Checked property changes. In addition to that, it will also be sent when the state changes from Checked to Indeterminate.

This concludes the events and properties of the RadioButton and CheckBox controls. But before looking at an example using these, let's take a look at the GroupBox control, which was mentioned earlier.

The GroupBox Control

The GroupBox control is often used to logically group a set of controls such as the RadioButton and CheckBox, and provide a caption and a frame around this set.

Using the group box is as simple as dragging it onto a form, and then dragging the controls it should contain onto it (but not the other way round — you can't lay a group box over some preexisting controls). The effect of this is that the parent of the controls becomes the group box, rather than the form, and it is, therefore, possible to have more than one RadioButton selected at any given time. Within the group box, however, only one RadioButton can be selected.

The relationship between parent and child probably needs to be explained a bit more. When a control is placed on a form, the form is said to become the parent of the control, and hence the control is the child of the form. When you place a GroupBox on a form, it becomes a child of a form. Because a group box can itself contain controls, it becomes the parent of these controls. The effect of this is that moving the GroupBox will move all of the controls placed on it.

Another effect of placing controls on a group box is that it allows you to affect the contained controls by setting the corresponding property on the group box. For instance, if you want to disable all the controls within a group box, you can simply set the Enabled property of the GroupBox to false.

The GroupBox control is demonstrated in the following Try It Out.

Try It Out   RadioButton and CheckBox Example

You'll modify the TextBoxTest example you created earlier with the demonstration of text boxes. In that example, the only possible occupation was Programmer. Instead of forcing users to type this out in full, you change this text box to a check box.

To demonstrate the RadioButton, you ask the user to provide one more piece of information: his or her gender.

Change the text box example like this:

1. Remove the label named labelOccupation and the text box named textBoxOccupation.

2. Add a CheckBox, a GroupBox and two RadioButton controls, and name the new controls as shown in Figure 14-12. Notice that the GroupBox control is located on the Containers tab in the Toolbox panel.

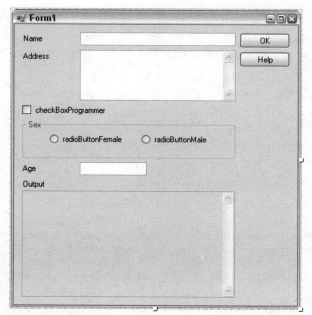

Figure 14-12

3. The `Text` property of the `RadioButton` and `CheckBox` controls should be the same as the names of the controls without the first three letters, and for the `GroupBox` the `Text` property should be `Sex`.

4. Set the `Checked` property of the `checkBoxProgrammer` check box to `true`.

5. Set the `Checked` property of either `radioButtonMale` or `radioButtonFemale` to `true`. Note that you cannot set both to `true`. If you try to do this with a second button, the value of the first `RadioButton` is automatically changed to `false`.

No more needs to be done on the visual part of the example, but there are a number of changes in the code. First, you need to remove all the references to the text box that you've removed. Go to the code and complete the following steps.

1. In the constructor of the form, remove the three lines that refer to `textBoxOccupation`. This includes subscriptions to the `Validating` and `TextChanged` events and the line that sets the `Tag` property to `false`.

2. Remove the `txtOccupation_Validating()` method entirely.

How It Works

The `txtBox_TextChanged` method included tests to see if the calling control was the `textBoxOccupation` `TextBox`. You now know for sure that it will not be (since you removed it), and so you change the method by removing the `else if` block and modify the `if` test as follows:

```
private void textBox_TextChanged(object sender, System.EventArgs e)
{
    // Cast the sender object to a Textbox.
    TextBox tb = (TextBox)sender;

    // Test if the data is valid and set the tag's background.
    // color accordingly.
    if (tb.Text.Length == 0)
    {
        tb.Tag = false;
        tb.BackColor = Color.Red;
    }
    else
    {
        tb.Tag = true;
        tb.BackColor = SystemColors.Window;
    }

    // Call ValidateOK to set the OK button.
    ValidateOK();
}
```

Another place in which you check the value of the text box you've removed is in the `ValidateOK()` method. Remove the check entirely so the code becomes:

```
private void ValidateOK()
{
```

```
        // Set the OK button to enabled if all the Tags are true.
        this.buttonOK.Enabled = ((bool)(this.textBoxAddress.Tag) &&
                                 (bool)(this.textBoxAge.Tag) &&
                                 (bool)(this.textBoxName.Tag));
}
```

Since you are using a check box rather than a text box, you know that the user cannot enter any invalid information, because he or she will always be either a programmer or not.

You also know that the user is either male or female, and because you set the property of one of the RadioButtons to true, the user is prevented from choosing an invalid value. Therefore, the only thing left to do is change the help text and the output. You do this in the button event handlers:

```
private void buttonHelp_Click(object sender, System.EventArgs e)
{
    // Write a short description of each TextBox in the Output TextBox.
    string output;

    output = "Name = Your name\r\n";
    output += "Address = Your address\r\n";
    output += "Programmer = Check 'Programmer' if you are a programmer\r\n";
    output += "Sex = Choose your sex\r\n";
    output += "Age = Your age";

    // Insert the new text.
    this.textBoxOutput.Text = output;
}
```

Only the help text is changed, so there is nothing surprising in the help method. It gets slightly more interesting in the OK method:

```
private void buttonOK_Click(object sender, EventArgs e)
{
    // No testing for invalid values is done, as that should
    // not be necessary.

    string output;

    // Concatenate the text values of the four TextBoxes.
    output = "Name: " + this.textBoxName.Text + "\r\n";
    output += "Address: " + this.textBoxAddress.Text + "\r\n";
    output += "Occupation: " + (string)(this.checkBoxProgrammer.Checked ?
            "Programmer" : "Not a programmer") + "\r\n";
    output += "Sex: " + (string)(this.radioButtonFemale.Checked ? "Female" :
                                                    "Male") + "\r\n";
    output += "Age: " + this.textBoxAge.Text;

    // Insert the new text.
    this.textBoxOutput.Text = output;
}
```

The first of the highlighted lines is the line in which the user's occupation is printed. You investigate the Checked property of the CheckBox, and if it is true, you write the string Programmer. If it is false, you write Not a programmer.

The second line examines only the radio button `rdoFemale`. If the `Checked` property is `true` on that control, you know that the user claims to be female. If it is `false` you know that the user claims to be male. It is possible to have radio buttons without any of them being checked when you start the program — but because you checked one of the radio buttons at design time, you know for sure that one of the two radio buttons will always be checked.

When you run the example now, you should get a result similar to that shown in Figure 14-13.

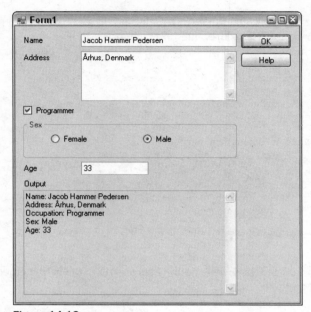

Figure 14-13

The RichTextBox Control

Like the normal `TextBox`, the `RichTextBox` control is derived from `TextBoxBase`. Because of this, it shares a number of features with the `TextBox`, but is much more diverse. Whereas a `TextBox` is commonly used with the purpose of obtaining short text strings from the user, the `RichTextBox` is used to display and enter formatted text (for example **bold**, underline, and *italic*). It does so using a standard for formatted text called Rich Text Format, or RTF.

In the previous example, you used a standard `TextBox`. You could just as well have used a `RichTextBox` to do the job. In fact, as you see in the example later, you can remove the `TextBox` name `textBoxOutput` and insert a `RichTextBox` in its place with the same name, and the example behaves exactly as it did before.

RichTextBox Properties

If this kind of text box is more advanced than the one you explored in the previous section, you'd expect there are new properties that can be used, and you'd be correct. The following table describes the most commonly used properties of the `RichTextBox`:

Name	Description
CanRedo	This property is `true` when the last undone operation can be reapplied using `Redo`.
CanUndo	This property is `true` if it is possible to undo the last action on the `RichTextBox`. Note that `CanUndo` is defined in `TextBoxBase`, so it is available to `TextBox` controls as well.
RedoActionName	This property holds the name of an action that would be performed by the `Redo` method.
DetectUrls	Set this property to `true` to make the control detect URLs and format them (underline as in a browser).
Rtf	This corresponds to the `Text` property, except that this holds the text in RTF.
SelectedRtf	Use this property to get or set the selected text in the control, in RTF. If you copy this text to another application, for example, Word, it will retain all formatting.
SelectedText	As with `SelectedRtf`, you can use this property to get or set the selected text. However, unlike the RTF version of the property, all formatting is lost.
SelectionAlignment	This represents the alignment of the selected text. It can be `Center`, `Left`, or `Right`.
SelectionBullet	Use this property to find out if the selection is formatted with a bullet in front of it, or use it to insert or remove bullets.
BulletIndent	Use this property to specify the number of pixels a bullet should be indented.
SelectionColor	This property allows you to change the color of the text in the selection.
SelectionFont	This property allows you to change the font of the text in the selection.
SelectionLength	Using this property, you either set or retrieve the length of a selection.
SelectionType	This property holds information about the selection. It will tell you if one or more OLE objects are selected or if only text is selected.
ShowSelectionMargin	If you set this property to `true`, a margin will be shown at the left of the `RichTextBox`. This will make it easier for the user to select text.
UndoActionName	Gets the name of the action that will be used if the user chooses to undo something.
SelectionProtected	You can specify that certain parts of the text should not be changed by setting this property to `true`.

As you can see from the preceding listing, most of the new properties have to do with a selection. This is so because any formatting you will be applying when a user is working on his or her text will probably be done on a selection made by that user. In case no selection is made, the formatting will start from the point in the text where the cursor is located, called the insertion point.

RichTextBox Events

Most of the events used by the `RichTextBox` are the same as those used by the `TextBox`. The following table presents a few new ones of interest, though.

Name	Description
LinkClicked	This event is sent when a user clicks on a link within the text.
Protected	This event is sent when a user attempts to modify text that has been marked as protected.
SelectionChanged	This event is sent when the selection changes. If for some reason you don't want the user to change the selection, you can prevent the change here.

In the next Try It Out, you create a very basic text editor. The example demonstrates how to change basic formatting of text and how to load and save the text from the `RichTextBox`. For the sake of simplicity, the example loads from and saves to a fixed file.

Try It Out   RichTextBox Example

As always, you start by designing the form:

1. Create a new C# Windows application called `RichTextBoxTest` in the `C:\BegVCSharp\Chapter14` directory.

2. Create the form as shown in Figure 14-14. The text box named `txtSize` should be a `TextBox` control. The text box named `RichTextBoxText` should be a `RichTextBox` control.

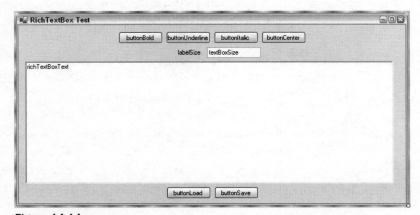

Figure 14-14

3. Name the controls as indicated in the picture.

4. Apart from the text boxes, set the `Text` of all controls to the same as the names except for the first part of the name that describes the type of the control.

5. Change the `Text` property of the `textBoxSize` text box to `10`.

6. Anchor the controls as in the following table.

Control name	Anchor value
`buttonLoad` and `buttonSave`	`Bottom`
`richTextBoxText`	`Top, Left, Bottom, Right`
All others	`Top`

7. Set the `MinimumSize` property of the form to the same as the `Size` property.

How It Works

That concludes the visual part of the example, and you'll move straight to the code. Double-click the `Bold` button to add the `Click` event handler to the code. Here is the code for the event:

```
private void buttonBold_Click(object sender, EventArgs e)
{
  Font oldFont;
  Font newFont;

  // Get the font that is being used in the selected text
  oldFont = this.richTextBoxText.SelectionFont;

  // If the font is using bold style now, we should remove the
  // Formatting.
  if (oldFont.Bold)
    newFont = new Font(oldFont, oldFont.Style & ~FontStyle.Bold);
  else
    newFont = new Font(oldFont, oldFont.Style | FontStyle.Bold);

  // Insert the new font and return focus to the RichTextBox.
  this.richTextBoxText.SelectionFont = newFont;
  this.richTextBoxText.Focus();
}
```

You start by getting the font that is being used in the current selection and assigning it to a local variable `oldFont`. Then you check if this selection is already bold. If it is, you want to remove the bold setting; otherwise, you want to set it. You create a new font using `oldFont` as the prototype but add or remove the bold style as needed.

Finally, you assign the new font to the selection and return focus to the `RichTextBox`—you look at the `Font` object more in Chapter 30.

The event handlers for `buttonItalic` and `buttonUnderline` are the same as the one above, except that you are checking the appropriate styles. Double-click the two buttons Italic and Underline and add this code:

```csharp
private void buttonUnderline_Click(object sender, EventArgs e)
{
  Font oldFont;
  Font newFont;

  // Get the font that is being used in the selected text.
  oldFont = this.richTextBoxText.SelectionFont;

  // If the font is using Underline style now, we should remove it.
  if (oldFont.Underline)
    newFont = new Font(oldFont, oldFont.Style & ~FontStyle.Underline);
  else
    newFont = new Font(oldFont, oldFont.Style | FontStyle.Underline);

  // Insert the new font.
  this.richTextBoxText.SelectionFont = newFont;
  this.richTextBoxText.Focus();
}

private void buttonItalic_Click(object sender, EventArgs e)
{
  Font oldFont;
  Font newFont;

  // Get the font that is being used in the selected text.
  oldFont = this.richTextBoxText.SelectionFont;

  // If the font is using Italic style now, we should remove it.
  if (oldFont.Italic)
    newFont = new Font(oldFont, oldFont.Style & ~FontStyle.Italic);
  else
    newFont = new Font(oldFont, oldFont.Style | FontStyle.Italic);

  // Insert the new font.
  this.richTextBoxText.SelectionFont = newFont;
  this.richTextBoxText.Focus();
}
```

Double-click the last of the formatting buttons, `Center`, and add the following code:

```csharp
private void buttonCenter_Click(object sender, EventArgs e)
{
  if (this.richTextBoxText.SelectionAlignment == HorizontalAlignment.Center)
    this.richTextBoxText.SelectionAlignment = HorizontalAlignment.Left;
  else
    this.richTextBoxText.SelectionAlignment = HorizontalAlignment.Center;
  this.richTextBoxText.Focus();
}
```

Here, you must check another property, `SelectionAlignment`, to see if the text in the selection is already centered. You do this because you want the button to behave like a toggle button — if the text is centered it becomes left-justified, otherwise it becomes centered. `HorizontalAlignment` is an enumeration with values `Left`, `Right`, `Center`, `Justify`, and `NotSet`. In this case, you simply check if `Center` is set, and if it is, you set the alignment to left. If it isn't you set it to `Center`.

The final formatting your little text editor will be able to perform is setting the size of text. You'll add two event handlers for the text box `Size`, one for controlling the input, and one to detect when the user has finished entering a value.

Find and double-click the `KeyPress` and `Validating` events for the `textBoxSize` control in the Properties panel to add the handlers to the code.

You saw these two event handlers in the previous example. Both of the events use a helper method called `ApplyTextSize` that takes a string with the size of the text.

```csharp
private void textBoxSize_KeyPress(object sender, KeyPressEventArgs e)
{
    // Remove all characters that are not numbers, backspace, or enter.
    if ((e.KeyChar < 48 || e.KeyChar > 57) &&
                                    e.KeyChar != 8 && e.KeyChar != 13)
    {
        e.Handled = true;
    }
    else if (e.KeyChar == 13)
    {
        // Apply size if the user hits enter
        TextBox txt = (TextBox)sender;

        if (txt.Text.Length > 0)
            ApplyTextSize(txt.Text);
        e.Handled = true;
        this.richTextBoxText.Focus();
    }
}


private void textBoxSize_Validating(object sender, CancelEventArgs e)
{
    TextBox txt = (TextBox)sender;

    ApplyTextSize(txt.Text);
    this.richTextBoxText.Focus();
}


private void ApplyTextSize(string textSize)
{
    // Convert the text to a float because we'll be needing a float shortly.
    float newSize = Convert.ToSingle(textSize);
    FontFamily currentFontFamily;
    Font newFont;

    // Create a new font of the same family but with the new size.
    currentFontFamily = this.richTextBoxText.SelectionFont.FontFamily;
```

```
        newFont = new Font(currentFontFamily, newSize);

        // Set the font of the selected text to the new font.
        this.richTextBoxText.SelectionFont = newFont;
    }
```

The work you are interested in takes place in the helper method `ApplyTextSize()`. It starts by converting the size from a string to a float. You prevented users from entering anything but integers, but when you create the new font, you need a `float`, so convert it to the correct type.

After that, you get the family to which the font belongs and create a new font from that family with the new size. Finally, you set the font of the selection to the new font.

That's all the formatting you can do, but some is handled by the `RichTextBox` itself. If you try to run the example now, you will be able to set the text to bold, italic, and underline, and you can center the text. That is what you expect, but there is something else that is interesting — try to type a Web address, for example `http://www.wrox.com` in the text. The text is recognized by the control as an Internet address, is underlined, and the mouse pointer changes to a hand when you move it over the text. If that leads you to believe that you can click it and be brought to the page, you are almost correct. You need to handle the event that is sent when the user clicks a link: `LinkClicked`.

Find the `LinkClicked` event in the Properties panel and double-click it to add an event handler to the code. You haven't seen this event handler before — it is used to provide the text of the link that was clicked. The handler is surprisingly simple and looks like this:

```
private void richTextBoxText_LinkClicked (object sender,
                            System.Windows.Forms.LinkClickedEventArgs e)
{
    System.Diagnostics.Process.Start(e.LinkText);
}
```

This code opens the default browser if it isn't open already and navigates to the site to which the link that was clicked is pointing.

The editing part of the application is now done. All that remains is to load and save the contents of the control. You use a fixed file to do this.

Double-click the Load button, and add the following code:

```
    private void buttonLoad_Click(object sender, EventArgs e)
    {
      // Load the file into the RichTextBox.
      try
      {
        richTextBoxText.LoadFile("Test.rtf");
      }
      catch (System.IO.FileNotFoundException)
      {
        MessageBox.Show("No file to load yet");
      }
    }
```

That's it! Nothing else has to be done. Because you are dealing with files, there is always a chance that you might encounter exceptions, and you have to handle these. In the `Load` method, you handle the exception that is thrown if the file doesn't exist. It is equally simple to save the file. Double-click the `Save` button and add this:

```
private void buttonSave_Click(object sender, EventArgs e)
{
  // Save the text.
  try
  {
    richTextBoxText.SaveFile("Test.rtf");
  }
  catch (System.Exception err)
  {
    MessageBox.Show(err.Message);
  }
}
```

Run the example now, format some text and click `Save`. Clear the text box and click `Load`, and the text you just saved should reappear.

This concludes the `RichTextBox` example. When you run it, you should be able to produce something like Figure 14-15.

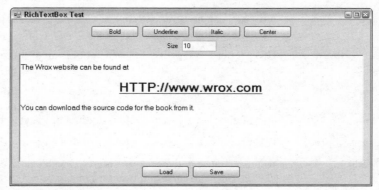

Figure 14-15

The ListBox and CheckedListBox Controls

List boxes are used to show a list of strings from which one or more can be selected at a time. Just like check boxes and radio buttons, the list box provides a means of asking users to make one or more selections. You should use a list box when at design time you don't know the actual number of values the user can choose from (an example could be a list of coworkers). Even if you know all the possible values at design time, you should consider using a list box if there are a great number of values.

425

The ListBox class is derived from the ListControl class, which provides the basic functionality for list-type controls that ship with the .NET Framework.

Another kind of list box available is called CheckedListBox and is derived from the ListBox class. It provides a list just like the ListBox, but in addition to the text strings it provides a check for each item in the list.

ListBox Properties

In the following table, all the properties exist in both the ListBox class and CheckedListBox class unless explicitly stated.

Name	Description
SelectedIndex	This value indicates the zero-based index of the selected item in the list box. If the list box can contain multiple selections at the same time, this property holds the index of the first item in the selected list.
ColumnWidth	In a list box with multiple columns, this property specifies the width of the columns.
Items	The Items collection contains all of the items in the list box. You use the properties of this collection to add and remove items.
MultiColumn	A list box can have more than one column. Use this property to get or set if values should be displayed in columns.
SelectedIndices	This property is a collection, which holds all of the zero-based indices of the selected items in the list box.
SelectedItem	In a list box where only one item can be selected, this property contains the selected item, if any. In a list box where more than one selection can be made, it will contain the first of the selected items.
SelectedItems	This property is a collection that contains all currently selected items.
SelectionMode	You can choose between four different modes of selection from the ListSelectionMode enumeration in a list box: None: No items can be selected. One: Only one item can be selected at any time. MultiSimple: Multiple items can be selected. With this style, when you click an item in the list it becomes selected and stays selected even if you click another item until you click it again. MultiExtended: Multiple items can be selected. You use the Ctrl, Shift, and arrows keys to make selections. Unlike MultiSimple, if you simply click an item and then another item afterwards, only the second item clicked will be selected.
Sorted	Setting this property to true will cause the ListBox to alphabetically sort the items it contains.

Name	Description
Text	You saw Text properties on a number of controls, but this one works differently from any you've seen so far. If you set the Text property of the list box control, it searches for an item that matches the text, and selects it. If you get the Text property, the value returned is the first selected item in the list. This property cannot be used if the SelectionMode is None.
CheckedIndices	(CheckedListBox only) This property is a collection which contains indexes of all the items in the CheckedListBox that have a checked or indeterminate state.
CheckedItems	(CheckedListBox only) This is a collection of all the items in a CheckedListBox that are in a checked or indeterminate state.
CheckOnClick	(CheckedListBox only) If this property is true, an item will change its state whenever the user clicks it.
ThreeDCheckBoxes	(CheckedListBox only) You can choose between CheckBoxes that are flat or normal by setting this property.

ListBox Methods

In order to work efficiently with a list box, you should know a number of methods that can be called. The following table lists the most common methods. Unless indicated, the methods belong to both the ListBox and CheckedListBox classes.

Name	Description
ClearSelected()	Clears all selections in the ListBox.
FindString()	Finds the first string in the ListBox beginning with a string you specify (for example, FindString("a") will find the first string in the ListBox beginning with a.
FindStringExact()	Like FindString, but the entire string must be matched.
GetSelected()	Returns a value that indicates whether an item is selected.
SetSelected()	Sets or clears the selection of an item.
ToString()	Returns the currently selected item.
GetItemChecked()	(CheckedListBox only) Returns a value indicating if an item is checked or not.
GetItemCheckState()	(CheckedListBox only) Returns a value indicating the check state of an item.
SetItemChecked()	(CheckedListBox only) Sets the item specified to a checked state.
SetItemCheckState()	(CheckedListBox only) Sets the check state of an item.

ListBox Events

Normally, the events you will want to be aware of when working with a `ListBox` or `CheckedListBox` are those that have to do with the selections that are being made by the user.

Name	Description
ItemCheck	(CheckedListBox only) Occurs when the check state of one of the list items changes.
SelectedIndexChanged	Occurs when the index of the selected item changes.

In the following Try It Out, you create a small example with both a `ListBox` and a `CheckedListBox`. Users can check items in the `CheckedListBox` and then click a button which moves the checked items to the normal `ListBox`.

Try It Out   ListBox Example

You create the dialog as follows:

1. Create a new Windows application called `Lists` in directory `C:\BegVCSharp\Chapter14`.

2. Add a `ListBox`, a `CheckedListBox`, and a button to the form and change the names as shown in Figure 14-16.

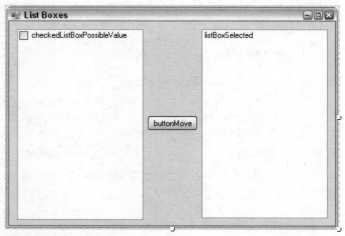

Figure 14-16

3. Change the `Text` property of the button to `Move`.

4. Change the `CheckOnClick` property of the `CheckedListBox` to `true`.

Adding the Event Handlers

Now, you are ready to add some code. When the user clicks the Move button, you want to find the items that are checked, and copy those into the right-hand list box.

Double-click the button and enter this code:

```
private void buttonMove_Click(object sender, EventArgs e)
{
    // Check if there are any checked items in the CheckedListBox.
    if (this.checkedListBoxPossibleValue.CheckedItems.Count > 0)
    {
        // Clear the ListBox we'll move the selections to
        this.listBoxSelected.Items.Clear();

        // Loop through the CheckedItems collection of the CheckedListBox
        // and add the items in the Selected ListBox
        foreach (string item in this.checkedListBoxPossibleValue.CheckedItems)
        {
            this.listBoxSelected.Items.Add(item.ToString());
        }

        // Clear all the checks in the CheckedListBox
        for (int i = 0; i < this.checkedListBoxPossibleValue.Items.Count; i++)
            this.checkedListBoxPossibleValue.SetItemChecked(i, false);
    }
}
```

How It Works

You start by checking the Count property of the CheckedItems collection. This will be greater than zero if any items in the collection are checked. You then clear all items in the listBoxSelected list box, and loop through the CheckedItems collection, adding each item to the listBoxSelected list box. Finally, you remove all the checks in the CheckedListBox.

Now, you just need something in the CheckedListBox to move. You can add the items while in design mode, by selecting the Items property in the Properties window and adding the items as shown in Figure 14-17:

Figure 14-17

Also you can add items in code, for example in the constructor of your form:

```
public Form1()
{
    //
    // Required for Windows Form designer support.
    //
    InitializeComponent();

    // Add a tenth element to the CheckedListBox.
    this.checkedListBoxPossibleValue.Items.Add("Ten");
}
```

Here you add a tenth element to the `CheckedListBox`, since you already have entered nine from the designer.

This concludes the list box example, and if you run it now, you will see something like Figure 14-18. Two, Four, and Six was selected and the Move button pressed to produce the image.

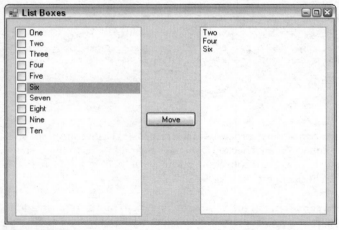

Figure 14-18

The ListView Control

Figure 14-19 below shows probably the most commonly known `ListView` in Windows; the list from which you select files to open in the standard dialog boxes in Windows is a `ListView` control. Everything you can do to the view in the standard list view dialog (Large icons, details view, and so on), you can do with the `ListView` control provided with the .NET Framework.

The list view is usually used to present data where the user is allowed some control over the detail and style of the presentation. It is possible to display the data contained in the control as columns and rows much like in a grid, as a single column or with varying icon representations. The most commonly used list view is like the one seen earlier, which is used to navigate the folders on a computer.

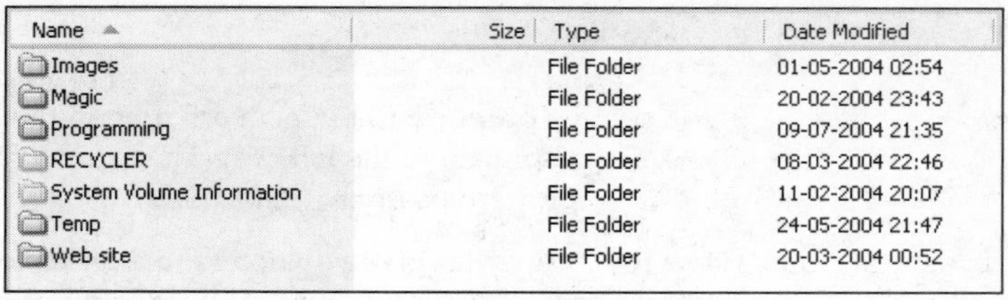

Figure 14-19

The ListView control is easily the most complex control you encounter in this chapter, and covering all of it is beyond the scope of this book. What this chapter does is provide a solid base for you to work on by writing an example that utilizes many of the most important features of the ListView control, and by a thorough description of the numerous properties, events, and methods that can be used. You also look at the ImageList control, which is used to store the images used in a ListView control.

ListView Properties

Name	Description
Activation	By using this property, you can control how a user activates an item in the list view. The possible values are: Standard: This setting is that which the user has chosen for his or her machine. OneClick: Clicking an item activates it. TwoClick: Double-clicking an item activates it.
Alignment	This property allows you to control how the items in the list view are aligned. The four possible values are: Default: If the user drags and drops an item it remains where he or she dropped it. Left: Items are aligned to the left edge of the ListView control. Top: Items are aligned to the top edge of the ListView control. SnapToGrid: The ListView control contains an invisible grid to which the items will snap.
AllowColumnReorder	If you set this property to true, you allow the user to change the order of the columns in a list view. If you do so, you should be sure that the routines that fill the list view are able to insert the items properly, even after the order of the columns is changed.
AutoArrange	If you set this property to true, items will automatically arrange themselves according to the Alignment property. If the user drags an item to the center of the list view, and Alignment is Left, then the item will automatically jump to the left of the list view. This property is only meaningful if the View property is LargeIcon or SmallIcon.

Table continued on following page

431

Name	Description
CheckBoxes	If you set this property to true, every item in the list view will have a CheckBox displayed to the left of it. This property is only meaningful if the View property is Details or List.
CheckedIndices CheckedItems	These two properties give you access to a collection of indices and items, respectively, containing the checked items in the list.
Columns	A list view can contain columns. This property gives you access to the collection of columns through which you can add or remove columns.
FocusedItem	This property holds the item that has focus in the list view. If nothing is selected, it is null.
FullRowSelect	When this property is true, and an item is clicked, the entire row in which the item resides will be highlighted. If it is false, only the item itself will be highlighted.
GridLines	Setting this property to true causes the list view to draw grid lines between rows and columns. This property is only meaningful when the View property is Details.
HeaderStyle	You can control how the column headers are displayed. There are three styles: Clickable: The column header works like a button. NonClickable: The column headers do not respond to mouse clicks. None: The column headers are not displayed.
HoverSelection	When this property is true, the user can select an item in the list view by hovering the mouse pointer over it.
Items	The collection of items in the list view.
LabelEdit	When this property is true, the user can edit the content of the first column in a Details view.
LabelWrap	If this property is true, labels will wrap over as many lines as needed to display all of the text.
LargeImageList	This property holds the ImageList, which holds large images. These images can be used when the View property is LargeIcon.
MultiSelect	Set this property to true to allow the user to select multiple items.
Scrollable	Set this property to true to display scrollbars.
SelectedIndices SelectedItems	These two properties contain the collections that hold the indices and items that are selected, respectively.
SmallImageList	When the View property is SmallIcon this property holds the ImageList that contain the images used.

Name	Description

Sorting	You can allow the list view to sort the items it contains. There are three possible modes:
	`Ascending`
	`Descending`
	`None`

StateImageList	The `ImageList` contains masks for images that are used as overlays on the `LargeImageList` and `SmallImageList` images to represent custom states.
TopItem	Returns the item at the top of the list view.
View	A list view can display its items in four different modes: `LargeIcon`: All items are displayed with a large icon (32×32) and a label. `SmallIcon`: All items are displayed with a small icon (16×16) and a label. `List`: Only one column is displayed. That column can contain an icon and a label. `Details`: Any number of columns can be displayed. Only the first column can contain an icon. `Tile` (only available on Windows XP and newer Windows platforms): Displays a large icon with a label and subitem information to the right of the icon.

ListView Methods

For a control as complex as the list view, there are surprisingly few methods specific to it. They are described in the following table.

Name	Description
BeginUpdate()	By calling this method you tell the list view to stop drawing updates until `EndUpdate()` is called. This is useful when you are inserting many items at once, because it stops the view from flickering and dramatically increases speed.
Clear()	Clears the list view completely. All items and columns are removed.
EndUpdate()	Call this method after calling `BeginUpdate`. When you call this method, the list view will draw all of its items.
EnsureVisible()	When you call this method, the list view will scroll itself to make the item with the index you specified visible.
GetItemAt()	Returns the `ListViewItem` at position `x, y` in the list view.

ListView Events

The ListView control events that you might want to handle are listed in the following table.

Name	Description
AfterLabelEdit	This event occurs after a label has been edited.
BeforeLabelEdit	This event occurs before a user begins editing a label.
ColumnClick	This event occurs when a column is clicked.
ItemActivate	This event occurs when an item is activated.

ListViewItem

An item in a list view is always an instance of the ListViewItem class. The ListViewItem holds information such as text and the index of the icon to display. ListViewItem objects have a SubItems property that holds instances of another class, ListViewSubItem. These subitems are displayed if the ListView control is in Details or tile mode. Each of the subitems represents a column in the list view. The main difference of the subitems and the main items is that a subitem cannot display an icon.

You add ListViewItems to the ListView through the Items collection, and ListViewSubItems to a ListViewItem through the SubItems collection on the ListViewItem.

ColumnHeader

To make a list view display column headers you add instances of a class called ColumnHeader to the Columns collection of the ListView. ColumnHeaders provide a caption for the columns that can be displayed when the ListView is in Details mode.

The ImageList Control

The ImageList control provides a collection that can be used to store images used in other controls on your form. You can store images of any size in an image list, but within each control every image must be of the same size. In the case of the ListView, this means that you need two ImageList controls to be able to display both large and small images.

The ImageList is the first control you visit in this chapter that does not display itself at runtime. When you drag it to a form you are developing, it is not placed on the form itself, but below it in a tray, which contains all such components. This nice feature is provided to stop controls that are not part of the user interface from clogging up the form designer. The control is manipulated in exactly the same way as any other control, except that you cannot move it around.

You can add images to the ImageList at both design time and runtime. If you know at design time what images you want to display, you can add the images by clicking the button at the right side of the Images property. This will bring up a dialog in which you can browse to the images you wish to insert. If you choose to add the images at runtime, you add them through the Images collection.

The best way of learning about using a `ListView` control and its associated image lists is through an example. In the following Try It Out, you create a dialog with a `ListView` and two `ImageLists`. The `ListView` will display files and folders on your hard drive. For the sake of simplicity, you will not extract the correct icons from the files and folders, but rather will use a standard folder icon for the folders and an information icon for files.

By double-clicking the folders you can browse into the folder tree and a Back button is provided to move up the tree. Five radio buttons are used to change the mode of the list view at runtime. If a file is double-clicked you'll attempt to execute it.

Try It Out   ListView Example

As always, you start by creating the user interface:

1. Create a new Windows application called `ListView` in the `C:\BegVCSharp\Chapter14` directory.

2. Add a `ListView`, a `Button`, a `Label`, and a `GroupBox` to the form. Then, add five radio buttons to the group box to get a form that looks like Figure 14-20. To set the width of the Label control you have to set its `AutoSize` property to `False`.

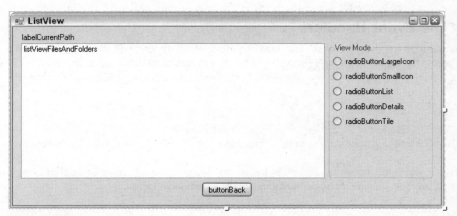

Figure 14-20

3. Name the controls as shown in Figure 14-20. The `ListView` will not display its name as in the picture above; I've added an extra item just to show the name here — you don't need to add this item.

4. Change the `Text` properties of the radio buttons and button to be the same as the name, except for the control names, and set the `Text` property of the form to `ListView`.

5. Clear the `Text` property of the label.

6. Add two `ImageList` controls to the form by double-clicking this control's icon in the Toolbox. You can find the ImageList control on the All Windows Forms tab in the Toolbox. Rename the controls `imageListSmall` and `imageListLarge`.

7. Change the `Size` property of the `ImageList` named `imageListLarge` to 32, 32.

8. Click the button to the right of the `Images` property of the `imageListLarge` image list to bring up the dialog on which you can browse to the images you want to insert.

9. Click `Add` and browse to the folder ListView in the code for this chapter. The files are:

   Folder 32x32.ico and Text 32x32.ico

10. Make sure that the folder icon is at the top of the list.

11. Repeat steps 8 and 9 with the other `ImageList`, `imageListSmall`, choosing the 16x16 versions of the icons.

12. Set the `Checked` property of the radio button `radioButtonDetails` to `true`.

13. Set the properties shown in the following table on the list view.

Property	Value
LargeImageList	imageListLarge
SmallImageList	imageListSmall
View	Details

Adding the Event Handlers

That concludes the user interface, and you can move on to the code. First of all, you need a field to hold the folders you browsed through in order to be able to return to them when the Back button is clicked. You will store the absolute path of the folders, so choose a `StringCollection` for the job:

```
partial class Form1 : Form
{
    // Member field to hold previous folders
    private System.Collections.Specialized.StringCollection folderCol;
```

You didn't create any column headers in the forms designer, so you have to do that now. You create them in a method called `CreateHeadersAndFillListView()`:

```
private void CreateHeadersAndFillListView()
{
    ColumnHeader colHead;

    // First header
    colHead = new ColumnHeader();
    colHead.Text = "Filename";
    this.listViewFilesAndFolders.Columns.Add(colHead); // Insert the header

    // Second header
    colHead = new ColumnHeader();
    colHead.Text = "Size";
    this.listViewFilesAndFolders.Columns.Add(colHead); // Insert the header

    // Third header
```

```
      colHead = new ColumnHeader();
      colHead.Text = "Last accessed";
      this.listViewFilesAndFolders.Columns.Add(colHead); // Insert the header
   }
```

You start by declaring a single variable, colHead, which is used to create the three column headers. For each of the three headers, you declare the variable as new and assign the Text to it before adding it to the Columns collection of the ListView.

The final initialization of the form as it is displayed the first time is to fill the list view with files and folders from your hard disk. This is done in another method:

```
private void PaintListView(string root)
{
  try
  {
    // Two local variables that are used to create the items to insert
    ListViewItem lvi;
    ListViewItem.ListViewSubItem lvsi;

    // If there's no root folder, we can't insert anything.
    if (root.CompareTo("") == 0)
      return;

    // Get information about the root folder.
    DirectoryInfo dir = new DirectoryInfo(root);

    // Retrieve the files and folders from the root folder.
    DirectoryInfo[] dirs = dir.GetDirectories(); // Folders
    FileInfo[] files = dir.GetFiles();           // Files

    // Clear the ListView. Note that we call the Clear method on the
    // Items collection rather than on the ListView itself.
    // The Clear method of the ListView remove everything, including column
    // headers, and we only want to remove the items from the view.
    this.listViewFilesAndFolders.Items.Clear();

    // Set the label with the current path.
    this.labelCurrentPath.Text = root;

    // Lock the ListView for updates.
    this.listViewFilesAndFolders.BeginUpdate();


    // Loop through all folders in the root folder and insert them.
    foreach (DirectoryInfo di in dirs)
    {
      // Create the main ListViewItem.
      lvi = new ListViewItem();
      lvi.Text = di.Name; // Folder name
      lvi.ImageIndex = 0; // The folder icon has index 0
      lvi.Tag = di.FullName; // Set the tag to the qualified path of the
      // folder
```

```
        // Create the two ListViewSubItems.
        lvsi = new ListViewItem.ListViewSubItem();
        lvsi.Text = ""; // Size - a folder has no size and so this column
        // is empty
        lvi.SubItems.Add(lvsi); // Add the subitem to the ListViewItem

        lvsi = new ListViewItem.ListViewSubItem();
        lvsi.Text = di.LastAccessTime.ToString(); // Last accessed column
        lvi.SubItems.Add(lvsi); // Add the subitem to the ListViewItem.

        // Add the ListViewItem to the Items collection of the ListView.
        this.listViewFilesAndFolders.Items.Add(lvi);
    }

    // Loop through all the files in the root folder.
    foreach (FileInfo fi in files)
    {
        // Create the main ListViewItem.
        lvi = new ListViewItem();
        lvi.Text = fi.Name; // Filename
        lvi.ImageIndex = 1; // The icon we use to represent a folder has
        // index 1.
        lvi.Tag = fi.FullName; // Set the tag to the qualified path of the
        // file.

        // Create the two subitems.
        lvsi = new ListViewItem.ListViewSubItem();
        lvsi.Text = fi.Length.ToString(); // Length of the file
        lvi.SubItems.Add(lvsi); // Add to the SubItems collection

        lvsi = new ListViewItem.ListViewSubItem();
        lvsi.Text = fi.LastAccessTime.ToString(); // Last Accessed Column
        lvi.SubItems.Add(lvsi); // Add to the SubItems collection

        // Add the item to the Items collection of the ListView.
        this.listViewFilesAndFolders.Items.Add(lvi);
    }

    // Unlock the ListView. The items that have been inserted will now
    // be displayed.
    this.listViewFilesAndFolders.EndUpdate();
}
catch (System.Exception err)
{
    MessageBox.Show("Error: " + err.Message);
}
}
```

How It Works

Before the first of the two foreach blocks, you call BeginUpdate() on the ListView control. Remember that the BeginUpdate() method on the ListView signals the ListView control to stop updating its visible area until EndUpdate() is called. If you did not call this method, filling the list view would be slower and the list may flicker as the items are added. Just after the second `foreach` block you call `EndUpdate()`, which makes the `ListView` control draw the items you filled it with.

The two `foreach` blocks contain the code you are interested in. You start by creating a new instance of a `ListViewItem` and then setting the `Text` property to the name of the file or folder you are going to insert. The `ImageIndex` of the `ListViewItem` refers to the index of an item in one of the `ImageLists`. Because of that, it is important that the icons have the same indexes in the two `ImageLists`. You use the `Tag` property to save the fully qualified path to both folders and files, for use when the user double-clicks the item.

Then, you create the two subitems. These are simply assigned the text to display and then added to the `SubItems` collection of the `ListViewItem`.

Finally, the `ListViewItem` is added to the `Items` collection of the `ListView`. The `ListView` is smart enough to simply ignore the subitems, if the view mode is anything but `Details`, so you add the subitems no matter what the view mode is now.

Note that there are some aspects of the code not discussed here — namely the lines that actually obtain information about the files:

```
// Get information about the root folder.
DirectoryInfo dir = new DirectoryInfo(root);

// Retrieve the files and folders from the root folder.
DirectoryInfo[] dirs = dir.GetDirectories(); // Folders
FileInfo[] files = dir.GetFiles();           // Files
```

These lines use classes from the `System.IO` namespace for accessing files, so you need to add the following to the using region at the top of the code:

```
#region Using directives

using System;
using System.Collections.Generic;
using System.ComponentModel;
using System.Data;
using System.Drawing;
using System.Windows.Forms;
using System.IO;

#endregion
```

You learn more about file access and `System.IO` in Chapter 22, but to give you an idea of what's going on, the `GetDirectories()` method of the `DirectoryInfo` object returns a collection of objects that represent the folders in the directory you're looking in, and the `GetFiles()` method returns a collection of objects that represent the files in the current directory. You can loop through these collections, as you did in the code above, using the object's `Name` property to return the name of the relevant directory or file, and create a `ListViewItem` to hold this string.

All that remains to be done for the list view to display the root folder is to call the two functions in the constructor of the form. At the same time, you instantiate the `folderCol StringCollection` with the root folder:

```
InitializeComponent();
```

```
// Init ListView and folder collection
folderCol = new System.Collections.Specialized.StringCollection();
CreateHeadersAndFillListView();
PaintListView(@"C:\");
folderCol.Add(@"C:\");
```

To allow users to double-click an item in the ListView to browse the folders, you need to subscribe to the ItemActivate event. Select the ListView in the designer and double-click the ItemActivate event in the properties panel.

The corresponding event handler looks like this:

```
private void listViewFilesAndFolders_ItemActivate(object sender, EventArgs e)
{
    // Cast the sender to a ListView and get the tag of the first selected
    // item.
    System.Windows.Forms.ListView lw = (System.Windows.Forms.ListView)sender;
    string filename = lw.SelectedItems[0].Tag.ToString();

    if (lw.SelectedItems[0].ImageIndex != 0)
    {
      try
      {
        // Attempt to run the file.
        System.Diagnostics.Process.Start(filename);
      }
      catch
      {
        // If the attempt fails we simply exit the method.
        return;
      }
    }
    else
    {
      // Insert the items.
      PaintListView(filename);
      folderCol.Add(filename);
    }
}
```

The Tag of the selected item contains the fully qualified path to the file or folder that was double-clicked. You know that the image with index 0 is a folder, so you can determine whether the item is a file or a folder by looking at that index. If it is a file, you attempt to load the file.

If it is a folder, you call PaintListView() with the new folder and then add the new folder to the folderCol collection.

Before you move on to the radio buttons, complete the browsing abilities by adding the Click event to the Back button. Double-click the button and fill the event handle with this code:

```
private void buttonBack_Click(object sender, EventArgs e)
{
  if (folderCol.Count > 1)
  {
    PaintListView(folderCol[folderCol.Count - 2].ToString());
    folderCol.RemoveAt(folderCol.Count - 1);


  }
  else
  {
    PaintListView(folderCol[0].ToString());
  }
}
```

If there is more than one item in the folderCol collection, then you are not at the root of the browser, and you call PaintListView() with the path to the previous folder. The last item in the folderCol collection is the current folder, which is why you need to take the second to last item. You then remove the last item in the collection and make the new last item the current folder. If there is only one item in the collection, you simply call PaintListView() with that item.

All that remains is to be able to change the view type of the list view. Double-click each of the radio buttons and add the following code:

```
private void radioButtonLargeIcon_CheckedChanged(object sender, EventArgs e)
{
  RadioButton rdb = (RadioButton)sender;
  if (rdb.Checked)
    this.listViewFilesAndFolders.View = View.LargeIcon;
}

private void radioButtonList_CheckedChanged(object sender, EventArgs e)
{
  RadioButton rdb = (RadioButton)sender;
  if (rdb.Checked)
    this.listViewFilesAndFolders.View = View.List;
}

private void radioButtonSmallIcon_CheckedChanged(object sender, EventArgs e)
{
  RadioButton rdb = (RadioButton)sender;
  if (rdb.Checked)
    this.listViewFilesAndFolders.View = View.SmallIcon;
}

private void radioButtonDetails_CheckedChanged(object sender, EventArgs e)
{
  RadioButton rdb = (RadioButton)sender;
  if (rdb.Checked)
    this.listViewFilesAndFolders.View = View.Details;
}
private void radioButtonTile_CheckedChanged(object sender, EventArgs e)
{
```

```
        RadioButton rdb = (RadioButton)sender;
        if (rdb.Checked)
            this.listViewFilesAndFolders.View = View.Tile;
    }
```

You check the radio button to see if it has been changed to Checked—if it has you set the View property of the ListView accordingly.

That concludes the ListView example. When you run it, you should see something like Figure 14-21.

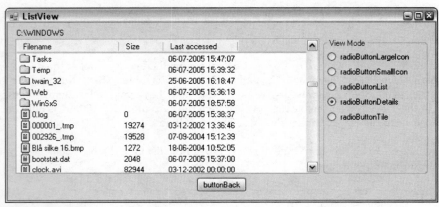

Figure 14-21

The TabControl Control

The TabControl provides an easy way of organizing a dialog into logical parts that can be accessed through tabs located at the top of the control. A TabControl contains TabPages that essentially work like a GroupBox control, in that they group controls together, although they are somewhat more complex.

Figure 14-22 shows the Options dialog in Word 2000 as it is typically configured, though it is a Danish language version of Office. Notice the two rows of tabs at the top of the dialog. Clicking each of them will show a different selection of controls in the rest of the dialog. This is a very good example of how to use a tab control to group related information, making it easier for the user to find the information he/she is looking for.

Using the tab control is easy. You simply add the number of tabs you want to display to the control's collection of TabPage objects and then drag the controls you want to display to the respective pages.

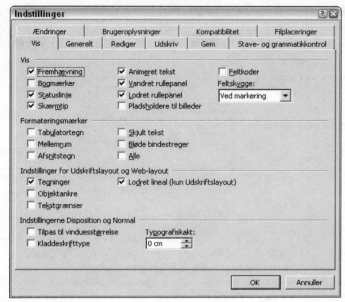

Figure 14-22

TabControl Properties

The properties of the TabControl (shown in the following table) are largely used to control the appearance of the container of TabPage objects, in particular the tabs displayed.

Name	Description
Alignment	This property controls where on the tab control the tabs are displayed. The default is at the top.
Appearance	The Appearance property controls how the tabs are displayed. The tabs can be displayed as normal buttons or with flat style.
HotTrack	If this property is set to true, the appearance of the tabs on the control changes as the mouse pointer passes over them.
Multiline	If this property is set to true, it is possible to have several rows of tabs.
RowCount	RowCount returns the number of rows of tabs currently displayed.
SelectedIndex	This property returns or sets the index of the selected tab.
SelectedTab	SelectedTab returns or sets the selected tab. Note that this property works on the actual instances of the TabPages.
TabCount	TabCount returns the total number of tabs.
TabPages	This property is the collection of TabPage objects in the control. Use this collection to add and remove TabPage objects.

Working with the TabControl

The TabControl works slightly differently from all other controls you've seen so far. The control itself is really little more than a container for the tab pages that is used to display the pages. When you double-click a TabControl in the Toolbox you are presented with a control that already has two TabPages added to it, as shown in Figure 14-23.

Figure 14-23

When the mouse moves over the control a small button with a triangle appears at the control's upper-right corner. When you click this button, a small window is unfolded. This is called the Actions Window and is designed to allow you to easily access selected properties and methods of the control. You may have noticed this earlier as many controls in Visual Studio include this feature, but the TabControl is the first of the controls in this chapter that actually allows you to do anything interesting in the Actions Window. The Actions Window of the TabControl allows you to easily add and remove TabPages at design time.

The procedure outlined in the preceding paragraph for adding tabs to the TabControl is provided in order for you to get up and running quickly with the control. If, on the other hand, you want to change the behavior or style of the tabs you should use the TabPages dialog — accessed through the button when you select TabPages in the Properties window. The TabPages property is also the collection used to access the individual pages on a tab control.

Once you've added the TabPages you need you can add controls to the pages in the same way you did earlier with the GroupBox.

In the following Try It Out, you create an example to demonstrate the basics of the control.

Try It Out   Working with Tab Pages

Follow these steps to create a Windows Application that demonstrates how to develop controls located on different pages on the tab control.

1. Create a new Windows application called TabControl in the directory C:\BegVCSharp\ Chapter14.

2. Drag a TabControl control from the Toolbox to the form. Like the GroupBox the TabControl is found on the Containers tab in the Toolbox.

3. Find the TabPages property, and click the button to the right of it after selecting it, to bring up the dialog shown in Figure 14-24.

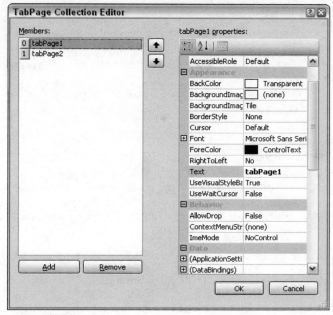

Figure 14-24

4. Change the `Text` property of the tab pages to `Tab One` and `Tab Two`, respectively, and click `OK` to close the dialog.

5. You can select the tab pages to work on by clicking on the tabs at the top of the control. Select the tab with the text `Tab One`. Drag a button on to the control. Be sure to place the button within the frame of the `TabControl`. If you place it outside then the button will be placed on the form rather than on the control.

6. Change the name of the button to `buttonShowMessage` and the `Text` of the button to `Show Message`.

7. Click on the tab with the `Text` property `Tab Two`. Drag a `TextBox` control onto the `TabControl` surface. Name this control `textBoxMessage` and clear the `Text` property.

8. The two tabs should look as shown in Figure 14-25 and Figure 14-26.

Figure 14-25

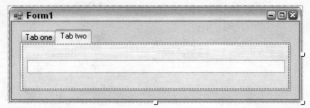

Figure 14-26

Adding the Event Handler

You are now ready to access the controls. If you run the code as it is, you will see the tab pages displayed properly. All that remains to do to demonstrate the tab control is to add some code such that when users click the Show Message button on one tab, the text entered in the other tab will be displayed in a message box. First, you add a handler for the Click event by double-clicking the button on the first tab and adding the following code:

```
private void buttonShowMessage_Click(object sender, EventArgs e)
{
    // Access the TextBox.

    MessageBox.Show(this.textBoxMessage.Text);
}
```

How It Works

You access a control on a tab just as you would any other control on the form. You get the Text property of the TextBox and display it in a message box.

Earlier in the chapter, you saw that it is only possible to have one radio button selected at a time on a form (unless you put them in group boxes). The TabPages work in precisely the same way as group boxes and it is, therefore, possible to have multiple sets of radio buttons on different tabs without the need to have group boxes. Also, as you saw in the buttonShowMessage_Click method, it is possible to access the controls that are located on other tabs than the one that the current control is on.

The last thing you must know to be able to work with a tab control is how to determine which tab is currently being displayed. There are two properties you can use for this purpose: SelectedTab and SelectedIndex. As the names imply, SelectedTab will return the TabPage object to you or null if no tab is selected, and SelectedIndex will return the index of the tab or –1 if no tab is selected. It is left to you in Exercise 2 to use these properties.

Summary

In this chapter, you visited some of the controls most commonly used for creating Windows applications, and you saw how they can be used to create simple, yet powerful, user interfaces. The chapter covered the properties and events of these controls, provided examples of their use, and explained how to add event handlers for the particular events of a control.

In this chapter, you learned how to:

❑ Use the `Label` and `LinkedLabel` controls to display information to users.

❑ Use the `Button` control and the corresponding `Click` event to allow the user to tell the application that they want some action to run.

❑ Use the `TextBox` and `RichTextBox` controls to allow the user to enter text either as plain or formatted text.

❑ Distinguish between the `CheckBox` and the `RaidioButton` and how to use them. You also learned how to group the two with the `GroupBox` control and how that affected the behavior of the controls.

❑ Use the `CheckedListBox` to provide lists from which the user can select items by clicking a check box. You also learned how to use the more common `ListBox` control to provide a list similar to that of the `CheckedListBox` control, but without the check boxes.

❑ Use the `ListView` and `ImageList` controls to provide a list that the users are able to view in a number of different ways.

❑ And finally you learned how to use the `TabControl` to group controls on different pages on the same form that the user is able to select at will.

In the next chapter, you look at some of the more complex controls and features of creating Windows Forms applications.

Exercises

1. In previous versions of Visual Studio, it was quite difficult to get your own applications to display their controls in the new Windows XP style — that changed in this version of Visual Studio. For this exercise, locate where, in a Windows Forms application, Windows XP styles are enabled in a new Windows Forms project. Experiment with enabling and disabling the styles and see how what you do affects the controls on the forms.

2. Modify the `TabControl` example by adding a couple of tab pages and display a message box with the text `You changed the current tab to <Text of the current tab> from <Text of the tab that was just left>`.

3. In the `ListView` example, you used the `tag` property to save the fully qualified path to the folders and files in the `ListView`. Change this behavior by creating a new class that is derived from `ListViewItem` and use instances of this new class as the items in the `ListView`. Store the information about the files and folders in the new class using a property named `FullyQualifiedPath`.

Advanced Windows Forms Features

In the previous chapter, you looked at some of the controls most commonly used in Windows application development. With controls such as these, it is possible to create impressive dialogs, but very few full-scale Windows applications have a user interface consisting solely of a single dialog. Rather, these applications use a Single Document Interface (SDI) or a Multiple Document Interface (MDI). Applications of either of these types usually make heavy use of menus and toolbars, neither of which were discussed in the previous chapter, but I'll make amends for that now.

This chapter begins where the last left off, by looking at controls, starting with the menu control and then moving on to toolbars, where you see how to link buttons on toolbars to specific menu items and vice versa. Then you move on to creating SDI and MDI applications, with the focus on MDI applications, because SDI applications are basically subsets of MDI applications.

So far, you've consumed only those controls that ship with the .NET Framework. These controls are, as you saw, very powerful and provide a wide range of functionality, but there are times when they are not sufficient. To overcome this, it is possible to create custom controls, and you look at how this is done toward the end of this chapter.

In this chapter, you will see how to:

- ❑ Use three common controls to create rich-looking menus, toolbars, and status bars
- ❑ Create MDI Applications
- ❑ Create your own controls

Menus and Toolbars

How many Windows applications can you think of that do not contain a menu or toolbar of some kind? The chances are that the number is very close to none. Menus and toolbars are, therefore, likely to be important parts of any application you will write for the Windows operating system.

To assist you in creating them for your applications, Visual Studio 2005 provides two controls that let you create, with very little difficulty, menus and toolbars that look like the menus you find in Visual Studio and Office.

Two Is One

The two controls you are going to look at over the following pages are new to Visual Studio 2005 and they represent a handsome boost of power to the casual developer and professional alike. Building applications with professional-looking toolbars and menus used to be reserved for those who would take the time to write custom paint handlers and those who bought third-party components. Creating what previously could take weeks is now a simple task that quite literally can be done in seconds.

Visual Studio 2005 introduces a family of controls that has the suffix `Strip`. They are the `ToolStrip`, `MenuStrip`, and `StatusStrip`. You return to the `StatusStrip` later in the chapter. If you want to look at it in its purest form, the `ToolStrip` and the `MenuStrip` are in fact the same control as `MenuStrip` derives directly from the `ToolStrip`. This means that anything the `ToolStrip` can do, the `MenuStrip` can do. Obviously, it also means that the two work really well together.

Before you examine the controls any more closely, I want to mention another control that you may find in your Toolbox in Visual Studio 2005: the `MainMenu` control. This is the control that was used to create menus in Visual Studio prior to 2005. The control is retained in this edition of Visual Studio for backward compatibility and for the rare occasion when you want to use a control that uses the Windows API menus. For most applications, you will be using the new controls and will focus on them, but to give you an idea of how the controls have improved, the File menu, using the `MainMenu` control, is shown in Figure 15-1 and the `MenuStrip` control is shown in Figure 15-2.

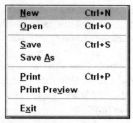

Figure 15-1

Figure 15-2

Using the MenuStrip Control

In addition to the `MenuStrip` control, there are a number of additional controls that are used to populate a menu. The three most common of these are the `ToolStripMenuItem`, `ToolStripDropDown`, and the `ToolStripSeparator`. All of these controls represent a particular way to view an item in a menu or toolbar. The `ToolStripMenuItem` represents a single entry in a menu, the `ToolStripDropDown` represents an item that when clicked displays a list of other items, and the `ToolStripSeparator` represents a horizontal or vertical dividing line in a menu or toolbar.

> *There is another kind of menu that is discussed briefly after the discussion of the* `MenuStrip` *— the* `ContextMenuStrip`. *A context menu appears when a user right-clicks on an item, and will typically display information relevant to that item.*

Without further ado, in the following Try It Out, you create the first example of the chapter.

Try It Out   Professional Menus in Five Seconds

This first example is very much a teaser, and you are simply going to introduce an aspect of the new controls that is truly wonderful if you want to create standard menus with the right look and feel.

1. Create a new Windows application and name it Professional Menus in the directory `C:\BegVCSharp\Chapter15`.
2. Draw an instance of the `MenuStrip` control from the Toolbox onto the design surface.
3. Click the triangle to the far right of the `MenuStrip` at the top of the dialog to display the Actions window.
4. Click the Insert Standard Items link.

That's it. If you drop down the File menu, you will see menu that was shown in Figure 15-2. There is no functionality behind the menu yet — you will have to fill that in. You can edit the menu as you see fit, and in order to do so, please read on.

Create Menus Manually

When you drag the `MenuStrip` control from the Toolbox to the design surface, you will see that this control places itself both on the form itself and in the control tray, but it can be edited directly on the form. To create new menu items, you simply place the pointer in the box marked Type Here in Figure 15-3.

When you enter the caption of the menu in the highlighted box, you may include an ampersand (&) in front of a letter that you want to function as the shortcut key character for the menu item — this is the character that appears underlined in the menu item and that can be selected pressing Alt and the key together.

Note that it is quite possible to create several menu items in the same menu with the same shortcut key character. The rule is that a character can be used for this purpose only once for each pop-up menu (for example, once in the Files pop-up menu, once in the View menu and so on). If you accidentally assign the same shortcut key character to multiple menu items in the same pop-up menu, you'll find that only the one closest to the top of the control will respond to the character.

Figure 15-3

When you select the item you will notice that the control automatically displays items under the current item and to the right of it. When you enter a caption into either of these controls, you create a new item in relation to the one you started out with. This is how you create drop-down menus.

To create the horizontal lines that divide menus into groups you must use the `ToolStripSeparator` control instead of the `ToolStripMenuItem`, but you don't actually insert a different control. Instead, you simply type a "-" (dash) as the only character as the caption of the item and Visual Studio will then automatically assume that the item is a separator and change the type of the control.

Finally, if you click the image icon to the far left of the item, you are presented with a dialog that allows you to select and import images to associate with the menus.

It is now time for you to try to create a menu without using Visual Studio to generate the items on it, in the following Try It Out.

Try It Out   Creating Menus from Scratch

In this example, you are going to create the File and Help menus from scratch, leaving the Edit and Tools menus for you to do by yourself.

1. Create a new Windows Application project, name it Manual Menus and save it to the `C:\` `BegVCSharp\Chapter15` folder.

2. Drag a `MenuStrip` control from the Toolbox onto the design surface.

3. Click in the text area of the `MenuStrip` control where it says Type Here and type **&File** and press the Enter key.

4. Type the following into the text areas below the File item:

   ❑ **&New**

   ❑ **&Open**

   ❑ -

   ❑ **&Save**

❑ **Save &As**

❑ **-**

❑ **&Print**

❑ **Print Preview**

❑ **-**

❑ **E&xit**

Your menu should look like that in Figure 15-4 now. Notice how the dashes are automatically changed by Visual Studio to a line that separates the elements.

Figure 15-4

5.   Click in the text area to the right of Files and type **&Help**.

6.   Type the following into the text areas below the Help item:

❑ **Contents**

❑ **Index**

❑ **Search**

❑ **-**

❑ **About**

7.   Your menu now looks like that in Figure 15-5.

8.   Now, return to the File menu and set the shortcut keys for the items. To do this, select the item you want to set, and find the `ShortcutKeys` property in the properties panel. When you click the drop-down arrow, you are presented with a small window where you can set the key combination you want to associate with the menu item. Because this menu is a standard menu, you should use the standard key combinations, but if you are creating something else, please feel free to select any other key combination. Set the `ShortcutKeys` properties in the File menu as shown in the following table.

Figure 15-5

Item Name	Properties and Values
&New	Ctrl + N
&Open	Ctrl + O
&Save	Ctrl + S
&Print	Ctrl + P

9. Now for the finishing touch: the images. Select the New item in the File menu and click on the ellipse (…) to the left of the Image property in the properties panel to bring up the Select Resource dialog.

Arguably the most difficult thing about creating these menus is obtaining the images you want to display. In this case, you can get the images by downloading the source code for this book at www.wrox.com, but normally you are going to have to draw them yourself or get them in some other way.

10. Because there are currently no resources in the project, the Entry list box is empty, so click Import. The images for this example can be found in the source code for this book under Chapter15\Manual Menus\Manual Menus\Images. Select all of the files there, and click Open. Remember that you are currently editing the New item, so select the New image in the Entry list and click OK.

11. Repeat step 10 for the images for the Open, Save, Save As, Print, and Print Preview buttons.

12. Run the project. Note that you can select the File menu by clicking it or by selecting Alt+F and the Help menu by hitting Alt+H.

Additional Properties of the ToolStripMenuItem

There are a few additional properties of the ToolStripMenuItem that you should be aware of when you are creating your menus. The list in the table that follows is in no way exhaustive — if you require a complete listing, please refer to .NET Framework SDK documentation.

Name	Description
Checked	This indicates whether the menu is checked.
CheckOnClick	When this property is true a check mark is placed in or removed from the position to the left of the text in the item that is otherwise occupied by an image. Use the Checked property to determine the state of the menu item.
Enabled	An item with Enabled set to false will be grayed and cannot be selected.
DropDownItems	This property returns a collection of items that is used as a drop-down menu in relation to the menu item.

Adding Functionality to Menus

Now, you are able to produce menus that look every bit as good as the ones you find in Visual Studio and Word, so the only thing left is to make something happen when you click on them. Obviously, what happens is pretty much up to you, and in the following Try It Out, you just create a very simple example that builds on the example you've just been through.

To respond to selections made by the user you should implement handlers for one of two events that the ToolStripMenuItems sends.

Event Name	Description
Click	This event is sent whenever the user clicks on an item. In most cases this is the event you want to respond to.
CheckedChanged	This event is sent when an item with the CheckOnClick property is clicked.

You are going to extend the Manual Menus example from the previous Try It Out by adding a text box to the dialog and implementing a few event handlers. You are also going to add another menu between Files and Help called Format.

Try It Out   Handling Menu Events

1. Drag a RichTextBox onto the design surface and change its name to **richTextBoxText**. Set its Dock property to Fill.

2. Select the MenuStrip and then enter **Format** into the text area next to the Help menu item and press the Enter key.

3. Select the Format menu item and drag it to a position between Files and Help.

4. Add a menu item to the Format menu with the text **Show Help Menu**.

5. Set the CheckOnClick property of the Show Help Menu to true. Also set its Checked property to true.

6. Change the name of these five menu items:

Menu Item	Name
New	MenuItemNew
Open	MenuItemOpen
Save	MenuItemSave
Show Help Menu	MenuItemShowHelpMenu
Help	MenuItemHelp

7. Select `MenuItemShowHelpMenu` and add an event handler for the `CheckedChanged` event by double-clicking the event in the Events part of the properties panel.

8. The event handler for this event should set the `Visible` property of the `MenuItemHelp` to `true` if the `Checked` property is `true`, otherwise it should be `false`. Add this code to the event handler:

```
private void MenuItemShowHelpMenu_Click(object sender, EventArgs e)
{
   ToolStripMenuItem item = (ToolStripMenuItem)sender;
   MenuItemHelp.Visible = item.Checked;
}
```

9. Double-click `MenuItemNew`, `MenuItemSave` and `MenuItemOpen`. Double-clicking a `ToolStripMenuItem` in Design View causes the `Click` event to be added to the code. The three event handlers clear the text in the rich text box, save the text in the rich text box to a predetermined file, and open said file, respectively. Enter this code:

```
private void MenuItemNew_Click(object sender, EventArgs e)
{
    richTextBoxText.Text = "";
}

private void MenuItemOpen_Click(object sender, EventArgs e)
{
    try
    {
      richTextBoxText.LoadFile(@".\Example.rtf");
    }
    catch
    {
      // Ignore errors
    }
}

private void MenuItemSave_Click(object sender, EventArgs e)
{
    try
    {
      richTextBoxText.SaveFile(@".\Example.rtf");
    }
    catch
```

```
          {
              // Ignore errors
          }
      }
```

10. Run the application. When you click the Show Help Menu, the Help menu disappears or appears, depending on the state of the `Checked` property, and you should be able to open, save, and clear the text in the text box.

Toolbars

While menus are great for providing access to a multitude of functionality in your application, some items benefit from being placed in a toolbar as well as on the menu. These items are those that are used frequently by the user, such as Open and Save, and a toolbar provides one-click access to such commonly used functionality.

Figure 15-6 shows the selection of toolbars that are visible as I'm writing this chapter in Word.

Figure 15-6

A button on a toolbar usually displays a picture and no text, though it is possible to have buttons with both. Examples of toolbars with no text are those found in Word (see above), and examples of toolbars that include text can be found in Internet Explorer. In addition to buttons, you will occasionally see combo boxes and text boxes in the toolbars too. If you let the mouse pointer rest above a button in a toolbar, it should display a tooltip, which provides some clue to the purpose of the button, especially when only an icon is displayed.

The `ToolStrip`, like the `MenuStrip`, has been made with a professional look and feel in mind. When users see a toolbar in an Office application, they expect to be able to move it around and position it wherever they want it. The `ToolStrip` enables users to do just that — that is, if *you* allow them to.

When you first add a `ToolStrip` to the design surface of your form it looks very similar to the `MenuStrip` you saw earlier, except for two things: To the far left are four vertical dots just as you know them from the menus in Visual Studio and Word. These dots indicate that the toolbar can be moved around and docked in the parent application window. The second difference is that by default a toolbar displays images rather than text and so the default of the items in the bar is a button. The toolbar displays a drop-down menu that allows you to select the type of the item.

One thing that is exactly like the `MenuStrip` is that the Action window includes a link called Insert Standard Items. When you click this, you don't get quite the same number of items as you did with the `MenuStrip`, but you get the buttons for New, Open, Save, Print, Cut, Copy, Paste, and Help. You won't go through a full Try It Out section as you did earlier; instead let's take a look at some of the properties of the `ToolStrip` itself and the controls used to populate it.

ToolStrip Properties

The properties of the ToolStrip control manage how and where the control is displayed. Remember that this control is actually the base for the MenuStrip control that you saw earlier and, therefore, there are many shared properties between them. Once again, the table that follows shows only a few properties of special interest—if you require a complete listing please refer to .NET Framework SDK documentation.

Name	Description
GripStyle	This property controls whether the four vertical dots are displayed by the far left of the toolbar. The effect of hiding the grip is that users can no longer move the toolbar.
LayoutStyle	By setting this property, you can control how the items in the toolbar are displayed. The default is horizontally.
Items	This property contains a collection of all the items in the toolbar.
ShowItemToolTip	This property allows you to determine if tooltips should be shown for the items in the toolbar.
Raft	This property allows you to specify the rafting container to contain the ToolStrip. This lets you position the ToolStrip in the dialog. The possible values are None, Top, Bottom, Left, and Right.
Stretch	By default a toolbar is only slightly wider or taller than the items contained within it. If you set the Stretch property to true the toolbar will fill the entire length of its container.

ToolStrip Items

There are a number of controls that can be used in a ToolStrip. Earlier, I mentioned that a toolbar should be able to contain buttons, combo boxes, and text boxes. As you would expect, there are controls for each of these items, but there are actually quite a few others, as described in the following table.

Name	Description
ToolStripButton	This control is used to represent a button. You use this for buttons with and without text.
ToolStripLabel	This control represents a label. It is important to realize that this control can also display images. What that means is that this control can be used to display a static image in front of another control that doesn't display information about itself such as a text box or combo box.

Name	Description
ToolStripSplitButton	This control displays a button with a drop-down button to the right that, when clicked, displays a menu below it. The menu does not unfold if the button part of the control is clicked.
ToolStripDropDownButton	This control is very similar to the ToolStripSplitButton. The only difference is that the drop-down button has been removed and replaced with an image of a down array. The menu part of the control unfolds when any part of the control is clicked.
ToolStripComboBox	As the name implies, this control displays a combo box.
ToolStripProgressBar	You can use this item to embed a progress bar in your toolbar.
ToolStripTextBox	Again, as the name implies, this control displays a text box.
ToolStripSeparator	You saw this control before, in the menus examples. It creates horizontal or vertical dividers for the items.

In the following Try It Out, you will extend your menus example to include a toolbar. The toolbar will contain the standard controls of a toolbar and three additional buttons: bold, italic, and underline. There will also be a combo box for selecting a font. (Note that the images you use here for the button that selects the font can be found in the code download.)

Try It Out   Toolbar Example

Follow these steps to extend the previous example with toolbars.

1. First, you need to remove the test ToolStripMenuItem that was used in the Format menu. Select the Show Help Menu and hit the Delete key. Then add three ToolStripMenuItems in its place and change each of their CheckOnClick properties to true:

   ❑   Bold

   ❑   Italic

   ❑   Underline

2. Name the three controls ToolStripMenuItemBold, ToolStripMenuItemItalic, and ToolStripMenuItemUnderline and set the CheckOnClick property on each of them to true.

3. Add a ToolStrip to the dialog. In the Actions Window, click Insert Standard Items. Select and delete the items for Cut, Copy, Paste, and the Separator after them.

4. Create three new buttons and a separator at the end of the toolbar by selecting Button three times and Separator once.

5. Now create the final two items by selecting ComboBox from the drop-down list first and then finally adding a separator as the last item.

6. Select the Help item and drag it from its current position to the position as the last item in the toolbar.

7. The first three buttons are going to be the bold, italic and underline buttons, respectively. Name the controls as shown in the following table.

ToolBarButton	Name
Bold button	ToolStripButtonBold
Italic button	ToolStripButtonItalic
Underline button	ToolStripButtonUnderline
ComboBox	ToolStripComboBoxFonts

8. Select the Bold button, click on the ellipse (...) in the `Image` property, select the Project resource file radio button and click the Import button. If you've downloaded the source code for this book, you should use the images found in the folder `Chapter15\Menus and Toolbars\ Manual Menus\Images`, where you will find three icons with the names `BLD.ICO`, `ITL.ICO`, and `UNDRLN.ICO`. Please note that the default extensions suggested by Visual Studio do not include `ICO`, so when browsing for the icons you will have to choose Show all files from the drop-down.

9. Select `BLD.ico` for the image of the Bold button.

10. Select the Italic button and change its image to `ITL.ico`.

11. Select the underline button and change its image to `UNDERLN.ico`.

12. Select the `ToolStripComboBox`. In the Properties panel, change the properties shown in the following table.

Name	Text
Items	MS Sans Serif Times New Roman
DropDownStyle	DropDownList

13. Set the `CheckOnClick` property for each of the Bold, Italic, and Underline buttons to `true`.

14. To select the initial item in the combo box, enter the following into the constructor of the class:

```
public Form1()
{
    InitializeComponent();

    this.ToolStripComboBoxFonts.SelectedIndex = 0;
}
```

15. Press F5 to run the example. You should see a dialog that looks like Figure 15-7.

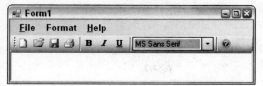

Figure 15-7

Adding Event Handlers

You are now ready to add the event handlers for the items on the menu and toolbars. You already have handlers for the Save, New, and Open items on the Menu, and obviously the buttons on the toolbar should behave in exactly the same way as the menus. This is easily achieved by assigning the `Click` events of the buttons on the toolbars to the same handlers that are used by the buttons on the menu. Set the events like this:

ToolStripButton	Text
New	MenuItemNew_Click
Open	MenuItemOpen_Click
Save	MenuItemSave_Click

Now it's time to add handlers for the bold, italic, and underline buttons. As these buttons are check buttons, you should use the `CheckedChanged` event instead of the `Click` event, so go ahead and add that event for each of the three buttons. Add the following code:

```
private void ToolStripButtonBold_CheckedChanged(object sender, EventArgs e)
{
    Font oldFont;
    Font newFont;

    bool checkState = ((ToolStripButton)sender).Checked;

    // Get the font that is being used in the selected text.
    oldFont = this.richTextBoxText.SelectionFont;

    if (!checkState)
      newFont = new Font(oldFont, oldFont.Style & ~FontStyle.Bold);
    else
      newFont = new Font(oldFont, oldFont.Style | FontStyle.Bold);

    // Insert the new font and return focus to the RichTextBox.
    this.richTextBoxText.SelectionFont = newFont;
    this.richTextBoxText.Focus();
```

```csharp
      this.ToolStripMenuItemBold.CheckedChanged -= new
EventHandler(ToolStripMenuItemBold_CheckedChanged);
      this.ToolStripMenuItemBold.Checked = checkState;
      this.ToolStripMenuItemBold.CheckedChanged += new
EventHandler(ToolStripMenuItemBold_CheckedChanged);
    }

    private void ToolStripButtonItalic_CheckedChanged(object sender, EventArgs e)
    {
      Font oldFont;
      Font newFont;

      bool checkState = ((ToolStripButton)sender).Checked;

      // Get the font that is being used in the selected text.
      oldFont = this.richTextBoxText.SelectionFont;

      if (!checkState)
        newFont = new Font(oldFont, oldFont.Style & ~FontStyle.Italic);
      else
        newFont = new Font(oldFont, oldFont.Style | FontStyle.Italic);

      // Insert the new font.
      this.richTextBoxText.SelectionFont = newFont;
      this.richTextBoxText.Focus();

      this.ToolStripMenuItemItalic.CheckedChanged -= new
EventHandler(ToolStripMenuItemItalic_CheckedChanged);
      this.ToolStripMenuItemItalic.Checked = checkState;
      this.ToolStripMenuItemItalic.CheckedChanged += new
EventHandler(ToolStripMenuItemItalic_CheckedChanged);
    }

    private void ToolStripButtonUnderline_CheckedChanged(object sender, EventArgs e)
    {
      Font oldFont;
      Font newFont;

      bool checkState = ((ToolStripButton)sender).Checked;

      // Get the font that is being used in the selected text.
      oldFont = this.richTextBoxText.SelectionFont;

      if (!checkState)
        newFont = new Font(oldFont, oldFont.Style & ~FontStyle.Underline);
      else
        newFont = new Font(oldFont, oldFont.Style | FontStyle.Underline);

      // Insert the new font.
      this.richTextBoxText.SelectionFont = newFont;
      this.richTextBoxText.Focus();
```

```
    this.ToolStripMenuItemUnderline.CheckedChanged -= new
EventHandler(ToolStripMenuItemUnderline_CheckedChanged);
    this.ToolStripMenuItemUnderline.Checked = checkState;
    this.ToolStripMenuItemUnderline.CheckedChanged += new
EventHandler(ToolStripMenuItemUnderline_CheckedChanged);
}
```

The event handlers simply set the correct style to the font used in the `RichTextBox`. The three last lines in each of the three methods all deal with the corresponding item in the menu. The first line removes the event handler from the menu item. This ensures that no events trigger when the next line runs, which sets the state of the `Checked` property to the same value as the toolbar button. Finally, the event handler is reinstated.

The event handlers for the menu items should simply set the `Checked` property of the buttons on the toolbar and allow the event handlers for the toolbar buttons to do the rest. Add the event handlers for the `CheckedChanged` event and enter this code:

```
private void ToolStripMenuItemBold_CheckedChanged(object sender, EventArgs e)
{
    this.ToolStripButtonBold.Checked = ToolStripMenuItemBold.Checked;
}

private void ToolStripMenuItemItalic_CheckedChanged(object sender, EventArgs e)
{
    this.ToolStripButtonItalic.Checked = ToolStripMenuItemItalic.Checked;
}

private void ToolStripMenuItemUnderline_CheckedChanged(object sender,
EventArgs e)
{
    this.ToolStripButtonUnderline.Checked = ToolStripMenuItemUnderline.Checked;
}
```

The only thing left to do is to allow the user to select a font family from the `ComboBox`. Whenever a user changes the selection in the `ComboBox` the `SelectedIndexChanged` is raised, so go ahead and add an event handler for that event. Enter the following code:

```
private void toolStripComboBoxFonts_SelectedIndexChanged(object sender,
EventArgs e)
{
    string text = ((ToolStripComboBox)sender).SelectedItem.ToString();

    // Create a new font with the correct font family.
    Font newFont = new Font(text, richTextBoxText.SelectionFont.Size,
                            richTextBoxText.SelectionFont.Style);
    richTextBoxText.SelectionFont = newFont;
}
```

Now run the code. You should be able to create a dialog that looks something like that shown in Figure 15-8. In the image, I've moved the toolbar a bit to the right to show the menu as well as the toolbar.

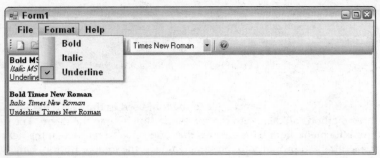

Figure 15-8

StatusStrip

The last of the small family of Strip controls is the StatusStrip. This control represents the bar that you will find at the bottom of the dialog in many applications. The bar is typically used to display brief information about the current state of the application—a good example is Word's displaying of the current page, column, line, and so on in the status bar as you are typing.

The StatusStrip is derived from the ToolStrip, and you should be quite familiar with the view that is presented to you as you drag the control onto your form. You will also notice that three of the four possible controls that can be used in the StatusStrip—ToolStripDropDownButton, ToolStripProgressBar, and ToolStripSplitButton—have been presented earlier. That leaves just one control that is specific to the StatusStrip: The StatusStripStatusLabel, which is also the default item you get.

StatusStripStatusLabel Properties

The StatusStripStatusLabel is used to present the user with information about the current state of the application with text and images. As the label is actually a pretty simple control I won't mention a lot of properties, concentrating instead on two that are actually not specific to the label, but nevertheless can and should be used with some effect.

Property	Value
AutoSize	AutoSize is on by default. This isn't really very intuitive because you don't want the labels in the status bar to jump back and forth because you changed the text in one of them. Unless the information in the label is static, you should always change this property to false.
DoubleClickEnable	With this property, you can specify whether the DoubleClick event will fire. This means that your users get a second place to change something in you application. An example of this is to allow users to double-click on a panel containing the word Bold to enable or disable bolding in the text.

In the following Try It Out, you are going to create a simple status bar for the example you've been working on. The status bar is going to have four panels, three of which will display an image and text, and the last one just text.

StatusStrip

Follow these steps to extend the small text editor you've been working on.

1. Double-click the `StatusStrip` in the `ToolBox` to add it to the dialog.

2. In the Properties panel, click the ellipse (...) in the `Items` property. This brings up the Items Collection Editor.

3. Click the Add button four times to add four panels to the `StaturStrip`. Set the following properties on the panels:

Panel	Property and Value
1	Name: `toolStripStatusLabelText` Text: Clear this property AutoSize: False DisplayStyle: Text Font: Arial; 8,25pt; style=Bold Size: 259,16 TextAlign: Middle Left
2	Name: `toolStripStatusLabelBold` Text: Bold DisplayStyle: ImageAndText Enabled: False Font: Arial; 8.25pt; style=Bold Size: 50, 16 Image: BLD ImageAlign: Middle-Center
3	Name: `toolStripStatusLabelItalic` Text: Italic DisplayStyle: ImageAndText Enabled: False Font: Arial; 8.25pt; style=Bold Size: 50, 16 Image: ITL ImageAlign: Middle-Center
4	Name: `toolStripStatusLabelUnderline` Text: Underline DisplayStyle: ImageAndText Enabled: False Font: Arial; 8.25pt; style=Bold Size: 70, 16 Image: UNDRLN ImageAlign: Middle-Center

4. Add this line of code to the event handler at the end of the `ToolStripButtonBold_CheckedChanged` method:

```
toolStripStatusLabelBold.Enabled = checkState;
```

5. Add this line of code to the event handler at the end of the `ToolStripButtonItalic_CheckedChanged` method:

```
toolStripStatusLabelItalic.Enabled = checkState;
```

6. Add this line of code to the event handler at the end of the `ToolStripButtonUnderline_CheckedChanged` method:

```
toolStripStatusLabelUnderline.Enabled = checkState;
```

7. Select the RichTextBox and add the TextChanged event to the code. Enter this:

```
private void richTextBoxText_TextChanged(object sender, EventArgs e)
{
    toolStripStatusLabelText.Text = "Number of characters: " +
richTextBoxText.Text.Length;
}
```

When you run the application you should be able to create a dialog that looks like that shown in Figure 15-9.

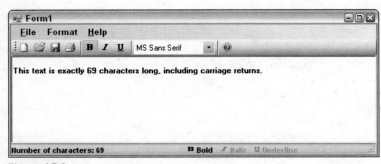

Figure 15-9

SDI and MDI Applications

Traditionally, there are three kinds of application that can be programmed for Windows. These are:

❑ **Dialog-based applications:** These present themselves to the user as a single dialog from which all functionality can be reached.

❑ **Single Document Interfaces (SDI):** These present themselves to the user with a menu, one or more toolbars, and one window in which the user can perform some task.

❑ **Multiple Document Interfaces (MDI):** These present themselves to the user in the same manner as an SDI does, but have the ability to hold multiple open windows at a time.

Dialog-based applications are usually small, single-purpose applications aimed at a specific task that needs a minimum of data to be entered by the user or that target a very specific type of data. An example of such an application is shown in Figure 15-10—the Calculator, which comes with Windows.

Figure 15-10

Single Document Interfaces are usually aimed at solving one specific task, because they allow the user to load a single document into the application to be worked on. This task, however, usually involves a lot of user interaction, and very often users will want the capability to save or load the result of their work. Good examples of SDI applications are WordPad (shown in Figure 15-11) and Paint, both of which come with Windows.

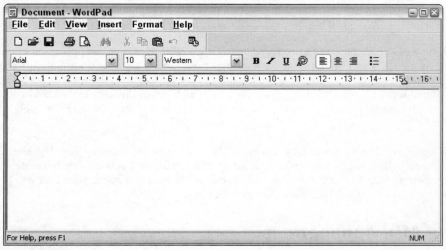

Figure 15-11

However, only one document can be open at any one time, so if a user wants to open a second document, a fresh instance of the SDI application will be opened and will have no reference to the first instance, so any configuration you do to one instance will not be carried over into the other. Thus, in one instance of Paint, you might set the drawing color to red, and if you open a second instance of Paint, the drawing color will be the default, which is black.

Multiple Document Interfaces are very much the same as SDI applications, except that they are able to hold more than one document open in different windows at any given time. A tell-tale sign of an MDI application is the inclusion of the Windows menu at the right-hand side of the menu bar, just before the Help menu. An example of an MDI application is Adobe Acrobat Reader, shown in Figure 15-12.

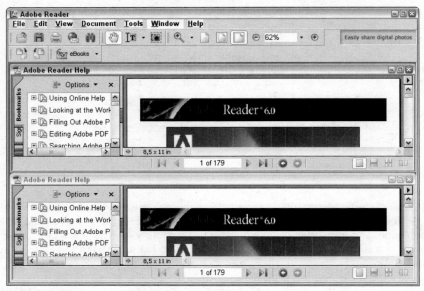

Figure 15-12

A fourth type of application was introduced with Office 2000. This type of application appears to be a cross between an SDI and MDI in that the windows presented to the user do not occupy the same area and each window shows up in the taskbar. Essentially the applications themselves are MDI applications because the main application will not shut down until all the windows are closed, and you can select which open document to view using the Window menu item, but the user interface itself is presented as an SDI.

In this chapter, you focus on the tasks necessary for creating an MDI application. The reasoning behind this is that any SDI application is basically a subset of an MDI, so if you are able to create an MDI you can also create an SDI. In fact in Chapter 16, you create a simple SDI application that will be used to demonstrate how to use the Windows Common Dialogs.

Building MDI Applications

What is involved in creating an MDI? First of all, the task you want the user to be able to accomplish should be one where he or she would want to have multiple documents open at a time. A good example of this is a text editor or, as in the screenshot above, a text viewer. Second, you should provide toolbars for the most commonly used tasks in the application, such as setting the font style, and loading and saving documents. Third, you should provide a menu that includes a Window menu item that allows the user to reposition the open windows relative to each other (tile and cascade) and that presents a list of all open windows. Another feature of MDI applications is that if a window is open and that window contains a menu, that menu should be integrated into the main menu of the application.

An MDI application consists of at least two distinct windows. The first window you create is called an *MDI container*. A window that can be displayed within that container is called an *MDI child*. I will refer to the MDI container as the MDI container or main window interchangeably and to the MDI child as the MDI child or child window.

To create an MDI application, you start out in the same way as you do for any other application—by creating a Windows Forms application in Visual Studio. To change the main window of the application from a form to an MDI container you simply set the `IsMdiContainer` property of the form to `true`. The background of the form changes color to indicate that it is now merely a background that you should not place visible controls on, although it is possible to do so, and it might even be reasonable to do so under certain circumstances.

To create a child window, add a new form to the project by choosing a Windows Form from the dialog brought up by selecting Project ➪ Add New Item. This form becomes a child window when you set the `MdiParent` property of the child window to a reference to the main window. You cannot set this property through the Properties panel, so you will have to do this using code.

Two things remain before the MDI application is able to display itself in its most basic mode. You must tell the MDI container which windows to display, and then you must display them. You do this simply by creating a new instance of the form you wish to display, and then calling `Show()` on it. The constructor of the form to display as a child should hook itself up with the parent container. You can arrange this by setting its `MdiParent` property to the instance of the MDI container.

The following Try It Out is a small example that takes you through these steps, before you move on to more complicated tasks.

Try It Out   Creating an MDI Application

1. Create a new Windows application called `MdiBasic` in the directory `C:\BegVCSharp\Chapter15`.

2. Select the form and set the following properties.

Property	Value
Name	frmContainer
IsMdiContainer	True
Text	MDI Basic
WindowState	Maximized

Add a new form to the solution by choosing Add Windows Form from the Project menu. Name the form `frmChild`.

How It Works

All the code that you need to display a child form is found in the constructors of the form. First, look at the constructor for the child window:

```
public frmChild(MdiBasic.frmContainer parent)
{
    InitializeComponent();

    // Set the parent of the form to the container.
    this.MdiParent = parent;
}
```

To bind a child form to the MDI container, the child must register itself with the container. This is done by setting the form's MdiParent property as shown in the preceding code. You will notice that the constructor you are using includes the parameter parent.

Because C# does not provide default constructors for a class that defines its own constructor, the preceding code prevents you from creating an instance of the form that is not bound to the MDI container.

Finally, you want to display the form. You do so in the constructor of the MDI container:

```
public frmContainer()
{
    InitializeComponent();

    // Create a new instance of the child form.
    MdiBasic.frmChild child = new MdiBasic.frmChild(this);

    // Show the form.
    child.Show();
}
```

You create a new instance of the child class and pass this to the constructor, where this represents the current instance of the MDI container class. Then you call Show() on the new instance of the child form and that's it. If you want to show more than one child window, all you have to do is repeat the two highlighted lines in the preceding code for each window.

If you run the code now, you should see something like Figure 15-13 (although the MDI Basic form will initially be maximized, I've resized it here to fit on the page).

It's not the most intriguing user interface ever designed, but it is clearly a solid start. In the next Try It Out, you produce a simple text editor, based on what you have already achieved in this chapter using menus, toolbars, and status bars.

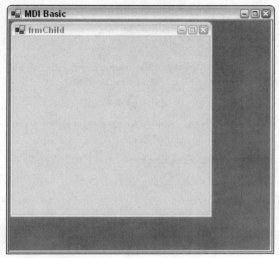

Figure 15-13

Try It Out | Creating an MDI Text Editor

Let's create the basic project first and then discuss what is happening:

1. Return to the earlier status bar example. Rename the form `frmEditor` and change its `Text` property to `Editor`.

2. Add a new form with the name `frmContainer.cs` to the project and set the following properties on it.

Properties	Value
Name	frmContainer
IsMdiParent	True
Text	Simple Text Editor
WindowState	Maximized

3. Open the `Program.cs` file and change the line containing the `Run` statement in the `Main` method to:

```
Application.Run(new frmContainer());
```

4. Change the constructor of the `frmEditor` form to:

```
public frmEditor(frmContainer parent)
{
    InitializeComponent();

    this.toolStripComboBoxFonts.SelectedIndex = 0;
```

471

```
        // Bind to the parent.
        this.MdiParent = parent;
}
```

5. Change the `MergeAction` property of the menu item with the text `&File` to `Replace` and the same property of the item with the text `&Format` to `MatchOnly`.

    Change the `AllowMerge` property of the toolbar to `False`.

6. Add a `MenuStrip` to the `frmContainer` form. Add a single item to the `MenuStrip` with the text `&File`

7. Change the constructor of the `frmContainer` form to:

```
public frmContainer()
{
    InitializeComponent();

    frmEditor newForm = new frmEditor(this);
    newForm.Show();
}
```

If you run the application now, you will see something like the example shown in Figure 15-14.

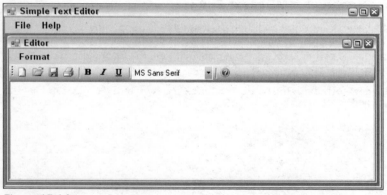

Figure 15-14

How It Works

Notice that a bit of magic has happened. The File menu and Help menu appear to have been removed from the `frmEditor`. If you select the File menu in the container window, you will see that the menu items from the `frmEditor` dialog can now be found there.

The menus that should be contained on child windows are those that are specific to that window. The File menu should be general for all windows and shouldn't be contained in the child windows as the only place it is found. The reason for this becomes apparent if you close the Editor window — the File menu now contains no items! What you really want is to be able to insert the items in the File menu that are specific to the child window when the child is in focus, and leave the rest of the items to the main window to display.

The properties that are controlling the behavior of menu items are these:

Name	Text
MergeAction	This property specifies how an item should behave when it is to be merged into another menu. The possible values are: Append: This causes the item to be placed last in the menu. Insert: Inserts the item immediately before the item that matches the criteria for where this is inserted. This criterion is either the text in the item or an index. MatchOnly: A match is required, but the item will not be inserted. Remove: Removes the item that matches the criteria for inserting the item. Replace: The matched item is replaced and the drop-down items are appended to the incoming item.
MergeIndex	The MergeIndex represents the position of a menu item in regard to other menu items that are being merged. You set this to a value greater than or equal to 0 if you want to control the order of the items that are being merged, otherwise you set it to –1. When merges are being performed, this value is checked and if it is not –1 this is used to match items rather than the text.
AllowMerge	Setting AllowMerge to false means the menus will not be merged.

In the following Try It Out, you continue with your text editor by changing how the menus are merged to reflect which menus belong where.

Try It Out   Merging Menus

Follow the steps below to change the text editor to use menus in both the container and child windows.

1. Add the following four menu items to the File menu on the frmContainer form. Notice the jump in MergeIndex values.

Name	Properties
&New	Name: ToolStripMenuItemNew MergeAction: MatchOnly MergeIndex: 0 ShortcutKeys: Ctrl + N
&Open	Name: ToolStripMenuItemOpen MergeAction: MatchOnly MergeIndex: 1 ShortcutKeys: Ctrl + O
-	MergeAction: MatchOnly MergeIndex: 10
E&xit	Name: ToolStripMenuItemNewExit MergeAction: MatchOnly MergeIndex: 11

2. You need a way to be able to add new windows, so double-click the menu item New and add the code below. It is the same code you entered into the constructor in order for the first dialog to be displayed:

```
private void ToolStripMenuItemNew_Click(object sender, EventArgs e)
{
    frmEditor newForm = new frmEditor(this);
    newForm.Show();
}
```

3. Go to the frmEditor form and delete the Open menu item from File menu, then change the properties of the other menu items to the following:

Name	Properties
&File	MergeAction: MatchOnly MergeIndex: -1
&New	MergeAction: MatchOnly MergeIndex: -1
-	MergeAction: Insert MergeIndex: 2
&Save	MergeAction: Insert MergeIndex: 3
Save &As	MergeAction: Insert MergeIndex: 4
-	MergeAction: Insert MergeIndex: 5
&Print	MergeAction: Insert MergeIndex: 6
Print Preview	MergeAction: Insert MergeIndex: 7
-	MergeAction: Insert MergeIndex: 8
E&xit	Name: ToolStripMenuItemClose Text: &Close MergeAction: Insert MergeIndex: 9

4. Run the application. You will now see that the two File menus have been merged, but there's still a File menu on the child dialog, containing just one item: New.

How It Works

The items that are set to MatchOnly are not moved between the menus, but in the case of the menu item with the text &File, the fact that the text of the two items matches means that their menu items are merged together.

The Items in the File menus are being merged together based on the MergedIndex properties for the items that you are interested in. The ones that should remain in place have their MergeAction property set to MatchOnly, the rest to Insert.

What is now very interesting is what happens when you click the menu items New and Save menus on the two different menus. Remember that the New menu on the child dialog just clears the text box where the other should create a new dialog. Not too surprisingly, because the two menus should belong to different windows, both work as expected, but what about the Save item? That has been moved off of the dialog and into its parent.

Try to open a few dialogs and enter some text into them, then click Save. Open a new dialog and click open (remember that Save always saves to the same file). Select one of the other windows and click save, then return to the new dialog and click Open again.

What you see is that the Save menu items always follow the dialog that is in focus. Every time a dialog is selected, the menus are merged again.

You just added a bit of code to the New menu item of the File menu in the frmContainer dialog, and you saw that the dialogs are created. One menu that is present in most if not all MDI applications is the Window menu. This lets you arrange the dialogs and often lists them in some way. In the following Try It Out, you will add this menu to your text editor.

Try It Out   Tracking Windows

Follow these steps to extend the application with the ability to display all open dialogs and arrange them.

1. Add a new top-level menu item to the frmContainer menu called &Window. Name this ToolStripMenuItemWindow.

2. Add the following three menu items to the new menu.

Name	Text
ToolStripMenuItemTile	&Tile
ToolStripMenuItemCascasde	&Cascade
-	-

3. Select the MenuStrip itself, not any of the items that are displayed in it, and change the MDIWindowListItem property to ToolStripMenuItemWindow.

4. Double-click first the tile item and then the cascade item to add the event handlers and enter the following code:

```
private void ToolStripMenuItemTile_Click(object sender, EventArgs e)
{
    LayoutMdi(MdiLayout.TileHorizontal);
}

private void ToolStripMenuItemCascasde_Click(object sender, EventArgs e)
{
    LayoutMdi(MdiLayout.Cascade);
}
```

5. Change the constructor of the `frmEditor` dialog to this:

```
public frmEditor(frmContainer parent, int counter)
{
    InitializeComponent();

    this.ToolStripComboBoxFonts.SelectedIndex = 0;

    // Bind to the parent.
    this.MdiParent = parent;
    this.Text = "Editor " + counter.ToString();
}
```

6. Add a private member variable to the top of the code for `frmContainer` and change the constructor and the event handler for the menu item New to the following:

```
public partial class frmContainer : Form
{
    private int mCounter;

    public frmContainer()
    {
        InitializeComponent();

        mCounter = 1;
        frmEditor newForm = new frmEditor(this, mCounter);
        newForm.Show();
    }

    private void ToolStripMenuItemNew_Click(object sender, EventArgs e)
    {
        frmEditor newForm = new frmEditor(this, ++mCounter);
        newForm.Show();
    }
```

How It Works

The most interesting part of this example concerns the Window menu. To have a menu display a list of all the dialogs that are opened in a MDI application, all you have to do is create a menu at the top level for it and set the `MdiWindowListItem` property to point to that menu.

The Framework will then append a menu item to the menu for each of the dialogs that are currently displayed. The item that represents the current dialog will have a check mark next to it, and you can select another dialog by clicking the list.

The other two menu items, the Tile and Cascade items, demonstrated a method of the form: MdiLayout. This method allows you to arrange the dialogs in a standard manner.

The changes to the constructors and New item simply ensure that the dialogs are numbered.

If you run the application now, you should see something like Figure 15-15.

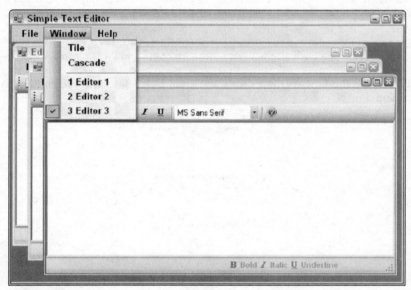

Figure 15-15

Creating Controls

There are times when the controls that ship with Visual Studio 2005 just don't meet your needs. The reasons for this can be many — the controls don't draw themselves in the way you want them to, the controls are restrictive in some way, or the control you need simply doesn't exist. Recognizing this, Microsoft has provided the means to create controls that meet your needs. Visual Studio provides a project type named Windows Control Library, which you use when you want to create a control yourself.

Two distinct kinds of home-made controls can be developed: user controls (or composite controls) and custom controls:

❑   **User or composite controls:** These controls build on the functionality of existing controls to create a new control. Such controls are generally made to encapsulate functionality with the user interface of the control, or to enhance the interface of a control by combining several other controls into one unit.

477

❑ **Custom controls:** These controls can be created when no control fits your needs, that is, you start from scratch. A custom control draws its entire user interface itself and no existing controls are used in the creation of the control. You will normally need to create a control like this when the user interface control you want to create is unlike that of any other available control.

In this chapter, you focus on user controls, because designing and drawing a custom control from scratch is beyond the scope of this book. Chapter 30 on GDI+ gives you the means to draw items by yourself, and you should then be able to move on to custom controls easily.

ActiveX controls as used in Visual Studio 6 existed in a special kind of file with the extension ocx. These files were essentially COM DLLs. In .NET, a control exists in exactly the same way as any other assembly, and because of that the ocx extension has disappeared and controls exist in DLLs.

User controls inherit from the System.Windows.Forms.UserControl class. This base class provides the control you are creating with all the basic features a control in .NET should include — leaving you only the task of creating the control. Virtually anything can be created as a control, ranging from a label with a nifty design to full-blown grid controls. In Figure 15-16, the box at the bottom, UserControl1, represents a new control.

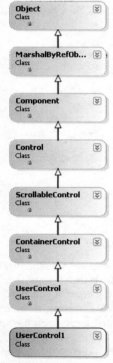

Figure 15-16

Unlike user controls, custom controls derive from the System.Windows.Forms.Control class rather than UserControl.

A number of things are taken for granted when working with controls. If your control doesn't fulfill those expectations, the chances are that people will be discouraged from using it. These criteria are:

❑ The behavior of the design-time control should be very similar to its behavior at runtime. This means that if the control consists of a `Label` and a `TextBox` that have been combined to create a `LabelTextbox`, the `Label` and `TextBox` should both be displayed at design time and the text entered for the `Label` should also be shown at design time. While this is fairly easy in this case it can present problems in more complex cases, where you'll need to find an appropriate compromise.

❑ Access to the properties of the control should be possible from the form designer in a logical manner. A good example of this is the `ImageList` control that presents a dialog from which you can browse to the images you want to include, and once the images are imported, they are shown in a list in the dialog.

The next few pages introduce you to the creation of controls by means of an example. The example creates the `LabelTextbox`, and it demonstrates the basics of creating a user control project, creating properties and events, and debugging controls.

As the name of the control in the following Try It Out implies, this control combines two existing controls to create a single one that performs, in one go, a task extremely common in Windows programming: adding a label to a form, then adding a text box to the same form and positioning the text box in relation to the label. Let's look at what a user of this control will expect it to do:

❑ It should be possible for the user to position the text box either to the right of the label or below it. If the text box is positioned to the right of the label, it should be possible to specify a fixed distance from the left edge of the control to the text box in order to align text boxes below each other.

❑ The usual properties and events of the text box and label should be available to the user.

Now that you know what you are up against, it is time to start Visual Studio and create a new project.

Try It Out   LabelTextbox Example

1. Create a new Windows Control Library project called `LabelTextbox` and save it in `C:\BegVCSharp\Chapter15`.

As you can see in Figure 15-17, the form designer presents you with a design surface that looks somewhat different from what you're used to. First of all, the surface is much smaller than normal, and second, it doesn't look like a dialog at all. You should not let this new look discourage you in any way — things still work as usual. The main difference is that up until now you have been placing controls on a form, but now you are creating a control to be placed on a form.

2. Click the design surface and bring up the properties for the control. Change the Name of the control to `ctlLabelTextbox`.

3. Double-click a `Label` in the Toolbox to add it to the control, placing it in the top left-hand corner of the surface. Change its Name property to `lblTextBox`. Set the Text property to `Label`.

4. Double-click a `TextBox` in the Toolbox. Change its Name property to `txtLabelText`.

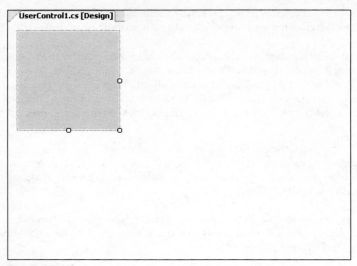

Figure 15-17

At design time, you do not know how the user will want to position these controls. Because of that you are going to write code that will position the Label and TextBox. That same code will determine the position of the controls when a LabelTextbox control is placed on a form.

Figure 15-18 shows that the design of the control looks anything but encouraging — not only is the TextBox obscuring part of the label, the surface is too large. However, this is of no consequence, because, unlike what you've been used to up until now, what you see is not what you get! The code you are about to add to the control will change the appearance of the control, but only when the control is added to a form.

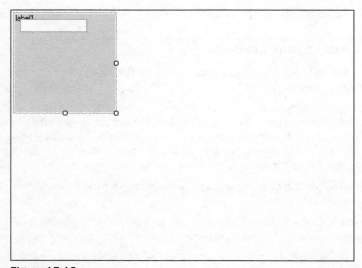

Figure 15-18

The first thing you want to do is position the controls relative to each other. The user should be able to decide how the controls are positioned and for that you add not one but two properties to the control. One property is called `Position` and gives the user a choice between two options: `Right` and `Below`. If the user chooses `Right` then the other property comes into play. This property is called `TextboxMargin` and is an `int` that represents the number of pixels from the left edge of the control to where the `TextBox` should be placed. If the user specifies `0`, the `TextBox` is placed with its right edge aligned with the right edge of the control.

Adding Properties

To give the user a choice between `Right` and `Below`, you start by defining an enumeration with these two values. Return to the control project, go to the code editor, and add this code:

```
public partial class ctlLabelTextbox : UserControl
{
    // Enumeration of the two possible positions
    public enum PositionEnum
    {
      Right,
      Below
    }
```

This is just a normal enumeration, as you saw in Chapter 5. Now for the magic — you want the position to be a property the user can set through code and the designer. You do this by adding a property to the `ctlLabelTextbox` class. First, however, you create two member fields that will hold the values the user selects:

```
// Member field that will hold the choices the user makes
private PositionEnum mPosition = PositionEnum.Right;
private int mTextboxMargin = 0;

public ctlLabelTextbox()
{
    ...
```

Then add the `Position` property as follows:

```
public PositionEnum Position
{
    get
    {
      return mPosition;
    }
    set
    {
      mPosition = value;
      MoveControls();
    }
}
```

The property is added to the class like any other property. If you are asked to return the property, you return the `mPosition` member field, and if you are asked to change the `Position`, you assign the value to `mPosition` and call the method `MoveControls()`. You return to `MoveControls()` in a short while—for now it is enough to know that this method positions the two controls by examining the values of `mPosition` and `mTextboxMargin`.

The `TextboxMargin` property is the same, except it works with an integer:

```
public int TextboxMargin
{
   get
   {
      return mTextboxMargin;
   }
   set
   {
      mTextboxMargin = value;
      MoveControls();
   }
}
```

Adding the Event Handlers

Before you move on to test the two properties, you add two event handlers as well. When the control is placed on the form, the `Load` event is called. You should use this event to initialize the control and any resources the control may use. You handle this event in order to move the controls and to size the control to fit neatly around the two controls it contains. The other event you add is the `SizeChanged` event. This event is called whenever the control is resized, and you should handle the event to allow the control to draw itself correctly. Select the control and add the two events: `SizeChanged` and `Load`.

Then you add the event handlers:

```
private void ctlLabelTextbox_Load(object sender, EventArgs e)
{
   lblTextBox.Text = this.Name; // Add a text to the label
   // Set the height of the control.
   this.Height = txtLabelText.Height > lblTextBox.Height ? txtLabelText.Height :
lblTextBox.Height;
   MoveControls(); // Move the controls.
}

private void ctlLabelTextbox_SizeChanged(object sender, System.EventArgs e)
{
   MoveControls();
}
```

Once again, you call `MoveControls()` to take care of the positioning of the controls. It is time to see this method, before you test the control again:

```
private void MoveControls()
{
   switch (mPosition)
   {
   case PositionEnum.Below:
      // Place the top of the Textbox just below the label.
```

```
                this.txtLabelText.Top = this.lblTextBox.Bottom;
                this.txtLabelText.Left = this.lblTextBox.Left;

                // Change the width of the Textbox to equal the width of the control.
                this.txtLabelText.Width = this.Width;
                this.Height = txtLabelText.Height + lblTextBox.Height;
                break;
            case PositionEnum.Right:
                // Set the top of the textbox to equal that of the label.
                txtLabelText.Top = lblTextBox.Top;

                // If the margin is zero, we'll place the text box next to the label.
                if (mTextboxMargin == 0)
                {
                    int width = this.Width-lblTextBox.Width-3;
                    txtLabelText.Left = lblTextBox.Right + 3;
                    txtLabelText.Width = width;
                }
                else
                {
                    // If the margin isn't zero, we place the text box where the user
                    // has specified.
                    txtLabelText.Left = mTextboxMargin;
                    txtLabelText.Width = this.Right-mTextboxMargin;
                }
                this.Height = txtLabelText.Height > lblTextBox.Height ?
                                    txtLabelText.Height : lblTextBox.Height;
                break;
        }
    }
```

The value in mPosition is tested in a switch statement to determine whether you should place the text box below or to the right of the label. If the user chooses Below, then move the top of the text box to the position that is the bottom of the label. You then move the left edge of the text box to the left edge of the control and set its width to the width of the control.

If the user chooses Right, then there are two possibilities. If the TextboxMargin is zero, then start by determining the width that is left in the control for the text box. You then set the left edge of the text box to just a nudge right of the text and set the width to fill the remaining space. If the user did specify a margin, then place the left edge of the text box at that position and set the width again.

You are now ready to test the control. Before moving on, build the project.

Debugging User Controls

Debugging a user control is quite different from debugging a Windows application. Normally, you would just add a breakpoint somewhere, press F5, and see what happens. If you are still unfamiliar with debugging, you should refer to Chapter 7 for a detailed explanation.

A control needs a container in which to display itself, and you will have to supply it with one. You do this in the following Try It Out by creating a Windows application project.

Debugging User Controls

1. From the File menu choose Add ➪ New Project... In the Add New Project dialog, create a new Windows application called `LabelTextboxTest`.

In Solution Explorer, you should now see two projects open. The first project you created, `LabelTextbox`, is written in boldface. This means that if you try to run the solution, the debugger will attempt to use the control project as the startup project. This will fail because the control isn't a stand-alone type of project. To fix this, right-click the name of the new project — `LabelTextboxTest` — and select Set as StartUp Project. If you run the solution now, the Windows application project will be run and no errors will occur.

2. At the top of the Toolbox you should now see a tab named LabelTextBox Components. Visual Studio has recognized that there is a Windows Control Library in the solution and the fact that it is likely that you want to use the controls provided by this library in other projects. Double-click on `ctlLabelTextBox` to add it to the form. Note that the References node in Solution Explorer is expanded. This happens because Visual Studio just added a reference to the `LabelTextBox` project for you.

3. While in the code, search for new `ctlLabel`. Search in the entire project. You will get a hit in the "behind the scenes" file `Form.Designer.cs` where Visual Studio hides most of the code it generates for you. Note that you should never edit this file directly.

4. Place a break point on this line:

```
this.ctlLabelTextbox1 = new LabelTextbox.ctlLabelTextbox();
```

5. Run the code. As you would expect, the code stops at the breakpoint you placed. Now step into the code (if you are using the default keyboard maps, then press F11 to do so). When you step into the code you are transferred to the constructor of your new control, which is exactly what you want in order to debug the component. You are also able to place breakpoints. Press F5 to allow the application to run.

Extending the LabelTextbox Control

Finally, you are ready to test the properties of the control. Go through the steps to create a project in a new instance of Visual Studio 2005 that includes the `LabelTextbox` control. As Figure 15-19 shows, you will see the label displaying the name of the control and the text box occupying the remaining area of the control. Also notice that the controls within the `LabelTextbox` control move to the correct positions when the control is added to the form.

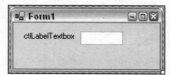

Figure 15-19

Adding More Properties

You can't do much with the control at the moment, as it is sadly missing the ability to change the text in the label and text box. You add two properties to handle this: `LabelText` and `TextboxText`. The properties are added in the same way as you did the two previous properties:

```
public string LabelText
{
   get
   {
      return mLabelText;
   }
   set
   {
       mLabelText = value;
       lblTextBox.Text = mLabelText;      MoveControls();
   }
}

public string TextboxText
{
   get
   {
      return txtLabelText.Text;
   }
   set
   {
      txtLabelText.Text = value;
   }
}
```

You also need to declare the member variable `mLabelText` to hold the text:

```
   private string mLabelText = "";

   public ctlLabelTextbox()
   {
```

You simply assign the text to the `Text` property of the `Label` and `TextBox` controls if you want to insert the text, and return the value of the `Text` properties. If the label text is changed, you need to call `MoveControls()`, because the label text may influence where the text box is positioned. Text inserted into the text box, on the other hand, does not move the controls, and if the text is longer than the text box, it will disappear out of sight.

Adding More Event Handlers

Now it is time to begin thinking about which events the control should provide. Because the control is derived from the `UserControl` class, it has inherited a lot of functionality that you don't need to worry about. There are, however, a number of events that you don't want to hand to the user in the standard way. Examples of this include the `KeyDown`, `KeyPress`, and `KeyUp` events. The reason you need to change these events is that users will expect them to be sent when they press a key in the text box. As they are now, the events are only sent when the control itself has focus and the user presses a key.

To change this behavior, you must handle the events sent by the text box, and pass them on to the user. Add the `KeyDown`, `KeyUp`, and `KeyPress` events for the text box and enter the following code:

```
private void txtLabelText_KeyDown(object sender, KeyEventArgs e)
{
    OnKeyDown(e);
}

private void txtLabelText_KeyUp(object sender, KeyEventArgs e)
{
    OnKeyUp(e);
}

private void txtLabelText_KeyPress(object sender, KeyPressEventArgs e)
{
    OnKeyPress(e);
}
```

Calling the `OnKeyXXX` method invokes a call to any methods that are subscribed to the event.

Adding a Custom Event Handler

When you want to create an event that does not exist in one of the base classes, you need to do a bit more work. You will create an event called `PositionChanged` that will occur when the `Position` property changes.

In order to create this event, you need three things:

❑   You need an appropriate delegate that can be used to invoke the methods the user assigns to the event.

❑   The user must be able to subscribe to the event by assigning a method to it.

❑   You must invoke the method the user has assigned to the event.

The delegate you use is the `EventHandler` delegate provided by the .NET Framework. As you learned in Chapter 12, this is a special kind of delegate that is declared by its very own keyword, `event`. The following line declares the event and enables the user to subscribe to it:

```
public event System.EventHandler PositionChanged;

// Constructor
public ctlLabelTextbox()
{
```

Now all that remains to do is raise the event. Because it should occur when the `Position` property changes, you raise the event in the `set` accessor of the `Position` property:

```
public PositionEnum Position
{
    get
    {
        return mPosition;
```

```
    }
    set
    {
        mPosition = value;
        MoveControls();
        if (PositionChanged != null) // Make sure there are subscribers
        {
            PositionChanged(this, new EventArgs());
        }
    }
}
```

First, you make sure that there are some subscribers by checking if `PositionChanged` is `null`. If it isn't you invoke the methods.

You subscribe to the new custom event as you would any other. Simply select the control on the form in the `LabelTextboxTest` project and double-click the `PositionChanged` event in the Events part of the Properties panel.

Your custom event handler doesn't really do anything sparkling — it simply points out that the position has changed!

```
private void ctlLabelTextbox1_PositionChanged(object sender, EventArgs e)
{
    MessageBox.Show("Changed");
}
```

Finally, add a button to the form and double-click it to add its `Click` event handler to the project and add this code:

```
private void buttonToggle_Click(object sender, EventArgs e)
{
    ctlLabelTextbox1.Position = ctlLabelTextbox1.Position ==
LabelTextbox.ctlLabelTextbox.PositionEnum.Right ?
LabelTextbox.ctlLabelTextbox.PositionEnum.Below :
LabelTextbox.ctlLabelTextbox.PositionEnum.Right;
}
```

When you run the application you can change the position of the text box at runtime. Every time the text box moves, the `PositionChanged` event is called and you get a `messagebox` displayed.

The example is now finished. It could be refined rather a bit, but I will leave that to you and the exercises.

Summary

In this chapter, you started where you left off in the previous chapter, by examining the `MainMenu` and `ToolBar` controls. You saw how to create MDI and SDI applications and how menus and toolbars are used in those applications. You then moved on to create a control of your own, designing properties, user interface, and events for the control. The next chapter will complete the discussion of Windows Forms by looking at the one special type of form only glossed over so far: the Windows common dialogs.

In this chapter, you learned to:

❑ Use the three Strip controls that allow you to work with menus, toolbars, and status bars in Windows Forms.

❑ Create MDI applications, which are used to extend the text editor even further.

❑ Create controls of your own by building on existing controls.

Exercise

1. Using the `LabelTextbox` example as the base, create a new property called `MaxLength` that stores the maximum number of characters that can be entered into the text box. Then create two new events called `MaxLengthChanged` and `MaxLengthReached`. The `MaxLengthChanged` event should be raised when the `MaxLength` property is changed, and `MaxLengthReached` should be raised when the user enters a character making the length of the text in the text box equal to the value of `MaxLength`.

Using Common Dialogs

The last three chapters looked at various aspects of programming Windows Forms applications, and how to implement such things as menus, toolbars, and SDI and MDI forms. Now you know how to display simple message boxes to get information from the user and how to create more sophisticated custom dialogs to ask the user for specific information. However, for common tasks such as opening and saving files, you can use prewritten dialog classes instead of having to create your own custom dialog.

This not only has the advantage of requiring less code, but also it uses the familiar Windows dialogs, giving your application a standard look and feel. The .NET Framework has classes that hook up to the Windows dialogs to open and create directories, to open and save files, to access printers, and to select colors and fonts.

In this chapter, you learn how to use these standard dialog classes. In particular, you will:

❑   Use `OpenFileDialog` and `SaveFileDialog` classes

❑   Learn about the .NET printing class hierarchy and use the `PrintDialog`, `PageSetupDialog`, and `PrintPreviewDialog` classes to implement printing and print preview

❑   Look at how to change fonts and colors with the `FontDialog` and `ColorDialog` classes

❑   Use the `FolderBrowserDialog` class that is new with .NET 2.0

Common Dialogs

A dialog is a window that is displayed within the context of another window. With a dialog, you can ask the user to enter some data before the flow of the program continues. A common dialog is a dialog used to get information from the user that most applications will typically require, such as the name of a file, and is a part of the Windows operating system.

The classes you get with the Microsoft .NET Framework are shown in Figure 16-1.

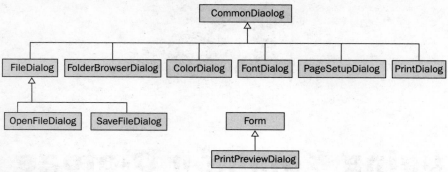

Figure 16-1

All these dialog classes, except the `PrintPreviewDialog`, derive from the abstract `CommonDialog` base class that has methods to manage a Windows common dialog.

The `CommonDialog` class defines the following methods and events common to all common dialog classes.

Public Instance Methods and Events	Description
ShowDialog()	This method is implemented from the derived class to display a common dialog.
Reset()	Every derived dialog class implements the Reset() method to set all properties of the dialog class to their default values.
HelpRequest	This event is thrown when the user clicks the Help button on a common dialog.

All these dialog classes wrap up a Windows common dialog to make the dialog available for .NET applications. `PrintPreviewDialog` is an exception because it adds its own elements to a Windows form to control the preview of a print, and hence is not really a dialog at all. The `OpenFileDialog` and `SaveFileDialog` classes derive from the abstract base class `FileDialog` that adds file features that are common to both the opening and closing file dialogs.

The following list provides an overview of how the different dialogs can be used:

❑ To let the user select and browse files to open, use the `OpenFileDialog`. This dialog can be configured to allow the selection of a single file or multiple files.

❑ With the `SaveFileDialog` the user can specify a filename and browse for a directory in which to save files.

❑ The `PrintDialog` is used to select a printer and set the printing options.

❑ To configure the margins of a page, the `PageSetupDialog` is usually used.

❑   The PrintPreviewDialog is one way to preview on the screen what is to be printed on paper, with options such as zoom.

❑   The FontDialog lists all installed Windows fonts with styles and sizes, and it provides a preview to select the font of choice.

❑   The ColorDialog class makes it easy to select a color.

❑   For selecting and creating directories, the dialog FolderBrowserDialog can be used. This dialog is new with .NET 2.0.

I have seen some applications developed (by the same company) where not only were common dialogs not reused, but also no style guide was used for building custom dialogs. The functionality of these dialogs was not consistent, with some buttons and other controls found in different locations, such as the OK and Cancel buttons being reversed between dialogs.

Sometimes that inconsistency can be found within one application. That's frustrating for the user, and it increases the time required to complete a task.

> **Be consistent in the dialogs you build and use! Consistency can be easily attained by using the common dialogs.**

How to Use Dialogs

As CommonDialog is the base class for the dialog classes, all the dialog classes can be used similarly. Public instance methods are ShowDialog() and Reset(). ShowDialog() invokes the protected RunDialog() instance method to display the dialog and finally returns a DialogResult instance with the information on how the user interacted with the dialog. Reset(), in contrast, sets properties of the dialog class to their default values.

The following code segment shows an example of how a dialog class can be used. Later, you take a more detailed look at each of the steps, but first you get an introduction explaining how dialogs can be used.

In the following code segment you can see how to use a dialog class:

```
OpenFileDialog dlg = new OpenFileDialog();
dlg.Title = "Sample";
dlg.ShowReadOnly = true;

if (dlg.ShowDialog() == DialogResult.OK)
{
    string filename = dlg.FileName;
}
```

❑   First a new instance of the dialog class is created.

❑   Next, you have to set some properties to enable and disable optional features and set dialog state. In this case, you set the Title property to "Sample", and the ShowReadOnly property to true.

❑ By calling the ShowDialog() method, the dialog is displayed, waiting for and reacting to user inputs.

❑ If the user presses the OK button, the dialog closes, and you check for the OK by comparing the result of the dialog with DialogResult.OK. After that you can get the values from the user input by querying for the specific property values. In this case, the value of the FileName property is stored in the filename variable.

It's really that easy! Of course, every dialog has its own configurable options, which you look at in the following sections.

If you use a dialog from within a Windows Forms application in Visual Studio, it's even easier than the few lines of code above. The Windows Forms designer creates the code to instantiate a new instance, and the property values can be set from the Properties window. You just have to call ShowDialog() and get to the changed values, as you shall see.

File Dialogs

With a file dialog, the user can select a drive and browse through the file system to select a file. From the file dialog, all you want returned is a filename from the user.

The OpenFileDialog enables users to select by name the file they want to open. The SaveFileDialog, in contrast, enables users to specify a name for a file they want to save. These dialog classes are similar because they derive from the same abstract base class, though there are some properties unique to each class. In this section, you look first at the features of the OpenFileDialog, then at where the SaveFileDialog differs, and you develop a sample application that uses both of them.

OpenFileDialog

The OpenFileDialog class enables users to select a file to open. As you saw in the preceding example, a new instance of the OpenFileDialog class is created before the ShowDialog() method is called.

```
OpenFileDialog dlg = new OpenFileDialog();
dlg.ShowDialog();
```

Running a Windows application program with these two code lines will result in the dialog shown in Figure 16-2.

As you have already seen, you can set the properties of this class before calling ShowDialog(), which changes the behavior and appearance of this dialog, or limits the files that can be opened. In the next sections you look at possible modifications.

> Note that if you want to use the OpenFileDialog with console applications, the System.Windows. Forms assembly must be referenced and the System.Windows.Forms namespace must be included.

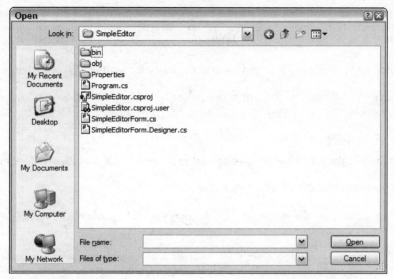

Figure 16-2

Dialog Title

The default title for the `OpenFileDialog` is Open. However, Open is not always the best name. For example, if in your application you want to analyze log files or get file sizes, perform whatever processing is required, and close the files immediately afterward, a title of Analyze Files would be better because the files don't stay open for the user. Fortunately, you can change the title of the dialog by setting the `Title` property. Visual Studio itself has different titles for the file open dialogs to differentiate the file types that are opened: Open Project, Open File, and Open Web Site.

This code segment shows how a different title can be set:

```
OpenFileDialog dlg = new OpenFileDialog();
dlg.Title = "Open File";
dlg.ShowDialog();
```

Specifying Directories

The directory that is opened by default is the directory that was opened by the user the last time the application was run. Setting the `InitialDirectory` property changes this behavior. The default value of `InitialDirectory` is an empty string representing the user's My Documents directory, which is shown the first time the dialog is used in the application. The second time that the dialog is opened, the directory shown is the same as for the previously opened file. The Windows common dialog called by the `OpenFileDialog` uses the Registry to locate the name of the previously opened file.

> You should never use a hard-coded directory string in your application because that directory might not exist on the user's system.

To get special system folders you can use the static method GetFolderPath() *of the* System .Environment *class. The* GetFolderPath() *method accepts an* Environment.SpecialFolder *enumeration member that defines which system directory you want the path for.*

In the following code example, the common user directory for templates is set as InitialDirectory.

```
string dir = Environment.GetFolderPath(Environment.SpecialFolder.Templates);
dlg.InitialDirectory = dir;
```

Setting the File Filter

The file filter defines the file types the user can select to open. A simple filter string can look like this:

```
Text Documents (*.txt)|*.txt|All Files|*.*
```

The filter is used to display the entries in the Files of type: list box. Microsoft WordPad displays the entries as shown in Figure 16-3.

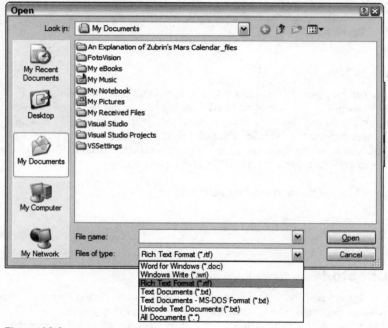

Figure 16-3

A filter has multiple segments separated with the pipe character (|). Two strings are required for each entry, so the number of segments should always be an even number. The first string for each entry defines the text presented in the list box; the second string specifies the extension of the files to be displayed in the dialog. You can set the filter string with the Filter property as in the following code:

```
dlg.Filter = "Text documents (*.txt)|*.txt|All Files|*.*";
```

A blank before or after the filter is not allowed.

A wrong `Filter` value results in a runtime exception — `System.ArgumentException` — with this error message: `The provided filter string is invalid`.

The `FilterIndex` property specifies the number of the default selection in the list box. With WordPad, the default selection is Rich Text Format (`*.rtf`) (highlighted in Figure 16-3). If you have multiple file types to choose from, you can set the `FilterIndex` to the default file type. It's worth paying attention to the fact that the `FilterIndex` is one-based!

Validation

The `OpenFileDialog` can do some automatic validation of the file before you attempt to open it. When the `ValidateNames` property is `true`, the filename entered by the user is checked to see if it is a valid Windows filename. Pressing the OK button of the dialog with an invalid filename displays the dialog shown in Figure 16-4, and the user must correct the filename or click Cancel to leave the `OpenFileDialog`. Invalid characters for a filename include characters such as `\\`, `/`, and `:`.

Figure 16-4

With `ValidateNames` set to `true`, you can use `CheckFileExists` and `CheckPathExists` for additional validation. With `CheckPathExists`, the *path* is validated, whereas `CheckFileExists` validates the *file*. If the file doesn't exist, the dialog shown in Figure 16-5 is displayed when the OK button is pressed.

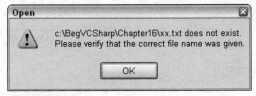

Figure 16-5

The default for these three properties is `true`, so the validation happens automatically.

Help

The `OpenFileDialog` class supports a Help button that is, by default, invisible. Setting the `ShowHelp` property to `true` makes this button visible, and you can add an event handler to the `HelpRequest` event to display help information to the user.

Results

The `ShowDialog()` method of the `OpenFileDialog` class returns a `DialogResult` enumeration value. The `DialogResult` enumeration defines the members `Abort`, `Cancel`, `Ignore`, `No`, `None`, `OK`, `Retry`, and `Yes`.

`None` is the default value that is set as long as the user hasn't closed the dialog. When a button is pressed, the corresponding result is returned. With the `OpenFileDialog`, only `DialogResult.OK` and `DialogResult.Cancel` are returned.

If the user presses the OK button, the selected filename can be accessed by using the `FileName` property. If the user canceled the dialog, the `FileName` is just an empty string. If the `Multiselect` property is set to `true` so that the user can select more than one file, you get all the selected filenames by accessing the `FileNames` property, which returns a string array.

Note that the `FileNames` property contains the files in the reverse order to which they were selected — thus the first string in the `FileNames` array is the last file selected. Also, the `FileNames` property always contains the filename of the *last* file that is selected.

This small code extract shows how multiple filenames can be retrieved from an `OpenFileDialog`:

```
OpenFileDialog dlg = new OpenFileDialog();
dlg.Multiselect = true;

if (dlg.ShowDialog() == DialogResult.OK)
{
    foreach (string s in dlg.FileNames)
    {
        // Now display the filenames in a list box.
        this.listBox1.Items.Add(s);
    }
}
```

The `ShowDialog()` method opens the dialog. Because the `Multiselect` property is set to `true`, the user can select multiple files. Pressing the OK button of the dialog ends the dialog if all goes well, and `DialogResult.OK` is returned. With the `foreach` statement, you go through all strings in the string array returned from the `FileNames` property to display every selected file.

OpenFileDialog Properties

In summary, Figure 16-6 shows the `OpenFileDialog` with its properties — you can easily see what properties influence which user interface elements.

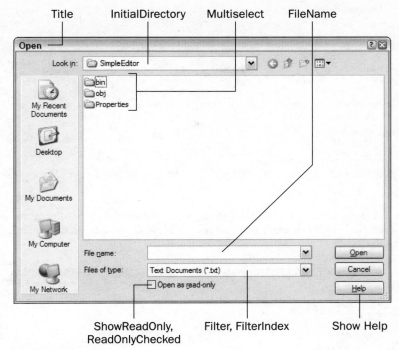

Figure 16-6

To demonstrate the use of the standard dialogs you create a simple text editor Windows application called `SimpleEditor` that will allow the user to load, save, and edit text files. As you progress further through the chapter, you will also see how to print the text file. In the following Try It Out, you start by seeing how to use the open and save file dialogs.

Try It Out   Creating the Simple Text Editor Windows Application

1. Create a new Windows application called `SimpleEditor` in the directory `C:\BegVCSharp\Chapter16`.

2. Rename the generated file `Form1.cs` to `SimpleEditorForm.cs`. Answer Yes to rename all references to the form. This way Visual Studio 2005 also changes the name of the class to `SimpleEditorForm`.

3. Set the `Text` property of the form to `Simple Editor`, and change its `Size` to `570;270`. A multiline text box will be the area to read and modify the data of the file, so add a `TextBox` from the Toolbox to the Windows Forms designer. The text box should be multiline and should cover the complete area of the application, so set these properties to the values specified in the following table.

Property	Value
(Name)	textBoxEdit
Text	
Multiline	True
Dock	Fill
ScrollBars	Both
AcceptsReturn	True
AcceptsTab	True

4. Next, add a MenuStrip to the application. Set the name of the MenuStrip to mainMenu. The menu should have a File entry with submenus New, Open..., Save, and Save As..., as Figure 16-7 demonstrates.

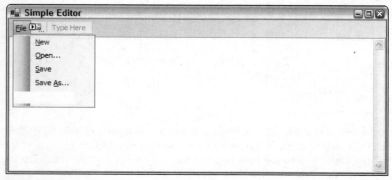

Figure 16-7

The . . . in the Text property of the Open and Save As menu entries advises the user that they will be asked for some data before the action happens. When choosing the File, New, and Save menus the action happens without additional intervention.

The table that follows lists the names of the menu items, as well as the values for the Text properties. Also define the Click event handler with names as shown in the table. To define the Click event handler you have to select the menu in the dialog, click the Events button in the Properties window, select the Click event, and enter the name of the handler method.

Menu item Name	Text	Handler Method
miFile	&File	
miFileNew	&New	OnFileNew
miFileOpen	&Open...	OnFileOpen
miFileSave	&Save	OnFileSave
miFileSaveAs	Save &As...	OnFileSaveAs

5. The handler for the menu entry &New should clear the data of the text box by calling the `Clear()` method of the `TextBox`:

```
private void OnFileNew(object sender, System.EventArgs e)
{
    filename = "Untitled";
    textBoxEdit.Clear();
}
```

6. Also, the `filename` member variable should be set to `Untitled`. You must declare and initialize this member variable in the `SimpleEditorForm` class:

```
public partial class SimpleEditorForm : Form
{
    private string filename = "Untitled";
```

With the `SimpleEditor` it should be possible to pass a filename as an argument when starting the application. The filename passed should be used to open the file and display it in the text box.

7. Change the implementation of the `SimpleEditorForm` constructor to use a string where the filename is passed:

```
public SimpleEditorForm(string filename)
{
    InitializeComponent();

    if (filename != null)
    {
        this.filename = filename;
        OpenFile();
    }
}
```

8. Now you can change the implementation of the `Main()` method in the file `Program.cs` so that an argument can be passed:

```
static void Main(string[] args)
{
    string filename = null;
    if (args.Length != 0)
        filename = args[0];

    Application.EnableVisualStyles();
    Application.Run(new SimpleEditorForm(filename));
}
```

9. And you have to implement the `OpenFile()` method that opens a file and fills the text box with data from the file.

Note that the `OpenFile()` *method actually accesses the file in question and uses methods not discussed at length here, but file access is covered fully in Chapter 22.*

```
protected void OpenFile()
{
    try
```

```
            {
                textBoxEdit.Clear();
                textBoxEdit.Text = File.ReadAllText(filename);
            }
            catch (IOException ex)
            {
                MessageBox.Show(ex.Message, "Simple Editor",
                    MessageBoxButtons.OK, MessageBoxIcon.Exclamation);
            }
        }
```

Here we use the File *class to read the file — this class is in the* System.IO *namespace, so you also need to add the following using directive at the beginning of the file* SimpleEditorForm.cs:

```
using System.IO;
```

The File class and the System.IO *namespace will be explored in Chapter 22 along with other file access classes.*

10. As you saw in Chapter 7, it's possible to define command-line parameters within Visual Studio for debugging purposes. In Solution Explorer, right-click on the project and select Properties. From the Properties dialog select the Debug tab along the left side. With the dialog shown here, you can enter the command-line arguments. For testing purposes here, enter the following:

```
C:\BegVCSharp\Chapter16\SimpleEditor\SimpleEditor\SimpleEditorForm.cs
```

11. Now you can run the application, and the SimpleEditorForm.cs file of your current project will be opened immediately and displayed, as can be seen in Figure 16-8.

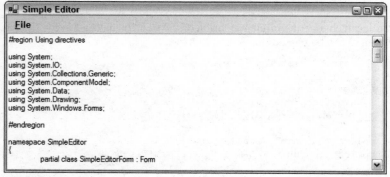

Figure 16-8

How It Works

The first six steps simply set up the form — you should be familiar with this process if you worked through the previous two chapters.

Step 7 is where the meat of the application begins. By adding the `string[]` to the parameters of the `Main()` method, you can use any command-line arguments that the user supplies when starting the application.

```
static void Main(string[] args)
```

In the `Main()` method, you check to see if arguments are passed by using the `Length` property. If at least one argument was passed, the first argument is set to the `filename` variable, which is then passed to the constructor of the `SimpleEditorForm`:

```
{
    string filename = null;
    if (args.Length != 0)
        filename = args[0];

    Application.EnableVisualStyles();
    Application.Run(new SimpleEditorForm(filename));
}
```

In the `SimpleEditorForm` constructor, you check if the `filename` variable already has a value set. If it has, the member variable `filename` is set and the method `OpenFile()` is invoked to open the file. You use a separate `OpenFile()` method, and don't write the calls to open the file and fill the text box directly in the constructor of the class, because `OpenFile()` can be used again in other parts of the program.

```
if (filename != null)
{
    this.filename = filename;
    OpenFile();
}
```

In the `OpenFile()` method you read the data from the file. You use the static method `ReadAllText()` of the `File` class to get all lines returned in an array of strings. The method `ReadAllText()` is new with .NET 2.0.

Because file operations can easily generate exceptions, caused, for example, by the user not having the right access permissions to the file, the code is wrapped in a `try` block. In the case of an IO exception, a message box shows up to inform the user about the problem, but the application keeps running.

```
protected void OpenFile()
{
    try
    {
        textBoxEdit.Clear();
        textBoxEdit.Text = File.ReadAllText(filename);
    }
    catch (IOException ex)
    {
        MessageBox.Show(ex.Message, "Simple Editor",
            MessageBoxButtons.OK, MessageBoxIcon.Exclamation);
    }
}
```

If you enter a nonexistent filename for the command-line argument when starting the application, the message box shown in Figure 16-9 is displayed.

Figure 16-9

Now, you can read files with the simple editor by passing a filename when starting the application. Of course, using common dialog classes is preferred, and you add those to the sample application in the following Try It Out.

Try It Out   Adding and Using an OpenFileDialog

1. In the Windows Forms category of the Toolbox, you can find the OpenFileDialog component. Drag this component from the Toolbox and drop it to the gray place on the bottom of the Windows Forms designer. Here, you change three properties: the name for the instance to dlgOpenFile, the Filter property to the following string, and the FilterIndex property to 2 to make Wrox Documents the default selection:

```
Text Documents (*.txt)|*.txt|Wrox Documents (*.wroxtext)|*.wroxtext|All
Files|*.*
```

2. Earlier you've added a click event handler named OnFileOpen to the Open menu entry. Now, you can add the implementation to this event handler. Using the Forms designer, double-click the Open menu entry, so you can add the implementation to the handler method. Here, the implementation the dialog is displayed and the selected file is read with this code:

```
private void OnFileOpen(object sender, System.EventArgs e)
{
    if (dlgOpenFile.ShowDialog() == DialogResult.OK)
    {
        filename = dlgOpenFile.FileName;
        OpenFile();
    }
}
```

How It Works

By adding the OpenFileDialog component to the Windows Forms designer, a new private member is added to the SimpleEditorForm class. You can see the private member in the file SimpleEditorForm.Designer.cs. This file only shows up when you click the button Show All Files in the Solution Explorer.

```
partial class SimpleEditorForm
{
    private System.Windows.Forms.TextBox textBoxEdit;
```

```
private System.Windows.Forms.MenuStrip mainMenu;
private System.Windows.Forms.ToolStripMenuItem miFile;
private System.Windows.Forms.ToolStripMenuItem miFileNew;
private System.Windows.Forms.ToolStripMenuItem miFileOpen;
private System.Windows.Forms.ToolStripMenuItem miFileSave;
private System.Windows.Forms.ToolStripMenuItem miFileSaveAs;
private System.Windows.Forms.OpenFileDialog dlgOpenFile;
```

In the region of designer code by the Windows Forms, in `InitializeComponent()`, a new instance of this `OpenFileDialog` class is created, and the specified properties are set. Click on the + character of the line Windows Forms Designer generated code and then on the + character of the line `private void InitializeComponent()` to see the following code:

```
private void InitializeComponent()
{
    this.textBoxEdit = new System.Windows.Forms.TextBox();
    this.mainMenu = new System.Windows.Forms.MenuStrip();
    this.miFile = new System.Windows.Forms.ToolStripMenuItem();
    this.miFileNew = new System.Windows.Forms.ToolStripMenuItem();
    this.miFileOpen = new System.Windows.Forms.ToolStripMenuItem();
    this.miFileSave = new System.Windows.Forms.ToolStripMenuItem();
    this.miFileSaveAs = new System.Windows.Forms.ToolStripMenuItem();
    this.dlgOpenFile = new System.Windows.Forms.OpenFileDialog();
    // ...
    //
    // dlgOpenFile
    //
    this.dlgOpenFile.Filter =
        "Text Documents (*.txt)|*.txt|Wrox Documents" +
            (*.wroxtext)|*.wroxtext|All Files|*.*";
    this.dlgOpenFile.FilterIndex = 2;
```

Of course, all that has happened here is exactly what you would expect if you dragged any another standard control onto the form, but with the support of the Windows Forms designer you have created a new instance of the `OpenFileDialog` and set the properties. Now you can display the dialog.

The `ShowDialog()` method displays the file open dialog and returns the button that the user pressed. Nothing should be done if the user presses anything other than the OK button. That's the reason to check for `DialogResult.OK` in the `if` statement. If the user cancels the dialog, just do nothing.

```
if (dlgOpenFile.ShowDialog() == DialogResult.OK)
{
```

Next, you get the selected filename by accessing the `FileName` property of the `OpenFileDialog` class and setting the member variable `filename` to this value. This is the value that's used by the `OpenFile()` method. It would also be possible to open the file directly with the `File` class, but because you already have an `OpenFile()` method that opens and reads a file, you will use this.

```
filename = dlgOpenFile.FileName;
OpenFile();
```

Now, you can start the simple editor program as shown in Figure 16-10. Only the New and Open… menu entries are functional at the moment. Save and Save As… will be implemented in the next section.

Figure 16-10

If you select the menu entry File ⇨ Open…, the OpenFileDialog shows up (see Figure 16-11) and you can select a file. I assume you currently don't have files with the file extension .wroxtext. Up to this time you have not been able to save files, so you can choose a different file type in the dialog editor to open a file, or you can copy a text file to a file with the extension .wroxtext.

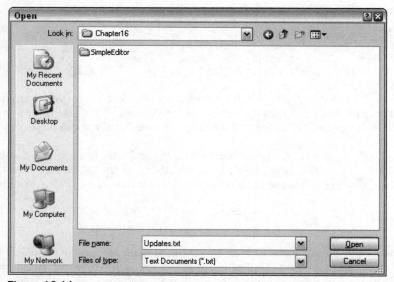

Figure 16-11

Select a text file, press the Open button, and the text shows up in the text box of the dialog. I selected a sample text file, Thinktecture.txt, on my local system, as you can see in Figure 16-12.

At this point, you can only read existing files. Now, it would be great to create new files and modify existing ones. You will use the SaveFileDialog to do this.

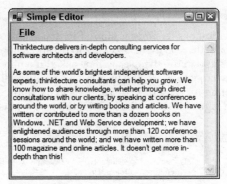

Figure 16-12

SaveFileDialog

The SaveFileDialog class is very similar to the OpenFileDialog, and they have a set of common properties — we will not talk about those properties that operate in the same way as those of the OpenFileDialog. Instead, we will focus on the properties specific to the save dialog properties and where the application of the common properties differs.

Dialog Title

With the Title property, you can set the title of the dialog similar to the OpenFileDialog. If nothing is set, the default title is Save As.

File Extensions

File extensions are used to associate files with applications. It is best to add a file extension to a file, otherwise Windows won't know which application should be used to open the file, and it's also likely that you would eventually forget this.

AddExtension is a Boolean property that automatically appends the file extension to the filename the user enters. The default value is true. If the user enters a file extension, no additional extension will be appended. Thus with AddExtension set to true, if the user enters the filename test, the filename test.txt will be stored. If the filename test.txt is entered, the filename will still be test.txt, and not test.txt.txt.

The DefaultExt property sets the file extension that will be used if the user doesn't enter one. If you leave the property blank, the file extension that's defined with the currently selected Filter will be used instead. If you set both a Filter and the DefaultExt, the DefaultExt will be used regardless of the Filter.

Validation

For automatic filename validation there are the properties ValidateNames, CheckFileExists, and CheckPathExists, similar to those for OpenFileDialog. The difference between OpenFileDialog and SaveFileDialog is that with the SaveFileDialog, the default value for CheckFileExists is false, which means that you can supply the name of a brand-new file to save.

505

Overwriting Existing Files

As you have seen, the validation of filenames is similar to that of the OpenFileDialog. However, for the SaveFileDialog class, there is more checking to do and some more properties to set. If the CreatePrompt property is set to true, the user will be asked if a new file is to be created. If the OverwritePrompt property is set to true, the user is asked if he really wants to overwrite an already existing file. The default setting for OverwritePrompt is true, and CreatePrompt is false. With this setting, the dialog shown in Figure 16-13 is displayed if the user wants to save an already existing file.

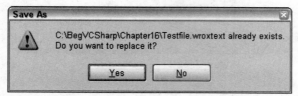

Figure 16-13

SaveFileDialog Properties

Figure 16-14 summarizes the properties of the SaveFileDialog.

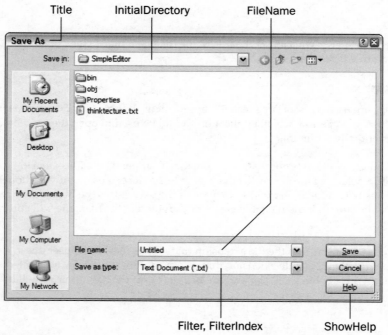

Figure 16-14

In the following Try It Out, you add a Save File dialog to the sample application.

Try It Out   Adding and Using a SaveFileDialog

1. In the same way that you added an `OpenFileDialog` to the form, you can add a
`SaveFileDialog`: select the `SaveFileDialog` component from the Toolbox and drop it
onto the gray area of the Forms Designer. Change the name to `dlgSaveFile`, `FileName` to
`Untitled`, the `FilterIndex` to 2, and the `Filter` property to the following string as you did
with the `OpenFileDialog` earlier. (Because you allow only the file extensions .txt and .wroxtext
to be saved with this editor, `*.*` will now be left out.)

```
Text Document (*.txt)|*.txt|Wrox Documents (*.wroxtext)|*.wroxtext
```

2. Add a handler to the `Click` event of the Save As menu entry with the name `OnFileSaveAs`. In
this code, you will display the `SaveFileDialog` with the `ShowDialog()` method. As with the
`OpenFileDialog`, you are only interested in the results if the user has pressed the OK button.
You call the `SaveFile()` method that stores the file to the disk. This method will have to be
implemented in the next step.

```csharp
private void OnFileSaveAs(object sender, EventArgs e)
{
    if (dlgSaveFile.ShowDialog() == DialogResult.OK)
    {
        filename = dlgSaveFile.FileName;
        SaveFile();
    }
}
```

3. Add the `SaveFile()` method to your file:

```csharp
protected void SaveFile()
{
    try
    {
        File.WriteAllText(filename, textBoxEdit.Text);
    }
    catch (IOException ex)
    {
        MessageBox.Show(ex.Message, "Simple Editor",
            MessageBoxButtons.OK, MessageBoxIcon.Exclamation);
    }
}
```

Similar to the `OpenFile()` method, here the `File` class is used. With .NET 2.0 this class offers
the new static method `WriteAll()` to write a string to a file. The first parameter defines the
name of the file, the second parameter defines the string that should be written to the file.

You can read more about the classes used for file access in Chapter 22.

4. After building the project, you can start the application using the Debug ⇨ Start menu of Visual
Studio. Write some text to the text box and choose the menu File ⇨ Save As... as shown in
Figure 16-15.

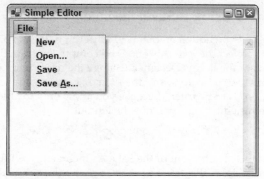

Figure 16-15

The `SaveFileDialog` (shown in Figure 16-16) will pop up. Now, you can save the file and open it again to make some more changes.

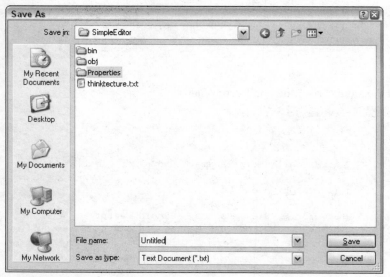

Figure 16-16

5. Now you can do a Save As, but the simple Save isn't available at the moment. Add a handler to the `Click` event of the Save menu entry and add this code:

```
private void OnFileSave(object sender, EventArgs e)
{
    if (filename == "Untitled")
    {
        OnFileSaveAs(sender, e);
    }
    else
```

```
        {
            SaveFile();
        }
    }
```

How It Works

With the Save menu, the file should be saved without opening any dialog. There's one exception to this rule. If the user creates a new document but does not supply a filename, then the Save handler should work as the Save As handler does and display the Save File dialog.

With the `filename` member variable you can easily check if a file is opened or if the filename is still set to the initial value `Untitled` after creating a new document. If the `if` statement returns `true`, the handler `OnFileSaveAs()` is called that you implemented previously for the Save As menu.

In the other case when a file was opened and the user now chooses the Save menu, the thread of execution passes into the `else` block. You can use the same `SaveFile()` method that you implemented previously.

With Notepad, Word, and other Windows applications, the name of the file that's currently edited is displayed in the title of the application. With the next Try It Out, you add this feature, too.

Try It Out **Setting the Title of the Form**

1. Create a new member function `SetFormTitle()` and add this implementation:

```
protected void SetFormTitle()
{
    FileInfo fileinfo = new FileInfo(filename);
    Text = fileinfo.Name + " - Simple Editor";
}
```

The `FileInfo` class is used to get the filename without the preceding path that's stored in the `filename` variable. The `FileInfo` class is covered in Chapter 22.

2. Add a call to this method in the `OnFileNew()`, `OnFileOpen`, and `OnFileSaveAs()` handler after setting the member variable `filename` as can be seen in the following code segments:

```
private void OnFileNew(object sender, System.EventArgs e)
{
    filename = "Untitled";
    SetFormTitle();
    textBoxEdit.Clear();
}
private void OnFileOpen(object sender, System.EventArgs e)
{
    if (dlgOpenFile.ShowDialog() == DialogResult.OK)
    {
        filename = dlgOpenFile.FileName;
        SetFormTitle();
        OpenFile();
    }
}
```

```
private void OnFileSaveAs(object sender, System.EventArgs e)
{
    if (dlgSaveFile.ShowDialog() == DialogResult.OK)
    {
        filename = dlgSaveFile.FileName;
        SetFormTitle();
        SaveFile();
    }
}
```

How It Works

Every time the filename changes, the `Text` property of the actual form will be changed to the filename appended with the name of the application.

The application now starts with the screen shown in Figure 16-17, where I'm editing the file `sample.txt.`, as you can see from the title of the form.

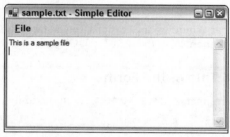

Figure 16-17

Now you have a simple editor — you can open, create, and save files (and edit them too). So, are we finished? Not really! Because the paperless office still doesn't exist, you should add some print functionality!

Printing

With printing there are many things to worry about, such as the selection of a printer, page settings, and how to print multiple pages. By using classes from the `System.Drawing.Printing` namespace, you can get a lot of help to solve these problems, and print documents from our own applications with ease.

Before looking at the `PrintDialog` class that makes it possible to select a printer, you must take a quick look at how .NET handles printing. The foundation of printing is the `PrintDocument` class, which has a `Print()` method that starts a chain of calls culminating in a call to `OnPrintPage()`, which is responsible for passing the output to the printer. However, before going deeper into how to implement printing code, first look a little bit more in detail at the .NET printing classes.

Printing Architecture

Figure 16-18 shows the major parts of the printing architecture to illustrate the relationship between the classes and some of the properties and methods.

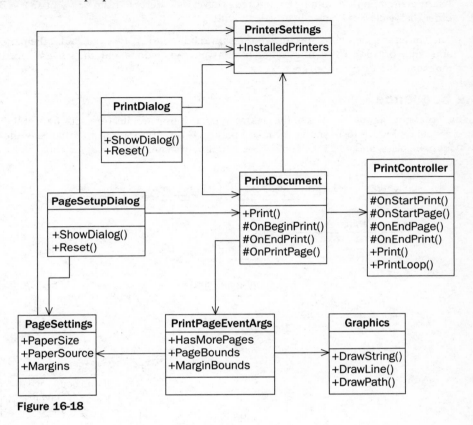

Figure 16-18

Let's look at the functionality of these classes.

❏   The `PrintDocument` class is the most important class. In Figure 16-18, you can see that nearly all other classes are related to this class. To print a document, an instance of `PrintDocument` is required. The following section looks at the printing sequence initiated by this class.

❏   The `PrintController` class controls the flow of a print job. The print controller has events for the start of the print, for each page, and for the end of the print. The class is abstract because the implementation of normal printing is different from that of print preview. Concrete classes that derive from `PrintController` are `StandardPrintController` and `PreviewPrintController`.

You will not find the methods `Print` and `PrintLoop` in the documentation, because these methods are internal to the assembly and can be invoked only by other classes in the same assembly, for example the `PrintDocument` class. However, these methods help you understand the printing process — that's why they are shown here.

❑ The `PrinterSettings` class can get and set the printer configurations such as duplex printing, landscape or portrait, and number of copies.

❑ The `PrintDialog` class contains options for selecting which printer to print to and how the `PrinterSettings` should be configured. This class is derived from `CommonDialog` like the other dialog classes I have already dealt with.

❑ The `PageSettings` class specifies the sizes and boundaries of a page, and if the page is in black and white or color. The configuration of this class can be done with the `PageSetupDialog` class that again is a `CommonDialog`.

Printing Sequence

Now, that you know about the roles of the classes in the printing architecture, let's look at the main printing sequence. Figure 16-19 shows the major players — our application, an instance of the `PrintDocument` class, and a `PrintController` in a timely sequence.

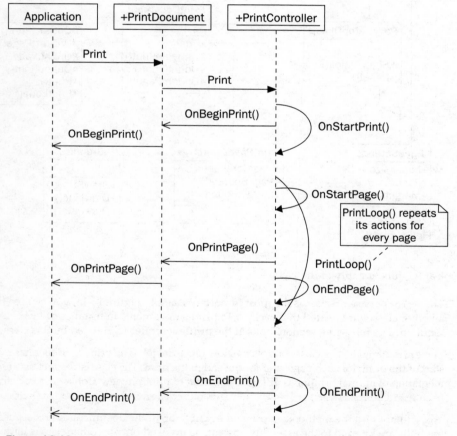

Figure 16-19

The application has to call the `Print()` method of the `PrintDocument`. This starts the printing sequence. As the `PrintDocument` itself is not responsible for the printing flow, the job is given to the `PrintController` by calling the `Print()` method of this class. The print controller now takes the action and informs the `PrintDocument` that the printing has started by calling `OnBeginPrint()`. If your application should do something at the start of a print job, you have to register an event handler in the `PrintDocument` so that you are informed in your application class. In the diagram in Figure 16-19, it is assumed that you registered the handler `OnBeginPrint()`, so this handler is called from the `PrintDocument` class.

After the beginning phase has ended, the `PrintController` goes into a `PrintLoop()` to call the `OnPrintPage()` method in the `PrintDocument` class for every page to print. `OnPrintPage()` invokes all `PrintPage` event handlers. You have to implement such a handler in every case; otherwise, nothing would be printed. In Figure 16-19 you can see the handler is called `OnPrintPage()`.

After the last page is printed the `PrintController` calls `OnEndPrint()` in the `PrintDocument` class. Optionally, we can implement a handler to be invoked here, too.

To summarize, the most important thing for us to know is that you can implement the printing code in the `PrintDocument.PrintPage` event handler. This handler will be called for every page that is to be printed. If there's printing code that should be called only once for a print job, you have to implement the `BeginPrint` and `EndPrint` event handlers.

PrintPage Event

So, what you know now is that you have to implement an event handler for the `PrintPage` event. The delegate `PrintPageEventHandler` defines the arguments of the handler:

```
public delegate void PrintPageEventHandler(object sender,
                                           PrintPageEventArgs e);
```

As you can see, you receive an object of type `PrintPageEventArgs`. You can have a look back to the class diagram to see the main properties of this class. This class has associations to the `PageSettings` and `Graphics` classes. The first enables you to set the paper size and the margins, and you can get device information from the printer. The `Graphics` class, on the other hand, makes it possible to access the device context of the printer and send such things as strings, lines, and curves to the printer.

> GDI (graphics device interface) makes it possible to do some graphical output to a device like the screen or a printer. GDI+ is the next generation of GDI that adds features like gradient brushes and alpha blending and is the drawing technology of the .NET Framework.
>
> In Chapter 30, you can read more about drawing with GDI+ and the `Graphics` class.

If at this point you think that printing is complex, don't be worried! The following example should convince you that adding printing features to an application is quite an easy task.

Before you can add the `PrintDialog`, you have to add some menu entries for printing. Add two separators and Print, Print Preview, Page Setup, and Exit menu items to the Simple Editor application.

The following table lists the `Name` and `Text` properties and handler methods of the new menu items.

Menu Item Name	Text	Handler
miFilePrint	&Print...	OnFilePrint
miFilePrintPreview	Print Pre&view...	OnFilePrintPreview
miFilePageSetup	Page Set&up...	OnFilePageSetup
miFileExit	E&xit	OnExit

The menu should look like Figure 16-20.

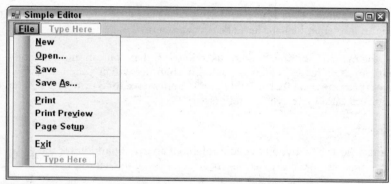

Figure 16-20

In the following Try It Out, you add printing functionality to the sample application by adding a `PrintDocument` component.

Try It Out   Adding a PrintDocument Component

1. Before you go any further, add the following `using` directive to the start of your code so that you can make use of the classes for printing:

```
using System.Drawing.Printing;
```

2. Drag a `PrintDocument` component from the Toolbox and drop it on the gray area below the form. Change the `Name` to `printDocument`, and add an event handler `OnPrintPage` to the `PrintPage` event by selecting the Events button in the Properties window. Then add the following code to the implementation of the event handler:

```
private void OnPrintPage(object sender, PrintPageEventArgs e)
{
    char[] param = { '\n' };
    string[] lines = textBoxEdit.Text.Split(param);

    int i = 0;
```

```
        char[] trimParam = { '\r' };
        foreach (string s in lines)
        {
            lines[i++] = s.TrimEnd(trimParam);
        }

        int x = 20;
        int y = 20;
        foreach (string line in lines)
        {
            e.Graphics.DrawString(line, new Font("Arial", 10),
                Brushes.Black, x, y);
            y += 15;
        }
    }
```

3. Next, add a handler to the `Click` event of the Print menu to call the `Print()` method of the `PrintDocument` class. In case there's no valid printer, an exception of type `InvalidPrinterException` is thrown that is caught to display an error message.

```
private void OnFilePrint(object sender, EventArgs e)
{
    try
    {
        printDocument.Print();
    }
    catch (InvalidPrinterException ex)
    {
        MessageBox.Show(ex.Message, "Simple Editor",
            MessageBoxButtons.OK, MessageBoxIcon.Error);
    }
}
```

4. Now you can build and start the application and print a document. Of course, you must have a printer installed for the example to work.

How It Works

The `printDocument` object's `Print()` method invokes the `PrintPage` event with the help of the `PrintController` class.

```
        printDocument.Print();
```

In the `OnPrintPage()` handler, you split up the text in the text box line by line using the `String.Split()` method and the newline character, `\n`. The resultant strings are written to the `string` array `lines`.

```
        char[] param = {'\n'};
        string[] lines = textBoxEdit.Text.Split(param);
```

Depending on how the text file was created, the lines are not only separated with the \n (newline) character, but also the \r (return) character. The `TrimEnd()` method of the `String` class removes the character \r from every string:

515

```
int i = 0;
char[] trimParam = {'\r'};
foreach(string s in lines)
{
    lines[i++] = s.TrimEnd(trimParam);
}
```

In the second `foreach` statement in the following code, you can see that you go through all lines and send every line to the printer by a call to `e.Graphics.DrawString()`. `e` is a variable of type `PrintPageEventArgs` where the property `Graphics` is connected to the printer context. The printer context makes it possible to draw to a printing device. The `Graphics` class has some methods to draw into this context.

You cannot yet select a printer, so the default printer (whose details are stored in the Windows Registry) is used.

With the `DrawString()` method, you use the Arial font with a size of 10 points and a black brush for the print output. The position for the output is defined with the x and y variables. The horizontal position is fixed to 20 pixels; the vertical position is incremented with every line.

```
int x = 20;
int y = 20;
foreach (string line in lines)
{
    e.Graphics.DrawString(line, new Font("Arial", 10),
                          Brushes.Black, x, y);
    y += 15;
}
```

The printing that was done so far has these problems:

❑   Printing multiple pages doesn't work. If the document to print spans multiple pages, only the first page gets printed. It would also be nice if a header (for example, the filename) and footer (for example, the page number) were printed.

❑   Page boundaries are fixed to hard-coded values in your program. To let the user set values for other page boundaries, you use the `PageSetupDialog` class.

❑   The print output is sent to the default printer set through the Control Panel by the user. It would be better if the application allows the user to choose a printer. You will use the `PrintDialog` class for this problem.

❑   The font is fixed. To enable the user to choose the font, you can use the `FontDialog` class, which you look at in more detail later.

So let's continue with the printing process to get these items fixed.

Printing Multiple Pages

The `PrintPage` event gets called for every page that prints. With the following Try It Out, you inform the `PrintController` that the current page printed was not the last page by setting the `HasMorePages` property of the `PrintPageEventArgs` class to `true`.

Try It Out   **Modifying OnPrintPage() for Multiple Pages**

1.   First, you must declare a member variable `lines` of type `string[]` and a variable `linesPrinted` of type `int` in the class `SimpleEditorForm`:

```
// Variables for printing
private string[] lines;
private int linesPrinted;
```

2.   Modify the `OnPrintPage()` handler. In the previous implementation of `OnPrintPage()` the text was split into lines. Because the `OnPrintPage()` method is called with every page, and splitting the text into lines is needed just once at the beginning of the printing operation, remove all the code from `OnPrintPage()` and replace it with the new implementation.

```
private void OnPrintPage(object sender, PrintPageEventArgs e)
{
    int x = 20;
    int y = 20;

    while (linesPrinted < lines.Length)
    {
        e.Graphics.DrawString (lines[linesPrinted++],
                new Font("Arial", 10), Brushes.Black, x, y);
        y += 15;
        if (y >= e.PageBounds.Height - 80)
        {
            e.HasMorePages = true;
            return;
        }
    }

    linesPrinted = 0;
    e.HasMorePages = false;
}
```

3.   Add an event handler to the `BeginPrint` event of the `printDocument` object called `OnBeginPrint`. `OnBeginPrint` is called just once for each print job and here you create your `lines` array.

```
private void OnBeginPrint(object sender, PrintEventArgs e)
{
    char[] param = { '\n' };
    lines = textBoxEdit.Text.Split(param);

    int i = 0;
    char[] trimParam = { '\r' };
    foreach (string s in lines)
    {
        lines[i++] = s.TrimEnd(trimParam);
    }
}
```

4.   Add an event handler to the `EndPrint` event of the `printDocument` called `OnEndPrint`. Here, you can release the resources that have been allocated in the `OnBeginPrint` method. With the sample an array of strings was allocated and referenced in the variable `lines`. In the `OnEndPrint` method the reference of the variable `lines` is set to `null`, so that the garbage collector can release the string array.

```
private void OnEndPrint(object sender, PrintEventArgs e)
{
    lines = null;
}
```

5. After building the project, you can start a print job for a multipage document.

How It Works

Starting the print job with the `Print()` method of the `PrintDocument` in turn calls `OnBeginPrint()` once and `OnPrintPage()` for every page.

In `OnBeginPrint()` you split up the text of the text box into a string array. Every string in the array represents a single line because you split it up at the newline (\n) character and removed the carriage return character (\r), as you've done before.

```
char[] param = {'\n'};
lines = textBoxEdit.Text.Split(param);
int i = 0;
char[] trimParam = {'\r'};
foreach (string s in lines)
{
    lines[i++] = s.TrimEnd(trimParam);
}
```

`OnPrintPage()` is called after `OnBeginPrint()`. You want to continue printing as long as the number of lines printed is less than the total number of lines you have to print. The `lines.Length` property returns the number of strings in the array `lines`. The `linesPrinted` variable gets incremented with every line you send to the printer.

```
while (linesPrinted < lines.Length)
{
    e.Graphics.DrawString(lines[linesPrinted++],
            new Font("Arial", 10), Brushes.Black, x, y);
```

After printing a line, you check if the newly calculated vertical position is outside of the page boundaries. Additionally, you decrement the boundaries by 80 pixels, because you don't really want to print to the very end of the paper, particularly since many printers can't do this anyway. If this position is reached, the `HasMorePages` property of the `PrintPageEventArgs` class is set to `true` in order to inform the controller that the `OnPrintPage()` method must be called once more, and another page needs to be printed—remember that `PrintController` has the `PrintLoop()` method that has a sequence for every page to print, and `PrintLoop()` will stop if `HasMorePages` is `false`. (The default value of the `HasMorePages` property is `false` so that only one page is printed.)

```
y += 15;
if (y >= e.PageBounds.Height - 80)
{
    e.HasMorePages = true;
    return;
}
```

PageSetupDialog

The margins of the page so far are hard-coded in the program. Let's modify the application to allow the user to set the margins on a page. To make this possible another dialog class is available: `PageSetupDialog`.

This class makes it possible to configure paper sizes and sources, orientation, and paper margins, and because these options depend on a printer, the selection of the printer can be done from this dialog too.

Figure 16-21 gives an overview about the properties that enable or disable specific options of this dialog and what properties can be used to access the values. I will discuss these properties in a moment.

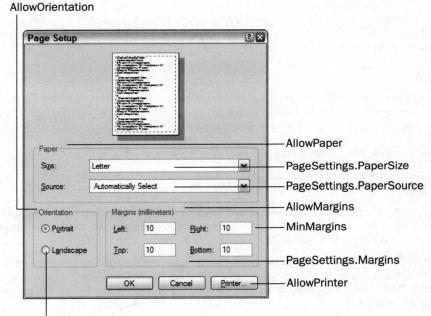

Figure 16-21

Paper

A value of true for the `AllowPaper` property means that the user can choose the paper size and paper source. The `PageSetupDialog.PageSettings.PaperSize` property returns a `PaperSize` instance where you can read the height, width, and name of the paper with the properties `Height`, `Width`, and `PaperName`. `PaperName` specifies names like Letter, and A4. The `Kind` property returns an enumeration where you can get a value of the `PaperKind` enumeration. The `PaperKind` enumeration consists of many different paper values that define the size of the paper, such as A3, A4, A5, Letter, LetterPlus, and `LetterRotated`.

The `PageSetupDialog.PageSettings.PaperSource` property returns a `PaperSource` instance where you can read the name of the printer paper source and the type of paper that fits in there (as long as the printer is correctly configured with the printer settings).

Margins

Setting the `AllowMargins` property to `true` allows the user to set the margin value for the printout. You can define minimum values for the user to enter by specifying the `MinMargins` property. To read the margins, use the `PageSetupDialog.PageSettings.Margins` property. The returned `Margins` object has `Bottom`, `Left`, `Right`, and `Top` properties.

Orientation

The `AllowOrientation` property defines whether or not the user can choose between portrait and landscape printing. The selected value can be read by querying the value of `PageSetupDialog.PageSettings.Landscape`, which is a Boolean value specifying landscape mode with `true` and portrait mode with `false`.

Printer

The `AllowPrinter` property defines whether or not the user can choose a printer. Depending on the value of this property the Printer button is enabled (`true`) or not (`false`). The handler to this button in turn opens up the `PrintDialog` that you will use next.

In the next Try It Out, you add the capability to configure page setup options for printing.

Try It Out   Adding a PageSetupDialog

1. Drag a `PageSetupDialog` component from the Toolbox and drop it onto the form in the Windows Forms designer. Set its `Name` to dlgPageSetup and the `Document` property to printDocument to associate the dialog with the document to print.

2. Now add a `Click` event handler to the Page Setup menu entry, and add the code below to display the dialog using the `ShowDialog()` method. It's not necessary to check the return value of `ShowDialog()` here because the implementation of the handler for the OK `Click` event already sets the new values in the associated `PrintDocument` object.

```
private void OnFilePageSetup(object sender, EventArgs e)
{
    dlgPageSetup.ShowDialog();
}
```

3. Now change the implementation of `OnPrintPage()` to use the margins that are set by the `PageSetupDialog`. In your code, the x and y variables are set to the properties `MarginBounds.Left` and `MarginBounds.Top` of the `PrintPageEventArgs` class. Check the boundary of a page with `MarginBounds.Bottom`.

```
private void OnPrintPage(object sender, PrintPageEventArgs e)
{
    int x = e.MarginBounds.Left;
    int y = e.MarginBounds.Top;
```

```
      while (linesPrinted < lines.Length)
      {
          e.Graphics.DrawString(lines[linesPrinted++],
              new Font("Arial", 10), Brushes.Black, x, y);

          y += 15;
          if (y >= e.MarginBounds.Bottom)
          {
              e.HasMorePages = true;
              return;
          }
      }

      linesPrinted = 0;
      e.HasMorePages = false;
  }
```

4. Now, you can build the project and run the application. Selecting File ➪ Page Setup displays the dialog shown in Figure 16-22. You can change the boundaries and print with the configured boundaries.

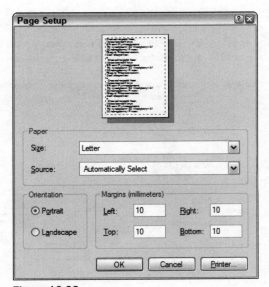

Figure 16-22

PrintDialog

The `PrintDialog` class allows the user to select a printer from the installed printers and choose a number of copies and some printer settings like the layout and paper sources of the printer. Because the `PrintDialog` is very easy to use, you will start immediately by adding the `PrintDialog` to the Editor application with the following Try It Out.

Try It Out   Adding a PrintDialog

1. Add a `PrintDialog` component from the Toolbox onto the form. Set the `Name` to `dlgPrint` and the `Document` property of this object to `printDocument`.

    Change the implementation of the event handler to the `Click` event of the Print menu to the following code:

```
private void OnFilePrint(object sender, EventArgs e)
{
    try
    {
        if (dlgPrint.ShowDialog() == DialogResult.OK)
        {
            printDocument.Print();
        }
    }
    catch (InvalidPrinterException ex)
    {
        MessageBox.Show(ex.Message, "Simple Editor",
            MessageboButtons.OK, MessageBoxIcon.Error);
    }
}
```

2. Build and run the application. Selecting File ➪ Print opens up the `PrintDialog`. Now you can select a printer to print the document, as shown in Figure 16-23.

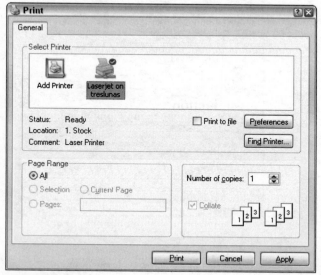

Figure 16-23

Options for the PrintDialog

In the SimpleEditor program you didn't change any of the properties of the `PrintDialog`. But this dialog has some options, too. In the dialog shown in Figure 16-23 you can see three groups: Printer, Print range, and Copies.

❑   In the Printer group not only the printer can be chosen, but there's also a Print to File option. By default this option is enabled, but it is not checked. Selecting this check box enables the user to write the printing output to a file instead of to the printer. You can disable this option by setting the `AllowPrintToFile` property to `false`.

❑   If the user selects this option, the dialog shown in Figure 16-24 is opened by the `printDocument.Print()` call to ask for an output filename for the printout.

Figure 16-24

❑   In the Print Range section of the dialog, only All can be selected — Pages and Selection are disabled by default. You look at how these options can be implemented in the following section.

❑   The Copies group allows the user to select the number of copies to be printed.

Printing Selected Text

Setting the `AllowSelection` property to `true` allows the user to print selected text, but you also have to change the printing code so that only the selected text gets printed. You add this functionality in the next Try It Out.

Try It Out   Adding a Print Selection

1.   Add the highlighted code to the `Click` handler of the Print button.

```
private void OnFilePrint(object sender, EventArgs e)
{
    if (textBoxEdit.SelectedText != "")
    {
        dlgPrint.AllowSelection = true;
    }
    if (dlgPrint.ShowDialog() == DialogResult.OK)
    {
        printDocument.Print();
    }
}
```

2.   In this program all the lines that will be printed are set up in the `OnBeginPrint()` handler. Change the implementation of this method:

```csharp
private void OnBeginPrint(object sender, PrintEventArgs e)
{
    char[] param = {'\n'};

    if (dlgPrint.PrinterSettings.PrintRange == PrintRange.Selection)
    {
        lines = textBoxEdit.SelectedText.Split(param);
    }
    else
    {
        lines = textBoxEdit.Text.Split(param);
    }

    int i = 0;
    char[] trimParam = {'\r'};
    foreach (string s in lines)
    {
        lines[i++] = s.TrimEnd(trimParam);
    }
}
```

3.　Now you can build and start the program. Open a file, select some text, start the print dialog with the menu File ⇨ Print, and select the Selection option button from the Print Range group. With this selected, pressing the Print button will print only the selected text.

How It Works

The `AllowSelection` property is set to `true` only if some text is selected. Before the `PrintDialog` is shown, a check must be done to determine if some text is selected. If some text is selected, the `SelectedText` property of the text box is not `null`. If there is some text selected, the property `AllowSelection` is set to `true`.

```csharp
if (textBoxEdit.SelectedText != "")
{
    dlgPrint.AllowSelection = true;
}
```

`OnBeginPrint()` is called at the start of every print job. Accessing the `printDialog.PrinterSettings.PrintRange` property, you discover whether the user has chosen the Selection option. The `PrintRange` property takes a value from the `PrintRange` enumeration: `AllPages`, `Selection`, or `SomePages`.

```csharp
if (printDialog.PrinterSettings.PrintRange == PrintRange.Selection)
{
```

If the option is indeed `PrintRange.Selection`, you get the selected text from the `SelectedText` property of the `TextBox`. This string is split up the same way as the complete text:

```csharp
lines = textBoxEdit.SelectedText.Split(param);
}
```

Printing Page Ranges

Printing a range of pages can be implemented similarly to printing a selection. The option button can be enabled by setting the `AllowSomePages` property to `true`. The user can now select the page range to print. However, where are the page boundaries in the Simple Editor? What's the last page? You should set the last page by setting the `PrintDialog.PrinterSettings.ToPage` property. How does the user know the page numbers he wants to print? With a document processing application like Microsoft Word, where the Print Layout can be selected to view the text on the screen, the user knows the page number. With the simple `TextBox` that's used with the Simple Editor, the number of pages is not known. That's why you will not implement this feature in your application.

Of course, you could implement page range printing capability as an exercise. What must be done? The `AllowSomePages` property must be set to `true`. Before displaying the `PrintDialog`, you can also set the `PrinterSettings.FromPage` to 1 and the `PrinterSettings.ToPage` to the maximum page number.

PrintDialog Properties

Figure 16-25 shows the properties discussed in this section and how they influence the `PrintDialog`'s layout.

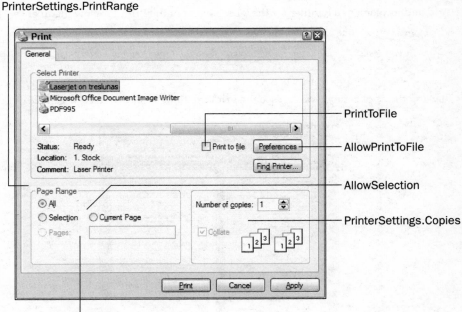

Figure 16-25

Print Preview

You can use Print Preview so that the user can see what the printout will look like. Implementing Print Preview can be easily done in .NET — you can use a `PrintPreviewControl` class that is used to preview the document inside a form to show how it will be printed. The `PrintPreviewDialog` is a dialog that wraps the control.

PrintPreviewDialog

If you look at the properties and inheritance list from the MSDN documentation of the `PrintPreviewDialog` class, you can see that it is actually a `Form` and not a wrapped common dialog — the class derives from `System.Windows.Forms.Form`, and you can work with it as with the forms you created in Chapter 15.

In the following Try It Out, you add a `PrintPreviewDialog` class to the Simple Editor application.

Try It Out   Adding a PrintPreviewDialog

1. Add a `PrintPreviewDialog` component from the Toolbox onto the Windows Forms designer. Set the `Name` to `dlgPrintPreview` and the `Document` property to `printDocument`.

2. Add and implement a handler for the `Click` event of the Print Preview menu entry.

    ```
    private void OnFilePrintPreview(object sender, EventArgs e)
    {
        dlgPrintPreview.ShowDialog();
    }
    ```

3. Starting the application, you can see the Print preview, as shown in Figure 16-26.

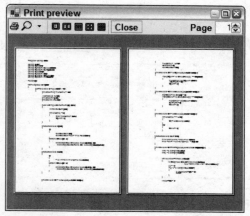

Figure 16-26

PrintPreviewControl

The print preview in Microsoft Word and WordPad is different from the `PrintPreviewDialog` in so far as the preview in these applications doesn't show up in its own dialog, but in the main window of the application.

To do the same, you can place the `PrintPreviewControl` class in your form. The `Document` property must be set to the `printDocument` object, and the `Visible` property to `false` — when you want to display the print preview, you simply set the `Visible` property to `true`. Then the `PrintPreviewControl` is in front of the other control, as shown in Figure 16-27.

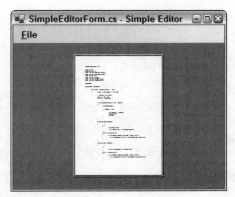

Figure 16-27

You can see from the title and the single File menu item that it is the main window of the Simple Editor application that is displayed. You still need to add some elements to control the `PrintPreviewControl` class to do zooming, printing, and to display several pages of text at once. A specific toolbar can be used to make these features available. The `PrintPreviewDialog` class already has this implemented as you can see from the four-page preview shown in Figure 16-28.

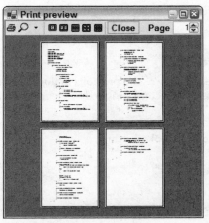

Figure 16-28

FontDialog and ColorDialog

The last dialogs you look at in this chapter are the `FontDialog` and the `ColorDialog`.

This chapter discusses these dialogs for setting font and color The Font *and* Color *classes are covered in Chapter 30.*

FontDialog

The `FontDialog` lets the user choose a font. The user can change the font, style, size, and color of the font.

Figure 16-29 shows the properties that change the behavior of the elements in the dialog.

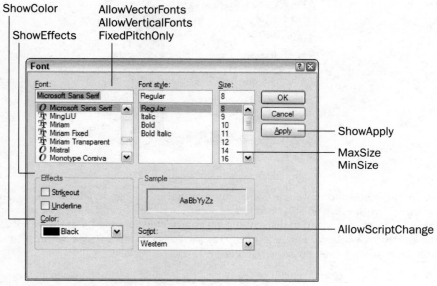

Figure 16-29

How to Use the FontDialog

The dialog can be used in the same way as the previous dialogs. In the Windows Forms designer the dialog can be dragged from the Toolbox and dropped to the form so that an instance of the `FontDialog` gets created.

The code to use the `FontDialog` can look like this:

```
if (dlgFont.ShowDialog() == DialogResult.OK)
{
    textBoxEdit.Font = dlgFont.Font;
}
```

The FontDialog is displayed by calling the ShowDialog() method. If the user presses the OK button, DialogResult.OK is returned from the method. The selected font can be read by using the Font property of the FontDialog class; this font is then passed to the Font property of the TextBox.

Properties of the FontDialog

You have already seen a picture with properties of the FontDialog class; but now let's see what these properties are used for.

Property	Description
AllowVectorFonts	Boolean value that defines if vector fonts can be selected in the font list. The default is true.
AllowVerticalFonts	Boolean value that defines if vertical fonts can be selected in the font list. Vertical texts are used in far eastern countries. There probably isn't a vertical font installed on your system. The default is true.
FixedPitchOnly	Setting the property FixedPitchOnly displays only fixed pitch fonts in the font list. With a fixed pitch font every character has the same size. The default is false.
MaxSize	Specifying a value for the MaxSize property defines the maximum font size the user can select.
MinSize	Similar to MaxSize you can set the minimum font size the user can select with MinSize.
ShowApply	If the Apply button should be displayed you have to set the ShowApply property to true. By pressing the Apply button the user can see an updated font in the application without leaving the font dialog.
ShowColor	By default the Color selection is not shown in the dialog. If you want the user to select the font color in the font dialog you just have to set the ShowColor property to true.
ShowEffects	By default the user can select the Strikeout and Underline check boxes to manipulate the font. If you don't want these options to be displayed you have to set the ShowEffects property to false.
AllowScriptChange	Setting the AllowScriptChange property to false prevents the user from changing the script of a font. The available scripts depend on the selected font. For example, the font Arial supports Western, Hebrew, Arabic, Greek, Turkish, Baltic, Central European, Cyrillic, Vietnamese scripts.

Enabling the Apply Button

An interesting difference from the other dialogs presented so far is that the FontDialog supports an Apply button, which is not displayed by default. If the user presses the Apply button the dialog stays opened, but the font should be applied.

By selecting the `FontDialog` in the Windows Forms designer you can set the `ShowApply` property in the Properties window to `true`. But how are you informed if the user now presses the Apply button? The dialog is still opened, so the `ShowDialog()` method will not return. Instead, you can add an event handler to the `Apply` event of the `FontDialog` class. You can do this by pressing the Events button in the Properties window, and by writing a handler name to the `Apply` event.

As you can see in the following code, I have entered the name `OnApplyFontDialog`. In this handler, you can access the selected font of the `FontDialog` using the member variable of the `FontDialog` class:

```
private void OnApplyFontDialog(object sender, System.EventArgs e)
{
    textBoxEdit.Font = dlgFont.Font;
}
```

ColorDialog

There isn't as much to configure in the `ColorDialog` as for the `FontDialog`. The `ColorDialog` makes it possible to configure custom colors if none of the basic colors are wanted. This is done by setting the `AllowFullOpen` property. The custom color configuration part of the dialog can also be automatically expanded with the `FullOpen` property. If `AllowFullOpen` is false, then the value of `FullOpen` will be ignored. The `SolidColorOnly` property specifies that only solid colors can be selected. The `CustomColors` property can be used to get and set the configured custom color values.

Figure 16-30 shows the color dialog with the properties that influence the dialog.

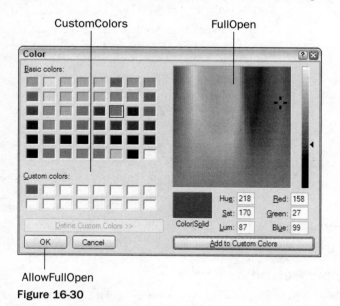

Figure 16-30

How to Use the ColorDialog

The `ColorDialog` can be dragged from the Toolbox and dropped onto the form in the Windows Forms designer, as you have done with the other dialogs. `ShowDialog()` displays the dialog until the user presses the OK or Cancel button. You can read the selected color by accessing the `Color` property of the dialog, as can be seen in the following code example:

```
if (dlgColor.ShowDialog() == DialogResult.OK)
{
   textBoxEdit.ForeColor = dlgColor.Color;
}
```

Properties of the ColorDialog

The properties to influence the look of the dialog are summarized in this table:

Properties	Description
AllowFullOpen	Setting this property to `false` disables the Define Custom Colors button, thus preventing the user from defining custom colors. The default value of this property is `true`.
FullOpen	Setting the `FullOpen` property to `true` before the dialog is displayed opens the dialog with the custom color selection automatically displayed.
AnyColor	Setting this property to `true` shows all available colors in the list of basic colors.
CustomColors	With the `CustomColors` property you can preset an array of custom colors, and you can read the custom colors defined by the user.
SolidColorOnly	By setting the `SolidColorOnly` property to `true` the user can only select solid colors.

FolderBrowserDialog

A new dialog with .NET 1.1 is a simple dialog to get directory names from the user or to create directories. The class of this dialog is `FolderBrowserDialog`. Just a few properties are available to configure this dialog as you can see in Figure 16-31.

The `Description` can be used to define the text above the tree view. `RootFolder` defines the folder where the user's search of the folder to select should start. With the `RootFolder` property, you can set a value from the enumeration `Environment.SpecialFolder`. `ShowNewFolderButton` defines if the user is allowed to create a new folder with the dialog.

Description   RootFolder

ShowNewFolderButton

Figure 16-31

How to Use the Folder Browser Dialog

The `FolderBrowserDialog` can be dragged from the Toolbox and dropped onto the form in the Windows Forms designer, as you have done with the other dialogs. `ShowDialog()` displays the dialog until the user presses the OK or Cancel button. You can read the path that is selected by the user using the `SelectedPath` property, as can be seen in the following code example:

```
dlgFolderBrowser.Description = "Select a directory";
if (dlgFolderBrowser.ShowDialog() == DialogResult.OK)
{
    MessageBox.Show("The folder " +
        dlgFolderBrowser.SelectedPath + " was selected");
}
```

Properties of the Folder Browser Dialog

The properties to influence the behavior of the dialog are summarized in the following table.

Properties	Description
Description	With the `Description` property you can define the text that shows up above the tree view of the dialog.
RootFolder	With the `RootFolder` property you can set the path where the browsing should start.

Properties	Description
SelectedPath	The property SelectedPath returns the path of the directory that is selected by the user.
ShowNewFolderButton	By setting the ShowNewFolderButton to true, the user can create a new folder.

Summary

In this chapter, you have seen how to use the dialog classes in applications. You looked at how to open and save files, and after reviewing the .NET Framework printing classes, this chapter showed you how to add printing capabilities to your applications. To summarize, in the Simple Editor application you used the following dialog classes:

❑   FileOpenDialog to ask the user for a file to open

❑   FileSaveDialog to ask for a filename to save the data

❑   PrintDialog to get the printer to print to and the printing configurations

❑   PageSetupDialog to modify the margins of the page where we do the print

❑   PrintPreviewDialog to view a preview of the print so that the user knows in advance how the print will look like

❑   FolderBrowserDialog to select and create directories

In the chapter, you've also seen the basics of the FontDialog and ColorDialog classes. In the exercises, you can extend the Simple Editor application to use these dialogs as well.

The next chapter shows how Windows applications such as the Simple Editor can be deployed on target systems using ClickOnce and the Windows installer.

Exercises

Because the FontDialog and the ColorDialog work in a similar way to the other dialogs discussed in this chapter, it's an easy job to add these dialogs to the Simple Editor application.

1.   Let the user change the font of the text box. To make this possible add a new menu entry to the main menu: F&ormat, and a submenu for Format: &Font.... Add a handler to this menu item. Add a FontDialog to the application with the help of the Windows Forms designer. Display this dialog in the menu handler, and set the Font property of the text box to the selected font.

You also have to change the implementation of the OnPrintPage() method to use the selected font for a printout. In the previous implementation you created a new Font object in the DrawString() method of the Graphics object. Now, use the font of the textBoxEdit object by accessing the Font property instead. You also have to be aware of a font location problem if the user chooses a big font. To avoid one line partly overwriting the one above/below, change the fixed value you used to change the vertical position of the lines. A better way to do this would be to use the size of the font to change the vertical increment: use the `Height` property of the `Font` class.

2. Another great extension to the Simple Editor application would be to change the font color. Add a second submenu to the Format menu entry: `Color....` Add a handler to this menu entry where you open up a `ColorDialog`. If the user presses the OK button, set the selected color of the `ColorDialog` to the `ForeColor` property of the text box.

    In the `OnPrintPage()` method make sure that the chosen color is used only if the printer supports colors. You can check the color support of the printer with the `PageSettings.Color` property of the `PrintPageEventArgs` argument. You can create a brush object with the color of the text box with this code:

```
Brush brush = new SolidBrush(textBoxEdit.ForeColor);
```

    This brush can then be used as an argument in the `DrawString()` method instead of the black brush you used in the example before.

Deploying Windows Applications

There are several ways to install Windows applications. Simple applications can be installed with a simple xcopy deployment, but for installation to hundreds of clients, an xcopy deployment is not really useful. For that situation, you have two options: you can use ClickOnce deployment, or you can install the application with the Microsoft installer.

With *ClickOnce* deployment the application is installed by clicking a link to a Website. In situations where the user should select a directory to install the application into, or when some Registry entries are required, the Windows Installer is the deployment option to use.

This chapter covers both options for installing Windows applications. In particular, you will look at:

❑ Deployment basics

❑ ClickOnce deployment

❑ Visual Studio Deployment and Setup Project types

❑ Features of the Windows Installer

❑ Creating Windows Installer Packages using Visual Studio 2005

Deployment Overview

Deployment is the process of installing applications to the target systems. Traditionally, such an installation has been done by invoking a setup program. If a hundred or thousand clients must be installed, the installation can be very time-consuming. To alleviate this, the system administrator can create batch scripts to automate this activity. However, particularly if the application logic changes regularly, problems can occur with clients that didn't have network access, along with incompatibilities among different library versions, resulting in a condition known as DLL hell.

DLL hell describes the problems that happen when each of several installed applications require different versions of the same DLL. If one application installs a DLL that overwrites a different version of the same DLL, applications requiring the overwritten DLL might break.

Because of these problems, many companies converted their intranet applications to Web applications, even though Windows applications can have a much richer user interface. Web applications just need to be deployed to the server, and the client automatically gets the up-to-date user interface.

With .NET, DLL hell is avoided by using private and shared assemblies. Private assemblies are copied with every application, so there cannot be a conflict with assemblies from other applications. Shared assemblies have a strong name that includes the version number. Multiple versions of the same assembly can coexist on the same system. Chapter 29 covers private and shared assemblies.

.NET 1.0 supported a technology known as no-touch deployment. With no-touch deployment, it was possible for the user to automatically install an application by clicking a link on a Web page. However, .NET 1.0 no-touch deployment had some complexity because of security issues, and it was missing many features that are required with many client applications — clearly this was a version 1 release. These issues are solved with the ClickOnce deployment technology that is new with .NET 2.0.

Similarly to no-touch deployment with ClickOnce deployment, the application can be installed by clicking a link inside a Web page. The user on the client system doesn't need administrative privileges, as the application is installed in a user-specific directory. With ClickOnce you can install applications with a rich user interface. The application is installed to the client, so there's no need to remain connected with the client system after the installation is completed. In other words, the application can be used offline. What's different to no-touch deployment, now an application icon is available from the Start menu, the security issues are easier to solve, and the application can easily be uninstalled.

A nice feature of ClickOnce is that updates can happen automatically when the client application starts or as a background task while the client application is running.

However, there are some restrictions accompanying ClickOnce deployment: ClickOnce cannot be used if you need to install shared components in the global assembly cache, or if the application needs COM components that require Registry settings, or if you want the user to decide in what directory the application should be installed. In such cases, you must use the Windows Installer. The Windows Installer is the traditional way to install Windows applications.

Let's start with ClickOnce deployment before working with Windows installer packages.

ClickOnce Deployment

With ClickOnce deployment there is no need to start a setup program on the client system. All the client system's user has to do is to click a link on a Web page, and the application is automatically installed. After the application is installed, the client can be offline — there's no need for the client to access the server where the application was installed from.

ClickOnce installation can be done from a Website, a UNC share, or a file location (for example, from a CD). With ClickOnce the application is installed on the client system, it is available with Start menu shortcuts, and it can be uninstalled from the Add/Remove Programs dialog.

ClickOnce deployment is described by manifest files. The application manifest describes the application and permissions required by the application. The deployment manifest describes deployment configuration such as update policies.

In the Try It Out sections of the ClickOnce section, you configure ClickOnce deployment for the Simple Editor you created in Chapter 16.

Successfully deploying the assembly across the network requires that the manifest that is used with the installation must have a certificate associated. The certificate shows for the user installing the application the organization that created the installation program. In the following Try It Out, you create a certificate that is associated with the ClickOnce manifests.

Try It Out   Sign the ClickOnce Manifests

1. Open the Simple Editor sample from Chapter 16 with Visual Studio. If you didn't create the sample by yourself, copy it from the downloadable files.

2. Select Properties for the project in the Solution Explorer, and select the Signing tab as shown in Figure 17-1.

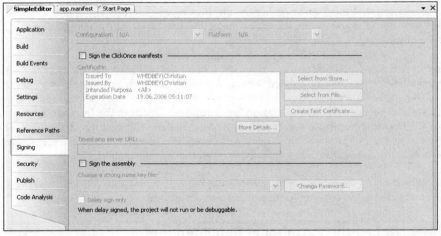

Figure 17-1

3. Check the checkbox Sign the ClickOnce manifests.

4. Click the button Create Test Certificate to create a test certificate that is associated with the ClickOnce manifests. Enter a password for the certificate as requested. You must remember the password for later settings. Then click the OK button.

5. With the Signing properties of the project you can see certificate information as shown in Figure 17-2.

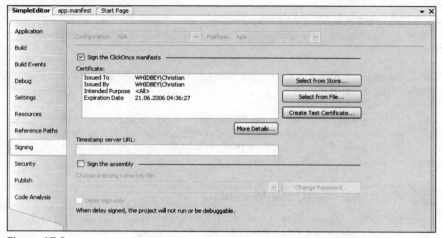

Figure 17-2

How It Works

A certificate is used that the user installing the application can identify the creator of the installation package. By reading the certificate, the user can decide if he can trust the installation to approve the security requirements.

With the test certificate you just created, the user doesn't get real trust information and receives a warning that this certificate cannot be trusted, as you will see later. Such a certificate is for testing only. Before you make the application ready for deployment, you have to get a real certificate from a certification authority such as Verisign. If the application is only deployed within the Intranet, you can also get a certificate from a local certificate server if there's one installed with your local network. The Microsoft certificate server can be installed with Windows Server 2003. If you have such a certificate, you can configure it by clicking the button Select from File... with the Signing options.

In the next Try It Out, you configure the permission requirements of the assembly. When the assembly is installed on the client, the required permissions must be approved.

Try It Out   Define the Permission Requirements

1. Select Properties for the project in the Solution Explorer and select Security, as shown in Figure 17-3.

2. Select Enable ClickOnce Security Settings.

3. Click the radio button This is a partial trust application.

4. Select the zone (Custom) as special security permissions are required by the application.

5. Click the Calculate Permissions button to calculate the permissions that are required by the application.

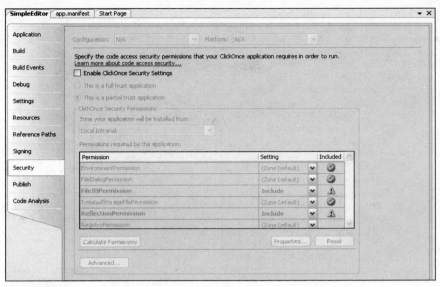

Figure 17-3

How It Works

Security is an important aspect of .NET applications. .NET uses evidence-based security to define what assemblies are allowed to do.

On one hand resources should be secured. Examples of such resources are files and directories, networking sockets, and environment variables. For all these resources, .NET permissions exist that allow access to them. One example is the `FileIOPermission` class, which can be used to allow access to the complete file system or to specific files and directories.

On the other hand you must define who is allowed to use these resources. Here, assemblies are grouped into different categories. Examples of such groups are assemblies that are installed locally, and assemblies that are loaded from the network. You can also define a category of assemblies from a specific manufacturer.

> *You can read the book* Professional C# 2005 (Wiley Publishing, Inc.) *for more information about evidence-based security.*

The Calculate Permissions button from the Security properties of Visual Studio analyzes the code used by the application to check the application's permission requirements. The result of this analysis is an application manifest that includes all required permissions. With Visual Studio 2005, you can see the application manifest with the name `app.manifest` below Properties in the Solution Explorer. The content of this file is shown here. The XML element `<applicationRequestMinimum>` defines all required permissions of the application. The `FileIOPermission` is required because the application reads and writes files using classes from the `System.IO` namespace.

```xml
<?xml version="1.0" encoding="utf-8"?>
<asmv1:assembly manifestVersion="1.0" xmlns="urn:schemas-microsoft-com:asm.v1"
xmlns:asmv1="urn:schemas-microsoft-com:asm.v1" xmlns:asmv2="urn:schemas-microsoft-
com:asm.v2" xmlns:xsi="http://www.w3.org/2001/XMLSchema-instance">
  <trustInfo xmlns="urn:schemas-microsoft-com:asm.v2">
    <security>
      <applicationRequestMinimum>
        <defaultAssemblyRequest permissionSetReference="Custom" />
        <PermissionSet class="System.Security.PermissionSet" version="1"
          ID="Custom" SameSite="site">
          <IPermission class="System.Security.Permissions.FileIOPermission,
            mscorlib, Version=2.0.0.0, Culture=neutral,
            PublicKeyToken=b77a5c561934e089" version="1" Unrestricted="true" />
          <IPermission class="System.Security.Permissions.ReflectionPermission,
            mscorlib, Version=2.0.0.0, Culture=neutral,
            PublicKeyToken=b77a5c561934e089" version="1" Flags="MemberAccess" />
          <IPermission class="System.Security.Permissions.SecurityPermission,
            mscorlib, Version=2.0.0.0, Culture=neutral,
            PublicKeyToken=b77a5c561934e089" version="1"
            Flags="Execution, ControlEvidence" />
          <IPermission class="System.Security.Permissions.UIPermission,
            mscorlib, Version=2.0.0.0, Culture=neutral,
            PublicKeyToken=b77a5c561934e089" version="1" Unrestricted="true" />
        </PermissionSet>
      </applicationRequestMinimum>
    </security>
  </trustInfo>
</asmv1:assembly>
```

By selecting a different zone in the Security dialog, you can verify if the application needs permissions that are not available within the zone.

With the defined security requirements, you can start to publish the application by creating a deployment manifest. This can easily be done with the Publish Wizard, as you see in the following Try It Out.

Try It Out   Using the Publish Wizard

1. Start the Publish Wizard by selecting the menu Build ➪ Publish Simple Editor. Enter a path to the Website http://localhost/SimpleEditor, as shown in Figure 17-4. Click the Next button.

2. At step 2 in the Publish Wizard select the option Yes, this application will be available online or offline, as shown in Figure 17-5. Click the Next button.

3. The last dialog gives summary information as you are Ready to Publish! (see Figure 17-6). Click the Finish button.

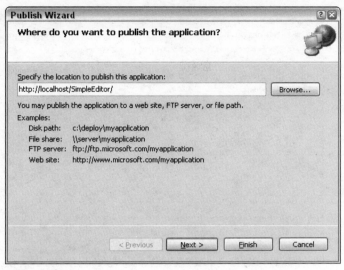

Figure 17-4

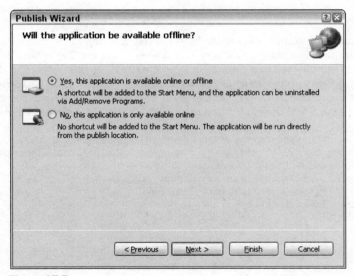

Figure 17-5

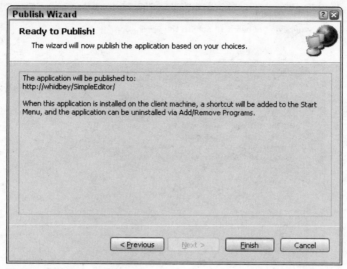

Figure 17-6

How It Works

The Publish Wizard creates a Website on the local Internet Information Services Web server. The assemblies of the application (executables and libraries) as well as the application and deployment manifests, a `setup.exe`, and a sample Web page, `publish.htm`, are copied to the Web server. The deployment manifest describes installation information as shown here. With Visual Studio, you can open the deployment manifest by opening the file `SimpleEditor.application` in the Solution Explorer. With this manifest you can see a dependency to the application manifest with the XML element `<dependentAssembly>`.

```
<assemblyIdentity name="SimpleEditor.application" version="1.0.0.12"
publicKeyToken="74fe8381193333a9" language="neutral" processorArchitecture="msil"
xmlns="urn:schemas-microsoft-com:asm.v1" />
  <description asmv2:publisher="Thinktecture" asmv2:product="SimpleEditor"
      xmlns="urn:schemas-microsoft-com:asm.v1" />
  <deployment install="true">
    <subscription>
      <update>
        <beforeApplicationStartup />
      </update>
    </subscription>
    <deploymentProvider
        codebase="http://cnagel/SimpleEditor/SimpleEditor.application" />
  </deployment>
  <dependency>
    <dependentAssembly dependencyType="install" allowDelayedBinding="true"
        codebase="SimpleEditor_1_0_0_1\SimpleEditor.exe.manifest"
        size="6789">
      <assemblyIdentity name="SimpleEditor.exe" version="1.0.0.1"
          publicKeyToken="74fe8381193333a9" language="neutral"
          processorArchitecture="msil" type="win32" />
      <hash>
```

```
        <dsig:Transforms>
          <dsig:Transform Algorithm=
              "urn:schemas-microsoft-com:HashTransforms.Identity" />
        </dsig:Transforms>
        <dsig:DigestMethod Algorithm="http://www.w3.org/2000/09/xmldsig#sha1" />
        <dsig:DigestValue>fL/kgd9/L3dmbuIfkSrU8AU1mbg=</dsig:DigestValue>
      </hash>
    </dependentAssembly>
  </dependency>
```

By selecting the option as shown in Figure 17-5, you've specified that the application will be available online and offline. This way the application is installed on the client system and can be accessed from the Start menu. You can also use Add/Remove Programs to uninstall the application. If you select that the application to be available only online, the user must always click the Website link to load the application from the server and start it locally.

The files that belong to the application are defined by the project output. You can see the application files with the Properties of the application in the Publish settings by clicking the button Application Files..., as shown in Figure 17-7.

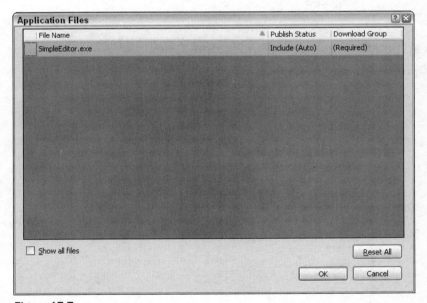

Figure 17-7

The prerequisites of the application are defined with the Prerequisites dialog (see Figure 17-8) that can be accessed by clicking the Prerequisites button. With .NET 2.0 applications, the prerequisite .NET Framework 2.0 is automatically detected, as the figure shows. You can select other prerequisites with this dialog.

Now, you can install the application by following the steps in the next Try It Out.

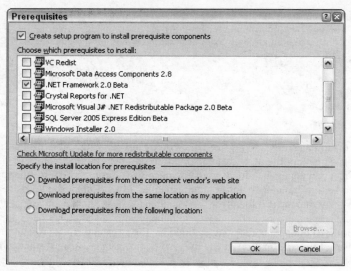

Figure 17-8

Installation of the Application

1. Open the Web page `publish.htm`, as shown in Figure 17-9.

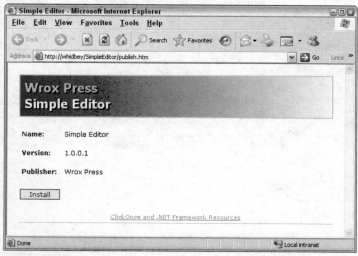

Figure 17-9

2. Click the Install button to install the application. Next, a security warning will pop up (see Figure 17-10).

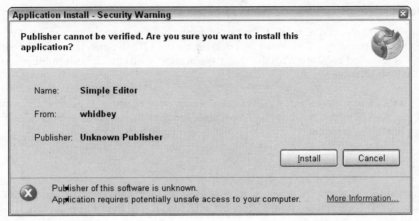

Figure 17-10

3. Click the More Information link to see the potential security issues with the application. Read the categories of this dialog, shown in Figure 17-11.

Figure 17-11

4. After reading the dialog information, click the OK button and press the Install button of the Application Install dialog.

How It Works

When the file `publish.htm` is opened, the target application is checked for version 2.0 of the .NET runtime. This check is done by a JavaScript function inside the HTML page. If the runtime is not installed, the runtime is installed together with the client application. With the default publish settings the runtime is copied to the Web server.

By clicking the link to install the application, the deployment manifest is opened to install the application. Next, the user is informed about some possible security issues of the application. If the user clicks OK, the application is installed.

Updates

With the default publish, the client application automatically checks the Web server for a new version. In the following Try It Out, you try such a scenario with the Simple Editor application.

Try It Out   Updating the Application

1. Make a change to the Simple Editor application that shows up immediately, like setting the background color of the text box.

2. Build the application and start the Publish Wizard once more using the same settings as before.

3. Do not click the link on the Web page `publish.htm`; instead, start the client application from the Start menu. When the application is started, the dialog shown in Figure 17-12 pops up asking if a new version should be downloaded. Click the OK button to download the new version. When the new version launches, you can see the application with the colored text box.

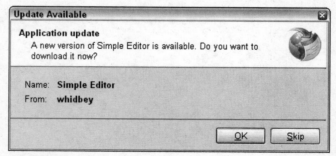

Figure 17-12

How It Works

The update policy is defined by a setting in the deployment manifest with the XML element `<update>`. You can change the update policy by clicking the Updates... button with the Publish settings. Remember to access the Publish settings with the properties of the project. The Application Updates dialog is shown in Figure 17-13.

With this dialog, you can define whether the client should look for updates at all. If updates should be checked, you can define whether the check should happen before the application starts or if the update should occur in the background while the application is running. If the update should occur in the background, you can set the time interval for them: with every start of the application, or with a specific number of hours, days, or weeks.

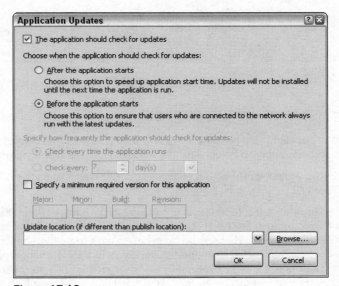

Figure 17-13

Visual Studio Setup and Deployment Project Types

Start the Visual Studio Add New Project dialog and select Setup and Deployment from the Project Types pane. The screen shown in Figure 17-14 is displayed.

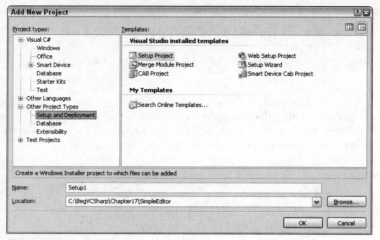

Figure 17-14

Here are the project types and what can be done with them:

❑ The Setup Project template is the one you will use. This template is used to create Windows Installer Packages, so it can be used for deploying Windows Applications.

❑ The Web Setup Project template can be used to install Web applications. This project template is used in Chapter 21.

❑ The Merge Module Project template is used to create Windows Installer merge modules. A merge module is an installer file that can be included in multiple Microsoft Installer installation packages. For components that should be installed with more than one installation program, a merge module can be created to include this module in the installation packages. One example of a merge module is the .NET runtime itself: it is delivered in a merge module; therefore, the .NET runtime can be included with the installer package of an application. You will use a merge module in the sample application.

❑ The Setup Wizard is a step-by-step way to choose the other templates. The first question to ask yourself is: Do you want to create a setup program to install an application or a redistributable package? Depending on your choice, a Windows Installer package, a merge module, or a CAB file is created.

❑ The Cab Project template allows you to create cabinet files. Cabinet files can be used to merge multiple assemblies into a single file and compress it. Since the cabinet files can be compressed, a Web client can download a smaller file from the server.

Creating components is not in the scope of this book, so you will not create cabinet projects. You can read Professional C# 2005 *(Wiley Publishing, Inc) for information on creating .NET components for download from a Web server.*

❑ The Smart Device Cab Project template can be used to create an installer package for smart device applications.

Microsoft Windows Installer Architecture

Before the Windows Installer existed, programmers had to create custom installation programs. Not only was it more work to build such installation programs, but many of them didn't follow the Windows rules. Often system DLLs were overwritten with older versions because the installation program didn't check the version. In addition, the directory where the application files were copied was often wrong. If, for example, a hard-coded directory string such as `C:\Program Files` was used and the system administrator changed the default drive letter or an international version of the operating system was used where this directory is named differently, the installation failed.

The first version of the Windows Installer was released as part of Microsoft Office 2000 and as a distributable package that could be included with other application packages. Version 1.1 was first released with Windows 2000 and added support to register COM+ components. Version 1.2 added support for the file protection mechanism of Windows ME. Version 2.0 was the first version that included support to install .NET assemblies, and it has support for the 64-bit release of Windows as well. With Visual Studio 2005, version 2.0 is used.

Windows Installer Terms

Working with the Windows Installer requires you to be familiar with some terms that are used with the Windows Installer technology: packages, features, and components.

> **Be aware of this about the term *component*. In the context of the Windows Installer, a component is not the same as a component in the .NET Framework. A Windows Installer component is just a single file (or multiple files that logically belong together). Such a file can be an executable, a DLL, or even a simple text file.**

As you can see in Figure 17-15, a *package* consists of one or more features. A package is a single Microsoft Installer (MSI) database. A *feature* is the user's view of the capabilities of a product and can consist of features and components. A *component* is the developer's view of the installation; it is the smallest unit of installation and consists of one or more files. The differentiation between features and components exists because a single component can be included in multiple features (as shown in Component 2 in the figure). A single feature cannot be included within multiple features.

Let's look at the features of a real-world example that you should already have: Visual Studio 2005. Using the Add/Remove Programs option in the Control Panel, you can change the installed features of Visual Studio after installation by pressing the Change/Remove button, as shown in Figure 17-16.

By pressing the Change/Remove button, you can visit the Visual Studio 2005 Maintenance Wizard. This is a good way to see features in action. Select Add or Remove Features to see the features of the Visual Studio 2005 package (see Figure 17-17).

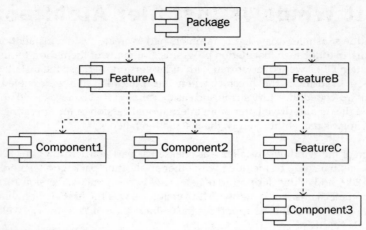

Figure 17-15

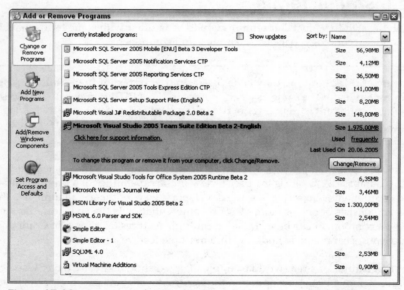

Figure 17-16

As you can see in Figure 17-17, the Visual Studio 2005 package includes the features Language Tools, .NET Framework SDK, Crystal Reports for Visual Studio 2005, Tools for Redistributing Applications, and Server Components. The Language Tools feature has the subfeatures Visual Basic, Visual C++, and Visual C#.

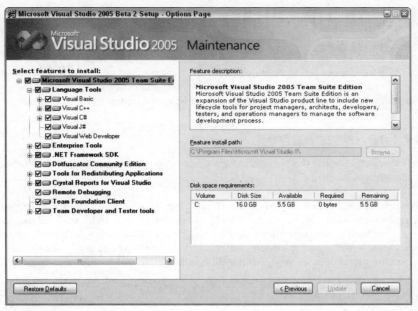

Figure 17-17

Advantages of the Windows Installer

The advantages of the Windows installer are:

❑ Features can be installed, not installed, or advertised. With *advertisement*, a feature of the package will be installed at first use. Maybe you have already seen the Windows Installer starting during your work with Microsoft Word. If you use an advertised feature of Word that was not installed, it will be installed automatically as soon as you use it.

❑ If an application becomes corrupt, it can *self-repair* through the repair feature of Windows Installer packages.

❑ An automatic *rollback* will be done if the installation fails. After the installation fails everything is left as before: no additional Registry keys, no files, and so on, are left on the system.

❑ With an *uninstall*, all the relevant files, Registry keys, and so on are removed — the application can be completely uninstalled. No temporary files are left out, and the Registry is also reinstated.

You can read the tables of the MSI database file to find information about such things as what files are copied and what Registry keys are written.

Creating an Installation Package for the Simple Editor

In this section, you will use the Simple Editor solution from Chapter 16 to create a Windows Installer Package using Visual Studio 2005. Of course, you can use any other Windows Forms application you have developed while you follow the steps; you just have to change some of the names used.

Planning the Installation

Before you can start building the installation program, you have to plan what you are going to put in it. There are some questions to be considered first:

❑ **What files are needed for the application?** Of course the executable and probably some component assemblies are required. It won't be necessary for you to identify all dependencies of these items because the dependencies will automatically be included. Maybe some other files are needed, too. What about a documentation file, a `readme.txt` file, a license file, a document template, pictures, and configuration files, among others? You have to know all required files.

For the Simple Editor that was developed in Chapter 16 an executable is needed, and you will also include the files `readme.rtf` and `license.rtf`, and a bitmap from Wrox Press to show in the installation dialogs.

❑ **What directories should be used?** Application files should be installed in `Program Files\ Application name`. The Program Files directory is named differently for each language variant of the operating system. Also, the administrator can choose different paths for this application. It is not necessary to know where this directory really is, because there's an API function call to get this directory. With the installer, you can use a special predefined folder to put files in the Program Files directory.

> It's worth making this point again — under no circumstances should the directories be hard-coded. With international versions these directories are named differently! Even if your application supports just English versions of Windows (which you really shouldn't do), the system administrator could have moved these directories to different drives.

The Simple Editor will have the executable in the default application directory unless the installing user selects a different path.

❑ **How should the user access the application?** You can put a shortcut to the executable in the Start menu, or place an icon on the desktop, for example. If you want to place an icon on the desktop, you should check whether the user is happy with that. With Windows XP, the guideline is to have the desktop as clean as possible.

The Simple Editor should be accessible from the Start menu.

❑ **What is the distribution media?** Do you want to put the installation packages on a CD, floppy disks, or a network share?

❏ **What questions should the user answer?** Should he or she accept license information, display a `ReadMe` file, or enter the path to install? Are some other options required for the installation?

The default dialogs supplied with the Visual Studio 2005 Installer are ample for the Windows Installer project you create over the remainder of the chapter. You will ask for the directory where the program should be installed (the setup may choose a path that is different from the default), show a `ReadMe` file, and ask the user to accept the license agreement.

Create the Project

Now that you know what should be in the installation package, you can use the Visual Studio 2005 installer to create an installer project and add all files that should be installed. In the following Try It Out, you use the Project Wizard and configure the project.

Try It Out **Creating a Windows Installer Project**

1. Open the solution file of the Simple Editor project you created in Chapter 16. You will add the installation project to the existing solution. If you didn't create the solution in Chapter 16 yourself (shame on you!), you'll find it in the downloadable code.

2. Add a Setup Project called `SimpleEditorSetup` to the solution with the File ➪ Add Project ➪ New Project menu, as shown in Figure 17-18, and click the OK button.

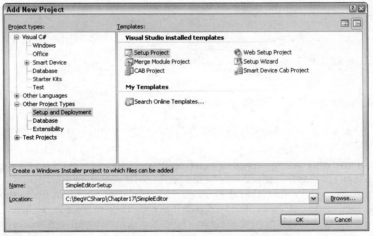

Figure 17-18

Project Properties

Up to this point, you have only a project file for the setup solution. The files to be installed must be defined. But you also have to configure the project properties. To do this, you have to know what the *Packaging* and *Bootstrapper* options mean.

Packaging

MSI is where the installation is started, but you can define how the files that are to be installed are packaged with three options in the dialog shown in Figure 17-19. This dialog opens if you right-click on the `SimpleEditorSetup` project and select Properties.

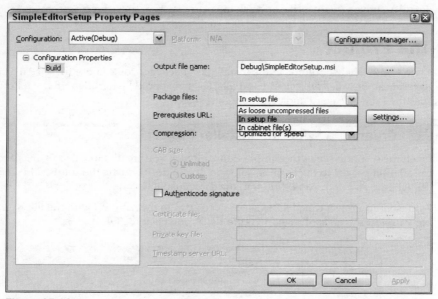

Figure 17-19

Look at options in the Package files drop-down list:

❑ The As loose uncompressed files option stores all program and data files as they are. No compressing takes place.

❑ The In setup file option merges and compresses all the files into the MSI file. This option can be overridden for single components in the package. If you put all your files into a single MSI file, you have to pay attention that the size of the installation program fits in the target you want to use, for example, CDs or floppy disks. If you have so many files to install that they exceed the capacity of a single floppy, you can try to change the compression option by selecting the Optimized for size option from the Compression drop-down list. If the files still don't fit you can choose the next option for packaging.

❑ The third way to package files is In cabinet file(s). With this method, the MSI file is used just to load and install the CAB files. With CAB files, it is possible to set file sizes that enable installations on CDs or floppy disks (you can set sizes of 1440 KB for installations from floppy disks).

Prerequisites

You can configure in the same dialog the prerequisites that must be installed before the application can be installed. When you click the Settings button near the Prerequisites URL text box, the Prerequisites dialog pops up, as shown in Figure 17-20. As you can see, the .NET Framework 2.0 is selected by default as a prerequisite. If the client system doesn't have the .NET Framework installed, it will be from the setup program. You can also select other prerequisite options, as shown in the following list:

❑ **Windows Installer 2.0:** Windows Installer 2.0 is required for installer packages created with Visual Studio 2005. If the target system is Windows XP or Windows Server 2003, the installer is already on the system. With older systems the correct version of the Windows Installer might not be there, so you can select this option to include Windows Installer 2.0 with the installation program.

❑ **Microsoft Visual J# .NET Redistributable Package:** If Visual J# assemblies are required for the application, you might select the Microsoft Visual J# .NET Redistributable Package to include with your setup program. Usually, this package is only needed if you develop Visual J# applications. However, it is also possible to use J# assemblies with other programming languages.

❑ **SQL Server 2005 Express Edition:** If you need a database on the client system, you can include the SQL Server 2005 Express edition with the setup program. Accessing SQL Server with ADO.NET is covered in Chapter 24.

❑ **Crystal Reports for .NET:** Crystal Reports allows you to create graphical reports. You can read more about Crystal Reports in the book *Professional Crystal Reports for Visual Studio .NET*, second edition by David McAmis (Wiley Publishing, Inc., April 2004).

❑ **Microsoft Data Access Components 2.8:** Microsoft Data Access Components (MDAC) includes the OLE DB provider, ODBC drivers, and the Microsoft SQL Server Network Libraries that are used to access databases. MDAC version 8.0 is part of Windows Server 2003. With .NET 2.0, MDAC is no longer needed; if you are using the .NET Data Provider for SQL Server, only the OLEDB and ODBC data providers require MDAC to be installed.

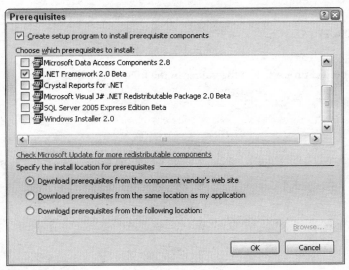

Figure 17-20

Try It Out   Configuring the Project

1. Change the Prerequisites option in the Property page that you just saw to include Windows Installer 2.0 so that the application can be installed on systems where the Windows Installer 2.0 is not available. Also change the output filename to `WroxSimpleEditor.msi`, as shown in Figure 17-21. Then click the OK button.

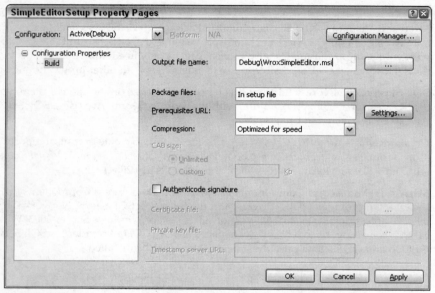

Figure 17-21

2. Set the project properties to the values in the following table.

Property	Value
Author	Wrox Press
Description	Simple Editor to print and edit text files.
Keywords	Installer, Wrox Press, Simple Editor
Manufacturer	Wrox Press
ManufacturerUrl	http://www.wrox.com
Product Name	Simple Editor
SupportUrl	http://p2p.wrox.com
Title	Installation Demo for Simple Editor
Version	1.0.0

Setup Editors

With a Visual Studio 2005 Setup Project you have six editors available. You can select the editor by opening a deployment project, and selecting the menu View ➪ Editor, as shown in Figure 17-22.

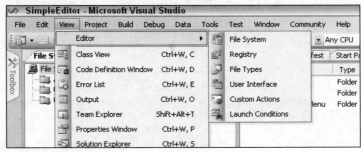

Figure 17-22

❑ The File System Editor is used to add files to the installation package.

❑ With the Registry Editor, you can create Registry keys for the application.

❑ The File Types Editor allows you to register specific file extensions for an application.

❑ With the User Interface Editor you can add and configure dialogs that are shown during installation of the product.

❑ The Custom Actions Editor allows you to start custom programs during installation and uninstallation.

❑ With the Launch Conditions Editor, you can specify requirements for your application, for example, that the .NET runtime already has to be in place.

File System Editor

With the File System Editor, you can add files to the installation package and configure the locations where they should be installed. This editor is opened with the menu options View ➪ Editor ➪ File System. Some of the predefined special folders are automatically opened, as shown in Figure 17-23.

Figure 17-23

❑ The Application Folder is used to store the executables and libraries. The location is defined as [ProgramFilesFolder]\[Manufacturer]\[ProductName]. On English language systems, [ProgramFilesFolder] is resolved to C:\Program Files. The directories for [Manufacturer] and [ProductName] are defined with the Manufacturer and ProductName project properties.

❑ If you want to place an icon on the desktop the User's Desktop folder can be used. The default path to this folder is `C:\Documents and Settings\`*username*`\Desktop` or `C:\Documents and Settings\All Users\Desktop`, depending on whether the installation is done for a single user or for all users.

❑ The user will usually start a program by starting it from the All Programs menu. The default path is `C:\Documents and Settings\`*username*`\Start Menu\`*Programs*. You can put a shortcut to the application in this menu. The shortcut should have a name that includes the company and the application name, so that the user can easily identify the application, for example, Microsoft Excel.

Some applications create a submenu where more than one application can be started, for example, Microsoft Visual Studio 2005. According to the Windows Guidelines, many programs do this for the wrong reason, listing programs which are not necessary: you shouldn't put an uninstall program in these menus, because this feature is available from Add/Remove Programs in the Control Panel and should be used from there. A help file should also not be placed in this menu because this should be available directly from the application. Thus, for many applications, it will be enough to place a shortcut to the application directly in the All Programs menu. The goal of these restrictions is to ensure that the Start menu doesn't get cluttered with too many items in it.

A great reference to this information can be found in "Application Specification for Microsoft Windows 2000." You can download this paper at `http://msdn.microsoft.com`, by following the Partners & Certification ⇨ Certified for Windows Program links.

There are other folders that you can add by right-clicking and selecting Add Special Folder. Some of these folders include:

❑ Global Assembly Cache Folder refers to the folder where you can install shared assemblies. The Global Assembly Cache is used for assemblies that should be shared between multiple applications. You can read more about sharing assemblies in Chapter 26.

❑ User's Personal Data Folder refers to the user's default folder where documents should be stored. `C:\Documents and Settings\username\My Documents` is the default path. This path is the default directory used by Visual Studio to store projects.

❑ The shortcuts placed in the *User's Send To Menu* extend the Send To context menu when a file is selected. With this context menu the user can typically send a file to the target location such as the floppy drive, a mail recipient, or the My Documents folder.

Adding Items to Special Folders

You can choose from a list to add items to a special folder by selecting a folder and choosing the menu Action ⇨ Add Special Folder, as shown in Figure 17-24.

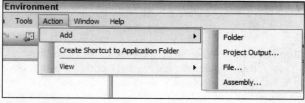

Figure 17-24

You can select Project Output, Folder, File, or Assembly. Adding the output of a project to a folder automatically adds the generated output files and a .dll or .exe, depending on whether the added project is a component library or an application. Selecting either Project Output or Assembly automatically adds all dependencies (all referenced assemblies) to the folder.

File Properties

If you select the properties of a file in a folder, you can set the following properties. Depending on the file types, some of these properties don't apply, and there are additional properties not listed in the following table.

Property	Description
Condition	A condition can be defined with this property to determine if the selected file should be installed. This can be useful if you want to add this file only for specific operating system versions or if the user must chose some selection in a dialog.
Exclude	Can be set to True if this file should not be installed. This way the file can stay in the project but doesn't install. You can exclude a file if you are sure that it's not a dependency or that it already exists on every system where the application is deployed.
PackageAs	With PackageAs, you can override the default way the file is added to the installer package. For example, if the project configuration says In Setup File, you can change the package configuration with this option to Loose for a specific file so that this file will not be added to the MSI database file. This is useful, for example, if you want to add a ReadMe file, which the user should read before starting the installation. Obviously, you would not compress this file even if all the others were compressed.
Permanent	Setting this property to True means that the file will stay on the target computer after uninstallation of the product. This can be used for configuration files. You might have already seen this when installing a new version of Microsoft Outlook: if you configure Microsoft Outlook, then uninstall the product and install it again, it's not necessary to configure it again because the configuration from the last install is not deleted.
ReadOnly	This property sets the read only file attribute at installation.
Vital	This property means that this file is essential for the installation of this product. If installation of this file fails, the complete installation is aborted and a rollback occurs.

In the next Try It Out you add files to the installer package.

Try It Out **Add Files to the Installer Package**

1. Add the primary output of the Simple Editor project to the installer project using the Project ⇨ Add ⇨ Project Output menu options. In the Add Project Output Group dialog, select the Primary Output, as shown in Figure 17-25.

Figure 17-25

Press the OK button to add the primary output of the `SimpleEditor` project to the Application folder in the automatically opened File System Editor. In this case, the primary output is `SimpleEditor.exe`.

2. Additional files to add are a logo, a license, and a `ReadMe` file. In the File System Editor create a subdirectory named Setup in the Application folder. You can do this by selecting the Application folder, and choosing the menu options Action ⇨ Add ⇨ Folder.

> The Action menu in Visual Studio is available only if you select items in the setup editors. If an item in the Solution Explorer or Class View is selected, the Action menu is not available.

3. Add the files `wroxlogo.bmp`, `wroxsetuplogo.bmp`, `readme.rtf`, and `license.rtf` to the folder setup by right-clicking on the `Setup` folder and selecting Add ⇨ File. These files are available with the code download for this chapter, but you can easily create these files yourself. You can fill the text files with license and ReadMe information. It is not necessary to change the properties of these files. These files will be used in the dialogs of the installation program.

The bitmap `wroxsetuplogo.bmp` should have a size of 500 pixels wide and 70 pixels high. The left 420 pixels of the bitmap should only have a background graphic because the text of the installation dialogs will cover this range.

4. Add the file `readme.txt` to the Application folder. You want this file to be available for the user to read before the installation is started. Set the property `PackageAs` to `vsdpaLoose` so that this file will not be compressed into the Installer package. Also set the `ReadOnly` property to `true` so that this file cannot be changed.

The project now includes two readme files, readme.txt and readme.rtf. The file readme.txt can be read by the user installing the application before the installation is started. The file readme.rtf is used to show some information in the installation dialogs.

5. Drag and drop the file `demo.wroxtext` to the User's Desktop folder. This file should only be installed after asking the user whether he or she really wants to install it. Therefore, set the `Condition` property of this file to CHECKBOXDEMO. CHECKBOXDEMO is the condition that can be set by the user. The value must be written in uppercase. The file will only be installed if the CHECKBOXDEMO condition is set to `true`. Later you define a dialog where this property will be set.

To make the program available from the Start ⇨ Programs menu, you need a shortcut to the `SimpleEditor` program.

6. Select the Primary output from `SimpleEditor` item in the Application folder and open the menu Action ⇨ Create Shortcut to Primary output from `SimpleEditor`. Set the `Name` property of the generated shortcut to `Wrox Simple Editor`, and drag and drop this shortcut to the User's Programs Menu.

File Types Editor

If your application uses custom file types and you want to register file extensions for files that should start your application when a user double-clicks them, you can use the File Types Editor. This editor can be started with View ⇨ Editor>File Types. Figure 17-26 shows the File Types Editor with a custom file extension added.

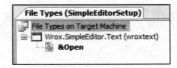

Figure 17-26

With the File Types Editor, you can configure a file extension that should be handled from your application. The file extension has the properties shown in the following table.

Property	Description
Name	Here, you should add a useful name describing the file type. This name is displayed in the File Types Editor and is also written to the Registry. The name should be unique. An example for .doc file types is `Word.Document.8`. It's not necessary to use a `ProgID` as in the Word example; simple text like `wordhtmlfile` as used for the .dochtml file extension can also be used.
Command	With the `Command` property you can specify the executable that should be started when the user opens a file with this type.
Description	Here you can add a description.

Table continued on following page

Property	Description
Extensions	This property is for the file extension where your application should be registered. The file extension will be registered in a section of the Registry.
Icon	Specify an icon to display for the file extension.

Create Actions

After creating the file types in the File Types Editor, you can add *actions*. The default action that is automatically added is Open. You can add additional actions like New and Print or whatever actions your program can do with files. Together with the actions, the Arguments and Verb properties must be defined. The Arguments property specifies the argument that is passed to the program, which is registered for the file extension. For example, %1 means that the filename is passed to the application. The Verb property specifies the action that should occur. With a print action a /print can be added if supported by the application.

In the next Try It Out, you add an action to the Simple Editor installation program. You want to register a file extension so that the Simple Editor application can be used from Windows Explorer to open files with the extension .wroxtext. After this registration you can double-click these files to open them, and the Simple Editor application will start automatically.

Try It Out   Set the File Extension

1. Start the File Types Editor with View ➪ Editor ➪ File Types. Add a new file type using the menu Action ➪ Add File Type with the properties set as shown in the following table. Because you don't want to change the ownership for Notepad of the .txt file extension, use the .wroxtext file extension.

Property	Value
(Name)	Wrox.SimpleEditor.Text
Command	Primary output from SimpleEditor
Description	Wrox Text Documents
Extensions	Wroxtext

You can also set the Icon property to define an icon for the opening of files.

Leave the properties of the Open action with the default values so that the filename is passed as an application argument.

Launch Condition Editor

With the Launch Condition Editor you can specify some requirements that the target system must have before the installation can take place. You can start the Launch Condition Editor by selecting the menu View ➪ Editor ➪ Launch Conditions, as shown in Figure 17-27.

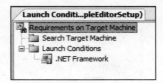

Figure 17-27

The editor has two sections to specify the requirements: Search Target Machine and Launch Conditions. In the first section, you can specify what specific file or Registry key to search for, and the second section defines the error message if the search is not successful.

Let's look into some of the launch conditions that you can define using the Action menu:

❑   The File Launch Condition searches the target system for a file you define before the installation starts.

❑   The Registry Launch Condition allows you to require a check of Registry keys before the installation starts.

❑   The Windows Installer Launch Condition makes it possible to search for Windows Installer components that must be present.

❑   The .NET Framework Launch Condition checks if the .NET Framework is already installed on the target system.

❑   The Internet Information Services Launch Condition checks for installed Internet Information Services. Adding this launch condition adds a Registry search for a specific Registry key that is defined when Internet Information Services is installed, and adds a condition to check for a specific version.

By default, a .NET Framework Launch Condition is included, and its properties have been set to predefined values: the `Message` property is set to `[VSDNETMSG]`, which is a predefined error message. If the .NET Framework is not installed, a message informing the user to install the .NET Framework pops up. `InstallUrl`, by default, is set to `http://go.microsoft.com/fwlink/?linkid=9832`, so the user can easily start the installation of the .NET Framework.

User Interface Editor

With the User Interface Editor, you can define the dialogs the user sees when configuring the installation. Here, you can inform the user about license agreements and ask for installation paths and other information to configure the application.

In the next Try It Out, you start the User Interface Editor, which will be used to configure the dialogs that are shown when the application is installed.

Try It Out   Start the User Interface Editor

1.   Start the User Interface Editor by selecting View ⇨ Editor ⇨ User Interface. You use the User Interface Editor to set properties for predefined dialog boxes. Figure 17-28 shows the automatically generated dialogs and two installation modes that you should see.

Figure 17-28

Install and Administrative Install

As you can see in Figure 17-28, there are two installation modes: Install and Administrative Install. The Install mode is typically used to install the application on a target system. With an Administrative Install you can install an image of the application on a network share. Afterward a user can install the application from the network.

Default Dialogs

Both installation modes have three sequences where dialogs can be shown: Start, Progress, and End. Let's look at the default dialogs:

❑ The Welcome dialog displays a welcome message to the user. You can replace the default welcome text with your own message. The user can only cancel the installation or press the next button.

❑ With the second dialog, Installation Folder, the user can choose the folder where the application should be installed. If you add custom dialogs (you look at this in a moment), you have to add them before this one.

❑ The Confirm Installation dialog is the last dialog before the installation starts.

❑ The Progress dialog displays a progress control so that the user can see the progress of the installation.

❑ When installation is finished, the Finished dialog shows up.

The default dialogs will show up automatically at installation time, even if you never opened the User Interface Editor in the solution. But you should configure these dialogs so that useful messages for your application are displayed.

In the next Try It Out, you configure the default dialogs that are shown when the application is installed. Here, the Administrative Install path will be ignored; only the typical installation path is configured.

Try It Out   Configuring the Default Dialogs

1. Select the Welcome dialog. In the Properties window, you can see three properties that can be changed for this dialog: BannerBitmap, CopyrightWarning, and WelcomeText. Select the BannerBitmap property by pressing (Browse...) in the combo box, and select the wroxsetuplogo.bmp file in the folder Application Folder\Setup. The bitmap stored in this file will show up on top of this dialog.

The default text for the property CopyrightWarning says:

```
WARNING: This computer program is protected by copyright law and international
treaties. Unauthorized duplication or distribution of this program, or any portion
of it, may result in severe civil or criminal penalties, and will be prosecuted to
the maximum extent possible under the law.
```

This text will show up in the Welcome dialog, too. Change this text if you want a stronger warning. The WelcomeText property defines more text that is displayed in the dialog. Its default value is:

```
The installer will guide you through the steps required to install [ProductName] on
your computer.
```

You can change this text, too. The string [ProductName] will be automatically replaced with the property ProductName that you defined in the properties of the project.

2. Select the Installation Folder dialog. This dialog has just two properties: BannerBitmap and InstallAllUsersVisible. The property InstallAllUsersVisible has a default value of true. If this value is set to false, the application can only be installed for the user that is logged on while the installation is running. Change the value of BannerBitmap to the wroxsetuplogo.bmp file as you did with the Welcome dialog. As each dialog can display a bitmap with this property, change the BannerBitmap property with all the other dialogs too.

Additional Dialogs

You cannot design a custom dialog and add it to the installation sequence with the Visual Studio installer. A more sophisticated tool such as InstallShield or Wise for Windows is required to do this — but with the Visual Studio installer, you can add and customize many of the predefined dialogs in the Add Dialog screen.

Selecting the Start sequence in the User Interface Editor and choosing the menu options Action ⇨ Add Dialog, causes the Add Dialog dialog to be displayed (see Figure 17-29). All these dialogs are configurable.

There are dialogs in which two, three, or four radio buttons appear, check box dialogs that show up to four check boxes, and text box dialogs that show up to four text boxes. You can configure these dialogs by setting their properties.

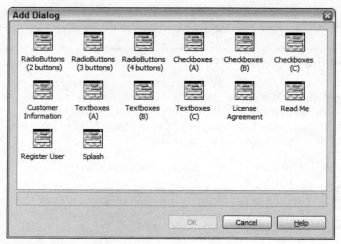

Figure 17-29

Here's a quick overview of some of the dialogs:

❑ The Customer Information dialog asks users for their name and company, and the product's serial number. If you don't provide a serial number with the product, you can hide the serial number text box by setting the ShowSerialNumber property to false.

❑ With the License Agreement dialog, users can accept a license before the installation starts. A license file is defined with the LicenseFile property.

❑ In the Register User dialog, users can press a Register Now button to launch a program defined with the Executable property. The custom program can send the data to an FTP server, or it can transfer the data by e-mail.

❑ The Splash dialog just displays a splash screen before the installation starts with a bitmap specified by the SplashBitmap property.

With the next Try It Out, you add some additional dialogs such as Read Me, License Agreement, and a Checkboxes dialog.

Try It Out   Adding Other Dialogs

1. Add a Read Me, a License Agreement, and a Checkboxes (A) dialog to the Start sequence with the menu options Action ⇨ Add Dialog. Define the order in the start sequence by dragging and dropping in this way:

```
Welcome - Read Me - License Agreement - Checkboxes (A) - Installation Folder -
Confirm Installation.
```

2. Configure the BannerBitmap property for all these dialogs as you did earlier. For the Read Me dialog, set the ReadmeFile property to readme.rtf, the file you added earlier to Application Folder\Setup.

3. For the License Agreement dialog, set the LicenseFile property to license.rtf.

4. The Checkboxes (A) dialog should be used to ask users if the file `demo.wroxtext` (which you have put into the user's Desktop folder) should be installed or not. Change the properties of this dialog according to the following table.

Property	Values
BannerText	Optional Files
BodyText	Installation of optional files
Checkbox1Label	Do you want a demo file put on to the desktop?
Checkbox1Property	CHECKBOXDEMO
Checkbox2Visible	False
Checkbox3Visible	False
Checkbox4Visible	False

The `Checkbox1Property` property is set to the same value as the `Condition` property of the file `demo.wroxtext` — you set this `Condition` value earlier when you added the file to the package using the File System Editor. If the user checks this check box, the value of CHECKBOXDEMO will be `true`, and the file will be installed; if the check box is not checked, the value will be `false`, and the file will not be installed.

The `CheckboxXVisible` property of the other check boxes is set to `false`, because you need only a single check box.

Building the Project

Now, complete the next Try It Out to start the build of the installer project.

Try It Out **Build the Project**

1. To create the Microsoft Installer Package, right-click the `SimpleEditorSetup` project and select Build. With a successful build you will find the files `setup.exe` and `WroxSimpleEditor.msi` as well as a `readme.txt` file in the `Debug` or `Release` directory (depending on your build settings).

`Setup.exe` will start the installation of the MSI database file `WroxSimpleEditor.msi`. All files that you have added to the installer project (with one exception) are merged and compressed into the MSI file because you have set the project properties to Package Files in Setup File. The exception to this is the `readme.txt` file, where the. `PackageAs` property was changed so that it can be read immediately before the application is installed. You can also find the installation package of the .NET Framework in the `DotNetFx` subdirectory.

Installation

Now, you can start installing the Simple Editor application. Double-click the `Setup.exe` file, or select the `WroxSimpleEditor.msi` file. Right-click to open the context menu and choose the Install option.

You can also start the installation from within Visual Studio 2005 by right-clicking the opened installation project in the Solution Explorer and selecting Install, as shown in Figure 17-30.

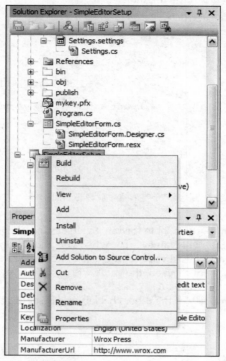

Figure 17-30

As you can see in the following screenshots, all the dialogs have the Wrox logo, and the inserted ReadMe and License Agreement dialogs appear with the configured files.

Let's walk through the installation sequence.

Welcome

The first dialog to be seen is the Welcome dialog (see Figure 17-31). In this dialog, you can see the Wrox logo that was inserted by setting the value of the BannerBitmap property. The text that can be seen is defined with the WelcomeText and CopyrightWarning properties. The title of this dialog results from the ProductName property that you set with the project properties.

Read Me

After pressing the Next button, you can see the Read Me dialog (see Figure 17-32). It shows the Rich Text file readme.rtf that was configured by setting the ReadmeFile property.

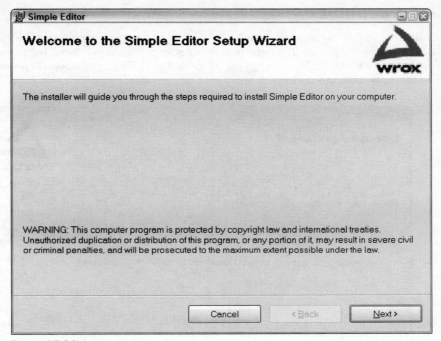

Figure 17-31

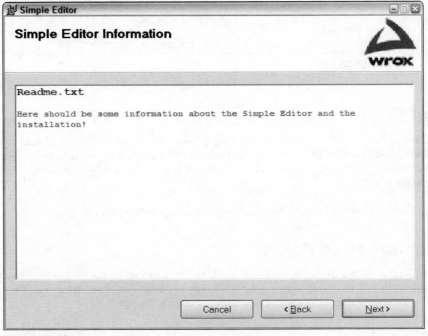

Figure 17-32

License Agreement

The third dialog to appear is the license agreement. Here, you have only configured the `BannerBitmap` and the `LicenseFile` properties. The radio buttons to agree to the license are added automatically. As you can see in Figure 17-33, the Next button stays disabled until the I agree button is pressed. This functionality is automatic with this dialog.

Figure 17-33

Optional Files

Agreeing to the license information and pressing the Next button displays the Checkboxes (A) dialog (see Figure 17-34). You should see the text that was defined with the `BannerText`, `BodyText`, and `Checkbox1Label` properties. The other check boxes are not visible because the specific `CheckboxVisible` property was set to `false`.

Selecting the check box will install the file `demo.wroxtext` to the desktop.

Select Installation Folder

In the Installation Folder dialog (see Figure 17-35) the user can select the path where the application should be installed. This dialog allowed us to set only the `BannerBitmap` property. The default path shown is `[Program Files]\[Manufacturer]\[Product Name]`.

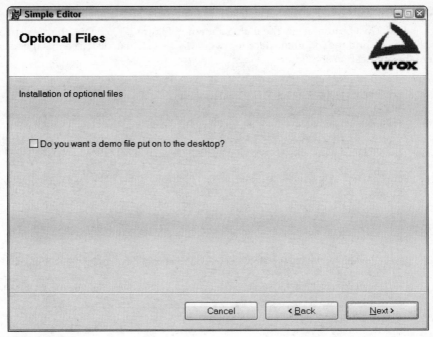

Figure 17-34

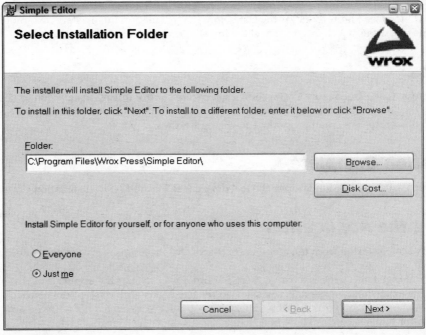

Figure 17-35

Disk Cost

Pressing the Disk Cost button opens the dialog shown in Figure 17-36. Here, the disk space of all hard drives is displayed, and the required space for every disk is calculated. This helps the user to choose a disk where the application should be installed.

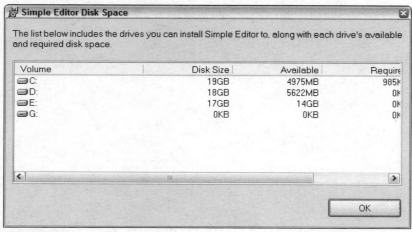

Figure 17-36

Confirm Installation

The next dialog (see Figure 17-37) is the last before the installation finally starts. No more questions are asked; this is just the last chance to cancel the installation before it really starts.

Progress

The Progress dialog (see Figure 17-38) shows a progress control during installation to keep the user informed that the installation is continuing and to give a rough idea of how long the installation will last. Since the editor is a small program, this dialog finishes very fast.

Installation Complete

After a successful installation you see the last dialog (see Figure 17-39): Installation Complete.

Running the Application

The editor can be started from the menu entry Start ➪ All Programs ➪ Wrox Simple Editor.

Because you registered a file extension, there's another way to start the application: double-click a file with the file extension .wroxtext. If you selected the check box with the Optional Files dialog, you can find demo.wroxtext on your desktop, otherwise you can create such a file with the now installed Simple Editor tool.

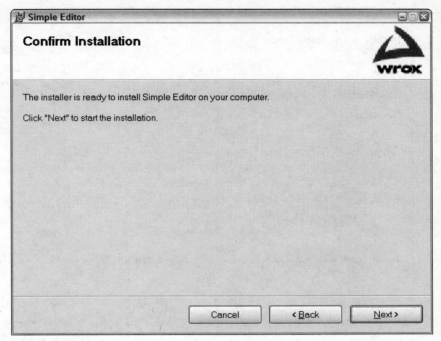

Figure 17-37

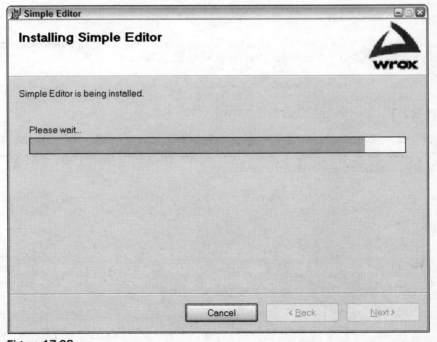

Figure 17-38

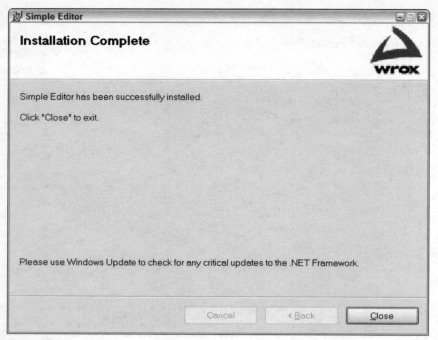

Figure 17-39

Uninstall

If you really want to get rid of the Wrox Simple Editor, you can use Add/Remove Programs from the Control Panel and press the Remove button for the Simple Editor.

Summary

This chapter covered how to use ClickOnce deployment and the functionality of the Windows Installer and how to create Installer packages using Visual Studio 2005. The Windows Installer makes it easy to do standardized installations, uninstalls, and repairs.

ClickOnce is a new technology that makes it easy to install Windows applications without the hassle of needing to be logged on as a system administrator. ClickOnce offers easy deployments as well as updates of client applications.

If more functionality than is available with ClickOnce is needed, the Windows Installer does a good job. The Visual Studio 2005 Installer is restricted in functionality and doesn't possess all the functionality of the Windows Installer, but for many applications the features of the Visual Studio 2005 Installer are more than enough. There are a lot of editors where the generated Windows Installer file can be configured. With the File System Editor, you specify all files and shortcuts; the Launch Conditions Editor can define some mandatory prerequisites; the File Types Editor is used to register file extensions for applications; and the User Interface Editor makes it easy to adapt the dialogs used for the installation.

In this chapter, you learned:

- ❑ About the features of and reasons to use ClickOnce deployment
- ❑ How to configure ClickOnce deployment for Windows applications
- ❑ How to create a setup project with Visual Studio
- ❑ How to use the file system, file types, launch condition, and user interface editors of a setup project

In the exercises in this chapter, you have to answer questions about ClickOnce deployment and the Windows Installer.

Exercises

1. What are advantages of ClickOnce deployment?

2. How are the required permissions defined with ClickOnce deployment?

3. What is defined with a ClickOnce manifest?

4. When is it necessary to use the Windows Installer?

5. What different editors can you use to create a Windows installer package using Visual Studio?

Part III
Web Programming

Basic Web Programming

Windows Forms is the technology for writing Windows applications; with ASP.NET, Web applications that are displayed in any browser can be built. ASP.NET allows you to write Web applications in a similar way to that in which Windows applications are developed. This is made possible by server-side controls that abstract the HTML code and mimic the behavior of the Windows controls. Of course, there are still many differences between Windows and Web applications because of the underlying technologies HTTP and HTML on which Web applications are based.

This chapter provides an overview of programming Web applications with ASP.NET, how to use Web controls, how to deal with state management (this is very different from how it's handled in Windows applications), how to perform authentication, and how to read and write data to and from a database.

In this chapter, you learn about:

- ❑ What happens on the server when a HTML request is sent from the client
- ❑ How to create a simple Web page
- ❑ Using Web server controls in a Web page (and seeing the HTML code they generate)
- ❑ Adding event handlers to act on user actions
- ❑ Using validation controls to validate user input
- ❑ State management with different methods such as ViewState, cookies, and session, application, and cache objects
- ❑ Authentication and authorization features that are offered with new ASP.NET 2.0 controls
- ❑ Displaying data from the database and updating data in the database

Overview

A Web application causes a Web server to send HTML code to a client. That code is displayed in a Web browser like Internet Explorer. When a user enters a URL string in the browser, an HTTP request is sent to the Web server. The HTTP request contains the filename that is requested along with additional information such as a string identifying the client application, the languages that the client supports, and additional data that belongs to the request. The Web server returns an HTTP response that contains HTML code, which is interpreted by the Web browser to display text boxes, buttons, and lists to the user.

You can read more about the HTTP protocol in Chapter 29.

ASP.NET is a technology for dynamically creating Web pages with server-side code. These Web pages can be developed with many similarities to client-side Windows programs. Instead of dealing directly with the HTTP request and response and manually creating HTML code to send to the client, you can use controls such as `TextBox`, `Label`, `ComboBox` and `Calendar`, which create HTML code themselves.

ASP.NET Runtime

Using ASP.NET for Web applications on the client system just a simple Web browser is needed. You can use Internet Explorer, Opera, Netscape Navigator, Firefox, or any other Web browser that supports HTML. The client system doesn't require .NET to be installed.

On the server system, the ASP.NET runtime is needed. If you have Internet Information Services (IIS) on the system, the ASP.NET runtime is configured with the server when the .NET Framework is installed. If you have Windows XP Home Edition on your developer system, IIS is not available. With Visual Studio 2005, this is not a problem anymore because the Visual Web Developer Web Server is part of Visual Studio and can be used to test your Web applications.

Let's look at a typical Web request from a browser to show how the ASP.NET runtime goes into action (see Figure 18-1). The client requests a file, for example `default.aspx`, from the server. All ASP.NET Web pages usually have the file extension .aspx. Because this file extension is registered with IIS, or known by the Visual Web Developer Web server, the ASP.NET runtime and the ASP.NET worker process get into the picture. With the first request to the file `default.aspx`, the ASP.NET parser is started, and the compiler compiles the file together with a C# file that is associated with the .aspx file and creates an assembly. Then the assembly is compiled to native code by the JIT compiler of the .NET runtime. The assembly contains a `Page` class that is invoked to return HTML code to the client. Then the `Page` object is destroyed. However, the assembly is kept for the next requests, so with the second request it is not necessary to compile the assembly again.

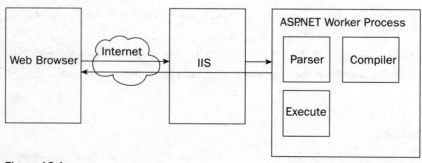

Figure 18-1

Creating a Simple Page

In the following Try It Out, you create a simple Web page. In the sample application dealt with in this and the next chapter, a simple Event Web site will be created where attendees can register for events.

Try It Out   **Create a Simple Web Page**

1. Create a new Web site by selecting File ⇨ New ⇨ Web Site with Visual Studio, as shown in Figure 18-2. Select Visual C# as the programming language, and set the Location combo box to File System. With the location, selecting HTTP means the IIS is used and a virtual directory is created. Name the Web site `EventRegistrationWeb`.

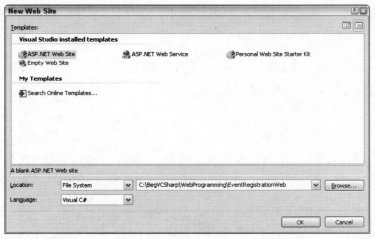

Figure 18-2

2. After having created the Web site, the file `default.aspx` is opened in the editor. Switch to the design view by clicking the Design button in the lower-left corner of the editor.

3. To arrange the controls a table is useful. Add a table by selecting the menu Layout ⇨ Insert Table. In the Insert Table dialog, set five rows and two columns, as shown in Figure 18-3.

4. Add four `Label`s, three `TextBox`es, a `DropDownList`, and a `Button` to the table, as shown in Figure 18-4.

5. Set the properties of the controls as shown in the following table.

Control Type	Name	Text
Label	labelEvent	Event:
Label	labelFirstname	Firstname:
Label	labelLastname	Lastname:

Table continued on following page

Control Type	Name	Text
Label	labelEmail	Email:
DropDownList	dropDownListEvents	
TextBox	textFirstname	
TextBox	textLastname	
TextBox	textEmail	
Button	buttonSubmit	Submit

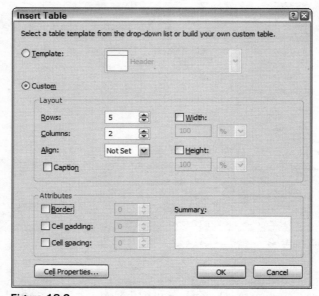

Figure 18-3

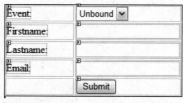

Figure 18-4

6. In the `DropDownList`, select the `Items` property in the Properties window, and enter the strings **SQL Server 2005 and XML, Office 2003 and XML**, and **Introduction to ASP.NET** in the `ListItem` Collection Editor, as shown in Figure 18-5.

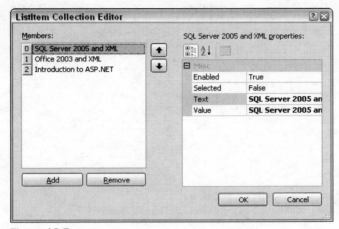

Figure 18-5

7. Switch the editor to the Source view and verify that the generated code looks similar to this:

```
<%@ Page Language="C#" AutoEventWireup="true" CodeFile="Default.aspx.cs"
    Inherits="_Default" %>

<!DOCTYPE html PUBLIC "-//W3C//DTD XHTML 1.1//EN"
"http://www.w3.org/TR/xhtml11/DTD/xhtml11.dtd">

<html xmlns="http://www.w3.org/1999/xhtml" >
<head runat="server">
  <title>Untitled Page</title>
</head>
<body>
  <form id="form1" runat="server">
    <div>
      <table>
       <tr>
         <td style="width: 100px">
           <asp:Label ID="labelEvent" Runat="server" Text="Event:"></asp:Label>
         </td>
         <td style="width: 100px">
           <asp:DropDownList ID="dropDownListEvents" Runat="server">
             <asp:ListItem>SQL Server 2005 and XML</asp:ListItem>
             <asp:ListItem>Office 2003 and XML</asp:ListItem>
             <asp:ListItem>Introduction to ASP.NET</asp:ListItem>
           </asp:DropDownList>
         </td>
       </tr>
```

```
          <tr>
            <td style="width: 100px">
              <asp:Label ID="labelFirstname" Runat="server"
                  Text="Firstname:"></asp:Label>
            </td>
            <td style="width: 100px">
              <asp:TextBox ID="textFirstname" Runat="server"></asp:TextBox>
            </td>
          </tr>
          <tr>
            <td style="width: 100px">
              <asp:Label ID="labelLastname" Runat="server"
                  Text="Lastname:"></asp:Label>
            </td>
            <td style="width: 100px">
              <asp:TextBox ID="textLastname" Runat="server"></asp:TextBox>
            </td>
          </tr>
          <tr>
            <td style="width: 100px">
              <asp:Label ID="labelEmail" Runat="server"
                  Text="Email:"></asp:Label>
            </td>
            <td style="width: 100px">
              <asp:TextBox ID="textEmail" Runat="server"></asp:TextBox>
            </td>
          </tr>
          <tr>
            <td style="width: 100px">
            </td>
            <td style="width: 100px">
              <asp:Button ID="buttonSubmit" Runat="server" Text="Submit" />
            </td>
          </tr>
        </table>

    </div>
  </form>
</body>
</html>
```

8. Start the Web application by selecting Debug ⇨ Start Without Debugging in the Visual Studio menu. When you start the application, the Visual Web Developer Web server is automatically started. You will find an icon for the Visual Web Developer Web server in the Windows Explorer taskbar. When you double-click this icon you can see a dialog similar to that shown in Figure 18-6. This dialog shows the physical and logical paths of the Web server, and the port the Web server is listening to. This dialog can also be used to stop the Web server.

Starting the application causes Internet Explorer to show the Web page, as you see in Figure 18-7. You can view the HTML code by selecting View ⇨ Source. You'll see that the server-side controls are converted to pure HTML code.

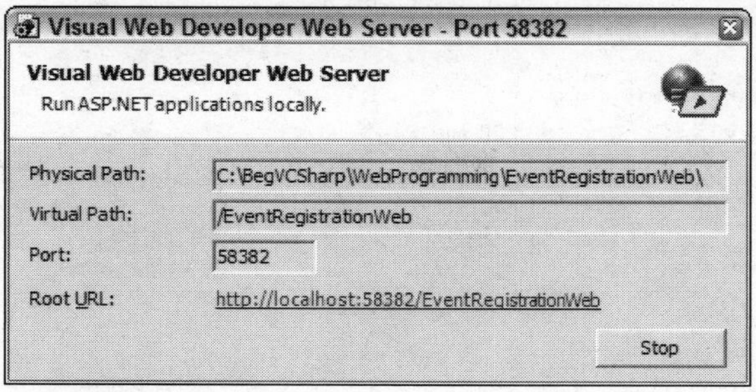

Figure 18-6

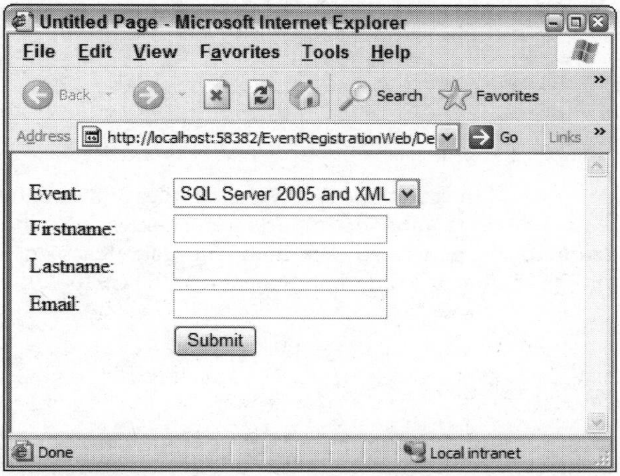

Figure 18-7

How It Works

The first line of the file `default.aspx` is the page directive. This directive defines the programming language and the classes that are used. The property `AutoEventWireup="true"` defines that event handlers for the page are automatically linked to specific method names, as will be shown later. `Inherits="Default_aspx"` means that the class that is dynamically generated from the ASPX file derives from the base class `Default_aspx`. This base class is in the code-behind file `Default.aspx.cs` as defined with the `CodeFile` property.

```
<%@ Page Language="C#" AutoEventWireup="true" CodeFile="Default.aspx.cs"
Inherits="_Default" %>
```

Visual Studio 2005 allows code behind with separate CS files or inline code where the C# code can be written directly into the ASPX file. When creating a new item with File ⇨ New ⇨ File, you can determine whether the code should be put into a separate file, as shown in Figure 18-8.

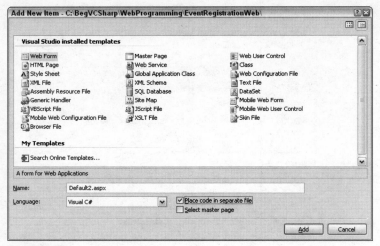

Figure 18-8

Separating the user interface and the code into ASPX and CS files allows better maintenance. The code that is generated in the file `Default.aspx.cs` imports some namespaces and includes a partial class: `Default_aspx`. The automatically generated class in the file Default.aspx derives from the class `Default_aspx`. Later in the chapter, you add handler code to the CS file.

```
using System;
using System.Data;
using System.Configuration;
using System.Web;
using System.Web.Security;
using System.Web.UI;
using System.Web.UI.WebControls;
using System.Web.UI.WebControls.WebParts;
using System.Web.UI.HtmlControls;

public partial class _Default: System.Web.UI.Page
{
    // Page events are wired up automatically to methods
    // with the following names:
    // Page_Load, Page_AbortTransaction, Page_CommitTransaction,
    // Page_DataBinding, Page_Disposed, Page_Error, Page_Init,
    // Page_InitComplete, Page_Load, Page_LoadComplete, Page_PreInit,
    // Page_PreLoad, Page_PreRender, Page_PreRenderComplete,
    // Page_SaveStateComplete, Page_Unload

    protected void Page_Load(object sender, EventArgs e)
    {
    }
}
```

The `partial` *keyword, used in the preceding code, is discussed in Chapter 10.*

Within the ASPX page, there's simple HTML code that is sent to the client as it is. Just the `runat="server"` attribute is removed from the `<head>` tag.

```
<html xmlns="http://www.w3.org/1999/xhtml" >
<head runat="server">
  <title>Untitled Page</title>
</head>
<body>
```

You will also find HTML elements with the attribute `runat=server`. A first example is the `<form>` element that includes this attribute. With the attribute `runat=server`, an ASP.NET server control is associated with the HTML tag. This control can be used to write server-side code. Behind the `<form>` element is an object of type `System.Web.UI.HtmlControls.HtmlForm`. The object has the variable name `form1` as defined with the `id` attribute. `form1` can be used to invoke methods and properties of the `HtmlForm` class.

The `HtmlForm` object creates a `<form>` tag that is sent to the client. Of course, the `runat` attribute is not sent to the client.

```
<form id="form1" runat="server">
```

The standard controls that you've dropped from the Toolbox to the form designer have elements that begin with `<asp:`. `<asp:Label>` and `<asp:DropDownList>` are server-side ASP.NET Web controls that are associated with .NET classes in the namespace `System.Web.UI.WebControls`. `<asp:Label>` is represented by the class `Label`, and `<asp:DropDownList>` is represented by the class `DropDownList`.

```
<td style="width: 100px">
  <asp:Label ID="labelEvent" Runat="server" Text="Event:"></asp:Label>
</td>
<td style="width: 100px">
  <asp:DropDownList ID="dropDownListEvents" Runat="server">
     <asp:ListItem>SQL Server 2005 and XML</asp:ListItem>
     <asp:ListItem>Office 2003 and XML</asp:ListItem>
     <asp:ListItem>Introduction to ASP.NET</asp:ListItem>
  </asp:DropDownList>
</td>
```

`<asp:Label>` doesn't send an `<asp:Label>` element to the client, because this is not a valid HTML element. Instead, the `<asp:Label>` returns a `<span>` tag. Similarly, the `<asp:DropDownList>` returns a `<select>` element, and the `<asp:TextBox>` returns the element `<input type="text">`.

ASP.NET has UI control classes in the namespaces `System.Web.UI.HtmlControls` and `System.Web.UI.WebControls`. Both of these namespaces have some similar controls, also known as HTML server controls and Web server controls. Examples are the HTML server control `HtmlInputText` and the Web server control `TextBox`. The HTML server controls offer methods and properties that are similar to the HTML controls, because they can be accessed from JavaScript in the HTML page on the client. The Web server controls offer methods and properties, as you know from your knowledge of Windows programming. Partly, it is a matter of taste for which control you use. However, with the Web server controls, you will find much more complex controls such as `Calendar`, `DataGrid`, and `Wizard`.

Server Controls

The following table lists some of the principal Web server controls available with .NET 2.0, and the HTML code that is returned by these controls.

Control	HTML	Description
Label	`<span>`	The Label control returns a span element containing text.
Literal	`static text`	If simple static text should be returned, the Literal control can be used. With this control, it is possible to transform the content depending on the client application.
TextBox	`<input type="text">`	The TextBox control returns HTML `<input type="text">` where the user can enter some values. You can write a server-side event handler when the text changes.
Button	`<input type="submit">`	The Button control is used to send form values to the server.
LinkButton	`<a href="javascript: __dopostback()>`	The LinkButton creates an anchor tag that includes JavaScript for doing a postback to the server.
ImageButton	`<input type="image">`	With the ImageButton control an input tag of type image is generated to show a referenced image.
HyperLink	`<a>`	The HyperLink control creates a simple anchor tag referencing a Web page.
DropDownList	`<select>`	The DropDownList creates a select tag where the user sees one item and can select one of multiple items by clicking on the drop-down selection.
ListBox	`<select size="">`	The ListBox control creates a select tag with a size attribute that shows multiple items at once.
CheckBox	`<input type="checkbox">`	The CheckBox control returns an input element of type check box to show a button that can be selected or deselected. Instead of using the CheckBox you can also use a CheckBoxList that creates a table consisting of multiple check box elements.
RadioButton	`<input type="radio">`	The RadioButton control returns an input element of type radio. With a radio button just one button of a group can be selected. Similar to the CheckBoxList, RadioButtonList provides a list of buttons.

Control	HTML	Description
Image	`<img src="">`	The `Image` control returns an img tag to display a gif or jpg file on the client.
Calendar	`<table>`	The `Calendar` control is a complex control to display a complete calendar where a date can be selected, the month can be changed, and so on. For output, an HTML table with JavaScript code is generated.
TreeView	`<div><table>`	The `TreeView` control returns a div tag that includes multiple table tags, depending on its content. JavaScript is used to open and close the tree on the client.

Event Handlers

You can add event handlers that are invoked on the server to Web server controls. The `Button` control can include a `Click` event; the `DropDownList` offers the event `SelectedIndexChanged`, and the `TextBox` offers the event `TextChanged`.

The events occur on the server only when a postback occurs. When a value in a text box changes, the `TextChanged` event doesn't occur immediately; instead, the `TextChanged` event only occurs when the form is submitted and sent to the server, which happens when the Submit button is clicked. The ASP.NET runtime verifies that the state of the control has changed to invoke the corresponding event handler. If the selection of the `DropDownList` has been changed, the `SelectedIndexChanged` event is invoked; the `TextChanged` event is invoked accordingly when the value of a text box changes.

> *If you want a change event immediately posted to the server (for example, when the selection of a* `DropDownList` *changes), you can set the* `AutoPostback` *property to* `true`. *This way a client-side JavaScript is used to submit the form data immediately to the server. Of course, network traffic is increased this way. Use this feature with care.*

Verification of the old values with the new values of the controls is done by the ViewState. ViewState is a hidden field that is sent with the page content to the browser. When sending the page to the client, the ViewState contains the same values as the controls within a form. With a postback to the server, the ViewState is sent to the server together with the new values of the controls. This way it can be verified if the values changed, and the event handler can be invoked.

Up to now, the sample application has sent only a simple page to the client. Now, you need to deal with the result from the user input. In the first example, the user input is displayed in the same page, and then a different page is used. In the following Try It Out, you display the user input.

Try It Out   Display the User Input

1.   Open the previously created Web application `EventRegistrationWeb` using Visual Studio 2005.

2.   To display user input for the event registration, add a label with the name `labelResult` to the Web page `Default.aspx`.

3. Double-click the Submit button to add a `Click` event handler to this button and add this code to the handler in the file `Default.aspx.cs`:

```
public partial class _Default: System.Web.UI.Page
{
    protected void buttonSubmit_Click(object sender, EventArgs e)
    {
        string selectedEvent = dropDownListEvents.SelectedValue;
        string firstname = textFirstname.Text;
        string lastname = textLastname.Text;
        string email = textEmail.Text;

        labelResult.Text = firstname + " " + lastname +
            "selected the event " + selectedEvent;
    }
}
```

4. Start the Web page using Visual Studio again. After you enter the data and click the Submit button, the same page will show up to display the user input in the new label.

How It Works

Double-clicking the Submit button adds the `OnClick` attribute to the `<asp:Button>` element in the file `Default.aspx`:

```
<asp:Button ID="buttonSubmit" Runat="server" Text="Submit"
    OnClick="buttonSubmit_Click" />
```

With the Web server control, `OnClick` defines the server-side `Click` event that will be invoked when the button is clicked.

Within the implementation of the `buttonSubmit_Click()` method, the values of the controls can be read by using properties. `dropDownListEvents` is the variable that references the `DropDownList` control. In the ASPX file, the ID is set to `dropDownListEvents`, so a variable is automatically created. The property `SelectedValue` returns the current selection. With the `TextBox` controls the `Text` property returns the strings that have been entered by the user.

```
        string selectedEvent = dropDownListEvents.SelectedValue;
        string firstname = textFirstname.Text;
        string lastname = textLastname.Text;
        string email = textEmail.Text;
```

The label `labelResult` again has a `Text` property where the result is set:

```
        labelResult.Text = firstname + " " + lastname +
            "selected the event " + selectedEvent;
```

Instead of displaying the results on the same page, NET 2.0 makes it easy to display the results in a different page, as you see in the following Try It Out.

Display the Results in a Second Page

1. Create a new `WebForm` with the name `ResultPage.aspx`.

2. Add a label to the `ResultPage` with the name `labelResult`.

3. Add code to the `Page_Load` method to the class `ResultPage_aspx` as shown here:

```
public partial class ResultPage: System.Web.UI.Page
{
    protected void Page_Load(object sender, EventArgs e)
    {
        try
        {
            DropDownList dropDownListEvents =
                (DropDownList)PreviousPage.FindControl("dropDownListEvents");

            string selectedEvent = dropDownListEvents.SelectedValue;

            string firstname =
                ((TextBox)PreviousPage.FindControl("textFirstname")).Text;
            string lastname =
                ((TextBox)PreviousPage.FindControl("textLastname")).Text;
            string email = ((TextBox)PreviousPage.FindControl("textEmail")).Text;

            labelResult.Text = firstname + " " + lastname
                    + " selected the event " + selectedEvent;
        }
        catch
        {
            labelResult.Text = "The originating page must contain " +
                    "textFirstname, textLastname, textEmail controls";
        }
    }
}
```

4. Set the `Default.aspx` page's Submit button's `PostbackUrl` property to `ResultPage.aspx`.

5. You can remove the `Click` event handler of the Submit button because it is not required anymore.

6. Start the `Default.aspx` page, fill in some data and click the Submit button. You will be redirected to the page `ResultPage.aspx`, where the entered data is displayed.

How It Works

With ASP.NET 2.0 the Button control has a new property `PostbackUrl` to define the page that should be requested from the Web server. This property creates client-side JavaScript code to request the defined page with the client-side `onclick` handler of the submit button:

```
<input type="submit" name="buttonSubmit" value="Submit"
    onclick="javascript:webForm_DoPostBackWithOptions(
        new WebForm_PostBackOptions(&quot;buttonSubmit&quot;,
            &quot;&quot;, false, &quot;&quot;, &quot;ResultPage.aspx&quot;,
            false, false))" id="buttonSubmit" />
```

The browser sends all the data from the form inside the first page to the new page. However, inside the newly requested page it is necessary to get the data from controls that have been defined with the previous page. With .NET 2.0 the Page class has a new property, PreviousPage, to access values from these controls. PreviousPage returns a Page object, where the controls of this page can be accessed using the FindControl() method. FindControl() is defined to return a Control object, so you must cast the return value to the control type that is searched.

```
DropDownList dropDownListEvents =
    (DropDownList)PreviousPage.FindControl("dropDownListEvents");
```

Instead of using the FindControl() method to access the values of the previous page, the access to the previous page can be strongly typed that is less error-prone during development. To make this possible, a custom struct that is returned with a property from the default_aspx class is defined in the next Try It Out.

Try It Out   Create a Strongly Typed PreviousPage

1. Create the App_Code folder in the Web application by selecting the Web folder in the Solution Explorer, and selecting the menu Website ⇨ Add ASP.NET Folder ⇨ App_Code.

2. In the Solution Explorer, select the App_Code folder and add a new C# file using Website ⇨ Add New Item ⇨ Class, with the name RegistrationInformation.cs.

3. Implement the struct RegistrationInformation in the file RegistrationInformation.cs as shown:

```
public struct RegistrationInformation
{
    private string firstname;
    public string Firstname
    {
        get { return firstname; }
        set { firstname = value; }
    }

    private string lastname;
    public string Lastname
    {
        get { return lastname; }
        set { lastname = value; }
    }

    private string email;
    public string Email
    {
        get { return email; }
        set { email = value; }
    }

    private string selectedEvent;
    public string SelectedEvent
    {
```

```
        get { return selectedEvent; }
        set { selectedEvent = value; }
    }
}
```

4. Add the public property `RegistrationInformation` to the class `Default_aspx` in the file `Default.aspx.cs`:

```
public RegistrationInformation RegistrationInformation
{
    get
    {
        RegistrationInformation ri = new RegistrationInformation();
        ri.Firstname = textFirstname.Text;
        ri.Lastname = textLastname.Text;
        ri.Email = textEmail.Text;
        ri.SelectedEvent = dropDownListEvents.SelectedValue;
        return ri;
    }
}
```

5. Add the `PreviousPageType` directive to the file `ResultPage.aspx` following the Page directive:

```
<%@ Page Language="C#" AutoEventWireup="true" CodeFile="ResultPage.aspx.cs"
    Inherits="ResultPage" %>
<%@ PreviousPageType VirtualPath="~/Default.aspx" %>
```

6. Within the `Page_Load()` method of the class `ResultPage_aspx` now the code can be simplified:

```
protected void Page_Load(object sender, EventArgs e)
{
    try
    {
        RegistrationInformation ri = PreviousPage.RegistrationInformation;

        labelResult.Text = ri.Firstname + " " + ri.Lastname
                + " selected the event " + ri.SelectedEvent;
    }
    catch
    {
        labelResult.Text = "The originating page must contain " +
                "textFirstname, textLastname, textEmail controls";
    }
}
```

Input Validation

When users enter data, it should be checked to see that the data is valid. The check can happen on the client and on the server. Checking the data on the client can be done by using JavaScript. However, if the data is checked on the client using JavaScript, it should also be checked on the server, because you can never fully trust the client. It is possible to disable JavaScript in the browser, and hackers can use different JavaScript functions. It is awfully necessary to check the data on the server. Checking the data on the client as well leads to better performance, as no round trips occur to the server until the data is validated on the client.

With ASP.NET it is not necessary to write the validation functions yourself. Many validation controls exist that create both client- and server-side validation.

This example shows the `RequiredFieldValidator` validation control that is associated with the text box `textFirstname`. All validator controls have in common the properties `ErrorMessage` and `ControlToValidate`. If the input is not correct, `ErrorMessage` defines the message that is displayed. The error message by default is displayed at the place where the validator control is positioned. The property `ControlToValidate` defines the control where the input is checked.

```
<asp:TextBox ID="textFirstname" Runat="server"></asp:TextBox>
<asp:RequiredFieldValidator ID="RequiredFieldValidator1" Runat="server"
    ErrorMessage="Enter your firstname" ControlToValidate="textFirstname">
</asp:RequiredFieldValidator>
```

The following table lists and describes all the validation controls.

Control	Description
RequiredFieldValidator	The `RequiredFieldValidator` defines that input is required with the control that is validated. If the control to validate has some initial value set, and the user has to change the initial value, you can set this initial value with the `InitialValue` property of the validator control.
RangeValidator	With the `RangeValidator` control you can define a minimum and maximum value that the user is allowed to enter. The specific properties of the control are `MinimumValue` and `MaximumValue`.
RegularExpressionValidator	With the `ValidationExpression` property a regular expression using Perl 5 syntax can be set to check the user input.
CompareValidator	For comparing multiple values (such as passwords), the `CompareValidator` can be used. Not only does this validator support comparing two values for equality, but there are also more options that can be set with the `Operator` property. The `Operator` property is of type `ValidationCompareOperator` that defines enumeration values such as `Equal`, `NotEqual`, `GreaterThan`, and `DataTypeCheck`. Using `DataTypeCheck`, the input value can be compared if it is of a specific data type, for example to see if it is a correct date input.

Control	Description
CustomValidator	If the other validator controls don't fulfill the requirements of the validation, the CustomValidator can be used. With the CustomValidator both a client- and server-side validation function can be defined.
ValidationSummary	With the ValidationSummary control, it is easy to write a summary for a page instead of writing error messages directly to the input controls.

With the sample application that you've done until now, the user can input firstname, lastname, and email address. In the following Try It Out the application will be extended by using validation controls.

Try It Out   Check for Required Input and Email Address

1. Open the previously created project EventRegistrationWeb with Visual Studio 2005.

2. Open the file default.aspx.

3. Add a new column to the table by selecting the right column in the design view of the editor, and by choosing the menu Layout ⇨ Insert ⇨ Column to the Right.

4. First name, last name, and e-mail address are required inputs. A check is done to determine if the e-mail address has the correct syntax. Add three RequiredFieldValidator controls and one RegularExpressionValidator control, as shown in Figure 18-9.

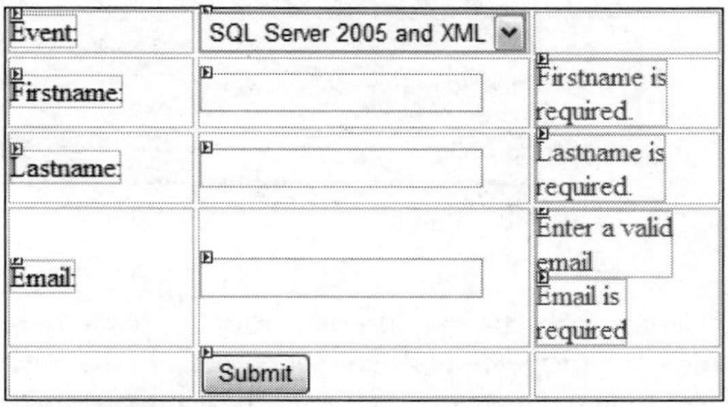

Figure 18-9

5. Configure the validation controls as defined in this table.

Validation Control	Property	Value
RequiredFieldValidator1	ErrorMessage	Firstname is required.
	ControlToValidate	textFirstname
RequiredFieldValidator2	ErrorMessage	Lastname is required.
	ControlToValidate	textLastname

Table continued on following page

Validation Control	Property	Value
RequiredFieldValidator3	ErrorMessage	Email is required.
	ControlToValidate	textEmail
RegularExpressionValidator1	ErrorMessage	Enter a valid email.
	ControlToValidate	textEmail
	ValidationExpression	\w+([-+.']\w+)*@\w+ ([-.]\w+)*\.\w+ ([-.]\w+)*
	Display	Dynamic

6. It is not necessary to enter the regular expression manually. Instead, you can click the ellipsis button of the `ValidationEpression` property in the property window to start the Regular Expression Editor, as shown in Figure 18-10. This editor makes some predefined regular expressions available where you can select the regular expression to check for an Internet E-Mail Address.

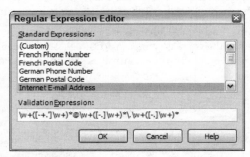

Figure 18-10

7. If a postback is done to a page that is different from the page that includes the validator controls (using the `PostBackUrl` property that was set earlier), in the new page you must verify that the result of the previous page was valid, using the `IsValid` property. Add this code to the `Page_Load` method of the `ResultPage_aspx` class:

```
protected void Page_Load(object sender, EventArgs e)
{
    try
    {
        if (!PreviousPage.IsValid)
        {
            labelResult.Text = "Error in previous page";
            return;
        }
        //...
```

8. Now you can start the application. When data is not entered or not correctly written, the validator controls show error messages, as you can see in Figure 18-11.

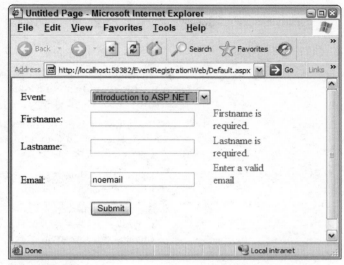

Figure 18-11

How It Works

The validator controls create both client-side JavaScript code to verify the input on the client and server-side code to validate the input on the server. It is also possible to turn JavaScript off by setting the validator property EnableClientScript to false. Instead of changing the property with every validator control, you can also turn off JavaScript by setting the property ClientTarget of the Page class.

Depending on the client type, the ASP.NET controls return JavaScript to the client or not. This behavior depends on the ClientTarget property. By default, the ClientTarget is set to "automatic", where, depending on the Web browser's functionality, scripting code is returned or not. If the ClientTarget is set to "downlevel", scripting code is not returned for any clients, while setting the ClientTarget property to "uplevel" always returns scripting code.

Setting the property ClientTarget can be done inside the Page_Load() method of the Page class:

```
protected void Page_Load(object sender, EventArgs e)
{
   ClientTarget = "downlevel";
}
```

State Management

The HTTP protocol is stateless. The connection that is initiated from the client to the server can be closed after every request. However, normally it is necessary to remember some client information from one page to the other. There are several ways to accomplish this.

The main difference among the various ways to keep state is whether the state is stored on the client or on the server. The following table shows an overview of state management techniques and how long the state can be valid.

State Type	Client or Server Resource	Time Valid
ViewState	Client	Just within a single page.
Cookie	Client	Temporary cookies are deleted when the browser is closed; permanent cookies are stored on the disk of the client system.
Session	Server	Session state is associated with a browser session. The session is invalidated with a timeout (by default 20 minutes).
Application	Server	Application state is shared among all clients. This state is valid until the server restarts.
Cache	Server	Similar to application state, cache is shared. However, there's much better control when the cache should be invalidated.

Now let's take a more detailed look at these techniques.

Client-Side State Management

First, you are going to step into client-side state management: ViewState and cookies.

ViewState

One technique to store state on the client was already discussed: ViewState. ViewState is used automatically by the Web server controls to make events work. The ViewState contains the same state as the control when sent to the client. When the browser sends the form back to the server, the ViewState contains the original values, but the values of the controls that are sent contain the new values. If there's a difference, the corresponding event handlers will be invoked.

The disadvantage to using ViewState is that data is always transferred from the server to the client, and vice versa, which increases network traffic. To reduce the network traffic, ViewState can be turned off. The ViewState can be turned off for all controls within the page by setting the `EnableViewState` property to `false` with the `Page` directive:

```
<%@ Page Language="C#" AutoEventWireUp="true" CodeFile="Default.aspx.cs"
    Inherits="Default_aspx" EnableViewState="false" %>
```

The ViewState can also be configured on a control by setting the `EnableViewState` property of a control. No matter what the page configuration says, when the `EnableViewState` property is defined for the control, the control value is used. The value of the page configuration is used only for these controls when the ViewState is not configured.

It is also possible to store custom data inside the ViewState. This can be done by using an indexer with the ViewState property of the Page class. You can define a name that is used to access the ViewState value with the index argument.

```
ViewState["mydata"] = "my data";
```

Reading the previously stored ViewState can be done as shown here:

```
string mydata = (string)ViewState["mydata"];
```

In the HTML code that is sent to the client you can see the ViewState of the complete page within a hidden field:

```
<input type="hidden" name="__VIEWSTATE"
    value="/wEPDwUKLTU4NzY5NTcwNw8WAh4HbXlzdGF0ZQUFbXl2YWwWAgIDD2QWAg
    IFDw8WAh4EVGV4dAUFbXl2YWxkZGTCdCywUOcAW97aKpcjt1tzJ7ByUA==" />
```

Using hidden fields has the advantage that every browser can use this feature, and the user cannot turn it off.

The ViewState is only remembered within a page. If the state should be valid across different pages, the use of cookies is an option for state on the client.

Cookies

A cookie is defined in the HTTP header. Use the HttpResponse class to send a cookie to the client. Response is a property of the Page class that returns an object of type HttpResponse. The HttpResponse class defines the Cookies property that returns an HttpCookieCollection. Multiple cookies can be returned to the client with the HttpCookieCollection.

The following sample code shows how a cookie can be sent to the client. First, an HttpCookie object is instantiated. In the constructor of this class, the name of the cookie is set—here it is mycookie. The HttpCookie class has a Values property to add multiple cookie values. If you just have one cookie value to return, you can use the Value property instead. However, if you plan to send multiple cookie values, it is better to add the values to a single cookie instead of using multiple cookies.

```
string myval = "myval";
HttpCookie cookie = new HttpCookie("mycookie");
cookie.Values.Add("mystate", myval);
Response.Cookies.Add(cookie);
```

Cookies can be temporary and valid within a browser session, or they can be stored on the client disk. To make the cookie permanent, the Expires property must be set with the HttpCookie object. With the Expires property the date is defined when the cookie is not valid anymore; here, it is set to a date three months from now.

Although a specific date can be set, there is no guarantee that the cookie is stored until the date is reached. The user can delete the cookies, and the browser application will also delete the cookie if there are too many cookies stored locally. The browser can have a limit of 20 cookies for a single server, and 300 cookies for all servers. When the limit is reached, the cookies that haven't been used for some time are deleted.

```
HttpCookie cookie = new HttpCookie("mycookie");
cookie.Values.Add("mystate", "myval");
cookie.Expires = DateTime.Now.AddMonths(3);
Response.Cookies.Add(cookie);
```

When the client requests a page from the server, and a cookie for this server is available on the client, the cookie is sent to the server as part of the HTTP request. Reading the cookie in the ASP.NET page can be done by accessing the cookies collection in the `HttpRequest` object.

Similarly to the HTTP response, the `Page` class has a `Request` property that returns an object of type `HttpRequest`. The property `Cookies` returns an `HttpCookieCollection` that can now be used to read the cookies that are sent by the client. A cookie can be accessed by its name with the indexer, and then the `Values` property of the `HttpCookie` is used to get the value from the cookie.

```
HttpCookie cookie = Request.Cookies["mycookie"];
string myval = cookie.Values["mystate"];
```

ASP.NET makes it easy to use cookies. However, you must be aware of the cookie's restrictions. As already discussed, a browser accepts just 20 cookies from a single server and 300 cookies for all servers. Also, there's a restriction in the size of a cookie. A cookie cannot store more then 4K of data. These restrictions are in place so the client disk won't be filled with cookies.

Server-Side State Management

Instead of remembering state with the client, it is also possible to remember state with the server. Using client-side state has the disadvantage that the data sent across the network increases. Using server-side state has the disadvantage that the server must allocate resources for its clients.

Let's look into the server-side state management techniques.

Session

Session state is associated with a browser session. A session starts when the client at first opens an ASP.NET page on the server, and ends when the client doesn't access the server for 20 minutes.

You can define your own code that should run when a session starts or ends within the Global Application Class. A Global Application Class can be created with the menu Website ⇨ Add New Item ⇨ Global Application Class. With a new Global Application Class, the file `global.asax` is created. Inside this file some event handler routines are defined:

```
<%@ Application Language="C#" %>

<script runat="server">

    void Application_Start(Object sender, EventArgs e) {
        // Code that runs on application startup
    }

    void Application_End(Object sender, EventArgs e) {
        //  Code that runs on application shutdown
    }
```

```
    void Application_Error(Object sender, EventArgs e) {
        // Code that runs when an unhandled error occurs
    }

    void Session_Start(Object sender, EventArgs e) {
        // Code that runs when a new session is started
    }

    void Session_End(Object sender, EventArgs e) {
        // Code that runs when a session ends.
        // Note: The Session_End event is raised only when the sessionstate mode
        // is set to InProc in the Web.config file. If session mode is set to
        // StateServer or SQLServer, the event is not raised.
    }

</script>
```

Session state can be stored within an HttpSessionState object. The session state object that is associated with the current HTTP context can be accessed with the Session property of the Page class. In the Session_Start() event handler, session variables can be initialized; in the example, the session state with the name mydata is initialized to 0.

```
    void Session_Start(Object sender, EventArgs e) {
        // Code that runs on application startup
        Session["mydata"] = 0;
    }
```

Reading session state, again, can be done with the Session property using the session state name:

```
    void Button1_Click(object sender, EventArgs e)
    {
        int val = (int)Session["mydata"];
        Label1.Text = val.ToString();
        val += 4;
        Session["mydata"] = val;
    }
```

To associate the client with its session variables, by default ASP.NET uses a temporary cookie with a session identifier. ASP.NET 2.0 also supports sessions without cookies where URL identifiers are used to map the HTTP requests to the same session.

Application

If data should be shared between different clients, application state can be used. Application state can be used in a manner that's very similar to how session state is used. With application state, the class HttpApplicationState is used, and it can be accessed with the Application property of the Page class.

In the example, the application variable with the name userCount is initialized when the Web application is started. Application_Start() is the event handler method in the file global.asax that gets invoked when the first ASP.NET page of the Website is started. This variable is used to count every user that is accessing the Website.

```
    void Application_Start(Object sender, EventArgs e) {
        // Code that runs on application startup
        Application["userCount"] = 0;
    }
```

In the `Session_Start()` event handler, the value of the application variable `userCount` is incremented. Before changing an application variable, the application object must be locked with the `Lock()` method; otherwise, threading problems can occur because multiple clients can access an application variable concurrently. After the value of the application variable was changed, the `Unlock()` method must be called. Be aware that the time between locking and unlocking is very short — you shouldn't read files or data from the database during that time. Otherwise, other clients must wait until the data access is completed.

```
    void Session_Start(Object sender, EventArgs e) {
        // Code that runs when a new session is started
        Application.Lock();
        Application["userCount"] = (int)Application["userCount"] + 1;
        Application.UnLock();
    }
```

Reading the data from the application state is as easy as it was with the session state:

```
    Label1.Text = Application["userCount"].ToString();
```

Don't store too much data in the application state, because the application state requires server resources until the server is stopped or restarted.

Cache

Cache is server-side state that is similar to application state in so far as it is shared with all clients. Cache is different from application state in that cache is much more flexible: there are many options to define when the state should be invalidated. Instead of reading a file with every request, or reading the database, the data can be stored inside the cache.

For the cache, the namespace `System.Web.Caching` and the class `Cache` are needed. Adding an object to the cache is shown here: the `Page` class has a `Cache` property that returns a `Cache` object. Using the `Add()` method of the `Cache` class, any object can be assigned to the cache. The first parameter of the `Add()` method defines the name of the cache item. The second parameter is the object that should be cached. With the third parameter dependencies can be defined, for example the cache item can be dependent on a file — when the file changes, the cache object is invalidated. With the sample there's no dependency because the `null` is set with this parameter. With parameters 4 and 5, a time can be set how long the cache item is valid. Parameter 4 defines an absolute time when the cache item should be invalidated, while parameter 5 requires a sliding time that invalidates the cache item after it hasn't been accessed for the time defined with the sliding expiration. Here, a sliding timespan is used so that the cache is invalidated after the cache item hasn't been used for 10 minutes. Parameter 6 defines a cache priority. `CacheItemPriority` is an enumeration for setting the cache priority. If the ASP.NET worker process has a high memory usage, the ASP.NET runtime removes cache items according to their priority. Items with a lower priority are removed first. With the last parameter, it is possible to define a method that should be invoked when the cache item is removed. An example of where this can be used is when the cache is dependent on a file. When the file changes, the cache item is removed and so the event handler is invoked. With the event handler the cache can be reloaded by reading the file once more.

```
Cache.Add("mycache", myobj, null, DateTime.MaxValue,
    TimeSpan.FromMinutes(10), CacheItemPriority.Normal, null);
```

Cache items can be read by using the indexer as you've already seen with the session and application state. Before using the object returned from the `Cache` property, always check whether the result is `null`, which happens when the cache is invalidated. When the returned value from the `Cache` indexer is not `null`, the returned object can be cast to the type that was used to store the cache item.

```
object o = Cache["mycache"];
if (o == null)
{
    // Reload the cache.
}
else
{
    // Use the cache.
    MyClass myObj = (MyClass)o;
    //...
}
```

Authentication and Authorization

To secure the Website, authentication is used to verify that the user has a valid logon, while authorization checks whether the user who was authenticated is allowed to use the resource.

ASP.NET offers Windows and Forms authentication. The most often used authentication technique for Web applications is Forms authentication, which will be covered here. ASP.NET 2.0 also has some great new features for Forms authentication. Windows authentication makes use of Windows accounts and IIS to authenticate the users.

ASP.NET 2.0 has many new classes for user authentication. Figure 18-12 shows the structure of the new architecture. With ASP.NET many new security controls such as a `Login` or `PasswordRecovery` are available. These controls make use of the Membership API. With the Membership API, it is possible to create and delete users, validate logon information, or get information about currently logged-in users. The Membership API itself makes use of a *membership provider*. With ASP.NET 2.0 different providers exist to access users in an Access database, the SQL Server database, or the Active Directory. It is also possible to create a custom provider that accesses an XML file or any custom store.

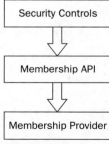

Figure 18-12

Authentication Configuration

In this chapter Forms authentication with a Membership provider will be demonstrated. In the following Try It Out, you configure security for the Web application and assign different access lists to different folders.

Try It Out   Security Configuration

1. Open the previously created Web application `EventRegistrationWeb` using Visual Studio 2005.

2. Create a new folder Intro by selecting the Web directory in the Solution Explorer, and selecting the menu Website ➪ New Folder. Name the folder Intro. This folder will be configured to be accessed by all users, while the main folder is only accessible by authenticated users.

3. Start the ASP.NET Web Application Administration by selecting the Visual Studio 2005 menu Website ➪ ASP.NET Configuration.

4. Select the Security tab, as shown in Figure 18-13.

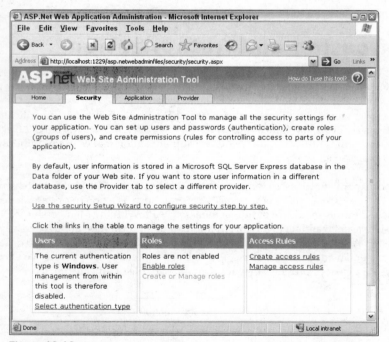

Figure 18-13

5. Click the link to the Security Setup Wizard. In the Welcome Screen click the Next button. From step 2 of the wizard, select the access method From the Internet, as shown in Figure 18-14.

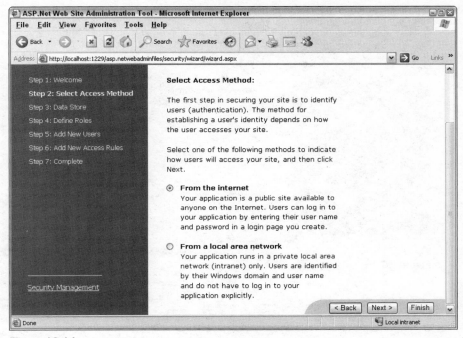

Figure 18-14

6. Clicking the Next button takes you to step 3, with information about the configured provider (see Figure 18-15). The default provider is SQL Server Express, where the user accounts are stored in a SQL Server database. This configuration cannot be changed in the Wizard mode, but you can change it afterward.

7. Click the Next button two times, which takes you to step 5, where you add new users. Create a new account, as shown in Figure 18-16.

8. After one user is successfully created, click the Next button for step 6 of the Wizard (see Figure 18-17). Here, you can configure which users are allowed or denied to use the Website or specific directories. Add a rule to deny anonymous users. Next, select the directory Intro and add a rule to allow anonymous users. Then click the Next button and finally the Finish button. Figure 18-18 shows the result of the Security tab after the Security Setup Wizard is finished.

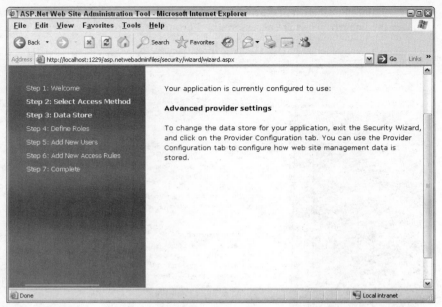

Figure 18-15

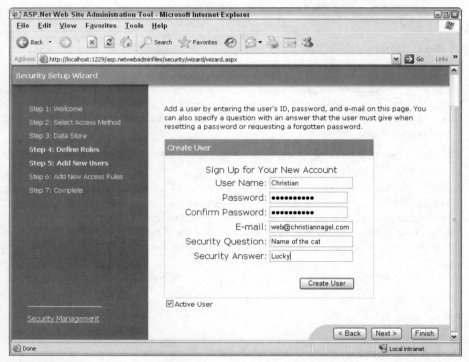

Figure 18-16

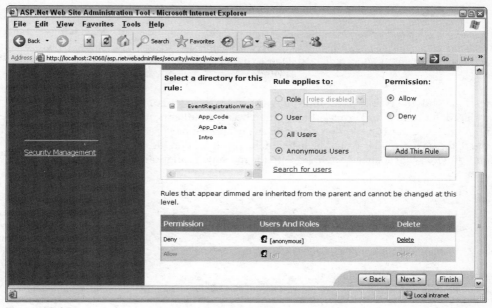

Figure 18-17

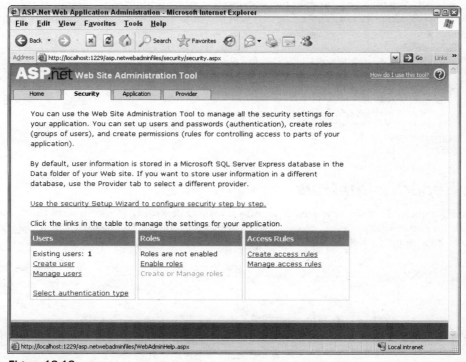

Figure 18-18

How It Works

After you complete the security configuration, a new Access database is created. Having refreshed the files in the Solution Explorer, you can see a new directory named Application_Data, which contains the Access database AspNetDB.mdb. This database contains tables that are used by the Access Membership provider.

Now, along with the Web application, you will also see the configuration file web.config. This file contains the configuration for Forms authentication because authentication across the Internet was selected, and the <authorization> section denies access to anonymous users. If the Membership provider is changed, the new provider would be listed in the configuration file. Because the Access provider is the default provider that is already defined with the machine configuration file, there is no need for it to be listed here.

```xml
<?xml version="1.0" encoding="utf-8"?>
<configuration>
  <system.web>
    <authorization>
      <deny users="?" />
    </authorization>
    <authentication mode="Forms" />
  </system.web>
</configuration>
```

Within the subfolder Intro, you can see another configuration file, web.config. The authentication section is missing from this configuration file, because the authentication configuration is taken from the parent directory. However, the authorization section is different. Here anonymous users are allowed with <allow users="?" />.

```xml
<?xml version="1.0" encoding="utf-8"?>
<configuration>
  <system.web>
    <authorization>
      <allow users="?" />
    </authorization>
  </system.web>
</configuration>
```

Using Security Controls

ASP.NET 2.0 includes many new security controls. Instead of writing a custom form to ask the user for a username and password, a ready-to-use Login control is available. The security controls and their functionality are listed in the following table.

Security Controls	Description
Login	The Login control is a composite control that includes controls to ask for username and password.
LoginStatus	The LoginStatus control includes hyperlinks to log in or logout, depending if the user is logged in or not.

Security Controls	Description
LoginName	The LoginName control displays the name of the user.
LoginView	With the LoginView control, different content can be displayed depending if the user is logged in or not.
PasswordRecovery	PasswordRecovery is a composite control to reset forgotten passwords. Depending on the security configurations, the user is asked for the answer to a previously set secret question or the password is sent by e-mail.
ChangePassword	ChangePassword is a composite control that allows logged in users to change their password.
CreateUserWizard	CreateUserWizard is a wizard to create a new user and write the user information to the Membership provider.

In the following Try It Out, you add a login page to the Web application.

Try It Out   Create a Login Page

If you tried to start the Website after it has been configured to deny anonymous users, you should have received an error because a login.aspx page is missing. If a specific login page is not configured with Forms authentication, login.aspx is used by default. You will now create a login.aspx page.

1. Add a new Web Form and name it login.aspx.

2. Add the Login control to the form. In the design view, you will see the control shown in Figure 18-19.

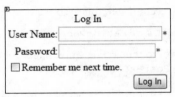

Figure 18-19

3. That's all that's necessary to create a login page. Now when you start the site default.aspx, you will be redirected to login.aspx, where you can enter the user credentials for the user you created earlier.

How It Works

After adding the Login control, you can see this code in the source view:

```
<asp:Login ID="Login1" Runat="server">
</asp:Login>
```

The properties for this control enable you to configure the text for the header, username, and password labels, and for the login button, too. You can make the check box Remember me next time visible by defining the DisplayRememberMe property.

If you want more control over the look and feel of the `Login` control, you can convert the control to a template. You can do this in the design view by clicking the smart tag and selecting Convert to Template. Next, when you click Edit Templates, you will get a view like that shown in Figure 18-20, where you can add and modify any controls.

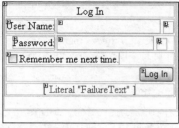

Figure 18-20

For verifying the user credentials, when the Login In button is clicked, the method `Membership.ValidateUser()` is invoked by the control, and you don't have to do this yourself.

When users don't have an account to login with the EventRegistration Website, they should create their own login. This can be done very easily with the `CreateUserWizard` control, as you will see with the next Try It Out.

Try It Out   Using the CreateUser Wizard

1. Add a new Web page named `CreateUser.aspx` in the `Intro` folder that was previously created. This folder is configured to be accessed from anonymous users.

2. Add a `CreateUserWizard` control to this Web page.

3. Set the property `ContinueDestinationPageUrl` to `~/Default.aspx`.

4. Add a `LinkButton` control to the `Login.aspx` page. Set the `Text` property of this control to `Register User`, and the `PostBackUrl` property of this control to the Web page `Intro/CreateUser.aspx`.

5. Now you can start the application. Clicking the link Register User on the `Login.aspx` page redirects to the page `CreateUser.aspx` where a new account will be created with the entered data.

How It Works

The `CreateUserWizard` control is a wizardlike control that consists of multiple wizard steps, which are defined with the element `<WizardSteps>`:

```
<asp:CreateUserWizard ID="CreateUserWizard1" Runat="server"
    ActiveStepIndex="1" ContinueDestinationPageUrl="~/Default.aspx">
  <WizardSteps>
    <asp:CreateUserWizardStep Runat="server"
        Title="Sign Up for Your New Account">
    </asp:CreateUserWizardStep>
    <asp:CompleteWizardStep Runat="server" Title="Complete">
```

```
        </asp:CompleteWizardStep>
    </WizardSteps>
</asp:CreateUserWizard>
```

These wizard steps can be configured in the designer. The smart tag of the control enables you to configure each of these steps separately. Figure 18-21 shows the configuration of step Sign Up for Your New Account, while Figure 18-22 shows the step Complete. You can also add custom steps with custom controls to add custom requirements, for example that the user should accept a contract before signing up for an account.

Figure 18-21

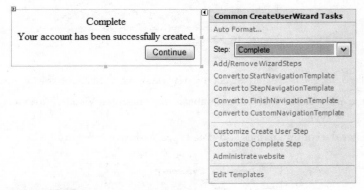

Figure 18-22

Reading and Writing a SQL Server Database

Most Web applications need access to a database to read data from and write data to it. In this section, you create a new database to store event information, and see how to use this database from ASP.NET.

First, you create a new SQL Server database in the next Try It Out. This can be done directly from within Visual Studio 2005.

Try It Out   **Create a New Database**

1. Open the previously created Web application `EventRegistrationWeb`, using Visual Studio 2005.

2. Open the Server Explorer. If you cannot already see it in Visual Studio, you can open the window using the menu options View ➪ Other Windows ➪ Server Explorer.

3. In the Server Explorer select Data Connections, right-click to open the context menu, and select Create New SQL Server Database....

4. The dialog shown in Figure 18-23 opens. Enter **localhost** for the server name, and **BegCSharpEvents** for the database name.

Figure 18-23

5. After the database is created, select the new database in Server Explorer.

6. Select the entry Tables below the database, and select the Visual Studio menu Data ➪ Add New ➪ Table.

7. Now enter the column names and data types as shown in Figure 18-24.

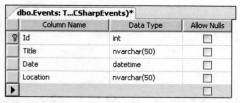

Figure 18-24

8. Configure the ID column as a primary key column with an identity increment of 1 and an identity seed of 1. All columns should be configured not to allow `null`s.

9. Save the table with the name Events.

10. Add a few events to the table with some sample titles, dates, and locations.

Displaying Data

To display and edit data there's a separate Data section in the Toolbox, representing data controls. The data controls can be categorized into two groups: data view and data source controls. A data source control is associated with a data source such as an XML file, a SQL database, or a .NET class; data views are connected with a data source to represent data.

The following table lists all the data controls.

Control	Description
GridView	The GridView control displays data with rows and columns.
DataList	The DataList control just displays a single column to display all items.
DetailsView	The DetailsView control can be used together with a GridView if you have a master/detail relationship with your data.
FormView	The FormView control is used to display a single row of the data source.
Repeater	With the Repeater control you have to define what HTML elements should be generated around the data from the data source.

The data source controls and their functionality are listed in the next table.

Control	Description
SqlDataSource	The SqlDataSource control accesses the SQL Server or any other ADO.NET provider (for example Oracle, ODBC, and OLEDB). Internally, it uses a DataSet or a DataReader class.
AccessDataSource	The AccessDataSource control enables you to use an Access database.
ObjectDataSource	The control ObjectDataSource allows you to use .NET classes as the data source.
XmlDataSource	XML files can be accessed with the XmlDataSource control. Using this data source, hierarchical structures can be displayed.
SiteMapDataSource	The SiteMapDataSource uses XML files to define a site structure for creating links and references with a Website. This feature is discussed in Chapter 19.

In the next Try It Out, you will use a GridView control to display and edit the data from the previously created database.

Try It Out   Using a GridView Control to Display Data

1.   In the Solution Explorer create a new regular folder `Admin`.

2.   Create a new Web page `EventsManagement.aspx` in the folder `Admin`.

3.   Add a `GridView` control to the Web page.

4.   In the Choose Data Source combo box of the control's smart tag, select <New data source...>.

5.   The dialog shown in Figure 18-25 now opens. Select Database and enter the name **EventsDataSource** for this new data source.

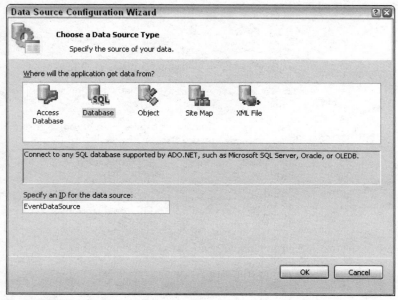

Figure 18-25

6.   Click the OK button to configure the data source. The Configure Data Source dialog will open. Click the New Connection button to create a new connection.

7.   With the Add Connection dialog shown in Figure 18-26 enter **localhost** as Server name, and select the previously created database `BegCSharpEvents`. Click the Test Connection button to verify that the connection is correctly configured. When you're satisfied that it is, click the OK button.

8.   The next dialog opens (to store the connection string, as shown in Figure 18-27). Click the check box to save the connection and enter the connection string name **EventsConnectionString**. Click the Next button.

Figure 18-26

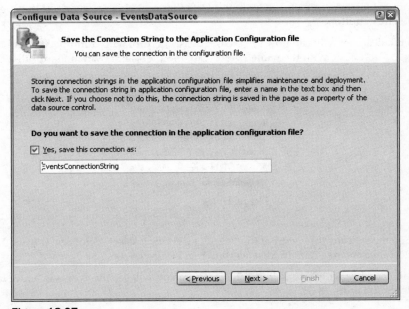

Figure 18-27

9. In the next dialog, select the Events table to read the data from this table, as shown in Figure 18-28. Select the ID, Title, Date, and Location columns to define the SQL command `SELECT [Id], [Title], [Date], [Location] From [Events]`. Click the Next button.

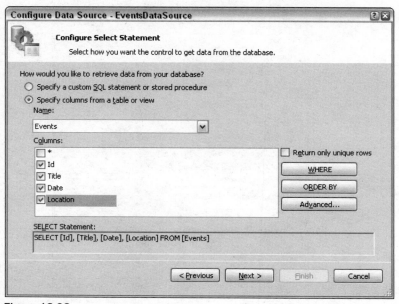

Figure 18-28

10. With the last window of the Configure Data Source dialog, you can test the query. Finally, press the Finish button.

11. In the designer, you can now see the `GridView` control with dummy data and the `SqlDataSource` with the name `EventsDatasource`, as shown in Figure 18-29.

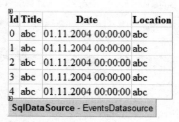

Figure 18-29

12. For a more beautiful layout of the `GridView` control, select AutoFormat from the smart tag and select the scheme Lilacs in Mist, as shown in Figure 18-30.

13. Start the page with Visual Studio 2005, where you will see the events in a nice table like that shown in Figure 18-31.

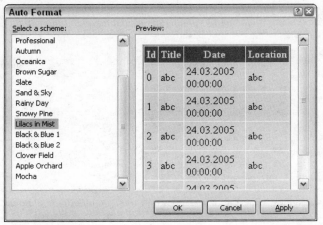

Figure 18-30

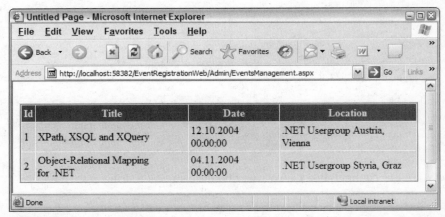

Figure 18-31

How It Works

After you add the GridView control, you can see its configuration in the source code. The DataSourceID attribute defines the association with the data source control that can be found after the grid control. Within the <Columns> element all bound columns for displaying data are shown. HeaderText defines the text of the header and DataField defines the field name within the data source.

The data source is defined with the <asp:SqlDataSource> element, where the SelectCommand defines how the data is read from the database, and the ConnectionString defines how to connect with the database. Because you selected to save the connection string in the configuration file, <%$ is used to make an association with a dynamically generated class from the configuration file.

```
<asp:GridView AutoGenerateColumns="False" BackColor="White"
    BorderColor="White" BorderStyle="Ridge"
    BorderWidth="2px" CellPadding="3" CellSpacing="1" DataKeyNames="Id"
    DataSourceID="EventsDataSource"
    GridLines="None" ID="GridView1" runat="server">
    <FooterStyle BackColor="#C6C3C6" ForeColor="Black" />
    <RowStyle BackColor="#DEDFDE" ForeColor="Black" />
    <Columns>
        <asp:BoundField DataField="Id" HeaderText="Id"
            InsertVisible="False" ReadOnly="True"
            SortExpression="Id"></asp:BoundField>
        <asp:BoundField DataField="Title" HeaderText="Title"
            SortExpression="Title"></asp:BoundField>
        <asp:BoundField DataField="Date" HeaderText="Date"
            SortExpression="Date"></asp:BoundField>
        <asp:BoundField DataField="Location" HeaderText="Location"
            SortExpression="Location"></asp:BoundField>
    </Columns>

    <PagerStyle BackColor="#C6C3C6" ForeColor="Black"
        HorizontalAlign="Right" />
    <SelectedRowStyle BackColor="#9471DE" Font-Bold="True"
        ForeColor="White" />
    <HeaderStyle BackColor="#4A3C8C" Font-Bold="True" ForeColor="#E7E7FF" />
    <EditRowStyle Font-Bold="False" Font-Italic="False" />
</asp:GridView>

<asp:SqlDataSource
    ConnectionString="<%$ ConnectionStrings:EventsConnectionString %>"
    ID="EventsDataSource" runat="server" SelectCommand=
    "SELECT [Id], [Title], [Date], [Location] FROM [Events]">
</asp:SqlDataSource>
```

In the web.config configuration file you can find the connection string to the database:

```
<connectionStrings>
  <add name="EventsConnectionString"
    connectionString="Data Source=localhost;
    Integrated Security=True;Initial Catalog=BegCSharpEvents;
    Pooling=False" providerName="System.Data.SqlClient" />
</connectionStrings>
```

Now the GridView control should be configured differently. In the next Try It Out, the ID will no longer be displayed to the user, and the date time display will only display the date.

Try It Out   Configure the GridView Control

1. Select the smart tag of the GridView control and select the Edit Columns menu. The Fields dialog, shown in Figure 18-32, shows up. Select the ID field, and change the Visible property to False. You can also arrange the columns with this dialog, and you can change the colors and define the header text.

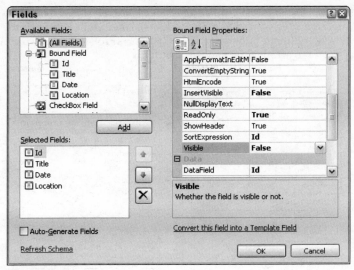

Figure 18-32

2. For editing the GridView, an update command must be defined with the data source. Select the `SqlDataSource` control with the name EventsDataSource, and select Configure Data Source... from the smart tag. With the Configure Data Source dialog click the Next button until you can see the previously configured SELECT command. Click the Advanced... button, and select the check box Generate INSERT, UPDATE, and DELETE statements as shown in Figure 18-33. Click the OK button. Then click the Next and Finish buttons.

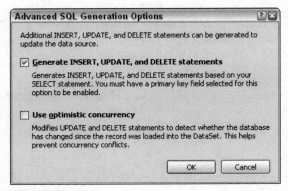

Figure 18-33

3. Select the smart tag of the `GridView` again. Now, there's a new item in the smart tag menu where you can enable editing (see Figure 18-34). After you've selected the check box to enable editing, a new column is added to the `GridView` control. You can also edit the columns with the smart tag menu to arrange the new `Edit` button.

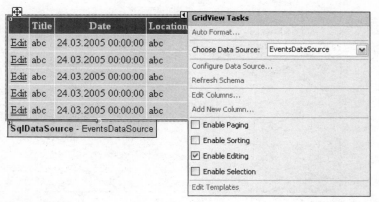

Figure 18-34

4. Now, you can start the application and edit the existing event records.

How It Works

No line of code had to be written manually, everything was possible by using ASP.NET Web controls. Behind the scenes, these controls make use of many features.

For example, the `SqlDataSource` control fills a `DataSet` with the help of a `SqlDataAdapter` with data from the database. The data that is used to fill the `DataSet` is defined with the connection string and the `SELECT` command. Just by changing a property of the `SqlDataSource`, the `SqlDataReader` can be used instead of the `DataSet`. Also, by setting the property `EnableCaching` to true, the `Cache` object (discussed earlier in the chapter) is used automatically.

You can read more about `DataSets`, the `SqlDataAdapter`, and the `SqlDataReader` in Chapter 24.

Summary

In this chapter, you've seen the architecture of ASP.NET, how to work with server-side controls and some base features of ASP.NET. ASP.NET 2.0 offers many big controls where not much code is necessary, as shown with login and data controls.

After learning about the base functionality of ASP.NET with server controls and event handling mechanism, you've learned how to do input validation, several methods for state management, authentication, and authorization, and displaying data from the database.

In this chapter, you learned to:

❑   Create a Web page with ASP.NET

❑   Use event handlers with Web server controls

❑   Verify user input with validation controls

❑   Deal with state management using different methods

❑   Configure authentication and authorization for Web applications

❑   Use ASP.NET 2.0 login controls

❑   Access and display values from a database with the `SqlDataSource` and `GridView` controls

The exercises that follow help you extend the Web application developed in this chapter. The next chapter will show more features of ASP.NET 2.0.

Exercises

1.   Add the username to the top of the ASP.NET pages you created in this chapter. You can use the `LoginName` control for this task.

2.   Add a page for password recovery. Add a link to the Web page `login.aspx`, so that the user can recover the password if the login fails.

3.   Change the data source of the `Default.aspx` page so that it uses the Events database for displaying the events.

19

Advanced Web Programming

In Chapter 18, you learned base features of ASP.NET, how server side controls can be used to render HTML code to the client, input validation, and state management. You've also seen how security can be added, and reading and writing data from the database. Now you will step into user interface elements and customizing Web pages with profiles and Web parts. Master pages are used to define a frame for multiple pages. You can use site navigation to define the structure of your Website for making menus to access all the pages. To reuse controls within multiple pages on the same Web, you can create user controls. The last section of the chapter shows Web parts. Web parts can be used to create a portal Website.

In this chapter, you will learn about:

- ❑ Master pages
- ❑ Creating and using user controls
- ❑ Navigation within Websites
- ❑ Profiles
- ❑ Using Web parts

Sample Site

With Visual Studio 2005, you get a sample Website which uses many ASP.NET 2.0 features that will be shown in this chapter. Now let's look into some of the concepts used with this Website.

Try It Out   Create a Personal Website

1. Create a new Website by selecting the menu File ➪ New ➪ Web Site. Select the Personal Web Site Starter Kit as shown in Figure 19-1.

2. View the page Default.aspx in the browser. You will see a page as shown in Figure 19-2.

3. Notice the links on top and bottom, and the YOUR NAME HERE text. This is defined by the master-page Default.master.

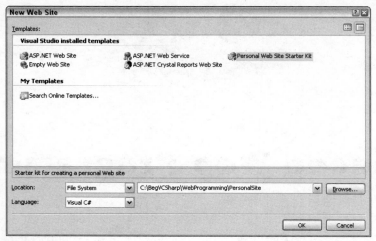

Figure 19-1

Figure 19-2

4. Click on the links Resume, Links, Albums. Notice how the navigation is shown in the second line of the page. The navigation is defined with the XML file web.sitemap.

5. Create an account and login to the site. Security is configured with the file web.config. Security controls as were discussed in the previous chapter are used with this site.

How you can implement the features from the Personal Website and more in your own site is shown in the next sections.

Master Pages

Most Websites reuse part of their content on every page—things like company logos and menus are often available on all pages. With ASP.NET 1.1, often just a single page is used where the content is replaced dynamically through user controls. With this concept for accessing different content, a URL parameter must be used, something like `http://www.ineta.org/DesktopDefault.aspx?tabindex=3`. Using different links to the pages would be more appealing: `http://www.ineta.org/Events.aspx` would be an easier to remember Web address. This is where master pages come into play.

With a master page the default content of a page (for example, the menus) is defined together with placeholders that are replaced by the Web pages using the master pages.

A master page has the file extension .master and uses the Master directive in the first line of the file, as shown here:

```
<%@ Master Language="C#" AutoEventWireup="true" CodeFile="MasterPage.master.cs"
   Inherits="MasterPage_master" %>
```

Only the master pages in the Website make use of `<html>`, `<head>`, `<body>`, and `<form>` HTML elements. The Web pages themselves contain only content that is embedded within the form element. The Web pages can embed their own content within the `ContentPlaceHolder` control. The master page can define default content for the `ContentPlaceHolder` if the Web page doesn't.

```
<html xmlns="http://www.w3.org/1999/xhtml>
<head runat="server">
  <title>Untitled Page</title>
</head>
<body>
  <form id="form1" runat="server">
    <div>
      <asp:contentplaceholder id="ContentPlaceHolder1" runat="server">
      </asp:contentplaceholder>
    </div>
  </form>
</body>
</html>
```

To use the master page, you must apply the `MasterPageFile` attribute to the `Page` directive. To replace the content of a master page, use the `Content` control. The Content control associates the `ContentPlaceHolder` with the `ContentPlaceHolderID`.

```
<%Page Language="C#" MasterPageFile="~/MasterPage.master"
    AutoEventWireUp="true" CodeFile="Default.aspx" Inherits="default"
    Title="Untitled Page" %>
<asp:Content ID="Content1" ContentPlaceHolderID="ContentPlaceHolder1"
    Runat="Server"></asp:Content>
```

Instead of defining the master page with the Page directive, you can assign a default master page to all Web pages with the <pages> element in the Web configuration file web.config:

```
<configuration xmlns="http://schemas.microsoft.com/.NetConfiguration/v2.0">
    <system.web>
      <pages masterPageFile="~/MasterPage.master" />
    </system.web>
</configuration>
```

With the master page file configured within web.config, the ASP.NET pages need a Content element configuration in the file as shown earlier; otherwise, the masterPageFile attribute would have no use. If you use both the Page directive's MasterPageFile attribute and the entry in web.config, the setting of the Page directive overrides the setting from web.config. This way it is possible to define a default master page file (with web.config), but override the default setting for specific Web pages.

It is also possible to programmatically change the master page. By doing so, different master pages can be used for different devices or different browser types. The last place the master page can be changed is in the Page_PreInit handler method. In the following sample code, the MasterPageFile property of the Page class is set to IE.master if the browser sends the MSIE string with the browser name (what is done by Microsoft Internet Explorer) or to Default.master for all other browsers.

```
public partial class changeMaster : System.Web.UI.Page
{
    void Page_Load(object sender, EventArgs e)
    {
    }

    void Page_PreInit(object sender, EventArgs e)
    {
        if (Request.UserAgent.Contains("MSIE")
        {
            this.MasterPageFile = "~/IE.master";
        }
        else
        {
            this.MasterPageFile = "~/Default.master";
        }
    }
}
```

Now, try creating your own master page in the following Try It Out. The sample master page here will have a heading and a body, and the main part of the master page will be replaced by individual pages.

Try It Out   Create a Master Page

1. Open the Website named `EventRegistrationWeb` that you've created in the previous chapter.

2. Add a new Master Page item, as shown in Figure 19-3, and name it `EventRegistration.master`.

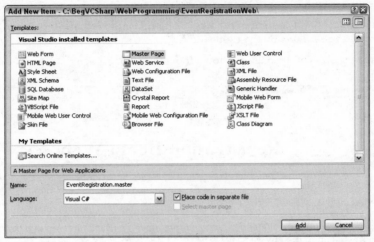

Figure 19-3

3. Remove the `ContentPlaceHolder` that was created automatically from the master page.

4. Insert a table in the page using the menu options Layout ⇨ Insert Table. In the Insert Table dialog select the template header, footer, and side, as shown in Figure 19-4.

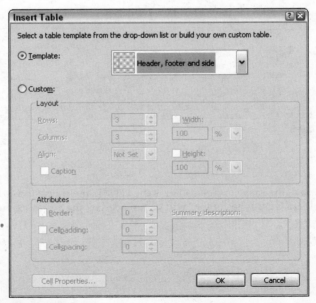

Figure 19-4

5. Add the text **Registration Demo Web** to the top of the master page, and a copyright notice to the bottom. You can place the text `Registration Demo Web` inside `<H1>` tags to make it larger. In addition, justify the text in the center.

6. In the second row add a `ContentPlaceHolder` to every column. Name the `ContentPlaceHolder` on the left side `ContentPlaceHolderMenu` and the one on the right side `ContentPlaceHolderMain`.

7. Add the text Default content of the **Registration Demo Web Master** to the `ContentPlaceHolder` on the right side.

8. Arrange the sizes of the page as shown in Figure 19-5.

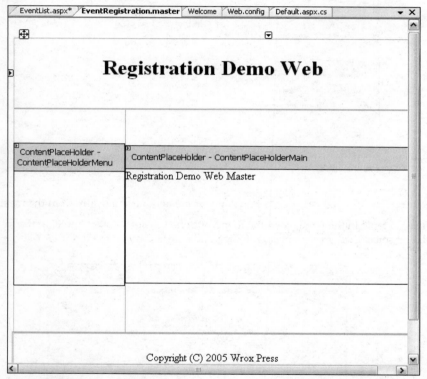

Figure 19-5

How It Works

As previously discussed, the master page contains the HTML, including the `<FORM>` tags that contain the content place holders where the content will be replaced by the pages that use the master page. The HTML table defines the layout of the page.

```
<%@ Master Language="C#" AutoEventWireup="true"
       CodeFile="EventRegistration.master.cs"
       Inherits="EventRegistration" %>

<!DOCTYPE html PUBLIC "-//W3C//DTD XHTML 1.1//EN"
"http://www.w3.org/TR/xhtml11/DTD/xhtml11.dtd">

<html xmlns="http://www.w3.org/1999/xhtml" >
<head runat="server">
  <title>Untitled Page</title>
</head>
<body>
  <form id="form1" runat="server">
  <div>
    <table border="0" cellpadding="0" cellspacing="0" style="width: 100%;
       height: 100%">
      <tr>
        <td colspan="2" style="height: 75px">
          <h1 style="text-align: center">Registration Demo Web</h1>
        </td>
      </tr>
      <tr>
        <td style="width: 166px;">
          <asp:ContentPlaceHolder ID="ContentPlaceHolderMenu" runat="server">
          </asp:ContentPlaceHolder>
        </td>
        <td>
          <asp:ContentPlaceHolder ID="ContentPlaceHolderMain" runat="server">
            Default content of the Registration Dem Web
          </asp:ContentPlaceHolder>
        </td>
      </tr>
      <tr>
        <td colspan="2" style="text-align: center" height="50">
          Copyright (C) 2005 Wrox Press</td>
      </tr>
    </table>
  </div>
  </form>
</body>
</html>
```

After you have created the master page, you can use it from a Web page, as shown in the following Try It Out.

Try It Out   Use a Master Page

1. Add a new item of type Web Form to the Web application and give it the name `EventList.aspx`. Click the check box Select master page.

2. With the check box Select a master page checked, click the Next button to open the dialog Select a Master Page, as shown in Figure 19-6. Select the previously created master page `EventRegistration.master` (see Figure 19-7), and click the OK button.

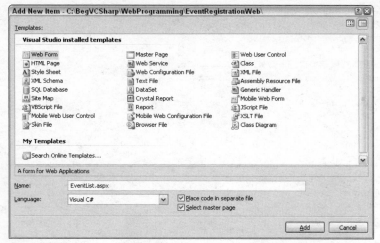

Figure 19-6

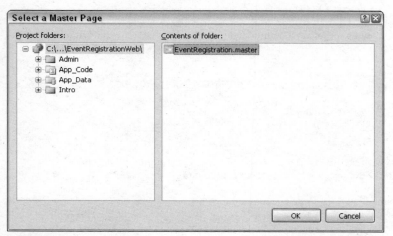

Figure 19-7

3. The source view of the file EventList.aspx shows just two Content controls after the Page directive that references the ContentPlaceHolder controls from the master page. Change the ID properties of the Content controls to ContentMenu and ContentMain.

```
<%@ Page Language="C#" MasterPageFile="~EventRegistration.master"
  AutoEventWireup="true" CodeFile="EventList.aspx.cs"
  Inherits="EventList" Title="Untitled Page" %>
<asp:Content ID="ContentMenu" ContentPlaceHolderID="ContentPlaceHolderMenu"
  Runat="Server"><asp:Content>
<asp:Content ID="ContentMain" ContentPlaceHolderID="ContentPlaceHolderMain"
  Runat="Server"><asp:Content>
```

4. Change to the design view in Visual Studio. This view shows you the content of the master page that cannot be changed from the page that includes the header and copyright information (see Figure 19-8).

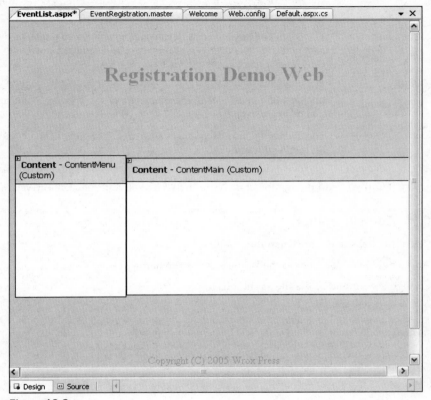

Figure 19-8

5. Add a table to the `ContentMain` control, where you add `Calendar` and `ListBox` controls. The content of the menu will be added later. When you open the source view you can see the table within the `Content` control.

6. View the page with the browser. The page includes the content from the Web page as well as the surroundings from the master page.

Site Navigation

For navigation between multiple pages on a Website, you can define an XML file that contains the structure of the Website, and use some UI controls to display the navigation options. The controls that are important with navigation are listed in the following table.

Control	Description
SiteMapDataSource	SiteMapDataSource control is a data source control that references any site map data provider. In the Visual Studio toolbox you can find this control in the Data section.
Menu	The Menu control is a control that displays links to pages as defined with a site map data source. The Menu can be displayed horizontally or vertically, and it has many options to configure its style.
SiteMapPath	The SiteMapPath control uses a minimal space to display the current position of a page within the hierarchy of the Website. You can display text or image hyperlinks.
TreeView	The TreeView control displays a hierarchical view of the Website in a hierarchical manner.

In the next Try It Out you add navigation controls to the Website EventRegistrationWeb.

Try It Out   Add Navigation

1. Open the Website EventRegistrationWeb.

2. Add a new Site Map item to the Website. Keep the name Web.sitemap.

3. Change the content of the file as shown:

```
<?xml version="1.0" encoding="utf-8" ?>
<sitemap xmlns=http://schemas.microsoft.com/AspNet/SiteMap-File-1.0 >
   <siteMapNode url="Default.aspx" title="Home" />
      <siteMapNode url="Register.aspx" title="Register" />
      <siteMapNode url="EventList.aspx" title="Events" />
   </siteMapNode>
</sitemap>
```

4. Open the file EventRegistration.master.

5. Add a SiteMapDataSource control to the page.

6. Add a Menu control below the title Registration Demo Web. Set the data source to SiteMapDataSource1.

7. Add a SiteMapPath control.

8. Open the file EventList.aspx in the browser. Notice the menu and the path that displays the position of the current file in the Website.

9. You can add other pages that are referenced in the file Web.sitemap as needed. You just have to reference the same master page to show the defined menus.

How It Works

The structure of the Website is defined by the Web pages listed in the file Web.sitemap. This XML file contains XML <siteMapNode> elements inside a <sitemap> root element. The <siteMapNode> element defines a Web page. The filename of the page is set with the url attribute, the title attribute specifies the name as it should appear on menus. The hierarchy of the pages is defined by writing `<siteMapNode>` elements as child elements of the page where the link to the children should happen.

The `SiteMapDataSource` control is a data source control with similarities to the data source controls shown in the previous chapter. This control can use different providers. By default the `XmlSiteMapProvider` class is used to get to the data. The `XmlSiteMapProvider` class by default uses the page `Web.sitemap`, that's why you've never configured this filename. In case you rename the XML file, the `siteMapFile` property of this provider must be set to a new filename.

With the `Menu` control you can edit menu items as needed that show up in the ASPX source; or you can add menu items programmatically. The easiest way for adding menu items is by using a site map data source by configuring the data source.

User Controls

If multiple Web controls that collaborate are used in several Web pages, you can create user controls. A user control has the file extension .ascx and contains parts of a form that can be included in several Web pages. Instead of creating the user interface and writing the code several times for every page where the same content is needed, the user control is just implemented once and used several times.

A user control can be added statically or dynamically to a Web page. Using the user control in a dynamic way, the controls shown can be changed during runtime.

A user control is represented by the `Control` directive in the first line of the source file. The `CodeFile` and `Inherits` attributes have the same usage as with the `Page` directive:

```
<%@ Control Language="C#" AutoEventWireup="true"
    CodeFile="DemoUserControl.ascx.cs" Inherits="DemoUserControl" %>
```

Normal HTML code that is part of a form follows the `Control` directive,. The `<HTML>` and `<FORM>` tags are not used within the user control, because the HTML code of the user control is embedded within a HTML form.

The user control can be added statically to the page as shown in the ASPX code sample. It is referenced with the `Register` directive. The `Src` attribute references the ASCX file of the user control, named `DemoUserControl.ascx` in this example. `TagPrefix` and `TagName` define the names of the control used within the page. `TagPrefix` is set to uc1 and `TagName` is set to `DemoUserControl`. That's why the control itself is referenced within the page using `<uc1:DemoUserControl>`. You can compare the uc1 prefix to the asp prefix that is used with ASP.NET Web server controls.

```
<%@ Page Language="C#" AutoEventWireup="true" CodeFile="DemoPage.aspx.cs"
    Inherits="DemoPage" %>
<%@ Register TagPrefix="uc1" TagName="DemoUserControl"
    Src="DemoUserControl.ascx" %>

<html xmlns="http://www.w3.org/1999/xhtml" >
...
<uc1:DemoUserControl ID="DemoUserControl1" runat="server" />
...
```

Instead of declaring a user control statically, you can load it dynamically. To implement a dynamic user control, put a PlaceHolder control on the page. User controls can be added within the controls collection of the placeholder. The Page_Load event handler shown demonstrates loading the user control DemoUserControl.ascx with the LoadControl method of the Page class. The returned control is added to the Controls collection of the PlaceHolder control named PlaceHolder1. Using such a technique, different user controls can be loaded according to user settings based on post data or URL strings.

```
void Page_Load(object sender, EventArgs e)
{
    Control c1 = LoadControl("DemoUserControl.ascx");
    PlaceHolder1.Controls.Add(c1);
}
```

User controls can be created and used very easily. You can immediately create one by following the instructions in the next Try It Out. Here, a new custom user control is created that is used to show a calendar and countries for events in a drop-down list.

Try It Out   Create a User Control

1. Open the previously created Website.

2. Add a new user control by selecting the menu Website ⇨ Add New Item, select the Web User Control template and name it ListEvents.ascx.

3. Add a table with two rows to the user control.

4. Use the designer to add a calendar control and a drop-down list to the user control, as shown in Figure 19-9. Name the calendar control EventCalendar and the drop-down list DropDownListCountries.

5. Set the AutoPostback property of the drop-down list to true. Fill the Items collection of the drop-down list with some countries.

Figure 19-9

6. Open the source file of the user control, ListEvents.ascx.cs. Add public method Configure(), as shown to initialize the elements of the user control. Public methods and properties can be invoked from the Web pages, using the control.

```
public void Configure(DateTime date, params string[] countries)
{
    DropDownListCountries.Items.Clear();

    EventCalendar.SelectedDate = date;
    ListItem[] items = new ListItem[countries.Length];
    for (int i = 0; i < countries.Length; i++)
    {
        items[i] = new ListItem(countries[i]);
    }
    DropDownListCountries.Items.AddRange(items);
}
```

The user control can now be used from within Web pages.

In the next Try It Out, you create a Web page that displays the user control as its content.

Try It Out   Using a User Control

1. Create a new Web page UseMyControl.aspx.

2. Open the Web page in design view. Drag and drop the user control from the Solution Explorer to the design surface. The content of the user control immediately shows up in the designer. When you check the ASPX code, you will see the Register directive and the user control code that have been added.

3. Open the source code to add initialization code for the user control by invoking the public method created earlier.

```
protected void Page_Load(object sender, EventArgs e)
{
    if (!Page.IsPostback)
    {
        ListEvents1.Configure(DateTime.Today, "Italy",
            "France", "Germany", "Spain");
    }
}
```

4. Now you can start the Web page. The calendar shows today's date selected, and the drop-down list has the list of countries available.

Profiles

Many commercial Websites let you can add products to a shopping cart, but if you take a coffee break before submitting your order, the session times out. The lesson to learn from this is that it's not a good idea to store orders only in session variables because session state is lost after the session timeout occurs.

ASP.NET 2.0 has a new concept for remembering user information persistently: profiles. Profiles are stored in the database, so they are also kept in cases where sessions end.

Profiles have the following characteristics:

❑   Profiles are stored persistently. The data store is managed by a profile provider. ASP.NET 2.0 includes profile providers for SQL Server and Access. Custom profile providers can be developed.

❑   Profiles are strongly typed. Session and application variables use an indexer, and casting is required to access the data. When you use profiles, properties with the name of the profile are generated automatically. The name and type of the properties are defined in the configuration file.

❑   Profiles can be used with both anonymous and authenticated users. With anonymous users the user identification can be stored inside the cookie. As soon as the user logs on to the Website, the state from the anonymous user can be converted to the state for the authenticated user.

In the next Try It Out, you create and use profile information.

Try It Out   Create Profile Information

1.   Open the previously created Web application.

2.   Open the file web.config that was created in the previous chapter. If you don't see a web.config file the Solution Explorer, create a new one by selecting the menu option Add New Item and select Web Configuration File.

3.   Add the <profile> XML element section containing the Country, Visits and LastVisit properties to the file web.config, as shown. The Country property is of type String (this is the default), the property Visits is of type Int32, and the property LastVisit is of type DateTime.

```
<configuration xmlns="http://schemas.microsoft.com/.NetConfiguration/v2.0">
   <system.web>
   <!-- ... -->

      <profile>
        <properties>
          <add name="Country" />
          <add name="Visits" type="System.Int32" defaultValue="0" />
          <add name="LastVisit" type="System.DateTime" />
        </properties>
      </profile>

   <!-- ... -->
   </system.web>
</configuration>
```

4.   Now, create a new Web page, ProfileDemo.aspx, and add three labels to display current values and a drop-down list to select a country.

5.   Add the following code to the Page_Load() event handler to display current values from the profile. Profile is a dynamically created property of the Page class that has properties defined within the configuration file. These properties are strongly typed — the name and type of the properties are the same as those defined in the configuration file.

```
void Page_Load(object sender, EventArgs e)
{
    LabelLastVisit.Text = Profile.LastVisit.ToLongTimeString();
    LabelVisitCount.Text = Profile.Visits.ToString();
    LabelSelectedCountry.Text = Profile.Country;

    Profile.Visits++;
    Profile.LastVisit = DateTime.Now;
}
```

6. Now you can start and view the Web page. Select a country from the list. Close the browser and start it again. You will see that profile information is remembered between sessions.

How It Works

The `Profile` property that you can use within the code of a Web page is dynamically created. You cannot find this property in the `Page` class in the MSDN documentation, because this property does not exist as part of the `Page` class. Instead because of the property configuration in the `web.config` configuration file, the `Profile` property is created dynamically. The type of the `Profile` property is a dynamically created class that derives from `ProfileBase` and contains properties as defined with the configuration file.

Profile Groups

Profiles can keep track of a lot of information, and that information can be grouped. A group of properties is defined with the element `<group>`, as shown here:

```
<configuration xmlns="http://schemas.microsoft.com/.NetConfiguration/v2.0">
    <system.web>
     <profile>
       <properties>
         <add name="Country" />
         <add name="Visits" type="System.Int32" defaultValue="0" />
         <add name="LastVisit" type="System.DateTime" />
         <group name="EventSelection" >
           <add name="Country" />
           <add name="City" />
           <add name="StartDate" type="System.DateTime" />
           <add name="EndDate" type="System.DateTime" />
         </group>
       </properties>
     </profile>

     <!-- ... -->
    </system.web>
</configuration>
```

So that you can access profile values that are defined within groups, a dynamic property is created that can be used to access the property values:

```
string country = Profile.EventSelection.Country;
string city = Profile.EventSelection.City;
DateTime startDate = Profile.EventSelection.StartDate;
DateTime endDate = Profile.EventSelection.EndDate;
```

Profiles with Components

Inside the code of components, profile information cannot be accessed with a `Profile` property. Instead, the profile is accessed with the help of `HttpContext`. Also, strong typing is not available. The example shows the accessing of the `Country` profile string defined earlier. `Current` is a static property of the `HttpContext` class that returns an `HttpContext` object that is associated with the client session. The property `Profile` returns an object of type `ProfileBase`, where every profile value can be accessed using an indexer. The indexer is defined to return objects of type `Object`, so a cast is needed to write the value to a variable.

```
string country = (string)HttpContext.Current.Profile["Country"];
```

Profiles with Custom Data Types

With profiles, you can store not only base data types such as `int`, `short`, `string`, and `DateTime` but also custom data types. The data type just has to support one serialization mechanism.

The following list explains the serialization mechanisms that are supported with profiles:

❑ **XML Serialization:** XML serialization is the default. With XML serialization all public properties and fields are stored. This serialization mechanism requires a default constructor. XML serialization is described in Chapter 23.

❑ **Binary Serialization:** With binary serialization the class must be marked with the attribute `[Serializable]`. Here, all private fields are serialized. Runtime serialization is described in Chapter 22.

❑ **String Serialization:** With string serialization a type converter class can be used to serialize the data. If there's no type converter class to do the serialization, the `ToString()` method is invoked to serialize the object as a string.

The serialization that is used is defined with the `serializeAs` attribute as shown. If this attribute is not set, XML serialization is used. The possible options with the `serializeAs` attribute are `Binary`, `Xml`, and `String`.

```
<profile>
  <properties>
    <add name="Demo" type="MyClass" serializeAs="Binary" />
  </properties>
</profile>
```

Profiles with Anonymous Users

By default, profiles are only enabled for authenticated users. To enable profiles for anonymous users, anonymous users must be enabled in the configuration file, and every profile property that should be available for anonymous users must be set individually.

```
<configuration>
  <system.web>
    <anonymousIdentification enabled="true" />
```

```
<profile>
  <properties>
    <add name="Country" allowAnonymous="true" />
  </properties>
</profile>
```

When a profile is accessed for an anonymous user, the anonymous user is created in the database of the profile provider. The anonymous user gets an ID similar to an authenticated user. The ID of the anonymous user by default is stored inside a cookie. However, it is also possible to use anonymous user identifiers within URL strings (*URL mungling*) instead of cookies.

Often anonymous profile information must be migrated to authenticated users. For example, a user might be able to add products to a shopping basket without being logged on, but to send the order, the user must log on to the system. In such a case all the profile information that was stored for the anonymous user must be migrated to the authenticated user.

For dealing with anonymous profiles, the following events can be acted on in `global.asax`.

Handler Name	Description
AnonymousIdentification_Create	When an anonymous user accesses the Website for the first time, an anonymous profile is created. This time the event handler `AnonymousIdentification_Create` is invoked.
AnonymousIdentification_Remove	When an authenticated user accesses the Web page, and the request of the authenticated user contains a profile identifier of an anonymous user, the anonymous user profile is removed and the event handler `AnonymousIdentification_Remove` is invoked.
Profile_MigrateAnonymous	After the `AnonymousIdentification_Remove` event handler, the event handler `Profile_MigrateAnonymous` is invoked. With this event handler an anonymous profile can be migrated to a profile for an authenticated user.

The implementation of the handler `Profile_MigrateAnonymous` in `global.asax` can look like the following sample. All profile values that are allowed for anonymous users can be migrated to the authenticated user configuration. The sample code migrates the Country profile value that is allowed for anonymous users in the configuration file. First `Profile.Country` is checked to determine whether it already has a value. `Profile.Country` will have a value if the user was already logged on to the system earlier when the profile value was created. It will not have a value if the user has been anonymous to the system before. Here, the method `GetProfile()` passing an ID of a user helps to access profile information from other users. Although the same person sits on the client, an authenticated user and an anonymous user always have different user IDs. When an anonymous user logs on the system and is now an authenticated user, the ID of the anonymous user is passed with the argument `ProfileMigrateEventArgs` of the method `Profile_MigrateAnonymous()`. The anonymous user ID (`e.AnonymousId`) is passed to the method `GetProfile()` to access the profile of the anonymous user. This profile information is now migrated to the profile information of the authenticated user by assigning profile value by value (such as the `Country` in the example).

```
void Profile_MigrateAnonymous(object sender, ProfileMigrateEventArgs e)
{
   if (Profile.Country == null)
   {
      Profile.Country = Profile.GetProfile(e.AnonymousId).Country;
   }
}
```

Web Parts

A really cool feature of ASP.NET 2.0 that allows customizing Web applications for every user is Web Parts. With Web Parts portal-style Web applications can be created easily. http://www.msn.com (see Figure 19-10) is an example of a portal-style application that offers news, shopping information, stocks, entertainment, and so on. With a personalized Web portal the user can configure what Web parts should be available.

Figure 19-10

The Web Parts framework is made up of zones and parts. The parts that can be inside a zone depend on the type of the zone; for example, a LayoutEditorPart can be a part inside the EditorZone.

The major zone is the Web Parts zone. A Web page can have multiple Web Parts zones to define the layout of the page. Inside this zone multiple Web parts, user controls, or Web server controls can be contained.

The catalog zone allows the user or administrator to choose Web parts from a catalog to be displayed within the Web page. For this zone the parts PageCatalogPart, ImportCatalogPart, and DeclarativeCatalogPart can be used.

With the Editor zone the user or administrator can edit the behavior and appearance of individual Web parts. The items that allow changing the look and feel of Web parts are AppearanceEditorPart, BehaviorEditorPart, and LayoutEditorPart.

The connections zone is used to connect multiple Web parts together. This way communication between multiple Web parts can be done. For example, if the user selects a month in one Web part another Web part that is displayed within the same page can know about the month and change its own behavior accordingly.

Now let's look into the Web Parts framework and start creating Web applications using Web Parts.

Web Parts Manager

A control that is required with every Web Parts–enabled site is the WebPartManager. This control is responsible for managing Web parts. With the WebPartManager Web Parts controls can be created, deleted, or moved.

All that's needed with a WebPartManager is that it be represented on a Web page as shown with this ASPX code:

```
<asp:WebPartManager ID="WebPartManager1" runat="server"></asp:WebPartManager>
```

This control doesn't have a user interface at runtime, and it's not necessary to configure any properties. With its properties you just can configure some warning messages when Web Parts controls are closed and deleted. What's more interesting with the WebPartManager is the methods that can optionally be used to change the display mode, as will be shown later.

Web Parts Zone

To make use of the Web Parts framework at least one WebPartZone must exist. A WebPartZone contains Web Parts controls and defines the layout and appearance of the Web Parts controls within the zone. As previously mentioned, the WebPartZone can contain user controls, Web parts, and Web server controls.

Within the ASPX page, the WebPartZone includes a ZoneTemplate that contains controls for display. The example here contains the previously created user control ListEvents.

```
<asp:WebPartZone ID="EventsZone" runat="server">
  <ZoneTemplate>
    <uc1:ListEvents ID="ListEvents1" runat="server" />
  </ZoneTemplate>
</asp:WebPartZone>
```

With the WebPartZone it is possible to define layout, coloring, and menus. The following sample shows the WebPartZone with the predefined professional layout to set colors and styles to the frame and the Web Parts menus.

```
<asp:WebPartZone BorderColor="#CCCCCC" Font-Names="Verdana"
    ID="EventZone" Padding="6" runat="server">
  <PartChromeStyle BackColor="#F7F6F3" BorderColor="#E2DED6"
      Font-Names="Verdana" ForeColor="White" />
  <MenuLabelHoverStyle ForeColor="#E2DED6" />
  <EmptyZoneTextStyle Font-Size="0.8em" />
  <MenuLabelStyle ForeColor="White" />
  <MenuVerbHoverStyle BackColor="#F7F6F3" BorderColor="#CCCCCC"
      BorderStyle="Solid" BorderWidth="1px" ForeColor="#333333" />
  <HeaderStyle Font-Size="0.7em" ForeColor="#CCCCCC"
      HorizontalAlign="Center" />
  <MenuVerbStyle BorderColor="#5D7B9D" BorderStyle="Solid"
      BorderWidth="1px" ForeColor="White" />
  <PartStyle Font-Size="0.8em" ForeColor="#333333" />
  <TitleBarVerbStyle Font-Size="0.6em" Font-Underline="False"
      ForeColor="White" />
  <MenuPopupStyle BackColor="#5D7B9D" BorderColor="#CCCCCC"
      BorderWidth="1px" Font-Names="Verdana" Font-Size="0.6em" />
  <PartTitleStyle BackColor="#5D7B9D" Font-Bold="True"
      Font-Size="0.8em" ForeColor="White" />
  <ZoneTemplate>
    <ucl:ListEvents ID="ListEvents1" runat="server" />
  </ZoneTemplate>
</asp:WebPartZone>
```

In the next Try It Out, you create the Web page `WebPartDemo.aspx` with the initial steps required to use the Web Parts framework. You will add two user controls to two different zones.

Try It Out   Create a Web Application Using Web Parts

1. Open the previously created Web application.

2. Add a new page named `WebPartsDemo.aspx`.

3. Add a `WebPartManager` control to this page.

4. Add a table with two columns and two rows to organize the layout of the Web parts.

5. Within each column of the second row add a `WebPartZone` control. Later, controls will be added to the first row. Set the `ID` of the first Web Part zone to `EventsZone` and the `ID` of the second zone to `WeatherZone`.

6. Using the smart tag of the first `WebPartZone` control in design view, select the Professional Auto Format. For easy differentiation of the second `WebPartZone`, select the Colorful Auto Format.

7. Set the `HeaderText` property of the first `WebPartZone` to `Events`, and set the same property of the second zone to `Weather`.

8. Add the user control `ListEvents.ascx`, which was created earlier, to the left `WebPartZone`.

9. Create a new user control `Weather.ascx` to show weather information based on a country. At this time the user control just needs one label named `LabelWeather`. You can use a random algorithm as shown if sun, cloudy, or rain should be displayed. Add this user control to the right `WebPartZone`.

```
public partial class Weather : System.Web.UI.UserControl
{
    protected void Page_Load(object sender, EventArgs e)
    {
```

```
        Random r = new Random();
        int n = r.Next(1, 3);

        switch (n)
        {
            case 1:
                LabelWeather.Text = "Sun";
                break;
            case 2:
                LabelWeather.Text = "Rain";
                break;
            case 3:
                LabelWeather.Text = "Cloudy";
                break;
        }
    }
}
```

10. Now you can start the Web page. You can see the user controls in Figure 19-11. Notice the frame around the user controls with the title Untitled and the small arrow (the Verb button) on the right side of the frame. This frame is known as the *chrome*. If you click the Verb button, you can see the menu entries Minimize and Close. Try to minimize the control and restore it again. However, don't click the Close menu entry, because as long as there's no catalog configured, it is not possible to reopen the closed controls.

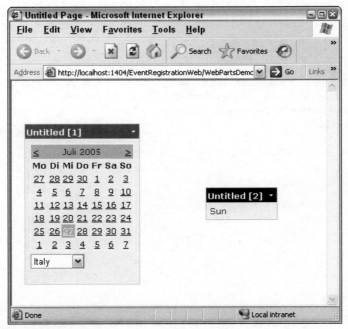

Figure 19-11

11. Next, you are going to make it impossible to close the controls. Open the Web page again in the designer and select a Web part. Open the `CloseVerb` property in the Property Editor. Set the `Enabled` option of this property to `false`. This setting makes it is impossible to select the `Close` menu item. To remove the menu entry, the `Visible` property can be set to `false`, too.

12. Open the Web page in the browser again. Notice that the Close menu entry cannot be selected.

Editor Zone

The Editor zone is used to change the appearance, behavior, and layout of the Web parts. For each of these activities different editor parts are available. The editor parts are active when a Web Parts control is set to Edit mode.

The Layout Editor part (see Figure 19-12) allows setting the chrome state, the zone where the Web part should be placed, and the order of a Web part inside a zone. The chrome state can be `Normal` or `Minimized`. When minimized chrome the Web part shows up only with a small icon so that it won't take up a lot of space within the Web page. The user can restore the Web part to a normal view by clicking this icon. The Zone combo box lists the names of all zones where the Web Parts controls can be placed.

Figure 19-12

The Appearance Editor part allows setting the title, chrome type, and size. Figure 19-13 shows all the possible settings of the Appearance Editor part. The title is used to give a Web part a new header. The chrome type defines the visibility of the title and the border. The height and width of the Web Parts control can also be specified.

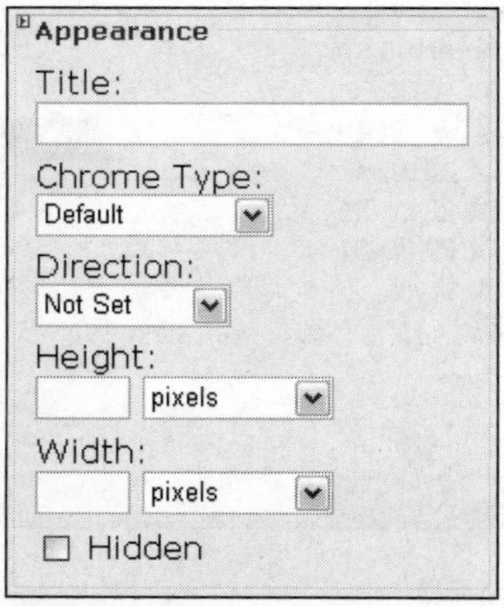

Figure 19-13

The Behavior Editor part (shown in Figure 19-14) allows setting title links and images, catalog links and images, and whether the Web Parts controls should be allowed to close, be edited, hide, and be minimized. The Export mode defines whether it is possible to export the Web Parts control information to the local disk of the user. Here, only the settings of the Web Parts control are exported to the local disk. This configuration can be used again to import the Web Parts control with any Website that offers the same Web Parts controls.

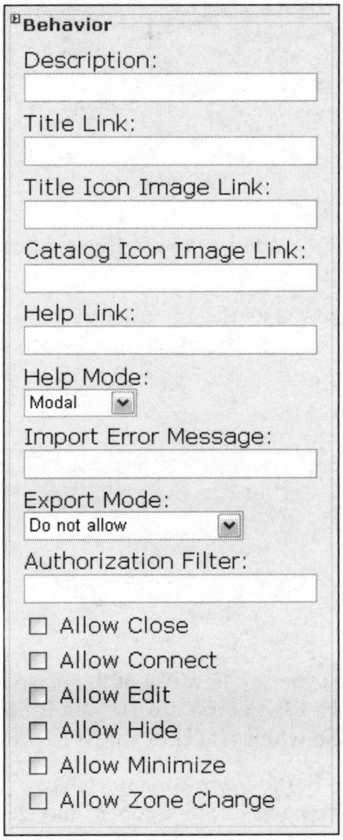

Behavior

Description:

Title Link:

Title Icon Image Link:

Catalog Icon Image Link:

Help Link:

Help Mode:
Modal

Import Error Message:

Export Mode:
Do not allow

Authorization Filter:

☐ Allow Close
☐ Allow Connect
☐ Allow Edit
☐ Allow Hide
☐ Allow Minimize
☐ Allow Zone Change

Figure 19-14

Try It Out   Add an Editor Zone

Adding an Editor zone makes it possible to change the appearance, behavior, and layout of the Web parts.

1. Open the previously created Web page `WebPartDemo.aspx`.

2. Add an `EditorZone` control to the first row of the table within the page.

3. Add an `AppearanceEditorPart` and a `LayoutEditorPart` to the Editor zone.

4. Add a `DropDownList` control to the top of the page. This control will be used to change from Browse mode to edit mode. Rename the `DropDownList` control to `DropDownListDisplayModes`.

5. Set the `AutoPostBack` property of the `DropDownListDisplayModes` control to `true`.

6. Add this code to the class `WebPartsDemo` in the file `WebPartsDemo.aspx.cs`. Here, all the display modes that are supported by the actual configuration of the `WebPartManager` are shown in the drop-down list.

```
protected void Page_Init(object sender, EventArgs e)
{
    foreach (WebPartDisplayMode mode in WebPartManager1.SupportedDisplayModes)
    {
        if (mode.IsEnabled(WebPartManager1))
        {
            DropDownListDisplayModes.Items.Add(new ListItem(mode.Name));
        }
    }
}
```

7. Add the method `OnChangeDisplayMode` to the `SelectedIndexChanged` event of the drop-down list `DropDownListDisplayModes`.

8. Add an implementation to the method `OnChangeDisplayMode()` to change the display mode of the `WebPartManager` to the mode that is selected in the drop-down list `DropDownListDisplayModes`:

```
protected void OnChangeDisplayMode(object sender, EventArgs e)
{
    string selectedMode = DropDownListDisplayModes.SelectedValue;
    WebPartDisplayMode mode = WebPartManager1.SupportedDisplayModes[selectedMode];
    if (mode != null)
    {
        WebPartManager1.DisplayMode = mode;
    }
}
```

9. Start the Web page in the browser. Because of the existence of an Editor zone there's an Edit selection in the drop-down list. Set the drop-down list to Edit the Page. Notice the Edit menu with the Web parts chrome when you click the Verb button.

10. Select the Edit menu. The Editor zone appears. Change the title and chrome type of the Web parts. Try to move the Web parts to other zones, and change the zone order.

11. Instead of using the Editor parts of the Editor zone to change the Web parts, you can also drag and drop a Web part from one zone to another—if the mode is set to Edit mode.

Catalog Zone

The Catalog zone is a real catalog—you can select Web parts from a catalog. Again, the Catalog zone is a zone similar to the other zones that manage Web parts. The Web parts that are managed by a Catalog zone are Catalog parts. ASP.NET 2.0 has three different kinds of catalogs: a page catalog, a declarative catalog, and an import catalog.

Figure 19-15 shows the `PageCatalogPart`. The page catalog lists all Web parts that are available within a Web page. All Web parts that have been closed by the user are listed within the `PageCatalogPart`. This way the user can reopen closed controls.

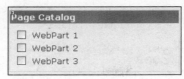

Figure 19-15

With the `DeclarativeCatalogPart` that is shown in Figure 19-16, the controls that should be available for selection must be explicitly defined within a `<WebPartsTemplate>` element. With the Visual Studio Designer, this can be done by clicking the smart tag of the control and clicking Edit Templates.

```
<asp:CatalogZone ID="CatalogZone1" runat="server">
  <ZoneTemplate>
    <asp:DeclarativeCatalogPart runat="server" ID="DeclarativeCatalogPart1">
      <WebPartsTemplate>
        <uc1:ListEvents ID="ListEvents2" runat="server" />
        <asp:Calendar ID="Calendar1" runat="server" />
      </WebPartsTemplate>
    </asp:DeclarativeCatalogPart>
  </ZoneTemplate>
</asp:CatalogZone>
```

```
Declarative Catalog
  ☐ Untitled
  ☐ Untitled
```

Figure 19-16

The `ImportCatalogPart` can be used to import Web parts that have been stored on the client system. As you can see in Figure 19-17, `ImportCatalogPart` includes Browse and Upload buttons. With the Browse button a locally stored Web part can be selected, and uploaded to the user's personalized settings on the Web server.

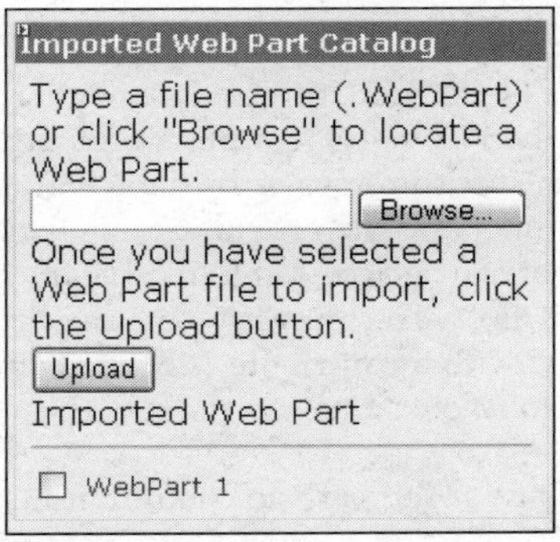

```
Imported Web Part Catalog
  Type a file name (.WebPart)
  or click "Browse" to locate a
  Web Part.
  [              ] [ Browse... ]
  Once you have selected a
  Web Part file to import, click
  the Upload button.
  [ Upload ]
  Imported Web Part

  ☐ WebPart 1
```

Figure 19-17

Adding a Catalog zone makes it possible to select Web parts that should be included with the Web page from a catalog. In the next Try It Out, you create a Catalog zone that includes multiple catalogs.

Try It Out   **Add a Catalog Zone**

1. Open the previously created Web page `WebPartDemo.aspx`.

2. Add a `CatalogZone` control to the second column of the first row of the table within the page.

3. Select a Professional Auto Format with the `CatalogZone` control.

4. Add a `PageCatalogPart` and a `DeclarativeCatalogPart` to the Catalog zone.

5. The `DeclarativeCatalogPart` requires some configuration. In the designer, click the smart tag of the `DeclarativeCatalogPart` control, and click Edit Templates. Now, you can add several controls (user controls or Web server controls) to the control. After you've completed adding the controls, click on End Template Editing.

6. Start the Web page in the browser. Close one or several Web Parts controls by clicking the Close menu. The Web Parts controls disappear. Of course you cannot close the controls of the zone you've set the `Enabled` property of `CloseVerb` to `false`.

7. Set the `DropDownList` to `Show the Catalog`. Because of the existence of the `CatalogZone`, the Catalog menu is added to the drop-down list. The Catalog zone opens.

8. Select Page Catalog from the catalog list. In the page catalog all Web parts that have been closed show up in a list. Select Web Parts from the list and add it to a zone.

9. Select Declarative Catalog from the catalog list. With the declarative catalog all Web parts that have been configured show up in the list. Select Web Parts from the list and add it to a zone.

10. Close the Catalog Zone.

Connections

Using the Connections zone, it is possible to send data from one Web Parts control to another Web Parts control on the same page. For example, if the user selects a city for weather information from the Weather Web part, the selected city can be sent to the News Web part that shows news from the same city.

The `WebPartManager` is responsible for initiating and managing the communication between the Web Parts. Communication between the Web parts requires a consumer and a provider to be differentiated. The provider offers some data; the consumer uses the data. Figure 19-18 shows the interaction of the `WebPartManager` with the consumer and the provider. First, the `WebPartManager` calls methods from the providers to get interfaces that can be accessed to receive the data. The providers are identified with the attribute `[ConnectionProvider]`. The `WebPartManager` then passes these interfaces to the consumers. Consumers are identified with the attribute `[ConnectionConsumer]`. Now, the consumer can invoke methods of the provider to receive data.

In the next Try It Out, you enable two Web parts to communicate, passing a selected country from the `ListEvents` Web part to another Web part.

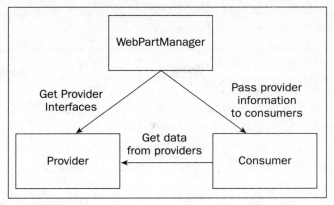

Figure 19-18

Create a Connection between Web Parts

1. Open the previously created Website `EventRegistrationWeb`.

2. Open the special folder `App_Code` in the Solution Explorer. If the folder does not exist, create a new one by selecting the menu Website ➪ Add Folder ➪ App_Code Folder.

3. Create a new C# file `ICountry.cs` to define the `ICountry` interface:

```
public interface ICountry
{
    string GetCountry();
}
```

4. Open the source code (`ListEvents.ascx.cs`) of the previously created user control `ListEvents`. With the class `ListEvents` implement the interface `ICountry`. The `GetCountry()` method is implemented to return the selected country to the caller.

```
public partial class ListEvents : System.Web.UI.UserControl, ICountry
{
    public string GetCountry()
    {
        return DropDownListCountries.SelectedItem.Value;
    }

    //...
```

5. The provider also needs a method that is marked with the attribute `[ConnectionProvider]`. The method must return an interface. Implement the method `GetCountryInterface()` to return a reference to the `ICountry` interface.

The attribute `[ConnectionProvider]` defines a friendly name (`Country`) and an actual name (`CountryProvider`) for the provider.

```
[ConnectionProvider("Country", "CountryProvider")]
public ICountry GetCountryInterface()
{
    return this;
}
```

6. Create a new user control named `Country.ascx` that acts as a consumer. This user control just needs a simple label to display the country.

7. Open the C# code of the user control `Country` to implement a consumer method that is marked with the attribute `[ConnectionConsumer]`. The method `SetCountry()` receives the `ICountry` interface that it uses to receive the data from the provider by calling the `GetCountry()` method. The returned string is assigned to the `Text` property of the label.

```csharp
[ConnectionConsumer("Country", "CountryConsumer")]
public void SetCountry(ICountry provider)
{
    string country = provider.GetCountry();
    if (!string.IsNullOrEmpty(country))
    {
        LabelCountry.Text = country;
    }
}
```

8. Open the Web page `WebPartDemo.aspx`. Add the new Country.ascx user control to a Web parts zone.

9. Select the `WebPartManager` and click the Ellipsis button with the `StaticConnections` property in the Property Editor. Add a new Connection with these settings:

Connection Properties	Value
ConsumerConnectionPointID	CountryConsumer
ConsumerID	Country1
ID	CountryConnection
ProviderConnectionPointID	CountryProvider
ProviderID	ListEvents1

Configuring the connections with the Property Editor adds the `<StaticConnections>` element to the `WebPartManager` control, as shown:

```xml
<asp:WebPartManager ID="WebPartManager1" Runat="server">
  <StaticConnections>
    <asp:Connection ID="CountryConnection" ProviderID="ListEvents1"
        ProviderConnectionPointID="CountryProvider" ConsumerID="Country1"
        ConsumerConnectionPointID="ListEvents1" />
  </StaticConnections>
</asp:WebPartManager>
```

10. Now you can start the Web page. With the connection setup, if you select a country with the `ListEvents` control, the country shows up in the `Country` control.

11. Instead of using static connections, with the possibility to change the Web parts shown during runtime, it is also necessary to configure connections during runtime. This can be done with the `ConnectionsZone` control. Add the `ConnectionsZone` control to the Web page and remove the static connections from the `WebPartManager`.

12. Start the Web page again. Select Connect Web Parts in the drop-down list.

13. Setting the `WebPartManager` to `ConnectDisplayMode` (what happens when the drop-down list is changed) causes the Verb button to offer the new verb Connect. Click this Connect menu entry of the `Country` control and create a dynamic connection with the `ListEvents` control.

14. As before, select a country with the `ListEvents` control, so that the selected country shows up in the `ListEvents` control.

Summary

In this chapter, many new features of ASP.NET 2.0 have been discussed. Among these new features are master pages, profiles, and Web Parts.

Master pages allow defining a common layout for all pages. Profiles are used to store user data persistently in a database. Contrary to session variables, where the state is lost when the session timeout occurs, profiles are stored in the database. Because profiles are strongly typed, it is easy to access the value using properties and Visual Studio IntelliSense. Web Parts are a mighty new feature of ASP.NET. Web Parts allow creating portal-style Web applications that can be customized for every user with just a few clicks. With the Web Parts framework you've seen different zone types; beside the `WebPartZone`, the Editor zone, Catalog zone, and Connections zone have been used.

User controls were also discussed, because these controls make it easy to reuse components with Web pages. User controls can be used within Web zones.

In this chapter, you've learned about:

❑ Creating and using master pages

❑ Creating a structure for your site to navigate different pages

❑ Creating user controls

❑ Storing user-specific data using profiles

❑ How to let the user customize a Web application using Web Parts

In the exercises in this chapter, you create a new Web application that uses the ASP.NET features demonstrated in this chapter and the previous chapter.

The next chapter gives you a start on how to write Web services with ASP.NET.

Exercises

1. Create a new portal-style personal Web application.

2. Create a user control to display your résumé.

3. Create a user control to display a list of links to your preferred Websites.

Chapter 19

4. Define Forms authentication as the authentication mechanism for the Website.

5. Create a user control where a user can register on the Website.

6. Create a master page that defines a common layout with top and bottom sections.

7. Define a sitemap to create links to all the Web pages on this Website.

8. Create a Web page that uses the Web Parts framework, where the user can define the layout of the page.

Web Services

You may have come across the term *Web services* before, though you may not be aware of what they are or how they fit into the way the Web operates — and will operate in the future. Suffice it to say that Web services provide the foundation of the new generation of Web applications. Whatever the client application is — whether it is a Windows application or an ASP.NET Web Forms application — and whatever system the client is running — whether it is Windows, Pocket Windows, or some other OS — they will regularly communicate over the Internet using a Web service. Web services are server-side programs that listen for messages from client applications and return specific information. This information may come from the Web service itself, from other components in the same domain, or from other Web services. While the whole of the Web service concept is evolving continuously, there are several different types of Web services that carry out different functions: some provide information specific to a particular industry such as manufacturing or healthcare; there are portal services that use services from different providers to offer information on a specific theme; there are services that are specific to single applications, and building block services that can be used by many different applications.

Web services give us the ability to combine, share, exchange, or plug in separate services from various vendors and developers to form entirely new services or custom applications created on the fly to meet the requirements of the client.

In this chapter, you look at:

- ❑ Predecessors of Web services
- ❑ What a Web service is
- ❑ Protocols used for Web services
- ❑ Creating an ASP.NET Web service
- ❑ Testing the Web service
- ❑ Building a client to use Web services
- ❑ Calling the Web service asynchronously
- ❑ Sending and receiving messages

This chapter will not go into the inner workings of Web services, especially the XML-based SOAP and WSDL formats, but you will get an overview of what these protocols are used for. After reading this chapter, you can start creating and consuming simple Web services with the help of Visual Studio.

Before Web Services

Connecting computers to transfer data was already an important concept in 1969 when just four computers were connected via telephone lines to form the ARPANET. In 1976 the TCP/IP protocol was invented. To make this protocol easy to use, the University of Berkeley created the socket model for network programming.

When programming with the Sockets API, the client had to initiate a connection to the server and then send and receive data. To call some operations on the server to get results, additional protocols are needed to describe request and response codes. Examples of such so-called application protocols are File Transfer Protocol (FTP), Telnet, and Hypertext Transfer Protocol (HTTP). The FTP protocol is used to get some files from the server and to put the files on the server. The FTP protocol supports request codes such as GET and PUT, which are sent across the wire from the client to the server. The server analyzes the data stream it receives, and, according to the request codes, invokes the corresponding method. The HTTP protocol works very similarly to the FTP protocol.

Remote Procedure Call (RPC)

With the Sockets API and the TCP/IP protocol calling custom methods on the server, the programmer would have had to create a means by which the server analyzes the data stream to invoke the corresponding method. To make all this work more easily, some companies created an *RPC (remote procedure calls)* protocol, an example of which is the still popular *DCE-RPC* protocol (Distributed Computing Environment – Remote Procedure Calls) from the Open Software Foundation (OSF), which later became the Open Group (www.opengroup.org). Using RPC, you defined methods in an *IDL* (Interface Definition Language) format, which the server has to implement, and which the client can call. You no longer have to define a custom protocol and parse the request codes to invoke the methods. This work is done by a special program, called a *stub*, generated by an interface compiler.

RPC is designed to invoke methods, which means that you have to do procedural programming. The RPC technology came in relatively late, when most developers had already started to work with the object-oriented paradigm. To bridge the technology gap, several technologies came into being, including CORBA and DCOM.

CORBA

In 1991 the Object Management Group (OMG, www.omg.org) initiated *CORBA* (Common Object Request Broker Architecture) to add object-orientation to network programming. Many vendors such as Digital Equipment, HP, IBM, and others implemented CORBA servers. Because the OMG didn't define a reference implementation though, only a specification, the servers of these vendors didn't really interoperate. The HP server needed an HP client, the IBM server an IBM client, and so on.

DCOM

With Windows NT 4, Microsoft extended the DCE-RPC protocol with object-oriented features. The *DCOM* (Distributed COM) protocol made it possible to call COM components across the network and is used in

COM+ applications. After some years in which Microsoft operating systems were a requirement for DCOM, Microsoft opened the protocol for others with The Active Group. DCOM was made available for Unix, VMS, and IBM systems. DCOM was heavily used in the Microsoft environments, but the initiative to bring it to other systems was not really successful. What IBM mainframe administrator wants to add Microsoft technology to his or her system?

RMI

Sun Microsystems took a different route with its Java technologies. In a pure Java world, the *RMI* (Remote Method Invocation) protocol can be used to call objects remotely. Sun added some bridges to the CORBA and COM world, but the major goal for Sun was to bring the masses to a Java-only solution.

SOAP

All the technologies that we have seen were used for application-to-application communication, but if you have a CORBA, a DCOM, and an RMI solution, it is hard to get these different technologies to talk together. Another problem with these technologies can be found in their architectures: because they are not designed for thousands of clients, they can't achieve the scalability required for Internet solutions.

As a result, several companies, including Microsoft and UserLand Software, (www.userland.com) created *SOAP* in 1999 as a completely new way of invoking objects over the Internet, one that builds upon already accepted standard protocols. SOAP uses an XML-based format to describe methods and parameters to make remote calls across the network. A SOAP server in the COM world could translate the SOAP messages to COM calls, whereas a SOAP server in the CORBA world translates them to CORBA calls. Originally, the SOAP definition made use of the HTTP protocol, so that SOAP calls could be done across the Internet.

With SOAP 1.2, Web services are independent of the HTTP protocol. Any transport protocol can be used. However, the most used transport protocol for Web services is still HTTP. In this chapter, the focus will be on Web services that can be created with the Visual Studio 2005 Project Wizard that makes use of SOAP and HTTP.

SOAP specifications can be found at www.w3.org/TR/SOAP.

Where to Use Web Services

To get another view of what Web services are, you can distinguish between *user-to-application* communication and *application-to-application* communication.

Let's start with a *user-to-application communication* example, getting some weather information from the Web. There are a large number of Websites, such as www.msnbc.com and www.weather.com, that present the weather information in an easy-to-digest format for a human reader. Normally, these pages are read directly by a user.

If you wanted to create a rich client application to display the weather (application-to-application communication) your application would have to connect to the Website with a URL string containing the city for which you want to know the weather. You would then have to parse the resulting HTML message returned from the Website to get the temperatures and weather conditions, and then you could finally display this information in an appropriate format for the rich client application.

That is a lot of work, considering that you just want to get some temperature readings for a particular city. And, the process of getting the data from the HTML is not trivial, because HTML data is designed to be displayed in the Web browser and is not meant to be used by any other client-side business application. Therefore, the data is embedded in the text and is not easily extracted, and you would have to rewrite or adapt the client application to retrieve different data information (such as rainfall) from the same Web page. Compared to using a Web browser, users can immediately pick out the data they need and can overlook what is not needed.

To get around the problem of processing HTML data, a Web service provides a useful means for returning only the data requested. Just call a method on the remote server, and get the information needed, which can be used directly by the client application. At no point do you have to deal with the preformatted text that is meant for the user interface, because the Web service presents the information in XML format, and tools already exist to process XML data. All that is required from the client application is to call some methods of the .NET Framework XML classes to get the information. Better still though, if you are writing a client in C# for a .NET Web service, you don't even need to write the code to do that—there are tools which will generate C# code for you!

This sort of weather application is one example of how Web services can be used, but there are a lot more.

A Hotel Travel Agency Application Scenario

How do you book your holiday? By going to a travel agency that does all the work for you. Have you already booked your holiday on the Internet? On an airline's Website, you can look for possible flights and book them. A Web search engine can be used to look for a hotel in the desired city. Maybe you are lucky and find a map showing how to get to the hotel. When you find the hotel's home page, you navigate to the booking form page, whereupon you can go ahead and book the room. Next you would search out a car rental firm, and so on.

A lot of the work you have to do today is to find the right Websites with the help of search engines, and then to navigate these sites. Instead of going through that, you could create a Home Travel Agency Application that uses Web services containing details about hotels, airlines, car rental firms, and so on. Then you can present the client with an easy-to-use interface to deal with all the holiday issues, including a not-to-be-forgotten early booking of a special musical event. With your Pocket PC on location during your holiday, you can use the same Web services to get a map to some leisure-time activities, and to get accurate information about cultural events or cinema programs, and so on.

A Book Distributor Application Scenario

Web services can also be useful for two companies that have a partnership. Assume that a book distributor wants to provide bookshops with information about books in stock. This can be accomplished with a Web service. An ASP.NET application using the Web service can be created to offer this service directly to users. Another client application of this service is a Windows application for the bookshop, where at first the local stock gets checked and then that of the distributor. The sales person can immediately answer questions about delivery dates without having to check different stock information in different applications.

Client Application Types

The client of a Web service can be a rich Windows application created using Windows Forms, or an ASP.NET application using Web Forms. A Windows PC, a Unix system, or a Pocket PC can be used to *consume* (use) the Web service. With the .NET Framework, Web services can be consumed in every application type: Windows Forms, Web Forms, or console applications.

Smart client is a new term for a rich client application that makes use of Web services. The smart client can operate without being connected to the Web service because it caches data locally. Microsoft Outlook is an example of a smart client as all the mail data is stored on the client system, and when the Exchange server can be connected the data is synchronized.

Application Architecture

What does an application using Web services actually look like? Regardless of whether you develop ASP.NET or Windows applications, or applications for small devices (as you have seen in the application scenarios presented here), Web services is an important technology.

Figure 20-1 illustrates a scenario showing how Web services can be used. Devices and browsers are connected through the Internet to an ASP.NET application developed with Web Forms. This ASP.NET application uses some local Web services and some other remote Web services that can be reached across the network: portal Web services, application-specific Web services, and building block Web services. The following list should help to elucidate the meaning of these service types:

❑ *Portal Web services* offer services from different companies with the same subject matter. This is an easy-to-use access point for multiple services.

❑ *Application-specific Web services* are created just for the use of a single application.

❑ *Building block Web services* are services that can easily be used within multiple applications.

The Windows application in Figure 20-1 can use the Web services directly without going through the ASP.NET application.

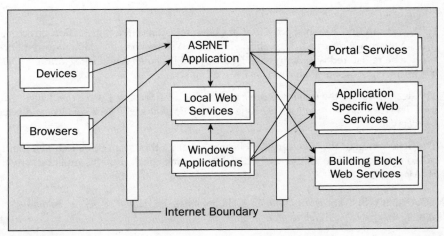

Figure 20-1

Web Services Architecture

Web services make use of the SOAP protocol, which is a standard defined by many companies. A big advantage of Web services is its platform-independence. However, Web services are not only a useful technology when multiple platforms need to cooperate. Web services are also a very useful technology for developing .NET applications on both the client and the server side. The advantage here is that the client and the server can emerge independently. A service description is done with a WSDL document (Web Service Description Language) that can be designed in a way to be independent of new versions of the Web service, and therefore the client needn't be changed.

If you want to use existing Web services, first you have to find one that meets your needs. If you know of a Web service that fits, you have to get the information on how to communicate with it. Figure 20-2 shows important mechanisms for calling Web services.

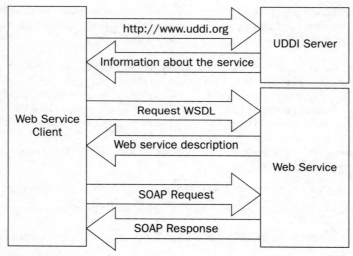

Figure 20-2

❑ First, you can find a Web service that has been registered in a registration directory service. This directory service returns information about the Web service. It's not a requirement that a Web service be registered with Universal Description, Discovery, and Integration (UDDI). You can get information about Web services from other sources.

❑ The description of the service is presented in the *Web Services Description Language* (WSDL) format. The description specifies the data that can be sent to the Web service, and what data can be received.

❑ The description of the Web service tells you what methods can be called. The methods will be called using SOAP, so all the method calls including the arguments must be converted to the SOAP protocol.

Both SOAP and WSDL are defined with an XML grammar. The UDDI server can be queried programmatically by using a UDDI Web service.

Let's look into the steps of the sequence in more detail.

Search Engine for Web Services

Maybe you can use a Web service that is already supported by another company. To search and find pre-existing Web services, Microsoft, IBM, and Ariba got together and initiated the www.uddi.org Website with the *UDDI* service. UDDI is a platform-independent, open framework for describing services, discovering businesses, and integrating business services using the Web as well as an operational registry. A company that wants to advertise its Web service can register it here. With the UDDI business registry and the UDDI API, it is possible to programmatically locate information about Web services.

Since the three companies mentioned earlier initiated UDDI, many more enterprises support the UDDI project; among them are Cisco Systems, Fujitsu, Intel, SAP, and Sun Microsystems.

To find an existing Web service, you can search by business name. After a successful search for a service you get its description, any information about its classification (for example, the groups it belongs to), and binding information.

In addition to using an open UDDI server for registration of services, you can install your own service if the service is only meant to be used within the company or by partners. Windows Server 2003 includes a UDDI server component that just needs to be configured.

In Visual Studio 2005, you can search for Web services by selecting Project ➪ Add Web Reference, as shown in Figure 20-3. You can select a Web service from the local solution, search for Web services on the local machine, browse UDDI servers on the local network, access the UDDI Directory from Microsoft, or make use of a Test UDDI Directory. If you know the path to the Web service, you can also enter it directly with the URL text box.

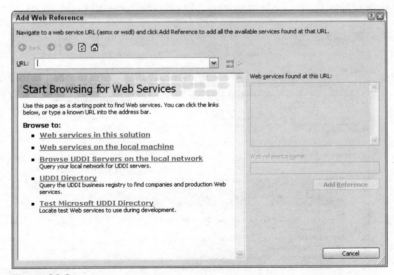

Figure 20-3

When you selecting the UDDI Directory link, Microsoft's UDDI server, http://uddi.microsoft.com, is opened, as shown in Figure 20-4. Here, you can specify search strings to find a registered Web service.

If the result of the search has binding information, a reference to the Web service can be added with the Add Reference button.

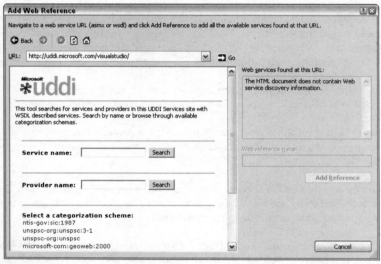

Figure 20-4

Entering the string `Continental` as provider name causes the server to list a Web service from Continental Airlines (see Figure 20-5) from which to get schedule and flight status information.

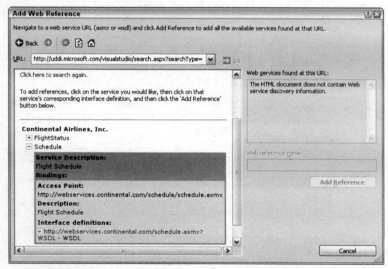

Figure 20-5

Besides UDDI servers, you can find many existing Web services at these Websites: www.xmethods.net and www.gotdotnet.com.

What Methods Can I Call?

A WSDL document has the information about the methods a Web service supports and how they can be called, parameter types passed to the service, and parameter types returned from the service. Figure 20-6 shows the WSDL that is generated from the ASP.NET runtime. Appending the string `?wsdl` to the .asmx file returns a WSDL document.

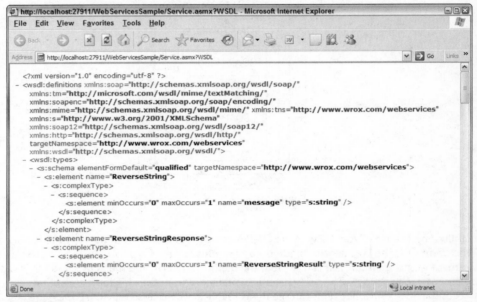

Figure 20-6

It is not necessary to deal with this information directly. The WSDL document will be generated dynamically with the `WebMethod` attribute; you look at this attribute later on. Adding the Web reference to the client application with Visual Studio causes a WSDL document to be requested. This WSDL document, in turn, is used to create a client proxy with the same methods and arguments. With this proxy, the client application has the advantage that it only needs to call the methods as they are implemented in the server, because the proxy converts them to SOAP calls to make the call across the network.

The WSDL specification is maintained by the World Wide Web Consortium (W3C). You can read the specification at the W3C Website www.w3.org/TR/wsdl.

Calling a Method

To call a method on a Web service, the call must be converted to the SOAP message as defined in the WSDL document.

A SOAP message is the basic unit of communication between a client and a server. Figure 20-7 demonstrates the parts of a SOAP message. A SOAP message includes a SOAP envelope, which, as you might guess, wraps all the SOAP information in a single block. The SOAP envelope itself consists of two parts:

a SOAP header and a SOAP body. The optional header defines how the client and server should process the body. The mandatory SOAP body includes the data that is sent. Usually information within this body is the method that is called together with the serialized parameter values. The SOAP server sends back the return values in the SOAP body of the SOAP message.

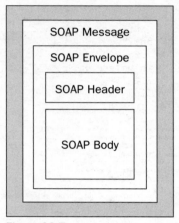

Figure 20-7

In the following example, you see what a SOAP message that is sent from the client to the server looks like. The client calls the Web service method `ReverseString()`. The string `Hello World!` is passed as an argument to this method. You can see that the method call is inside the SOAP body, it is within the XML element `<soap:Body>`. The body itself is contained within the envelope `<soap:Envelope>`. Before the start of the SOAP message, you can see the HTTP header, because the SOAP message is sent with an HTTP POST request.

It is not necessary to create such a message, because that is done by the client proxy:

```
POST /WebServiceSample/Service1.asmx HTTP/1.1
Host: localhost
Content-Type: text/xml; charset=utf-8
Content-Length: 508
SOAPAction: "http://www.wrox.com/webservices/ReverseString"

<?xml version="1.0" encoding="utf-8"?>
<soap:Envelope xmlns:xsi="http://www.w3.org/2001/XMLSchema-instance"
    xmlns:xsd="http://www.w3.org/2001/XMLSchema"
    xmlns:soap="http://schemas.xmlsoap.org/soap/envelope/">
  <soap:Body>
    <ReverseString xmlns="http://www.wrox.com/webservices">
      <message>Hello World!</message>
    </ReverseString>
  </soap:Body>
</soap:Envelope>
```

The server answers with the SOAP message !dlroW olleH, as can be seen with the
ReverseStringResult XML element:

```
HTTP/1.1 200 OK
Content-Type: text/xml; charset=utf-8
Content-Length: 446

<?xml version="1.0" encoding="utf-8"?>
<soap:Envelope xmlns:xsi="http://www.w3.org/2001/XMLSchema-instance"
    xmlns:xsd="http://www.w3.org/2001/XMLSchema"
    xmlns:soap="http://schemas.xmlsoap.org/soap/envelope/">
  <soap:Body>
    <ReverseStringResponse xmlns="http://www.wrox.com/webservices">
      <ReverseStringResult>!dlroW olleH</ReverseStringResult>
    </ReverseStringResponse>
  </soap:Body>
</soap:Envelope>
```

The SOAP specification is maintained by the XML Protocol Working Group of the W3C (www.w3.org/
TR/soap).

SOAP and Firewalls

System administrators often ask if the SOAP protocol breaks the security boundaries of the firewalls—
in other words, does SOAP violate the concept of firewalls? In reality, there are no more security issues
to consider than for normal Web servers. With normal Web server firewalls, the system administrator
opens HTTP port 80 to allow the server to communicate with the outside world. Users on the Internet
can have direct access to these servers even though they sit behind the firewall. A user can request an
HTML file with an HTTP request and the server returns either a static page, or a page created on the fly
using ASP or CGI scripts. Web services are just another type of server-side application that communi-
cates using HTTP, though instead of receiving simple HTTP GET or POST requests, it receives an HTTP
POST request containing an embedded SOAP message, and instead of returning HTML, it returns an
HTTP response containing the SOAP response message. As far as the firewall is concerned, the communication is through HTTP and hence it will be allowed through port 80.

However, if this Web service does not behave as it should, such as leaking confidential data or breaking
the server, then there is a problem, but such problems are common to all server-side applications whether
they be traditional Web pages, server-side business objects, or Web services.

If the firewall's system administrator is still worried about the security implications of Web services, he
or she can use an application filter to not allow SOAP calls with an HTTP request.

WS-I Basic Profile

The SOAP specification emerged over time. That's the reason why sometimes it is hard to get interaction with Web services from different vendors. To cover this issue, the Web Services Interoperability
Organization (http://ws-i.org) was formed. This organization defined the requirements for a Web
service with the WS-I Basic Profile specification.

You can read the WS-I Basic Profile specification at www.ws-i.org/Profiles/BasicProfile-1.1.html.

Web Services and the .NET Framework

With the .NET Framework, it is easy to create and consume Web services. The three major namespaces that deal with Web services are:

❑   The classes in the namespace `System.Web.Services` are used to create Web services.

❑   With the namespace `System.Web.Services.Description`, you can describe Web services via WSDL.

❑   With `System.Web.Services.Protocols` you can create SOAP requests and responses.

Creating a Web Service

To implement a Web service, you can derive the Web service class from `System.Web.Services.WebService`. The `WebService` class provides access to ASP.NET `Application` and `Session` objects. Using this class is optional, and you have to derive from it only if you need easy access to the properties the class offers.

WebService Property	Description
Application	Returns an `HttpApplicationState` object for the current request.
Context	Returns an `HttpContext` object that encapsulates HTTP specific information. With this context the HTTP header information can be read.
Server	Returns an `HttpServerUtility` object. This class has some helper methods to do URL encoding and decoding.
Session	Returns an `HttpSessionState` object to store some state for the client.
User	Returns a user object implementing the `IPrincipal` interface. With this interface, you can get the name of the user and the authentication type.
SoapVersion	Returns the SOAP version that is used with the Web service. The SOAP version is encapsulated in the enumeration `SoapProtocolVersion`.

When creating Web services with ASP.NET, it is not a requirement that they be derived from the base class `WebService`. *This base class is required only if you want to have easy access to the HTTP context with the properties of the* `WebService` *class.*

WebService Attribute

The subclass of `WebService` should be marked with the `WebService` attribute. The class `WebServiceAttribute` has the following properties:

Property	Description
Description	A description of the service that will be used in the WSDL document.
Name	Gets or sets the name of the Web service.
Namespace	Gets or sets the XML namespace for the Web service. The default value is http://tempuri.org, which is okay for testing, but before you make the service public you should change the namespace.

Attributes are covered in more detail in Chapter 27.

WebMethod Attribute

All methods available from the Web service must be marked with the WebMethod attribute. Of course, the service can have other methods that are not marked using WebMethod. Such methods can be called from the WebMethods, but they cannot be called from the client. With the attribute class WebMethodAttribute, the method will be callable from remote clients, and you can define whether the response is buffered, for how long the cache should be valid, and whether the session state should be stored with named parameters. The following table lists the properties of the WebMethodAttribute class.

Property	Description
BufferResponse	Gets or sets a flag indicating whether the response should be buffered. The default is true. With a buffered response, only the finished package is sent to the client.
CacheDuration	With this property you can set the length of time that the result should be cached. If the same request is made a second time, only the cached value will be returned if the request is made during the period set by this property. The default value is 0; which means that the result will not be cached.
Description	The description is used for the generation of service help pages for prospective consumers.
EnableSession	A Boolean value indicating whether the session state is valid. The default is false, so that the Session property of the WebService class cannot be used for storing session state.
MessageName	By default, the name of the message is set to the name of the method.
TransactionOption	This property indicates the transaction support for the method. The default value is Disabled.

WebServiceBinding Attribute

.NET 2.0 has a new attribute for Web services: WebServiceBinding. This attribute is used to mark the Web services interoperability conformance level of the Web service.

Property	Description
ConformanceClaims	The conformance level of the Web service can be set to a value of the WsiClaims enumeration. WsiClaims can have two values: BP10 when the Web service conforms to Basic Profile 1.0, or None when no conformance is defined.
EmitConformanceClaims	EmitConformanceClaims is a Boolean property that defines whether the conformance claims that are specified with the ConformanceClaims property should be transmitted to the generated WSDL documentation.
Name	With the Name property, the name of the binding can be defined. By default, the name is the same as the name of the Web services with the string Soap appended.
Location	The Location property defines the location of the binding information, for example http://www.wrox.com/DemoWebservice.asmx?wsdl.
Namespace	The Namespace property defines the XML namespace of the binding.

Client

To call a method, the client has to create an HTTP connection to the server of the Web service, and send an HTTP request to pass a SOAP message. The method call must be converted to a SOAP message. All this is done by the client proxy. The implementation of the client proxy is in the SoapHttpClientProtocol class.

SoapHttpClientProtocol

The class System.Web.Services.Protocols.SoapHttpClientProtocol is the base class for the client proxy. The Invoke() method converts the arguments to build a SOAP message that is sent to the Web service. Which Web service is called is defined with the Url property.

The SoapHttpClientProtocol class also supports asynchronous calls with the BeginInvoke() and EndInvoke() methods.

Alternative Client Protocols

Instead of using the SoapHttpClientProtocol class, other proxy classes can be used. HttpGetClientProtocol and HttpPostClientProtocol just do a simple HTTP GET or HTTP POST request without the overhead of a SOAP call.

> The HttpGetClientProtocol and HttpPostClientProtocol classes can be used if your solution uses .NET on the client and the server. If you want to support different technologies, you have to use the SOAP protocol.

Compare the HTTP POST request below with the SOAP call you saw earlier in this chapter:

```
POST /WebServiceSample/Service1.asmx/ReverseString HTTP/1.1
Host: localhost
Content-Type: application/x-www-form-urlencoded
Content-Length: length

message=string
```

The HTTP GET request is even shorter. The disadvantage of the GET request is that the size of the parameters sent is limited. If the size goes beyond 1K, you should consider using POST:

```
GET /WebServiceSample/Service1.asmx/ReverseString?message=string HTTP/1.1
Host: localhost
```

The overhead of the HttpGetClientProtocol and the HttpPostClientProtocol is smaller than that of SOAP methods; the disadvantage here is that there is no support from Web services on other platforms and no support for sending anything other than simple data.

Creating a Simple ASP.NET Web Service

In the following Try It Out, you create a simple Web service with Visual Studio.

Try It Out   Creating a Web Service Project

1.   Create a new Web Service with File ⇨ New ⇨ Web Site..., choose the ASP.NET Web Service template as shown in Figure 20-8, name the project WebServiceSample, and click the OK button.

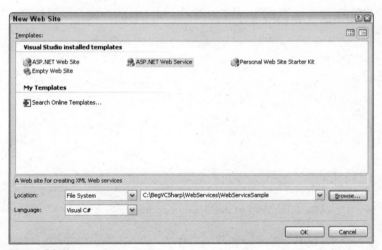

Figure 20-8

Generated Files

The files generated by the wizard are listed here:

❑   `Service.asmx` holds your Web service class. All ASP.NET Web services are identified with the `.asmx` extension. The file that has the source code is `Service.cs`, as the code-beside feature is used with Visual Studio 2005. This file can be found in the `App_Code` directory.

❑   The wizard generates a class `Service` that derives from `System.Web.Services.WebService`. In the `Service.cs` file, you can also see some sample code showing how a method for a Web service should be coded — it should be public and marked with the `WebMethod` attribute:

```
using System.Web;
using System.Web.Services;
using System.Web.Services.Protocols;

[WebService(Namespace = http://tempuri.org)]
[WebServiceBinding(ConformsTo=WsiProfile.BasicProfile1_1)]
public class Service : System.Web.Services.WebService
{
    [WebMethod]
    public string HelloWorld()
    {
      return "Hello World";
    }
}
```

Adding a Web Method

The next thing you should do is add a custom method to your Web service. In the following Try It Out, you add a simple method `ReverseString()` that receives a string and returns the reversed string to the client.

Try It Out   Adding a Method

1.   Remove the method `HelloWorld()` with the complete implementation. Add the following code to the file `Service.cs`:

```
[WebMethod]
public string ReverseString(string message)
{
    char[] arr = message.ToCharArray();
    Array.Reverse(arr);
    message = new string(arr);

    return message;
}
```

To use the `Array` class, you must import the `System` namespace.

To uniquely identify the XML elements in the generated description of the Web service, a namespace should be added. Add the `WebService` attribute with the namespace `http://www.wrox.com/webservices` to the class `Service`. Of course, you can use any other string that uniquely identifies the XML elements. You can use the URL link to your company's page. It is not necessary that the Web link really exist; it is just used for unique identification. If you use a namespace based on your company's Web address, you can almost guarantee that no other company is using the very same namespace.

If you don't change the namespace, the default namespace used is `http://tempuri.org`. For learning purposes, this default namespace is good enough, but you shouldn't deploy a production Web service using it.

2. So, modify the example code as follows:

```
[WebService(Namespace="http://www.wrox.com/webservices")]
[WebServiceBinding(ConformsTo=WsiProfile.BasicProfile1_1)]
public class Service : System.Web.Services.WebService
{
```

3. Now compile the project.

Testing the Web Service

Now, you can test the service. Opening the file `Service1.asmx` in the browser (you can start it from within Visual Studio 2005 by going to Debug ⇨ Start Without Debugging) lists all methods of the service, as can be seen in Figure 20-9. In your service the only method is `ReverseString()`.

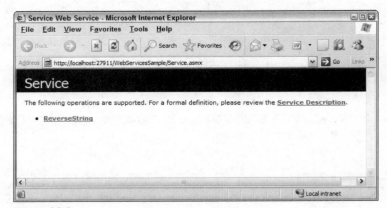

Figure 20-9

When you choose the link to the `ReverseString` method, you see a dialog to test the Web service. The test dialog has edit fields for every parameter you can pass with this method; here it is only a single parameter.

In this page, you also get information about what the SOAP calls from the client and the responses from the server will look like (see Figure 20-10). The examples show SOAP and HTTP `POST` requests.

Pressing the Invoke button after entering the string `Hello Web Services!` into the text box, you receive the result from the server shown in Figure 20-11.

The result is of type `string`, and, as expected, it is the reverse of the entered string.

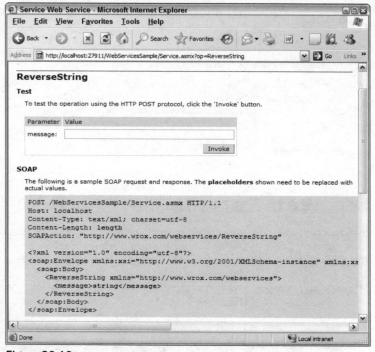

Figure 20-10

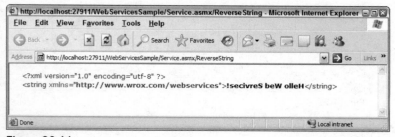

Figure 20-11

Implementing a Windows Client

The test is working, but you want to create a Windows client that uses the Web service. The client must create a SOAP message that will be sent across an HTTP channel. It is not necessary to make this message ourselves. The `System.Web.Services.Protocols.SoapHttpClientProtocol` class does all the work behind the scenes.

Try It Out   Creating a Client Windows Application

1. Create a new C# Windows Application, call it `SimpleClient`, and add two text boxes and a button to the form (see Figure 20-12). You will use the button's `Click` handler to invoke the Web service.

Figure 20-12

2. Add a Web reference using the Project ⇨ Add Web Reference... menu and enter the URL of the Web service that was just generated. Then, you can view the contract and documentation. Before pressing the Add Reference button, change the Web reference name to `WebServicesSample`, as shown in Figure 20-13.

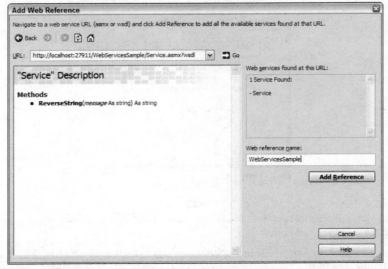

Figure 20-13

3. In the Solution Explorer you can now see a new Web Reference, `WebServicesSample`. When you click the Show All Files button, you can see the WSDL document and the file `reference.cs` that includes the source code of the proxy (see Figure 20-14).

671

Figure 20-14

What the Solution Explorer shows only when the Show All Files button is clicked can be shown more easily in the Class View (the new class that implements the client proxy). This class converts method calls to the SOAP format. In Class View (see Figure 20-15), you will find a new namespace with the name that was defined with the Web Reference name. In this case, `WebServicesSample` was created. The class `Service` derives from `SoapHttpClientProtocol` and implements the method of the Web service, `ReverseString()`.

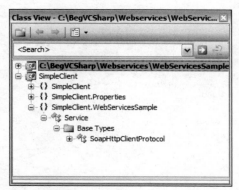

Figure 20-15

Double-click the `Service` class to open the auto-generated `reference.cs` file. Let's look into this wizard-generated code.

The `Service` class derives from the `SoapHttpClientProtocol` class. This base class creates a SOAP message in the `Invoke()` method. The `WebServiceBindingAttribute` attribute sets binding values to the Web service:

```
[System.Diagnostics.DebuggerStepThroughAttribute()]
[System.ComponentModel.DesignerCategoryAttribute("code")]
[System.Web.Services.WebServiceBindingAttribute(Name="ServiceSoap",
   Namespace="http://www.wrox.com/webservices")]
public partial class Service :
   System.Web.Services.Protocols.SoapHttpClientProtocol {
```

In the constructor, the `Url` property is set to the Web service. This property will be used from the `SoapHttpClientProtocol` class to request a service:

```
public Service() {
    this.Url =
SimpleClient.Properties.Settings.Default.SimpleClient_WebServicesSample_Service;
}
```

The most important method is the method that the Web service supplies: `ReverseString()`. The method here has the same parameter that you implemented on the server. The implementation of the client-side version of `ReverseString()` calls the `Invoke()` method of the base class `SoapHttpClientProtocol`. `Invoke()` creates a SOAP message using the method name `ReverseString` and the parameter `message`:

```
[System.Web.Services.Protocols.SoapDocumentMethodAttribute(
    "http://www.wrox.com/webservices/ReverseString",
    RequestNamespace="http://www.wrox.com/webservices",
    ResponseNamespace="http://www.wrox.com/webservices",
    Use=System.Web.Services.Description.SoapBindingUse.Literal,
    ParameterStyle=
        System.Web.Services.Protocols.SoapParameterStyle.Wrapped)]
public string ReverseString(string message) {
    object[] results = this.Invoke("ReverseString", new object[]
        { message});
    return ((string)(results[0]));
}
```

Until now you have not written a single line of code for the client. You designed a small user interface, and used the Add Web Reference menu to create a proxy class. Now you just have to create the link between the two.

4. Add a `Click` event handler to the button and add these two lines of code:

```
private void button1_Click(object sender, EventArgs e)
{
    WebServicesSample.Service ws = new WebServicesSample.Service();
    textBox2.Text = ws.ReverseString(textBox1.Text);
}
```

How It Works

With the following line, you create a new instance of the proxy class. As you saw in the implementation of the constructor, the `Url` property is set to the Web service:

```
    WebServicesSample.Service ws = new WebServicesSample.Service();
```

As a result of calling the `ReverseString()` method of the proxy class, a SOAP message is sent to the server, and so the Web service is called:

```
    textBox2.Text = ws.ReverseString(textBox1.Text);
```

Running the program produces output like that shown in Figure 20-16.

Figure 20-16

Calling the Service Asynchronously

When you send a message across the network, you always have to be aware of the network latency. If the Web service is invoked synchronously, the client application is blocked until the call returns. This may be fast enough in a local network; however, you must pay attention to the production system's network infrastructure.

You can send messages to the Web service asynchronously. The client proxy creates not only synchronous methods but also asynchronous methods. However, there's a special issue with Windows applications. Because every Windows control is bound to a single thread, methods, and properties of Windows controls may only be called from within the creation thread. The proxy class of .NET 2.0 has some special features for this issue as you can see with the generated proxy code.

Here you can see the asynchronous version of the method `ReverseString()`. With the asynchronous implementation of the proxy class, there's always a method that can be invoked asynchronously, and an event where you can define what method should be invoked when the Web service method is finished. Let's get into this with more detail. The method `ReverseStringAsync()` only has the parameters that are sent to the server. The data that are received from the client can be read by assigning an event handler to the event `ReverseStringCompleted`. This event is of type `ReverseStringCompletedEventHandler`. `ReverseStringCompletedEventHandler` is a delegate where the second parameter (`ReverseStringCompletedEventArgs`) is created from the input parameters of the `ReverseString()` method. The class `ReverseStringCompletedEventArgs` contains the return data from the Web service in the `Result` property. Why this implementation works is with the `SendOrPostCallback` delegate. This delegate forwards the call to the correct thread of the Windows Forms control.

```
public event ReverseStringCompletedEventHandler ReverseStringCompleted;

public void ReverseStringAsync(string message) {
    this.ReverseStringAsync(message, null);
}

public void ReverseStringAsync(string message, object userState) {
    if ((this.ReverseStringOperationCompleted == null)) {
        this.ReverseStringOperationCompleted =
            new System.Threading.SendOrPostCallback(
```

```
                    this.OnReverseStringOperationCompleted);
        }
        this.InvokeAsync("ReverseString", new object[] {
            message), this.ReverseStringOperationCompleted, userState);
}

public void OnReverseStringOperationCompleted(object arg) {
    if ((this.ReverseStringCompleted != null)) {
        System.Web.Services.Protocols.InvokeCompledtedEventArgs invokeArgs =
            ((System.Web.Services.Protocols.InvokeCompletedEventArgs)(arg));
        this.ReverseStringCompleted(this,
            new ReverseStringCompletedEventArgs(invokeArgs.Results,
                invokeArgs.Error, invokeArgs.Cancelled, invokeArgs.UserState);
    }
}

public delegate void ReverseStringCompletedEventHandler(object sender,
    ReverseStringCompletedEventArgs e);

public partial class ReverseStringCompletedEvenArgs :
    System.ComponentModel.AsyncCompletedEventArgs
{
    private object[] results;

    internal ReverseStringCompletedEventArgs(object[] results,
        System.Exception exception, bool cancelled, object userState) :
        base(exception, cancelled, userState) {
        this.results = results;
    }

    public string Result
    {
        get {
            this.RaiseExceptionIfNecessary();
            return ((string)(ths.results[0]));
        }
    }
}
```

Now let's use the asynchronous implementation of the proxy class.

1. Create a handler method with the name `WebServicesResult` that has the same signature as is defined by the delegate `ReverseStringCompletedEventHandler`. This method will be invoked when the Web service call is completed. With the implementation the `Result` property of the `ReverseStringComletedEventArgs` parameter is passed to the `Text` property of `textBox2`:

```
private void WebServicesResult(object sender,
    WebServicesSample.ReverseStringCompletedEventArgs e)
{
    textBox2.Text = e.Result;
}
```

2. To invoke the Web service asynchronously, change the implementation of the method `button1_Click`. After the proxy is instantiated, add the previous created method `WebServicesResult` to the event `ReverseStringCompleted`. Next you can invoke the asynchronous method of the proxy `ReverseStringAsync`, and pass the `Text` property from `textBox1`. With the asnyc method a thread is created that does the call to the Web service.

```
private void button1_Click(object sender, EventArgs e)
{
    // asynchronous version
    WebServicesSample.Service ws = new WebServicesSample.Service();
    ws.ReverseStringCompleted += WebServicesresult;
    ws.ReverseStringAsync(textBox1.Text);
}
```

Now you can run the client once more. You can also add a sleep interval to the Web service implementation, so you can see that the UI of the client application is not stalled while the Web service is invoked.

Implementing an ASP.NET Client

The same service now can be used from an ASP.NET Client application. Referencing the Web service can be done the same way as with the Windows application.

Creating an ASP.NET Client Application

1. Create a new C# ASP.NET Website, call it `ASPNETClient`, and add two text boxes and a button to the Web form, as shown in Figure 20-17.

Figure 20-17

2. Add a Web reference to `http://localhost/webservicesample/service.asmx` in the same way you did with the Windows application.

3. With the Web reference added, a client proxy class was again generated. Add a click handler to the button and write the following lines of code for this handler:

```
private void Button1_Click(object sender, System.EventArgs e)
{
    WebServicesSample.Service ws =
        new WebServicesSample.Service();
    TextBox2.Text = ws.ReverseString(TextBox1.Text);
}
```

4. Now build the project and with Debug ⇨ Start, you can start the browser and enter a test message in the first text box. When you press the button, the Web service is invoked, and you get the reversed message returned in the second text box, as shown in Figure 20-18. With a multi-project solution, you have to set the startup project to the project you want started.

Figure 20-18

As you have just seen, using Web services is as easy in Web applications as it is in Windows applications!

Passing Data

With the simple Web service developed earlier only a simple string has been passed to the Web service. Now you are going to add a method where weather information is requested from the Web service. This information requires more complex data to be sent to and from the Web service.

Try It Out   **Creating Passing Data with a Web Service**

1. Open the previously created Web service project using Visual Studio. With this Web service, define the `GetWeatherRequest` and `GetWeatherResponse` classes that define the documents to be sent to and from the Web service. The enumerations `TemperatureType` and `TemperatureCondition` are used within these classes.

ASP.NET Web services use XML serialization to convert objects to an XML representation. You can use attributes from the namespace `System.Xml.Serialization` to influence how the generated XML format should look. (You can read more about XML serialization in Chapter 23.)

```
public enum TemperatureType
{
   Fahrenheit,
   Celsius
}

public enum TemparatureCondition
{
```

```
    Rainy,
    Sunny,
    Cloudy,
    Thunderstorm
}

public class GetWeatherRequest
{
    public string City;
    public TemperatureType TemperatureType;
}

public class GetWeatherResponse
{
    public TemparatureCondition Condition;
    public int Temperature;
}
```

2. Add the Web service method `GetWeather()`. This method receives the data defined with `GetWeatherRequest` and returns data defined with `GetWeatherResponse`. Within the implementation a random weather condition is returned — with the exception of the home of Microsoft, Redmond, where it rains all week. For random weather generation, the class `Random` from the `System` namespace is used.

```
[WebMethod]
public GetWeatherResponse GetWeather(GetWeatherRequest req)
{
    GetWeatherResponse resp = new GetWeatherResponse();
    Random r = new Random();
    int celsius = r.Next(-20, 50);

    if (req.TemperatureType == TemperatureType.Celsius)
        resp.Temperature = celsius;
    else
        resp.Temperature = (212-32)/100 * celsius + 32;

    if (req.City == "Redmond")
        resp.Condition = TemparatureCondition.Rainy;
    else
        resp.Condition = (TemparatureCondition)r.Next(0, 3);

    return resp;
}
```

3. After building the Web service, create a new project of type using the Windows Forms template and name the application `WeatherClient`.

4. Modify the main dialog like that shown in Figure 20-19. The control embeds two radio buttons where the temperature type (Celsius or Fahrenheit) can be selected, and the city can be entered. Clicking the Get Weather button will invoke the Web service, where the result of the Web service is shown in the Weather Condition and the Temperature text box controls.

Figure 20-19

The controls with their names and the value for the Text property are listed in this table:

Control	Name	Text Property
RadioButton	radioButtonCelsius	Celsius
RadioButton	radioButtonFahrenheit	Fahrenheit
Button	buttonGetWeather	Get Weather
Label	labelWeatherCondition	
TextBox	textCity	
TextBox	textWeatherCondition	
TextBox	textTemperature	
Label	labelCity	City
Label	labelWeatherCondition	Weather Condition
Label	labelTemperature	Temperature
GroupBox	groupBox1	

5. Add a reference to the Web service, similar to how it was done with the earlier client application projects. Name the reference WeatherService.

6. Import the namespace WeatherClient.WeatherService with the client application.

7. Add a Click event handler to the button buttonGetWeather with the name OnGetWeather using the Property dialog of the button.

8. Add the implementation to the OnGetWeather() method as shown. First a GetWeatherRequest object is created that defines the request sent to the Web service. The Web service is invoked by

calling the `GetWeather()` method. This method returns a `GetWeatherResponse` object with values that are read for display in the user interface.

```csharp
private void OnGetWeather(object sender, EventArgs e)
{
    GetWeatherRequest req = new GetWeatherRequest();
    if (radioButtonCelsius.Checked)
        req.TemperatureType = TemperatureType.Celsius;
    else
        req.TemperatureType = TemperatureType.Fahrenheit;
    req.City = textCity.Text;

    Service ws = new Service();

    GetWeatherResponse resp = ws.GetWeather(req);

    textWeatherCondition.Text = resp.Condition.ToString();
    textTemperature.Text = resp.Temperature.ToString();
}
```

9. Start the client application. Enter a city and click the Get Weather button. If you are lucky, the real weather is shown (see Figure 20-20).

Figure 20-20

Summary

In this chapter you saw what Web services are, and you briefly looked at the protocols used with them. To locate and run Web services, you have to use some or all of the following:

❑ **Directory:** Find a Web service by UDDI.

❑ **Description:** WSDL describes the methods and arguments.

❑ **Calling:** Platform-independent method calls are done with the SOAP protocol.

You have seen how easy it is to create Web services with Visual Studio 2005, where the `WebService` class is used to define some methods with the `WebMethod` attribute. Creating the client that consumes Web services is as easy as creating Web services — you add a Web reference to the client project and use the proxy. The heart of the client is the `SoapHttpClientProtocol` class that converts the method call to a SOAP message. The client proxy you created offers both asynchronous and synchronous methods. The client interface is not blocked when you use asynchronous methods until the Web service method completes. You have seen how to create custom classes that define the data passed when you want to transfer more than simple data. The next chapter shows how Web applications and Web services can be deployed.

Exercises

The following exercises help you use the knowledge you gained in this chapter to create a new Web service that offers a seat reservation system for a cinema.

1. Create a new Web service named `CinemaReservation`.

2. The `ReserveSeatRequest` and `ReserveSeatResponse` classes are needed to define the data sent to and from the Web service. The `ReserveSeatRequest` class needs a member `Name` of type `string` to send a name and two members of type `int` to send a request for a seat defined with `Row` and `Seat`. The class `ReserveSeatResponse` defines the data to be sent back to the client — that is, the name for the reservation and the seat that is really reserved.

3. Create a Web method `ReserveSeat` that requires a `ReserveSeatRequest` as a parameter and returns a `ReserveSeatResponse`. Within the implementation of the Web service, you can use a `Cache` object (see Chapter 18) to remember the seats that already have been reserved. If the seat that is requested is available, return the seat and reserve it in the `Cache` object. If it is not available, take the next free seat. For the seats in the `Cache` object you can use a two-dimensional array, as was shown in Chapter 5.

4. Create a Windows client application that uses the Web service to reserve a seat in the cinema.

21

Deploying Web Applications

In the previous three chapters you learned to develop Web applications and Web services with ASP.NET. For all these application types, different deployment options exist. You can copy the Web pages, publish the Website, or create an installation program. This chapter covers the advantages and disadvantages of the different options, and how to accomplish these tasks.

In this chapter, you learn about:

- ❑ Internet Information Services
- ❑ IIS configuration
- ❑ Copy Websites
- ❑ Precompiling Websites
- ❑ Windows Installer

Internet Information Services

Internet Information Services (IIS) needn't be installed for developing Web applications with Visual Studio 2005 because Studio 2005 has its own Web server: the Visual Web Developer Web Server. This is a simple Web server that runs only on the local machine. On the production system, IIS is needed to run the Web application.

Now look at how IIS and ASP.NET fit together. Figure 21-1 shows Windows XP's process model. IIS is running in the `inetinfo.exe` process. This process has an ISAPI extension for ASP.NET that uses configured file extensions to pass requests from the client to the ASP.NET process `aspnet_wp.exe`. By default, IIS's processes run with System account privileges, while the ASP.NET runtime runs with the nonprivileged user *aspnet*.

An ISAPI extension is a DLL that is running in the process of the Web server.

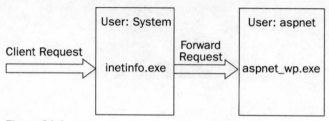

Figure 21-1

Figure 21-2 shows the IIS file configuration for referencing the ASP.NET runtime. Each ASP.NET file extension is configured to a specific version of the ASP.NET runtime. Different Websites can use different versions of the runtime. Later, you see how to configure a specific runtime for a Website.

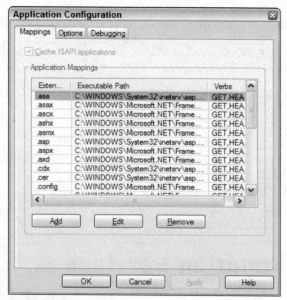

Figure 21-2

The process model for a Web application running with Windows Server 2003 looks different. Windows Server 2003 has IIS version 6, while Windows XP is delivered with IIS version 5. Version 5 of IIS was available before ASP.NET. Windows Server 2003 is delivered with .NET 1.1, so ASP.NET is better integrated.

Figure 21-3 shows the IIS 6 process model. With IIS 6, application domains can be configured so that different worker processes (`w3wp.exe`) can be configured for different Web applications. As before, `inetinfo.exe` forwards the request to an ASP.NET page to a worker process. Using multiple worker processes has the advantage of better scalability, and it is also possible that every worker process runs with a different user identity.

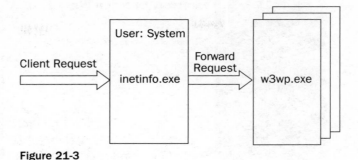

Figure 21-3

IIS Configuration

IIS must be configured before you run a Web application with it. In the following Try It Out, you create a Website with the Internet Information Services Admin tool. To begin, your Website needs a virtual directory, which is the directory used by the client accessing the Web application. For example, `http://server/mydirectory`, `mydirectory` is a virtual directory. The virtual directory is completely independent of the physical directory where the files are stored on the disk. For example, the physical directory for `mydirectory` can be `d:\someotherdirectory`.

To configure a Website with IIS, you first have to create a new virtual directory, which you do in the following Try It Out.

Try It Out   **Create a New Website**

1.   Start the Internet Information Services Admin tool. You can find this tool in the Control Panel, in Administrative Tools.

2.   Open the Default Web Site in the tree view of the IIS tool.

3.   Select the menu Action ⇨ New ⇨ Virtual Directory.... The Virtual Directory Creation Wizard starts (see Figure 21-4).

4.   After clicking the Next button, you can select the name for the virtual directory (see Figure 21-5). Enter the name **BegVCSharpWebsite** in the Alias text box. This is how the directory is accessed from the browser (`http://servername/BegVCSharpWebsite`). Click the Next button.

5.   In the next dialog (see Figure 21-6), you can select the physical directory that is referenced by the virtual directory's name. Select an empty directory for the Website. You can also create a new directory. If you click the Browse button, you will find the button Make New Folder to create a new physical directory.

Figure 21-4

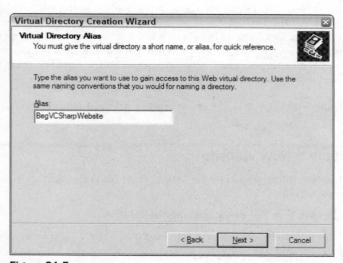

Figure 21-5

6. You configure the access permissions with the dialog shown in Figure 21-7. For ASP.NET applications, permissions for reading and running scripts are usually enough. Write permission allows users to write files to the Website. If want users to be able to upload files to the Website, you should configure a separate directory where users have write permissions. If Browse is enabled, the user gets a listing of the files on the directory.

7. Click the Next button, read the configuration summary, and click the Finish button.

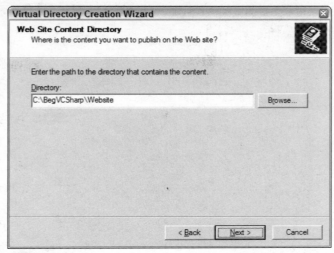

Figure 21-6

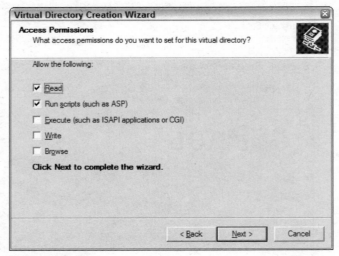

Figure 21-7

8. After the Virtual Directory is created, you can see the properties of the Website. Select BegVCSharpWebsite in the tree view of the IIS Admin tool. You might have to refresh the view before this virtual directory shows up. Then select the menu options Action ⇨ Properties. You can see the virtual directory configuration (shown in Figure 21-8).

9. Select the ASP.NET tab in this configuration (see Figure 21-9). Here you have to configure the version of the ASP.NET runtime that should be used for the Website.

Now the virtual directory is configured, and it is possible to copy or publish the Web application to this Website.

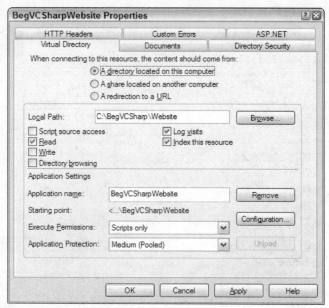

Figure 21-8

Figure 21-9

Copying a Web Site

With Visual Studio 2005, you can copy files from a source Website to a remote Website. The source Website is the Website of your Web application that has been opened with Visual Studio. This Website is accessed either from the local file system or from IIS—depending on how the Web application was created. The remote Website to which the files should be copied can be accessed using the file system, the FTP protocol, or FrontPage Server Extensions on IIS.

Copying files can happen in both directions: from the source Website to the remote Website and vice versa.

In the next Try It Out, you use Visual Studio to copy the Web application from Chapter 19 to the Website you configured earlier.

Try It Out   Copy a Web Site

1. Open the Web application from Chapter 19.
2. Select the menu options Website ⇨ Copy Web Site. The dialog shown in Figure 21-10 will appear.

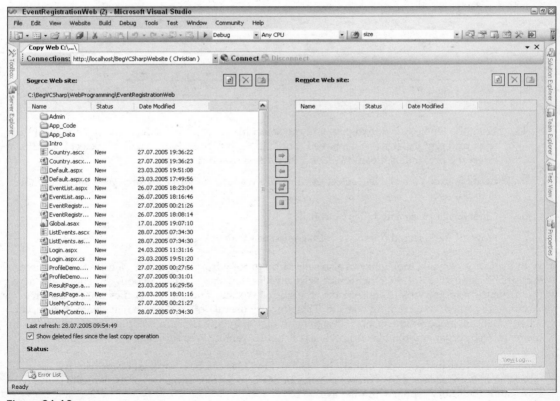

Figure 21-10

3. Select the button Connect to a remote site that is located next to the Connect to drop-down list. The dialog in Figure 21-11 appears.

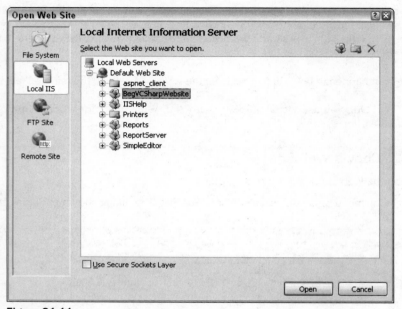

Figure 21-11

4. From the Open Web Site dialog, you can select files to copy to the local file system, local IIS, FTP sites, and remote sites (which have FrontPage Server Extensions installed). Select Local IIS, and select the previously created Website, BegVCSharpWebsite.

5. In the Source Web site list, select the files you want to copy from Source Web Site to Remote Web Site.

6. Click the Copy selected files button.

7. Now all the selected files have been copied to the new Website.

With the Copy Web Site tool, you can also select files to copy from the remote Website to the source Website. Selecting the button Synchronize selected files that shows errors in both directions, the newer files from the remote Website are copied to the source Website, and the newer files from the source Website are copied to the remote Website. This is a very useful option if you have a team Web server where other developers synchronize files. Synchronizing in both directions copies your newer files to the team Web server and the files from your colleagues' remote Web server to your local site.

When the files are just copied, you cannot be sure if the files can be compiled. Compilation happens when the files are accessed by a browser. You can perform a precompilation of the Website using the command-line utility aspnet_compiler.exe.

If you start the command

```
aspnet_compiler -v /BegVCSharpWebsite
```

the Website BegVCSharpWebsite is precompiled. This way the first user doesn't have to wait until the ASPX pages are compiled as they already are.

You can find this utility in the directory of the .NET runtime.

Precompiling a Web Site

Instead of copying all files to the target Website, you can precompile the Website. With precompiling, the assemblies are created before the files are copied to the target Website. This way, source files are not copied to the target Website.

In the next Try It Out, you publish the Web application from Chapter 19 using Visual Studio.

Try It Out   **Precompiling a Website for Deployment**

1. Open the Web application from Chapter 19 with Visual Studio.

2. Start the Visual Studio 2005 command prompt.

3. Create a new directory for the precompiled Website, e.g., `c:/precompiledWeb`.

4. In the Visual Studio command prompt enter this command:

```
aspnet_compiler -p c:/BegVCSharp/WebProgramming/EventRegistrationWeb
    -v / c:/precompiledWeb
```

The option -p references the physical path of the source files from the Website that should be precompiled. The option -v / specifies how root references within the Web pages should be resolved. The last option c:/precompiledWeb specifies the target path where the precompiled files should be stored.

5. After the publishing is completed, check the created files on the target site. You will find ASXP files, but when you check the content of these files, you'll find only this text:

```
This is a marker file generated by the precompilation tool,
and should not be deleted!
```

You can find the generated assemblies in the `bin` directory. The `bin` directory contains XML files (with the extension .compiled) that map the ASPX files to assemblies. Each Web page will have one assembly with the file extension `.dll`.

> **Precompiling Websites has the advantage that the source files are not copied to the target Website, which means that the Web administrator cannot change the source files on the server.**

Windows Installer

You can also create a Windows installer program to install the Web application. Creating installation programs is required if shared assemblies are needed by the Web application. Also, using installation programs has the advantage that the virtual directory is configured with IIS, and you're not required to create a virtual directory manually. The person installing the Web application can start a setup.exe program, and the complete setup is done automatically. Of course, administrative privileges are required to start this program.

Shared assemblies are discussed in Chapter 26.

Creating a Setup Program

Visual Studio 2005 ships with the project type Web Setup Project to create installation programs for Web applications. With the Web Setup Project, the following editors are available: File System, Registry, File Types, User Interface, and Custom Action and Launch Conditions. Not all these editors will be discussed here — this already has been done in Chapter 17 with Windows applications. Only the tasks needed for Web applications are shown.

In the next Try It Out, you create a setup program that installs a Web application.

Try It Out   **Create a Setup Program**

1.   Open the Web application from Chapter 19 using Visual Studio 2005.

2.   Add a new project of type Web Setup Project, as shown in Figure 21-12. Name the project **EventRegistrationWeb**. Click the OK button.

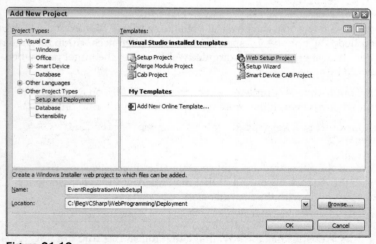

Figure 21-12

3. After you click the OK button, the file system editor is displayed. Select File System on Target Machine, and select the menu Project ⇨ Add ⇨ Project Output. From the Project Output dialog, select Content Files of the Web application and click the OK button.

4. In the file system editor, select Web Application Folder. You can now configure the Web application with the properties editor. The table below shows the properties and their descriptions.

Web Application Folder Property	Description
`AllowDirectoryBrowsing`	`AllowDirectoryBrowsing` is one of the options discussed in the IIS configuration section earlier in the chapter (see Figure 21-7). Setting this option to `true` allows browsing for files on the Website. The default value is `false`.
`AllowReadAccess`	This option is set by default to `true`. To access ASPX pages, read access is required.
`AllowScriptSourceAccess`	By default, script source access is denied with the `AllowScriptSourceAccess` property set to `false`.
`AllowWriteAccess`	Write access is denied by default.
`DefaultDocument`	The `DefaultDocument` property sets the home page of the Website, for example `Default.aspx`.
`ExecutePermissions`	The default value of `ExecutePermissions` is set to `vsdepScriptsOnly`, which allows access to ASP.NET pages, but does not allow custom executables to run on the server. If custom executables should be allowed to run on the server, this option can be set to `vsdepScriptsAndExecutables`.
`LogVisits`	With `LogVisits` set to `true`, client access logging is configured.
`VirtualDirectory`	With this property, you can set the name of the virtual directory that is configured with IIS.

5. Open the Launch Conditions editor with the menu View ⇨ Editor ⇨ Launch Conditions. Launch conditions define what products must be installed on the target system before the installation can be done.

6. Check the launch conditions that are configured. The Search for IIS configuration verifies if IIS is installed on the target system by checking the registry key `SYSTEM\CurrentControlSet\Services\W3SVC\Parameters` to get the IIS version. The launch condition IIS Condition checks that the IIS version is at least 4. For ASP.NET 2.0 Web applications, you can change this value to 5 to require at least IIS 5.

7. Build the setup application by selecting the menu Build ⇨ Build EventRegistrationWebSetup.

8. In the directory of the setup project you will find the `setup.exe` file and an installation package named `EventRegistrationWebSetup.msi`.

Installing the Web Application

By starting the setup.exe program, you can install the Web application.

Try It Out   **Installing a Web Application**

1.   Click setup.exe to start installing the Web application. The Web Setup Wizard will display the dialog shown in Figure 21-13.

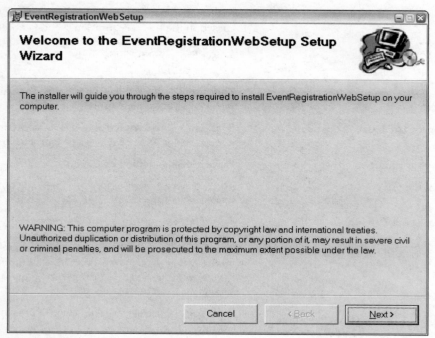

Figure 21-13

2.   Click the Next button. With the second dialog (see Figure 21-14) you can select the installation address. Rename the Virtual directory to a name that's not already configured with IIS.

3.   Click the Next button. At the Confirm Installation dialog, you can confirm the installation by clicking the Next button (see Figure 21-15).

4.   While the installation is running, a progress bar is shown (see Figure 21-16).

5.   After a successful installation, you see the Installation Complete dialog (see Figure 21-17). Click the Close button.

6.   Now you can start the Website from the new virtual directory.

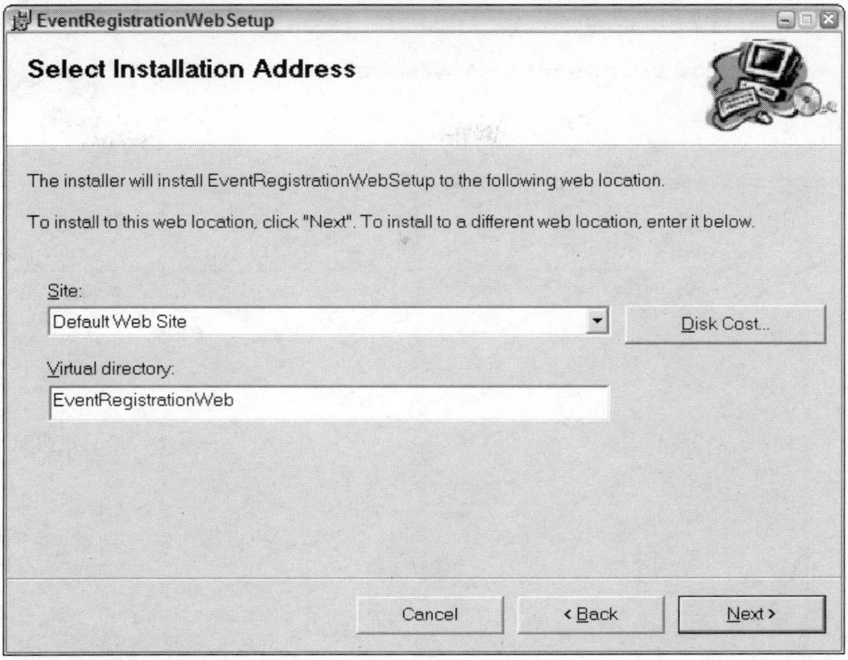

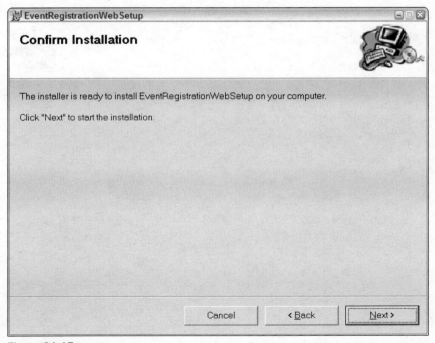

Figure 21-14

Figure 21-15

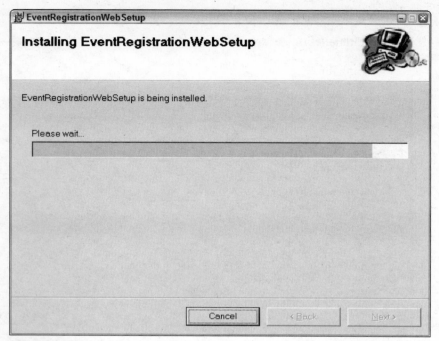

Figure 21-16

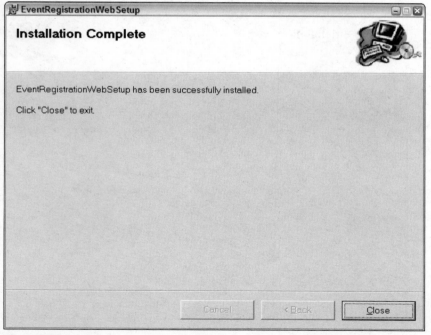

Figure 21-17

Summary

In this chapter, you saw different options for deploying Web applications. The Copy Web Site tool enables you to copy files to Web servers by using file shares, FTP, or FrontPage Server Extensions. Synchronization of files can happen in both directions. Publishing Websites is a new feature where just the assemblies are deployed to existing virtual directories. The Web administrator no longer has access to the sources. Finally, creating a setup project not only copies the ASP.NET pages and assemblies, but also creates a virtual directory with IIS.

In this chapter, you learned

❑   How to create a new Virtual Directory with IIS

❑   How to copy a Web Site with Visual Studio

❑   How to publish a Web Site with Visual Studio

❑   How to create a Setup Program for the installation of a Web application

The exercises following ask questions about topics you've learned with this chapter.

The next chapter is the first chapter in a series that deals with data access, starting with the file system.

Exercises

1.   What is the difference between copying and precompiling a Web application? When should you use what?

2.   When is using a Setup program preferred compared copying a site?

3.   What must be done before a Website can be published?

4.   Publish the Web service from Chapter 20 to a virtual directory that you define with IIS.

Part IV
Data Access

File System Data

In this chapter, you learn how to read and write files, an essential aspect of many .NET applications. You touch on the major classes used to create, read from, and write to files, and the supporting classes used to manipulate the file system from C# code. Although you won't cover all of the classes in detail, this chapter will go into enough depth to give you a good idea of the concepts and fundamentals.

Files can be a great way to store data between instances of your application, or they can be used to transfer data between applications. User and application configuration settings can be stored to be retrieved the next time your application is run. Delimited text files, such as comma-separated files, are used by many legacy systems, and to interoperate with such systems you will need to know how to work with delimited data. As you will see, the .NET Framework provides you with the tools to use files effectively in your applications.

By the end of this chapter, you will have learned:

- ❏ What a stream is and how .NET uses stream classes to access files
- ❏ How to use the `File` object to manipulate the file structure
- ❏ How to write to a file
- ❏ How to read from a file
- ❏ How to read and write formatted data from and to files
- ❏ How to read and write compressed files
- ❏ How to serialize and deserialize objects
- ❏ How to monitor files and directories for changes

Streams

All input and output in the .NET Framework involves the use of *streams*. A stream is an abstract representation of a *serial device*. A serial device is something that stores data in a linear manner and is accessed the same way: 1 byte at a time. This device can be a disk file, a network channel, a memory location, or any other object that supports reading and writing to it in a linear manner. Keeping the device abstract means that the underlying destination/source of the stream can be hidden. This level of abstraction enables code reuse and allows you to write more generic routines, since you don't have to worry about the specifics of how data transfer actually occurs. Therefore, similar code can be transferred and reused when the application is reading from a file input stream, a network input stream, or any other kind of stream. Because you can ignore the physical mechanics of each device, you don't need to worry about, for example, hard disk heads or memory allocation when dealing with a file stream.

There are two types of stream:

- **Output streams:** These are used when data is written to some external destination. This can be a physical disk file, a network location, a printer, or another program. Understanding stream programming opens many advanced possibilities. In this chapter, you are concentrating on file system data, so you'll only be looking at writing to disk files.

- **Input streams:** These are used to read data into memory or variables that your program can access. The most common form of input stream you have worked with so far is the keyboard. An input stream can come from almost any source, but in this chapter you concentrate on reading disk files. The concepts applied to reading/writing disk files will apply to most devices, so you'll gain a basic understanding of streams and see a proven approach that can be applied to many situations.

The Classes for Input and Output

The `System.IO` namespace contains almost all of the classes that you will be covering in this chapter. `System.IO` contains the classes for reading and writing data to and from files, and you must reference this namespace in your C# application to gain access to these classes. There are quite a few classes contained in `System.IO`, as you can see in Figure 22-1, but you will only be covering the primary classes needed for file input and output.

The classes you look at in this chapter are:

- `File`: A static utility class that exposes many static methods for moving, copying, and deleting files.

- `Directory`: A static utility class that exposes many static methods for moving, copying, and deleting directories.

- `Path`: A utility class used to manipulate path names.

- `FileInfo`: Represents a physical file on disk, and has methods to manipulate this file. For any reading and writing to the file, a `Stream` object must be created.

- `DirectoryInfo`: Represents a physical directory on disk and has methods to manipulate this directory.

- `FileSystemInfo`: Serves as the base class for both `FileInfo` and `Directory` info, making it possible to deal with files and directories at the same time using polymorphism.

- `FileStream`: Represents a file that can be written to or read from, or both. This file can be written to and read from asynchronously or synchronously.

❑ `StreamReader`: Reads character data from a stream and can be created by using a `FileStream` as a base.

❑ `StreamWriter`: Writes character data to a stream and can be created by using a `FileStream` as a base.

❑ `FileSystemWatcher`: The `FileSystemWatcher` is the most advanced class you will be examining in this chapter. It is used to monitor files and directories, and exposes events that your application can catch when changes occur in these locations. This functionality has always been missing from Windows programming, but now the .NET Framework makes it much easier to respond to file system events.

You'll also look at the `System.IO.Compression` namespace in this chapter, which allows you to read and write compressed files, using either GZIP compression or the Deflate compression scheme:

❑ `DeflateStream`: Represents a stream where data is compressed automatically when writing, or uncompressed automatically when reading. Compression is achieved using the Deflate algorithm.

❑ `GZipStream`: Represents a stream where data is compressed automatically when writing or uncompressed automatically when reading. Compression is achieved using the GZIP algorithm.

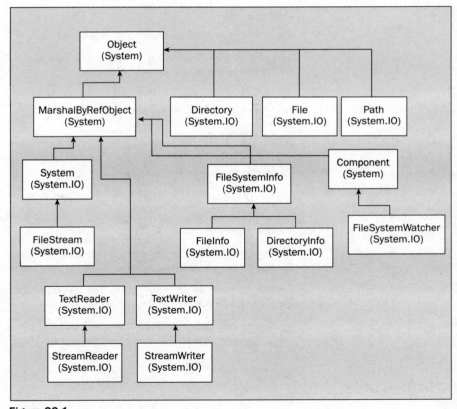

Figure 22-1

Finally, you'll look at object serialization using the `System.Runtime.Serialization` namespace and its child namespaces. You'll primarily be looking at the `BinaryFormatter` class in the `System.Runtime.Serialization.Formatters.Binary` namespace, which enables you to serialize objects to a stream as binary data, and deserialize them again.

The File and Directory Classes

The `File` and `Directory` utility classes expose many static methods for manipulating, surprisingly enough, files and directories. These methods make it possible to move files, query, and update attributes, and create `FileStream` objects. As you learned in Chapter 8, static methods can be called on classes without having to create instances of them.

Some of the most useful static methods of the `File` class are shown in the following table.

Method	Description
Copy()	Copies a file from a source location to a target location.
Create()	Creates a file in the specified path.
Delete()	Deletes a file.
Open()	Returns a `FileStream` object at the specified path.
Move()	Moves a specified file to a new location. You can specify a different name for the file in the new location.

Some useful static methods of the `Directory` class are shown in the next table.

Method	Description
CreateDirectory()	Creates a directory with the specified path.
Delete()	Deletes the specified directory and all the files within it.
GetDirectories()	Returns an array of `string` objects that represent the names of the directories below the specified directory.
GetFiles()	Returns an array of `string` objects that represent the names of the files in the specified directory.
GetFileSystemEntries()	Returns an array of `string` objects that represent the names of the files and directories in the specified directory.
Move()	Moves the specified directory to a new location. You can specify a new name for the folder in the new location.

The FileInfo Class

Unlike the `File` class, the `FileInfo` class is not static and does not have static methods. This class is only useful when instantiated. A `FileInfo` object represents a file on a disk or network location, and you can create one by supplying a path to a file, for example:

```
FileInfo aFile = new FileInfo(@"C:\Log.txt");
```

Since you will be working with strings representing the path of a file throughout this chapter, which will mean a lot of \ characters in your strings, it's worth reminding yourself that the @ that prefixes the string above means that this string will be interpreted literally. Thus \ will be interpreted as \, and not as an escape character. Without the @ prefix, you would need to use \\ instead of \ to avoid having this character be interpreted as an escape character. In this chapter you'll stick to the @ prefix for your strings.

You can also pass the name of a directory to the `FileInfo` constructor, although in practical terms this isn't particularly useful. Doing this causes the base class of `FileInfo`, which is `FileSystemInfo`, to be initialized with all the directory information, but none of the `FileInfo` methods or properties relating specifically to files will work.

Many of the methods exposed by the `FileInfo` class are similar to those of the `File` class, but because `File` is a static class, it requires a string parameter specifying the file location for every method call. Therefore, the following calls do the same thing:

```
FileInfo aFile = new FileInfo("Data.txt");

if (aFile.Exists)
    Console.WriteLine("File Exists");

if (File.Exists("Data.txt"))
    Console.WriteLine("File Exists");
```

In this code a check is made to see if the file `Data.txt` exists. Note that no directory information is specified here, meaning that the current *working directory* is the only location examined. This directory is the one containing the application that calls this code. You'll look at this in more detail a little later, in the section "Pathnames and Relative Paths."

Most of the `FileInfo` methods mirror the `File` methods in this manner. In most cases it doesn't matter which technique you use, although the following criteria may help you to decide which is more appropriate:

❑ It makes sense to use methods on the static `File` class if you are only making a single method call — the single call will be faster because the .NET Framework will not have to go through the process of instantiating a new object and then calling the method.

❑ If your application is performing several operations on a file, it makes more sense to instantiate a `FileInfo` object and use its methods — this will save time because the object will already be referencing the correct file on the file system, whereas the static class will have to find it every time.

The `FileInfo` class also exposes properties relating to the underlying file, some of which can be manipulated to update the file. Many of these properties are inherited from `FileSystemInfo`, and thus apply to both the `File` and `Directory` classes. The properties of `FileSystemInfo` are shown in the following table.

Property	Description
Attributes	Gets or sets the attributes of the current file or directory, using the `FileAttributes` enumeration.
CreationTime	Gets or sets the creation date and time of the current file.
Extension	Retrieves the extension of the file. This property is read-only.
Exists	Determines whether a file exists. This is a read-only abstract property, and is overridden in `FileInfo` and `DirectoryInfo`.
FullName	Retrieves the full path of the file. This property is read-only.
LastAccessTime	Gets or sets the date and time that the current file was last accessed.
LastWriteTime	Gets or sets the date and time that the current file was last written to.
Name	Retrieves the full path of the file. This is a read-only abstract property, and is overridden in `FileInfo` and `DirectoryInfo`.

The properties specific to `FileInfo` are shown in the next table.

Property	Description
Directory	Retrieves a `DirectoryInfo` object representing the directory containing the current file. This property is read-only.
DirectoryName	Returns the path to the file's directory. This property is read-only.
IsReadOnly	Shortcut to the read-only attribute of the file. This property is also accessible via `Attributes`.
Length	Gets the size of the file in bytes, returned as a `long` value. This property is read-only.

Note that a FileInfo object doesn't in itself represent a stream. To read or write to a file, a `Stream` object has to be created. The `FileInfo` object aids you in doing this by exposing several methods that return instantiated `Stream` objects.

The DirectoryInfo Class

The `DirectoryInfo` class works exactly like the `FileInfo` class. It is an instantiated object that represents a single directory on a machine. Like the `FileInfo` class, many of the method calls are duplicated across `Directory` and `DirectoryInfo`. The guidelines for choosing whether to use the methods of `File` or `FileInfo` also apply to `DirectoryInfo` methods:

❏   If you are making a single call, use the static `Directory` class.

❏   If you are making a series of calls, use an instantiated `DirectoryInfo` object.

The `DirectoryInfo` class inherits most of its properties from `FileSystemInfo`, as does `FileInfo`, although these properties operate on directories instead of files. There are also two `DirectoryInfo`-specific properties, shown in the following table.

Property	Description
Parent	Retrieves a `DirectoryInfo` object representing the directory containing the current directory. This property is read-only.
Root	Retrieves a `DirectoryInfo` object representing the root directory of the current volume, for example the `C:\` directory. This property is read-only.

Path Names and Relative Paths

When specifying a path name in .NET code, you can use either absolute or relative path names. An *absolute* path name explicitly specifies where a file or directory is from a known location — like the `C:` drive. An example of this would be `C:\Work\LogFile.txt`. Note that this path defines exactly where the file is, with no ambiguity.

Relative path names are relative to a starting location. By using relative path names, no drive or known location needs to be specified. You saw this earlier, where the current working directory was the starting point — which is the default behavior for relative path names. For example, if your application is running in the `C:\Development\FileDemo` directory and uses the relative path `LogFile.txt`, the file references would be `C:\Development\FileDemo\LogFile.txt`. To move "up" a directory the `..` string is used. Thus, in the same application, the path `..\Log.txt` points to the file `C:\Development\Log.txt`.

As you saw earlier, the working directory is initially set to the directory in which your application is running. When you are developing with Visual Studio 2005, this means the application is several directories beneath the project folder you created. It is usually located in `ProjectName\bin\Debug`. This means that to access a file in the root folder of the project, you will have to move up *two* directories with `..\..\` — you will see this happen often in the chapter.

Should you need to, you can find out what the working directory is currently set to using `Directory.GetCurrentDirectory()`, or you can set it to a new path using `Directory.SetCurrentDirectory()`.

The FileStream Object

The `FileStream` object represents a stream pointing to a file on a disk or a network path. While the class does expose methods for reading and writing bytes from and to the files, most often you will use a `StreamReader` or `StreamWriter` to perform these functions. This is because the `FileStream` class operates on bytes and byte arrays, while the `Stream` classes operate on character data. Character data is easier to work with, but you will see that there are certain operations, such as random file access (access to data at some point in the middle of a file), that can only be performed by a `FileStream` object. You'll examine this subject later in the chapter.

There are several ways to create a `FileStream` object. The constructor has many different overloads but the simplest takes just two arguments: the filename and a `FileMode` enumeration value.

```
FileStream aFile = new FileStream(filename, FileMode.Member);
```

The `FileMode` enumeration has several members that specify how the file is opened or created. You'll see the possibilities shortly. Another commonly used constructer is as follows:

```
FileStream aFile = new FileStream(filename, FileMode.Member, FileAccess.Member);
```

The third parameter is a member of the `FileAccess` enumeration and is a way of specifying the purpose of the stream. The members of the `FileAccess` enumeration are shown in the following table.

Member	Description
Read	Opens the file for reading only
Write	Opens the file for writing only
ReadWrite	Opens the file for reading or writing only

Attempting to perform an action other than that specified by the `FileAccess` enumeration member will result in an exception being thrown. This property is often used as a way of varying user access to the file based on the authorization level of the user.

In the version of the `FileStream` constructor that doesn't use a `FileAccess` enumeration parameter, the default value is used, which is `FileAccess.ReadWrite`.

The `FileMode` enumeration members are shown in the next table. What actually happens when each of these values is used depends on whether the filename specified refers to an existing file. Note that the entries in this table refer to the position in the file that the stream points to when it is created, a subject you'll examine in more detail in the next section. Unless otherwise stated, the stream will point to the beginning of a file.

Member	File Exists Behavior	No File Exists Behavior
Append	The file is opened, with the stream positioned at the end of the file. Can only be used in conjunction with `FileAccess.Write`.	A new file is created. Can only be used in conjunction with `FileAccess.Write`.
Create	The file is destroyed, then a new file is created in its place.	A new file is created.
CreateNew	An exception is thrown.	A new file is created.
Open	The file is opened, with the stream positioned at the beginning of the file.	An exception is thrown.
OpenOrCreate	The file is opened, with the stream positioned at the beginning of the file.	A new file is created.
Truncate	The file is opened and erased. The stream is positioned at the beginning of the file. The original file creation date is retained.	An exception is thrown.

Both the `File` and `FileInfo` classes expose `OpenRead()` and `OpenWrite()` methods that make it easier to create `FileStream` objects. The first opens the file for read-only access, and the second allows you write-only access. These methods provide shortcuts, so you do not have to provide all the information required in the form of parameters to the `FileStream` constructor. For example, the following line of code opens the `Data.txt` file for read-only access:

```
FileStream aFile = File.OpenRead("Data.txt");
```

Note that the following code performs the same function:

```
FileInfo aFileInfo = new FileInfo("Data.txt");
FileStream aFile = aFileInfo.OpenRead();
```

File Position

The `FileStream` class maintains an internal file pointer. This points to the location within the file where the next read or write operation will occur. In most cases, when a file is opened it points to the beginning of the file, but this pointer can be modified. This allows an application to read or write anywhere within the file. This allows for random access to a file and the ability to jump directly to a specific location in the file. This can be very time saving when dealing with very large files, because you can instantly move to the location you want.

The method that implements this functionality is the `Seek()` method, which takes two parameters. The first parameter specifies how far to move the file pointer, in bytes. The second parameter specifies where to start counting from, in the form of a value from the `SeekOrigin` enumeration. The `SeekOrigin` enumeration contains three values: `Begin`, `Current`, and `End`.

For example, the following line would move the file pointer to the eighth byte in the file, starting from the very first byte in the file:

```
aFile.Seek(8, SeekOrigin.Begin);
```

The following line would move the file pointer 2 bytes forward, starting from the current position. If this were executed directly after the previous line, the file pointer would now point to the tenth byte in the file:

```
aFile.Seek(2, SeekOrigin.Current);
```

Note that when you read from or write to a file the file pointer changes as well. After you have read 10 bytes, the file pointer will point to the byte after the tenth byte read.

You can specify negative seek positions as well, which could be combined with the `SeekOrigin.End` enumeration value to seek near the end of the file. The following line will seek to the fifth byte from the end of the file:

```
aFile.Seek(-5, SeekOrigin.End);
```

Files accessed in this manner are sometimes referred to as random access files, because an application can access any position within the file. The `Stream` classes you will look at later access files sequentially, and they do not allow you to manipulate the file pointer in this way.

Reading Data

Reading data using the `FileStream` class is not as easy as using the `StreamReader` class, which you will look at later in this chapter. This is because the `FileStream` class deals exclusively with raw bytes. Working in raw bytes makes the `FileStream` class useful for any kind of data file, not just text files. By reading byte data, the `FileStream` object can be used to read files such as images or sound files. The cost of this flexibility is that you cannot use a `FileStream` to read data directly into a string as you can with the `StreamReader` class. However, there are several conversion classes that make it fairly easy to convert byte arrays into character arrays and vice versa.

The `FileStream.Read()` method is the primary means to access data from a file that a `FileStream` object points to. This method *reads* the data from a file and then *writes* this data into a `byte` array. There are three parameters, the first parameter being a `byte` array passed in to accept data from the `FileStream` object. The second parameter is the position in the `byte` array to begin writing data to — this will normally be zero to begin writing data from the file at the beginning of the array. The last parameter specifies how many bytes to read from the file.

The following Try It Out demonstrates reading data from a random access file. The file you will read from will actually be the class file you create for the example.

Try It Out   Reading Data from Random Access Files

1. Create a new console application called `ReadFile` in the directory `C:\BegVCSharp\Chapter22`.

2. Add the following `using` directive to the top of the `Program.cs` file.

```
using System;
using System.Collections.Generic;
using System.Text;
using System.IO;
```

3. Add the following code to the `Main()` method:

```
static void Main(string[] args)
{
    byte[] byData = new byte[200];
    char[] charData = new Char[200];

    try
    {
        FileStream aFile = new FileStream("../../Program.cs", FileMode.Open);
        aFile.Seek(135, SeekOrigin.Begin);
        aFile.Read(byData, 0, 200);
    }
    catch(IOException e)
    {
        Console.WriteLine("An IO exception has been thrown!");
        Console.WriteLine(e.ToString());
        Console.ReadKey();
        return;
    }
```

```
            Decoder d = Encoding.UTF8.GetDecoder();
            d.GetChars(byData, 0, byData.Length, charData, 0);

            Console.WriteLine(charData);
            Console.ReadKey();
    }
```

4.   Run the application. The result is shown in Figure 22-2.

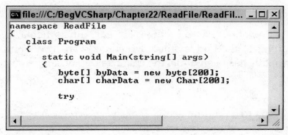

Figure 22-2

How It Works

This application opens its own .cs file to read from. It does this by navigating two directories up the file structure with the `..` string in the following line:

```
FileStream aFile = new FileStream("../../Program.cs", FileMode.Open);
```

The two lines that implement the actual seeking and reading from a specific point in the file are:

```
aFile.Seek(135, SeekOrigin.Begin);
aFile.Read(byData, 0, 200);
```

The first line moves the file pointer to byte number 135 in the file. This is the "n" of namespace in the `Program.cs` file; the 135 characters preceding it are the `using` directives and associated `#region`. The second line reads the next 200 bytes into the `byte` array `byData`.

Note that these two lines were enclosed in `try...catch` blocks to handle any exceptions that may be thrown:

```
try
{
    aFile.Seek(135, SeekOrigin.Begin);
    aFile.Read(byData,0,100);
}
catch(IOException e)
{
    Console.WriteLine("An IO exception has been thrown!");
    Console.WriteLine(e.ToString());
    Console.ReadKey();
    return;
}
```

Almost all operations involving file IO can throw an exception of type `IOException`. All production code must contain error handling, especially when dealing with the file system. The examples in this chapter will all have a basic form of error handling.

Once you have the `byte` array from the file, you then need to convert it into a character array so that you can display it to the console. To do this you use the `Decoder` class from the `System.Text` namespace. This class is designed to convert raw bytes into more useful items, such as characters:

```
Decoder d = Encoding.UTF8.GetDecoder();
d.GetChars(byData, 0, byData.Length, charData, 0);
```

These lines create a `Decoder` object based on the UTF8 encoding schema, which is the Unicode encoding schema. Then the `GetChars()` method is called, which takes an array of bytes and converts it to an array of characters. Once this has been done, the character array can be written to the console.

Writing Data

The process for writing data to a random access file is very similar. A byte array must be created; the easiest way to do this is to first build the character array you wish to write to the file. Next, use the `Encoder` object to convert it to a byte array, very much like you used the `Decoder` object. Last, call the `Write()` method to send the array to the file.

Here's a simple example to demonstrate how this is done.

Try It Out   Writing Data to Random Access Files

1. Create a new console application called `WriteFile` in the directory `C:\BegVCSharp\Chapter22`.

2. Just like before, add the following `using` directive to the top of the `Program.cs` file:

```
using System;
using System.Collections.Generic;
using System.Text;
using System.IO;
```

3. Add the following code to the `Main()` method:

```
static void Main(string[] args)
{
    byte[] byData;
    char[] charData;

    try
    {
        FileStream aFile = new FileStream("Temp.txt", FileMode.Create);
        charData = "My pink half of the drainpipe.".ToCharArray();
        byData = new byte[charData.Length];
        Encoder e = Encoding.UTF8.GetEncoder();
        e.GetBytes(charData, 0, charData.Length, byData, 0, true);

        // Move file pointer to beginning of file.
        aFile.Seek(0, SeekOrigin.Begin);
        aFile.Write(byData, 0, byData.Length);
```

```
    }
    catch (IOException ex)
    {
        Console.WriteLine("An IO exception has been thrown!");
        Console.WriteLine(ex.ToString());
        Console.ReadKey();
        return;
    }
}
```

4. Run the application. It should run briefly, then close.

5. Navigate to the application directory — the file will have been saved there because you used a relative path. This is located in the `WriteFile\bin\Debug` folder. Open the `Temp.txt` file. You should see text in the file as shown in Figure 22-3.

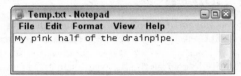

Figure 22-3

How It Works

This application opens up a file in its own directory and writes a simple string to it. In structure, this example is very similar to the previous example, except you use `Write()` instead of `Read()`, and `Encoder` instead of `Decoder`.

The following line creates a character array by using the `ToCharArray()` static method of the `String` class. Because everything in C# is an object, the text `"My pink half of the drainpipe."` is actually a `string` object (albeit a slightly odd one), so these static methods can be called even on a string of characters.

```
CharData = "My pink half of the drainpipe.".ToCharArray();
```

The following lines show how to convert the character array to the correct byte array needed by the `FileStream` object.

```
Encoder e = Endoding.UTF8.GetEncoder();
e.GetBytes(charData, 0, charData.Length, byData, 0, true);
```

This time, an `Encoder` object is created based on the UTF8 encoding. You used Unicode for the decoding as well, and this time you need to encode the character data into the correct byte format before you can write to the stream. The `GetBytes()` method is where the magic happens. This converts the character array to the byte array. It accepts a character array as the first parameter (`charData` in your example), and the index to start in that array as the second parameter (0 for the start of the array). The third parameter is the number of characters to convert (`charData.Length` — the number of elements in the `charData` array). The fourth parameter is the byte array to place the data into (`byData`), and the fifth parameter is the index to start writing in the byte array (0 for the start of the `byData` array).

The sixth and final parameter determines if the `Encoder` object should flush its state after completion. This refers to the fact that the `Encoder` object retains an in-memory record of where it was in the byte array. This aids in subsequent calls to the `Encoder` object, but is meaningless when only a single call is made. The final call to the `Encoder` must set this parameter to `true` to clear its memory and free the object for garbage collection.

After this it is a simple matter of writing the byte array to the `FileStream` using the `Write()` method:

```
aFile.Seek(0, SeekOrigin.Begin);
aFile.Write(byData, 0, byData.Length);
```

Like the `Read()` method, the `Write()` method has three parameters: the array to write from, the index in the array to start writing from, and the number of bytes to write.

The StreamWriter Object

Working with arrays of bytes is not most people's idea of fun—having worked with the `FileStream` object, you may be wondering if there is an easier way. Fear not, for once you have a `FileStream` object you will usually wrap it in a `StreamWriter` or `StreamReader` and use their methods to manipulate the file. If you do not need the ability to change the file pointer to any arbitrary position, then these classes make working with files much easier.

The `StreamWriter` class allows you to write characters and strings to a file, with the class handling the underlying conversions and writing to the `FileStream` object for you.

There are many ways to create a `StreamWriter` object. If you already have a `FileStream` object, then you can use this to create a `StreamWriter`:

```
FileStream aFile = new FileStream("Log.txt", FileMode.CreateNew);
StreamWriter sw = new StreamWriter(aFile);
```

A `StreamWriter` object can also be created directly from a file:

```
StreamWriter sw = new StreamWriter("Log.txt", true);
```

This constructor takes the file name, and a Boolean value that specifies whether to append to the file or create a new one:

❑ If this is set to `false`, then a new file is created or the existing file is truncated and then opened.

❑ If it is set to `true`, then the file is opened, and the data is retained. If there is no file, a new one is created.

Unlike when creating a `FileStream` object, creating a `StreamWriter` does not provide you with a similar range of options—other than the Boolean value to append or create a new file, you have no option for specifying the `FileMode` property as you did with the `FileStream` class. Also, you do not have an option of setting the `FileAccess` property, so you will always have read/write privileges to the file. To use any of the advanced parameters, you must first specify them in the `FileStream` constructor and then create a `StreamWriter` from the `FileStream` object, as you do in the following Try It Out.

Try It Out   Output Stream

1. Create a new console application called StreamWrite in the directory C:\BegVCSharp\ Chapter22.

2. You will be using the System.IO namespace again, so add the following using directive near the top of the Program.cs file:

```
using System;
using System.Collections.Generic;
using System.Text;
using System.IO;
```

3. Add the following code to the Main() method:

```
static void Main(string[] args)
{
    try
    {
        FileStream aFile = new FileStream("Log.txt", FileMode.OpenOrCreate);
        StreamWriter sw = new StreamWriter(aFile);

        bool truth = true;
        // Write data to file.
        sw.WriteLine("Hello to you.");
        sw.WriteLine("It is now {0} and things are looking good.",
                    DateTime.Now.ToLongDateString());
        sw.Write("More than that,");
        sw.Write(" it's {0} that C# is fun.", truth);
        sw.Close();
    }
    catch(IOException e)
    {
        Console.WriteLine("An IO exception has been thrown!");
        Console.WriteLine(e.ToString());
        Console.ReadLine();
        return;
    }
}
```

4. Build and run the project. If no errors are found, it should quickly run and close. Since you are not displaying anything on the console, it is not a very exciting program to watch.

5. Go to the application directory and find the Log.txt file. This is located in the StreamWrite\ bin\Debug folder because you used a relative path.

6. Open up the file, and you should see the text shown in Figure 22-4.

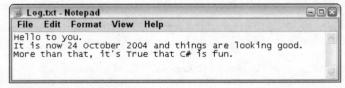

Figure 22-4

How It Works

This simple application demonstrates the two most important methods of the `StreamWriter` class, `Write()` and `WriteLine()`. Both of them have many overloaded versions for performing more advanced file output, but you used basic string output in this example.

The `WriteLine()` method will write the string passed to it, followed immediately by a newline character. You can see in the example that this causes the next write operation to begin on a new line.

Just as you can write formatted data to the console, so you can also do this to files. For example, you can write out the value of variables to the file using standard format parameters:

```
sw.WriteLine("It is now {0} and things are looking good.",
             DateTime.Now.ToLongDateString());
```

`DateTime.Now` holds the current date, the `ToLongDateString()` method is used to convert this date into an easy-to-read form.

The `Write()` method simply writes the string passed to it to the file, without a newline character appended, allowing you to write a complete sentence or paragraph using more than one `Write()` statement.

```
sw.Write("More than that,");
sw.Write(" it's {0} that C# is fun.", truth);
```

Here again, you use format parameters, this time with `Write()` to display the Boolean value `truth`— you set this variable to `true` earlier, and its value is automatically converted into the string `"True"` for the formatting.

You can use `Write()` and format parameters to write comma-separated files:

```
[StreamWriter object].Write("{0},{1},{2}", 100, "A nice product", 10.50);
```

In a more sophisticated example, this data could come from a database or other data source.

The StreamReader Object

Input streams are used to read data from an external source. Many times this will be a file on a disk or network location. But remember that this source could be almost anything that can send data, such as a network application, Web service, or even the console.

The `StreamReader` class is the one that you will be using to read data from files. Like the `StreamWriter` class, this is a generic class that can be used with any stream. In the next Try It Out, you will again be constructing it around a `FileStream` object so that it points to the correct file.

`StreamReader` objects are created in much the same way as `StreamWriter` objects. The most common way to create one is to use a previously created `FileStream` object:

```
FileStream aFile = new FileStream("Log.txt", FileMode.Open);
StreamReader sr = new StreamReader(aFile);
```

Like the `StreamWriter`, the `StreamReader` class can be created directly from a string containing the path to a particular file:

```
StreamReader sr = new StreamReader("Log.txt");
```

Try It Out   Stream Input

1. Create a new console application called `StreamRead` in the directory `C:\BegVCSharp\Chapter22`.

2. Again you must import the `System.IO` namespace, so place the following line of code near the top of `Program.cs`:

```
using System;
using System.Collections.Generic;
using System.Text;
using System.IO;
```

3. Add the following code to the `Main()` method:

```
static void Main(string[] args)
{
    string strLine;

    try
    {
        FileStream aFile = new FileStream("Log.txt", FileMode.Open);
        StreamReader sr = new StreamReader(aFile);
        strLine = sr.ReadLine();
        // Read data in line by line.
        while(strLine != null)
        {
            Console.WriteLine(strLine);
            strLine = sr.ReadLine();
        }
        sr.Close();
    }
    catch(IOException e)
    {
        Console.WriteLine("An IO exception has been thrown!");
        Console.WriteLine(e.ToString());
        return;
    }
    Console.ReadKey();
}
```

4. Copy the `Log.txt` file, created in the previous example, into the `StreamRead\bin\Debug` directory. If you don't have a file named `Log.txt`, the `FileStream` constructor will throw an exception when it doesn't find the file.

5. Run the application—you should see the text of the file written to the console. The result is shown in Figure 22-5.

Figure 22-5

How It Works

This application is very similar to the previous one, with the obvious difference being that it is reading a file rather than writing one. As before you must import the System.IO namespace to be able to access the necessary classes.

You use the ReadLine() method to read text from the file. This method reads text until a carriage return is found, and returns the resulting text as a string. The method returns a null when the end of the file has been reached, which you use to test for the end of the file. Note that you use a while loop, which checks to be sure that the line read isn't null *before* any code in the body of the loop is executed — this way only the genuine contents of the file are displayed:

```
strLine = sr.ReadLine();
while(strLine != null)
{
    Console.WriteLine(strLine);
    strLine = sr.ReadLine();
}
```

Reading Data

The ReadLine() method is not the only way you have of accessing data in a file. The StreamReader class has many methods for reading data.

The simplest of the reading methods is Read(). This method returns the next character from the stream as a positive integer value or a –1 if it has reached the end. This value can be converted into a character by using the Convert utility class. In the example above the main parts of the program could be rewritten as follows:

```
StreamReader sr = new StreamReader(aFile);
int nChar;
nChar = sr.Read();
while(nChar != -1)
{
    Console.Write(Convert.ToChar(nChar));
    nChar = sr.Read();
}
sr.Close();
```

A very convenient method to use with smaller files is the ReadToEnd() method. This method reads the entire file and returns it as a string. In this case, the earlier application could be simplified to this:

```
StreamReader sr = new StreamReader(aFile);
strLine = sr.ReadToEnd();
Console.WriteLine(strLine);
sr.Close();
```

While this may seem very easy and convenient, care must be taken. By reading all the data into a string object, you are forcing the data in the file to exist in memory. Depending on the size of the data file, this can be prohibitive. If the data file is extremely large, it is better to leave the data in the file and access it with the methods of the `StreamReader`.

Delimited Files

Delimited files are a common form of data storage and are used by many legacy systems — if your application must interoperate with such a system, then you will encounter the delimited data format quite often. A particularly common form of delimiter is a comma — for example, the data in an Excel spreadsheet, an Access database, or a SQL Server database can be exported as a comma-separated value (CSV) file.

You've seen how to use the `StreamWriter` class to write such files using this approach — it is also easy to read comma-separated files. If you cast your mind back to Chapter 5, you may remember that you saw the `Split()` method of the `String` class, that is used to convert a string into an array based on a supplied separator character. If you specify a comma as the separator, it will create a correctly dimensioned string array containing all of the data in the original comma-separated string.

In the next Try It Out, you see how useful this can be. The example deals with comma-separated values, loading them into a `List<Dictionary<string, string>>` object. This useful example is quite generic, and you may find yourself using this technique in your own applications if you need to work with comma-separated values.

Try It Out   Comma-Separated Values

1. Create a new console application called `CommaValues` in the directory `C:\BegVCSharp\Chapter22`.

2. Place the following line of code near the top of `Program.cs`. You need to import the `System.IO` namespace for your file handling:

```
using System;
using System.Collections.Generic;
using System.Text;
using System.IO;
```

3. Add the following `GetData()` method into the body of `Program.cs`, before the `Main()` method:

```
private static List<Dictionary<string, string>> GetData(out List<string> columns)
{
    string strLine;
    string[] strArray;
    char[] charArray = new char[] {','};
    List<Dictionary<string, string>> data = new List<Dictionary<string, string>>();
    columns = new List<string>();

    try
    {
        FileStream aFile = new FileStream("../../../SomeData.txt", FileMode.Open);
```

```
            StreamReader sr = new StreamReader(aFile);

            // Obtain the columns from the first line.

            // Split row of data into string array
            strLine = sr.ReadLine();
            strArray = strLine.Split(charArray);

            for (int x = 0; x <= strArray.GetUpperBound(0); x++)
            {
                columns.Add(strArray[x]);
            }

            strLine = sr.ReadLine();
            while (strLine != null)
            {
                // Split row of data into string array
                strArray = strLine.Split(charArray);
                Dictionary<string, string> dataRow = new Dictionary<string, string>();

                for (int x = 0; x <= strArray.GetUpperBound(0); x++)
                {
                    dataRow.Add(columns[x], strArray[x]);
                }

                data.Add(dataRow);

                strLine = sr.ReadLine();
            }

            sr.Close();
            return data;
        }
        catch (IOException ex)
        {
            Console.WriteLine("An IO exception has been thrown!");
            Console.WriteLine(ex.ToString());
            Console.ReadLine();
            return data;
        }
    }
```

4. Now add the following code to the `Main()` method:

```
static void Main(string[] args)
{
    List<string> columns;
    List<Dictionary<string, string>> myData = GetData(out columns);

    foreach (string column in columns)
    {
        Console.Write("{0,-20}", column);
    }
    Console.WriteLine();
```

```
        foreach (Dictionary<string, string> row in myData)
        {
            foreach (string column in columns)
            {
                Console.Write("{0,-20}", row[column]);
            }
            Console.WriteLine();
        }
        Console.ReadKey();
    }
```

5. In VS, create a new text file by choosing `Text File` from the `File` ⇨ `New` ⇨ `File` dialog.

6. Enter the following text into this new text file:

```
ProductID,Name,Price
1,Spiky Pung,1000
2,Gloop Galloop Soup,25
4,Hat Sauce,12
```

7. Save the file as `SomeData.txt` in the `CommaValues` project directory.

8. Run the application — you should see the text of the file written to the console, as shown in Figure 22-6.

Figure 22-6

How It Works

Like the previous example, this application reads the file line by line into a string. However, since you know this is a file containing comma-separated text values, you are going to handle it differently. Not only that, but you will actually store the values you read in a data structure.

First, you need to look at some of the comma-separated data itself:

```
ProductID,Name,Price
1,Spiky Pung,1000
```

Note that the first line holds the names of the columns of data and subsequent lines hold the data. Thus, your procedure will be to obtain the column names from the first line of the file and then proceed to retrieve the data in the remaining lines.

Now look at the `GetData()` method — this method is declared as `static`, so you can call this method without creating an instance of your class. This method returns a `List<Dictionary<string, string>>` object that you will create and then populate with data from the comma-separated text file. It also returns a `List<string>` object containing the header names. The following lines initialize these objects:

```
List<Dictionary<string, string>> data = new List<Dictionary<string, string>>();
columns = new List<string>();
```

`columns` will contain the column names from the first row of the comma-separated text file, and `data` will hold the values on subsequent rows.

You start by creating a `FileStream` object and then construct a `StreamReader` around that as you did in earlier examples. Now you can read the first line of the file and create an array of strings from that one string:

```
strLine = sr.ReadLine();
strArray = strLine.Split(charArray);
```

You saw the `Split()` method in Chapter 5 — it accepts a character array, in this case consisting of just "," so that `strArray` will hold the array of strings formed from splitting `strLine` at each instance of ",". Since you are currently reading from the first line of the file, and this line holds the names of the columns of data, you need to loop through each string in `strArray` and add it to `columns`:

```
for (int x = 0; x <= strArray.GetUpperBound(0); x++)
{
    columns.Add(strArray[x]);
}
```

Now that you have the names of the columns for your data, you can read in the data. The code for this is essentially the same as that for the earlier `StreamRead` example, except for the presence of the code required to add `Dictionary<string, string>` objects to `data`:

```
strLine = sr.ReadLine();
while (strLine != null)
{
    // Split row of data into string array.
    strArray = strLine.Split(charArray);
    Dictionary<string, string> dataRow = new Dictionary<string, string>();

    for (int x = 0; x <= strArray.GetUpperBound(0); x++)
    {
        dataRow.Add(columns[x], strArray[x]);
    }

    data.Add(dataRow);

    strLine = sr.ReadLine();
}
```

For each line in the file, you create a new `Dictionary<string, string>` object and fill it with a row of data. Each entry in this collection has a key corresponding to a column name and a value that is the value of the column for that row. The keys are extracted from the `columns` object you created earlier, and the values come from the string array obtained using `Split()` for the line of text extracted from the data file.

Once you've read all the data in from the file, you close the `StreamReader` and return your data.

The code in the `Main()` method obtains the data from the `GetData()` method in variables called `myData` and `columns`, and displays this information to the console. First, the name of each column is displayed:

```
foreach (string column in columns)
{
    Console.Write("{0,-20}", column);
}
Console.WriteLine();
```

The `-20` part of the formatting string `{0,-20}` ensures that the name you display is left-aligned in a column of 20 characters — this will help to format the display.

Finally, you loop through each `Dictionary<string, string>` object in the `myData` collection and display the values in that row, once again using the formatting string to format your output.

```
foreach (Dictionary<string, string> row in myData)
{
    foreach (string column in columns)
    {
        Console.Write("{0,-20}", row[column]);
    }
    Console.WriteLine();
}
```

As you can see, it is very simple to extract meaningful data from comma-separated value (CSV) files using the .NET Framework. This technique is also easy to combine with the data access techniques you will see in Chapter 24, meaning that data from a CSV file can be manipulated just like any other data source (such as a database). However, there is no information about the data types of the data extracted from the CSV file. Currently you've just been treating all data as strings, but for an enterprise-level business application, you will need to go the extra step of adding type information to the data you extract. This could come from additional information stored in the CSV file, it could be configured manually, or it could be inferred from the strings in the file, all depending on the specific application

Even though XML, which you'll be looking at in the next chapter, is a superior method of storing and transporting data, you will find that CSV files are still very common and will be for quite some time. Delimited files such as comma-separated files also have the advantage of being very terse and, therefore, smaller than their XML counterparts.

Reading and Writing Compressed Files

Often when dealing with files you will find that quite a lot of space is used up on your hard disk. This is particularly true for graphics and sound files. You've probably come across utilities that enable you to compress and decompress files, which comes in handy when you want to move them around or e-mail them to your friends. The `System.IO.Compression` namespace contains classes that enable you to compress files from your code, either using the GZIP or Deflate algorithm — both of which are publicly available and free for anyone to use.

There is a little bit more to compressing files than just compressing them though. Commercial applications will allow multiple files to be placed in a single compressed file and so on. What you'll be looking at in this section is much simpler — you'll just be saving text data to a compressed file. You are unlikely to be able to access this file in an external utility. However, the file will be much smaller than its uncompressed equivalent!

The two compression stream classes in the `System.IO.Compression` namespace that you'll look at here, `DeflateStream` and `GZipStream`, work in very similar ways. In both cases, you initialize them with an existing stream, which in the case of files will be a `FileStream` object. After this you can use them with `StreamReader` and `StreamWriter` just like any other stream. All you need to specify on top of that is whether the stream will be used for compression (saving files) or decompression (loading files) so that the class knows what to do with the data that passes through it.

This is best illustrated with the following example.

Try It Out   Compressed Data

1. Create a new console application called `Compressor` in the directory `C:\BegVCSharp\Chapter22`.

2. Place the following lines of code near the top of `Program.cs`. You need to import the `System.IO` namespace for your file handling and `System.IO.Compression` to use the compression classes:

```
using System;
using System.Collections.Generic;
using System.Text;
using System.IO;
using System.IO.Compression;
```

3. Now add the following methods into the body of `Program.cs`, before the `Main()` method:

```
static void SaveCompressedFile(string filename, string data)
{
   FileStream fileStream =
      new FileStream(filename, FileMode.Create, FileAccess.Write);
   GZipStream compressionStream =
      new GZipStream(fileStream, CompressionMode.Compress);
   StreamWriter writer = new StreamWriter(compressionStream);
   writer.Write(data);
   writer.Close();
}

static string LoadCompressedFile(string filename)
{
   FileStream fileStream =
      new FileStream(filename, FileMode.Open, FileAccess.Read);
   GZipStream compressionStream =
      new GZipStream(fileStream, CompressionMode.Decompress);
   StreamReader reader = new StreamReader(compressionStream);
   string data = reader.ReadToEnd();
   reader.Close();
   return data;
}
```

4. Now add the following code to the `Main()` method:

```csharp
static void Main(string[] args)
{
    try
    {
        string filename = "compressedFile.txt";

        Console.WriteLine(
            "Enter a string to compress (will be repeated 1000 times):");
        string sourceString = Console.ReadLine();
        StringBuilder sourceStringMultiplier =
            new StringBuilder(sourceString.Length * 100);
        for (int i = 0; i < 100; i++)
        {
            sourceStringMultiplier.Append(sourceString);
        }
        sourceString = sourceStringMultiplier.ToString();
        Console.WriteLine("Source data is {0} bytes long.", sourceString.Length);

        SaveCompressedFile(filename, sourceString);
        Console.WriteLine("\nData saved to {0}.", filename);

        FileInfo compressedFileData = new FileInfo(filename);
        Console.WriteLine("Compressed file is {0} bytes long.",
                          compressedFileData.Length);

        string recoveredString = LoadCompressedFile(filename);
        recoveredString = recoveredString.Substring(0, recoveredString.Length / 100);
        Console.WriteLine("\nRecovered data: {0}", recoveredString);

        Console.ReadKey();
    }
    catch (IOException ex)
    {
        Console.WriteLine("An IO exception has been thrown!");
        Console.WriteLine(ex.ToString());
        Console.ReadKey();
    }
}
```

5. Run the application and enter a suitably long string. The result is shown in Figure 22-7.

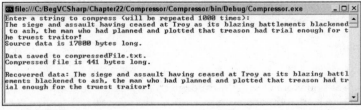

Figure 22-7

6. Open `compressedFile.txt` in Notepad. The text is shown in Figure 22-8.

Chapter 22

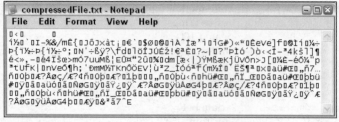

Figure 22-8

How It Works

In this example, you define two methods for saving and loading a compressed text file. The first of these, `SaveCompressedFile()`, is as follows:

```
static void SaveCompressedFile(string filename, string data)
{
    FileStream fileStream =
        new FileStream(filename, FileMode.Create, FileAccess.Write);
    GZipStream compressionStream =
        new GZipStream(fileStream, CompressionMode.Compress);
    StreamWriter writer = new StreamWriter(compressionStream);
    writer.Write(data);
    writer.Close();
}
```

The code starts by creating a `FileStream` object, then uses this to create a `GZipStream` object. Note that you could replace all occurrences of `GZipStream` in this code with `DeflateStream`—the classes work in the same way. You use the `CompressionMode.Compress` enumeration value to specify that data is to be compressed, and then use a `StreamWriter` to write data to the file.

`LoadCompressedFile()` mirrors `SaveCompressedFile()` method. Instead of saving to a filename, this method loads a compressed file into a string:

```
static string LoadCompressedFile(string filename)
{
    FileStream fileStream =
        new FileStream(filename, FileMode.Open, FileAccess.Read);
    GZipStream compressionStream =
        new GZipStream(fileStream, CompressionMode.Decompress);
    StreamReader reader = new StreamReader(compressionStream);
    string data = reader.ReadToEnd();
    reader.Close();
    return data;
}
```

The differences are as you would expect—different `FileMode`, `FileAccess`, and `CompressionMode` enumeration values to load and uncompress data, and the use of a `StreamReader` to get the uncompressed text out of the file.

The code in `Main()` is a simple test of these methods. It simply asks for a string, duplicates the string 100 times to make things interesting, compresses it to a file, then retrieves it. In the example the opening stanza of Sir Gawain and the Green Knight repeated 100 times is 17,800 characters long, but when compressed only takes up 441 bytes; a compression ration of around 40:1. Admittedly, this is a bit of a cheat — the GZIP algorithm works particularly well with repetitive data, but this does illustrate compression in action.

You also looked at the text stored in the compressed file. Obviously, it isn't easily readable. This has implications, should you wish to share data between applications for example. However, since the file has been compressed with a known algorithm at least you know that it is possible for applications to uncompress it.

Serialized Objects

Applications, as you have seen, often need to store data on a hard disk. So far in this chapter, you've looked at constructing text and data files piece by piece, but often that isn't the most convenient way of doing things. Sometimes it's better to store data in the form that it is used in, namely objects.

The .NET Framework provides the infrastructure to serialize objects in the `System.Runtime .Serialization` and `System.Runtime.Serialization.Formatters` namespaces, with specific classes implementing this infrastructure in namespaces below the latter. There are two implementations available to you in the Framework:

❑   `System.Runtime.Serialization.Formatters.Binary`: This namespace contains the class `BinaryFormatter`, which is capable of serializing objects into binary data, and vice versa.

❑   `System.Runtime.Serialization.Formatters.Soap`: This namespace contains the class `SoapFormatter`, which is capable of serializing objects into SOAP format XML data, and vice versa.

In this chapter, you just look at `BinaryFormatter`, since you have yet to learn about XML data. However, since these classes implement the `IFormatter` interface much of the discussion applies equally to both.

The `IFormatter` interface provides the methods shown in the following table.

Method	Description
`void Serialize(Stream stream, object source)`	Serializes source into stream
`object Deserialize(Stream stream)`	Deserializes the data in stream and returns the resultant object

Importantly, and conveniently for this chapter, these methods work with streams. This makes it easy to tie these methods into the file access techniques you've already seen in this chapter — you can use `FileStream` objects.

So, serializing using `BinaryFormatter` is as simple as this:

```
IFormatter serializer = new BinaryFormatter();
serializer.Serialize(myStream, myObject);
```

Deserializing is equally easy:

```
IFormatter serializer = new BinaryFormatter();
MyObjectType myNewObject = serializer.Deserialize(myStream) as MyObjectType;
```

Obviously, you need streams and objects to work with, but the preceding holds true for pretty much all circumstances. In the following Try It Out, you'll se this working in practice.

Try It Out   Object Serialization

1. Create a new console application called ObjectStore in the directory C:\BegVCSharp\Chapter22.

2. Add a new class called Product to the project, and modify the code as follows:

```
namespace ObjectStore
{
    public class Product
    {
        public long Id;
        public string Name;
        public double Price;

        [NonSerialized]
        string Notes;

        public Product(long id, string name, double price, string notes)
        {
            Id = id;
            Name = name;
            Price = price;
            Notes = notes;
        }

        public override string ToString()
        {
            return string.Format("{0}: {1} (${2:F2}) {3}", Id, Name, Price, Notes);
        }
    }
}
```

3. Place the following lines of code near the top of Program.cs. You need to import the System.IO namespace for your file handling and the other namespaces for serialization:

```
using System;
using System.Collections.Generic;
using System.Text;
using System.IO;
using System.Runtime.Serialization;
using System.Runtime.Serialization.Formatters.Binary;
```

4. Now add the following code to the Main() method in Program.cs:

```csharp
static void Main(string[] args)
{
    try
    {
        // Create products.
        List<Product> products = new List<Product>();
        products.Add(new Product(1, "Spiky Pung", 1000.0, "Good stuff."));
        products.Add(new Product(2, "Gloop Galloop Soup", 25.0, "Tasty."));
        products.Add(new Product(4, "Hat Sauce", 12.0, "One for the kids."));

        Console.WriteLine("Products to save:");
        foreach (Product product in products)
        {
            Console.WriteLine(product);
        }
        Console.WriteLine();

        // Get serializer.
        IFormatter serializer = new BinaryFormatter();

        // Serialize products.
        FileStream saveFile =
          new FileStream("Products.bin", FileMode.Create, FileAccess.Write);
        serializer.Serialize(saveFile, products);
        saveFile.Close();

        // Deserialize products.
        FileStream loadFile =
          new FileStream("Products.bin", FileMode.Open, FileAccess.Read);
        List<Product> savedProducts =
            serializer.Deserialize(loadFile) as List<Product>;
        loadFile.Close();

        Console.WriteLine("Products loaded:");
        foreach (Product product in savedProducts)
        {
            Console.WriteLine(product);
        }
    }
    catch (SerializationException e)
    {
        Console.WriteLine("A serialization exception has been thrown!");
        Console.WriteLine(e.Message);
    }
    catch (IOException e)
    {
        Console.WriteLine("An IO exception has been thrown!");
        Console.WriteLine(e.ToString());
    }

    Console.ReadKey();
}
```

5. Run the application. The result is shown in Figure 22-9.

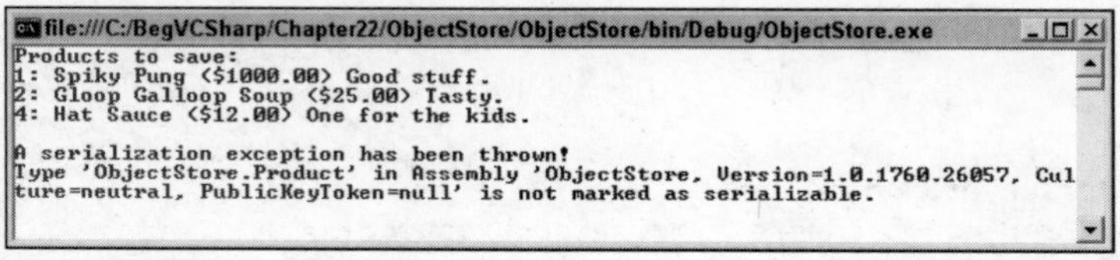

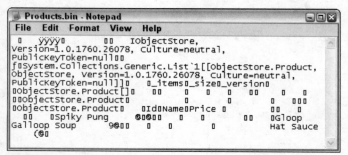

Figure 22-9

6. Modify the code in `Product.cs` as follows:

```
namespace ObjectStore
{
    [Serializable]
    public class Product
    {
        ...
    }
```

7. Run the application again. The result is shown in Figure 22-10.

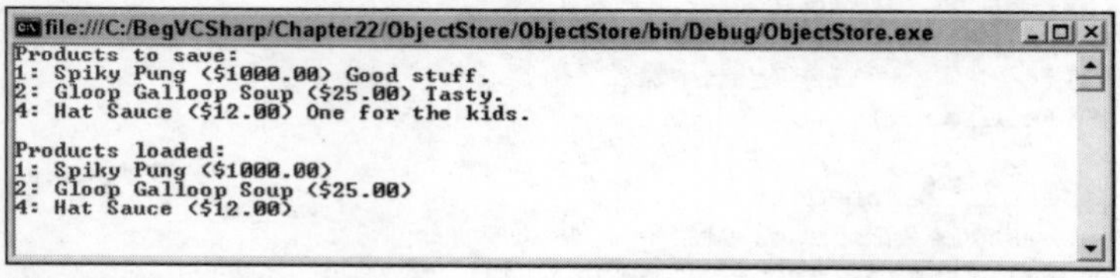

Figure 22-10

8. Open `Products.bin` in Notepad. The text is shown in Figure 22-11.

Figure 22-11

How It Works

In this example, you have created a collection of `Product` objects, saved the collection to disk, then reloaded it. The first time you ran the application, though, an exception was thrown, because the `Product` object was not marked as *serializable*.

The .NET Framework forces you to mark objects as serializable to enable them to be serialized. There are a number of reasons for this, including:

- ❑ Some objects don't serialize very well. They may require references to local data that only exists while they are in memory, for example.

- ❑ Some objects might contain sensitive data that you wouldn't want to be saved in an insecure way or transferred to another process.

As you saw in the example, marking an object as serializable is a matter of moments, using the `Serializable` attribute:

```
namespace ObjectStore
{
    [Serializable]
    public class Product
    {
        ...
    }
}
```

An important point to note here is that this attribute is not inherited by derived classes. It must be applied to each and every class that you want to be able to serialize. Also, it is worth pointing out that the `List<T>` class you used to generate a collection of `Product` objects has this attribute — otherwise, applying it to `Product` wouldn't have helped to make the collection serializable.

When the `products` collection was successfully serialized and deserialized (on the second attempt), another important fact came to light. Only the `Id`, `Name`, and `Price` fields were reconstituted. This is because of another attribute being used, `NonSerialized`:

```
        [NonSerialized]
        string Notes;
```

Any member can be marked with this attribute and will not be saved with other members. This can be useful, for example, if just one field or property contains sensitive data.

You also looked at the resultant saved data in the example. Note that some of the data here is human-readable, which may not be what you desire — or expect. The `BinaryFormatter` class makes no serious attempt to shield your data from prying eyes. Of course, since you are using streams it is a relatively easy act to intercept the data as it is saved to disk or loaded and apply your own obfuscating or encryption algorithms. The same applies to compression — using the techniques from the last section you could quite easily compress object data as it is saved to disk.

There is a lot more to the subject of serialization, but you've covered enough information to get the basics. One of the more advanced techniques that you might like to investigate is custom serialization using the `ISerializable` interface, which enables you to customize exactly what data is serialized. This can be important, for example, when upgrading classes subsequent to release. Changing the members exposed to serialization can cause existing saved data to become unreadable, unless you provide your own logic to save and retrieve data.

Monitoring the File Structure

Sometimes, an application must do more than just read and write files to the file system. Sometimes, it is important to know when files or directories are being modified. The .NET Framework has made it easy to create custom applications that do just that.

The class that helps you to do this is the `FileSystemWatcher` class. This class exposes several events that your application can catch. This enables your application to respond to file system events.

The basic procedure for using the `FileSystemWatcher` is simple. First you must set a handful of properties, which specify where to monitor, what to monitor, and when it should raise the event that your application will handle. Then you give it the addresses of your custom event handlers, so that it can call these when significant events occur. Then you turn it on and wait for the events.

The properties that must be set before a `FileSystemWatcher` object is enabled are shown in the following table.

Property	Description
Path	This must be set to the file location or directory to monitor.
NotifyFilter	This is a combination of `NotifyFilters` enumeration values that specify what to watch for within the monitored files. These represent properties of the file or folders being monitored. If any of the specified properties change, an event is raised. The possible enumeration values are: `Attributes`, `CreationTime`, `DirectoryName`, `FileName`, `LastAccess`, `LastWrite`, `Security`, `Size`. Note that these can be combined using the binary OR operator.
Filter	A filter on which files to monitor, for example *.txt.

Once these settings have been set, you must write event handlers for the four events, `Changed`, `Created`, `Deleted`, and `Renamed`. As you saw in Chapter 13, this is simply a matter of creating your own method and assigning it to the object's event. By assigning your own event handler to these methods, your method will be called when the event is fired. Each event will fire when a file or directory matching the `Path`, `NotifyFilter`, and `Filter` property is modified.

Once you have set the properties and the events, set the `EnableRaisingEvents` property to `true` to begin the monitoring. In the following Try It Out, you'll use `FileSystemWatcher` in a simple client application to keep tabs on a directory of your choice.

Try It Out   Monitoring the File System

Here's a more sophisticated example utilizing much of what you have learned in this chapter.

1. Create a new Windows application called `FileWatch` in the directory `C:\BegVCSharp\Chapter22`.

2. Set the various form properties using those shown in the following table.

Property	Setting
FormBorderStyle	FixedDialog
MaximizeBox	False
MinimizeBox	False
Size	302, 160
StartPosition	CenterScreen
Text	File Monitor

3. Using the properties from the preceding table, add the required controls to the form and set the appropriate properties.

Control	Name	Location	Size	Text
TextBox	txtLocation	8, 24	184,20	
Button	cmdBrowse	208, 24	64, 24	Browse...
Button	cmdWatch	88, 56	80, 32	Watch!
Label	lblWatch	8, 104	0, 0	

Ensure that you see the `Enabled` property of the `cmdWatch` Button to `False`, since you can't watch a file before one has been specified, and the `AutoSize` property of `lblWatch` to `True` so that you'll be able to see its contents. Also add an `OpenFileDialog` control to the form, set its `Name` to `FileDialog`, and its `Filter` to `All Files|*.*`. When you are finished, your form should look like Figure 22-12.

Figure 22-12

4. Now that the form looks good, you can add some code to make it do some work. The first thing you need to do is add your usual `using` directive for the `System.IO` namespace to the existing list of `using` directives:

```
#region Using directives

using System;
using System.Collections.Generic;
using System.ComponentModel;
```

```
using System.Data;
using System.Drawing;
using System.Windows.Forms;
using System.IO;

#endregion
```

5. Now you must add the `FileSystemWatcher` class to the `Form1` class, as well as a delegate to facilitate changing the text of `lblWatch` from different threads. Add the following code to `Form1.cs`:

```
namespace FileWatch
{
    partial class Form1 : Form
    {
        //File System Watcher object.
        private FileSystemWatcher watcher;
        private delegate void UpdateWatchTextDelegate(string newText);
```

6. You need to add some code to the form constructor. Just after the `InitializeComponent()` method call add the following code. This code is needed to initialize the `FileSystemWatcher` object and associate the events to methods that you are going to create next:

```
public Form1()
{
    InitializeComponent();

    this.watcher = new System.IO.FileSystemWatcher();
    this.watcher.Deleted +=
        new System.IO.FileSystemEventHandler(this.OnDelete);
    this.watcher.Renamed +=
        new System.IO.RenamedEventHandler(this.OnRenamed);
    this.watcher.Changed +=
        new System.IO.FileSystemEventHandler(this.OnChanged);
    this.watcher.Created +=
        new System.IO.FileSystemEventHandler(this.OnCreate);
}
```

7. Add the following five methods to the `Form1` class. The first method will be used to update the text in `lblWatch` asynchronously from the threads that will run the event handlers for the `FileSystemWatcher` events, and the other methods are the event handlers themselves:

```
// Utility method to update watch text.
public void UpdateWatchText(string newText)
{
    lblWatch.Text = newText;
}

// Define the event handlers.
public void OnChanged(object source, FileSystemEventArgs e)
{
    try
    {
        StreamWriter sw =
            new StreamWriter("C:/FileLogs/Log.txt", true);
        sw.WriteLine("File: {0} {1}", e.FullPath,
```

```
                             e.ChangeType.ToString());
            sw.Close();
            this.BeginInvoke(new UpdateWatchTextDelegate(UpdateWatchText),
                "Wrote change event to log");
        }
        catch (IOException)
        {
            this.BeginInvoke(new UpdateWatchTextDelegate(UpdateWatchText),
                "Error Writing to log");
        }
    }
    public void OnRenamed(object source, RenamedEventArgs e)
    {
        try
        {
            StreamWriter sw =
                new StreamWriter("C:/FileLogs/Log.txt", true);
            sw.WriteLine("File renamed from {0} to {1}", e.OldName,
                        e.FullPath);
            sw.Close();
            this.BeginInvoke(new UpdateWatchTextDelegate(UpdateWatchText),
                "Wrote renamed event to log");
        }
        catch (IOException)
        {
            this.BeginInvoke(new UpdateWatchTextDelegate(UpdateWatchText),
                "Error Writing to log");
        }
    }
    public void OnDelete(object source, FileSystemEventArgs e)
    {
        try
        {
            StreamWriter sw =
                new StreamWriter("C:/FileLogs/Log.txt", true);
            sw.WriteLine("File: {0} Deleted", e.FullPath);
            sw.Close();
            this.BeginInvoke(new UpdateWatchTextDelegate(UpdateWatchText),
                "Wrote delete event to log");
        }
        catch (IOException)
        {
            this.BeginInvoke(new UpdateWatchTextDelegate(UpdateWatchText),
                "Error Writing to log");
        }
    }

    public void OnCreate(object source, FileSystemEventArgs e)
    {
        try
        {
            StreamWriter sw =
                new StreamWriter("C:/FileLogs/Log.txt", true);
            sw.WriteLine("File: {0} Created", e.FullPath);
            sw.Close();
            this.BeginInvoke(new UpdateWatchTextDelegate(UpdateWatchText),
```

```
                        "Wrote create event to log");
        }
        catch (IOException)
        {
            this.BeginInvoke(new UpdateWatchTextDelegate(UpdateWatchText),
                "Error Writing to log");
        }
    }
```

8. You will now add the `Click` event handler for the `Browse...` button. The code in this event handler will open the Open File dialog, allowing the user to select a file to monitor. Double-click the `Browse...` button and enter the following code:

```
private void cmdBrowse_Click(object sender, EventArgs e)
{
    if (FileDialog.ShowDialog() != DialogResult.Cancel )
    {
        txtLocation.Text = FileDialog.FileName;
        cmdWatch.Enabled = true;
    }
}
```

The `ShowDialog()` method returns a `DialogResult` enumeration value representing how the user exited the File Open dialog. The user could have clicked OK or hit the `Cancel` button. You need to check that the user did not click the `Cancel` button, so you compare the result from the method call to the `DialogResult.Cancel` enumeration value before saving the user's file selection to the `TextBox`. Finally, you set the `Enabled` property of the `Watch` button to true so that you can watch the file.

9. Now for the last bit of code. Follow the same procedure as above with the `Watch` button. Add the following code to launch the `FileSystemWatcher`:

```
private void cmdWatch_Click(object sender, EventArgs e)
{
    watcher.Path =Path.GetDirectoryName(txtLocation.Text);
    watcher.Filter = Path.GetFileName(txtLocation.Text);
    watcher.NotifyFilter = NotifyFilters.LastWrite |
        NotifyFilters.FileName | NotifyFilters.Size;
    lblWatch.Text = "Watching " + txtLocation.Text;
    // Begin watching.
    watcher.EnableRaisingEvents = true;
}
```

10. You need to make sure the `FileLogs` directory exists for you to write data to. Add the following code to the `Form1` constructor that will check to see if the directory exists, and create the directory if it does not already exist.

```
public Form1()
{
    ...

    DirectoryInfo aDir = new DirectoryInfo(@"C:\\FileLogs");
    if (!aDir.Exists)
        aDir.Create();
}
```

11. Create a directory called `C:\TempWatch` and a file in this directory called `temp.txt`.

12. Build the project. If everything builds successfully click the `Browse` button and select `C:\TempWatch\temp.txt`.

13. Click the `Watch` button to begin monitoring the file. The only change you will see in your application is the label control showing the file is being watched.

14. Using Windows Explorer navigate to `C:\TempWatch`. Open `temp.txt` in Notepad and add some text to the file. Save the file.

15. Rename the file.

16. You can now check the log file to see the changes. Navigate to the `C:\FileLogs\Log.txt` file and open it in Notepad. You should see a description of the changes to the file you selected to watch, shown in Figure 22-13.

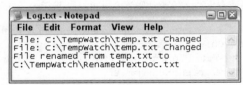

Figure 22-13

How It Works

This application is fairly simple, but it demonstrates how the `FileSystemWatcher` works. Try playing with the string you put into the monitor text box. If you specify `*.*` in a directory it will monitor all changes in the directory.

Most of the code in the application is based around setting up the `FileSystemWatcher` object to watch the correct location:

```
watcher.Path =Path.GetDirectoryName(txtLocation.Text);
watcher.Filter = Path.GetFileName(txtLocation.Text);
watcher.NotifyFilter = NotifyFilters.LastWrite |
    NotifyFilters.FileName | NotifyFilters.Size;
lblWatch.Text = "Watching " + txtLocation.Text;
// Begin watching.
watcher.EnableRaisingEvents = true;
```

The code first sets the path to the directory to monitor. This uses a new object you have not looked at yet: the `System.IO.Path` object. This is a static class, very much like the static `File` object. It exposes many static methods to manipulate and extract information out of file location strings. You first use it to extract the directory name the user typed in from the text box, using the `GetDirectoryName()` method.

The next line sets the filter for the object. This can be an actual file, in which case it would only monitor the file, or it could be something like `*.txt`, in which case it would monitor all the `.txt` files in the directory specified. Again, you use the `Path` static object to extract the information from the supplied file location.

The `NotifyFilter` is a combination of `NotifyFilters` enumeration values that specify what constitutes a change. In this example, you have said that if the last write timestamp, the filename, or the size of
the file changes then your application will be notified of the change. After updating the UI, you set the
`EnableRaisingEvents` property to `true` to begin monitoring.

But before this you have to create the object and set the event handlers:

```
this.watcher = new System.IO.FileSystemWatcher();
this.watcher.Deleted +=
    new System.IO.FileSystemEventHandler(this.OnDelete);
this.watcher.Renamed +=
    new System.IO.RenamedEventHandler(this.OnRenamed);
this.watcher.Changed +=
    new System.IO.FileSystemEventHandler(this.OnChanged);
this.watcher.Created +=
    new System.IO.FileSystemEventHandler(this.OnCreate);
```

This is how you hook up the event handlers for the watcher object with the private methods you have
created. Here, you will have event handlers for the event raised by the watcher object when a file is
deleted, renamed, changed or created. In your own methods, you decide how to handle the actual event.
Note that you are notified *after* the event takes place.

In the actual event handler methods, you simply write the event to a log file. Obviously, this could be a
more sophisticated response, depending on your application. When a file is added to a directory you
could move it somewhere else or read the contents and fire off a new process using the information. The
possibilities are endless!

Summary

In this chapter, you learned about streams and why they are used in the .NET Framework to access files
and other serial devices. You looked at the basic classes in the `System.IO` namespace, including:

❑   `File`

❑   `FileInfo`

❑   `FileStream`

You saw that the `File` class exposes many static methods for moving, copying, and deleting files,
`FileInfo` represents a physical file on disk, and has methods to manipulate this file. A `FileStream`
object represents a file that can be written to, or read from, or both. You also explored `StreamReader`
and `StreamWriter` classes and saw how useful they were for writing to streams. You saw how to read
and write to random files using the `FileStream` class. Building on this knowledge, you used classes in
the `System.IO.Compression` namespace to compress streams as you write them to disk and also saw
how to serialize objects to files. Finally, you built an entire application to monitor files and directories
using the `FileSystemWatcher` class.

In summary, you covered

- ❏   Opening a file
- ❏   Reading from a file
- ❏   Writing to a file
- ❏   The difference between the `StreamWriter` and `StreamReader` classes and the `FileStream` class
- ❏   Working with delimited files to populate a data structure
- ❏   Compressing and decompressing streams
- ❏   Serializing and deserializing objects
- ❏   Monitoring the file system with the `FileSystemWatcher` class

Exercises

1.   What is the namespace that must be imported to allow an application to work with files?

2.   When would you use a `FileStream` object to write to a file instead of using a `StreamWriter` object?

3.   What methods of the `StreamReader` class allow you to read data from files and what does each one do?

4.   What class would you use to compress a stream using the Deflate algorithm?

5.   How would you prevent a class you have created from being serialized?

6.   What events does the `FileSystemWatcher` class expose and what are they for?

7.   Modify the `FileWatch` application you built in this chapter. Add the ability to turn the file system monitoring on and off without exiting the application.

XML

Extensible Markup Language (XML as it is commonly called) is a technology that has been receiving great attention for the past few years. XML is not new, and it was certainly not invented by Microsoft for use in the .NET environment, but Microsoft recognized the possibilities of XML early in its development. Because of that you will see it performing a large number of duties in .NET, from describing the configuration of your applications to transporting information between Web services.

XML is a way of storing data in a simple text format, which means that it can be read by pretty well any computer. As you've seen in some of the earlier chapters about Web programming, this makes it a perfect format for transferring data over the Internet. It's even not too difficult for humans to read!

The ins and outs of XML can be very complicated, so you won't look at every single detail here. However, the basic format is very simple, and most of the time you won't require a detailed knowledge of XML, because Visual Studio will normally take care of most of the work for you — you will rarely have to write an XML document by hand. Having said that, XML is hugely important in the .NET world, because it's used as the default format for transferring data, so it's vital to understand the basics.

In this chapter, you learn about:

❑ The structure and elements of XML

❑ XML Schema

❑ Using XML in your applications

If you need a fuller understanding of XML, please check out Beginning XML, *3rd Edition (Wiley Publishing, Inc., ISBN 0-7645-7077-3).*

XML Documents

A complete set of data in XML is known as an *XML document*. An XML document could be a physical file on your computer or just a string in memory. However, it has to be complete in itself, and it must obey certain rules (you see what these are shortly). An XML document is made up of a number of different parts. The most important of these are *XML elements*, which contain the actual data of the document.

XML Elements

XML elements consist of an opening tag (the name of the element enclosed in angled brackets, such as `<myElement>`), the data within the element, and a closing tag (the same as the opening tag, but with a forward slash after the opening bracket: `</myElement>`).

For example, you might define an element to hold the title of a book like this:

```
<book>Tristram Shandy</book>
```

If you already know some HTML, you might be thinking that this looks very similar — and you'd be right! In fact, HTML and XML share much of the same syntax. The big difference is that XML doesn't have any predefined elements — you choose the names of our own elements, so there's no limit to the number of elements you can have. The most important point to remember is that XML — despite its name — isn't actually a language at all. Rather, it's a standard for defining languages (known as *XML applications*). Each of these languages has its own distinct vocabulary — a specific set of elements that can be used in the document and the structure these elements are allowed to take. As you'll shortly see, you can explicitly limit the elements allowed in the XML document. Alternatively, you can allow any elements, and allow the program using the document to work out for itself what the structure is.

Element names are case-sensitive, so `<book>` and `<Book>` are counted as different elements. This means that if you attempt to close a `<book>` element using a closing tag that doesn't have identical casing (for example, `</BOOK>`), your XML document won't be legal. Programs that read XML documents and analyze them by examining their individual elements are known as *XML parsers,* and they will reject any document that contains illegal XML.

Elements can also contain other elements, so you could modify this `<book>` element to include the author as well as the title by adding two subelements:

```
<book>
    <title>Tristram Shandy</title>
    <author>Lawrence Sterne</author>
</book>
```

However, overlapping elements aren't allowed, so you must close all subelements before the closing tag of the parent element. This means, for example, that you can't do this:

```
<book>
    <title>Tristram Shandy
    <author>Lawrence Sterne
    </title></author>
</book>
```

This is illegal, because the `<author>` element is opened within the `<title>` element, but the closing `</title>` tag comes before the closing `</author>` tag.

There's one exception to the rule that all elements must have a closing element. It's possible to have "empty" elements, with no nested data or text. In this case, you can simply add the closing tag straight after the opening element, as shown above, or you can use a shorthand syntax, adding the slash of the closing element to the end of the opening element:

```
<book />
```

This is identical to the full syntax:

```
<book></book>
```

Attributes

As well as storing data within the body of the element, you can also store data within attributes, which are added within the opening tag of an element. Attributes are in the form

```
name="value"
```

where the value of the attribute *must* be enclosed in either single or double quotes. For example:

```
<book title="Tristram Shandy"></book>
```

or

```
<book title='Tristram Shandy'></book>
```

These are both legal, but this is not:

```
<book title=Tristram Shandy></book>
```

At this point, you may be wondering why you need both ways of storing data in XML. What's the difference between

```
<book>
    <title>Tristram Shandy</title>
</book>
```

and

```
<book title="Tristram Shandy"></book>
```

The honest answer is that there isn't any earth-shatteringly fundamental difference between the two. There isn't really any big advantage to using either. Elements are a better choice if there's a possibility that you'll need to add more information about that piece of data later — you can always add a subelement or an attribute to an element, but you can't do that for attributes. Arguably, elements are more readable and more elegant (but that's really a matter of personal taste). On the other hand, attributes consume less bandwidth if the document is sent over a network without compression (with compression there's not much difference) and are convenient for holding information that isn't essential to every user of the document. Probably the best advice is to use both, selecting whichever you're most comfortable with for storing a particular item of data,. but there really are no hard and fast rules.

The XML Declaration

In addition to elements and attributes, XML documents can contain a number of constituent parts. These individual parts of an XML document are known as *nodes*; elements, the text within elements, and attributes are all nodes of the XML document. Many of these are important only if you really want to delve deeply into XML. However, one type of node occurs in almost every XML document. It is the *XML declaration*, and if you include it, it must occur as the first node of the document.

The XML declaration is similar in format to an element, but has question marks inside the angled brackets. It always has the name xml, and it always has an attribute named version; currently, the only possible value for this is "1.0". The simplest possible form of the XML declaration is, therefore:

```
<?xml version="1.0"?>
```

As of February 2004 W3C (www.w3c.org) has released a recommendation for XML 1.1, but at the time of this writing there are few or no real-life implementations of this recommendation.

Optionally, it can also contain the attributes encoding (with a value indicating the character set that should be used to read the document, such as "UTF-16" to indicate that the document uses the 16-bit Unicode character set) and standalone (with the value "yes" or "no" to indicate whether the XML document depends on any other files). However, these attributes are not required, and you will probably include only the version attribute in your own XML files.

Structure of an XML Document

One of the most important things about XML is that it offers a way of structuring data that is very different from relational databases. Most modern database systems store data in tables that are related to each other through values in individual columns. Each table stores data in rows and columns—each row represents a single record, and each column a particular item of data about that record. In contrast, XML data is structured hierarchically, a little like the folders and files in Windows Explorer. Each document must have a single *root element* within which all elements and text data is contained. If there is more than one element at the top level of the document, the document will not be legal XML. However, you can include other XML nodes at the top level—notably the XML declaration. So this is a legal XML document:

```
<?xml version="1.0"?>
<books>
    <book>Tristram Shandy</book>
    <book>Moby Dick</book>
    <book>Ulysses</book>
</books>
```

But this isn't:

```
<?xml version="1.0"?>
<book>Tristram Shandy</book>
<book>Moby Dick</book>
<book>Ulysses</book>
```

Under this root element, you have a great deal of flexibility about how you structure the data. Unlike relational data, in which every row has the same number of columns, there's no restriction on the number of subelements an element can have. And, although XML documents are often structured similarly to relational data, with an element for each record, XML documents don't need any predefined structure at all. This is one of the major differences between traditional relational databases and XML. Where relational databases always define the structure of the information before any data can be added, information can be stored in XML without this initial overhead, which makes it a very convenient way to store small blocks of data. As you will see shortly, it is quite possible to provide a structure for your XML, but unlike the relational databases, no one will enforce this structure unless you ask for it explicitly.

XML Namespaces

As you learned in Chapter 9, everyone can define their own C# classes, and everyone can define their own XML elements, and this gives rise to exactly the same problem — how do you know which elements belong to which vocabulary? As you might gather from the title of this section, this question is answered in a similar way. Just as you define namespaces to organize your C# types, you use XML namespaces to define our XML vocabularies. This allows you to include elements from a number of different vocabularies within a single XML document, without the risk of misinterpreting elements because (for example) two different vocabularies define a `<customer>` element.

XML namespaces can be quite complex, so I won't go into great detail here, but the basic syntax is simple. Specific elements or attributes are associated with a specific namespace using a prefix, followed by a colon. For example, `<wrox:book>` represents a `<book>` element that resides in the `wrox` namespace. But how do you know what namespace `wrox` represents? For this approach to work, you need to be able to guarantee that every namespace is unique. The easiest way to do this is to map the prefixes to something that's already known to be unique. And this is exactly what happens: somewhere in your XML document you need to associate any namespace prefixes with a *Uniform Resource Identifier* (URI). URIs come in several flavors, but the most common type is simply a Web address, such as `"http://www.wrox.com"`.

To identify a prefix with a specific namespace, use the `xmlns:prefix` attribute within an element, setting its value to the unique URI that identifies that namespace. The prefix can then be used anywhere within that element, including any nested child elements. For example:

```
<?xml version="1.0"?>
<books>
   <book xmlns:wrox="http://www.wrox.com">
      <wrox:title>Beginning C#</wrox:title>
      <wrox:author>Karli Watson</wrox:author>
   </book>
</books>
```

Here, you can use the `wrox:` prefix with the `<title>` and `<author>` elements, because they are within the `<book>` element, where the prefix is defined. However, if you tried to add this prefix to the `<books>` element, the XML would be illegal, as the prefix isn't defined for this element.

You can also define a default namespace for an element using the `xmlns` attribute:

```
<?xml version="1.0"?>
<books>
   <book xmlns="http://www.wrox.com">
      <title>Beginning Visual C#</title>
      <author>Karli Watson</author>
      <html:img src="begvcsharp.gif"
```

```
                    xmlns:html="http://www.w3.org/1999/xhtml" />
     </book>
  </books>
```

Here, the default namespace for the `<book>` element is defined as `"http://www.wrox.com"`. Everything within this element will, therefore, belong to this namespace, unless you explicitly request otherwise by adding a different namespace prefix, as you do for the `<img>` element (you set it to the namespace used by XML-compatible HTML documents).

Well-Formed and Valid XML

I've been talking up until now about *legal* XML. In fact, XML distinguishes between two forms of legality. Documents that obey all the rules required by the XML standard itself are said to be *well-formed*. If an XML document is not well-formed, parsers will be unable to interpret it correctly, and will reject the document. To be well-formed, a document must:

❑   Have one and only one root element

❑   Have closing tags for every element (except for the shorthand syntax mentioned previously)

❑   Not have any overlapping elements — all child elements must be fully nested within the parent

❑   Have all attributes enclosed in quotes

This isn't a complete list, by any means, but it does highlight the most common pitfalls made by programmers who are new to XML.

However, XML documents can obey all these rules and still not be *valid*. Remember that I said earlier that XML is not itself a language, but a standard for defining XML applications. Well-formed XML documents simply comply with the XML standard; to be valid, they also need to conform to any rules specified for the XML application. Not all parsers check whether documents are valid; those that do are said to be *validating parsers*. But to check whether a document adheres to the rules of the application, you first need a way to specify what those rules are.

Validating XML Documents

XML supports two ways of defining which elements and attributes can be placed in a document and in what order: *Document Type Definitions* (DTDs) and *schemas*. DTDs use a non-XML syntax inherited from the parent of XML and are gradually being replaced by schemas. DTDs don't allow you to specify the data types of the elements and attributes and so are relatively inflexible and not used that much in the context of the .NET Framework. Schemas, on the other hand, are used frequently — they do allow you to specify data types, and they are written in an XML-compatible syntax. However schemas are unfortunately very complex, and there are different formats for defining them — even within the .NET world!

Schemas

There are two separate formats for schemas supported by .NET — XML Schema Definition language (XSD) and XML-Data Reduced schemas (XDR). Schemas can be either included within your XML document or kept in a separate file. These formats are mutually incompatible, and you really need to be very familiar with XML before you attempt to write one, so I won't go into great detail here. It is, however, useful to be able to recognize the main elements in a schema, so I will explain the basic principles. To do this, you look at sample XSD and XDR schemas for this simple XML document, which contains basic details about a couple of Wrox's C# books:

```xml
<?xml version="1.0"?>
<books>
    <book>
        <title>Beginning Visual C#</title>
        <author>Karli Watson</author>
        <code>7582</code>
    </book>
    <book>
        <title>Professional C# 2nd Edition</title>
        <author>Simon Robinson</author>
        <code>7043</code>
    </book>
</books>
```

XSD Schemas

Elements in XSD schemas must belong to the namespace `http://www.w3.org/2001/XMLSchema`. If this namespace isn't included, the schema elements won't be recognized.

To associate the XML document with an XSD schema in another file, you need to add a `schema-location` element to the root element:

```xml
<?xml version="1.0"?>
<books schemalocation="file://C:\BegVCSharp\XML\books.xsd">
    ...
</books>
```

Take a quick look at an example XSD schema:

```xml
<schema xmlns="http://www.w3.org/2001/XMLSchema">
    <element name="books">
        <complexType>
            <choice maxOccurs="unbounded">
                <element name="book">
                    <complexType>
                        <sequence>
                            <element name="title" />
                            <element name="author" />
                            <element name="code" />
                        </sequence>
                    </complexType>
                </element>
            </choice>
            <attribute name="schemalocation" />
        </complexType>
    </element>
</schema>
```

The first thing to notice here is that the default namespace is set to the XSD namespace. This tells the parser that all the elements in the document belong to the schema. If you don't specify this namespace, the parser will think that the elements are just normal XML elements and won't realize that it needs to use them for validation.

The entire schema is contained within an element called <schema> (with a lowercase "s" — remember that case is important!). Each element that can occur within the document must be represented by an <element> element. This element has a name attribute that indicates the name of the element. If the element is to contain nested child elements, you must include the <element> tags for these within a <complexType> element. Inside this, you specify how the child elements must occur. For example, you use a <choice> element to specify that any selection of the child elements can occur or <sequence> to specify that the child elements must appear in the same order as they are listed in the schema. If an element can appear more than once (as the <book> element does), you need to include a maxOccurs attribute within its parent element. Setting this to "unbounded" means that the element can occur as often as you like. Finally, any attributes must be represented by <attribute> elements, including your schemalocation attribute that tells the parser where to find the schema. Place this after the end of the list of child elements.

XDR Schemas

To attach an external XDR schema to an XML document, you specify a namespace for the document with the value "x-schema:<schema_filename>":

```
<?xml version="1.0"?>
<books xmlns="x-schema:books.xdr">
   ...
</books>
```

The schema that follows is the XDR equivalent of the XSD schema you just looked at. As you can see, it is very different:

```
<Schema xmlns="urn:schemas-microsoft-com:xml-data">
    <ElementType name="title" content="textOnly" />
    <ElementType name="author" content="textOnly" />
    <ElementType name="code" content="textOnly" />
    <ElementType name="book" content="eltOnly">
        <group order="seq">
            <element type="title" />
            <element type="author" />
            <element type="code" />
        </group>
    </ElementType>
    <ElementType name="books" content="eltOnly">
        <element type="book" />
    </ElementType>
</Schema>
```

Again, the default namespace is set to tell the parser that all elements in the document belong to the schema definition, this time to "urn:schemas-microsoft-com:xml-data". Notice that (unlike XSD schemas) this is a proprietary format, so it won't work at all with non-Microsoft products. In fact, XDR schemas are particularly useful when working with SQL Server, Microsoft's database server, because it has in-built support for XDR.

This time our root element is `<Schema>` with a *capital* "S." This root element again contains the entire schema definition (remember that XML documents must have a single root element). After this, though, there's a big difference — the elements that will appear in your document are defined *in reverse order*! The reason for this is that each element in the document is represented in the schema by an `<ElementType>` element, and this contains an `<element>` element (note the lowercase *e* here) for each child element. Within the `<element>` tags, the `type` attribute is set to point to an `<ElementType>` element — and this must already have been defined. If you want to restrict how child elements can appear, you can use a `<group>` element within the `<ElementType>` and set its `order` attribute. In the case, it is set to `"seq"` to specify that the elements occur in the same sequence as in the schema — just like the `<sequence>` tag in the XSD schema!

Now you've covered the basic theory behind XML, so in the following Try It Out, you can have a go at creating XML documents. Fortunately, VS does a lot of the hard work for you, and it will even create an XSD schema based on your XML document without you having to write a single line of code!

Try It Out   Creating an XML Document in Visual Studio

Follow these steps to create an XML document.

1. Open VS and select File ⇨ New ⇨ File... from the menu. (you don't need to have a project already open).

2. In the New File menu, select XML File and click Open. VS will create a new XML document for you. As Figure 23-1 shows, VS adds the XML declaration, complete with an `encoding` attribute (it also colors the attributes and elements, but this won't show up well in black and white print):

```
XMLFile1.xml
    <?xml version="1.0" encoding="utf-8" ?>
```

Figure 23-1

3. Save the file by pressing Ctrl+S or by selecting File ⇨ Save XMLFile1.xml from the menu. VS will ask you where to save the file and what to call the file; save it in the `BegCSharp\Chapter23` folder as `GhostStories.xml`.

4. Move the cursor to the line underneath the XML declaration, and type the text `<stories>`. Notice how VS automatically puts the end tag in as soon as you type the greater than sign to close the opening tag.

5. Type in this XML file:

```xml
<?xml version="1.0" encoding="utf-8" ?>
<stories>
    <story>
        <title>A House in Aungier Street</title>
        <author>
            <name>Sheridan Le Fanu</name>
            <nationality>Irish</nationality>
        </author>
        <rating>eerie</rating>
    </story>
```

```
    <story>
       <title>The Signalman</title>
       <author>
           <name>Charles Dickens</name>
           <nationality>English</nationality>
       </author>
       <rating>atmospheric</rating>
    </story>
    <story>
       <title>The Turn of the Screw</title>
       <author>
           <name>Henry James</name>
           <nationality>American</nationality>
       </author>
       <rating>a bit dull</rating>
    </story>
</stories>
```

6. Right-click on the XML in the code window and select View Data Grid from the pop-up menu. Visual Studio displays the data from the XML file in a tabular format, as shown in Figure 23-2, as though it came from a relational database.

Visual Studio is now displaying two tabs with the same caption (GhostStories.xml). These two windows represent two different views for the same file — if you change something in one it is immediately reflected in the other.

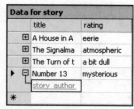

Figure 23-2

7. You can actually edit the data in this table, so you can modify our XML document here without even having to type the tags. Click on the box for the title column in the empty row at the bottom of the grid, and type Number 13. Now move to the rating box beside it, and type mysterious. This enters a new story, but you still need to enter the author. To do this, click on the plus sign next to the new row. This will bring up a link for the <author> element, as shown in Figure 23-3.

Figure 23-3

8. Click this link and another table will be displayed where you can enter the name and nationality of the author. Enter MR James and English in the two columns (make sure that you press Enter after typing the nationality, or the data will be lost). You should now see the information shown in Figure 23-4.

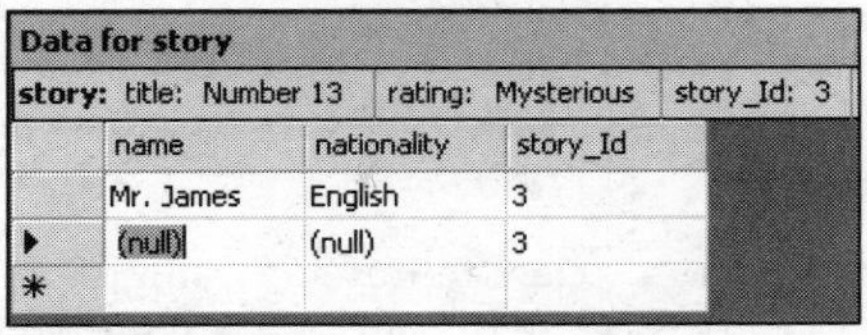

Data for story			
story: title: Number 13	rating: Mysterious		story_Id: 3
name	nationality	story_Id	
Mr. James	English	3	
(null)	(null)	3	

Figure 23-4

9. Now return to the first tab labeled GhostStories.xml. A new <story> element should have been added just before the closing </stories> tag:

```
<story>
    <title>Number 13</title>
    <rating>mysterious</rating>
    <author>
        <name>MR James</name>
        <nationality>English</nationality>
    </author>
</story>
```

10. As its final party trick, you get VS to create an XSD schema for this XML document. On the XML Menu, click Create Schema to have VS create a new XSD schema file for you that represents the data in the original XML document.

Using XML in Your Application

Now that you know how to create XML documents, it is time to put this knowledge to use. The .NET Framework includes a number of namespaces and classes that makes it quite simple to read, manipulate, and write XML. The following pages cover at a number of these classes and examine how you can use them to create and manipulate XML programmatically.

XML Document Object Model

The XML Document Object Model (XML DOM) is a set of classes used to access and manipulate XML in a very intuitive way. The DOM is perhaps not the quickest way to read XML data, but as soon as you understand the relationship between the classes and the elements of an XML document, you are going to find it very easy to use.

The classes that make up the DOM can be found in the namespace System.Xml. The are a number of classes and namespaces in this namespace, but in this chapter you are going to focus on only a few of the classes that allow you to easily manipulate XML. The classes you are going to examine and use are described in the following table.

Class Name	Description
XmlNode	This class represents a single node in a document tree. It is the base of many of the classes you'll see in this chapter. If this node represents the root of an XML document, you will be able to navigate to any position in the document from it.
XmlDocument	The XmlDocument class extends the XmlNode class, but is often the first object you use when using XML. This is because this class is used to load and save data from disk or elsewhere.
XmlElement	The XmlElement class represents a single element in the XML document. The XmlElement is derived from XmlLinkedNode, which in turn is derived from XmlNode.
XmlAttribute	This class represents a single attribute. Like the XmlDocument class, it is derived from the XmlNode class.
XmlText	Represents the text between a beginning and closing tag.
XmlComment	Represents a special kind of node that is not regarded as part of the document other than to provide information to the reader about parts of the document.
XmlNodeList	The XmlNodeList class represents a collection of nodes.

XmlDocument Class

Usually, the first thing your application will want to do with XML is to read it from disk. As described in the preceding table, this is the domain of the XmlDocument class. You can think of the XmlDocument as an in-memory representation of the file on disk. Once you have used the XmlDocument class to load a file into memory, you can obtain the root node of the document from it and start reading and manipulating the XML:

```
using System.Xml;
.
.
.
XmlDocument document = new XmlDocument();
document.Load(@"C:\Beginning Visual C#\Chapter 23\books.xml");
```

The two lines of code create a new instance of the XmlDocument class and load the file books.xml into it. Remember that the XmlDocument class is located in the System.Xml namespace, and you should insert a using System.Xml; in the using section at the beginning of the code.

In addition to loading and saving the XML, the XmlDocument class is also responsible for maintaining the XML structure itself. Because of this you will find a large number of methods on this class that are used to create, alter, and delete nodes in the tree. You will look at some of those methods shortly, but to present the methods properly, you need to know a bit more about another class, the XmlElement.

XmlElement Class

Now that the document has been loaded into memory, you want to do something with it. The DocumentElement property of the XmlDocument instance you created in the preceding code will return an instance of an XmlElement that represents the root element of the XmlDocument. This element is important because once you have that, you have access to every bit of information in the document:

```
XmlDocument document = new XmlDocument();
document.Load(@"C:\Beginning Visual C#\Chapter 23\books.xml");
XmlElement element = document.DocumentElement;
```

After you've got the root element of the document, you are ready to use the information. The XmlElement class contains methods and properties for manipulating the nodes and attributes of the tree. Let's examine the methods for navigating the XML elements first.

Property Name	Description
FirstChild	This property returns the first child element after this one. If you recall the books.xml file from earlier in the chapter, the root node of the document was called "books" and the next node after that was "book." In that document, then, the first child of the root node "books" is "book."
	`<books>` ← Root node `<book>` ← FirstChild
	nodeFirstChild returns an XmlNode object, and you should test for the type of the returned node as it is unlikely to always be an XmlElement instance. In the books example, the child of the Title element is, in fact, an XmlText node that represents the text Beginning Visual C#.
LastChild	This property operates exactly like the FirstChild property, except that it returns the last child of the current node. In the case, of the books example, the last child of the "books" node will still be a "book" node, but it will be the node representing the "Professional C# 2nd Edition" book.

	`<books>` ← Root node
	   `<book>` ← FirstChild
	      `<title>Beginning Visual C#</title>`
	      `<author>Karli Watson</author>`
	      `<code>7582</code>`
	   `</book>`
	   `<book>` ← LastChild
	      `<title>Professional C# 2nd Edition</title>`
	      `<author>Simon Robinson</author>`
	      `<code>7043</code>`
	   `</book>`
	`</books>`

ParentNode	This property returns the parent of the current node. In the books example, the "books" node is the parent of both of the "book" nodes.
NextSibling	Where the FirstChild and LastChild properties returned the leaf node of the current node, the NextSibling node returns the next node that has the same parent node. In the case of the books example, this means that getting the NextSibling of the title element will return the author element and calling NextSibling on that will return the code element.

Table continued on following page

Property Name	Description
HasChildNodes	This handy property allows you to check if the current element has child elements without actually getting the value from `FirstChild` and examining that against `null`.

Using the four properties from the preceding table, it is possible to run through an entire `XmlDocument`, as shown in the following Try It Out.

Try It Out Looping through All Nodes in an XML Document

In this example, you are going to create a small Windows Forms application that loops through all the nodes of an XML document and prints out the name of the element or the text contained in the element in the case of an `XmlText` element.

1. Begin by creating a new Windows Form project by selecting File ➪ New ➪ Project... In the dialog, select Windows Application. Name the project `LoopThroughXmlDocument` and press Enter.

2. Design the form as shown in Figure 23-5 by dragging a `ListBox` and a `Button` control onto the form.

Figure 23-5

3. Name the `ListBox` `listBoxXmlNodes` and the button `buttonLoopThroughDocument`.

4. Double-click the button and enter the code that follows. Don't forget to add `using System.Xml;` to the using section at the top of the file:

```
private void buttonLoopThroughDocument_Click(object sender, EventArgs e)
{
    // Clear ListBox
    listBoxXmlNodes.Items.Clear();

    // Load the XML document
    XmlDocument document = new XmlDocument();
```

```
        document.Load(@"C:\Beginning Visual C#\Chapter 23\Books.xml");

        // Use recursion to loop through the document.
        RecurseXmlDocument((XmlNode)document.DocumentElement, 0);
    }
```

```
private void RecurseXmlDocument(XmlNode root, int indent)
    {
        // Make sure we don't do anything if the root is null.
        if (root == null)
          return;

        if (root is XmlElement) // Root is an XmlElement type
        {
          // first, print the name
          listBoxXmlNodes.Items.Add(root.Name.PadLeft(root.Name.Length + indent));

          // Then check if there are any child nodes and if there are, call this
          // method again to print them.
          if (root.HasChildNodes)
            RecurseXmlDocument(root.FirstChild, indent + 2);

          // Finally check to see if there are any siblings and if there are
          // call this method again to have them printed.
          if (root.NextSibling != null)
            RecurseXmlDocument(root.NextSibling, indent);
        }
        else if (root is XmlText)
        {
          // Print the text.
          string text = ((XmlText)root).Value;
          listBoxXmlNodes.Items.Add(text.PadLeft(text.Length + indent));
        }
    }
```

5. Run the application and click Loop. You should get a result like that shown in Figure 23-6.

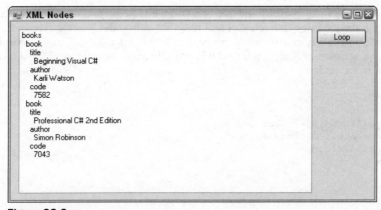

Figure 23-6

You'll notice the output doesn't look like it is valid XML, and obviously it isn't. The thing to notice is that when you ran through the elements of the XML document, you didn't encounter a single closing tag. In other words, you never have to worry whether the current element is a starting tag or a closing tag — the XmlNode or XmlElement instance represents the entire node, not just the text representation of a tag.

How It Works

When you click the button the first thing that happens is the XmlDocument method Load is called. This method loads the XML from a file into the XmlDocument instance, which can then be used to access the elements of the XML. Then you call a method that will allow you to loop through the XML recursively, passing the root node of the XML document to the method. The root element is obtained with the property DocumentElement of the XmlDocument class. Aside from the check for null on the root parameter that is passed into the RecurseXmlDocument method the first line of notice is the if sentence:

```
if (root is XmlElement) // Root is an XmlElement type
{
  ...
}
else if (root is XmlText)
{
  ...
}
```

Recall that the is operator lets you examine the type of an object and returns true if the instance is of the specified type. Even though the root node is declared as an Xmlnode, that is merely the base type of the objects you are going to work with. But using the is operator to test the type of the objects you are able to determine the type of the objects runtime and behave accordingly.

Inside the two if blocks you add the appropriate text to the list view. Notice that the reason you have to know the type of the current instance of root is that the information you want to display is obtained differently for different elements: You want to display the name of XmlElements and the value of XmlText elements. The reason you only call RecurseXmlDocument recursively if the node is an XmlElement is that XmlText nodes never have child nodes.

Changing the Values of Nodes

Before you examine how to change the value of a node, it is important to realize that very rarely is the value of a node a simple thing. In fact, you will find that although all of the classes that derive from XmlNode include a property called Value, it very rarely returns anything useful to you. While this can feel like a bit of a letdown at first, you'll find it is actually quite logical that it must be so. Examine the books example from earlier:

```
<books>
  <book>
    <title>Beginning Visual C#</title>
    <author>Karli Watson</author>
    <code>7582</code>
  </book>
  <book>
</books>
```

Every single one of the tag pairs in the document resolves into a node in the DOM. Remember that when you looped through all the nodes in the document, you encountered a number of `XmlElement` nodes and three `XmlText` nodes. The `XmlElement` nodes in the XML above are `<books>`, `<book>`, `<title>`, `<author>`, and `<code>`. The `XmlText` nodes are the text between the starting and closing tags of title, author, and code. Though it could be argued that the value of title, author, and code is the text between the tags, that text is itself a node and it is that node that actually holds the value. The other tags clearly have no value associated with them other than other nodes.

If you look toward the bottom of the code in the `RecurseXmlDocument` method above, you will find the following line in the if block that executes when the current node is an `XmlText` node:

```
string text = ((XmlText)root).Value;
```

Here, you see that the `Value` property of the `XmlText` node instance is used to get the value of the node.

Nodes of the type `XmlElement` will return `null` if you use their `Value` property, but it is possible to get the information between the starting and closing tags of an `XmlElement` if you use one of two other methods: `InnerText` and `InnerXml`. This means that you are able to manipulate the value of nodes using two methods and a property, as described in the following table.

Property Name	Description
InnerText	This property gets the text of all the child nodes of the current node and returns it as a single concatenated string. This means that if you get the value of `InnerText` from the book node in the XML above, you will see the string `"Beginning Visual C#Karli Watson7582"` returned. If you get the `InnerText` of the title node, only `"Beginnning Visual C#"` is returned. You can set the text using this method, but be careful if you do so, because it is quite possible to overwrite information you did not want to change if you set the text of a wrong node.
InnerXml	The `InnerXml` property returns the text like `InnerText`, but it also returns all of the tags. This means that if you get the value of `InnerXml` on the book node the result is the following string: `<title>Beginning Visual C#</title><author>Karli Watson</author><code>7582</code>` As you can see, this can be quite useful if you have a string containing XML that you want to inject directly into your XML document. However, you are entirely responsible for the string yourself, and if you insert badly formed XML the application will generate an exception.

Value	The `Value` property is the "cleanest" way to manipulate information in the document, but as mentioned earlier, only a few of the classes actually return anything useful to you when you get the value. The classes that will return the desired text are:
	
	`XmlText`
	`XmlComment`
	`XmlAttribute`

Inserting New Nodes

Now that you've seen that you can move around in the XML document and even get the values of the elements, let's examine how to change the structure of the document by adding nodes to the books document you've been using until now.

To insert new elements in the list, you are going to need to examine the new methods that are placed on the XmlDocument and XmlNode classes, shown in the following table. The XmlDocument class has methods that allow you to create new XmlNode and XmlElement instances, which is nice because both of these classes have only a protected constructor, which means you cannot create an instance of either directly with new.

Method Name	Description
CreateNode	The CreateNode method can be used to create any kind of node. There are three overloads of the method, two of which allow you to create nodes of the type found in the XmlNodeType enumeration and one that allows you to specify the type of node to use as a string. Unless you are quite sure about specifying a node type other than those in the enumeration, I strongly recommend using the two overloads that use the enumeration.
	The method returns an instance of XmlNode that can then be cast to the appropriate type explicitly.
CreateElement	This method is simply a version of CreateNode that can only create nodes of the XmlDocument variety.
CreateAttribute	Again, this is simply a version of CreateNode that can only create nodes of the XmlAttribute variety.
CreateTextNode	CreateTextNode method creates, yes, you guessed it, nodes of the type XmlTextNode.
CreateComment	I've included this method in this list to show how diverse are the types of nodes that can be created. This method doesn't create a node that is actually part of the data represented by the XML document, but rather it is a comment meant for any human eyes that might have to read the data. You can pick up comments when reading the document in your applications as well.

The methods in the preceding table are all used to create the nodes themselves, but after calling any of them you really have to do something with them before they become interesting. Immediately after creation the nodes have no additional information about them, and they are not yet inserted into the document. To do either you should use methods that are found on any class derived from XmlNode (including XmlDocument and XmlElement). They following table describes those methods.

Method Name	Description
AppendChild	This simple-to-use method appends a child node to a node of type XmlNode or derived type. It is important to remember that the node you append appears at the bottom of the list of children of the node on which the method is called. If you don't care about the order of the children there's no problem, but if you do you should remember to append the nodes in the correct sequence.
InsertAfter	By using the InsertAfter method, you can control exactly where you want to insert the new node. The method takes two parameters, one of which is the new node and the second of which is the node after which the new node should be inserted.
InsertBefore	This method works exactly like InsertAfter, except that the new node is inserted before the node you supply as a reference.

In the Following Try It Out, you build on the previous example and insert a book node in the books.xml document. There is no code in the example to clean the document (yet), so if you run it several times you will probably end up with a lot of identical nodes.

Try It Out   **Creating Nodes**

Follow these steps to add a node to the books.xml document.

1. Add a button beneath the existing button on the form and name it buttonCreateNode. Change its Text property to Create Node.

2. Double-click the new button, and enter the following code:

```
private void buttonCreateNode_Click(object sender, EventArgs e)
{
    // Load the XML document.
    XmlDocument document = new XmlDocument();
    document.Load(@"C:\Beginning Visual C#\Chapter 23\Books.xml");

    // Get the root element.
    XmlElement root = document.DocumentElement;

    // Create the new nodes.
    XmlElement newBook = document.CreateElement("book");
    XmlElement newTitle = document.CreateElement("title");
    XmlElement newAuthor = document.CreateElement("author");
    XmlElement newCode = document.CreateElement("code");
    XmlText title = document.CreateTextNode("Beginning Visual C# 3rd Edition");
    XmlText author = document.CreateTextNode("Karli Watson et al");
    XmlText code = document.CreateTextNode("1234567890");
    XmlComment comment = document.CreateComment("This book is the book you are reading");

    // Insert the elements.
    newBook.AppendChild(comment);
    newBook.AppendChild(newTitle);
```

```
    newBook.AppendChild(newAuthor);
    newBook.AppendChild(newCode);
    newTitle.AppendChild(title);
    newAuthor.AppendChild(author);
    newCode.AppendChild(code);
    root.InsertAfter(newBook, root.FirstChild);

    document.Save(@"C:\Beginning Visual C#\Chapter 23\Books.xml");
}
```

3. Add the following code to the end of the `RecurseXmlDocument` method:

```
else if (root is XmlComment)
{
  // Print text.
  string text = root.Value;
  listBoxXmlNodes.Items.Add(text.PadLeft(text.Length + indent));

  // Then check if there are any child nodes, and if there are call this
  // method again to print them.
  if (root.HasChildNodes)
    RecurseXmlDocument(root.FirstChild, indent + 2);

  // Finally, check to see if there are any siblings, and if there are
  // call this method again to have them printed.
  if (root.NextSibling != null)
    RecurseXmlDocument(root.NextSibling, indent);
}
```

4. Run the application and click Create Node. Then click Loop, and you should see the dialog shown in Figure 23-7.

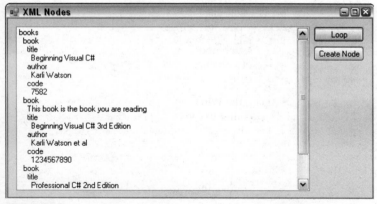

Figure 23-7

There is one important type of node that you didn't create in the preceding example: the `XmlAttribute`. I will leave this for an exercise at the end of the chapter.

How It Works

The code in the `buttonCreateNode_Click` method is where all the creation of nodes happens. It creates eight new nodes, four of which are of type `XmlElement`, three of type `XmlText`, and finally one of type `XmlComment`.

All of the nodes are created with the method of the encapsulating `XmlDocument` instance. The `XmlElement` nodes are created with the `CreateElement` method, the `XmlText` nodes are created with the `CreateTextNode` method, and the `XmlComment` node is created with the `CreateComment` method.

After the nodes have been created, they still need to be inserted into the XML tree. This is done with the `AppendChild` method on the element to which the new node should become a child. The only exception to this is the book node that is the root node of all of the new nodes. This node is inserted into the tree using the `InsertAfter` method of the root object. Whereas all of the nodes that are inserted using `AppendChild` always become the last of the list of child nodes, `InsertAfter` allows you to position the node where you want it.

Deleting Nodes

Now that you've seen how to create new nodes, all that is left is to learn how to delete them again. All classes derived from `XmlNode` include a number of methods, shown in the following table, that allow you to remove nodes from the document.

Method Name	Description
RemoveAll	Rather unsurprisingly, this method will remove all child nodes in the node on which it is called. What is slightly less obvious is that it will also remove all attributes on the node, because they are regarded as child nodes as well.
RemoveChild	This method will remove a single child in the node on which it is called. The method returns the node that has been removed from the document, but you can reinsert it if you change your mind.

The following short Try It Out extends the Windows Forms application you've been creating over the past two examples to include the capability to delete nodes. For now, all that it does is find the last instance of the book node and remove it.

Try It Out   Removing Nodes

The following steps let you find and remove the final instance of the book node.

1. Add a new button below the two that already exist and name it `buttonDeleteNode`. Set its Text property to `Delete Node`.

2. Double-click the new button and enter the following code:

```
private void buttonDeleteNode_Click(object sender, EventArgs e)
{
  // Load the XML document.
  XmlDocument document = new XmlDocument();
  document.Load(@"C:\Beginning Visual C#\Chapter 23\Books.xml");

  // Get the root element.
  XmlElement root = document.DocumentElement;

  // Find the node. root is the <books> tag, so its last child
  // which will be the last <book> node.
  if (root.HasChildNodes)
  {
    XmlNode book = root.LastChild;

    // Delete the child.
    root.RemoveChild(book);

    // Save the document back to disk.
    document.Save(@"C:\Beginning Visual C#\Chapter 23\Books.xml");
  }
}
```

3. Run the application. Note that when you click the Delete Node button and then the Loop button, the last node in the tree will disappear.

How It Works

After the initial steps to load the XML into the XmlDocument object, you examine the root element to see if there are any child elements in the XML you loaded. If there are, you use the LastChild property of the XmlElement class to get the last child. After that, removing the element is as simple as calling RemoveChild, passing in the instance of the element that you wish to remove, in this case the last child of the root element.

Selecting Nodes

You now know how to move back and forth in an XML document, how to manipulate the values of the document, how to create new nodes, and how to delete them again. Only one thing remains in this chapter: how to select nodes without having to traverse the entire tree.

The XmlNode class includes two methods commonly used to select nodes from the document without running through every node in it. These are SelectSingleNode and SelectNodes (described in the following table), both of which use a special query language, called XPath, to select the nodes. You learn about that shortly.

Method Name	Description
SelectSingleNode	This method is used to select a single node. If you create a query that fetches more than one node, only the first node will be returned.
SelectNodes	This method returns a node collection in the form of an XmlNodesList class.

XPath

XPath is a query language for XML documents much as SQL is for relational databases. It is used by the two methods described in the previous table to let you avoid the hassle of walking the entire tree of an XML document. It does take a little getting used to, however, because the syntax is nothing like SQL or C#.

XPath is quite extensive, and only a small part of it is covered here to allow you to start selecting nodes. If you are interested in learning more, you should take a look at www.w3.org/TR/xpath *and the Visual Studio help pages.*

To properly see the XPath in action, you are going to use a slightly extended version of the books.xml file. It is listed in its entirety in the "Selecting Nodes" Try It Out example later in the chapter, and it can be found on this book's Website as XPathQuery.xml.

The following table lists some of the most common operations you can perform with XPath. If nothing else is stated, then the XPath query example will make a selection that is relative to the node on which it is performed. Where it is necessary to have a name of a node, you can assume that the current node is the <book> node in the XML document above.

Purpose	XPath Query Example
Select the current node.	.
Select the parent of the current node.	..
Select all child nodes of the current node.	*
Select all child nodes with a specific name—in this case title.	title
Select an attribute of the current node.	@pages
Select all attributes of the current node.	@*
Select a child node by index—in this case the second author node.	author[2]
Select all the text nodes of the current node.	text()
Select one or more grandchildren of the current node.	author/text()
Select all nodes in the document with a particular name—in this case all title nodes.	//title
Select all nodes in the document with a particular name and particular parent name—in this case the parent name is book and node name is title.	//book/title
Select a node where a value criteria is met—in this case, the books where the author Jacob Hammer Pedersen participated.	//book[author='Jacob Hammer Pedersen']
Select a node where an attribute value criteria is met—in this case the pages attribute = 1000.	//book[@pages='1000']

In the following Try It Out, you'll create a small application that will allow you to execute and see the results of a number of predefined queries, as well as allow you to enter your own queries.

Selecting Nodes

As previously mentioned, this example uses an extended version of the `books.xml` file seen earlier in this chapter. You can download the file from the book's Website or type it in from the listing here:

```
<?xml version="1.0"?>
<books>
  <book pages="944">
    <title>Beginning Visual C#</title>
    <author>Karli Watson</author>
    <author>Jacob Hammer Pedersen</author>
    <author>Christian Nagel</author>
    <author>David Espinosa</author>
    <author>Zach Greenvoss</author>
    <author>Jon D. Reid</author>
    <author>Matthew Reynolds</author>
    <author>Morgan Skinner</author>
    <author>Eric White</author>
    <code>7582</code>
  </book>
  <book pages="1000">
    <title>Beginning Visual C# 3rd Edition</title>
    <author>Karli Watson</author>
    <author>Jacob Hammer Pedersen</author>
    <author>Christian Nagel</author>
    <author>Jon D. Reid</author>
    <author>Morgan Skinner</author>
    <author>Eric White</author>
    <code>1234567890</code>
  </book>
  <book pages="1272">
    <title>Professional C# 2nd Edition</title>
    <author>Simon Robinson</author>
    <author>Scott Allen</author>
    <author>Ollie Cornes</author>
    <author>Jay Glynn</author>
    <author>Zach Greenvoss</author>
    <author>Burton Harvey</author>
    <author>Christian Nagel</author>
    <author>Morgan Skinner</author>
    <author>Karli Watson</author>
    <code>7043</code>
  </book>
</books>
```

Save the XML file as `XPathQuery.xml`. Remember to change the path to the file in the code that follows.

Follow these steps to create a Windows Forms application with querying capability.

1. Create a new Windows Forms application and name it `XmlQueryExample`.

2. Create the dialog shown in Figure 23-8. Name the `TextBox` `textBoxQuery`. All the other controls should be named with their type followed by their text property (that is, the name of the radio button "Set Book as current" is `radioButtonSetBookAsCurrent` and the Close button is `buttonClose`).

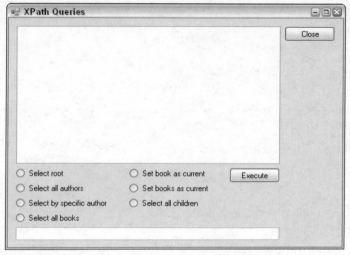

Figure 23-8

3. Right-click the form and choose View Code. The first thing is to include the `using` directive:

```
using System.Xml;
```

4. Next, add two private fields to hold the document and current node, and initialize them in the constructor:

```
private XmlDocument mDocument;
private XmlNode mCurrentNode;

public Form1()
{
   InitializeComponent();

   mDocument = new XmlDocument();
   mDocument.Load(@"C:\Beginning Visual C#\Chapter 23\XPathQuery.xml");
   mCurrentNode = mDocument.DocumentElement;
   ClearListBox();
}
```

5. Next, you need a few helper methods to display the result of the queries in the list box:

```
private void DisplayList(XmlNodeList nodeList)
{
   foreach (XmlNode node in nodeList)
   {
      RecurseXmlDocumentNoSiblings(node, 0);
   }
}

private void RecurseXmlDocumentNoSiblings(XmlNode root, int indent)
{
   // Make sure we don't do anything if the root is null.
```

```
      if (root == null)
        return;

      if (root is XmlElement) // Root is an XmlElement type
      {
        // First, print the name.
        listBoxResult.Items.Add(root.Name.PadLeft(root.Name.Length + indent));

        // Then check if there are any child nodes and if there are, call this
        // method again to print them.
        if (root.HasChildNodes)
          RecurseXmlDocument(root.FirstChild, indent + 2);
      }
      else if (root is XmlText)
      {
        // Print the text.
        string text = ((XmlText)root).Value;
        listBoxResult.Items.Add(text.PadLeft(text.Length + indent));
      }
      else if (root is XmlComment)
      {
        // Print text.
        string text = root.Value;
        listBoxResult.Items.Add(text.PadLeft(text.Length + indent));

        // Then check if there are any child nodes and if there are, call this
        // method again to print them.
        if (root.HasChildNodes)
          RecurseXmlDocument(root.FirstChild, indent + 2);
      }
    }

    private void RecurseXmlDocument(XmlNode root, int indent)
    {
      // Make sure we don't do anything if the root is null.
      if (root == null)
        return;

      if (root is XmlElement) // Root is an XmlElement type.
      {
        // First, print the name.
        listBoxResult.Items.Add(root.Name.PadLeft(root.Name.Length + indent));

        // Then check if there are any child nodes and if there are, call this
        // method again to print them.
        if (root.HasChildNodes)
          RecurseXmlDocument(root.FirstChild, indent + 2);

        // Finally check to see if there are any siblings, and if there are
        // call this method again to have them printed.
        if (root.NextSibling != null)
          RecurseXmlDocument(root.NextSibling, indent);
      }
      else if (root is XmlText)
      {
```

```
      // Print the text.
      string text = ((XmlText)root).Value;
      listBoxResult.Items.Add(text.PadLeft(text.Length + indent));
    }
    else if (root is XmlComment)
    {
      // Print text.
      string text = root.Value;
      listBoxResult.Items.Add(text.PadLeft(text.Length + indent));

      // Then check if there are any child nodes. and if there are call this
      // method again to print them.
      if (root.HasChildNodes)
        RecurseXmlDocument(root.FirstChild, indent + 2);

      // Finally, check to see if there are any siblings, and if there are
      // call this method again to have them printed.
      if (root.NextSibling != null)
        RecurseXmlDocument(root.NextSibling, indent);
    }
  }

private void ClearListBox()
{
  listBoxResult.Items.Clear();
}

private void buttonClose_Click(object sender, EventArgs e)
{
  Application.Exit();
}
```

6. Next, insert the code to perform the queries on the XML into the SelectionChange event of the radio buttons:

```
private void radioButtonSelectRoot_CheckedChanged(object sender, EventArgs e)
{
  mCurrentNode = mDocument.DocumentElement.SelectSingleNode("//books");
  ClearListBox();
  RecurseXmlDocument(mCurrentNode, 0);
}

private void radioButtonSelectAllAuthors_CheckedChanged(object sender,
EventArgs e)
{
  if (mCurrentNode != null)
  {
    XmlNodeList nodeList = mCurrentNode.SelectNodes("//book/author");
    ClearListBox();
    DisplayList(nodeList);
  }
  else
    ClearListBox();
}
```

```csharp
    private void radioButtonSelectBySpecificAuthor_CheckedChanged(object sender,
EventArgs e)
    {
      if (mCurrentNode != null)
      {
        XmlNodeList nodeList = mCurrentNode.SelectNodes("//book[author='Jacob
Hammer Pedersen']");
        ClearListBox();
        DisplayList(nodeList);
      }
      else
        ClearListBox();
    }

    private void radioButtonSelectAllBooks_CheckedChanged(object sender, EventArgs e)
    {
      if (mCurrentNode != null)
      {
        XmlNodeList nodeList = mCurrentNode.SelectNodes("//book");
        ClearListBox();
        DisplayList(nodeList);
      }
      else
        ClearListBox();
    }

    private void radioButtonSetBookAsCurrent_CheckedChanged(object sender,
EventArgs e)
    {
      if (mCurrentNode != null)
      {
        mCurrentNode = mCurrentNode.SelectSingleNode("book[title='Beginning Visual
C#']");
        ClearListBox();
        RecurseXmlDocumentNoSiblings(mCurrentNode, 0);
      }
      else
        ClearListBox();
    }

    private void radioButtonSetBooksAsCurrent_CheckedChanged(object sender,
EventArgs e)
    {
      if (mCurrentNode != null)
      {
        mCurrentNode = mCurrentNode.SelectSingleNode("//books");
        ClearListBox();
        RecurseXmlDocumentNoSiblings(mCurrentNode, 0);
      }
      else
        ClearListBox();
    }

    private void radioButtonSelectAllChildren_CheckedChanged(object sender,
EventArgs e)
```

```
    {
      if (mCurrentNode != null)
      {
        XmlNodeList nodeList = mCurrentNode.SelectNodes("*");
        ClearListBox();
        DisplayList(nodeList);
      }
      else
        ClearListBox();
    }
```

7. Finally, insert the code that executes whatever the user has entered in the `TextBox` and the code that closes the application when the buttonClose button is clicked:

```
    private void buttonExecute_Click(object sender, EventArgs e)
    {
      if (textBoxQuery.Text == "")
        return;

      try
      {
        XmlNodeList nodeList = mCurrentNode.SelectNodes(textBoxQuery.Text);
        ClearListBox();
        DisplayList(nodeList);
      }
      catch (System.Exception err)
      {
        MessageBox.Show(err.Message);
      }
    }

    private void buttonClose_Click(object sender, EventArgs e)
    {
      Application.Exit();
    }
```

8. Run the application. Note how the values change as you click the radio buttons.

How It Works

The first two methods, `RecurseXmlDocumentNoSiblings` and `RecurseXmlDocument`, and `DisplayList` are used to make the listings in the list box. The reason you need more than one of these methods is that you want to be able to more tightly control the output.

The code that does the actual searching in the XML is all found in the code in steps 6 and 7. The method `SelectNodes` of the `XmlNode` class is used to execute searches that can or should return multiple nodes. This method returns an `XmlNodeList` object, which is then passed to the `DisplayList` helper method.

The other method that is used to search through the XML is `SelectSingleNode`. This method, as the name suggests, returns a single node, which you pass to the `RecurseXmlNodeNoSiblings` helper method to display the current node and its child nodes.

The following table lists the XPath queries that are used in the methods and what they do.

XPath	Description
`//book/author`	This selects all the nodes in the XML that have the name `author` and the parent `book`.
`//book[author='Jacob Hammer Pedersen']`	Selects all the `book` nodes in the XML that have a child node with the name `author` that has the value `Jacob Hammer Pedersen`.
`//book`	Selects all the book nodes in the XML.
`book[title='Beginning Visual C#']`	Selects the book node with the title node that equals `Beginning Visual C#`.
`//books`	Selects all books nodes.
`*`	Selects all child nodes of the current node.

Summary

In this chapter you learned about Extensible Markup Language (XML), a text format for storing and retrieving data. We looked at the rules we need to obey to ensure that XML documents are well-formed, and you saw how to validate them against XSD and XDR schemas.

After learning about the basics of XML you saw how XML can be utilized through code using C# and Visual Studio, and finally you saw how to use XPath to make queries in the XML.

The topics we covered were:

❑ How to read and write Extensible Markup Language (XML)

❑ The rules that apply to well-formed XML

❑ How to validate your XML documents against two types of Schema: XSD and XDR

❑ How to use .NET to use XML in your programs

❑ How to search through XML documents using XPath queries

In the next chapter you will learn how to access databases in .Net using ADO.Net. Before you move on you should try the exercises below.

Exercises

1. Change the Insert example in the "Creating Nodes" Try It Out section to insert an attribute called `Pages` with the value `1000` on the book node.

2. Currently, the last example about XPath doesn't have built-in capability to search for an attribute. Add a radio button and make a query for all books where the `pages` attribute of the book node equals 1000.

3. Change the methods that write to the listbox (`RecurseXmlDocument` and `RecurseXmlDocumentNoSiblings`) in the XPath example so that they're able to display attributes.

Databases and ADO.NET

This chapter shows you how to access relational databases with C#. Because this is a C# book, this is a largely code-based chapter, showing how ADO.NET (the data access classes in .NET) is structured and how to accomplish basic data access with C# code. In the next chapter, you look at how Visual Studio 2005 can generate much of the data access code for you and how to use that generated code in many common business situations. However, it is important that you have the background information necessary to understand what the wizard-generated code is doing for you and how you can combine your own code with what Visual Studio 2005 generates to provide maximum flexibility and productivity when accessing relational data. That background is provided in this chapter. In particular, you look at:

❑   An overview of ADO.NET, and the structure of its main classes

❑   Reading data with a `DataReader` and with a `DataSet`

❑   Updating the database, adding records and deleting records

❑   Working with relationships in ADO.NET

❑   Reading and writing XML documents in ADO.NET

❑   Direct execution of SQL commands from ADO.NET

❑   Execution of stored procedures from ADO.NET

First, you get an overview of ADO.NET and learn the concepts behind it. Then you can create some simple projects and start using the ADO.NET classes.

What Is ADO.NET?

ADO.NET is the name for the set of classes you use with C# and the .NET Framework to access data in a relational, table-oriented format. This includes relational databases such as Microsoft SQL Server and Microsoft Access, as well as other databases and even nonrelational data sources. ADO.NET is integrated into the .NET Framework and is designed to be used with any .NET language, especially C#.

ADO.NET includes all of the `System.Data` namespace and its nested namespaces such as `System.Data.SqlClient` and `System.Data.OleDb`, plus some specific data-related classes from the `System.Xml` namespace. You looked at XML in Chapter 23; in this chapter you see ADO.NET's support for XML. Physically, the ADO.NET classes are contained in the `System.Data.dll` assembly and related `System.Data.xxx.dll` assemblies, again with some exceptions such as XML.

Why Is It Called ADO.NET?

You might ask, why does this part of the .NET Framework get its own weird moniker, ADO.NET? Why not just call it `System.Data` and be done with it? ADO.NET takes its name from ADO (ActiveX Data Objects), a widely used set of classes used for data access in the previous generation of Microsoft technologies. The ADO.NET name is used because Microsoft wants to make it clear that this is the preferred data access interface in the .NET programming environment.

ADO.NET serves the same purpose as ADO, providing an easy-to-use set of classes for data access, updated and enhanced for the .NET programming environment. While it fulfills the same role as ADO, the classes, properties, and methods in ADO.NET are quite different from those in ADO.

If you are interested in more details of how this developed historically and where it fits in with other Microsoft database interfaces such as ODBC and OLE DB, see the following brief history. Otherwise, skip to the next section to start learning about ADO.NET!

A (Very) Brief History of Data Access

When the first database systems, such as Oracle and IBM's DB2, were written, any developers who wanted their programs to access the data in them needed to use sets of functions that were specific to that database system. Each system had its own library of functions, such as the Oracle Call Interface (OCI) for Oracle, or DBLib for Sybase's SQL Server (later bought by Microsoft). This allowed the programs to have fast access to the data, because their programs communicated directly with the database. However, it meant that programmers had to be familiar with a different library for every database they worked with, so the task of writing data-driven applications was very complicated. It also meant that if a company changed the database system it used, its applications had to be completely rewritten.

This problem was solved by *Open Database Connectivity (ODBC)*. ODBC was developed by Microsoft in collaboration with other companies in the early 1990s. ODBC provided a common set of functions that developers could use against any database system. These functions were translated into database-specific function calls by drivers for that specific database system.

This solved the main problems of the proprietary database libraries — developers only needed to know how to use one set of functions (the ODBC functions), and if a company changed its database system, all it needed to change in its applications was the code to connect to the database. However, there was still one problem. While the *paperless office* is still largely a myth, companies do have a vast amount of electronic data stored in a whole variety of places — e-mails, Web pages, Project 2000 files, and so on. ODBC was fine for accessing data in traditional databases, but it couldn't access other types of data, which aren't stored in nice neat columns and rows and don't necessarily have a coherent structure at all.

The answer to this problem was provided by *OLE DB*. OLE DB works in a similar way to ODBC, providing a layer of abstraction between the database and applications that need access to the data. Client applications communicate with the data source, which can be a traditional database or any other place where data is held, through an OLE DB provider for that data source. Data from any source is exposed to the application in table format — just as if it came from a database. And because OLE DB allowed access to data exposed by the existing ODBC drivers, it could be used to access all the databases supported by ODBC. As you will see shortly, ADO.NET supports both OLE DB and ODBC in a very similar way.

The last *legacy* data access technology to mention is *ActiveX Data Objects (ADO)*. ADO is simply a thin layer, which sits on top of OLE DB, and allows programs written in high-level languages such as Visual Basic to access OLE DB data.

Design Goals of ADO.NET

Let's quickly look at the design goals of ADO.NET. These include:

❑ Simple access to relational and nonrelational data

❑ Extensibility to support even more data sources than its predecessor technologies

❑ Support for multitier applications across the Internet

❑ Unification of XML and relational data access

Simple Access to Relational Data

The primary goal of ADO.NET is to provide simple access to relational data. Straightforward, easy-to-use classes represent the tables, columns, and rows within relational databases. Additionally, ADO.NET introduces the `DataSet` class, which represents a set of data from related tables encapsulated as a single unit, preserving the integrity of the relationships between them. This is a new concept in ADO.NET that significantly extends the capabilities of the data access interface.

Extensibility

ADO.NET is *extensible* — it provides a framework for plug-in .NET data providers (also called *managed providers*) that can be built to read and write data from any data source. ADO.NET comes with several built-in .NET data providers, including one for the Microsoft SQL Server database, one for Oracle, one each for the generic database interfaces ODBC (the Microsoft Open DataBase Connectivity database API) and OLE DB (Microsoft's COM-based Object Linking and Embedding DataBase API). Almost every database and data file format has an ODBC or OLE DB provider available for it, including Microsoft Access, third-party databases, and nonrelational data; thus, ADO.NET can be used to interface to almost any database or data format through one of the built-in data providers. Many database vendors such as MySQL and Oracle also provide native .NET data providers for their offerings.

Support for Multitier Applications

ADO.NET is designed for multitier applications. This is the most common architecture today for business and e-commerce applications. In multitier architecture, different parts of the application logic are separated into layers, or tiers, and communicate only with the layer around them.

One of the most common approaches is the 3-tier model, which consists of the following:

❑ **Data tier:** Contains the database and data access code.

❑ **Business tier:** Contains the business logic, which defines the unique functionality of this application, and abstracts this away from other tiers. This tier is sometimes referred to as the *middle tier*.

❑ **Presentation tier:** Provides the user interface and control of process flow to the application, as well as such things as the validation of user input.

ADO.NET uses the open Internet-standard XML format for communications between the tiers, allowing data to pass through Internet firewalls and allowing the possibility of a non-Microsoft implementation of one or more tiers.

Unification of XML and Relational Data Access

Another important goal of ADO.NET is to provide a bridge between relational data in rows and columns, and XML documents, which have a hierarchical data structure. The .NET technology is built around XML, and ADO.NET makes extensive use of it.

Now that you've seen what ADO.NET's goals are, let's look at the actual ADO.NET classes themselves.

Overview of ADO.NET Classes and Objects

The diagram in Figure 24-1 shows the basic classes in ADO.NET. Note that this is not an inheritance diagram but rather shows the relationships between the most commonly used classes.

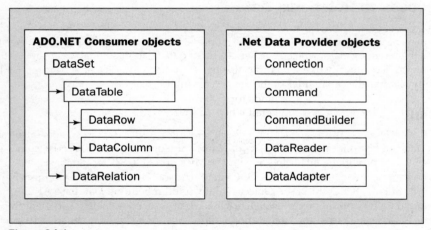

Figure 24-1

Here the classes are divided into .NET data provider objects and consumer objects.

❑ *Provider objects* are specific to each type of data source — the actual reading and writing to and from the data source is done with the provider-specific objects.

❑ *Consumer objects* are what you use to access and manipulate the data once you have read it into memory.

The provider objects require an active connection. You use these first to read the data, then depending on your needs, you may work with the data in memory using the consumer objects. You can also update the data in the data source using the provider objects to write the changes back to the data source. Thus, the consumer objects operate in a disconnected fashion; you can work with the data in memory even if the database connection is down.

Provider Objects

These are the objects defined in each .NET data provider. The names are prefaced with a name unique to the provider; so for example the actual connection object for the OLE DB provider is `OleDbConnection`; the class for the SQL Server .NET provider is `SqlConnection`.

Connection Object

The connection object is typically the first object that you will use, before using most of the other ADO.NET objects — it provides the basic connection to your data source. If you are using a database that requires a user and password or one on a remote network server, the connection object takes care of the details of establishing the connection and logging in.

If you are familiar with classic ADO, you'll note that Connection and other objects that serve a similar function in classic ADO have similar names in ADO.NET.

Command Object

You use this object to give a command to a data source, such as `SELECT * FROM Customers` to query the data in the `Customers` table.

The provider-specific names include `SqlCommand` for SQL Server, `OdbcCommand` for ODBC, and `OleDbCommand` for OLE DB.

CommandBuilder Object

This object is used to build SQL commands for data modification from objects based on a single-table query. You look at this object in more detail when you study how to update data.

The provider-specific names include `SqlCommandBuilder` for SQL Server, `OdbcCommandBuilder` for ODBC, and `OleDbCommandBuilder` for OLE DB.

DataReader Object

This is a fast, simple-to-use object that reads a forward-only read-only stream of data (such as the set of customers found) from a data source. This object gives the maximum performance for simply reading data; the first example will demonstrate how to use this object.

The provider-specific names include `SqlDataReader` for SQL Server, `OdbcDataReader` for ODBC, and `OleDbDataReader` for OLE DB.

DataAdapter Object

This is a general-purpose class that performs various operations specific to the data source, including updating changed data, filling `DataSet` objects (see the "DataSet Object" section) and other operations, which you see in the following examples.

The provider-specific names include `SqlDataAdapter` for SQL Server, `OdbcDataAdapter` for ODBC, and `OleDbAdapter` for OLE DB.

Consumer Objects

These are the objects defined for the disconnected, consumer side of ADO.NET. These aren't related to any specific .NET data provider and live within the `System.Data` namespace.

DataSet Object

The `DataSet` is the king of consumer objects. The `DataSet` represents a set of related tables referenced as one unit in your application. For example, `Customers`, `Orders`, and `Products` might all be tables in one `DataSet` representing each customer and the products he or she ordered from your company. With this object, you can get all the data you need from each table quickly, examine and change it while you're disconnected from the server, and then update the server with the changes in one efficient operation.

The `DataSet` has features that let you access lower-level objects that represent individual tables and relationships. These objects, the `DataTable` object and the `DataRelation` object, are covered in the following sections.

DataTable Object

This object represents one of the tables in the `DataSet`, such as `Customers`, `Orders`, or `Products`.

The `DataTable` object has features that allow you to access its rows and columns:

❑   **DataColumn object:** This represents one column in the table, for example `OrderID` or `CustomerName`.

❑   **DataRow object:** This represents one row of related data from a table; for example, a particular customer's `CustomerID`, name, address, and so on.

DataRelation Object

This object represents the relationship between two tables via a shared column; for example, the `Orders` table might have a `CustomerID` column identifying the customer who placed the order. A `DataRelation` object might be created representing the relationship between `Customers` and `Orders` via the shared column `CustomerID`.

You now have an idea of the overall structure of the objects in ADO.NET. There are more objects than the ones just listed, but let's skip the details for now and get into some examples that show how this all works.

Using the System.Data Namespace

The first step in using ADO.NET within your C# code is to reference the `System.Data` namespace, in which all the ADO.NET classes are located. Put the following `using` directive at the beginning of any program using ADO.NET:

```
using System.Data;
```

Next, you need to reference the .NET data provider for the specific data source you'll be using.

SQL Server .NET Data Provider

If you are using the SQL Server database (version 7 or greater), including the desktop engine (SQL Express or MSDE), the best performance and most direct access to the underlying features is available with the native (SQL Server–specific) .NET data provider, referenced with this `using` directive:

```
using System.Data.SqlClient;
```

Oracle .NET Data Provider

If you are using the Oracle database, a native Oracle .NET driver is the best choice; one is provided with the .NET Framework, referenced with this `using` directive:

```
using System.Data.OracleClient;
```

Oracle itself also provides a .NET data provider, referenced as `Oracle.DataAccess.Client`. This is a separate download that you have to get from Oracle. Whether you use a .NET data provider from the database vendor or just use the one provided with the .NET Framework is your choice. Generally, a provider from the vendor will make more use of the database product's special features, but for basic or beginning usage this is unlikely to matter much. Either provider will work; use the one that you prefer.

OLE DB .NET Data Provider

For data sources other than SQL Server or Oracle (such as Microsoft Access), you can use the OLE DB .NET data provider, referenced with this `using` directive:

```
using System.Data.OleDb;
```

This provider uses an OLE DB provider DLL for the specific database you are accessing; OLE DB providers for many common databases are installed with Windows, notably Microsoft Access, which you will use in the following examples.

ODBC .NET Data Provider

If you have a data source for which no native or OLE DB provider is available, the ODBC .NET data provider is a good alternative because most databases provide an ODBC interface. It is referenced with this `using` directive:

```
using System.Data.Odbc;
```

Other Native .NET Data Providers

If there is a native .NET data provider available specifically for your database, then you may want to use that .NET data provider instead. Many other database vendors and third-party companies provide native .NET data providers; the choice between using the native provider and using something generic like the ODBC provider will depend on your circumstances. If you value portability over performance, then go generic. If you want to get the best performance or make the best use of a particular database's features, go native.

Install SQL Server and the Northwind Sample Data

To run the examples shown in this chapter, you must install either Microsoft SQL Server or one of its lightweight equivalents (SQL Express or MSDE).

While ADO.NET can work with many different database products, the details differ with the database used. The examples in this chapter and Chapter 25 are based on the Microsoft SQL Server database, except where a different database is specifically noted, so one of the first tasks is to install SQL Server!

Install SQL Express

Visual Studio 2005 includes a copy of SQL Express, the lightweight desktop engine version of SQL Server 2005. If you are familiar with previous versions of SQL Server, you may have known this lightweight version as the Microsoft SQL Desktop Engine (MSDE).

If you have already installed SQL Server 2000 or the desktop engine version of SQL Server 2000 (MSDE) on your system, you can use your existing installation and skip the following steps for installing SQL Express.

Note that if you use your existing installation of SQL Server, you need to change the instance name as used in the examples from SQLExpress to the name of your server.

SQL Express is offered as one of the packages to install with VS2005, but is not checked by default. If you did not check the option to install SQL Express, you can install it by browsing to the directory:

```
C:\Program Files\Microsoft Visual Studio 8\SDK\v2.0\Bootstrapper\Packages\
SqlExpress\en
```

Execute the installation executable in this location:

```
Sqlexpr32.exe
```

Be sure to check the client command-line tools in order to include osql.exe as part of the installation.

Install the Northwind Sample Database

The Northwind sample database for SQL Server is included with the Quickstart samples of Visual Studio 2005 in the .NET Framework v2.0 SDK samples setup area. If you did not select the Quickstart samples as one of the features to install, run the VS2005 setup again and select .NET Framework SDK ➪ Quickstart Samples.

To install the Northwind sample into your SQL Express instance after installing the Quickstart samples, execute a command prompt (Start ➪ Run ➪ cmd) and change directory to the samples setup area:

```
cd "C:\Program Files\Microsoft Visual Studio 8\SDK\v2.0\Samples\Setup"
```

Assuming that you have installed SQL Express on your computer as noted earlier, run the osql utility (located in C:\Program Files\Microsoft SQL Server\90\Tools\Binn) to install the sample data:

```
osql -E -S (local)\sqlexpress -i instnwnd.sql
```

The –E flag tells osql to use the built-in Windows security (your Windows login) as the SQL Server user. The –S flag identifies the name of the SQL Server, which consists of a server name and an instance name. The sqlexpress name is an instance name; you may have multiple versions of SQL Server running on one machine, identified by a unique instance name; sqlexpress is the default instance created by the SQL Express installation. The server name (local) is a generic name for a local server; that is, the SQL Server running on the same machine as osql or VS2005 (your desktop computer). You may substitute the actual name of your machine for (local); for example, my laptop is called roadrunner, so I could also invoke osql with –S roadrunner\sqlexpress, which would refer to the sqlexpress instance of SQL Server running on the machine named roadrunner.

This completes the installation of SQL Server (SQL Express) and the sample data needed for this chapter. Now let's go on to have some fun with Visual Studio 2005!

Reading Data with the DataReader

In the following Try It Out, you just get some data from one table, the `Customers` table in the SQL Server/MSDE `Northwind` sample database (you look at this database again in Chapter 25). The `Customers` table contains rows and columns with data about the customers of Northwind traders. The first example here uses a `DataReader` to retrieve the `CustomerID` and `CompanyName` columns from this table.

Try It Out   Reading Data with the DataReader

Follow these steps to create the example in Visual Studio 2005:

1. Create a new console application called `DataReading` in the directory `C:\BegVCSharp\Chapter24`.

2. Begin by adding the `using` directives for the ADO.NET classes you will be using:

```
#region Using Directives
using System;
using System.Data;              // Use ADO.NET namespace
using System.Data.SqlClient;    // Use SQL Server data provider namespace
using System.Collections.Generic;
using System.Text;
#endregion
```

3. Now add the following code to the `Main()` method:

```
static void Main(string[] args)
{
    // Specify SQL Server-specific connection string
    SqlConnection thisConnection = new SqlConnection(
        @"Server=(local)\sqlexpress;Integrated Security=True;" +
        "Database=northwind");

    // Open connection
    thisConnection.Open();

    // Create command for this connection
    SqlCommand thisCommand = thisConnection.CreateCommand();
```

```
    // Specify SQL query for this command
    thisCommand.CommandText =
        "SELECT CustomerID, CompanyName from Customers";

    // Execute DataReader for specified command
    SqlDataReader thisReader = thisCommand.ExecuteReader();

    // While there are rows to read
    while (thisReader.Read())
    {
        // Output ID and name columns
        Console.WriteLine("\t{0}\t{1}",
        thisReader["CustomerID"], thisReader["CompanyName"]);
    }

    // Close reader
    thisReader.Close();

    // Close connection
    thisConnection.Close();

    Console.Write("Program finished, press Enter/Return to continue:");
    Console.ReadLine();
}
```

4. Compile and execute this program. You will see a list of customer IDs and company names, as shown in Figure 24-2. If you don't see the output below, don't worry, you come to the possible problems in a moment.

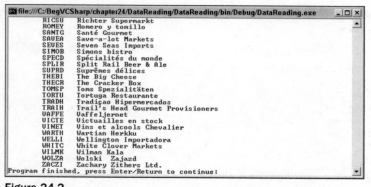

Figure 24-2

How It Works

The first step is to reference the `System.Data` namespace and your provider as described before. You're going to use the SQL Server .NET provider in these examples, so you need the following lines at the start of your program:

```
using System.Data;
using System.Data.SqlClient;
```

There are five steps to retrieving the data from the program:

1. Connect to the data source.

2. Open the connection.

3. Issue a SQL query.

4. Read and display the data with the `DataReader`.

5. Close the `DataReader` and the connection.

You look at each of these steps in turn.

First, you need to connect to your data source. This is done by creating a connection object using a connection string. The connection string is just a character string containing the name of the provider for the database you want to connect to, the login information (database user, password, and so on), and the name of the particular database you want to use. Let's look at the specific elements of this connection string; however, keep in mind that these strings differ significantly between data providers, so you need to look up the specific connection information for your data provider if it is different from this example (the connection information for Access is shown a little later in the chapter).

The line where you create the connection object looks like this:

```
SqlConnection thisConnection = new SqlConnection(
    @"Server=(local)\sqlexpress;Integrated Security=True;" +
    "Database=northwind");
```

`SqlConnection` is the name of the connection object for the SQL .NET data provider; if you were using OLE DB you would create an `OleDbConnection`, but you see this in the next example. The connection string consists of named entries separated by semicolons; let's look at each one. The first is:

```
Server=(local)\sqlexpress;
```

This is just the name of the SQL Server you are accessing, in the form `computername\instancename`. The computer name `(local)` is a handy SQL Server shorthand name that refers to the server instance running on the current machine. You can also substitute the actual network name of your computer; for example, my laptop computer is `\\roadrunner`, so I could also use `roadrunner\sqlexpress` as my server name.

`sqlexpress` is the SQL Server *instance* name. There can be multiple copies of SQL Server installed on one machine, and the instance name, set at installation time, is a how you tell SQL Server which one you want. `Sqlexpress` is the default instance name used when you install SQL Express. If you have another version of SQL Server installed, the instance name will differ — there may be no instance name (in which case you would use `(local)` or your machine name by itself), or it may be a different name, such as `(local)\NetSDK` used for the MSDE installations with previous versions .NET Framework.

Note that the @ sign prefacing the connection string indicates a string literal, making the backslash in this name work; otherwise double backslashes (\\) are necessary to escape the backslash character inside a C# string.

If you installed the SQL Server you are working with, you know the name of the SQL Server instance. Otherwise, you have to check with your SQL Server or network administrator to find out what name to use.

The next part of the connection string specifies how to log in to the database; here, you use the integrated security of the Windows login so no separate user and password need to be specified:

```
Integrated Security=True;
```

This clause specifies the standard built-in security for SQL Server and Windows. Alternatively, instead of the Integrated Security clause you could specify a username and password clause, as in User=sa; PWD=secret. Using the built-in security of your Windows login is preferable to using hard-coded usernames and passwords in connection strings!

Finally, the particular database you want to use is specified, in this case, the Northwind sample:

```
Database=northwind
```

You must have installed the Northwind sample for this database to be found; it may already be present if you are using an existing SQL Server installation, though many database administrators choose to omit it to save space.

Anyway, you now have a connection object that is configured for your machine and database (but the connection is not yet active; to do this you must open it).

Once you have a connection object, you can move on to the second step. The first thing you want to do with the connection object is open it, which establishes the connection to the database:

```
thisConnection.Open();
```

If the Open() method fails, for example if the SQL Server cannot be found, a SqlException exception will be thrown and you will see a message like that shown in Figure 24-3.

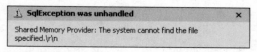

Figure 24-3

This particular message indicates that the program couldn't find the SQL Server database or server. Check that the server name in the connection string is correct and that the server is running.

The third step is to create a command object and give it a SQL command to perform a database operation (such as retrieving some data). The code to do this is as follows:

```
SqlCommand thisCommand = thisConnection.CreateCommand();
thisCommand.CommandText = "SELECT CustomerID, CompanyName from Customers";
```

The connection object has a method called CreateCommand() to create a command associated with this connection, so you will use this to get your command object. The command itself is assigned to the CommandText property of the command object. You're going to get a list of the customer IDs and the company names from the Northwind database, so that is the basis for your SQL query command:

```
SELECT CustomerID, CompanyName from Customers
```

The SELECT command is the SQL command to get the data from one or more tables. A common error is to mistype the name of one of the tables, resulting in another exception:

```
thisCommand.CommandText = "SELECT CustomerID, CompanyName from Customer";
```

Whoops! I forgot the "s" in Customers—I get the exception shown in Figure 24-4.

Figure 24-4

Fix the typo, rebuild, and move on.

The fourth step is to read and display the data. First, you have to read the data—you do this with a DataReader. The DataReader is a lightweight, fast object for quickly getting the results of a query. It is read-only, so you can't use it to update data—you get to that after you finish this example. As you saw in the previous section, you use a method from the last object you created, the command object, to create an associated instance of the object you need next—in this case, the DataReader:

```
SqlDataReader thisReader = thisCommand.ExecuteReader();
```

ExecuteReader() executes the SQL command at the database, so any database errors are generated here; it also creates the reader object for reading the generated results—here you assign it to thisReader.

There are several methods for getting the results out of the reader, but the following is the usual process. The Read() method of DataReader reads a single row of the data resulting from the query, and returns true while there is more data to read, false if there is not. So, you set up a while loop to read data with the Read() method and print out the results as you get them on each iteration:

```
while (thisReader.Read())
{
    Console.WriteLine("\t{0}\t{1}",
                    thisReader["CustomerID"], thisReader["CompanyName"]);
}
```

So, while Read() returns true, Console.WriteLine("\t{0}\t{1}", ...) writes out a line with two pieces of data separated by tab characters (\t). The DataReader object provides an indexer property (see Chapter 11 for a discussion of indexers). The indexer is overloaded, and allows you to reference the columns as an array reference by column name: thisReader["CustomerID"], thisReader["CompanyName"], or by an integer: thisReader[0], thisReader[1].

When Read() returns false at the end of the results, the while loop ends.

The fifth and final step is to close the objects you opened, which include the reader object and the connection object. Each of these objects has a Close() method, which you call before exiting the program:

```
thisReader.Close();
thisConnection.Close();
```

That's all there is to accessing a single table!

The same program can be written with just a few simple changes to use the Microsoft Access version of this database (nwind.mdb). This can be found in the C:\Program Files\Microsoft Office\Office\Samples directory (if you have Office). Make a copy of the file (in a temporary directory such as C:\tmp\nwind.mdb), so you can always go back to the original.

If you do not have Office already, download Nwind.exe from:

> www.microsoft.com/downloads/details.aspx?familyid=c6661372-8dbe-422b-8676-c632d66c529c&displaylang=en

Execute Nwind.exe to install the sample database; it prompts you for a directory, so you can place it wherever you want to, such as in c:\tmp. Except for the details of the connection string, the changes you make in the following Try It Out will work for any other OLE DB data source.

Try It Out   Reading from an Access Database

1. Create a new console application called ReadingAccessData in the directory C:\BegVCSharp\Chapter24.

2. Begin by adding the using directives for the OLE DB provider classes you will be using:

```
#region Using Directives
using System;
using System.Data;              // Use ADO.NET namespace
using System.Data.OleDb;        // Use namespace for OLE DB .NET Data Provider
using System.Collections.Generic;
using System.Text;
#endregion
```

3. Now add the following code to the Main() method:

```
static void Main(string[] args)
{
    // Create connection object for Microsoft Access OLE DB Provider;
    // note @ sign prefacing string literal so backslashes in path name;
    // work
    OleDbConnection thisConnection = new OleDbConnection(
        @"Provider=Microsoft.Jet.OLEDB.4.0;Data Source=C:\tmp\nwind.mdb");

    // Open connection object
    thisConnection.Open();

    // Create SQL command object on this connection
    OleDbCommand thisCommand = thisConnection.CreateCommand();

    // Initialize SQL SELECT command to retrieve desired data
    thisCommand.CommandText =
        "SELECT CustomerID, CompanyName FROM Customers";

    // Create a DataReader object based on previously defined command object
    OleDbDataReader thisReader = thisCommand.ExecuteReader();
```

```
        while (thisReader.Read())
        {
            Console.WriteLine("\t{0}\t{1}",
            thisReader["CustomerID"], thisReader["CompanyName"]);
        }
        thisReader.Close();
        thisConnection.Close();

        Console.Write("Program finished, press Enter/Return to continue:");
        Console.ReadLine();
    }
```

How It Works

Instead of the SqlConnection, SqlCommand, and SqlDataReader objects, you create OleDbConnection, OleDbCommand, and OleDbDataReader objects. These objects work essentially the same way as their SQL Server counterparts.

Accordingly, you change the using directive that specifies the data provider from

```
using System.Data.SqlClient;
```

to

```
using System.Data.OleDb;
```

The only other difference is in the connection string, which you need to change completely. The first part of an OLE DB connection string, the Provider clause, specifies the name of the OLE DB provider for this type of database. For Microsoft Access databases, this is always the following name (Jet is the name of the database engine included in Access):

```
Provider=Microsoft.Jet.OLEDB.4.0;
```

If you are using a different OLE DB provider for a different database or data format, then specify the name of that provider in the Provider clause.

The second part of the connection string is the Data Source clause, and in the OLE DB/Microsoft Access case, this simply specifies the name of the Microsoft Access database file (.mdb file) you are going to open:

```
Data Source=C:\tmp\nwind.mdb
```

Once again, you have the @ sign preceding the connection string to specify a string literal, so that the backslashes in the path name work; otherwise, double backslashes (\\) would be necessary to escape the filename in C#.

Reading Data with the DataSet

You've just seen how to read data with a DataReader, so now let's look at how to accomplish the same task with the DataSet. First, let's take a detailed look at the structure of the DataSet.

The DataSet is the central object in ADO.NET; all operations of any complexity use it.

A DataSet contains a set of DataTable objects representing the database tables that you are working with.

> *Note: It can be just one DataTable.*

Each DataTable object has children DataRow and DataColumn objects representing the rows and columns of the database table. You can get to all the individual elements of the tables, rows, and columns through these objects, as you see in a moment.

Filling the DataSet with Data

Your favorite activity with the DataSet will probably be to fill it with data using the Fill() method of a data adapter object.

Why is Fill() a method of the data adapter and not the DataSet? This is because the DataSet is an abstract representation of data in memory, while the data adapter is the object that ties the DataSet to a particular database. Fill() has many overloads, but the one you will be using in this chapter takes two parameters — the first specifies the DataSet you want filled, and the second is the name of the DataTable within the DataSet that will contain the data you want loaded.

Accessing Tables, Rows, and Columns in the DataSet

The DataSet object has a property named Tables that is a collection of all the DataTable objects within the DataSet. Tables is of type DataTableCollection and has an overloaded indexer, which means that you can access each individual DataTable in one of two possible ways:

❑ **By table name:** thisDataSet.Tables["Customers"] specifies the DataTable called Customers.

❑ **By index (the index is zero-based):** thisDataSet.Tables[0] specifies the first DataTable in the DataSet.

Within each DataTable, there is a Rows property that is a collection of the individual DataRow objects. Rows is of type DataRowCollection, and is an ordered list, indexed by row number. Thus

```
myDataSet.Tables["Customers"].Rows[n]
```

specifies row number n - 1 (remember the index is zero-based) in the Customers DataTable of thisDataSet. (Of course, you could have used the alternative index syntax to specify the DataTable as well.)

You might expect `DataRow` to have a property of type `DataColumnCollection`, but it's not as simple as that, because you want to take advantage of the data type of the individual columns in each row, so that a column containing character data becomes a string, a column containing an integer becomes an integer object, and so on.

The `DataRow` object itself has an indexer property that is overloaded, allowing you to access individual columns by name, and also by number. Thus

```
thisDataSet.Tables["Customers"].Rows[n]["CompanyName"]
```

specifies the `CompanyName` column of row number n - 1 in the `Customers DataTable` of `thisDataSet` — the `DataRow` object here is `thisDataSet.Tables["Customers"].Rows[n]`.

The structure just discussed is a little confusing, but Figure 24-5 gives you a picture of it.

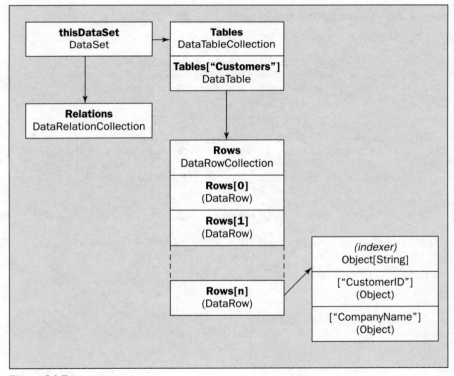

Figure 24-5

In the following Try It Out you see all of this in practice by creating a program that uses the DataSet and its child classes. Let's start with a program that simply reads data. It is similar in function to the DataReading program, but accomplishes its task via the DataSet instead.

Try It Out   Reading Data with the DataSet

Follow these steps to create the DataSetRead program in Visual Studio 2005.

1. Create a new console application called DataSetRead in the directory C:\BegVCSharp\ Chapter24.

2. Begin by adding the using directives for the ADO.NET classes you will be using:

```
#region Using Directives
using System;
using System.Data;              // Use ADO.NET namespace
using System.Data.SqlClient;    // Use SQL Server data provider namespace
using System.Collections.Generic;
using System.Text;
#endregion
```

3. Now add the following code to the Main() method:

```
static void Main(string[] args)
{
    // Specify SQL Server-specific connection string
    SqlConnection thisConnection = new SqlConnection(
        @"Server=(local)\sqlexpress;Integrated Security=True;" +
        "Database=northwind");

    // Create DataAdapter object
    SqlDataAdapter thisAdapter = new SqlDataAdapter(
        "SELECT CustomerID, ContactName FROM Customers", thisConnection);

    // Create DataSet to contain related data tables, rows, and columns
    DataSet thisDataSet = new DataSet();

    // Fill DataSet using query defined previously for DataAdapter
    thisAdapter.Fill(thisDataSet, "Customers");
    foreach (DataRow theRow in thisDataSet.Tables["Customers"].Rows)
    {
        Console.WriteLine(theRow["CustomerID"] + "\t" +
                                        theRow["ContactName"]);
    }

    thisConnection.Close();
    Console.Write("Program finished, press Enter/Return to continue:");
    Console.ReadLine();
}
```

4. Compile and execute this program. You will see the list of customer IDs and company names, as shown in Figure 24-6.

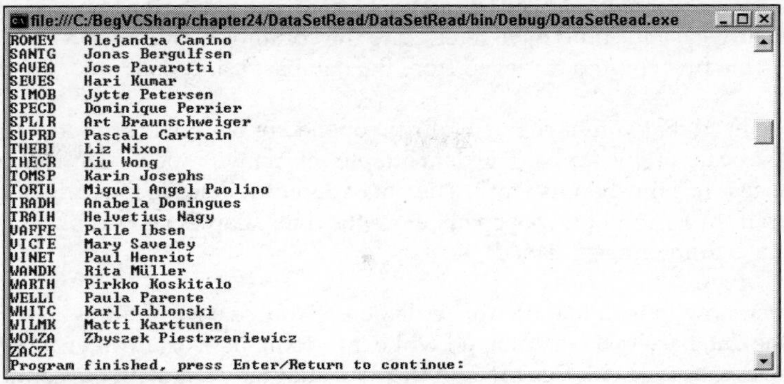

Figure 24-6

How It Works

First, you create a connection, and then use this connection to create a `SqlDataAdapter` object:

```
SqlConnection thisConnection = new SqlConnection(
    @"Server=(local)\sqlexpress;Integrated Security=True;" +
    "Database=northwind");

SqlDataAdapter thisAdapter = new SqlDataAdapter(
    "SELECT CustomerID, ContactName FROM Customers", thisConnection);
```

The next step is to create the `DataSet` that you want filled with data:

```
DataSet thisDataSet = new DataSet();
```

Now that you have your `DataSet` and your data adapter object in place (`SqlDataAdapter` here, since you are using the SQL Server provider), you can proceed to fill a `DataTable` in the `DataSet`:

```
thisAdapter.Fill(thisDataSet, "Customers");
```

A `DataTable` named `Customers` will be created in this `DataSet`. Note that this occurrence of the word `Customers` does not refer to the `Customers` table in the `Northwind` database—it specifies the name of the `DataTable` in the `DataSet` to be created and filled with data.

Now that the `DataSet` has been filled, you can access the individual rows and columns. The process for this is straightforward—you loop through all the `DataRow` objects in the `Rows` collection of the `Customers` `DataTable`. For each `DataRow`, you retrieve the values in the `CustomerID` and `ContactName` column:

```
foreach (DataRow theRow in thisDataSet.Tables["Customers"].Rows)
{
    Console.WriteLine(theRow["CustomerID"] + "\t" +
                              theRow["ContactName"]);
}
```

I mentioned earlier that the `DataRow` object has an indexer property that lets you access its individual columns by name and also by number. Thus, `theRow["CustomerID"]` specifies the `CustomerID` column of theRow DataRow, and theRow["ContactName"] specifies the ContactName column of theRow DataRow. Alternatively, you could have referred to the columns by number — CustomerID would be theRow[0] (it is the first column retrieved from the database), and ContactName as theRow[1].

You may have noticed that you have not explicitly opened or closed a connection in this example — the data adapter takes care of this for us. The data adapter object will open a connection as needed and close it again once it has finished its work. The data adapter will leave the state of the connection unchanged — so if the connection was open before the data adapter started its work, it will be still be open after the data adapter has finished.

Okay, you've seen how to read in data from a database. You've used a DataReader, which requires a connection to the database to be maintained while it is doing its work. You've also just used the data adapter to fill a DataSet — with this method the data adapter deals with the connection for you, opening it and closing it as needed. The DataReader also reads in a forward-only manner — it can navigate through records or jump to a given record. As its name suggests, the DataReader only *reads* data — the DataSet offers tremendous flexibility for *reading* and *writing* data, and working with data from different sources. You see the power of the DataSet unfold as you move through the chapter.

Reading data is only going to be half of what you want — you will usually want to modify data, add new data, or delete data. So let's get on with that. Your next step is to look at updating a database.

Updating the Database

Now that you can read data from databases, how do you change it? This section provides a very simple example, again using just one table, and at the same time introduces a few new objects you will use later in the chapter.

All the actions you typically wish to perform on the database (updating, inserting, and deleting records) can be accomplished with the same pattern:

1. Fill a DataSet with the data from the database you wish to work with.
2. Modify the data held in the DataSet (update, insert, or delete records for example).
3. Once all the modifications are made, persist the DataSet changes back to the database.

You will see this theme recurring as you move through the examples — there is no need to worry about the exact SQL syntax for updating the database, say, and all the modifications to the data in the database can be performed at one time.

In the following Try It Out, you begin by looking at how to update data in a database before moving on to add and delete records.

Try It Out   Updating the Database

Imagine that one of your customers, Bottom-Dollar Markets, has changed its name to Acme, Inc. You need to change the company's name in your databases. Again, you use the SQL Server/MSDE version of the Northwind database.

1. Create a new console application called `UpdatingData` in the directory `C:\BegVCSharp\Chapter24`.

2. Begin by adding the `using` directives for the ADO.NET classes you will be using:

```
#region Using Directives
using System;
using System.Data;                 // Use ADO.NET namespace
using System.Data.SqlClient;   // Use SQL Server data provider namespace
using System.Collections.Generic;
using System.Text;
#endregion
```

3. Add the following code to the `Main()` method:

```
static void Main(string[] args)
{
    // Specify SQL Server-specific connection string
    SqlConnection thisConnection = new SqlConnection(
        @"Server=(local)\sqlexpress;Integrated Security=True;" +
        "Database=northwind");
    // Create DataAdapter object for update and other operations
    SqlDataAdapter thisAdapter = new SqlDataAdapter(
        "SELECT CustomerID, CompanyName FROM Customers", thisConnection);

    // Create CommandBuilder object to build SQL commands
    SqlCommandBuilder thisBuilder = new SqlCommandBuilder(thisAdapter);
    // Create DataSet to contain related data tables, rows, and columns
    DataSet thisDataSet = new DataSet();

    // Fill DataSet using query defined previously for DataAdapter
    thisAdapter.Fill(thisDataSet, "Customers");

    // Show data before change
    Console.WriteLine("name before change: {0}",
        thisDataSet.Tables["Customers"].Rows[9]["CompanyName"]);

    // Change data in Customers table, row 9, CompanyName column
    thisDataSet.Tables["Customers"].Rows[9]["CompanyName"] = "Acme, Inc.";

    // Call Update command to mark change in table
    thisAdapter.Update(thisDataSet, "Customers");

    Console.WriteLine("name after change: {0}",
        thisDataSet.Tables["Customers"].Rows[9]["CompanyName"]);

    thisConnection.Close();
    Console.Write("Program finished, press Enter/Return to continue:");
    Console.ReadLine();
}
```

4. Running the program produces the output shown in Figure 24-7.

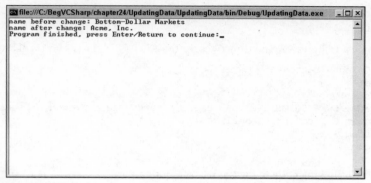

Figure 24-7

How It Works

The first part of the program is similar to the previous SQL Server example; you create a connection object using a connection string:

```
SqlConnection thisConnection = new SqlConnection(
@"Server=(local)\sqlexpress;Integrated Security=True;" +
 "Database=northwind");
```

Then you create a `SqlDataAdapter` object with the next statement:

```
SqlDataAdapter thisAdapter = new SqlDataAdapter(
    "SELECT CustomerID, CompanyName FROM Customers", thisConnection);
```

Next, you want to create the correct SQL statements to update the database — you don't have to do this yourself, the `SqlCommandBuilder` will take care of this:

```
SqlCommandBuilder thisBuilder = new SqlCommandBuilder(thisAdapter);
```

Note that you pass `thisAdapter` to the `SqlCommandBuilder` constructor as an argument. The correct SQL commands are generated and associated with the passed data adapter by the constructor when the `SqlCommandBuilder` object is created. A bit later in the chapter you look at different SQL statements; but for now the SQL has been taken care of for you.

Now you create your illustrious `DataSet` object and fill it with data:

```
DataSet thisDataSet = new DataSet();
thisAdapter.Fill(thisDataSet, "Customers");
```

In this case, it is the `Customers` table you want, so you call the associated `DataTable` in the `DataSet` by the same name. Now that the `DataSet` has been filled, you can access the individual rows and columns.

Before you change the data, you output a *before* picture of the data you want to change:

```
Console.WriteLine("name before change: {0}",
    thisDataSet.Tables["Customers"].Rows[9]["CompanyName"]);
```

What are you doing here? You are printing the value in the `CompanyName` column in the row with index number nine in the `Customers` table. This whole line outputs the following:

```
name before change: Bottom-Dollar Markets
```

You're cheating a little bit here; you just happen to know that you are interested in the row with index number nine (which is actually the tenth since the indexer is zero-based — the first row is `Rows[0]`). In a real program, rather than an example, you would have probably put a qualifier in your SQL query to select just the rows you were interested in, rather than having to know to go to the row with an index number of nine. In the next example I discuss how to find only the rows you are interested in.

Another way to understand what is going on with all of this is to look at an equivalent example that breaks out each separate object in the expression:

```
// Example using multiple objects
DataTable customerTable = thisDataSet.Tables["Customers"];
DataRow rowTen = customerTable.Rows[9];
object companyName = rowTen["CompanyName"];
Console.WriteLine("name before change: {0}", companyName);
```

In this example, you declare `customerTable` as a `DataTable` and assign the `Customers` table from the `Tables` property of `thisDataSet`. You declare `rowTen` as a `DataRow` and to it you assign the tenth element of the `Rows` property of `customerTable`. Finally, you declare `companyName` as an `object` and use the indexer property of `rowTen` to assign the `CompanyName` field to it.

This example helps you follow the process as you follow the chain of related objects, but it is often simpler to use the one-line expression, which gives the same result:

```
Console.WriteLine("name before change: {0}",
                thisDataSet.Tables["Customers"].Rows[9]["CompanyName"]);
```

If the code using multiple objects is more understandable to you, by all means use this method. For a one-time reference like this one, it is potentially inefficient to create variables for each object and assign to them every time; however, if the objects are going to be reused the multiple-object method may be more efficient. The compiler's optimizer may compensate for any inefficiency in one way of coding over another; therefore it's often best to code in the most readable manner.

Back to the example — you've displayed the value of the column before you make a change, so now let's make a change to the column. To change the value of a `DataColumn`, simply assign to it, as in the next line of the example:

```
thisDataSet.Tables["Customers"].Rows[9]["CompanyName"] = "Acme, Inc.";
```

This line changes the value of the `CompanyName` column in the row with index number nine of `Customers` to `"Acme, Inc."`.

However this change only changes the value of the column in the `DataSet` *in memory, not in the database itself.*

The `DataSet`, `DataTable`, `DataRow`, and `DataColumn` are in-memory representations of the data in the table. To update the database, you need to call the `Update()` method.

Update() is a method of the data adapter object. To call it, specify the DataSet you want the update to be based on and the name of the DataTable in the DataSet to update. It's important that the DataTable name ("Customers") match the one you used when calling the Fill() method previously:

```
thisAdapter.Update(thisDataSet, "Customers");
```

The Update() method automatically goes through the rows in the DataTable to check for changes that need to be made to the database. Each DataRow object in the Rows collection has a property, RowState, that tracks whether this row is deleted, added, modified, or is unchanged. Any changes made are reflected in the database.

Now you confirm the change by printing out the *after* state of the data:

```
Console.WriteLine("name after change: {0}",
    thisDataSet.Tables["Customers"].Rows[9]["CompanyName"]);
```

That's all there is to it!

Before moving on, let's have a quick reminder of the new characters you met here:

❑   SqlCommandBuilder: The SqlCommandBuilder object takes care of the correct SQL statements for updating the database — you don't have to craft these statements ourselves.

❑   SqlDataAdapter.Update(): This method goes through the rows in a DataTable to check for changes that need to be made to the database. Each DataRow object in the Rows collection has a property, RowState,, tracking whether this row is deleted, added, modified, or is unchanged. Any changes made are reflected in the database.

These, of course, are the SQL Server provider versions — there are corresponding OLE DB provider versions that work in the same way.

Adding Rows to the Database

In the previous example you updated values in existing rows, and your next step is to add an entirely new row. Your procedure to add a new record to the database involves, exactly like the update example earlier, adding a new row to an existing DataSet (this is where most of the work is required), and then persisting this change back to the database.

The process for adding a new row to the database is straightforward:

1. Create a new DataRow.
2. Populate it with some data.
3. Add it to the Rows collection of the DataSet.
4. Persist this change back to the database by calling the Update() method of the data adapter.

Sounds like a perfectly sensible scheme. In the following Try It Out, you see exactly how it's done.

Try It Out   **Adding Rows**

Follow the steps below to create the AddingData example in Visual Studio 2005.

1. Create a new console application called AddingData in the directory C:\BegVCSharp\Chapter24.

2. Begin by adding the usual using directives for the ADO.NET classes, you will be using:

```
#region Using Directives
using System;
using System.Data;              // Use ADO.NET namespace
using System.Data.SqlClient;    // Use SQL Server data provider namespace
using System.Collections.Generic;
using System.Text;
#endregion
```

3. Now add the following code to the Main() method:

```
static void Main(string[] args)
{
    // Specify SQL Server-specific connection string
    SqlConnection thisConnection = new SqlConnection(
        @"Server=(local)\sqlexpress;Integrated Security=True;" +
        "Database=northwind");

    // Create DataAdapter object for update and other operations
    SqlDataAdapter thisAdapter = new SqlDataAdapter(
        "SELECT CustomerID, CompanyName FROM Customers", thisConnection);

    // Create CommandBuilder object to build SQL commands
    SqlCommandBuilder thisBuilder = new SqlCommandBuilder(thisAdapter);

    // Create DataSet to contain related data tables, rows, and columns
    DataSet thisDataSet = new DataSet();
    // Fill DataSet using query defined previously for DataAdapter
    thisAdapter.Fill(thisDataSet, "Customers");

    Console.WriteLine("# rows before change: {0}",
                    thisDataSet.Tables["Customers"].Rows.Count);

    DataRow thisRow = thisDataSet.Tables["Customers"].NewRow();
    thisRow["CustomerID"] = "ZACZI";
    thisRow["CompanyName"] = "Zachary Zithers Ltd.";
    thisDataSet.Tables["Customers"].Rows.Add(thisRow);

    Console.WriteLine("# rows after change: {0}",
                    thisDataSet.Tables["Customers"].Rows.Count);

    // Call Update command to mark change in table
    thisAdapter.Update(thisDataSet, "Customers");

    thisConnection.Close();
    Console.Write("Program finished, press Enter/Return to continue:");
    Console.ReadLine();
}
```

4. On executing, the output of this example is as shown in Figure 24-8.

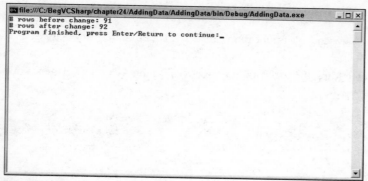

```
file:///C:/BegVCSharp/chapter24/AddingData/AddingData/bin/Debug/AddingData.exe
# rows before change: 91
# rows after change: 92
Program finished, press Enter/Return to continue:_
```

Figure 24-8

How It Works

The lines of interest here are the lines between the `thisAdapter.Fill()` and `thisAdapter.Update()` method calls.

First, to see the *before* picture you introduce a new property of the `Rows` collection: `Count`. This gives you a count of how many rows are in this table:

```
Console.WriteLine("# rows before change: {0}",
    thisDataSet.Tables["Customers"].Rows.Count);
```

Next, you create the new row object, using the `NewRow()` method of the `DataTable` object:

```
DataRow thisRow = thisDataSet.Tables["Customers"].NewRow();
```

Note that this creates a new row object using the same columns as the `Customers` table, but does not actually add it to the `DataSet`; you need to assign some values to the columns before that can be done:

```
thisRow["CustomerID"] = "ZACZI";
thisRow["CompanyName"] = "Zachary Zithers Ltd.";
```

Now, you can actually add the row using the `Add()` method of the `Rows` collection:

```
thisDataSet.Tables["Customers"].Rows.Add(thisRow);
```

If you check the `Count` property again after calling `Add()`, you see that you have indeed added one row:

```
Console.WriteLine("# rows after change: {0}",
            thisDataSet.Tables["Customers"].Rows.Count);
```

The output shows 92 rows, one more than the *before change* output. As with the previous example, the call to `Update()` is needed to actually add the new row to the database on disk:

```
thisAdapter.Update (thisDataSet, "Customers");
```

Remember, the `DataSet` is an in-memory, disconnected copy of the data; it is the `DataAdapter` which is actually connected to the database on disk and, therefore, its `Update()` method needs to be called to synchronize the in-memory data in the `DataSet` with the database on disk.

If you look at the table in the VS2005 Server Explorer after executing this program, you can see that you have indeed successfully added a row by scrolling to the bottom of the table display, as shown in Figure 24-9.

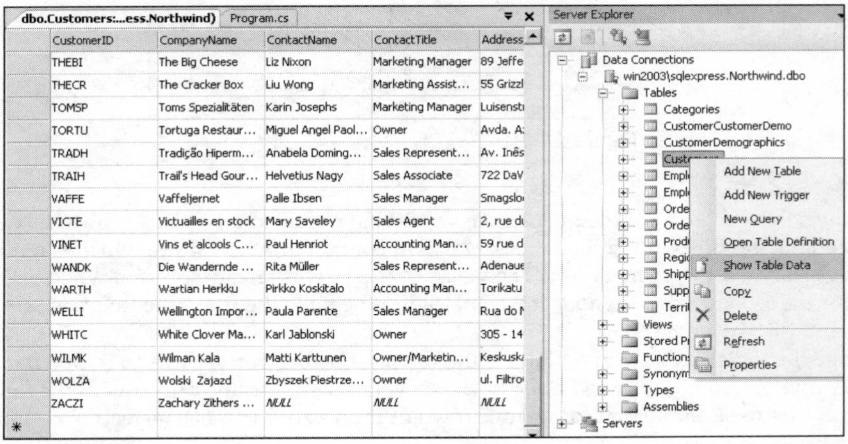

Figure 24-9

Notice that only the `Customer ID` and `Company Name` columns are filled, since that's all you used in your program. The remaining columns are blank (actually, they contain the value `NULL` in SQL terms). You might think filling in, say, `Contact Name` is simply a matter of adding the line to the code:

```
thisRow["ContactName"] = "Zylla Zithers";
```

However, this is not the only step you must perform. Recall that when you made the original query, you built the `DataSet` specifying just two columns `CustomerID` and `CompanyName`:

```
SqlDataAdapter thisAdapter = new SqlDataAdapter(
    "SELECT CustomerID, CompanyName FROM Customers", thisConnection);
```

The reference to `ContactName` would cause an error, because there is no such column in the `DataSet` that you built. You could rectify this by adding the `ContactName` column to the original SQL query:

```
SqlDataAdapter thisAdapter = new SqlDataAdapter(
    "SELECT CustomerID, ContactName, CompanyName FROM Customers",
    thisConnection);
```

Or you could select all the columns from `Customers` using this command:

```
SqlDataAdapter thisAdapter = new SqlDataAdapter("SELECT * FROM Customers",
                                    thisConnection);
```

The asterisk (*) in a SQL SELECT command is a shorthand for all the columns in the table; with this change, you can add values for any of the columns in the database. However, getting all the columns when you are only working with two or three is inefficient; this is something you should generally avoid.

Finding Rows

If you tried to run the previous example more than once, you would have seen a message like the one shown in Figure 24-10.

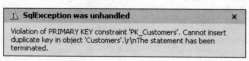

Figure 24-10

This indicates that the Add() failed because it would have created a duplicate row. The definition of the Customers table requires that the CustomerID field contain unique values, which is required when a column is designated the primary key. The value "ZACZI" was already present when you tried to run the code for the second time, because it was placed in the table the first time that you ran the sample.

Let's change the logic so that you search for the row first before you try to add it. The DataTable Rows collection provides a method called Find() that is very useful for this purpose. In the following Try It Out, you rewrite the logic surrounding your row addition to use Find() instead of counting rows.

Try It Out   **Finding Rows**

Follow these steps to create FindingData example in Visual Studio 2005:

1. Create a new console application called FindingData in the directory C:\BegVCSharp\ Chapter24.

2. Begin by adding the usual using directives for the ADO.NET classes you will be using:

```
#region Using Directives
using System;
using System.Data;              // Use ADO.NET namespace
using System.Data.SqlClient;   // Use SQL Server data provider namespace
using System.Collections.Generic;
using System.Text;
#endregion
```

3. Now add the following code to the Main() method:

```
static void Main(string[] args)
{
    // Specify SQL Server-specific connection string
    SqlConnection thisConnection = new SqlConnection(
        @"Server=(local)\sqlexpress;Integrated Security=True;" +
          "Database=northwind");

    // Create DataAdapter object for update and other operations
    SqlDataAdapter thisAdapter = new SqlDataAdapter(
```

```
          "SELECT CustomerID, CompanyName FROM Customers", thisConnection);
// Create CommandBuilder object to build SQL commands
SqlCommandBuilder thisBuilder = new SqlCommandBuilder(thisAdapter);

// Create DataSet to contain related data tables, rows, and columns
DataSet thisDataSet = new DataSet();

// Fill DataSet using query defined previously for DataAdapter
 thisAdapter.Fill(thisDataSet, "Customers");

Console.WriteLine("# rows before change: {0}",
     thisDataSet.Tables["Customers"].Rows.Count);

// Set up keys object for defining primary key
DataColumn[] keys = new DataColumn[1];
keys[0] = thisDataSet.Tables["Customers"].Columns["CustomerID"];
thisDataSet.Tables["Customers"].PrimaryKey = keys;

DataRow findRow = thisDataSet.Tables["Customers"].Rows.Find("ZACZI");

if (findRow == null)
{
   Console.WriteLine("ZACZI not found, will add to Customers table");

   DataRow thisRow = thisDataSet.Tables["Customers"].NewRow();
   thisRow["CustomerID"] = "ZACZI";
   thisRow["CompanyName"] = "Zachary Zithers Ltd.";
   thisDataSet.Tables["Customers"].Rows.Add(thisRow);
   if ((findRow =
        thisDataSet.Tables["Customers"].Rows.Find("ZACZI")) != null)
   {
      Console.WriteLine("ZACZI successfully added to Customers table");
   }
}
else
{
   Console.WriteLine("ZACZI already present in database");
}

thisAdapter.Update(thisDataSet, "Customers");

Console.WriteLine("# rows after change: {0}",
thisDataSet.Tables["Customers"].Rows.Count);

thisConnection.Close();
Console.Write("Program finished, press Enter/Return to continue:");
Console.ReadLine();
}
```

How It Works

The beginning of the program up to the `Fill()` method call is the same as previous examples. You use the `Count` property to output the number of rows currently existing, then proceed to use `Find()` to check that the row you want to add is already present.

Before you can use `Find()` you need to set up a primary key. The primary key is what you will use when searching; it is made of one or more of the columns of the table and contains a value or set of values that uniquely identifies this particular row in the table, so that when you search by the key you will find one and only one row. The `Customers` table in the `Northwind` database uses the `CustomerID` column as its primary key:

```
DataColumn[] keys = new DataColumn[1];
keys[0] = thisDataSet.Tables["Customers"].Columns["CustomerID"];
thisDataSet.Tables["Customers"].PrimaryKey = keys;
```

First, you create a `DataColumn` array — since the key can consist of one or more columns, an array is the natural structure to use; you call your `DataColumn` array keys. Next, you assign the first element of the keys array, `keys[0]`, to the `CustomerID` column in your `Customers` table. Finally, you assign keys to the `PrimaryKey` property of the `Customers` `DataTable` object.

Alternatively, it is possible to load primary key information directly from the database, which is not done by default. You can explicitly tell ADO.NET to load the primary key information by setting the `DataAdapter` `MissingSchemaAction` property before filling the `DataSet`, as follows:

```
thisAdapter.MissingSchemaAction = MissingSchemaAction.AddWithKey;
thisAdapter.Fill(thisDataSet, "Customers");
```

This accomplishes the same primary key setup by initializing the `PrimaryKey` property of the `DataTable` implicitly.

In any case, now you're ready to find a row!

```
DataRow findRow = thisDataSet.Tables["Customers"].Rows.Find("ZACZI");
```

`Find()` returns a `DataRow`, so you set up a `DataRow` object named `findRow` to get the result. `Find()` takes a parameter, which is the value to look up; this can be an array of objects for a multicolumn primary key, but in this case with only one primary key column, you need just one value which you pass as a string containing the value `ZACZI` — this is the `CustomerID` you want to look up.

If `Find()` locates a matching row, it returns the `DataRow` matching that row; if it does not find a match, it returns a `null` reference, which you can check for:

```
if (findRow == null)
{
    Console.WriteLine("ZACZI not found, will add to Customers table");

    DataRow thisRow = thisDataSet.Tables["Customers"].NewRow();
    thisRow["CustomerID"] = "ZACZI";
    thisRow["CompanyName"] = "Zachary Zithers Ltd.";
    thisDataSet.Tables["Customers"].Rows.Add(thisRow);
    if ((findRow = thisDataSet.Tables["Customers"].Rows.Find("ZACZI")) != null)
    {
        Console.WriteLine("ZACZI successfully added to Customers table");
    }
}
else
```

```
    {
        Console.WriteLine("ZACZI already present in database");
    }
```

If `findRow` is `null`, you go ahead and add the row as in the previous example. Just to make sure that the `Add()` was successful, you do a `Find()` again immediately after the add operation to prove that it worked.

As mentioned at the start of this section, this version using `Find()` is repeatable; you can run it multiple times without errors. However, it never executes the `Add()` code once the `"ZACZI"` row is in the database. Let's look at how to make it repeat that part of the program also.

Deleting Rows

Once you can add rows to the `DataSet` and to the database, it is logical to follow with the opposite action, removing rows.

The `DataRow` object has a `Delete()` method that deletes the current row. The following Try It Out changes the sense of the `if` statement on `findRow` so that you test for `findRow` *not* equal to null (in other words, the row you were searching for was found). Then you remove the row by calling `Delete()` on `findRow`.

Try It Out   Deleting Rows

Follow these steps to create the `DeletingData` example in Visual Studio 2005:

1. Create a new console application called `DeletingData` in the directory `C:\BegVCSharp\Chapter24`.

2. As usual, begin by adding the `using` directives for the ADO.NET classes you will be using:

```
#region Using Directives
using System;
using System.Data;              // Use ADO.NET namespace
using System.Data.SqlClient;  // Use SQL Server data provider namespace
using System.Collections.Generic;
using System.Text;
#endregion
```

3. Now add the following code to the `Main()` method:

```
static void Main(string[] args)
{
    // Specify SQL Server-specific connection string
    SqlConnection thisConnection = new SqlConnection(
        @"Server=(local)\sqlexpress;Integrated Security=True;" +
        "Database=northwind");

    // Create DataAdapter object for update and other operations
    SqlDataAdapter thisAdapter = new SqlDataAdapter(
        "SELECT CustomerID, CompanyName FROM Customers", thisConnection);
```

```
      // Create CommandBuilder object to build SQL commands
      SqlCommandBuilder thisBuilder = new SqlCommandBuilder(thisAdapter);

      // Create DataSet to contain related data tables, rows, and columns
      DataSet thisDataSet = new DataSet();

      // Fill DataSet using query defined previously for DataAdapter
      thisAdapter.Fill(thisDataSet, "Customers");

      Console.WriteLine("# rows before change: {0}",
          thisDataSet.Tables["Customers"].Rows.Count);
      // Set up keys object for defining primary key
      DataColumn[] keys = new DataColumn[1];
      keys[0] = thisDataSet.Tables["Customers"].Columns["CustomerID"];
      thisDataSet.Tables["Customers"].PrimaryKey = keys;

      DataRow findRow = thisDataSet.Tables["Customers"].Rows.Find("ZACZI");

      if (findRow != null)
      {
         Console.WriteLine("ZACZI already in Customers table");
         Console.WriteLine("Removing ZACZI  . . .");

         findRow.Delete();

         thisAdapter.Update(thisDataSet, "Customers");
      }

      Console.WriteLine("# rows after change: {0}",
          thisDataSet.Tables["Customers"].Rows.Count);
      thisConnection.Close();
      Console.Write("Program finished, press Enter/Return to continue:");
      Console.ReadLine();
   }
```

How It Works

The code to create the DataSet and the data adapter objects is standard — you've seen it before several times in this chapter so you won't go through it again.

The difference between this code and the previous example is that if the row is found, it is deleted! Note that when Delete() is called it doesn't remove the row in the database until Update is called to commit the change.

The Delete() method doesn't actually delete a row, it just marks it for deletion.

Each DataRow object in the Rows collection has a property, RowState, that tracks whether this row is deleted, added, modified, or is unchanged. The Delete() method sets the RowState of the row to Deleted, and then Update() deletes any rows it finds in the Rows collection marked as Deleted from the database.

A word of caution about calling the `AcceptChanges()` method of the `DataSet` after `Delete()` — doing so will remove the row from the `DataSet`, which means that there will be no effect on the row in the actual database, because `Update()` acts only on the rows it finds in the `Rows` collection, and a missing row is simply ignored.

This same issue applies to the `Remove()` method; call this only if you want to remove rows from the `Rows` collection of the `DataSet`, but not from the database itself.

Accessing Multiple Tables in a DataSet

One of the big advantages of the ADO.NET model over previous data access models lies in the fact that the `DataSet` object tracks multiple tables and the relationships between them all within itself. This means that you can pass an entire set of related data between parts of your program in one operation, and the architecture inherently maintains the integrity of the relationships between the data.

Relationships in ADO.NET

The `DataRelation` object is used to describe the relationships between multiple `DataTable` objects in a `DataSet`. Each `DataSet` has a `Relations` collection of `DataRelations` that enables you to find and manipulate related tables.

Let's start with just the `Customers` and `Orders` tables. Each customer may place several orders; how can you see the orders placed by each customer? Each row of the `Orders` table contains the `CustomerID` of the customer placing the order; you match all the order rows containing a particular `CustomerID` with that customer's row in the `Customers` table, as shown in Figure 24-11.

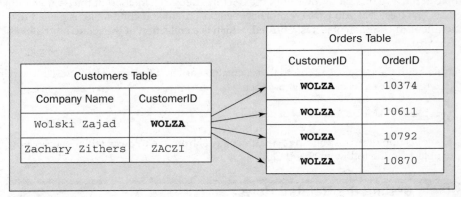

Figure 24-11

The matching `CustomerID` fields in the two tables define a one-to-many relationship between `Customers` table and the `Orders` table. You can use that relationship in ADO.NET by creating a `DataRelation` object to represent it.

Creating a DataRelation Object

The `DataSet` has a `Relations` property that is a collection of all the `DataRelation` objects representing relationships between tables in this `DataSet`.

To create a new `DataRelation`, use the `Add()` method of `Relations` which accepts a string name for the relationship and two `DataColumns` — the parent column, followed by the child column. Thus, to create the relationship described above between the `CustomerID` column of the `Customers` table and the `CustomerID` table of the `Orders` table, you would use the following syntax, giving the relationship the name `CustOrders`:

```
DataRelation custOrderRel = thisDataSet.Relations.Add("CustOrders",
    thisDataSet.Tables["Customers"].Columns["CustomerID"],
    thisDataSet.Tables["Orders"].Columns["CustomerID"]);
```

You see this syntax again in the next example.

Navigating with Relationships

To use the relationship, you need to go from a row of one of your tables to the related rows in the other table. This is called navigating the relationship. Often navigations consist of traveling from a parent row in the first table to the related children in the other table. In the diagram shown earlier, the row in the `Customers` table can be considered the parent row and each of the related rows in the `Orders` table can be considered children. Navigations can also go in the opposite direction.

Fetching the Child Rows

Given a row in the parent table, how do you obtain all the rows in the child table that correspond to this row? You can retrieve this set of rows with the `GetChildRows()` method of the `DataRow` object. The `DataRelation` object that you have created between the parent and child tables is passed to the method, and a `DataRowCollection` object is returned, which is a collection of the related `DataRow` objects in the child `DataTable`.

For example, with the `DataRelation` that you created earlier, if the given `DataRow` in the parent `DataTable` (`Customers`) is `customerRow`, then

```
customerRow.GetChildRows(custOrderRel);
```

returns the collection of corresponding `DataRow` objects from the `Orders` table. You see how to handle this set of objects in the following Try It Out.

Try It Out   **Getting the Related Rows**

Follow these steps to create the `DataRelationExample` program in Visual Studio 2005:

1.   Create a new console application called `DataRelationExample` in the directory `C:\BegVCSharp\Chapter24`.

2.   Begin by adding the using directives for the ADO.NET classes you will be using:

```
#region Using Directives
using System;
using System.Data;           // Use ADO.NET namespace
using System.Data.SqlClient; // Use SQL Server data provider namespace
using System.Collections.Generic;
using System.Text;
#endregion
```

3. Now add the following code to the `Main()` method:

```
static void Main(string[] args)
{
    // Specify SQL Server-specific connection string
    SqlConnection thisConnection = new SqlConnection(
        @"Server=(local)\sqlexpress;Integrated Security=True;" +
        "Database=northwind");

    // Create DataAdapter object for update and other operations
    SqlDataAdapter thisAdapter = new SqlDataAdapter(
        "SELECT CustomerID, CompanyName FROM Customers", thisConnection);
    // Create CommandBuilder object to build SQL commands
    SqlCommandBuilder thisBuilder = new SqlCommandBuilder(thisAdapter);

    // Create DataSet to contain related data tables, rows, and columns
    DataSet thisDataSet = new DataSet();

    // Set up DataAdapter objects for each table and fill
    SqlDataAdapter custAdapter = new SqlDataAdapter(
        "SELECT * FROM Customers", thisConnection);
    SqlDataAdapter orderAdapter = new SqlDataAdapter(
        "SELECT * FROM Orders", thisConnection);
    custAdapter.Fill(thisDataSet, "Customers");
    orderAdapter.Fill(thisDataSet, "Orders");

    // Set up DataRelation between customers and orders
    DataRelation custOrderRel = thisDataSet.Relations.Add("CustOrders",
        thisDataSet.Tables["Customers"].Columns["CustomerID"],
        thisDataSet.Tables["Orders"].Columns["CustomerID"]);

    // Print out nested customers and their order ids
    foreach (DataRow custRow in thisDataSet.Tables["Customers"].Rows)
    {
        Console.WriteLine("Customer ID: " + custRow["CustomerID"] +
                          " Name: " + custRow["CompanyName"]);
        foreach (DataRow orderRow in custRow.GetChildRows(custOrderRel))
        {
            Console.WriteLine("  Order ID: " + orderRow["OrderID"]);
        }
    }
    thisConnection.Close();
    Console.Write("Program finished, press Enter/Return to continue:");
    Console.ReadLine();
}
```

4. Execute the application, and you will see the output shown in Figure 24-12.

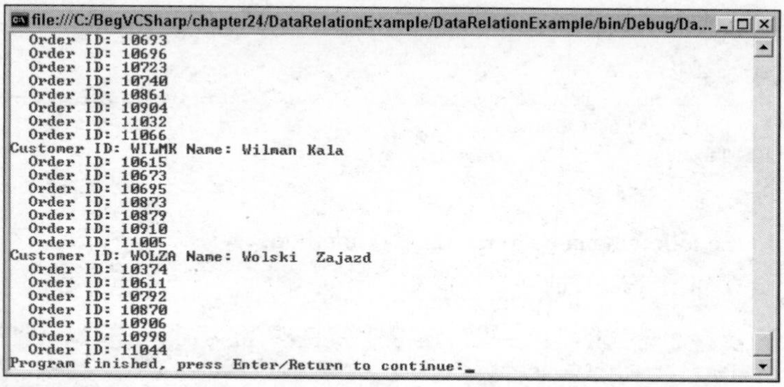

```
file:///C:/BegVCSharp/chapter24/DataRelationExample/DataRelationExample/bin/Debug/Da... _ □ ×
  Order ID: 10693
  Order ID: 10696
  Order ID: 10723
  Order ID: 10740
  Order ID: 10861
  Order ID: 10904
  Order ID: 11032
  Order ID: 11066
Customer ID: WILMK Name: Wilman Kala
  Order ID: 10615
  Order ID: 10673
  Order ID: 10695
  Order ID: 10873
  Order ID: 10879
  Order ID: 10910
  Order ID: 11005
Customer ID: WOLZA Name: Wolski  Zajazd
  Order ID: 10374
  Order ID: 10611
  Order ID: 10792
  Order ID: 10870
  Order ID: 10906
  Order ID: 10998
  Order ID: 11044
Program finished, press Enter/Return to continue:_
```

Figure 24-12

How It Works

Before you construct the `DataRelation`, you need to create the `DataSet` object and link the database tables you are going to use with it, as shown here:

```
DataSet thisDataSet = new DataSet();
SqlDataAdapter custAdapter = new SqlDataAdapter(
    "SELECT * FROM Customers", thisConnection);
SqlDataAdapter orderAdapter = new SqlDataAdapter(
    "SELECT * FROM Orders", thisConnection);
custAdapter.Fill(thisDataSet, "Customers");
orderAdapter.Fill(thisDataSet, "Orders");
```

You create a `DataAdapter` object for each table you will reference. You then fill the `DataSet` with data from the columns you're going to work with; in this case, you're not worried about efficiency, so you just use all of the available columns (SELECT * FROM <table>).

Next, you make the `DataRelation` object and link it to the `DataSet`:

```
DataRelation custOrderRel = thisDataSet.Relations.Add("CustOrders",
    thisDataSet.Tables["Customers"].Columns["CustomerID"],
    thisDataSet.Tables["Orders"].Columns["CustomerID"]);
```

Now you're ready to find the customers and orders. First, let's set up a `foreach` loop to display the customer information for each customer:

```
foreach (DataRow custRow in thisDataSet.Tables["Customers"].Rows)
{
    Console.WriteLine("Customer ID: " + custRow["CustomerID"] +
                " Name: " + custRow["CompanyName"]);
```

You're just looping through the `Rows` collection of the `Customers` table, printing the `CustomerID` and `CompanyName` for each customer. Once you've displayed the customer, you'd like to display the related orders for that customer.

To do that, you add a nested `foreach` loop, initialized by calling the `GetChildRows()` method of `DataRow`. You pass your `DataRelation` object to `GetChildRows()`, and it returns a `DataRowCollection` containing just the related rows in the `Orders` table for this customer. To display these related rows, simply loop through each `DataRow` in this collection with your `foreach` loop:

```
foreach (DataRow orderRow in custRow.GetChildRows(custOrderRel))
{
    Console.WriteLine("  Order ID: " + orderRow["OrderID"]);
}
}
```

Now you repeat the process for each customer. You added some leading spaces to the display of the `OrderID`, so the orders for each customer are displayed indented underneath the customer information. With the indented display, you can see the parent-child relationship between each customer and its orders more clearly. Customer ID "`Zachary Zithers Ltd.`" has no `Orders` because you just added it to the table in the previous examples.

That's one relation between two tables—let's go further and look at relations between more tables. Let's extend this program to see what specific items each customer is placing in each order and what the names of the products are. This information is available through the other tables in the `Northwind` database. Let's review these relationships; an easy way to see these is to look at a database diagram for the `Northwind` database, as shown in Figure 24-13.

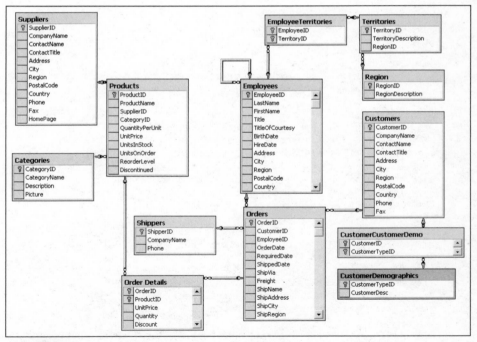

Figure 24-13

The lines between the tables represent the relationships, with the line on each side going to the column that identifies the relationship. A primary key-foreign key relationship is shown with a key symbol by the parent column and an infinity symbol by the child column.

In the next Try It Out, you're going to display the details of each customer order, including the product names, by following the relationships between four tables in the diagram above: Customers, Orders, Order Details, and Products tables.

Try It Out   Working with Multiple Relations

Follow these steps to create the ManyRelations program in Visual Studio 2005:

1. Create a new console application called ManyRelations in the directory C:\BegVCSharp\ Chapter24.

2. Begin by adding the using directives for the ADO.NET classes you will be using:

```
#region Using Directives
using System;
using System.Data;              // Use ADO.NET namespace
using System.Data.SqlClient;   // Use SQL Server data provider namespace
using System.Collections.Generic;
using System.Text;
#endregion
```

3. Now add the following code to the Main() method:

```
static void Main(string[] args)
{
    // Specify SQL Server-specific connection string

    SqlConnection thisConnection = new SqlConnection(
        @"Server=(local)\sqlexpress;Integrated Security=True;" +
          "Database=northwind");

    DataSet thisDataSet = new DataSet();
    SqlDataAdapter custAdapter = new SqlDataAdapter(
        "SELECT * FROM Customers", thisConnection);
    custAdapter.Fill(thisDataSet, "Customers");

    SqlDataAdapter orderAdapter = new SqlDataAdapter(
        "SELECT * FROM Orders", thisConnection);
    orderAdapter.Fill(thisDataSet, "Orders");

    SqlDataAdapter detailAdapter = new SqlDataAdapter(
        "SELECT * FROM [Order Details]", thisConnection);
    detailAdapter.Fill(thisDataSet, "Order Details");

    SqlDataAdapter prodAdapter = new SqlDataAdapter(
        "SELECT * FROM Products", thisConnection);
    prodAdapter.Fill(thisDataSet, "Products");

    DataRelation custOrderRel = thisDataSet.Relations.Add("CustOrders",
            thisDataSet.Tables["Customers"].Columns["CustomerID"],
            thisDataSet.Tables["Orders"].Columns["CustomerID"]);

    DataRelation orderDetailRel = thisDataSet.Relations.Add("OrderDetail",
            thisDataSet.Tables["Orders"].Columns["OrderID"],
            thisDataSet.Tables["Order Details"].Columns["OrderID"]);
```

```
        DataRelation orderProductRel = thisDataSet.Relations.Add(
          "OrderProducts",thisDataSet.Tables["Products"].Columns["ProductID"],
          thisDataSet.Tables["Order Details"].Columns["ProductID"]);

        foreach (DataRow custRow in thisDataSet.Tables["Customers"].Rows)
        {
            Console.WriteLine("Customer ID: " + custRow["CustomerID"]);

            foreach (DataRow orderRow in custRow.GetChildRows(custOrderRel))
            {
                Console.WriteLine("\tOrder ID: " + orderRow["OrderID"]);
                Console.WriteLine("\t\tOrder Date: " + orderRow["OrderDate"]);

                foreach (DataRow detailRow in
                        orderRow.GetChildRows(orderDetailRel))
                {
                    Console.WriteLine("\t\tProduct: " +
                    detailRow.GetParentRow(orderProductRel)["ProductName"]);
                    Console.WriteLine("\t\tQuantity: " + detailRow["Quantity"]);
                }
            }
        }
        thisConnection.Close();
        Console.Write("Program finished, press Enter/Return to continue:");
        Console.ReadLine();
    }
```

4.   Execute the application, and you will see output like the following (I've shown an abbreviated version here, with only the last part of the output):

```
Customer ID: WOLZA
        ...
        Order ID: 10998
                Order Date: 4/3/1998 12:00:00 AM
                Product: Guaraná Fantástica
                Quantity: 12
                Product: Sirop d'érable
                Quantity: 7
                Product: Longlife Tofu
                Quantity: 20
                Product: Rhönbräu Klosterbier
                Quantity: 30
        Order ID: 11044
                Order Date: 4/23/1998 12:00:00 AM
                Product: Tarte au sucre
                Quantity: 12
Customer ID: ZACZI
```

How It Works

As usual, you begin by initializing a connection and then creating a new DataSet. Next, you create a data adapter for each of the four tables that will be used:

```
SqlDataAdapter custAdapter = new SqlDataAdapter(
    "SELECT * FROM Customers", thisConnection);
custAdapter.Fill(thisDataSet, "Customers");

SqlDataAdapter orderAdapter = new SqlDataAdapter(
    "SELECT * FROM Orders", thisConnection);
orderAdapter.Fill(thisDataSet, "Orders");

SqlDataAdapter detailAdapter = new SqlDataAdapter(
    "SELECT * FROM [Order Details]", thisConnection);
detailAdapter.Fill(thisDataSet, "Order Details");

SqlDataAdapter prodAdapter = new SqlDataAdapter(
    "SELECT * FROM Products", thisConnection);
prodAdapter.Fill(thisDataSet, "Products");
```

Next, you build `DataRelation` objects for each of the relationships between the four tables:

```
DataRelation custOrderRel = thisDataSet.Relations.Add("CustOrders",
        thisDataSet.Tables["Customers"].Columns["CustomerID"],
        thisDataSet.Tables["Orders"].Columns["CustomerID"]);

DataRelation orderDetailRel = thisDataSet.Relations.Add("OrderDetail",
        thisDataSet.Tables["Orders"].Columns["OrderID"],
        thisDataSet.Tables["Order Details"].Columns["OrderID"]);

DataRelation orderProductRel = thisDataSet.Relations.Add(
    "OrderProducts",thisDataSet.Tables["Products"].Columns["ProductID"],
    thisDataSet.Tables["Order Details"].Columns["ProductID"]);
```

The first relationship is exactly the same as in the previous example. The next one adds the relationship between `Orders` and `Order Details`, using the `OrderID` as the linking column. The last relationship is the one between `Order Details` and `Products`, using `ProductID` as the linking column. Notice that in this relationship, `Products` is actually the parent table (second of the three parameters). This is because it is the *one* side of the one-to-many relation (one `Product` may appear in many `Orders`).

Now that you've set up the relationships you can do processing with them. Again, the basic structure is a nested `foreach` loop, this time with three nested levels:

```
foreach (DataRow custRow in thisDataSet.Tables["Customers"].Rows)
{
    Console.WriteLine("Customer ID: " + custRow["CustomerID"]);

    foreach (DataRow orderRow in custRow.GetChildRows(custOrderRel))
    {
        Console.WriteLine("\tOrder ID: " + orderRow["OrderID"]);
        Console.WriteLine("\t\tOrder Date: " + orderRow["OrderDate"]);

        foreach (DataRow detailRow in
                orderRow.GetChildRows(orderDetailRel))
        {
            Console.WriteLine("\t\tProduct: " +
```

```
                            detailRow.GetParentRow(orderProductRel)["ProductName"]);
                            Console.WriteLine("\t\tQuantity: " + detailRow["Quantity"]);
                    }
                }
            }
```

Just as before, you output the data for the parent row, then use `GetChildRows()` to obtain the child rows related to this parent. The outer loop is the same as the previous example. Next, you print out the additional detail of the `OrderDate` to the `OrderID` and then get the `OrderDetails` for this `OrderID`.

The innermost loop is different; to get the `Product` row, you call `GetParentRow()`, which gets the parent object, going from the *many* side to the *one* side of the relationship. Sometimes, this navigation from child to parent is called navigating *upstream*, as opposed to the normal parent-to-child *downstream* navigation. Upstream navigation requires the `GetParentRow()` call.

The output of the program shows all the details of the orders processed for each customer, indented to show the parent and child hierarchy. Again, the Customer ID `ZACZI` has no orders because you just added it to the table in the previous examples.

XML and ADO.NET

As stated in the introduction, XML support is one of the major design goals of ADO.NET and is also central to ADO.NET's internal implementation. Therefore, it makes sense that ADO.NET would have lots of support for XML built into its object model. XML was introduced in Chapter 23, and you are now going to learn about the support for it in ADO.NET.

XML Support in ADO.NET DataSets

The XML support in ADO.NET is centered around the `DataSet` object, because XML is all about relationships and hierarchically structured data. The `DataSet` has several methods that process XML, and one of the easiest to use is `WriteXml()`, which writes out the contents of the `DataSet` as an XML document.

To use `WriteXml()`, simply construct a `DataSet` from existing data using the same code as in the previous examples; use the `Fill()` method of a data adapter to load the data, define `DataRelation` objects for the relationships, and so on. Then, simply call `WriteXml()` on the `DataSet` you have constructed:

```
        thisDataSet.WriteXml("nwinddata.xml");
```

`WriteXml()` can write to various targets; this version of the method simply writes the XML to a file. An external program that accepts XML as an input format can easily read and process the XML.

A `ReadXml()` method is available also to read the contents of an XML file into a `DataSet`.

This example takes the code from the `DataRelationExample` and simply writes out the data in the `DataSet` to an XML file—the nested `foreach` loops are simply replaced by the single call to `WriteXml()`. You will need to ensure that you have a directory named `C:\tmp` before running this program.

Try It Out   Writing XML from a DataSet

Follow these steps to modify the `DataRelationExample` program to write XML:

1. Open the `DataRelationExample` project, and replace the `foreach` loop

```
// Print out nested customers and their order IDs
foreach (DataRow custRow in thisDataSet.Tables["Customers"].Rows)
{
    ...
}
```

with the following code:

```
custOrderRel.Nested = true;

thisDataSet.WriteXml(@"c:\tmp\nwinddata.xml");
Console.WriteLine(
    @"Successfully wrote XML output to file c:\tmp\nwinddata.xml");
```

2. Open Internet Explorer, and browse the `C:\tmp\nwinddata.xml` file, as shown in Figure 24-14.

Figure 24-14

How It Works

The `Nested` property of the `DataRelation` objects tells the `WriteXml()` method to nest the order details and orders underneath each parent customer in the XML output. The file `nwinddata.xml` contains all the data in your tables (including all the columns since you specified `SELECT * FROM` when filling the `DataSet`). It is in human-readable, easy-to-parse XML format, and the file can be browsed directly in Microsoft Internet Explorer.

So, the `DataSet` has a `WriteXml()` — guess what, it also has a `ReadXml()` method! The `ReadXml()` method creates and populates a `DataTable` in a `DataSet` with the data from an XML file. Furthermore, the `DataTable` created is given the name of the root element in the XML document.

Having just created an XML file in the previous example, in the next Try It Out you read it back in and display it!

Try It Out   **Reading XML into a DataSet**

Follow these steps to create the `ReadingXML` example in Visual Studio 2005:

1. Create a new console application called `ReadingXML` in the directory `C:\BegVCSharp\Chapter24`.

2. Add a using directive for the `System.Data` namespace to the top of the code:

```
using System.Data;
```

3. Add the following code to the `Main()` method:

```
static void Main(string[] args)
{
    DataSet thisDataSet = new DataSet();
    thisDataSet.ReadXml(@"c:\tmp\nwinddata.xml");

    foreach (DataRow custRow in thisDataSet.Tables["Customers"].Rows)
    {
        Console.WriteLine("Customer ID: " + custRow["CustomerID"] +
                          " Name: " + custRow["CompanyName"]);
    }

    Console.WriteLine("Table created by ReadXml is called {0}",
                      thisDataSet.Tables[0].TableName);

    Console.Write("Program finished, press Enter/Return to continue:");
    Console.ReadLine();
}
```

4. Execute the application, and you should see output like that shown in Figure 24-15, provided that you ran the previous example to create the `C:\tmp\nwinddata.xml` file.

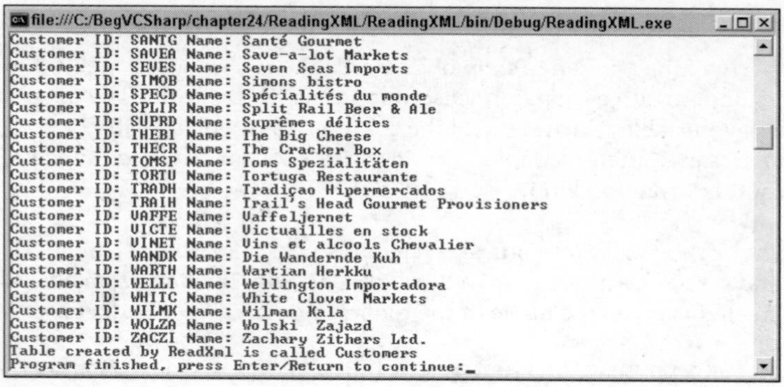

Figure 24-15

How It Works

Note that you are only using one data namespace here — System.Data. You aren't using any database access so you don't have any need for the System.Data.SqlClient or System.Data.OleDb. All you do is create a new DataSet and then use the ReadXml() method to load the data from the C:\tmp\ nwinddata.xml file. The overload of ReadXml() that you use here simply requires you to specify the name of the XML file:

```
DataSet thisDataSet = new DataSet();
thisDataSet.ReadXml(@"c:\tmp\nwinddata.xml");
```

Next, you output the contents of the Customers table — this code should be familiar from the DataRelationExample code — you loop through each DataRow in the Rows collection of the Customers table, and display the value of the CustomerID and CompanyName columns:

```
foreach (DataRow custRow in thisDataSet.Tables["Customers"].Rows)
{
    Console.WriteLine("Customer ID: " + custRow["CustomerID"] +
                      " Name: " + custRow["CompanyName"]);
}
```

How did you know the table was called Customers? As mentioned earlier, the DataTable is named from the root node of the XML document that is read in — if you look back at the screenshot for the WriteXml() method, you will see that the root node of the XML document produced is indeed Customers. Just to prove the point, write out the name of the first DataTable in the Tables collection of the DataSet, using the TableName property of the DataTable:

```
Console.WriteLine("Table created by ReadXml is called {0}",
                  thisDataSet.Tables[0].TableName);
```

SQL Support in ADO.NET

This chapter has covered the basic ADO.NET operations without your having to know anything about the SQL database query language. All ADO.NET commands that read and write from the data source are translated to SQL commands that execute the raw database operations.

Practical use of ADO.NET in real-life working situations will require some knowledge of SQL; for a much more complete introduction to SQL than there is space for here, refer to a good book on SQL such as *Beginning SQL Server 2005 Programming* (ISBN 0-7645-8433-2) or *Professional SQL Server 2005 Programming* (ISBN 0-7645-8434-0), both from Wiley Publishing, Inc.

That said, there are a few basics to cover here.

SQL Commands in Data Adapters

In the examples given earlier, you used SQL SELECT commands that return all the rows of a table, such as:

```
SqlDataAdapter thisAdapter = new SqlDataAdapter(
    "SELECT * FROM Customers", thisConnection);
```

This SELECT command returns all the rows and columns of the customer table when the Fill() method is called, and loads them into the memory of your program. This is fine for a small table like the Customers table of Northwind, which has only 11 columns and less than 100 rows of data; however, it is not likely to work well for a large table typical of those encountered in many business applications with 100,000 or even 1,000,000 rows.

You need to construct the SELECT command so that it only brings in the data you actually need to process. One way is to limit the number of columns used if your program really only interacts with some of the columns, with a SELECT statement specifying only the desired columns, such as:

```
SELECT CustomerID, CompanyName FROM Customers
```

However, you typically don't want to do this when adding rows, because you will want to specify values for all columns.

Use of WHERE with SELECT

Another technique for minimizing the amount of data loaded into memory is to always specify a WHERE clause on the SQL SELECT statement, which limits the number of rows selected. For example, the statement

```
SELECT * FROM Customers WHERE CustomerID = 'ZACZI'
```

will load only the one row containing Zachary Zithers into memory, using a fraction of the memory required to load the entire table. A range can be specified with WHERE clauses as well, so a statement like

```
SELECT * FROM Orders WHERE OrderID BETWEEN 10900 AND 10999
```

will only load the rows with OrderID in the range shown.

If you can limit the number of rows being loaded from a large table with a WHERE clause, always do so. Never load all the rows of a table into your DataSet and then search them with a foreach loop; use the SELECT statement with WHERE to do this kind of search instead.

Your goal is to find the most effective balance between processing data locally on the client where your ADO.NET program is executing and processing on the server where the SQL is executed. The ADO.NET object model and C# are better suited than SQL for complex calculations or navigational logic. Fill your

`DataSet` with the data from the tables you want to process, and execute this kind of logic on the client. However, limiting the number of rows selected from each table with appropriate conditions will greatly increase the performance (especially if the data is being transferred across a network) and decrease the memory usage.

Viewing SQL SELECT, UPDATE, INSERT, and DELETE Commands

SQL uses four basic commands for querying, updating, adding, and deleting rows from a table. These are, respectively, the `SELECT`, `UPDATE`, `INSERT`, and `DELETE` commands. In earlier examples, you have used the `CommandBuilder` object to create the SQL commands used to update the database:

```
SqlDataAdapter thisAdapter =
    new SqlDataAdapter("SELECT CustomerID from Customers", thisConnection);

SqlCommandBuilder thisBuilder = new SqlCommandBuilder(thisAdapter);
```

The command builder generates the SQL commands for modifying the data (`UPDATE`, `INSERT`, and `DELETE`) based on the `SELECT` command.

In the program, you create in the following Try It Out, you can see the generated commands with the `GetUpdateCommand()`, `GetInsertCommand()`, and `GetDeleteCommand()` methods of the `CommandBuilder` object.

Try It Out   Show SQL Example

Follow these steps to create the `ShowSQL` example in Visual Studio 2005:

1. Create a new console application called `ShowSQL` in the `C:\BegVCSharp\Chapter24` directory, and add the usual `using` directives to the top of the code:

```
#region Using Directives
using System;
using System.Data;               // Use ADO.NET namespace
using System.Data.SqlClient;     // Use SQL Server data provider namespace
using System.Collections.Generic;
using System.Text;
#endregion
```

2. Now add the following code to the `Main()` method:

```
static void Main(string[] args)
{
    // Specify SQL Server-specific connection string
    SqlConnection thisConnection = new SqlConnection(
        @"Server=(local)\sqlexpress;Integrated Security=True;" +
        "Database=northwind");

    thisConnection.Open();

    SqlDataAdapter thisAdapter = new
      SqlDataAdapter("SELECT CustomerID from Customers", thisConnection);

    SqlCommandBuilder thisBuilder = new SqlCommandBuilder(thisAdapter);
```

```
                Console.WriteLine("SQL SELECT Command is:\n{0}\n",
                            thisAdapter.SelectCommand.CommandText);

                SqlCommand updateCommand = thisBuilder.GetUpdateCommand();
                Console.WriteLine("SQL UPDATE Command is:\n{0}\n",
                            updateCommand.CommandText);

                SqlCommand insertCommand = thisBuilder.GetInsertCommand();
                Console.WriteLine("SQL INSERT Command is:\n{0}\n",
                            insertCommand.CommandText);

                SqlCommand deleteCommand = thisBuilder.GetDeleteCommand();
                Console.WriteLine("SQL DELETE Command is:\n{0}",
                            deleteCommand.CommandText);

                thisConnection.Close();

                Console.Write("Program finished, press Enter/Return to continue:");
                Console.ReadLine();
        }
```

The output of this example is shown in Figure 24-16.

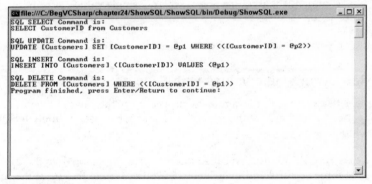

Figure 24-16

How It Works

Note that the UPDATE and DELETE commands use a WHERE clause that was generated by the CommandBuilder object.

The question marks (?) are markers for parameters, where the ADO.NET runtime will substitute an actual value into the command; for example, when you used the Delete() method to delete the row containing CustomerID ZACZI, at the time Update() was called, the command

```
DELETE FROM Customers WHERE ( CustomerID = 'ZACZI' )
```

was executed to remove the ZACZI row.

Notice that to output the SELECT command you used the SelectCommand property to get the command directly from the DataAdapter. The DataAdapter also has the UpdateCommand, InsertCommand, and DeleteCommand properties to get or set the SQL commands used at update time directly. A developer familiar with SQL can optimize these commands to perform better than the commands automatically generated by CommandBuilder, especially when all columns are included in the SQL SELECT statement.

Direct Execution of SQL Commands

If your program needs to perform a set-oriented operation such as deleting or updating all rows meeting a certain condition, it is much more efficient, especially for large tables, to do this as a single SQL command than to do extended processing in C# code.

ADO.NET provides the SqlCommand or OleDbCommand objects for executing SQL commands. These objects provide methods for executing SQL commands directly. You used the ExecuteReader() method at the beginning of the chapter when you looked at the DataReader object. Here, you look at the other methods for executing SQL statements—ExecuteScalar() and ExecuteNonQuery().

Retrieving Single Values

On many occasions, it is necessary to return a single result from a SQL query, such as the number of records in a given table. The ExecuteScalar() method allows you to achieve this—this method is used to execute SQL commands that return only a scalar (a single value), as opposed to returning multiple rows, as with ExecuteReader().

In the next Try It Out, you use the ExecuteScalar() method of SqlCommand to execute the query.

Try It Out   **Retrieving Single Values with ExecuteScalar()**

As a first example, let's consider a program that gets a count of the rows in the Customers table. This is similar to the DataReader example at the start of the chapter, but uses a different SQL statement and method of execution.

1. Create a new console application called ExecuteScalarExample in the C:\BegVCSharp\ Chapter24 directory, and add the usual using directives to the top of the code:

```
#region Using Directives
using System;
using System.Data;              // Use ADO.NET namespace
using System.Data.SqlClient;    // Use SQL Server data provider namespace
. . .
```

2. Now add the following code to the Main() method:

```
static void Main(string[] args)
{
    SqlConnection thisConnection = new
    SqlConnection(@"Server=(local)\sqlexpress;Integrated Security=True;" +
                   "Database=northwind");
    thisConnection.Open();
    SqlCommand thisCommand = thisConnection.CreateCommand();
    thisCommand.CommandText = "SELECT COUNT(*) FROM Customers";
    Object countResult = thisCommand.ExecuteScalar();
    Console.WriteLine("Count of Customers = {0}", countResult);
```

```
                thisConnection.Close();
                Console.Write("Program finished, press Enter/Return to continue:");
                Console.ReadLine();
        }
```

How It Works

This program uses the SQL Server .NET data provider. The core of the program is the same as the first example in this chapter, opening a connection to SQL Server on the local machine with integrated security and the Northwind database.

You create a SqlCommand object and assign the SELECT COUNT(*) command to its CommandText property. COUNT() is a SQL function that returns the count of rows that match the WHERE condition. Then you call the ExecuteScalar() method of SqlCommand to execute the query to retrieve the count. You display the count and exit. When executed against the Northwind database, the program displays:

```
    Count of Customers = 91
```

(Provided that you've deleted Zachary Zithers Ltd!) This is equivalent to loading the Customers table into the DataTable object and using the Count property of the Rows object as in earlier examples. Why would you want to do the job this way? It depends on the structure of your data and what else you are doing in your program. If you have a small amount of data, or are loading all the rows into your DataSet for any other reason, it makes sense to just use DataTable.Rows.Count. However, if you wanted to count the exact number of rows in a very large table with 1,000,000 rows, it is much more efficient to issue a SELECT COUNT(*) query with the ExecuteScalar() method rather than trying to load 1,000,000 rows into memory.

Retrieving No Data

A rather strange heading, but bear in mind that data modification operations such as SQL INSERT, UPDATE, and DELETE do not return data. What is interesting for these commands is the number of rows affected. This number is returned by the ExecuteNonQuery() method.

Assume that one of your suppliers has increased all prices by 5 percent for all of its products. The following Try It Out shows how to use the SqlCommand object to execute a SQL UPDATE command to increase all the prices by 5 percent for products supplied by that supplier.

Try It Out   Data Modification with ExecuteNonQuery

Follow these steps to create the ExecuteNonQueryExample in Visual Studio 2005:

1.   Create a new console application called ExecuteNonQueryExample in the C:\BegVCSharp\ Chapter24 directory, and add the usual using directives to the top of the code:

```
#region Using Directives
using System;
using System.Data;            // Use ADO.NET namespace
using System.Data.SqlClient;  // Use SQL Server data provider namespace
. . .
```

2.   Next add the following code to the Main() method:

```
static void Main(string[] args)
{
    SqlConnection thisConnection = new SqlConnection(
        @"Server=(local)\sqlexpress;Integrated Security=True;" +
        "Database=northwind");
    thisConnection.Open();

    SqlCommand thisCommand = thisConnection.CreateCommand();
    thisCommand.CommandText = "UPDATE Products SET " +
        "UnitPrice=UnitPrice*1.05 WHERE SupplierId=12";
    int rowsAffected = thisCommand.ExecuteNonQuery();
    Console.WriteLine("Rows Updated = {0}", rowsAffected);
    thisConnection.Close();

    Console.Write("Program finished, press Enter/Return to continue:");
    Console.ReadLine();
}
```

How It Works

This program opens the connection just as in the previous example. You create a `SqlCommand` object and assign the `UPDATE` command shown as the text of the command. Then you call the `ExecuteNonQuery()` method of `SqlCommand` to execute the query, returning the number of rows affected in the database. You display the number of rows and exit. When executed against the `Northwind` database, the program displays

```
Rows Updated = 5
```

indicating that the prices were adjusted for five products.

Calling a SQL Stored Procedure

Finally, here's an example of calling a SQL stored procedure, which is a procedure written in SQL and stored in the database. Stored procedures encapsulate complex SQL queries and database procedures in a single unit that can be called by multiple application programs or directly by users; the database administrator can be sure that the exact same steps are followed whenever a stored procedure is called, ensuring consistent use of the database. Users and application developers don't have to remember complex SQL query syntax; all they have to do is know the name of the stored procedure and what it does. Northwind contains several stored procedures. You will call the Ten Most Expensive Products procedure, which you can see in the Server Explorer, as shown in Figure 24-17.

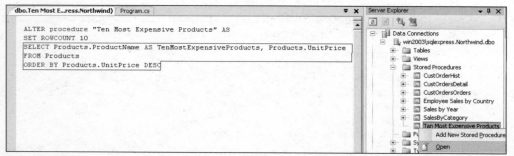

Figure 24-17

As you can see, it returns two columns, TenMostExpensiveProducts and UnitPrice. Let's try it out!

Try It Out   Calling a Stored Procedure

Essentially, this program is a variation on the very first example in this chapter, DataReading. Just like SQL commands, stored procedures can return single values, in which case you would use ExecuteScalar or ExecuteNonQuery, as you just saw with regular SQL commands. Alternately, they can return query results that are read with a DataReader, like this example in this Try It Out.

1. Create a new console application called SQLStoredProcedure in the C:\BegVCSharp\ Chapter24 directory, and add the usual using directives to the top of the code:

```
#region Using Directives
using System;
using System.Data;          // Use ADO.NET namespace
using System.Data.SqlClient;  // Use SQL Server data provider namespace
. . .
```

2. Next, make the Main() method look like the following (note that it is just the same as DataReading except for the highlighted differences):

```
static void Main(string[] args)
{
        // Specify SQL Server-specific connection string
        SqlConnection thisConnection = new SqlConnection(
          @"Server=(local)\sqlexpress;Integrated Security=True;" +
          "Database=northwind");

        // Open connection
        thisConnection.Open();

        // Create command for this connection
        SqlCommand thisCommand = thisConnection.CreateCommand();

        // Set command to Stored Procedure type.
        thisCommand.CommandType = CommandType.StoredProcedure;
        thisCommand.CommandText =
                "Ten Most Expensive Products";

        // Execute DataReader for specified command
        SqlDataReader thisReader = thisCommand.ExecuteReader();

        // While there are rows to read
        while (thisReader.Read())
        {
        // Output product name and price columns
        Console.WriteLine("\t{0}\t{1}",
        thisReader["TenMostExpensiveProducts"], thisReader["UnitPrice"]);
        }

        // Close reader
        thisReader.Close();

        // Close connection
        thisConnection.Close();
```

```
            Console.Write("Program finished, press Enter/Return to continue:");
            Console.ReadLine();
        }
```

Press F5 to execute in the debugger; you see the results shown in Figure 24-18.

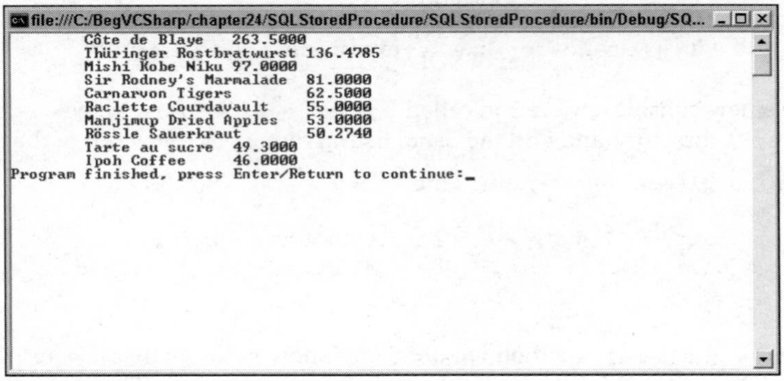

Figure 24-18

How It Works

This program opens the connection just as in previous examples. You create a SqlCommand object set the CommandType parameter to CommandType.StoredProcedure, an enumeration within ADO.NET for the purpose of supporting stored procedure calls. When CommandType is set to StoredProcedure, the CommandText holds the name of the stored procedure, not a SQL command. The rest of the program is exactly the same as if a SQL command were executed. The columns returned have different names, so the printout of the values differs slightly only for that reason.

Summary

In this chapter, you learned:

❑ That ADO.NET is the part of the .NET Framework that enables access to relational databases and other data sources. ADO.NET is designed to provide a simple, flexible framework for data access. It is designed for multitier application architectures and integrates relational data with XML.

❑ That the ADO.NET classes are contained in the System.Data namespace. You reviewed the object model of ADO.NET and learned the roles of its major objects, including the connection, command, DataReader, data adapter, DataSet, DataTable, DataRow, and DataColumn objects.

❑ That .NET data providers give access to specific data sources, and that ADO.NET can be extended to new data sources by writing .NET data providers for the new data source. You examined the .NET data providers included with ADO.NET for Microsoft SQL Server and OLE DB data sources and learned that these are contained in the System.Data.SqlClient and System.Data.OleDb namespaces, respectively.

❑ How to implement quick read-only access to data via the `DataReader` object, and how to write an equivalent program for both the `SqlClient` and `OleDb` .NET data providers. You learned how to update data and add rows via the `DataSet`, data adapter, and `CommandBuilder` objects. You saw how to find rows using the primary key, and also how to delete rows.

❑ How to access multiple tables in a `DataSet` via the `DataRelation` object and how to generate an XML view of that data. Finally, you looked briefly at how to take advantage of the SQL database language support within ADO.NET, including display of automatically generated SQL commands, direction execution of SQL, and how to call a SQL stored procedure.

As you have seen, creating database code can be quite complex as you start to build more than a simple application. In the next chapter, you look at the tools in VS2005 that create much of this complex code for you and make database development much more fun!

Exercises

1. Modify the program given in the first sample to use the `Employees` table in the `Northwind` database. Retrieve the `EmployeeID` and `LastName` columns.

2. Modify the first program showing the `Update()` method to change the company name back to Bottom-Dollar Markets.

3. Write a program that asks the user for a Customer ID.

4. Write a program to create some orders for the customer `Zachary Zithers`; use the sample programs to view the orders.

5. Write a program to display a different part of the relationship hierarchies in the `Northwind` database than the one used in this chapter; for example, `Products`, `Suppliers`, and `Categories`.

6. Write out the data generated in the previous exercise as an XML document.

7. Change the program used to print all customer order details and products to use a WHERE clause in the SELECT statement for `Customers`, limiting the customers processed.

8. Modify the program shown to print out UPDATE, INSERT, and DELETE statements to use `"SELECT * FROM Customers"` as the SQL SELECT command. Note the complexity of the generated statements.

25

Data Binding

The heart of any business application is data. Think of all the data a company holds describing employee details, such as salary and job descriptions, customer details, and so on. Most of the programs you write will access external data like this in some way, whether the program is a simple data-entry application that allows personnel staff to enter and edit employee details in their database or a full-blown e-commerce Web site that reads the product catalog and customer details such as credit card numbers and shipping addresses from a back-end database.

Chapter 24 gave you a detailed overview of ADO.NET, its class structure, and component parts. However, the good news is that you don't have to write all this detailed code to get a database application up and running.

In this chapter, you will learn:

❑   How to use VS2005 to connect to a database

❑   How to browse database objects with the Server Explorer

❑   How to get VS2005 to do almost all of the hard work of writing business applications for databases

❑   How to use VS2005's powerful features to write a simple data-driven application without having to worry too much about the C# ADO.NET code, which VS2005 generates for you

❑   How to use VS2005 to make *data binding*, the process of writing user interface objects that are bound to an underlying database connection, very easy!

For those of you who love to write pages upon pages of code to get even the simplest task done, this chapter is not for you! For those of you who enjoy getting your job done well but quickly in order to have a life, welcome!

Installing SQL Server and Sample Data

As with Chapter 24, the examples in this chapter depend on your having a version of SQL Server available containing the Northwind sample database. The SQL Express or MSDE engines are okay for this chapter's examples, but the Northwind data must be loaded. Carefully follow the steps listed in the section "Install SQL Server and the Northwind Sample Data" at the beginning of Chapter 24 to ensure that both SQL Server and the sample Northwind database are installed before you begin.

Creating Your VS Database Project

Fire up Visual Studio .NET, create a new Windows application In the C:\BegVCSharp\Chapter25 directory, name it GettingData (also change the Name and Text properties of Form1 to GettingData), and use the following Try It Out to connect to a database!

Try It Out   **Connecting to a Database**

After VS2005 is open, follow these steps to create your connection:

1.   Open Server Explorer by choosing Tools ⇨ Connect to Database... as shown in Figure 25-1.

Figure 25-1

2.   Click Connect to Database to bring up the Choose Data Source window, shown in Figure 25-2.

Figure 25-2

For this example we want to choose Microsoft SQL Server using the .NET Framework Provider for SQL Server as shown in Figure 25-2. However, if you want to use another database such as Oracle, you would choose the data source appropriate for that database and select the appropriate .NET data provider for your database.

3. Now the Add Connection dialog appears, shown in Figure 25-3. Here you fill out all the information VS2005 needs to connect to your database.

First of all, in the Server name combo box, either type the name of the SQL Server you wish to connect to, or select the server name from the drop-down list. SQL Server names consist of the server (machine) name and an instance name, which is needed in case there is more than one installation of SQL Server on the same machine.

Assuming that you installed SQL Express with the default options, use the name `(local)\ SQLEXPRESS`. As described in Chapter 24, the server name `(local)` is a generic alias for your local desktop machine. `SQLEXPRESS` is the default instance name used when SQL Express is installed; if you specified a different server or instance name during installation, use that instead.

4. Next, you need to specify the user account you want to use to connect to the database. If you select Use Windows Authentication, VS will attempt to connect to the database with the same user account that you used to log on to Windows.

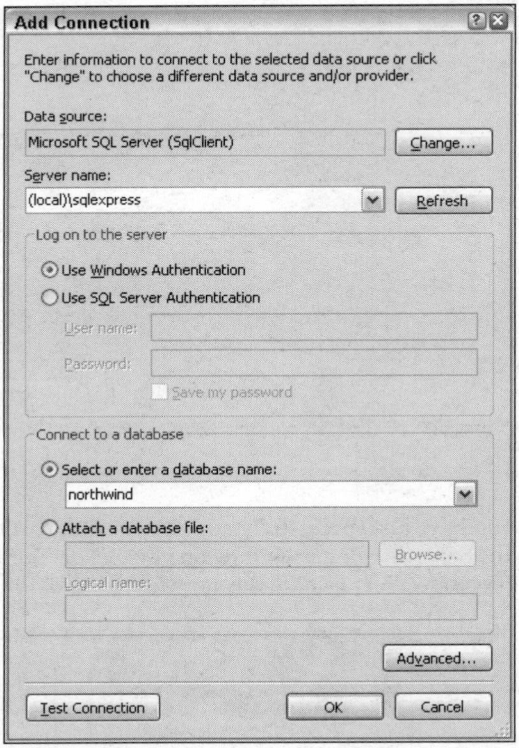

Figure 25-3

SQL Express is installed with Windows integrated security as the default security option, so you will want to choose this option unless you know you use a different username and password to connect to your SQL Server, in which case you would select the next option (Use a specific user ID and password), and enter them in the appropriate boxes.

5. Finally, select the Northwind database from the "Select or enter a database" drop-down list. If Northwind doesn't appear in the list, see the section "Install SQL Server and the Northwind Sample Data" in Chapter 24 for details on how to install the Northwind sample database.

6. When you've finished entering this information, click on the Test Connection button. Hopefully, you will now see a dialog box like that shown in Figure 25-4, saying that the connection succeeded.

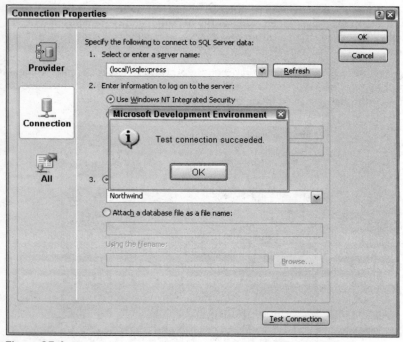

Figure 25-4

Congratulations, you have just successfully added your first ADO.NET database connection! You will now see the Server Explorer window on your Visual Studio 2005 screen, as shown in Figure 25-5, and the connection just added is now nested under the Data Connections node.

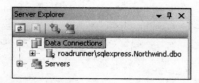

Figure 25-5

You now have access to the database and all the data in it, without even leaving VS! Note that the actual server machine name (`roadrunner`, in my case) appears instead of (`local`). Let's have a look at this data to see how it's structured.

Database Objects

In the Server Explorer, click on the node beside the connection you just made and examine what kinds of objects can be viewed here, as shown in Figure 25-6.

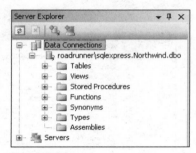

Figure 25-6

Relational databases such as SQL Server and Oracle contain a number of different kinds of objects, which the Server Explorer allows you to examine interactively.

- ❑ *Tables* contain the actual database data, stored in rows and columns.

- ❑ *Views* look like tables, but contain alternate views of the data, possibly including combinations of the data from several tables (the view changes when the data in its underlying table changes).

- ❑ *Stored procedures* contain code that is stored within the database. Traditionally, stored procedures have been written in the SQL database language, but with SQL Server 2005 and Visual Studio 2005, you can now write database stored procedures in C# or other .NET Framework languages. However, that is a topic beyond the scope of a beginning book such as this one.

- ❑ *Functions* are like stored procedures but return a data value, like a method in C# that returns a particular data type such as an `int` or `string`. In contrast, a stored procedure is like a method with a `void` return type.

- ❑ *Synonyms* are a new object type found only in SQL Server 2005 (and SQL Express); they are alternate names for database objects such as tables, views, procedures, and functions.

- ❑ *Types* are also new, found only in SQL Server 2005 (and SQL Express); these are user-defined data types that extend the data type system of the SQL database language, making it somewhat object-oriented. User-defined types are implemented in C# or another .NET Framework language, unless they are simply alternate names for an existing SQL data type.

- ❑ *Assemblies*, also new to SQL Server 2005 (and SQL Express), are the .NET binary assemblies (compiled from C# or other .NET language source code), implement a user-defined type, .NET stored procedure, or .NET function. See Chapter 26 for more information on .NET assemblies in general; the ones shown here are assemblies registered with SQL Server 2005 to extend its functionality.

You may see other object types listed also, depending on which edition of Visual Studio 2005 and what database product you have. Let's look now at some of the objects in the Northwind database, starting with the tables.

Browsing Database Tables and Relationships

In the Server Explorer, open up the Tables node underneath the connection you just added. You should now see a list of the tables in the Northwind database, as shown in Figure 25-7.

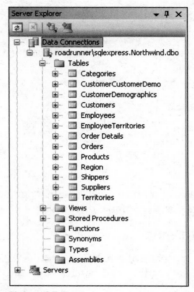

Figure 25-7

As stated earlier, relational databases store data within a series of related tables. These tables consist of rows and columns; each row represents a record within the database, and the columns represent the individual fields for each record. To see a visual representation of this, right-click on the Customers node in the Server Explorer, and select Show Table Data. VS2005 will now load and display the data from the Customers table in the Northwind database, as shown in Figure 25-8.

The Northwind sample database contains the data for a fictional food wholesaler that supplies various restaurants and food shops. The Customers table contains the details about each of these customers. Each row in this table represents a specific company that Northwind supplies, and each column contains a specific piece of data about the company, such as the company's name, its address, and the name of Northwind's contact in the company.

Each row in the table is distinguished by a unique five-character ID code, which is stored in the CustomerID field. This distinguishing field is known as the *primary key* and is vital for relating the Customers table to the other tables in the database. To see how this works, right-click on the Orders node, and again select Show Table Data, which displays the rows from the Orders table, as shown in Figure 25-9.

dbo.Customers...ess.Northwind)

CustomerID	CompanyName	ContactName	ContactTitle	Address	City
ALFKI	Alfreds Futterkiste	Maria Anders	Sales Represent...	Obere Str. 57	Berlin
ANATR	Ana Trujillo Emp...	Ana Trujillo	Owner	Avda. de la Con...	México D.F.
ANTON	Antonio Moreno ...	Antonio Moreno	Owner	Mataderos 2312	México D.F.
AROUT	Around the Horn	Thomas Hardy	Sales Represent...	120 Hanover Sq.	London
BERGS	Berglunds snabb...	Christina Berglund	Order Administrator	Berguvsvägen 8	Luleå
BLAUS	Blauer See Delik...	Hanna Moos	Sales Represent...	Forsterstr. 57	Mannheim
BLONP	Blondesddsl père ...	Frédérique Citeaux	Marketing Manager	24, place Kléber	Strasbourg
BOLID	Bólido Comidas p...	Martín Sommer	Owner	C/ Araquil, 67	Madrid
BONAP	Bon app'	Laurence Lebihan	Owner	12, rue des Bouc...	Marseille
BOTTM	Bottom-Dollar M...	Elizabeth Lincoln	Accounting Man...	23 Tsawassen Bl...	Tsawassen
BSBEV	B's Beverages	Victoria Ashworth	Sales Represent...	Fauntleroy Circus	London
CACTU	Cactus Comidas ...	Patricio Simpson	Sales Agent	Cerrito 333	Buenos Aires
CENTC	Centro comercial ...	Francisco Chang	Marketing Manager	Sierras de Grana...	México D.F.
CHOPS	Chop-suey Chinese	Yang Wang	Owner	Hauptstr. 29	Bern
COMMI	Comércio Mineiro	Pedro Afonso	Sales Associate	Av. dos Lusíadas...	Sao Paulo

1 of 91

Figure 25-8

dbo.Orders: Ta...ess.Northwind) dbo.Customers...ess.Northwind)

OrderID	CustomerID	EmployeeID	OrderDate	RequiredDate	ShippedDate
10248	VINET	5	7/4/1996 12:00:...	8/1/1996 12:00:...	7/16/1996 12:
10249	TOMSP	6	7/5/1996 12:00:...	8/16/1996 12:00...	7/10/1996 12:
10250	HANAR	4	7/8/1996 12:00:...	8/5/1996 12:00:...	7/12/1996 12:
10251	VICTE	3	7/8/1996 12:00:...	8/5/1996 12:00:...	7/15/1996 12:
10252	SUPRD	4	7/9/1996 12:00:...	8/6/1996 12:00:...	7/11/1996 12:
10253	HANAR	3	7/10/1996 12:00...	7/24/1996 12:00...	7/16/1996 12:
10254	CHOPS	5	7/11/1996 12:00...	8/8/1996 12:00:...	7/23/1996 12:
10255	RICSU	9	7/12/1996 12:00...	8/9/1996 12:00:...	7/15/1996 12:
10256	WELLI	3	7/15/1996 12:00...	8/12/1996 12:00...	7/17/1996 12:
10257	HILAA	4	7/16/1996 12:00...	8/13/1996 12:00...	7/22/1996 12:
10258	ERNSH	1	7/17/1996 12:00...	8/14/1996 12:00...	7/23/1996 12:
10259	CENTC	4	7/18/1996 12:00...	8/15/1996 12:00...	7/25/1996 12:
10260	OTTIK	4	7/19/1996 12:00...	8/16/1996 12:00...	7/29/1996 12:
10261	QUEDE	4	7/19/1996 12:00...	8/16/1996 12:00...	7/30/1996 12:
10262	RATTC	8	7/22/1996 12:00...	8/19/1996 12:00...	7/25/1996 12:

1 of 830

Figure 25-9

This table represents the orders received by the Northwind company. Again, each row represents one order. Notice that this table also has a `CustomerID` field with the same five-character ID codes as in the `Customers` table. The values in this column serve as a pointer to the row in the `Customers` table where more information about the customer can be found. This type of column is known as a *foreign key*.

You will use tables related through their primary and foreign keys in queries that fill the data structures and forms in the example applications. The ability to browse the database is very handy for developing database applications, because you can check your work against the database as you go (now what is the name of that column again?).

However, you didn't buy VS to use it as a front end for your database, so let's see how to use the connection from your C# programs!

Adding a Data Source to an Application

Go back to the design view for Form1 in the GettingData project. Change the form's name to GettingData, then go to the Data menu and choose Add New Data Source... as shown in Figure 25-10.

Figure 25-10

This brings up the Data Source Configuration Wizard.

The Data Source Configuration Wizard

Adding a data source brings up the Data Source Configuration Wizard, shown in Figure 25-11.

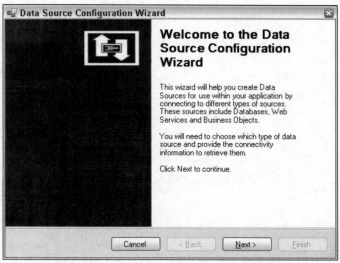

Figure 25-11

A data source is a generic connection to a database or other source of data for your application. The data source can be a database, a file, a Web service, or a generic object, which is why pressing Next brings you to the Choose Data Source Type dialog, shown in Figure 25-12.

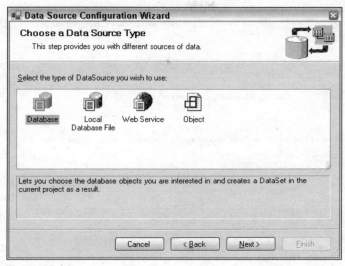

Figure 25-12

The default choice, Database, is the type of data source that you want, so simply press Next. The next screen, shown in Figure 25-13, lets you choose the data connection you want.

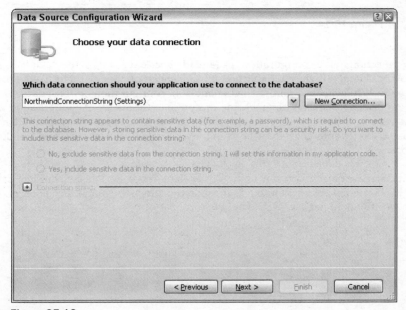

Figure 25-13

Since you have only one connection configured (the one you set up earlier to access the Northwind database), this is the only one available in the list. If you had not built one yet, you could also select New Connection... and add it here. Click on this connection in the drop-down list. Note that it creates the Connection string for you, based on the choices you made in setting up the connection. You saw connection strings in Chapter 24; this dialog makes it very easy to manage them. Click Next to move on to the next screen (see Figure 25-14), where you are prompted to save the connection in the application configuration file.

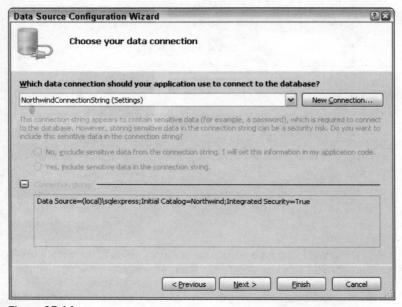

Figure 25-14

Saving the connection in the configuration file (already checked as this is the default) is a good idea, because it can be changed in the configuration file at installation time without having to rebuild the application code. While all applications can benefit from configuration options, database apps are particularly notorious for always having some exception to the standard configuration when deployed to the field, such as a different server name or different network setup. Next, specify what data from your database is loaded into your application in the Choose Your Database Objects dialog, shown in Figure 25-15.

These are the database objects you saw in the Server Explorer earlier; this wizard lets you do some exploration to choose the objects of interest. To begin this process, expand the Tables node to show the tables in the Northwind database, as shown in Figure 25-16.

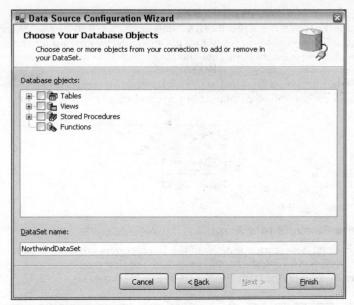

Figure 25-15

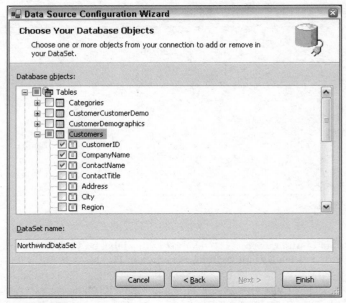

Figure 25-16

You see the Customers table as before. Expand the Customers node to see the individual data columns. Check the boxes for the first three, CustomerID, CompanyName, and ContactName. These are what you will display on your form. While you could pick all the fields, that would make for a crowded form to say the least; these will be enough! Now click the Finish button to finish creating the data source.

Now, to use the data source you just created, go back to the Data menu and choose Show Data Sources, so the Data Source window will be displayed in your project, as shown in Figure 25-17.

Figure 25-17

Adding Data-Bound Controls to a Form

Now your newly added data source appears in the Data Sources window. Expand the Customers node so that the three columns you selected appear. Click on the first one, CustomerID, to select it. Then, drag the CustomerID control onto the GettingData form, as shown in Figure 25-18.

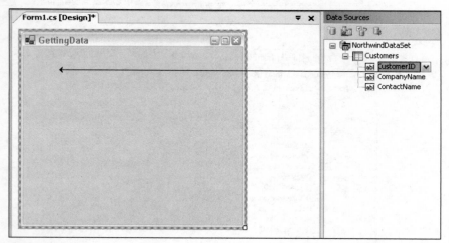

Figure 25-18

This will create a data-bound CustomerID text box with a label on your form, and several nongraphic data controls are added as well, at the bottom, as shown in Figure 25-19.

What are these strange pseudocontrols at the bottom of your form, northwindDataSet, customersBindingSource, customersTableAdapter, and customersBindingNavigator? They do not seem to appear on the screen if you run the application.

Actually, one of the new objects *does* appear on the form. This is the customersBindingNavigator, a navigation bar at the top of your form for moving through the rows in the database, as shown in Figure 25-20.

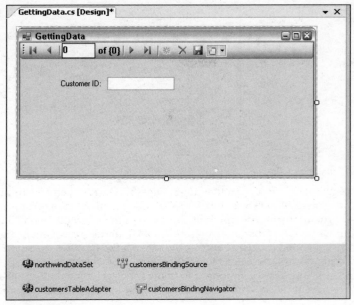

Figure 25-19

Figure 25-20

It has buttons to move to the first row in the table, the previous row, the next row, the last row, and so on. You look at this control in just a bit.

VS2005-Generated ADO.NET Objects

The other objects you see at the bottom of your form design window are not actually visible on the form, but are wizard-created ADO.NET objects, automatically added to your project by VS2005.

The `northwindDataSet` object is a *strongly typed* `DataSet`. As you learned in Chapter 24, the `DataSet` is one of the primary ADO.NET classes, allowing you to bring in data from various data sources, store it in application memory, and manipulate and convert it to various formats.

What you may not have noticed is the addition to the Solution Explorer. If you look, a new file has been added to your project, named `NorthwindDataSet.xsd`, as shown in Figure 25-21.

Figure 25-21

This file is the schema for the `northwindDataSet`. The XSD (XML Schema Definition) schema is a document by which you can verify the structure of an XML document. XML, a text format used to represent data, has become particularly important with the growth of the Internet. The XSD schema is an important tool for ADO.NET because a `DataSet` object uses XML under the covers to organize and structure data. Automatically generated by Visual Studio, the schema file specifies the structure of the `DataSet`, each table, and all relationships between tables. XML and XSD schemas are described more fully in Chapter 23 of this book, but what is important to know for developing data applications is Visual Studio 2005 uses XML to represent the structure of a `DataSet`, and luckily VS2005 can generate this representation for you!

Two other ADO.NET objects added to your project connect the `DataSet` to the database; these are the `customersTableAdapter` and `customersBindingSource`. The table adapter contains the basic information for the data that you can expect to return from the database. Think of the adapter as the bridge between the `DataSet` and the database. The table adapter is a single-table version of the more general `DataAdapter` object, which you worked with in the previous chapter as one of the components of a .NET data provider. It is used to fill a `DataSet` with data from the database and to send changes made in the `DataSet` back to the database. The `customersDataConnection` object contains all the information that ADO.NET needs to connect to your database.

However, you don't need to know the details, you have a running data-based application already as you shall see! Use the following Try It Out to run the application you have created.

Try It Out   Compile and Run the Database Application

Follow these steps to run the `GettingData` program:

1. Just to make the application look more interesting when it runs, drag the other two columns from the data source (`CompanyName` and `ContactName`) onto your form. You might play around with the alignment of the forms and labels to make them look neat and clean.

2. Press F5 to build the `GettingData` project and run it in the debugger, and you will see your form contains the data from the first row of the Customers table in the Northwind database, as shown in Figure 25-22.

Figure 25-22

3. There are indeed 91 customers in the Northwind database, as shown in the customersBindingNavigator bar at the top of the form. Note the full set of navigational buttons. Press the left-arrow button a few times to go forward through a few records, then press the left-arrow+bar (End) button to go to the last record, as shown in Figure 25-23.

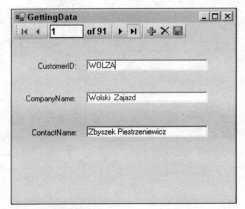

Figure 25-23

Cool! And you didn't have to write any of the code that does the heavy lifting!

4. Press the X (Close) button in the upper-right corner to stop the application, or press Shift+F5 to stop debugger.

Of course, there is still a fair amount of work involved. You had to drag the individual data fields from the data source three times, and then the user has to click on the navigator buttons a bunch of times to get to the record of interest; can you make it any easier? You can indeed with a DataGridView control!

Adding a DataGridView

The DataGridView displays all of the records in a spreadsheet-like format. Although not typically added to a form that is as complete as yours, the DataGridView is a fast and convenient object that can be added to Windows forms to display data and even provide a user interface for changes.

To add the DataGridView, first make the GettingData form larger, keeping the three fields you've already defined at the top.

Then simply drag the Customers table itself from the Data Source window to the area you've added at the bottom, as shown in Figure 25-24.

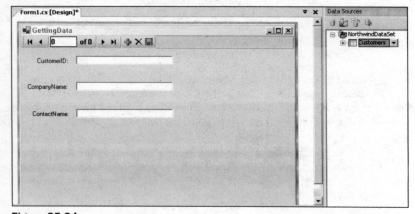

Figure 25-24

Resize the grid to fill the bottom of the form and line up nicely, and your form should now look something like that shown in Figure 25-25.

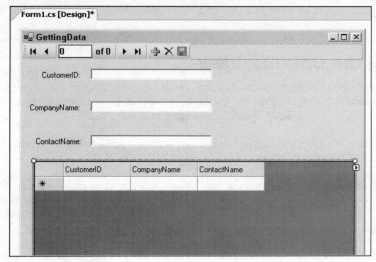

Figure 25-25

Go ahead and run the program now in the debugger by pressing F5. You can see that the `DataGridView` is already connected with the database, and if you click on a particular row in the grid the data in the other controls change to match the selected row (see Figure 25-26).

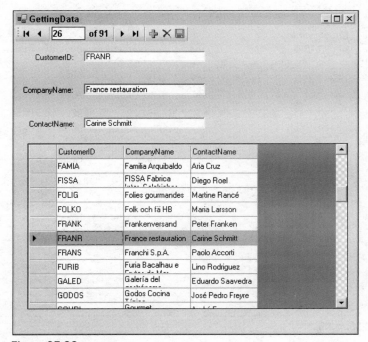

Figure 25-26

You'd expect that you'd have to write some code to synchronize all the controls, but VS2005 has already done that for you. What could be simpler?

Formatting the DataGridView

The formatting of the `DataGridView` does leave a little bit to be desired. For example, the default column widths as shown don't make for the prettiest formatting. You can change this by right-clicking the `DataGridView` and choosing Edit Columns, as shown in Figure 25-27.

Try setting the default width for the `CustomerID` column to 75, the width for `CompanyName` to 200, and `ContactName` to 150. Run the program again with F5 — doesn't that look nicer?

You can also change the default appearance of the `DataGridView` to make your application look more polished. The easiest way to do this is simply to apply one of the many templates built into the object. For example, if you do not like the basic blue and gray, you can modify the template. Begin by right-clicking the `DataGridView` and selecting Auto Format, as shown in Figure 25-28.

Within the Auto Format dialog, you can select any of the predefined templates to spruce up your `DataGridView`. However, if you'd prefer to alter the look manually, you can adjust all the properties for the background colors or font styles — for example if you have a corporate color scheme you would like to match. You can go into quite elaborate detail, all without touching a line of code.

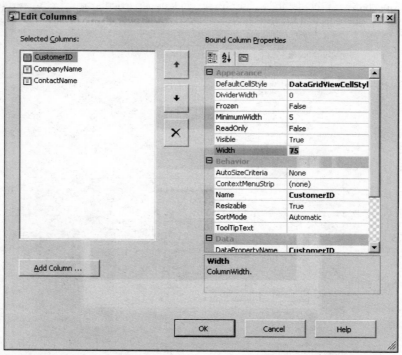

Figure 25-27

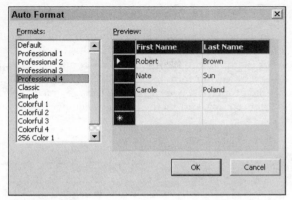

Figure 25-28

For example, let's change the background color for the column headers. Right-click again on the `DataGridView` and choose Properties. Scroll through the properties until you find `ColumnHeadersDefaultCellStyle`. This brings up the CellStyle Builder, in which you can click the `BackColor` property. Within the color dialog, you will see a color list with three tabs: Custom, Web, and System, as shown in Figure 25-29.

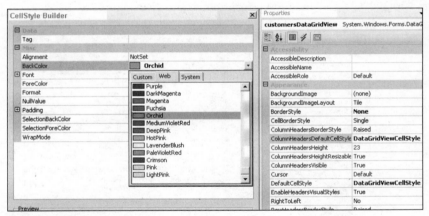

Figure 25-29

The System has predefined colors, supplied by Windows. For example, if you select the color Desktop from System, this color will change if the user alters the color of his or her desktop. This can sometimes cause unexpected side effects, such as poor legibility. Therefore, be careful when you alter these values. For now, select the color Orchid on the Web tab. The color across the top of the grid will turn to this interesting shade of purple.

Adding Different Types of Controls

Data-bound controls are not limited to controls created by dragging items off the data source. You can also bind any control you create with the Toolbox by setting its data binding properties in the Data section of its properties. For example, you can create a data-bound `ListBox` by selecting ListBox from the Toolbox, dragging it onto your form to create ListBox1, then right-clicking to view its properties. In the Data section of the properties, you can set the Data Source property to your existing customerDataConnection data source, and set the Display Member property to the CustomerID column, as shown in Figure 25-30.

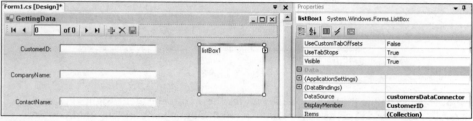

Figure 25-30

This creates a data-bound list box, which will display the CustomerID synchronized with the current row just as with the data grid and text box controls, as shown in Figure 25-31.

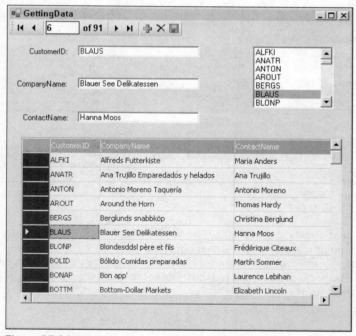

Figure 25-31

You could fiddle with properties and colors all day long, but that's quite enough to make the point. You can accomplish a tremendous amount of what would otherwise be laborious work through VS2005's data wizards and data-bound control properties.

A Quick Look at the Generated Code

Just to see the work you're missing, choose File ⇨ Open ⇨ File, and open the file NorthwindDataSet. Designer.cs in your project directory. This C# code is generated from your project form (via the NorthwindDataSet.xsd file mentioned earlier). Choose Edit ⇨ Find and search for partial class; you'll see class definitions for NorthwindDataSet, CustomersDataTable, CustomersTableAdapter, and so on:

```
namespace GettingData {
    .
    .
    .

    public partial class NorthwindDataSet : System.Data.DataSet {

        private CustomersDataTable tableCustomers;

        public NorthwindDataSet() {
            this.BeginInit();
            this.InitClass();
    .
    .
    .
    public partial class CustomersDataTable : System.Data.DataTable
    .
    .
    .
    public partial class CustomersTableAdapter : . . . ICustomersTableAdapter {
```

This is several hundred lines of database code that you didn't have to write! Similarly, there are several hundred lines generated in Form1.Designer.cs as well that would have been murder to write by hand! You've gone about as far as you can without writing code, but you will see how adding just a few lines of code to what VS2005 has done can get you that much closer to having exactly the application behavior you want.

Updating the Database

So far, you can read the data from the database, and you can change it in the text boxes and the DataGridView, but that's not much use if you can't save the changes you make to the database itself. You may have noticed that any changes you type into the text boxes or data grid disappear when you exit the application and restart it.

Therefore, you will quickly see how to update and validate the data in the database with the data in your DataSet. For this portion, you use a little bit of your own code, in addition to the wizard-generated code.

The `BindingNavigator` bar has a Save Data button at the right, as shown on Figure 25-32.

Figure 25-32

In an early beta of VS2005 the Save button was disabled and additional code needed to be added to enable the save functionality. In the final edition of VS2005 the Save code is generated automatically so this additional code is not necessary. However, you may want to add additional code to validate any data changes made by your user before saving the changes to the database. Let's look at a simple example of this so that you can see how easy it is to modify the code generated by VS2005.

For example, suppose that the user types a change into the `CustomerID` text box. The values for the `CustomerID` columns in the Northwind database must each be exactly 5 characters long. You can add a handler to the Save button to ensure that the `CustomerID` entered by the user conforms to this requirement. To do this, go up to the Save Data button and double-click it.

The VS2005-generated `bindingNavigatorSaveItem_Click` method appears in the code view window It begins with an `if` statement calling the form's `Validate` method, followed by a call to the `customersBindingSource EndEdit` method and `customersTableAdapter Update` method. To enter your own validation logic, type in the following code at the beginning of `bindingNavigatorSaveItem_Click`, before the `if` statement calling Validate:

```
private void bindingNavigatorSaveItem_Click(object sender, EventArgs e)
{
        if (this.customerIDTextBox.Text.Length != 5))
        {
           MessageBox.Show(this, "CustomerID must be 5 characters long", "Save");
           return;
        }
        if (this.Validate())
        {
           this.customersBindingSource.EndEdit();
           this.customersTableAdapter.Update(this.northwindDataSet.Customers);
        }
}
```

Now, build and run the application and attempt to change the customer ID in the `CustomerID` text box for one of the records. If you enter a value less than 5 characters long the message shown in the code appears and the change is not saved to the database.

Any changes made to the `DataSet` will be passed back to the database with the `Update()` method when the Save button is pressed. You used the `Update()` method with the `DataAdapter` in Chapter 24; the `customersTableAdapter` inherits the `Update()` method from the parent `DataAdapter` class.

You would need to add similar handling for all the text box controls, of course, to fully flesh out the application. I'll leave that as an exercise for you!

Summary

Visual Studio.NET provides you with a whole range of tools for quickly creating applications that connect to databases, requiring only a small amount of code to be written by hand. Throughout this chapter, you looked at several mechanisms for displaying data. From the basic `TextBox`, to the more advanced `DataGridView`, they all rely on the power and flexibility of ADO.NET and the `BindingContext` object inherent to all Windows forms.

In this chapter, you learned:

- ❑ How to browse database objects with the Server Explorer
- ❑ How to add a data source to your VS2005 project to connect to a database
- ❑ How to use VS2005 to add data-bound controls to a form that work "right out of the box" with no handwritten data access code
- ❑ How to modify the properties of a standard control from the Toolbox to bind it to a database field
- ❑ How to create a DataGridView and modify the VS2005-generated code to update the database

Remember, automatically generated code is never quite as efficient as handwritten code, so the techniques you learned in Chapter 24 for writing your own ADO.NET code can be combined with what you learned in this chapter to modify the VS2005-generated code to produce exactly the results you want for your end user and to optimize the performance of the generated code.

This finishes the discussion of databases. In the next chapter you learn about assemblies, which are how the .NET runtime packages your compiled C# code.

Exercises

1. Modify the first example by adding the column `ContactTitle` to the data source `NorthwindDataSet`.

2. Add a text box to the form that will display the `ContactTitle` information.

3. Create a new application that displays data from the `Products` table of the `Northwind` database.

4. Modify the code for the "Updating the Database" example to validate changes to all the data fields, not just the `CustomerID`.

Part V
Additional Techniques

.NET Assemblies

If you are reading this book just to learn about the C# language, you can now skip to the next chapter. This chapter is an "under-the-hood" look at how the Microsoft C# compiler packages your C# code when it is compiled into an executable format. The chapter will help you understand how your C# code makes calls into the .NET Framework system classes and how other programs can call your code when you make a class library. Also, if you are planning to make a C# program that will be distributed as a commercial software product or even deployed on many computers within your organization, then the material in this chapter will be very important to understand. But if you are just making a C# program for a student project or your own personal use, then much of what follows here will be interesting, but not necessary to your use of Visual C#.

When your C# program is compiled, it is packaged into an *assembly*. An assembly is a .NET executable program (or part of an executable program) delivered as a single unit. It is a file or set of files containing a .NET program or resources supporting a program. When you build a C# Windows or console application, the .exe file produced is an assembly. If you build a class library, the DLL (Dynamic Link Library) file produced is also an assembly.

All the code in an assembly is built, delivered, and assigned a version number as a single unit. The assembly makes the public classes, properties, and methods visible to other programs. Everything private to your program is kept inside the assembly.

This chapter explores assemblies. In particular, you look at:

- ❏ A brief review of components
- ❏ Features of an assembly, including its self-description ability
- ❏ The structure of an assembly, and how to view its contents
- ❏ Assembly versioning
- ❏ Private and shared assemblies
- ❏ Signing assemblies and the Global Assembly Cache

While every C# program is packaged as an assembly, many of the features of assemblies are designed to make it easy to deliver a special class of programs called components. Understanding components is essential to understanding the benefits of assemblies, so let's review what a component is.

Components

A component is a subprogram or part of a program designed to be used by other programs. In addition, a component is a *binary* unit (executable code as opposed to source code) that can be used by other programs without having to recompile either the source code of the component itself or the program using the component. This means that third-party suppliers don't have to provide the source code for their components.

In the loosest sense, a component includes any binary subprogram; thus, any DLL is by definition a component, since it is a subprogram containing executable code.

A stricter definition of a component requires it to provide a means of advertising its contents to other programs. Assemblies provide this advertising ability within .NET.

In strictest definition of a component in the .NET Framework, a component must implement the System.ComponentModel.IComponent interface, which includes methods that can be called by other components to release no-longer-used system resources and to support integration with design tools.

To aid your understanding of the benefits of assemblies, this chapter uses the less strict definition, including the requirement of advertising the contents of the component.

Benefits of Components

Components provide improved reusability, flexibility, and delivery of subprograms. In addition, binary reuse saves time and increases reliability.

For example, consider a class named Shapes that contains objects for representing circles, triangles, or other shapes. It might contain methods for calculating the area of a shape or performing other operations with shapes. Many kinds of programs might use a Shapes class: painting/drawing programs, engineering, architecture/building design, computer-aided design, games, and others.

Wouldn't it be great if the routines for drawing and manipulating shapes could be defined just once and reused by all these programs? This is the reusability benefit.

What if this reuse could be accomplished without having to recompile and link the Shapes class library for every program that uses it? This saves time and helps reliability, since it removes the possibility of introducing problems each time you compile and link.

Even better, maybe some other person or company has already written a shapes component that does what you want, then you can use the component (by downloading and/or purchasing it) without having to write it yourself. If you could share components at the binary level, you wouldn't have to worry about what programming language was used to develop the component. The .NET Framework and assemblies provide all of these benefits.

A Brief History of Components

For different programs to reuse components at the binary level, there must be some standard for implementing the way classes and objects are named and used at the binary level. The standard for doing this in Microsoft-based products has evolved over time.

Microsoft Windows introduced the DLL (Dynamic Link Library) where one or more programs could use a chunk of code stored in a separate file. This worked at a very basic level if the programs were written in the same language (typically C). However, programs needed to know a lot in advance about the DLLs they used, and DLLs did not enable programs to use one another's data.

To exchange data, DDE (Dynamic Data Exchange) was developed. This defined a format and mechanism for piping data from one program to another, but was not flexible. OLE 1.0 (Object Linking and Embedding) followed, which enabled a document such as a Word document to actually contain a document from another program (such as Excel). This was something like components, but OLE 1.0 was not truly a general-purpose component standard.

Microsoft defined its first true component standard with the COM (Component Object Model) standard implemented in Windows in the mid-1990s. OLE version 2 and many successor technologies were built on COM. DCOM (Distributed COM) introduced the ability for COM components to interact over a network, and COM+ added services that components could call on to ensure high performance in multitier environments.

COM works well but is difficult to learn (especially when used from C++) and to use. COM requires information about components to be inserted into the Windows system Registry, making installation more complex and component removal more difficult.

COM was originally designed for use with C/C++; it was enhanced so that Visual Basic could use it (Automation) and indeed this works well, but it became even harder for the C/C++ programmer to make components compatible with Visual Basic (you still could not inherit from a class defined in another language, for example).

Additionally, as users installed multiple versions of DLLs and COM components from Microsoft and other companies over time, problems arose with programs using different versions of the same shared DLL. It was very easy for one program to install a different version of a DLL already used by another program, and this would cause the original program to break (this phenomenon was the infamous DLL hell). The burden of tracking all the information about the different DLLs installed on a system made it very hard to upgrade and maintain components.

The .NET programming model brings a new standard that addresses these problems, the .NET assembly.

.NET Assembly Features

Before looking at the structure of an assembly, let's discuss some of the features of .NET assemblies.

Self-Description

The most important aspect of .NET assemblies, which distinguishes them from their predecessors, is that they are fully self-describing. The description is contained within the assembly, so the system or calling program does not have to look up information in the Registry or elsewhere about the objects contained within the assembly.

The self-description of .NET assemblies goes beyond names of objects and methods, and the data types of parameters; it also includes information about what version the objects are (think of Shapes 1.0 followed by Shapes 1.1 or Shapes 2.0), and controls the security for the contained objects. All of this information is contained within the assembly itself — there is no need to look up information elsewhere. This makes installation of a .NET component much easier and more straightforward than with the existing Windows technologies. In fact, it can be literally as easy as copying the assemblies onto the disk of the target system.

.NET Assemblies and the .NET Framework Class Library

Every .NET program, including all C# programs, makes extensive use of the .NET Framework Class Library. You are using these classes whenever you call a method from the System namespace with the using System directive — all the System namespaces (System.Data, System.Drawing, and so on) belong to the .NET Framework Class Library.

Each class within this library is part of a self-describing assembly. The drawing classes, for example, are contained in the System.Drawing.dll assembly. If you add a reference to this assembly in Visual Studio 2005, the compiler will include a reference to that assembly when it builds the assembly for your program. At runtime, the CLR reads the metadata in your program's assembly to see what other assemblies it needs, then locates and loads those assemblies for your program to use. Assemblies referenced by your program may reference other assemblies, so that even a simple program with a single using directive may actually reference several different assemblies. The self-description in each assembly keeps track of all these references, without you having to be aware of it.

I should clarify something here so as to not cause confusion later on.

> The correspondence between namespaces and assemblies is not necessarily one-to-one. In other words, an assembly may contain information from more than one namespace, and conversely, a single namespace may be spread across several assemblies.

For example, the System.Data.dll assembly actually contains some functionality from both the System.Data and System.Xml namespaces, while other functionality in the System.Xml namespace is implemented in the System.Xml.dll assembly. Within your program, you are referring to a namespace when specifying the using directive; the references in your Visual Studio 2005 project specify the actual assemblies used.

Cross-Language Programming

One additional benefit of assemblies and .NET is that they enable cross-language programming, since components can be called from any .NET language, regardless of the language they were originally written in.

.NET provides a number of features that enable cross-language programming:

❑ The Common Language Runtime (CLR), which manages the execution of all .NET assemblies.

❑ MSIL (Microsoft Intermediate Language), generated by all the .NET language compilers. This is a common standard for the binary code generated by the compilers and is what is executed by the CLR. The CLR also defines the format for storing an assembly's metadata, and this means that all assemblies, whatever language they were written in, share a common format for storing their metadata.

❑ The Common Language Specification (CLS), provided so that programs written in C#, the .NET versions of Visual Basic and Visual C++, or any other .NET language that is CLS-compliant can share components with full inheritance across language boundaries. The CLS defines the features that languages must support in order to support interoperability with other .NET languages. It is possible to use features that are not in the CLS, but there is no guarantee that these will be supported by other languages.

The Common Type System (CTS), which defines the basic types used by all .NET languages and rules for defining your own classes. This prevents languages implementing, say, the String type in incompatible ways.

By following the CLS specification, you can write a component in C#, and the assembly containing the component can be used by a program written in another .NET language, such as Visual Basic .NET, because both the C# and Visual Basic .NET components will be executed by the CLR. Similarly, C# programs can use components written in Visual Basic .NET, Visual C++.NET, and so on. At the assembly level, all classes, objects, and data types used by .NET languages are shared, so you can inherit classes and make full use of components no matter what language they are written in.

Interoperation with COM and Other Legacy Code

The .NET Framework also allows components or libraries written using COM and other *legacy* technologies to be used with C# and other .NET languages.

This mechanism also works via self-describing assemblies. A wrapper assembly is created for the legacy code that allows it to describe itself to the .NET runtime and convert the COM data types to .NET data types, and allows calls back and forth from the .NET languages to the legacy code and vice versa. Visual Studio 2005 automatically creates a wrapper assembly when you add a reference to a COM component (using the COM tab in the Add Reference dialog).

This diagram shows such a wrapper (also called a Runtime Callable Wrapper) in use. Calls made by the .NET client assembly go through the wrapper to get to the COM component. From the .NET assembly's point of view, the wrapper *is* the component, as shown in Figure 26-1.

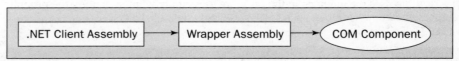

Figure 26-1

There are difficulties in interoperating with legacy technologies such as COM, but that subject is beyond the scope of this book.

Structure of Assemblies

The parts of an assembly provide the means for .NET programs to find out about one another and resolve the references between programs and components.

An assembly contains the executable code for a program or class library, along with metadata (data describing other data), which enables other programs to look up classes, methods, and properties of the objects defined within the assembly. The metadata acts in two ways: as a table of contents, describing what is contained inside the assembly and as a bibliography describing references to data outside the assembly. Let's look at this in more detail.

Single-file .NET assemblies have the following general format, shown in Figure 26-2.

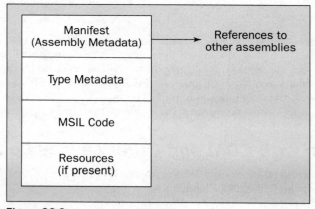

Figure 26-2

Each assembly contains a manifest, which describes the contents of the assembly (like a manifest for a shipment of goods). The manifest is also called the assembly metadata, because it describes the assembly itself — what modules it contains, what other assemblies it references, and so on. You examine this in more detail later on in this chapter when you view the contents of an assembly you create. Previous component technologies such as COM have no in-built concept like the manifest; the manifest is the heart of the self-description built into .NET assemblies.

The .NET runtime uses the manifest in the program's assembly when executing the program for resolving references to other assemblies, such as `System`, that contains the `Console.WriteLine()` method for printing out Hello, World!.

The manifest is followed by the type metadata — the description of the classes, properties, methods, and so on contained within the assembly along with the data types for their parameters and return values. This is followed by the actual binary code for each of the types, stored as machine-independent MSIL code. Finally, there are any resources that form part of the assembly. Resources are nonexecutable parts of your program (specified in .Resources files) such as images, icons, or message files.

Although an assembly often consists of only one file, it can also be composed of several files, as shown in Figure 26-3.

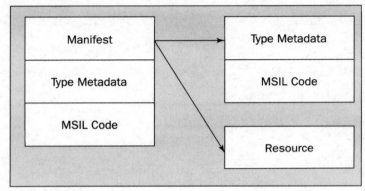

Figure 26-3

From the .NET runtime's point of view, a multiple-file assembly is a single logical DLL or EXE that just happens to consist of multiple files. Only one file contains the manifest. The manifest points to the other files that make up the multiple-file assembly. The files that contain executable code are called modules; these contain type metadata and MSIL code. There may also be resource files containing no executable code.

Multiple-file assemblies are usually needed only in certain advanced applications. A module or resource is loaded only when it is actually executed or brought into use, so you can save download time and memory when modules and resources that are rarely used are stored in separate files. For example, an application delivered internationally may have modules or resources written in different languages. You would separate these so that only the module for the language actually in use was loaded into memory.

Now that you've seen what assemblies are, you'll create one and look at its properties. First, you need to create a simple class library in C# that you refer to in the rest of this chapter. In the following Try It Out, you make a simple version of the Shapes component imagined in the first part of the chapter.

Try It Out   **Creating the Shapes Component**

To create the Shapes class library component that you will use as an example assembly in the rest of this chapter, follow these steps:

1.   Create a new class library project called Shapes in the directory C:\BegVCSharp\Chapter26.

2.   Rename the Class1.cs file created by default to Shapes.cs, and type in the source code shown below. The binary file built from Shapes.cs will be Shapes.dll, and you will use that as the example of an assembly.

3. Enter the following code into the Shapes namespace:

```
namespace Shapes
{
    public class Circle
    {
        double Radius;

        public Circle()
        {
            Radius = 0;
        }
        public Circle(double givenRadius)
        {
            Radius = givenRadius;
        }
        public double Area()
        {
            // area = pi r squared
            return System.Math.PI * (Radius * Radius);
        }
    }

    public class Triangle
    {
        double Base;
        double Height;

        public Triangle()
        {
            Base = 0;
            Height = 0;
        }

        public Triangle(double givenBase, double givenHeight)
        {
            Base = givenBase;
            Height = givenHeight;
        }

        public double Area()
        {
            return 0.5F * Base * Height;  // area = 1/2 base * height
        }
    }
}
```

The code is very simple and obviously not a complete implementation of everything you might want to do with a set of shapes, but it will do for your purposes. The one bit of complexity is that the Circle and Triangle classes each have two constructors, one that takes no parameters and another that takes parameters to initialize the instance variables. You see this again later on when you examine the contents of the assembly that is produced.

4. Before moving on, build the Shapes project with Build ⇨ Build Solution (Ctrl-Shift-B).

Viewing the Contents of an Assembly

Let's view the contents of the assembly you just created using the self-description in the `shapes.dll` assembly. The tool you can use to view the contents of an assembly is `Ildasm`, the .NET Framework *Intermediate Language Disassembler* tool. This is a handy tool for viewing and understanding the internal structure of assemblies and can also be used by the curious to view the contents of the System assemblies. However, it is not something you will need to use in day-to-day development of C# programs; don't feel that you have to memorize the details of using it.

Executing Ildasm from the Visual Studio Command Line

The quickest way to execute `Ildasm` is to go the Start ⇨ All Programs ⇨ Microsoft Visual Studio 2005 ⇨ Visual Studio Tools ⇨ Visual Studio Command Prompt and simply enter **Ildasm** at the command prompt. The Visual Studio 2005 command prompt has the PATH set to the Visual Studio 2005 tools.

Adding Ildasm as an External Tool to Visual Studio 2005

Another way to execute `Ildasm` is to add it as an external tool to the Visual Studio 2005 development environment; this makes it easier to go back and execute it again without having to leave Visual Studio 2005. To do this, go to the Tools ⇨ External Tools... menu in Visual Studio 2005. Click the Add button in this dialog. You will see [New Tool 1] in the Menu Contents list and the Title entry box; type in **Ildasm** in the Title entry box, then click on the browse button (...) to the right of the Command entry box. In the Open dialog that appears, navigate to this path:

```
C:\Program Files\Microsoft Visual Studio 8\SDK\v2.0\Bin
```

Click on `Ildasm.exe` in the `Bin` directory, and then click Open. `Ildasm` will now appear in the Menu Contents list, as shown in Figure 26-4.

Figure 26-4

Click OK, and Ildasm will appear as a choice in the Tools menu of Visual Studio 2005.

Now that you have this tool easily available on the Tools menu, you can try it out!

Try It Out   Viewing the Contents of an Assembly with Ildasm

To try out the Ildasm tool, follow these steps:

1. Now that Ildasm has been added to Visual Studio 2005, open it by selecting Tools ➪ Ildasm. Ildasm will appear in a separate window, as shown in Figure 26-5.

Figure 26-5

2. Use the File ➪ Open menu to find the directory containing Shapes.dll and open it. Shapes.dll will be located in the bin subdirectory of your project (C:\BegVCSharp\Chapter26\Shapes\ Shapes\bin), probably in the Debug subdirectory if you built the default configuration.

3. Once you have located Shapes.dll, click on the Open button. The view of the assembly then appears in the Ildasm main window, as shown in Figure 26-6.

    You can see the manifest and the Shapes class in the display. The manifest is the assembly information; you look at that in a bit. The Shapes shield icon represents the Shapes namespace; it comes from the type metadata for this assembly.

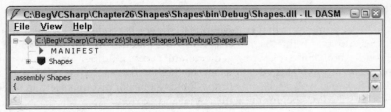

Figure 26-6

4. Expand the tree view by clicking on the + sign in front of the Shapes shield icon. You now see the two classes defined in your source file, `Circle` and `Triangle`, as shown in Figure 26-7.

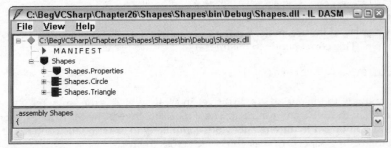

Figure 26-7

5. Expand the view of each class by clicking on the + signs in front of Circle and Triangle, as shown in Figure 26-8.

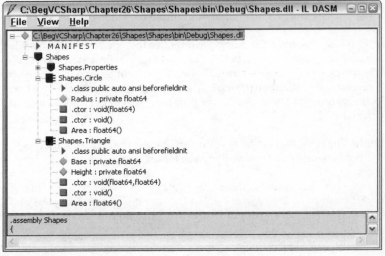

Figure 26-8

How It Works

Now you begin to see something that corresponds to the source code you created. You can see the class instance variables `Radius` for the `Circle` class and `Base` and `Height` for the `Triangle` class, as well as the `Area` method for both. Since `private` is the default access modifier for class instance variables such as `Radius` and `Base`, this explains why you can see these variables marked with private in the screen-shot in Figure 26-8. You can also see some funny-looking lines of text that seem to be additional to the source code, such as the lines beginning with `.ctor` and `.class`.

If you look closely, you notice that the `.ctor` lines actually correspond to the constructors defined for `Circle` and `Triangle`. There are two constructors for each, one that takes no parameters and another that takes parameters to initialize the instance variables. In `Circle`'s case, the constructor with parameters takes one `float` value, which corresponds to the line

```
.ctor void(float64)
```

in the `Ildasm` display of the assembly. For the `Triangle` class, the parameterized constructor takes two `float` parameters. This corresponds to the line:

```
.ctor void(float64, float64)
```

The lines beginning with the period are directives in MSIL, which is the language C# code is compiled into for execution in the .NET environment. The `.ctor` directive is the MSIL instruction to make a class constructor. You don't need to understand MSIL completely to examine the contents of assemblies; I'll just point out interesting aspects of it as you come across them.

You also see the line at the top that is labeled MANIFEST; let's talk a little bit about that now.

Manifests

The manifest of an assembly was discussed earlier — it describes each file or module within the assembly (remember that an assembly could consist of multiple files though typically it is just one file).

More importantly, it also describes the *external* assemblies that are referenced by this assembly. For example, if your program uses `System.Data.dll`, that fact is reflected in the manifest. This makes it much easier to keep track of the dependencies between assemblies, making deployment and verification of a program's correct installation much easier. The manifest also tracks the version number of the assembly, making upgrading to new versions of programs easier. Let's take a look at the manifest of the assembly you just created.

Double-click on the line labeled MANIFEST at the top of the `Ildasm` listing for `shapes.dll`. This opens a new window with the manifest details, as shown in Figure 26-9.

The manifest for `Shapes.dll` contains three `.assembly` directives and a number of other directives, including a `.module` directive. Don't worry about the contents of the `.assembly` blocks; that is, ignore everything inside the curly braces `{}` for now. The first line you can see is:

```
.assembly extern mscorlib
```

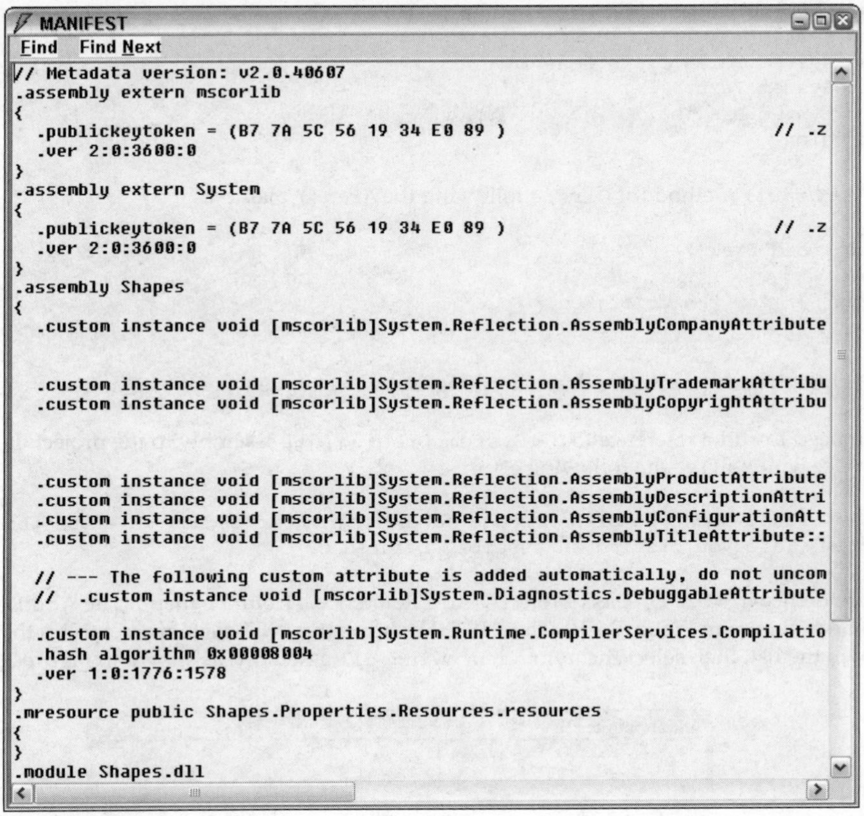

Figure 26-9

This is an external assembly reference to the mscorlib.dll, which is the core library for the Microsoft .NET Framework. The most basic System classes in the .NET Framework are defined here. This external reference is also needed for every .NET program. The next assembly directive is:

```
.assembly extern System
```

This is an external assembly reference to the System.dll, which is where some (but not all) of the base System classes in the .NET Framework are defined. This external reference is needed for every C# and .NET program that uses the classes in the System namespace.

The .assembly Shapes line is the declaration of the Shapes assembly itself. This is followed by a .module declaration for the shapes.dll file. Your assembly has just one file, so there is a single .module declaration for that file.

Let's see what happens when an additional reference is added to the source file. Suppose that you wanted to draw a shape using some of the methods from the System.Drawing namespace. Close Ildasm and go back to the Shapes project in Visual Studio 2005. Modify Shapes.cs as follows. First, expand the Using directives region at the top of the Shapes.cs source file add a using directive referencing the System.Drawing namespace:

```
#region Using directives
using System;
using System.Collections.Generic;
using System.Text;
using System.Drawing;
#endregion
```

Then, add a `Draw()` method for `Circle` following the `Area()` method:

```
public void Draw()
{
    Pen p = new Pen(Color.Red);
}
```

This isn't enough code to actually draw anything, but you can see where it's going!

Now, you need to add a reference to the `System.Drawing.dll` assembly to the project. If you don't add this reference, you will see the following error:

```
error CS0234: The type or namespace name 'Drawing' does not exist in the namespace
'System' (are you missing an assembly reference?)
```

To add a reference in VS2005, select Project ⇨ Add Reference... from the menu. The Add Reference dialog will appear as shown in Figure 26-10. The .NET tab shows the .NET system assemblies that are available. Scroll down the list, then select the `System.Drawing.dll` assembly, as shown in Figure 26-6.

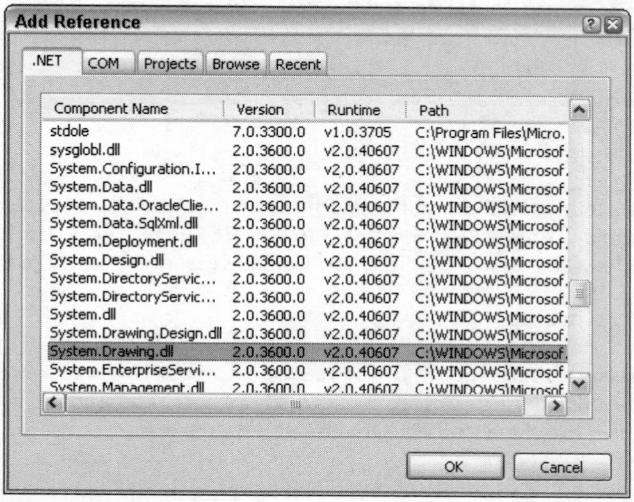

Figure 26-10

Now press OK to add the reference. This adds the `System.Drawing.dll` reference to the `Shapes.dll` file. Save your source file changes, close `Ildasm` if you did not do so already (otherwise, you'll get a compiler error because `Ildasm` has `Shapes.dll` open), and then recompile `Shapes.cs` with the above changes.

Start Ildasm again and open Shapes.dll. You'll notice the Draw() method under the Circles object, as shown in Figure 26-11.

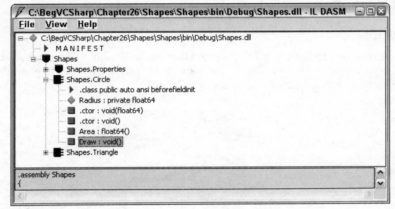

Figure 26-11

Double-click on MANIFEST again to see the changes you have made to it. There is now an external assembly reference to the System.Drawing assembly, as shown in Figure 26-12.

```
MANIFEST
Find   Find Next
// Metadata version: v2.0.40607
.assembly extern mscorlib
{
  .publickeytoken = (B7 7A 5C 56 19 34 E0 89 )           // .z
  .ver 2:0:3600:0
}
.assembly extern System
{
  .publickeytoken = (B7 7A 5C 56 19 34 E0 89 )           // .z
  .ver 2:0:3600:0
}
.assembly extern System.Drawing
{
  .publickeytoken = (B0 3F 5F 7F 11 D5 0A 3A )           // .?
  .ver 2:0:3600:0
}
.assembly Shapes
{
  .custom instance void [mscorlib]System.Reflection.AssemblyCompanyAttribute
```

Figure 26-12

The Shapes assembly will inform the system that it requires the System.Drawing assembly whenever Shapes itself is referenced. You look at how another program makes use of the Shapes assembly in just a bit, but after looking at the screen in Figure 26-12, your curiosity about the stuff inside the .assembly directives (that I told you to ignore earlier) is probably getting to be too great. Let's put you out of your misery and discuss that information now.

Chapter 26

Assembly Attributes

Besides the external assembly references, the manifest of an assembly contains information that pertains to the assembly itself. These are called assembly attributes.

AssemblyInfo.cs

When building your project, you may have noticed that Visual Studio 2005 creates a second C# source file as part of your project, inside the Projects folder of the Solution Explorer. Expand the Projects folder to see this file, called `AssemblyInfo.cs`, as shown in Figure 26-13.

Figure 26-13

`AssemblyInfo.cs` is used to set properties of the assembly in the manifest. Double-click on the file to open it, and look at the contents (some comments have been removed to save space):

```
//
// General Information about an assembly is controlled through the following
// set of attributes. Change these attribute values to modify the information
// associated with an assembly.
//
[assembly: AssemblyTitle("Shapes")]
[assembly: AssemblyDescription("")]
[assembly: AssemblyConfiguration("")]
[assembly: AssemblyCompany("My Company, Inc.")]
[assembly: AssemblyProduct("Shapes")]
[assembly: AssemblyCopyright("Copyright @ My Company, Inc. 2005")]
[assembly: AssemblyTrademark("")]
[assembly: AssemblyCulture("")]

//
// Version information for an assembly consists of the following four values:
//
//      Major Version
//      Minor Version
//      Build Number
//      Revision
//
// You can specify all the values or you can default the Revision and
// Build Numbers by using the '*' as shown below:

[assembly: AssemblyVersion("1.0.*")]
```

Each of the statements in square brackets that looks like [assembly: Assembly...] is an *attribute*, a special syntax in C# that is covered in more depth in Chapter 27. For our purposes here, it's enough for you to know that each of these statements sets a particular property of the assembly. The word assembly: at the beginning of each attribute tells the system that the directive following is targeted at the assembly itself, not a class, method, or other part of the program.

Visual Studio 2005 supplies this file containing the assembly attributes as a template for you to fill in with the properties you want your assembly to have. Most of the attributes such as title, company, and so on are purely informational and can be filled in with any descriptive value you want associated with your component, such as:

```
[assembly: AssemblyTitle("MyCompany Shapes Class Library")]
[assembly: AssemblyDescription("Classes for Manipulation of Shapes")]
[assembly: AssemblyConfiguration("Enterprise Version")]
[assembly: AssemblyCompany("MyCompany, Inc.")]
[assembly: AssemblyProduct("Shapes")]
[assembly: AssemblyCopyright("Copyright 2005, MyCompany, Inc.")]
[assembly: AssemblyTrademark("Shapes is a trademark of MyCompany, Inc.")]
```

When a source file containing assembly attributes is built, the attributes are incorporated into the assembly's manifest. For example, if you change the AssemblyTitle attribute, build, and look again at the manifest for Shapes.dll with Ildasm, you'll see this line within the .assembly Shapes section:

```
.custom instance void [mscorlib]System.Reflection.AssemblyTitleAttribute::
.ctor(string) =
    ( 01 00 1E 4D 79 43 6F 6D 70 61 6E 79 20 53 68 61   // ...MyCompany Sha
      70 65 73 20 43 6C 61 73 73 20 4C 69 62 72 61 72   // pes Class Librar
      79 00 00 )                                         // y..
```

This line indicates that the assembly contains an AssemblyTitle attribute, and it indicates the value of this attribute.

Assembly Culture

The line following the company and trademark attributes is the AssemblyCulture attribute:

```
[assembly: AssemblyCulture("")]
```

This sets the national language used for this assembly (English, French, Chinese, and so on) and if it is specified, it is a special abbreviation following an international standard. For more information, see the System.Globalization namespace and culture topics in the .NET Framework online documentation.

You don't need to set the culture unless you're distributing different language versions of a component; if you are doing this then the .NET runtime will automatically search for the version of your assembly that matches the current culture, so that, for example, in France you display the French messages (using your French message resources and/or code) and in Britain you display English messages (using your English message resources and/or code). You mark the appropriate assembly with the correct culture attribute for this to happen.

Version Numbers

The line following the culture attribute is the `AssemblyVersion` attribute:

```
[assembly: AssemblyVersion("1.0.*")]
```

Before I explain this assembly version attribute specifically, let's examine how assembly version numbers work in .NET. The version for a .NET assembly has four parts, as shown here:

```
Major version . Minor version . Build Number . Revision
```

The first two parts are probably familiar to you if you are a user of consumer software—they are a major version number and a minor version number, as in Shapes version 1.0 (where 1 is the major version and 0 the minor version).

The next two parts take the versioning to a finer level of detail. The build number indicates which build of the assembly this is; the build number would typically change every time the assembly is rebuilt.

The revision number goes one level deeper and is designed to be used for a patch or a "hot fix" to an assembly that is exactly the same as its predecessor, except for this one bug fix.

Version Attributes

You can see an assembly's version attributes in `Ildasm`. Look in the manifest of the `shapes.dll` file, and you will see that each referenced assembly has a `.ver` directive inside the `.assembly` block for that assembly.

You may also notice that the version information for the external assembly references, such as the references to the `mscorlib` and `System` assemblies, are all the same. This is because the .NET runtime uses assembly version numbers for compatibility checking. I'll talk more about this when I discuss version compatibility.

When looking at an assembly created with Visual Studio 2005, you will see a version number that probably looks something like this:

```
.ver 1:0:486:7484
```

Visual Studio 2005 assigns version numbers automatically as projects are built, depending on what information is set in the `AssemblyVersion` attribute, which you look at next.

Note: If you were to look at the version number of an assembly created outside of VS2005 with the .NET Framework command-line C# compiler (csc), the `.ver` directive for the shapes assembly would have all zeros in it, like this: `.ver 0:0:0:0`. This is because the command-line compiler does not automatically create an assemblyinfo.cs file with an AssemblyVersion attribute, as described in the next section. Just another little detail VS2005 takes care of for you!

AssemblyVersion attribute

Within the `AssemblyInfo.cs` file created by Visual Studio 2005, the version number is set with the `AssemblyVersion` attribute:

```
[assembly: AssemblyVersion("1.0.*")]
```

The `AssemblyVersion` attribute allows an asterisk (*) to be specified for the last two parts of the version number. This directs Visual Studio 2005 to set the build and revision numbers automatically. You can also specify the asterisk just for the revision number (as in `1.1.1.*`) but not the major and minor version numbers (`1.*` is not allowed). If you look at the assembly version number with `Ildasm`, you'll see that the actual version number Visual Studio 2005 sets will be something like:

```
.ver 1:0:585:24784
```

If you change some code in your classes and build again; you'll see the number change automatically to something like:

```
.ver 1:0:585:25005
```

You can directly set all the parts of the version by specifying a specific number instead of the asterisk:

```
[assembly: AssemblyVersion("1.0.1.2")]
```

This will force Visual Studio 2005 to produce an assembly with this specific major, minor, build, and revision number.

If you are just developing a program for your own use, you won't need to set or care about version numbers. However, if you are releasing software to other end users, you will want to change major and minor version numbers as you add significant new functionality to your releases: 1.0 for the first production release, 1.1 for a release introducing minor enhancements, 2.0 for major changes, and so on. It's okay to let Visual Studio 2005 set the build/revision numbers automatically, and you won't even need to be aware of them most of the time.

It is handy to be able to use `Ildasm` to check the full version number. For example, if an end user reports a bug, you can compare the version of the assembly on your computer and the one installed on the end-user's computer. You can tell exactly which version that user has; with the revision and build numbers you can even distinguish between the build made this morning and the one made just before noon.

Version Compatibility

The .NET runtime checks version numbers when loading assemblies to determine version compatibility. This is done only for shared assemblies, which you look at later in this chapter. However, the way version checking works with version numbers is described here.

You'll recall that the manifest of an assembly contains the version number of the current assembly as well as the version numbers of referenced external assemblies. When the .NET runtime loads a referenced assembly, it checks the version in that assembly's manifest and compares it to the version stored in the reference to make sure the versions are compatible.

If the assemblies have different major or minor version numbers, they are assumed to be incompatible, and the referenced assembly will not load — for example, Shapes version 1.1 is not compatible with a program referencing Shapes version 1.0, 1.2, or 2.0.

What if you have program A that uses Shapes 1.0 and program B that uses Shapes 1.1 on the same system? This is actually taken care of in the .NET runtime; there is a feature called side-by-side execution, which enables Shapes 1.0 and Shapes 1.1 to both be installed on the same computer and each to be available to the programs that need that version.

The next two parts of the version number take the versioning to a finer level of detail. The build number indicates which build of the assembly this is; this typically changes every time the assembly is rebuilt. Two assemblies with the same major/minor version number and a differing build number may or may not be compatible; the runtime assumes that they are compatible so that they are allowed to load. It is up to the developer to make sure to change the major or minor version if incompatible changes are introduced.

You'll notice in earlier examples that the version number of the mscorlib assembly and the System .Drawing assembly were both version 2.0 with a build number of 3600; that is the build number of the .NET System assemblies currently on my system as I write this. If one of these libraries were updated to build number 3302 or even 9999 the .NET runtime would try to use the new build; however, the build number is not guaranteed to be compatible.

The revision number goes one more level, enabling you to specify a very specific patch or fix to a particular build number. 2.0.3600.0 and 2.0.3600.1 are assumed to be totally compatible. In the side-by-side scenario, if the major and minor versions of two coexisting assemblies match and differ only by build number and/or revision, the system will execute the newer assembly (namely, the one with a higher build/revision number).

Calling Assemblies

Now let's look at what happens when Shapesis referenced by a program.

In the following Try It Out, you'll make a simple client for Shapes named ShapeUser, and take a look at this client in Ildasm before executing it.

Try It Out   Creating a Shapes Client

To create the client program that uses the Shapes assembly, follow these steps:

1. Create a new console application project named ShapeUser in the directory C:\BegVCSharp\ Chapter26. (See Figure 26-14.)

2. Rename the Program.cs source file to ShapeUser.cs, and enter the following code:

```
#region Using directives
using System;
using System.Collections.Generic;
using System.Text;
using Shapes;
#endregion

namespace ShapeUser
{
    public class ShapeUser
    {
        public static void Main()
        {
            Circle c = new Circle(1.0F);

            Console.WriteLine("Area of Circle(1.0) is {0}", c.Area());
```

```
            Console.ReadKey(); // press a key to exit program
        }
    }
}
```

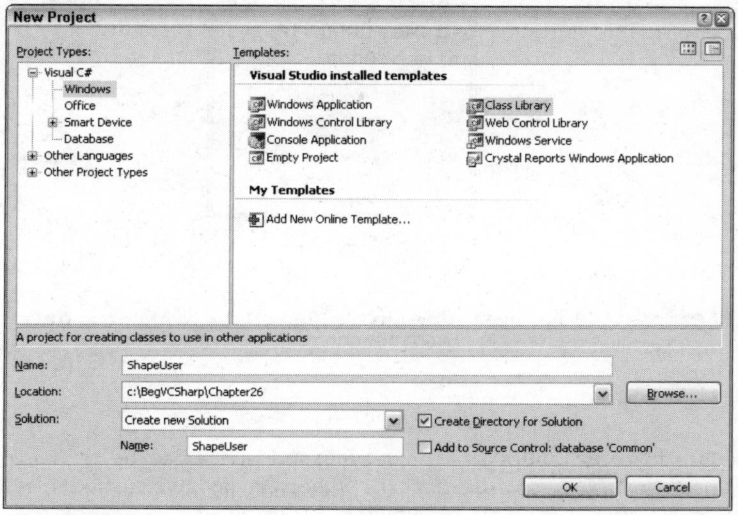

Figure 26-14

This project will need a reference to the Shapes project to build correctly, so choose Add Reference... from the Project menu (or right-click on References in the Solution Explorer and select Add Reference...), and the Add Reference dialog will appear. Select the Browse tab in this dialog, then navigate to the Shapes.dll file in the Shapes\bin\Debug directory under C:\BegVCSharp\Chapter26\Shapes (or wherever you have created it), as shown in Figure 26-15.

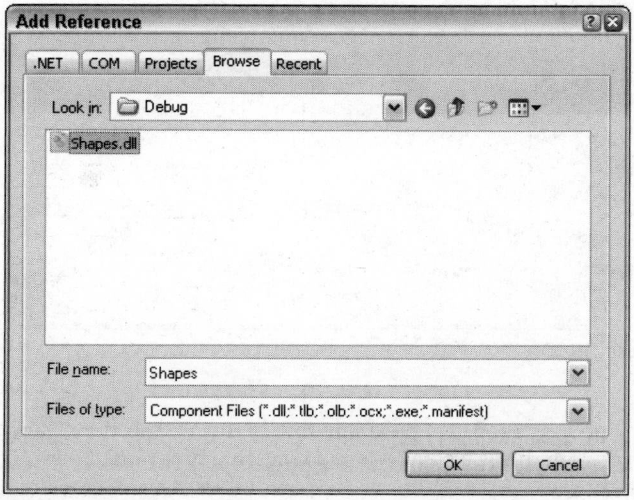

Figure 26-15

Click the OK button. Shapes is added to the list of references for the ShapesUser project, as shown in Figure 26-16.

Figure 26-16

A private copy of Shapes.dll has been added to the ShapeUser bin\Debug directory — I'll discuss this more in the next section.

Build the ShapeUser application.

Now that ShapeUser has been built, start Ildasm again and navigate to the C:\BegVCSharp\Chapter26\ShapeUser\ShapeUser\bin\Debug directory (or wherever you have created it, again) and open ShapeUser.exe to examine its contents, as shown in Figure 26-17.

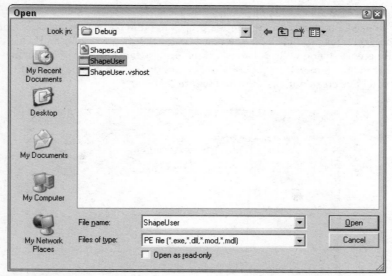

Figure 26-17

Note the private copy of Shapes.dll; I'll explain that in the next section. Click the Open button to proceed. Note that even though this is a stand-alone executable program, it has metadata just like a class library does. Double-click on MANIFEST to see the external reference to the Shapes component, as shown in Figure 26-18.

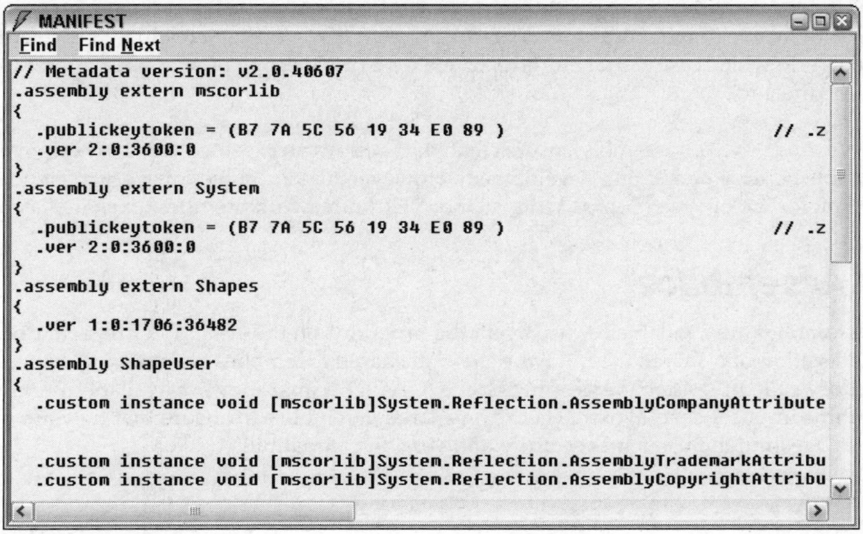

Figure 26-18

Finally, to see the assemblies run together, close Ildasm, then execute ShapeUser.exe by pressing F5 to execute in Debug mode. ShapeUser.exe will create a Circle object using the class defined in Shapes.dll, and will call the Area method to get its area. The output appears in a separate Console window, as shown in Figure 26-19.

Figure 26-19

Press a key to exit the program (or press Shift-F5 to stop debugging), and now you can move on to learn about private and shared assemblies.

Private and Shared Assemblies

Up to now you have been dealing only with private assemblies — assemblies that are deployed as part of a single application. However, the .NET Framework also has special facilities to provide for shared assemblies that are used by multiple programs simultaneously.

Private Assemblies

By default, an assembly is private to your project. Private assemblies *must* be in the same directory as the application.

The `Shapes.dll` assembly is private; in order to refer to it from the `ShapeUser` project you had to browse into the `Shapes` development directory from the `ShapeUser` project when adding the reference in Visual Studio 2005 — in which case Visual Studio 2005 makes a private copy of `Shapes.dll` and places it in the `ShapeUser` directory.

Copying the `Shapes.dll` assembly ensures that `ShapeUser` can execute even if the original `Shapes.dll` is unavailable because of ongoing development. However, making copies of every referenced DLL is not very efficient for widely used components, so the .NET Framework provides for shared assemblies.

Shared Assemblies

Shared assemblies are available for use by all the programs on the system. A program does not need to know the location of a shared assembly because all shared assemblies are stored in a special .NET system directory called the Global Assembly Cache (GAC). Because they are available systemwide, the .NET runtime imposes several extra checks on shared assemblies to ensure that they are valid for the program requesting them, such as security and version compatibility.

Strong Names

A shared assembly must have some means of distinguishing it from other assemblies that may have the same name. Also, for assemblies shared across the system, it is desirable for security to have a means of uniquely identifying an assembly as originating from you, the developer, and prevent the assembly from being replaced with another assembly using the same name and version, or prevent it from being altered in any way, for example by a virus.

Requiring that a shared assembly be signed with a cryptographic key does this. The key uniquely identifies your assembly and protects not only against a security breach but also against a simple name/version collision due to two components having the same name and version number.

> *If the keys are different, the components are considered to be different even if they have the same name.*

The unique combination of the assembly name, version, and key is called a strong name.

Strong names are required for shared assemblies installed with ClickOnce deployment or installed into the Global Assembly Cache, described in the next section. You do not generally want to add a strong name for an application executable, as it might interfere with that application's use of private assemblies. For example, it does not make sense for us to sign `ShapeUser.exe` with a strong name, but it does make sense to sign `Shapes.dll` with a strong name for use by multiple applications.

Global Assembly Cache

The Global Assembly Cache is a special directory, located in the `WINDOWS\assembly` directory (on Windows XP) or the `WINNT\assembly` directory (on Windows 2000/2003). All shared assemblies, including the .NET Framework `System` assemblies supplied by Microsoft, are located and loaded from here. If you browse this directory with the Windows Explorer, a special Windows shell extension displays the properties of the assemblies, including the key incorporated into the strong name of each.

The Windows shell extension (called `shfusion.dll`) plugs into Windows Explorer and extends its capabilities beyond a normal file listing. This screenshot shows the GAC viewed in Windows Explorer. The name, version, key, and other properties of the assemblies are listed in Figure 26-20.

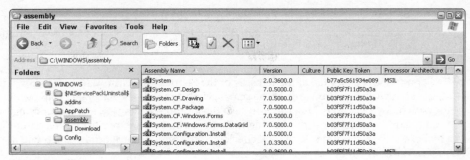

Figure 26-20

The Windows shell extension enforces the security policy for the Global Assembly Cache, enabling assemblies to be copied into this directory via drag and drop, but only if the rules are adhered to. Let's look at the rules you have to follow to allow you to place an assembly into the Global Assembly Cache.

Creating a Shared Assembly

In order to create a shared assembly with a strong name, you must generate a public/private key pair that is used to sign an assembly. Public/private key cryptographic systems use a private key known only to the originator of the information to be encrypted, and a public key published to the world. The .NET environment uses this same mechanism to ensure that a referenced shared assembly is really the assembly wanted (assemblies from different companies could have the same name and version number, for example, or a hacker could try to *spoof* a program by creating an assembly with the same name/version, or try to tamper with an existing assembly). The keys in the reference to the assembly and the key in the (signed) shared assembly itself are checked to make sure they match; if they do not, the shared assembly will not load.

The combination of the assembly name, version, and public key are guaranteed to be unique; this combination is called a strong name.

The .NET Framework provides a tool for generating the strong name called sn.exe (sn stands for *strong name*).

Executing sn.exe from the Visual Studio Command Line

Sn.exe is an external .NET Framework utility like Ildasm. As with Ildasm, you can execute it from the Visual Studio Command Prompt. To do this, go to go the Start ➪ All Programs ➪ Microsoft Visual Studio 2005 ➪ Visual Studio Tools ➪ Visual Studio Command Prompt menu and start a command prompt to try the steps in the following Try It Out. Because you must pass command-line arguments to Sn.exe it is not really practical to add it as an external tool to Visual Studio 2005 as you did with Ildasm.

Try It Out   Signing the Shapes Assembly

Follow these steps to sign the Shapes assembly:

1.   From the command line, change the directory to C:\BegVCSharp\Chapter26\Shapes\ Shapes. Use the following command to generate a key file, giving a filename (usually with the .snk extension) that you will reference from your assembly:

```
sn -k Shapes.snk
```

This creates the key file `Shapes.snk` in the current directory.

2. Now, to sign `Shapes.dll` with this key file, right-click on the Shapes C# project in the Solution Explorer (highlighted in the Solution Explorer on the right side of Figure 26-21), and choose Properties.

3. Click on to the Signing tab at the left side of the Shapes project properties, as shown in Figure 26-21. In the Key Selection area of the screen, click on the Use a Key File radio button, type in the path name to `Shapes.snk` (or browse to the location of `Shapes.snk` by choosing <Browse...> from the drop-down list — the key file will appear in the directory list with a padlock icon). Finally, check the Sign the Assembly check box; the Signing properties screen will appear as shown in Figure 26-21.

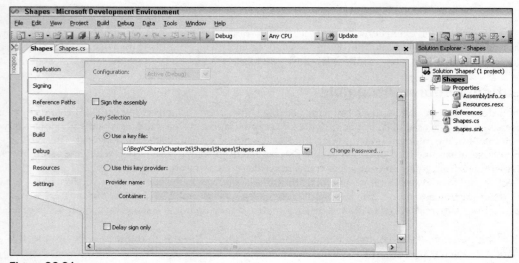

Figure 26-21

4. Now recompile the `Shapes.dll` assembly. If Visual Studio 2005 can't find the `Shapes.snk` file, the project won't compile, and you will get an error such as:

```
Cryptographic failure while signing assembly
'C:\BegVCSharp\Chapter26\Shapes\Shapes\obj\Debug\Shapes.dll' --
'Error reading key file 'Shapes.snk' -- The system cannot find the file specified.'
```

This tells you exactly where Visual Studio 2005 is looking for the key file, and you can either move the file to that directory or specify a directory relative to it.

Once you have successfully rebuilt the project, the assembly is signed.

5. Open up `Ildasm`, and examine the manifest of the `Shapes.dll` assembly — you can see that a public key has been generated and embedded with a `.publickey` statement toward the bottom of the manifest, as shown in Figure 26-22.

6. You need to recompile `ShapeUser.cs` to update the external assembly reference inside `ShapeUser.exe` with the signed version of `Shapes.dll`. Once recompiled, it works just as before, still using the local copy of `Shapes.dll`.

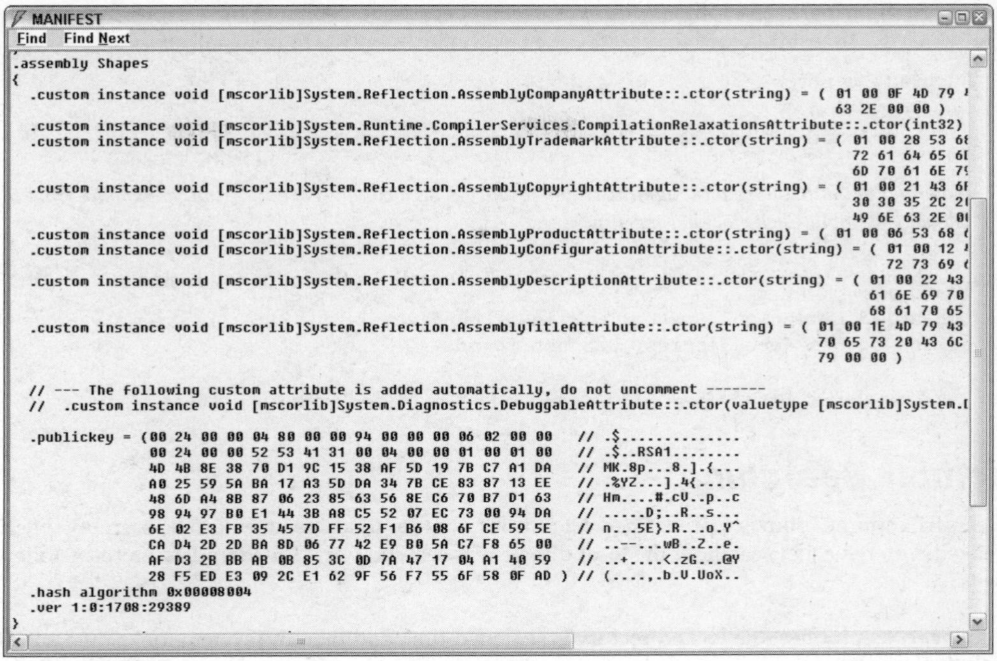

Figure 26-22

7. Now that your assembly is signed, you are able to install it into the Global Assembly Cache. This can be done simply by dragging and dropping the .dll file into the GAC folder located in `WINDOWS\assembly` (on Windows XP) or `WINNT\assembly` (on Windows 2000/2003), or alternatively, you can use a Visual Studio 2005 command-line tool called `Gacutil` (Global Assembly Cache Utility). To install `Shapes.dll` into the Global Assembly Cache, use the `Gacutil` with the `/i` option from a command-line prompt:

```
Gacutil /i Shapes.dll
```

The message "Assembly successfully added to the cache" will indicate successful installation of the assembly.

Note that for deployment of a commercial application, the preferred way to add a shared assembly to the Global Assembly Cache is to use the Windows Installer.

8. To prove that `Shapes.dll` is in the cache, delete the copy of `Shapes.dll` in the current directory. Now, from the command line, go to the directory containing the `ShapeUser` executable, which is

```
C:\BegVCSharp\Chapter26\ShapeUser\ShapeUser\bin\Debug
```

and run `ShapeUser.exe`. You should see the output:

```
Area of Circle(1.0) is 3.14159265358979
```

It still runs, even with `Shapes.dll` absent, because it is loading the `Shapes` assembly from the GAC. To test this further, use `Gacutil` with the `/u` option to uninstall shapes:

```
Gacutil /u shapes
```

Note that the .dll extension is omitted for the uninstall option.

Note that you must have local administrator privileges on a computer to uninstall assemblies from the Global Assembly Cache for that machine.

9. Now try to run `ShapeUser` as above, and you will see the following message:

```
Unhandled Exception: System.IO.FileNotFoundException: File or assembly name Shapes,
or one of its dependencies, was not found.
```

This shows that `Shapes.dll` was indeed being loaded from the GAC.

Assembly Searching

The .NET runtime follows a predefined set of rules in order to locate an external assembly when it is referenced. You have just seen how the local directory is searched first for shared assemblies, followed by the GAC.

For private assemblies, the local directory is searched first, and then the system looks for a subdirectory with the same name as the assembly. The runtime also looks for either a DLL or EXE file with the same name as the requested assembly. For the `Shapes` class the combination of these results in the following set of searches:

```
./Shapes.dll.
./Shapes/Shapes.dll
./Shapes/Shapes.exe
./Shapes.exe
```

If the assembly has a specific culture defined, a subdirectory with the name of the culture (for example, `de` for German) would be searched, also. Additional search paths or even URLs for downloading an assembly from a remote location via the Internet may be specified with a configuration file. Configuration files for an assembly are XML-format files that specify rules for the .NET runtime to apply when searching for an assembly. Configuration files can also override the default behavior for version checking. The details of configuration files and XML are quite complex and beyond the scope of this book.

Summary

In this chapter, you learned:

❑ That C# programs and class libraries are delivered as assemblies, which have many features that ease the delivery of components in the Microsoft .NET Framework. Components provide for binary reuse of objects.

❑ That the essential feature of .NET components is self-description; this distinguishes them from their historical ancestors (such as COM components).

❑ That self-description has a number of benefits, including ease of installation and integration with the Common Language Runtime (CLR) to provide cross-language and legacy support, as well as C# development.

❑ How to create a C# class library component and compile it into an assembly. You then created a C# application that used this component, and learned how to view the contents of assemblies using Ildasm.

❑ About the various parts of an assembly, including the manifest.

❑ About the assembly version number and other assembly attributes. Besides helping you to understand the structure, you learned how to compare version numbers in external references for debugging purposes.

❑ That assemblies can be either private assemblies local to an application, or shared assemblies, which are available systemwide.

❑ How to create shared assemblies by creating a key file and signing the project to create a strong name for the assembly. You also learned about version checking for shared assemblies, and looked at the Global Assembly Cache (GAC) where shared assemblies are stored.

❑ How references to assemblies are searched and resolved in the .NET runtime. These features of assemblies all help to make delivery of applications in the .NET environment much easier.

In the next chapter, you learn more about attributes and how they apply to classes and methods as well as assemblies.

Exercises

1. Change the version number and other assembly attributes in AssemblyInfo.cs or Shapes.cs, and view the resulting changes in Shapes.dll using Ildasm.

2. Make a new MoreShapes assembly with a Square class in addition to Circle and Triangle, and then examine its properties with Ildasm.

3. Change the assembly reference in ShapeUser.exe to use MoreShapes.dll, and then view the changed properties in Ildasm.

4. Make your own client for MoreShapes that uses the Square and Triangle objects as well as Circle. Examine the assembly for this client with Ildasm.

5. Display the command options for Gacutil with the /? flag, then use its options to list the properties of all the global assemblies on your system.

6. Create a strong name for MoreShapes and sign the assembly. View the results with Ildasm. Try executing your client program, then recompile it to reference the signed assembly.

7. Install MoreShapes.dll into the Global Assembly Cache using Gacutil, and experiment with ShapeUser and your own client by running with and without the MoreShapes assembly present in the local directory and/or GAC.

Attributes

This chapter introduces the subject of attributes, describing what they are and what they can be used for. You also find examples showing you the workings of several attributes available with the .NET Framework. Custom attributes — attributes you can write yourself to extend the system — are covered as well, along with several working examples. You'll also learn how the Intermediate Language Disassembler (Ildasm) can be used to discover the attributes of existing assemblies.

Attributes are one of the most useful features of the .NET Framework, and they are used frequently by Microsoft. To use them effectively, you need to make a significant investment of time, but it is worth the effort. In this chapter, you'll learn how to:

❑   Use attributes to define sections of code that are only included in Debug builds

❑   Use attributes to define information about an assembly, such as the copyright information

❑   Use attributes to mark sections of code as obsolete, so that over time you can revise your assemblies

❑   Create your own attributes and how to use these for testing code

The final section of this chapter describes in detail how to write your own attributes that extend the system, and it provides two working examples of custom attributes. By the end of the chapter, you should have enough knowledge of attributes to apply these to your own projects.

What Is an Attribute?

It's difficult to define an attribute in a single sentence — it's best to learn by examining how they are used. For now I'll define an attribute as extra information that can be applied to chunks of code within an assembly — such as a class, method, or property. This information is accessible to any other class that uses the assembly.

Chapter 27

Chapter 26 discussed assemblies and mentioned the `AssemblyInfo.cs` file. Let's have a look at this file—create a new Windows application called `AttributePeek` in the `C:\BegVCSharp\Chapter27` folder, and open the Solution Explorer. Expand the Properties node, as shown in Figure 27-1.

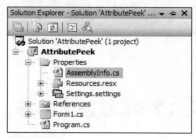

Figure 27-1

If you double-click on this file, and you'll see some code created by Visual Studio. Part of this code is shown here:

```
using System.Reflection;
using System.Runtime.CompilerServices;

//
// General Information about an assembly is controlled through the following
// set of attributes. Change these attribute values to modify
// the information associated with an assembly.
//
[assembly: AssemblyTitle("AttributePeek")]
[assembly: AssemblyDescription("")]
[assembly: AssemblyConfiguration("")]
[assembly: AssemblyCompany("MorganSkinner.com")]
[assembly: AssemblyProduct("AttributePeek")]
[assembly: AssemblyCopyright("Copyright MorganSkinner.com 2005")]
[assembly: AssemblyTrademark("")]
[assembly: AssemblyCulture("")]
```

For brevity, only part of the file is shown here. Within this file there are a number of lines beginning `[assembly:` — these are attribute definitions. When the file is compiled, any attributes defined are saved into the resulting assembly — this process is known as *pickling*. To see this in action, modify one of the preceding attributes — say the `AssemblyTitle` attribute — and compile your assembly:

```
[assembly: AssemblyTitle("AttributePeek - by ME")]
```

Once it is compiled, right-click on the assembly (which you can find in the project `\bin\Debug` directory) in Windows Explorer and select `Properties`. Figure 27-2 shows the `Version` information tab in Windows XP. The `Description` field contains the description contained in the `AssemblyTitle` attribute.

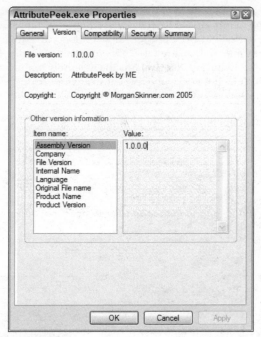

Figure 27-2

The assembly attributes and their corresponding names on the Version information tab are listed in the following table.

Attribute	Version Information
AssemblyTitle	Description
AssemblyDescription	Comments
AssemblyCompany	Company name
AssemblyTrademark	Legal trademarks
AssemblyVersion	Assembly version and product version
AssemblyCopyright	Copyright
AssemblyProduct	Product name

You may have noticed that the list of attributes available through the assembly Properties sheet is fewer than the list of attributes defined within the assembly — one example being the AssemblyConfiguration attribute. Microsoft has mapped some of the most common attributes onto the Properties sheet, but to get at the other attributes you'll either have to write code (shown in the upcoming "Reflection" section) or use the Ildasm or Reflector tools.

To find all attributes on a given assembly, you can use Ildasm to inspect the assembly and look for the attribute(s) defined. You were introduced to Ildasm in Chapter 26 and saw how to add it as an external tool to Visual Studio 2005. If you haven't done so, now is a good time to go back and see how to do this. Open Ildasm and select the assembly using File ➪ Open. Double-clicking the highlighted MANIFEST section will open a secondary window that contains the assembly manifest, as described in Chapter 26. Scrolling down the file a little will reveal some lines of strange-looking code — this code is the IL produced from the C# compiler:

```
.assembly AttributePeek
{
  .custom instance void
  [mscorlib]System.Reflection.AssemblyCopyrightAttribute::.ctor(string)
     = (01 00 00 00 00)

  .custom instance void
  [mscorlib]System.Reflection.AssemblyKeyNameAttribute::.ctor(string)
     = (01 00 00 00 00)

  ...

  .custom instance void
    [mscorlib]System.Reflection.AssemblyTitleAttribute::.ctor(string) =
       ( 01 00 13 41 74 74 72 69 62 75 74 65 50 65 65 6B    // ...AttributePeek
         20 62 79 20 4D 45 00 00 )                          //  by ME..
  .hash algorithm 0x00008004
  .ver 1:0:0:0
}
```

Looking down through the file, you'll notice a number of declarations that look something like type declarations:

```
[mscorlib]System.Reflection.AssemblyTitleAttribute::.ctor(string) =
   ( 01 00 13 41 74 74 72 69 62 75 74 65 50 65 65 6B    // ...AttributePeek
```

The AssemblyTitle that you typed in has been persisted into the assembly manifest — if you get your hex/ASCII conversion tables out, you'll see that the set of characters after 01 00 0A are the ASCII codes for AttributePeek. Just in case you are curious, the prolog bytes 01 00 are a 2-byte ID, and 13 is the length of the string (18 characters). As mentioned earlier, this process of storing the attribute within the assembly is known as pickling, and you may come across this if you look at some of the background material on .NET available on the Web.

You may have noticed that in the code snippet from AssemblyInfo.cs, the term AssemblyTitle was used; however, in the IL code you just looked at, this is shown as AssemblyTitleAttribute. The C# compiler will look up an attribute class called AssemblyTitle first, and if it is not found it will then append the word Attribute and search again. So, whether you type the whole class name or omit the final Attribute, the same code is generated. Throughout this chapter the Attribute suffix has been dropped.

The attribute declaration persisted (pickled) into the manifest looks suspiciously like an object and its constructor. The bytes in parentheses are the parameters passed to the constructor.

Having examined the background, you can now understand the following attribute definition:

An *attribute* is a class that can include additional data within an assembly, concerning the assembly, or any type within that assembly. Given that an attribute is a class, and in the manifest the attribute is stored in the format shown above, let's revisit the attribute definition from earlier in the chapter:

```
[assembly: AssemblyTitle("AttributePeek by ME")]
```

The syntax is a little different from normal C#, because there are square brackets enclosing the attribute. The `assembly:` tag defines the scope of the attribute (which is covered later in the chapter), and the rest of the code declares the attribute. The `AssemblyTitle` attribute has a constructor that takes only one argument—a string value. The compiler includes this value in the assembly. This value can be accessed by the standard Windows Explorer `Properties` sheet, by viewing the assembly within `Ildasm`, or programmatically by *reflection*—discussed in the following section.

In addition to the simple attributes dealing with assembly information, the .NET Framework defines nearly two hundred attributes used for things as diverse as debugging, design-time control behavior, serialization, and much more. You'll see some standard attributes after the "Reflection" section and then continue by seeing how to extend .NET with your own custom attributes.

Reflection

Unless you have a grounding in Java, reflection is probably a new topic, so I will spend a couple of pages defining it and showing how it can be used.

Reflection allows you to programmatically inspect and get information about an assembly, including all object types contained within it. This information includes the attributes you have added to those types. The reflection objects reside within the `System.Reflection` namespace.

In addition to reading the types defined within a given assembly, you can also generate (emit) your own assemblies and types using the services of `System.Reflection.Emit` or `System.CodeDom`. This topic is a little too hectic for a beginning book on C#, but if you are interested, then MSDN contains some information on emitting dynamic assemblies.

The first example in this section inspects an assembly and displays a list of all attributes defined on the assembly—this should produce a list similar to that shown earlier.

> *In this chapter, I'm going to be a bit more relaxed about the format of the code examples, since if you've gotten to this point in the book you must be pretty confident of what you're doing! All of the code can be found in the `Chapter27` folder of the code download—some examples in this chapter might show you only the most important parts of the code, so don't forget to look through the downloaded code to see the whole picture.*

This first example can be found in the `Chapter27\FindAttributes` directory. The entire source file is reproduced here:

```
// Import types from the System and System.Reflection assemblies
using System;
using System.Reflection;

namespace FindAttributes
```

```
{
    class Program
    {
        /// <summary>
        /// Main .exe entry point
        /// </summary>
        /// <param name="args">Command line args - the name of an assembly</param>
        static void Main(string[] args)
        {
            // Output usage information if necessary.
            if (args.Length == 0)
                Usage();
            else if ((args.Length == 1) && (args[0] == "/?"))
                Usage();
            else
            {
                // Load the assembly.
                string assemblyName = null;

                // Loop through the arguments passed to the console application.
                // I'm doing this as if you specify a full path name including
                // spaces you end up with several arguments - I'm just stitching
                // them back together again to make one filename...
                foreach (string arg in args)
                {
                    if (assemblyName == null)
                        assemblyName = arg;
                    else
                        assemblyName = string.Format("{0} {1}", assemblyName, arg);
                }

                try
                {
                    // Attempt to load the named assembly.
                    Assembly a = Assembly.LoadFrom(assemblyName);

                    // Now find the attributes on the assembly.
                    // The parameter is ignored, so I chose true.
                    object[] attributes = a.GetCustomAttributes(true);

                    // If there were any attributes defined...
                    if (attributes.Length > 0)
                    {
                        Console.WriteLine("Assembly attributes for '{0}'...",
                                        assemblyName);

                        // Dump them out...
                        foreach (object o in attributes)
                            Console.WriteLine("  {0}", o.ToString());
                    }
                    else
                        Console.WriteLine("Assembly {0} contains no Attributes.",
                                        assemblyName);
                }
```

```
                        catch (Exception ex)
                        {
                            Console.WriteLine("Exception thrown loading assembly {0}...",
                                              assemblyName);
                            Console.WriteLine();
                            Console.WriteLine(ex.ToString());
                        }
                    }
                }


            /// <summary>
            /// Display usage information for the .exe.
            /// </summary>
            static void Usage()
            {
                Console.WriteLine("Usage:");
                Console.WriteLine("   FindAttributes <Assembly>");
            }
        }
    }
```

Now, build the executable in Visual Studio 2005, or if you prefer use the command-line compiler:

>csc FindAttributes.cs

This will compile the file and produce a console executable, which you can then call.

To run the FindAttributes application, you need to supply the name of an assembly to inspect. For now, you can use the FindAttributes.exe assembly itself, which is shown in Figure 27-3.

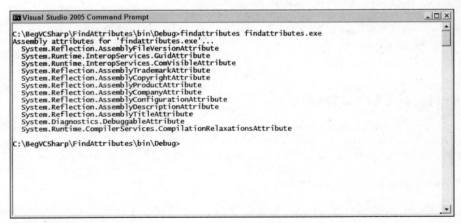

Figure 27-3

The example code first checks the parameters passed to the command line — if none are supplied, or if the user types FindAttributes /? then the Usage() method will be called, which will display a simple command usage summary:

```
      if (args.Length == 0)
        Usage ();
      else if ((args.Length == 1) && (args[0] ==  "/?"))
        Usage ();
```

Next, reconstitute the command-line arguments into a single string. The reason for this is that it's common to have spaces in directory names, such as `Program Files`, and the space would cause it to be considered as two arguments. So, iterate through all the arguments, stitching them back into a single string, and use this as the name of the assembly to load:

```
      foreach (string arg in args)
      {
        if (assemblyName == null)
          assemblyName = arg;
        else
          assemblyName = string.Format ("{0} {1}" , assemblyName , arg);
      }
```

Then attempt to load the assembly and retrieve all custom attributes defined on that assembly with the `GetCustomAttributes()` method:

```
      Assembly a = Assembly.LoadFrom (assemblyName);

      // Now find the attributes on the assembly.
      object[]  attributes = a.GetCustomAttributes(true);
```

Any attributes found are output to the console. When you tested the program against the `FindAttributes.exe` file, an attribute called `DebuggableAttribute` was displayed. Although you have not specified the `DebuggableAttribute`, it has been added by the C# compiler, and you will find that most of your executables have this attribute.

You return to reflection later in the chapter, to see how to retrieve attributes on classes and methods defined within an assembly.

Built-In Attributes

You saw in previous sections that the .NET Framework includes a number of attributes, such as `DebuggableAttribute` and `AssemblyTitleAttribute`. This section discusses some of the more common attributes defined in the .NET Framework, and when you might want to use them.

The attributes covered in this section are:

❑ `System.Diagnostics.ConditionalAttribute`

❑ `System.ObsoleteAttribute`

❑ `System.SerializableAttribute`

❑ `System.Reflection.AssemblyDelaySignAttribute`

There is more information about the other attributes that ship with the .NET Framework in the .NET Framework SDK documentation.

Another extremely useful tool when working with .NET is a program called *Reflector* and is download-able from www.aisto.com/roeder/dotnet. This tool uses reflection to inspect assemblies. You can use it to find, with a few mouse clicks, all classes that derive from System.Attribute. It's one tool you shouldn't be without.

System.Diagnostics.ConditionalAttribute

This is one of the most useful attributes of all, because it permits sections of code to be included or excluded based on the definition of a symbol at compilation time. This attribute is contained within the System.Diagnostics namespace, which includes classes for debug and trace output, event logging, performance counters, and process information. The following code is an example of how to use this attribute:

```
using System;
using System.Diagnostics;

namespace TestConditional
{
    class Program
    {
        static void Main(string[] args)
        {
            // Call a method only available if DEBUG is defined...
            Program.DebugOnly();
        }

        // This method is atributed and will ONLY be included in
        // the emitted code if the DEBUG symbol is defined when
        // the program is compiled.
        [Conditional("DEBUG")]
        public static void DebugOnly()
        {
            // This line will only be displayed in debug builds...
            Console.WriteLine("This string only displays in Debug");
        }
    }
}
```

The source code for this example is available in the Chapter27/Conditional directory. The code calls the static DebugOnly() method, which is attributed with the Conditional attribute. This function just displays a line of text on the console.

When a C# source file is compiled, you can define symbols on the command line. The Conditional attribute will prevent calls to a method that is conditional on a symbol that is not present.

The DEBUG symbol will be set automatically for you if you compile a Debug build within Visual Studio 2005. If you want to define or refine the symbols for a particular project then display the project Properties dialog and navigate to the Build option of Configuration Properties, as shown in Figure 27-4.

Notice that the defaults for a Debug build are to check both the DEBUG and TRACE options.

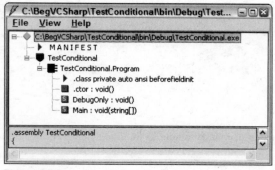

Figure 27-4

To define a symbol on the command line, you use the `/d:` switch (the short form for `/define:` — you can type the entire string if you wish):

```
>csc /d:DEBUG conditional.cs
```

If you compile and run the file with the command line shown, you'll see the output string `This string only displays in Debug`. If you compile the code without defining the `DEBUG` symbol on the command line, then the program will display nothing. Note that the options for `csc` are case-sensitive.

To get a clearer picture of what is happening within the generated code, use `Ildasm` to view the generated code, as shown in Figure 27-5.

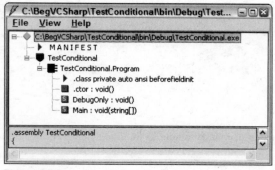

Figure 27-5

When the `DEBUG` symbol is not defined, the IL generated for the `Main()` method is:

```
.method private hidebysig static void  Main(string[] args) cil managed
{
    .entrypoint
    // Code size        1 (0x1)
    .maxstack  8
    IL_0000:  ret
} // end of method Program::Main
```

This code simply returns from the `Main` method.

If, however, you compile the file with the `/d:DEBUG` switch, you'll see the following code:

```
.method private hidebysig static void  Main(string[] args) cil managed
{
  .entrypoint
  // Code size        8  (0x8)
  .maxstack  8
  IL_0000:  nop
  IL_0001:  call        void TestConditional.Program::DebugOnly()
  IL_0006:  nop
  IL_0007:  ret
} // end of method Program::Main
```

The line highlighted is the call to the conditionally compiled method. Use of `Conditional()` will remove calls to a method, but not the method itself.

> The `Conditional` attribute can be used only on methods that return void — otherwise removing the call would mean that no value was returned; however, you can attribute a method that has `out` or `ref` parameters — the variables will retain their original value.

System.ObsoleteAttribute

This attribute shows the attention to detail that the Microsoft engineers have put into the .NET Framework. The `Obsolete` attribute can be used to mark a class, method, or any other entry in an assembly as being no longer used.

This attribute would be useful, for example, when publishing a library of classes. It is inevitable that through the course of developing a set of classes, some of those classes/methods/properties will be superseded. This attribute can be used to prepare the users of your code for the eventual withdrawal of a particular feature.

Suppose that in version one of your application, you have a class like this:

```
public class Coder
{
    public Coder ()
    {
    }

    public void CodeInCPlusPlus ()
    {
    }
}
```

You compile and use this class for several years, but then something new comes along to replace the old functionality:

```
public void CodeInCSharp ()
{
}
```

Naturally, you want to allow the users of your library to use `CodeInCPlusPlus()` for some time, but you would also like to alert them to the fact that there is a newer method by displaying a warning message at compile time, informing your users of the existence of `CodeInCSharp()`. To do this, all you need to add is the `Obsolete` attribute, as shown here:

```
[Obsolete("CodeInCSharp instead.")]
public void CodeInCPlusPlus ()
{
}
```

When you compile again, for Debug or Release, you'll receive a warning from the C# compiler that you are using an obsolete (or soon to be obsolete) method:

```
Obsolete.cs(20,1): warning CS0618: 'Developer.CodeInCPlusPlus()' is obsolete:
        'CodeInCSharp instead.'
```

Over the course of time, everyone will become tired of seeing this warning message each time the code is compiled, so eventually everyone (well, almost everyone) will utilize `CodeInCSharp()`. Eventually, you'll want to entirely drop support for `CodeInCPlusPlus()`, so you add an extra parameter to the `Obsolete` attribute:

```
[Obsolete("You must CodeInCSharp instead.", true)]
public void CodeInCPlusPlus()
{
}
```

When a user attempts to compile this method, the compiler will generate an error and halt the compilation with the following message:

```
Obsolete.cs(20,1): error CS0619: 'Developer.CodeInCPlusPlus()' is obsolete:
        'You must CodeInCSharp instead.'
```

Using this attribute provides users of your class with help in modifying applications that use your class, as the class evolves.

For binary classes, such as components that you purchase without source code, this isn't a good way to do versioning — the .NET Framework has excellent built-in versioning capabilities that you looked at in Chapter 26. But the `Obsolete` attribute does provide a useful way to hint that a particular feature of your classes should no longer be used.

System.SerializableAttribute

Serialization is the name for storing and retrieving an object, either in a disk file, memory, or anywhere else you can think of. When serialized, all instance data is persisted to the storage medium, and when deserialized, the object is reconstructed and is indistinguishable from its original instance.

For any of you who have programmed in MFC, ATL, or VB before, and had to worry about storing and retrieving instance data, this attribute will save you a great deal of typing. Suppose that you have a C# object instance that you would like to store in a file, such as:

```csharp
public class Person
{
    public Person ()
    {
    }

    public int Age;
    public int WeightInPounds;
}
```

In C# (and indeed any of the languages built on the .NET Framework), you can serialize an instance's members without writing any code—well almost. All you need to do is add the Serializable attribute to the class, and the .NET runtime will do the rest for you.

When the runtime receives a request to serialize an object, it checks if the object's class implements the ISerializable interface, and if it does not then the runtime checks if the class is attributed with the Serializable attribute. I won't discuss ISerializable any further here—it is an advanced topic.

If the Serializable attribute is found on the class, then .NET uses reflection to get all instance data—whether public, protected, or private—and to store this as the representation of the object. Deserialization is the opposite process—data is read from the storage medium, and this data is assigned to instance variables of the class.

The following code shows a class marked with the Serializable attribute:

```csharp
[Serializable]
public class Person
{
    public Person ()
    {
    }

    public int Age;
    public int WeightInPounds;
}
```

The entire code for this example is available in the Chapter27/Serialize subdirectory. To store an instance of this Person class, use a Formatter object—which converts the data stored within your class into a stream of bytes. The system comes with two default formatters, BinaryFormatter and SoapFormatter (these have their own namespaces below System.Runtime.Serialization .Formatters). The following code shows how to use the BinaryFormatter to store a person object:

```csharp
using System;
using System.Runtime.Serialization.Formatters.Binary;
using System.IO;

    public static void Serialize ()
    {
```

```
        // Construct a person object.
        Person  me = new Person ();

        // Set the data that is to be serialized.
        me.Age = 38;
        me.WeightInPounds = 200;

        // Create a disk file to store the object to...
        Stream  s = File.Open ("Me.dat" , FileMode.Create);

        // And use a BinaryFormatted to write the object to the stream...
        BinaryFormatter bf = new BinaryFormatter ();

        // Serialize the object.
        bf.Serialize (s , me);

        // And close the stream.
        s.Close ();
    }
```

The code first creates the person object and sets the Age and WeightInPounds data, and then it constructs a stream on a file called Me.dat. The binary formatter utilizes the stream to store the instance of the person class into Me.dat, and the stream is closed.

The default serialization code will store all the public contents of the object, which in most cases is what you would want. But under some circumstances you may wish to define one or more fields that should not be serialized. That's easy too:

```
[Serializable]
public class Person
{
    public Person ()
    {
    }

    public int Age;

    [NonSerialized]
    public int WeightInPounds;
}
```

When this class is serialized, only the Age member will be stored — the WeightInPounds member will not be persisted and so will not be retrieved on deserialization.

Deserialization is basically the opposite of the preceding serialization code. The example that follows opens a stream on the Me.dat file created earlier, constructs a BinaryFormatter to read the object, and calls its Deserialize method to retrieve the object. It then casts this into a Person and writes the age and weight to the console:

```
public static void DeSerialize ()
{
    // Open the file this time.
    Stream  s = File.Open ("Me.dat" , FileMode.Open);
```

```
        // And use BinaryFormatted to read object(s) from the stream.
        BinaryFormatter bf = new BinaryFormatter ();

        // Deserialize the object.
        object  o = bf.Deserialize (s);

        // Ensure it is of the correct type...
        Person  p = o as Person;

        if (p != null)
          Console.WriteLine ("DeSerialized Person aged: {0} weight: {1}" ,
                            p.Age , p.WeightInPounds);

        // And close the stream.
        s.Close ();
    }
```

You can use the `NonSerialized` attribute to mark data that does not need to be serialized, such as data that can be recomputed or calculated when necessary. An example is a class that computes prime numbers—you may well cache primes to speed up response times while using the class; however, serializing and deserializing a list of primes is unnecessary because they can simply be recomputed on request. At other times, the member may be relevant only to that specific use of the object. For example, in an object representing a word processor document, you would want to serialize the content of the document but usually not the position of the insertion point—when the document next loads you simply place the insertion point at the start of the document.

If you want yet more control over how an object is serialized, you can implement the `ISerializable` interface. This is an advanced topic, and I won't take this discussion any further in this book.

System.Reflection.AssemblyDelaySignAttribute

The `System.Reflection` namespace provides a number of attributes, some of which have been shown earlier in the chapter. One of the more complex to use is `AssemblyDelaySign`. In Chapter 26, you learned about building assemblies, creating shared assemblies, and registering them in the Global Assembly Cache (GAC). The .NET Framework also permits you to delay-sign an assembly, which means that you can register it in the GAC for testing without a private key.

One scenario in which you might use delayed signing is when developing commercial software. Each assembly that is developed in-house needs to be signed with your company's private key before being shipped to your customers. So, when you compile your assembly you reference the key file before you can register the assembly in the GAC.

However, many organizations would not want their private key to be on every developer's machine. For this reason, the runtime enables you to partially sign the assembly and tweak a few settings so that your assembly can be registered within the GAC. When fully tested, it can be signed by whoever holds the private key file. This may be your QA department, one or more trusted individuals, or the marketing department.

The following Try It Out shows how you can delay-sign a typical assembly, register it in the GAC for testing, and finally complete the signing by adding in the private key.

Try It Out   Extracting the Public Key

1.   First, you need to create a key file with the `sn.exe` utility. The key file will contain the public and private keys, so call it `Company.Key`:

```
>sn -k Company.Key
```

2.   Then you need to extract the public key portion for use by developers with the –p option:

```
>sn -p Company.Key Company.Public
```

This command will produce a key file `Company.Public` with only the public part of the key. This public key file can be copied onto all machines and doesn't need to be kept safe — it's the private key file that needs to be secure. Store the `Company.Key` file somewhere safe, because it only needs to be used when you wish to finally sign your assemblies.

3.   In order to delay-sign an assembly and register that assembly within the GAC, you also need to obtain the public key token — this is basically a shorter version of the public key, used when registering assemblies. You can obtain the token in one of two ways:

❏   From the public key file itself:

```
>sn -t Company.Public
```

❏   From any assembly signed with the key:

```
>sn -T <assembly>
```

Both of these methods will display a hashed version of the public key and are case-sensitive. I'll explain this further when you register the assembly.

Delay-Signing the Assembly

The following code shows how to attribute an assembly for delayed signing. It is available in the `Chapter27/DelaySign` directory:

```
using System;
using System.Reflection;

// Define the file that contains the public key.
[assembly: AssemblyKeyFile ("Company.Public") ]
// And that this assembly is to be delay signed.
[assembly: AssemblyDelaySign (true) ]

public class DelayedSigning
{
  public DelayedSigning ()
  {
  }
}
```

The `AssemblyKeyFile` attribute defines the file where the key is to be found. This can be either the public key file, or for more trusted individuals, the file containing both public and private keys. The `AssemblyDelaySign` attribute defines whether the assembly will be fully signed (`false`) or delay-signed (`true`). Note that you can also set the key file and delay sign option from the user interface in Visual Studio 2005, as shown in Figure 27-6 — this is a portion of the Project Properties window.

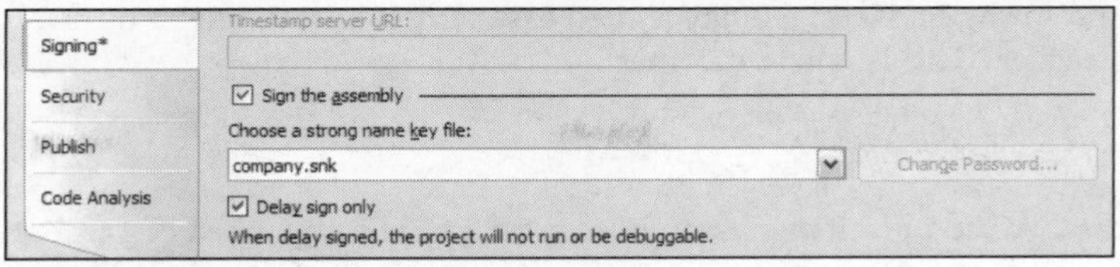

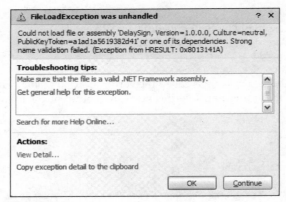

Figure 27-6

As an alternative to setting this from the user interface, you can also alter the `AssemblyInfo.cs` file and define the `AssemblyDelaySign` and `assemblyKeyFile` attributes there.

When compiled, the assembly will contain an entry in the manifest for the public key. In fact, the manifest will also contain enough room for the private key too, so re-signing the assembly will not change it in any way (other than writing a few extra bytes into the manifest). If you try to run the assembly you will receive the error shown in Figure 27-7.

Figure 27-7

This is so because, by default, the .NET runtime will only load unsigned assemblies (where no key file has been defined) or run fully signed assemblies that contain both the public and private key pairs. The section that follows on registering an assembly in the GAC also shows how to load partially signed assemblies using a process called skip verification.

Registering in the GAC

Attempting to use the `Gacutil` tool (which you met in Chapter 26) to register a delay-signed assembly in the GAC will generate an error message similar to this:

```
Microsoft (R) .NET Global Assembly Cache Utility.  Version 2.0.50214.0
Copyright (C) Microsoft Corporation. All rights reserved.

Failure adding assembly to the cache: Strong name signature could not be verified.
Was the assembly built delay-signed?
```

The assembly is only partially signed at the moment, and by default the GAC and Visual Studio .NET will only accept assemblies with a complete strong name. You can, however, instruct the GAC to skip verification of the strong name on a delay signed assembly by using the sn utility. Remember the public key token from earlier? This is where it comes into play.

```
>sn -Vr *,34AAA4146EE01E4A
```

This instructs the GAC to permit any assemblies with a public key token of 34AAA4146EE01E4A4A to be registered. Typing this at the command prompt will generate the following message:

```
Microsoft (R) .NET Framework Strong Name Utility  Version 2.0.50214.0
Copyright (C) Microsoft Corporation. All rights reserved.

Verification entry added for assembly '*,34AAA4146EE01E4A4A'
```

Attempting to install the assembly into the GAC with Gacutil will now succeed. You don't need to use the public key value when adding a verification entry for your assembly — you can specify that all assemblies can be registered by using:

```
>sn -Vr *
```

Or you can specify the assembly by typing its full name, like this:

```
>sn -Vr DelaySign.dll
```

This data is permanently held in what is called the verification skip table, which is a file stored on disk. To obtain a list of the entries in the verification skip table, type the following (these commands are case-sensitive):

```
>sn -Vl
```

This is the output on my machine:

```
Microsoft (R) .NET Framework Strong Name Utility   Version 2.0.50214.0
Copyright (C) Microsoft Corporation. All rights reserved.

Assembly/Strong Name                        Users
============================================
*,03689116d3a4ae33                          All users
*,33aea4d316916803                          All users
*,34AAA4146EE01E4A                          All users
*,631223CD18E5C371                          All users
*,b03f5f7f11d50a3a                          All users
*,b77a5c561934e089                          All users
```

Notice the Users column — you can define that a given assembly can be loaded into the GAC by a subset of all users. Check out the sn.exe documentation for further details of this and other assembly naming options.

Completing the Strong Name

The last stage in the process is to compile the public and private keys into the assembly — an assembly with both entries is said to be strongly named and can be registered in the GAC without a skip verification entry.

Once again, use the `sn.exe` utility, this time with the `-R` switch. The `-R` switch means that you want to re-sign the assembly and add in the private key portion:

```
>sn -R delaysign.dll Company.Key
```

This will display the following:

```
Microsoft (R) .NET Framework Strong Name Utility  Version 2.0.50214.0
Copyright (C) Microsoft Corporation. All rights reserved.

Assembly 'delaysign.dll' successfully re-signed
```

The other parameters along with the `-R` switch are the name of the assembly to be re-signed and the key file that contains the public and private keys.

Custom Attributes

The first half of this chapter concentrated on some of the attributes contained within the .NET Framework. That's not the whole story though — you can also create your own attributes.

In this section, you will only scratch the surface of what can be done with custom attributes. You will look at the following (invented) attributes:

❏   **TestCaseAttribute:** Links the code used to test a class to the class itself

❏   **BugFixAttribute:** Records who altered what and when within the source code

❏   **DatabaseTableAttribute and DatabaseColumnAttribute:** Shows how to produce database schemas from .NET classes

A custom attribute is simply a special class that must comply with these two specifications:

❏   A custom attribute must derive from `System.Attribute`.

❏   The constructor(s) for an attribute may only contain types that can be resolved at compile time — such as strings and integers.

The restriction on the types of parameters allowable on the attribute constructor(s) is due to the way that attributes are persisted into the assembly metadata. When you use an attribute within code, you are using the attribute's constructor inline. For example:

```
[assembly: AssemblyKeyFile ("Company.Public") ]
```

This attribute is persisted into the assembly metadata as an instruction to call a constructor of `AssemblyKeyFileAttribute`, which accepts a string. In the preceding example that string is `Company.Public`. If you define a custom attribute, users of the attribute are basically writing parameters to the constructor of the class.

The first example, `TestCaseAttribute`, shows how test classes can be coupled with the code that they test.

TestCaseAttribute

When unit testing software it is common to define a set of test classes that exercise your classes to ensure that they perform as expected. This is especially true in regression testing, where you want to ensure that by fixing a bug or adding extra functionality, you have not broken something else.

When working with regulated customers (such as producing software for pharmaceutical companies who work under strict controls from government agencies), it is necessary to provide cross-references between code and tests. The TestCaseAttribute presented here can help to trace between a class and its test class.

The full source code is available in the Chapter27/TestCase directory.

To create a custom attribute class, you must:

❑   Create a class derived from System.Attribute

❑   Create the constructor(s) and public properties as required

❑   Attribute the class to define where it is valid to use your custom attribute

Each of these steps is discussed in turn in the following sections.

Creating the Custom Attribute Class

This is the simplest step. All you need to do here is create a class derived from System.Attribute:

```
public class TestCaseAttribute : Attribute
{
}
```

Creating Constructors and Properties

As mentioned earlier, when the user uses an attribute he or she is effectively calling the attribute's constructor. For the test case attribute, you want to define the type of object used to test a given class, so you'll use a String value, as this permits the tested assembly to be deployed separately from the testing assembly:

```
using System;
public class TestCaseAttribute : Attribute
{
    /// <summary>
    /// Constructor for the class
    /// </summary>
    /// <param name="testCase">The object which contains
    /// the test case code</param>
    public TestCaseAttribute (string testCase)
    {
        _testCase = testCase;
    }
    /// <summary>
    /// Perform the test.
    /// </summary>
    public void Test ()
    {
```

```
      // Create an instance of the class under test.
      // The test case object created is assumed to
      // test the object in its constructor.
      object o = Activator.CreateInstance (TestCase);
   }


   /// <summary>
   /// Get the test case type object.
   /// </summary>
   /// <value>Returns the type of object that runs the test</value>
   public Type TestCase
   {
     get
     {
       if (null == _testType)
       {
         _testType = Type.GetType(_testCase);
       }
       return _testType;
     }
   }


   /// <summary>
   /// Store the test case object name.
   /// </summary>
   private string  _testCase;

   /// <summary>
   /// Cache the type object for the test case.
   /// </summary>
   private Type     _testType = null ;
}
```

This defines a single constructor and a read-only member variable TestCase. The Test method is used to instantiate the test case; this simple example will perform the tests within the constructor of the test case class.

Attributing the Class for Usage

The last thing you need to do is attribute your attribute class to indicate where it can be used. For the test case attribute you want to say "this attribute is only valid on classes." You can decide where an attribute that you create is valid. This will be explained in more detail later in the chapter:

```
[AttributeUsage(AttributeTargets.Class,
                AllowMultiple=false,
                Inherited=true)]
public class TestCaseAttribute : Attribute
...
```

The AttributeUsage attribute has a single constructor, which takes a value from the AttributeTargets enum (described in full later in this section). Here, you have stated that the only valid place to put a TestCase attribute is on a class. You can specify several values in this enum using the | symbol for a logical OR — so other attributes might be valid on classes, or constructors, or properties.

The definition of the attribute here also utilized two properties of that attribute — `AllowMultiple` and `Inherited`. I will discuss these properties more fully later in the section.

Now, you need an object to test with a test case. There's nothing particularly magic about this class:

```
[TestCase ("TestCase.TestAnObject, TestCase")]
public class SomeCodeOrOther
{
    public SomeCodeOrOther ()
    {
    }

    public int Do ()
    {
        return 999;
    }
}
```

The class is prefixed with the `TestCase` attribute and uses a `string` to define the class used to test the code in question. To complete this example, you need to write the test class. The object used to exercise an instance of the code under test is presented here:

```
public class TestAnObject
{
    public TestAnObject ()
    {
        // Exercise the class under test.
        SomeCodeOrOther scooby = new SomeCodeOrOther ();

        if (scooby.Do () != 999)
            throw new Exception ("Pesky Kids");
    }
}
```

This class simply instantiates the class under test, calls a method, and throws an exception if the returned value is not what was expected. A more complete test case would exercise the object under test completely, by calling all methods on that class, passing in values out of range to check for error conditions, and possibly setting up some other classes used for contextual information — if testing a class that accesses a database, you might pass in a connection object.

Now for the main code. This class will loop through all types in the assembly, looking for those that have the `TestCaseAttribute` defined. When found, the attribute is retrieved and the `Test()` method called:

```
using System;
using System.Reflection;

[AttributeUsage(AttributeTargets.Class,AllowMultiple=false,Inherited=true)]
public class TestCaseAttribute : Attribute
{
    // Code removed for brevity
}
```

```
/// <summary>
/// A class that uses the TestCase attribute
/// </summary>
[TestCaseAttribute("TestCase.TestAnObject, TestCase")]
public class SomeCodeOrOther
{
    // Code removed for brevity
}
```

```
// Main program class
public class UnitTesting
{
  public static void Main ()
  {
    // Find any classes with test cases in the current assembly.
    Assembly a = Assembly.GetExecutingAssembly ();

    // Loop through the types in the assembly and test them if necessary.
    System.Type[] types = a.GetExportedTypes ();

    foreach (System.Type t in types)
    {
      // Output the name of the type...
      Console.WriteLine ("Checking type {0}", t.ToString ());

      // Does the type include the TestCaseAttribute custom attribute?
      object[] atts = t.GetCustomAttributes(typeof(TestCaseAttribute),
                                            false);
      if (1 == atts.Length)
      {
        Console.WriteLine (" Found TestCaseAttribute: Running Tests");

        // OK, this class has a test case. Run it...
        TestCaseAttribute tca = atts[0] as TestCaseAttribute;

        try
        {
          // Perform the test...
          tca.Test ();
          Console.WriteLine ("  PASSED!");
        }
        catch (Exception ex)
        {
          Console.WriteLine ("  FAILED!");
          Console.WriteLine (ex.ToString ());
        }
      }
    }
  }
}
```

The new section of code is highlighted. When run, the program gets the executing assembly via the static `GetExecutingAssembly()` method of the `Assembly` class. It then calls `GetExportedTypes()` on that assembly to find a list of all object types publicly accessible in the assembly.

It then checks each exported type in the assembly to see if it includes the TestCase attribute. It retrieves the attribute if it exists (which internally constructs the attribute instance, passing the parameters used within the code to the constructor of the object) and calls the Test method, which tests the code.

When run, the output from the program is:

```
Checking type TestCaseAttribute
Checking type SomeCodeOrOther
    Found TestCaseAttribute: Running Tests
    PASSED!
Checking type TestAnObject
Checking type UnitTesting
```

System.AttributeUsageAttribute

When you're defining a custom attribute class, you must define the type or types on which the attribute can be used. In the preceding example, the TestCase attribute is valid only for use on classes. To define where an attribute can be placed, you add another attribute — AttributeUsage.

In its simplest form, this can be used as shown here:

```
[AttributeUsage(AttributeTargets.Class)]
```

The single parameter is an enumeration defining where your attribute is valid. If you attempt to attribute a method with the TestCase attribute, you'll receive an error message from the compiler. An invalid usage could be:

```
public class TestAnObject
{
    [TestCase ("TestCase.TestAnObject, TestCase")]   // Invalid here
    public TestAnObject ()
    {
        etc...
    }
}
```

The error reported is:

```
TestCase.cs(54,4): error CS0592: Attribute 'TestCase' is not valid on this
        declaration type. It is valid on 'class' declarations only.
```

The AttributeTargets enum defines the following members, which can be combined together using the or operator (|) to define a set of elements that this attribute is valid on.

AttributeTargets Value	Description
All	The attribute is valid on anything within the assembly.
Assembly	The attribute is valid on the assembly — an example is the AssemblyTitle attribute shown earlier in the chapter.

AttributeTargets Value	Description
Class	The attribute is valid on a class definition. The TestCase attribute used this value. Another example is the Serializable attribute.
Constructor	The attribute is valid only on class constructors.
Delegate	The attribute is valid only on a delegate.
Enum	The attribute can be added to enumerated values. One example of this attribute is the System.FlagsAttribute, which when applied to an enum defines that the user can use the bitwise or operator to combine values from the enumeration. The AttributeTargets enum uses this attribute.
Event	The attribute is valid on event definitions.
Field	The attribute can be placed on a field, such as an internal member variable. An example of this is the NonSerialized attribute, which was used earlier to define that a particular value should not be stored when the class was serialized.
Interface	The attribute is valid on an interface. One example of this is the GuidAttribute defined within System.Runtime.InteropServices, which permits you to explicitly define the GUID for an interface.
Method	The attribute is valid on a method. The OneWay attribute from System.Runtime.Remoting.Messaging uses this value.
Module	The attribute is valid on a module. An assembly may be created from a number of code modules, so you can use this to place the attribute on an individual module and not the whole assembly.
Parameter	The attribute can be applied to a parameter within a method definition.
Property	The attribute can be applied to a property.
ReturnValue	The attribute is associated with the return value of a function.
Struct	The attribute is valid on a structure.

Attribute Scope

In the first examples in the chapter you saw the Assembly* attributes, which all included syntax similar to the following:

```
[assembly: AssemblyTitle("AttributePeek")]
```

The assembly: string defines the scope of the attribute, which in this case tells the compiler that the AssemblyTitle attribute should be applied to the assembly itself. You need to use only the scope modifier when the compiler cannot work out the scope itself. For example, if you wish to add an attribute to the return value of a function:

```
[MyAttribute ()]
public long DoSomething ()
{
    ...
}
```

When the compiler reaches this attribute, it takes an educated guess that you are applying the attribute to the method itself, which is not what you want here, so you can add a modifier to indicate exactly what the attribute is attached to:

```
[return:MyAttribute ()]
public long DoSomething ()
{
    ...
}
```

If you wish to define the scope of the attribute, choose one of the following values:

- ❑ `assembly`: The attribute applies to the assembly.
- ❑ `field`: The attribute applies to a field of an `enum` or class.
- ❑ `event`: The attribute applies to an event.
- ❑ `method`: The attribute applies to the method it precedes.
- ❑ `module`: The attribute is stored in the module.
- ❑ `param`: The attribute applies to a parameter.
- ❑ `property`: The attribute is stored against the property.
- ❑ `return`: The apply the attribute to the return value of a function.
- ❑ `type`: The attribute applies to a class, interface, or struct.

Many of these are rarely used, because the scope is not normally ambiguous. However, for `assembly`, `module`, and `return` values you will have to use the scope flag. If there is some ambiguity as to where the attribute is defined, the compiler will choose which object the attribute will be assigned to. This is most common when attributing the return value of a function, as shown here:

```
[SomeAttribute]
public string DoSomething ();
```

Here, the compiler guesses that the attribute applies to the method and not the return value. You need to define the scope in the following way to get the desired effect:

```
[return:SomeAttribute]
public string DoSomething ();
```

AttributeUsage.AllowMultiple

This attribute defines whether the user can add one or more of the same attributes to the element. For example, you could create an attribute that lists all of the bug fixes applied to a section of code. As the assembly evolves, you may want to supply details of several bug fixes on a method.

BugFixAttribute

The code that follows defines a simple `BugFixAttribute` and uses the `AllowMultiple` flag so that the attribute can be used more than once on any given chunk of code:

```
[AttributeUsage (AttributeTargets.Class | AttributeTargets.Property |
                 AttributeTargets.Method | AttributeTargets.Constructor ,
                 AllowMultiple=true)]
public class BugFixAttribute : Attribute
{
   public BugFixAttribute (string bugNumber , string comments)
   {
      BugNumber = bugNumber;
      Comments = comments;
   }

   public readonly string BugNumber;
   public readonly string Comments;
}
```

The `BugFix` attribute constructor takes a bug number and a comment string and is marked with `AllowMultiple=true` to indicate that it can be used as follows:

```
[BugFix("101","Created some methods")]
public class MyBuggyCode
{
   [BugFix("90125","Removed call to base()")]
   public MyBuggyCode ()
   {
   }

   [BugFix("2112","Returned a non null string")]
   [BugFix("38382","Returned OK")]
   public string DoSomething ()
   {
      return "OK";
   }
}
```

The syntax for setting the `AllowMultiple` flag is a little strange. The constructor for `AttributeUsage` only takes a single parameter — the list of flags where the attribute can be used. `AllowMultiple` is a property on the `AttributeUsage` attribute, and so the syntax that follows means "construct the attribute, and then set the value of the `AllowMultiple` property to `true`":

```
[AttributeUsage (AttributeTargets.Class | AttributeTargets.Property |
                 AttributeTargets.Method | AttributeTargets.Constructor ,
                 AllowMultiple=true)]
public class BugFixAttribute : Attribute
{
   ...
}
```

A similar method is used to set the `Inherited` property. If a custom attribute has properties, you can set these in the same manner. One example might be to add on the name of the person who fixed the bug:

```
public readonly string BugNumber;
public readonly string Comments;
public string Author = null;

public override string ToString ()
{
   if (null == Author)
      return string.Format ("BugFix {0} : {1}" ,
                                 BugNumber , Comments);
   else
      return string.Format ("BugFix {0} by {1} : {2}" ,
                                 BugNumber , Author , Comments);
}
```

This adds the `Author` property, and an overridden `ToString()` implementation that will display the full details if the `Author` property is set. If the `Author` property is not defined when you attribute your code, the output from the `BugFix` attribute just shows the bug number and comments. The `ToString()` method would be used to display a list of bug fixes for a given section of code—perhaps to print and file away somewhere. Once you have written the `BugFix` attribute, you need some way to report the fixes made on a class and the members of that class.

The method of reporting bug fixes for a class is to pass the class type (again a `System.Type`) to the `DisplayFixes` function shown below. This also uses reflection to find any bug fixes applied to the class, and then iterates through all methods of that class looking for bug fix attributes.

This example can be found in the `Chapter22\BugFix` directory:

```
public static void DisplayFixes (System.Type t)
{
  // Get all bug fixes for the given type,
  // which is assumed to be a class.
  object[] fixes = t.GetCustomAttributes (typeof (BugFixAttribute) , false);

  Console.WriteLine ("Displaying fixes for {0}" , t);

  // Display the big fix information.
  foreach (BugFixAttribute bugFix in fixes)
    Console.WriteLine (" {0}" , bugFix);

  // Now get all members (i.e., functions) of the class.
  foreach (MemberInfo member in t.GetMembers (BindingFlags.Instance |
                                              BindingFlags.Public |
                                              BindingFlags.NonPublic |
                                              BindingFlags.Static))
  {
    // And find any big fixes applied to these too.
    object[] memberFixes = member.GetCustomAttributes(typeof(BugFixAttribute)
                                                        , false);

    if (memberFixes.Length > 0)
    {
      Console.WriteLine (" {0}" , member.Name);
```

```
            // Loop through and display these.
            foreach (BugFixAttribute memberFix in memberFixes)
                Console.WriteLine ("     {0}" , memberFix);
        }
    }
}
```

The first thing the code does is to retrieve all `BugFix` attributes from the type itself:

```
object[] fixes = t.GetCustomAttributes (typeof (BugFixAttribute) ,
                                                    false);
```

These are enumerated and displayed. The code then loops through all members defined on the class, by using the `GetMembers()` method:

```
foreach (MemberInfo member in t.GetMembers (
        BindingFlags.Instance | BindingFlags.Public |
        BindingFlags.NonPublic | BindingFlags.Static))
```

`GetMembers` retrieves properties, methods, and fields from a given type. To limit the list of members that are returned, the `BindingFlags` enum is used (which is defined within `System.Reflection`).

The binding flags passed to this method indicate which members you are interested in — in this case, you'd like all instance and static members, regardless of visibility, so you specify `Instance` and `Static`, together with `Public` and `NonPublic` members.

After getting all members, you loop through these, finding any `BugFix` attributes associated with the particular member, and output these to the console. To output a list of bug fixes for a given class, all you do is call the static `DisplayFixes()` method, passing in the class type:

```
BugFixAttribute.DisplayFixes (typeof (MyBuggyCode));
```

For the `MyBuggyCode` class presented earlier, this results in the following output:

```
Displaying fixes for MyBuggyCode
    BugFix 101 : Created some methods
    DoSomething
        BugFix 2112 : Returned a non-null string
        BugFix 38382 : Returned OK
    .ctor
        BugFix 90125 : Removed call to base()
```

If you wanted to display fixes for all classes in a given assembly, you could use reflection to get all the types from the assembly, and pass each one to the static `BugFixAttribute.DisplayFixes` method.

AttributeUsage.Inherited

An attribute may be defined as inheritable by setting this flag when defining the custom attribute:

```
[AttributeUsage (AttributeTargets.Class,
                 Inherited = true)]
public class BugFixAttribute { ... }
```

This indicates that the `BugFix` attribute will be inherited by any subclasses of the class using the attribute, which may or may not be desirable. In the case of the `BugFix` attribute, this behavior would probably not be desirable, because a bug fix normally applies to a single class and not the derived classes.

Say that you have the following abstract class with a bug fix applied:

```
[BugFix("38383","Fixed that abstract bug")]
public abstract class GenericRow : DataRow
{
    public GenericRow (System.Data.DataRowBuilder builder) : base (builder)
    {
    }
}
```

If you created a subclass from this class, you wouldn't want the same `BugFix` attribute to be reflected in the subclass — the subclass has not had that fix done on it. However, if you were defining a set of attributes that linked members of a class to fields in a database table, then you probably would want to inherit these attributes.

It's fairly common when defining database schema to come up with a set of standard columns that most tables include, such as `Name` and `Description`. You could code a base class with these fields and include a custom attribute that links a property in the class with a database column. Further subclasses could add more fields in as appropriate.

In the following example, you create `DatabaseTable` and `DatabaseColumn` attributes that can be applied to a class so that a database table suitable for persisting that class can be generated automatically.

Generating Database Tables Using Attributes

This final example shows how attributes can be used from .NET classes to generate the database schema — a database design including tables, columns, and data types — so that .NET objects can create their own database tables to be persisted into. You will see how to extract this schema information to generate the SQL to create the tables in a database and to construct in-memory `DataTable` objects.

As you saw in Chapter 24, you use `DataSet`, `DataTable`, `DataRow`, and `DataAdapter` objects to access data in ADO.NET. It is important to keep your use of these objects in synch with the underlying database structure. If a database structure changes over time, then you need to ensure that updates to tables, such as adding in new columns, are reflected in the classes that access the database.

In this example, you create subclasses of `DataRow` that are designed specifically for storing data from a particular database table. In cases where the underlying database schema will not change often, this can provide a very effective way to access databases. If your schema is likely to change frequently, or if you permit users to modify the database structure, it might be better to generate the `DataTable` objects dynamically by requesting schema information from the database and building the data tables on the fly.

Figure 27-8 shows the relationship between the ADO.NET classes and the underlying database table.

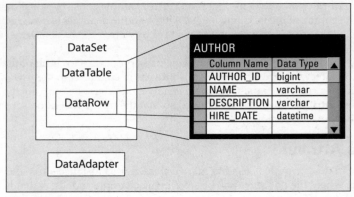

Figure 27-8

The `DataSet` consists of one or more `DataTable` objects, each one having `DataRow` objects that map to a single row within the database table. The data adapter is used to retrieve data from the database into the `DataTable` and to write data from the `DataTable` back to the database.

The `DataTable` consists largely of boilerplate code, so you will define a base class `DataTable` object that can serve as a generic container for `DataRow` objects. The `DataRow`, however, needs to provide type-safe access to columns within the database, so you will subclass it. The relationship between this object and the underlying table is shown in Figure 27-9:

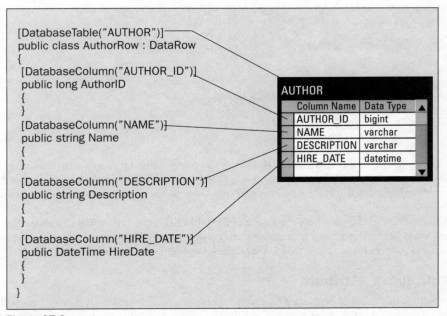

Figure 27-9

This example concentrates on `Books` and `Authors`. The example consists of just these two tables, which are shown over the course of the next few pages. Although the example is designed to work with SQL Server, you could alter the code to work with Oracle or any other database engine.

The `AuthorRow` class derives from `DataRow` and includes properties for each of the columns within the underlying `Author` table. A `DatabaseTable` attribute has been added to the row class, and for each property that links to a column in the table there is now a `DatabaseColumn` attribute. Some of the parameters to these attributes have been removed so that the image will fit on screen. The full details will appear in the following sections.

DatabaseTable Attribute

The first attribute in this example is used to mark a class, in this instance a `DataRow`, with the name of the database table where the `DataRow` will be saved. The example code is available in the `Chapter27/DatabaseAttributes` directory:

```
// Excerpt from DatabaseAttributes.cs
/// <summary>
/// Attribute to be used on a class to define which database table is used
/// </summary>
[AttributeUsage (AttributeTargets.Class , Inherited = false ,
                 AllowMultiple=false)]
public class DatabaseTableAttribute : Attribute
{
  /// <summary>
  /// Construct the attribute.
  /// </summary>
  /// <param name="tableName">The name of the database table</param>
  public DatabaseTableAttribute (string tableName)
  {
    TableName = tableName;
  }

  /// <summary>
  /// Return the name of the database table.
  /// </summary>
  public readonly string TableName;
}
```

The attribute consists of a constructor that accepts the name of the table as a string and is marked with the `Inherited=false` and `AllowMultiple=false` modifiers. It's unlikely that you would want any subclasses to inherit this attribute, and it is marked as single use as a class will only link to a single table.

Within the attribute class, you store the name of the table as a field rather than a property. This is a matter of personal choice. In this instance, there is no method to alter the value of the table name, so a read-only field will suffice. If you prefer using properties, then feel free to alter the example code.

DatabaseColumn Attribute

This attribute is designed to be placed on public properties of the `DataRow` class and is used to define the name of the column that the property will link to, together with such things as whether the column can contain a null value:

```csharp
// Excerpt from DatabaseAttributes.cs
/// <summary>
/// Attribute to be used on all properties exposed as database columns
/// </summary>
[AttributeUsage (AttributeTargets.Property , Inherited=true ,
                 AllowMultiple=false) ]
public class DatabaseColumnAttribute : Attribute
{
  /// <summary>
  /// Construct a database column attribute.
  /// </summary>
  /// <param name="column">The name of the column</param>
  /// <param name="dataType">The datatype of the column</param>
  public DatabaseColumnAttribute (string column , ColumnDomain dataType)
  {
    ColumnName = column;
    DataType = dataType;
    Order = GenerateOrderNumber ();
  }

  /// <summary>
  /// Return the column name.
  /// </summary>
  public readonly string ColumnName;
  /// <summary>
  /// Return the column domain.
  /// </summary>
  public readonly ColumnDomain DataType;
  /// <summary>
  /// Get/Set the nullable flag. A property might be better
  /// </summary>
  public bool Nullable = false;
  /// <summary>
  /// Get/Set the Order number. Again a property might be better.
  /// </summary>
  public int Order;
  /// <summary>
  /// Get/Set the Size of the column (useful for text columns).
  /// </summary>
  public int Size;

  /// <summary>
  /// Generate an ascending order number for columns.
  /// </summary>
  /// <returns></returns>
  public static int GenerateOrderNumber ()
  {
    return nextOrder++;
  }

  /// <summary>
  /// Private value used while generating the order number
  /// </summary>
  private static int nextOrder = 100;
}
```

```
/// <summary>
/// Enumerated list of column data types
/// </summary>
public enum ColumnDomain
{
  /// <summary>
  /// 32 bit
  /// </summary>
  Integer,
  /// <summary>
  /// 64 bit
  /// </summary>
  Long,
  /// <summary>
  /// A string column
  /// </summary>
  String,
  /// <summary>
  /// A date time column
  /// </summary>
  DateTime
}
```

This class is again marked with `AllowMultiple=false`, because there is always a one-to-one correspondence between a property of a `DataRow` and the column to which it is linked.

This attribute is marked as inheritable so that you can create a class hierarchy for database rows, because it is likely that you will have some similar columns throughout each table within the schema.

The constructor accepts two arguments. The first is the name of the column that is to be defined within the database. The second argument is an enumerated value from the `ColumnDomain` enumeration, which consists of four values for this example, but which would be insufficient for production code.

The attribute also has three other properties, which are summarized here:

❑   `Nullable`: Defaulting to `false`, this property is used when the column is generated to define whether the database value can be set to `null`.

❑   `Order`: Defines the order number of the column within the table. When the table is generated, the columns will be output in ascending order. The default is to generate an incrementing value, which is done within the constructor. You can naturally override this value as necessary.

❑   `Size`: Defines the maximum number of characters allowed in a string type.

To define a `Name` column, you can use the following code:

```
[DatabaseColumn("NAME",ColumnDomain.String,Order=10,Size=64)]
public string Name
{
   get { return (string) this ["NAME"]; }
   set { this["NAME"] = value; }
}
```

This defines a field called NAME, and it will be generated as a VARCHAR(64) because the column domain is set to String and the size parameter has been set to 64. It sets the order number to 10 — you will see why later in the chapter. The column will also not allow null values, because the default for the Nullable property is false (thus, the column will be generated as non-null).

The DataRow class has an indexer that takes the name of a field (or ordinal) as the parameter. This returns an object, which is cast to a string before returning it in the get accessor shown above.

Creating Database Rows

The point of this example is to produce a set of strongly typed DataRow objects. In this example you create two classes, Author and Book, which derive from a common base class because they shares some common fields. (See Figure 27-10.)

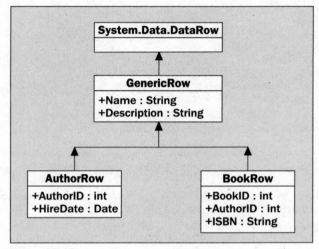

Figure 27-10

The GenericRow class defines the Name and Description properties, and the code for this follows. It is derived from DataRow, the base class for all database rows in the Framework.

For the example, two classes derive from GenericRow — one to represent an Author (AuthorRow) and another representing a Book (BookRow). These both contain additional properties, which are linked to fields within the database:

```
// Excerpt from DatabaseTables.cs
/// <summary>
/// Base class row - defines Name and Description columns
/// </summary>
public abstract class GenericRow : DataRow
{
    /// <summary>
    /// Construct the object.
    /// </summary>
    /// <param name="builder">Passed in from System.Data</param>
    public GenericRow (System.Data.DataRowBuilder builder)
```

```
        : base (builder)
    {
    }

    /// <summary>
    /// A column for the record name
    /// </summary>
    [DatabaseColumn("NAME",ColumnDomain.String,Order=10,Size=64)]
    public string Name
    {
      get { return (string) this["NAME"]; }
      set { this["NAME"] = value; }
    }

    /// <summary>
    /// A column for the description, which may be null
    /// </summary>
    [DatabaseColumn("DESCRIPTION",ColumnDomain.String,Nullable=true,Order=11,
                    Size=1000)]
    public string Description
    {
      get { return (string) this["DESCRIPTION"]; }
      set { this["DESCRIPTION"] = value; }
    }
  }
```

Deriving from `DataRow` requires that you create a constructor that accepts a single parameter, a `DataRowBuilder`. This class is internal to the `System.Data` assembly.

Two properties are then defined, `Name` and `Description`, and each of these is attributed accordingly. The name field is attributed as follows:

```
[DatabaseColumn("NAME",ColumnDomain.String,Order=10,Size=64)]
```

This defines the column name as NAME, defines its domain as a string of size 64 characters, and sets its order number to 10. I've chosen this because when creating database tables I always prefer the primary key fields to be emitted before any other fields within the table. Setting this value to 10 provides space for numerous identity fields. Any more than 10 fields in a primary key will require a redesign!

The description column is also given a name, domain, and size. The `Nullable` property is set to `true` so that you are not forced to define a description column. The other option would be to define a `default` property and set this to an empty string, which would avoid the use of `null` in the database. The order number is set to 11, so that the name and description columns are always kept together in the generated schema:

```
[DatabaseColumn("DESCRIPTION",ColumnDomain.String,Nullable=true,
                                        Order=11,Size=1000)]
```

Each property accessor defines a `get` and `set` method for the value of the property, and these are strongly typed so that in the case of a string column, a `string` value is returned to the caller:

```
        get { return (string) this["NAME"]; }
        set { this["NAME"] = value; }
```

There is some duplication of code here, because the attribute defines the name of the column, so you could use reflection within these methods to retrieve the value of the appropriate column. However, reflection is not the most efficient of API's — because these classes are used to access the underlying columns, you want them to be as fast as possible. To squeeze every last ounce of performance from these accessors, you could use numeric indexes for the columns, since using strings involves a look up for the numeric index value. Be careful when using numeric indexers because they are slightly more difficult to maintain, especially in the instance where a subclass is defined.

The `Author` row is constructed as follows:

```
// Excerpt from DatabaseTables.cs
/// <summary>
/// Author table, derived from GenericRow
/// </summary>
[DatabaseTable("AUTHOR")]
public class AuthorRow : GenericRow
{
  public AuthorRow (DataRowBuilder builder)
    : base (builder)
  {
  }

  /// <summary>
  /// Primary key field
  /// </summary>
  [DatabaseColumn("AUTHOR_ID",ColumnDomain.Long,Order=1)]
  public long AuthorID
  {
    get { return (long) this["AUTHOR_ID"]; }
    set { this["AUTHOR_ID"] = value; }
  }

  /// <summary>
  /// Date the author was hired
  /// </summary>
  [DatabaseColumn("HIRE_DATE",ColumnDomain.DateTime,Nullable=true)]
  public DateTime HireDate
  {
    get { return (DateTime) this["HIRE_DATE"]; }
    set { this["HIRE_DATE"] = value; }
  }
}
```

Here, the `GenericRow` class has been subclassed, and `AuthorID` and `HireDate` properties are added in. Note the order number chosen for the `AUTHOR_ID` column — it is set to one so that it appears as the first column within the emitted table. The `HireDate` property has no such order number, so its value is generated by the attribute, and these generated values all start from 100; thus, the table will be laid out as `AUTHOR_ID`, `NAME`, `DESCRIPTION`, and finally `HIRE_DATE`.

The `BookRow` class again derives from `GenericRow`, so as to include the name and description properties. It adds `BookID`, `PublishDate` and `ISBN` properties:

```
// Excerpt from DatabaseTables.cs
/// <summary>
/// Table for holding books
/// </summary>
[DatabaseTable("BOOK")]
public class BookRow : GenericRow
{
  public BookRow (DataRowBuilder builder)
    : base (builder)
  {
  }

  /// <summary>
  /// Primary key column
  /// </summary>
  [DatabaseColumn("BOOK_ID",ColumnDomain.Long,Order=1)]
  public long BookID
  {
    get { return (long) this["BOOK_ID"]; }
    set { this["BOOK_ID"] = value; }
  }

  /// <summary>
  /// Author who wrote the book
  /// </summary>
  [DatabaseColumn("AUTHOR_ID",ColumnDomain.Long,Order=2)]
  public long AuthorID
  {
    get { return (long) this["AUTHOR_ID"]; }
    set { this["AUTHOR_ID"] = value; }
  }

  /// <summary>
  /// Date the book was published
  /// </summary>
  [DatabaseColumn("PUBLISH_DATE",ColumnDomain.DateTime,Nullable=true)]
  public DateTime PublishDate
  {
    get { return (DateTime) this["PUBLISH_DATE"]; }
    set { this["PUBLISH_DATE"] = value; }
  }

  /// <summary>
  /// ISBN for the book
  /// </summary>
  [DatabaseColumn("ISBN",ColumnDomain.String,Nullable=true,Size=10)]
  public string ISBN
  {
    get { return (string) this["ISBN"]; }
    set { this["ISBN"] = value; }
  }
}
```

Generating the SQL

Now that the database rows have been defined, it's time for the code that will generate a database schema from these classes. The example dumps its output to the console, so you could for example pipe the output to a text file by running the .exe from a command prompt.

The following class calls `OutputTable` for each type that you wish to create a database table for:

```
public class DatabaseTest
{
   public static void Main ()
   {
      OutputTable (typeof (AuthorRow));
      OutputTable (typeof (BookRow));
   }
   public static void OutputTable (System.Type t)
   {
      // Code in full below
   }
}
```

You could utilize reflection to loop through each class in the assembly, check if it is derived from `GenericRow`, and output the classes automatically. For simplicity's sake the name of the tables that are to be generated are hard-coded: `AuthorRow` and `BookRow`.

The `OutputTable` method is:

```
// Excerpt from Database.cs
/// <summary>
/// Produce SQL Server-style SQL for the passed type.
/// </summary>
/// <param name="t"></param>
public static void OutputTable (System.Type t)
{
   // Get the DatabaseTable attribute from the type.
   object[]  tableAttributes = t.GetCustomAttributes
                (typeof (DatabaseTableAttribute) , true) ;

   // Check there is one...
   if (tableAttributes.Length == 1)
   {
      // If so output some SQL
      Console.WriteLine ("CREATE TABLE {0}" ,
         ((DatabaseTableAttribute)tableAttributes[0]).TableName);
      Console.WriteLine ("(");
      SortedList columns = new SortedList ();

      // Roll through each property.
      foreach (PropertyInfo prop in t.GetProperties ())
      {
         // And get any DatabaseColumnAttribute that is defined.
         object[]  columnAttributes = prop.GetCustomAttributes
            (typeof (DatabaseColumnAttribute) , true);
```

```
                // If there is a DatabaseColumnAttribute
                if (columnAttributes.Length == 1)
                {
                    DatabaseColumnAttribute dca = columnAttributes[0]
                                            as DatabaseColumnAttribute;

                    // Convert the ColumnDomain into a SQL Server data type.
                    string  dataType = ConvertDataType (dca);

                    // And add this column SQL into the sorted list - I want the
                    // columns to come out in ascending order of order number.
                    columns.Add (dca.Order, string.Format (" {0,-31}{1,-20}{2,8}," ,
                        dca.ColumnName ,
                        dataType ,
                        dca.Nullable ? "NULL" : "NOT NULL"));
                }
            }
            // Now loop through the SortedList of columns.
            foreach (DictionaryEntry e in columns)
                // And output the string...
                Console.WriteLine (e.Value);

            // Then terminate the SQL.
            Console.WriteLine (")");
            Console.WriteLine ("GO");
            Console.WriteLine ();
        }
    }
```

This code reflects over the type passed in and looks for the DatabaseTable attribute. If the DatabaseTable attribute is found, it writes a CREATE TABLE clause to the console, including the name of the table from the attribute.

You then loop through all properties of the type to find any DatabaseColumn attributes. Any property that has this attribute will become a column in the generated table:

```
        foreach (PropertyInfo prop in t.GetProperties ())
        {
            object[] columnAttributes = prop.GetCustomAttributes (
                            typeof (DatabaseColumnAttribute) , true);
```

The string representation of the column is constructed by calling the ConvertDataType() method, shown in a moment. This is stored within a sorted collection so that the columns are generated based on the value of the Order property of the attribute.

After looping through all attributes and creating entries within the sorted list, you then loop through the sorted list and write each value to the console:

```
        foreach (DictionaryEntry e in columns)
            Console.WriteLine(e.Value);
```

Finally, you add the closing bracket and a GO command, which will instruct SQL Server to execute the batch of statements and thereby create the table.

The last function in this assembly, `ConvertDataType()`, converts values from the `ColumnDomain` enumeration into a database specific data type. In addition, for string columns, you create the column representation to include the size of the column, so for instance the `Name` property from the generic base class is constructed as `VARCHAR(64)`. This column type represents a varying array of characters up to 64 characters in length.

```
// Excerpt from Database.cs
/// <summary>
/// Convert a ColumnDomain to a SQL Server data type.
/// </summary>
/// <param name="dca">The column attribute</param>
/// <returns>A string representing the data type</returns>
private static string ConvertDataType (DatabaseColumnAttribute dca)
{
  string dataType = null;

  switch (dca.DataType)
  {
    case ColumnDomain.DateTime:
    {
      dataType = "DATETIME";
      break;
    }
    case ColumnDomain.Integer:
    {
      dataType = "INT";
      break;
    }
    case ColumnDomain.Long:
    {
      dataType = "BIGINT";
      break;
    }
    case ColumnDomain.String:
    {
      // Include the size of the string...
      dataType = string.Format ("VARCHAR({0})" , dca.Size);
      break;
    }
  }

  return dataType;
}
```

For each member of the enumeration, you create a column string appropriate for SQL Server. The SQL emitted for the `Author` and `Book` classes from this example is:

```
CREATE TABLE AUTHOR
(
    AUTHOR_ID           BIGINT              NOT NULL,
    NAME                VARCHAR(64)         NOT NULL,
    DESCRIPTION         VARCHAR(1000)       NULL,
    HIRE_DATE           DATETIME            NULL,
)
```

```
GO

CREATE TABLE BOOK
(
    BOOK_ID                 BIGINT                  NOT NULL,
    AUTHOR_ID               BIGINT                  NOT NULL,
    NAME                    VARCHAR(64)             NOT NULL,
    DESCRIPTION             VARCHAR(1000)           NULL,
    PUBLISH_DATE            DATETIME                NULL,
    ISBN                    VARCHAR(10)             NULL,
)
GO
```

This SQL can be run against an empty or preexisting SQL Server database to create the tables. The DataRow classes created can be used to provide type safe access to the data within these tables.

To utilize the derived DataRow classes, you need to provide some code such as the following. This class overrides the minimum set of functions from DataTable and is passed the type of the row in the constructor:

```csharp
// Excerpt from DatabaseTables.cs
/// <summary>
/// Boilerplate data table class
/// </summary>
public class MyDataTable : DataTable
{
    /// <summary>
    /// Construct this object based on a DataRow.
    /// </summary>
    /// <param name="rowType">A class derived from DataRow</param>
    public MyDataTable (System.Type rowType)
    {
        m_rowType = rowType;
        ConstructColumns ();
    }


    /// <summary>
    /// Construct the DataColumns for this table.
    /// </summary>
    private void ConstructColumns ()
    {
        SortedList columns = new SortedList ();

        // Loop through all properties.
        foreach (PropertyInfo prop in m_rowType.GetProperties ())
        {
            object[] columnAttributes = prop.GetCustomAttributes
                (typeof (DatabaseColumnAttribute) , true);

            // If it has a DatabaseColumnAttribute
            if (columnAttributes.Length == 1)
            {
                DatabaseColumnAttribute dca = columnAttributes[0]
                                        as DatabaseColumnAttribute;
```

```
       // Create a DataColumn.
       DataColumn  dc = new DataColumn (dca.ColumnName ,
                                        prop.PropertyType);
       // Set its nullable flag.
       dc.AllowDBNull = dca.Nullable;
       // And add it to a temporary column collection
       columns.Add (dca.Order , dc);
     }
   }

  // Add the columns in ascending order.
  foreach (DictionaryEntry e in columns)
    this.Columns.Add (e.Value as DataColumn);
}


/// <summary>
/// Called from within System.Data
/// </summary>
/// <returns>The type of the rows that this table holds</returns>
protected override System.Type GetRowType ()
{
  return m_rowType;
}


/// <summary>
/// Construct a new DataRow
/// </summary>
/// <param name="builder">Passed in from System.Data</param>
/// <returns>A type safe DataRow</returns>
protected override DataRow NewRowFromBuilder (DataRowBuilder builder)
{
  // Construct a new instance of my row type class.
  return (DataRow) Activator.CreateInstance (GetRowType() ,
                                    new object[1] { builder });
}

/// <summary>
/// Store the row type.
/// </summary>
private System.Type m_rowType;
}
```

The ConstructColumns() function, called from the constructor, will generate a DataColumn array for the DataTable — these are again retrieved using reflection. The other methods, GetRowType() and NewRowFromBuilder(), override methods in the base DataTable class.

Once you have this derived MyDataTable class, you can easily use it in your own code. The following is an example of adding a couple of author records into the Author table, then outputting these rows to an XML file:

```
    DataSet      ds = new DataSet ();
    MyDataTable t = new MyDataTable (typeof (AuthorRow));

    ds.Tables.Add (t);
    AuthorRow   author = (AuthorRow)t.NewRow ();
```

```
        author.AuthorID = 1;
        author.Name = "Me";
        author.HireDate = new System.DateTime (2000,12,9,3,30,0);

        t.Rows.Add (author);

        author = (AuthorRow) t.NewRow ();
        author.AuthorID = 2;
        author.Name = "Paul";
        author.HireDate = new System.DateTime (2001,06,06,23,56,33);

        t.Rows.Add (author);

        t.DataSet.WriteXml (@"c:\BegVCSharp\Chapter22\authors.xml");
```

When run, this code produces the following output:

```
<?xml version="1.0" standalone="yes"?>
<NewDataSet>
  <Table1>
    <AUTHOR_ID>1</AUTHOR_ID>
    <NAME>Me</NAME>
    <HIRE_DATE>2000-12-09T03:30:00.0000000-00:00</HIRE_DATE>
  </Table1>
  <Table1>
    <AUTHOR_ID>2</AUTHOR_ID>
    <NAME>Paul</NAME>
    <HIRE_DATE>2001-06-06T23:56:33.0000000+01:00</HIRE_DATE>
  </Table1>
</NewDataSet>
```

This example is a practical example of using custom attributes in your code. If you don't mind coupling the database structure into the classes that access the database then this is a good starting point. Tying database tables to classes is acceptable if your schema doesn't change very often, but for more dynamic back ends it may be better to work in a way that keeps data access classes in step with the database tables accessed.

In a full implementation, you might also include attributes to define some or all of the following:

❑   Primary key columns

❑   Constraints — foreign key and check

❑   Versions — a version number on each column attribute and table attribute simplifies the generation of upgrade scripts — you can in fact generate the whole upgrade based on attributes

❑   Default values for columns

Summary

This chapter described what attributes are and discussed some of the attributes defined within the Framework. There are many more attribute classes within the Framework, and the best way to find out what they are used for is to take a look through the .NET Framework SDK documentation.

In this chapter, you learned about the following attribute-related topics:

❑   Using the Conditional attribute to exclude debugging code from release mode binaries

❑   Using the Obsolete attribute to revise libraries over time

❑   How serialization uses attributes to specify what should and what should not be serialized

❑   How to delay-sign an assembly

❑   How to create custom attributes

Attributes are a powerful way to add extra, out-of-band information into your assemblies. You can create your own attributes to add extra information to your classes as appropriate. This chapter described how to create a `TestCase` attribute, which could be used to link your code to the test cases that exercise that code. There are many other uses of attributes — I encourage you to look into the Framework for other attribute classes.

The next chapter discusses one of the most onerous tasks a developer generally has to face — that of creating documentation. It's often an afterthought, but .NET makes this process much easier and integrates the comments into the code, so there's no excuse for letting the documentation lag behind the code since they can both be generated together.

XML Documentation

Up to this point in this book, you've seen the entire C# language and a whole bunch of things you can do with it, including both Web and Windows programming. Along the way you've seen, and made extensive use of, the IntelliSense feature in Visual Studio. This helpful tool dramatically cuts down on the amount of typing you have to do, because it suggests keywords, type names, variable names, and parameters as you type. It also makes it easier to remember what methods and properties you have at your disposal and often tells you exactly how to use them.

However, the classes you have made have suffered slightly here. While the classes and member names are suggested for you, no handy hints pop up telling you how to do things. To achieve the kind of behavior that you see with the .NET Framework types, you need to use *XML documentation*. XML documentation enables you to include syntax, help, and examples for the classes you create at the source code level. This information may then be used to provide IntelliSense information for Visual Studio as discussed above, but there are other possibilities. You can use XML documentation as a starting point for full, MSDN-link documentation of your projects. Or you can style the XML documentation using XSLT to obtain instant HTML documentation with very little effort. You have seen in earlier chapters just how versatile XML is, and you can use all of its power in the development and production lifecycle of your applications.

Documentation is particularly important when you are working as part of a team, since it allows you to show exactly how your types work. It can also be very useful to end users if you are creating an SDK or similar product where you expect people to use your classes from their code. Having the facility to create this documentation built into the tool you use to develop code is a very powerful feature. Despite the fact that it can be time-consuming to add XML documentation to your code, the end result is well worth it. Dropping text in as you develop can make things easier in the long run and also give you a handy quick reference that will help to avoid confusion when the amount of classes in your project starts getting out of hand.

In this chapter, you will learn:

- ❑ How to add and view basic XML documentation
- ❑ How to use XML documentation

Adding XML Documentation

Adding XML documentation to your code is a remarkably simple thing to do. As with attributes, which you examined in the last chapter, you can apply XML documentation to any type or member by placing it on lines just before the member. XML documentation is added using an extended version of C# comment syntax, with three front slashes instead of two. For example, the following code shows how to place XML documentation in a source code file for a class called `MyClass`, and a method of that class `MyMethod()`:

```
/// (XML Documentation goes here.)
class MyClass
{
    /// (And here.)
    public void MyMethod()
    {
        ...
    }
    ...
}
```

Note that XML documentation cannot be applied to namespace declarations.

Typically, XML documentation will span multiple lines and be marked up using the XML documentation vocabulary:

```
/// <XMLDocElement>
/// Content.
/// More content.
/// </XMLDocElement>
class MyClass
{
    ...
```

Here `<XMLDocElement>` is one of several available elements that are available and may contain nested elements, some of which use attributes to further specify functionality. Note that the `///` parts of the lines of code containing XML documentation are completely ignored and treated as whitespace. The only reason they are necessary is to prevent the compiler from thinking that the lines of documentation can be interpreted as code, which would lead to compiler errors.

The most basic element for XML documentation is `<summary>`, and it provides a short description of a type or member. Before moving on to anything more complicated, you should take a look at the following example, which illustrates this element and how the results become visible.

Try It Out   Adding and Viewing Basic XML Documentation

1. Create a new console application called `FirstXMLDocumentation` in the directory `C:\BegVCSharp\Chapter28`.

2. Add a class called `DocumentedClass`.

3. Open the code for `DocumentedClass`, add a new line before the class declaration, and type `///` (three front slashes).

4. Note that VS auto-completion adds the following code, placing the cursor inside the `<summary>` element.

```
namespace FirstXMLDocumentation
{
    /// <summary>
    ///
    /// </summary>
    public class DocumentedClass
    {
```

5. Add the following text to the `<summary>` element:

```
namespace FirstXMLDocumentation
{
    /// <summary>
    /// This is a summary description for the DocumentedClass class.
    /// </summary>
    public class DocumentedClass
    {
```

6. In `Program.cs`, type `doc` in the `Main()` method and note the IntelliSense information that pops up, shown in Figure 28-1.

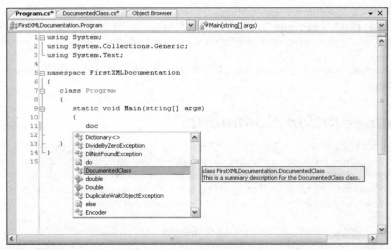

Figure 28-1

7. Open the Object Browser widow and expand the entry for the `FirstXMLDocumentation` project until you can click on `DocumentedClass`. Note the summary information displayed in the bottom right. This is shown in Figure 28-2.

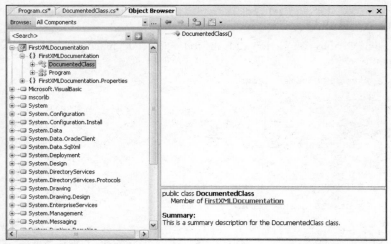

Figure 28-2

How It Works

This example demonstrates the basic technique for adding XML documentation and how this documentation is used in Visual Studio.

When adding the basic summary information for your `DocumentedClass` class, you saw how VS dynamically detects what you have in mind and fills out the basic code for you. Next, you saw how IntelliSense and the object browser detect the documentation you added without even having to compile the project.

These basic techniques apply to all aspects of XML documentation and make it easy to add and consume this information.

XML Documentation Comments

You can in fact add any XML you like to the XML documentation of a target (by target we mean *type* or *member*). However, there are some recommended elements and attributes that will help your documentation to meet standard guidelines. You'll find that the recommended XML is enough for most situations, and following this standard will mean that tools that consume XML documentation (including IntelliSense and the Object Browser) will be able to interpret your documentation effectively.

Brief descriptions of the basic elements for XML documentation are shown in the following table. You'll look at each of these in more depth in subsequent sections.

Element	Description
`<c>`	Formats text in code font. Use this for individual code words embedded in other text.
`<code>`	Formats text in code font. Use this for multiple lines of code, not embedded in other text.

Element	Description
`<description>`	Marks text as being an item description. Used as a child element of `<item>` or `<listheader>` in lists.
`<example>`	Marks text as an example usage of the target.
`<exception>`	Specifies an exception that may be thrown by the target.
`<include>`	Gets XML documentation from an external file.
`<item>`	Represents an item in a list. Is used as a child of `<list>`, and can have `<description>` and `<term>` children.
`<list>`	Defines a list. Can have `<listheader>` and `<item>` children.
`<listheader>`	Represents the header row of a tabular list. Is used as a child of `<list>`, and can have `<description>` and `<term>` children.
`<para>`	Used to break text into separate paragraphs.
`<param>`	Describes a parameter of target.
`<paramref>`	References a method parameter.
`<permission>`	Specifies the permissions required for target.
`<remarks>`	Additional information concerning target.
`<returns>`	Description of the return value of target, used with methods.
`<see>`	Reference to another target, used in the body of an element such as `<summary>`.
`<seealso>`	Reference to another target, usually used outside of other elements, or at the end of, for example, `<summary>`.
`<summary>`	Summary information concerning target.
`<term>`	Marks text as being an item definition. Used as a child element of `<item>` or `<listheader>` in lists.
`<typeparam>`	Describes a type parameter for a generic target.
`<typeparamref>`	References a type parameter.
`<value>`	Description of the return value of target, used with properties.

Text Formatting Elements

Many of the elements shown in the preceding table are intended for formatting the text within other elements. A `<summary>` element, for example, might contain a combination of other elements that specify the text to display. The text formatting elements are `<c>`, `<code>`, `<list>` and its associated elements, `<para>`, `<paramref>`, and `<see>`. `<seealso>` are a special case that you can also include in this list, since it can be included in a body of text, although it will usually occur at the end.

<para>

The `<para>` element is used to separate text into paragraphs, for example:

```
/// <summary>
/// <para>1st paragraph of summary.</para>
/// <para>2nd paragraph of summary.</para>
/// </summary>
```

<c> and <code>

The `<c>` and `<code>` elements are both used to format text in a code font, typically a monospaced font such as Courier. The difference is that `<c>` can be thought of as "code in text," that is, code words that appear in the middle of sentences, while `<code>` is used for sections of code outside of text. `<c>` and `<code>` might be used as follows:

```
/// <summary>
/// <para>
/// This summary is about a <c>class</c> that does interesting things. Try this:
/// </para>
/// <code>
/// MyPoet poet = new MyPoet("Homer");
/// poet.AddMuse("Thalia");
/// poet.WriteMeAnEpic();
/// </code>
/// </summary>
```

<see>, <seealso>, <paramref>, and <typeparamref>

These four elements are all used to refer to other entries in the XML documentation for a project or to external MSDN entries. Commonly, each of these will be rendered as a hyperlink allowing documentation browsers to jump to other entries.

`<see>` and `<seealso>` specify their target via a `cref` attribute, where the target can be any type or member of any class, in the project or elsewhere. `<paramref>` and `<typeparamref>` use a `name` attribute to reference a parameter of the current target. For example:

```
/// <summary>
/// <para>
/// This method uses <paramref name="museName" /> to choose a muse.
/// For more details, see <see cref="MyPoet" />.
/// </para>
/// <seealso cref="MyParchment />
/// <seealso cref="MyTheme />
/// </summary>
```

`<see>` can be particularly useful to refer to C# keywords using an alternative attribute, `langword`. For example:

```
/// <summary>
/// For more information, see <see langword="null" />.
/// </summary>
```

The benefit here is that since you have specified a language-specific keyword it is possible to refactor the documentation for other languages, such as Visual Basic. The null keyword in C# is equivalent to Nothing in Visual Basic, so it would be possible to cater to both languages — assuming that the tool you use to format the XML documentation is aware of such things.

Note that the elements don't include the text to display, which will typically be constructed from the name, cref, or langword attribute. You should bear this in mind to avoid repetition of text, for example:

```
/// This method uses <paramref name="museName" /> museName to choose a muse.
```

Here the word museName is likely to be repeated.

<list> and associated elements

The <list> element is the most complicated text formatting element, because it can be used in different ways. It has an attribute called type that can be any of the following:

- ❑ bullet —Formats a bulleted list
- ❑ number — Formats a numbered list
- ❑ table — Formats a table

A <list> element will typically have a single <listheader> element child and several <item> children. Each of these may have <term> and <description> children. The exact choice of which children to use will depend on the type of the list and the way your chosen tool formats lists. <term>, for example, is optional in table format lists, while <listheader> might only make sense in a table. For bulleted lists you could use something like:

```
/// <summary>
/// <para>
/// This method uses <paramref name="museName" /> to choose a muse.
/// </para>
/// <para>
/// Try the following muses:
/// <list type="bullet">
/// <listheader>
/// <term>Muse name</term>
/// <description>Muse's favorite pizza</description>
/// </listheader>
/// <item>
/// <term>Calliope</term>
/// <description>Ham &amp; Mushroom</description>
/// </item>
/// <item>
/// <term>Clio</term>
/// <description>Four Seasons</description>
/// </item>
/// <item>
/// <term>Erato</term>
/// <description>Meat Feast</description>
/// </item>
/// </list>
/// </para>
/// </summary>
```

Since the exact behavior of the formatting with these elements may vary, it's best to experiment a bit. Note that whatever you do with these elements, you won't see any difference in the Object Browser, which ignores them.

Major Structural Elements

Several of the elements in the previous table are intended for use as top-level elements in the description of a given target. `<summary>` is a good example of this, as you saw in the earlier example. The `<summary>` element should never be contained in another element, and it is always used to give summary information about the target. The other elements that fit this description are `<example>`, `<exception>`, `<param>`, `<permission>`, `<remarks>`, `<returns>`, and `<value>`. `<seealso>` is a special case that can be either a top-level element or a child of another element, and `<include>` is another special case, because it effectively overrides other elements by fetching XML from an external file.

You'll look at each of these elements in turn.

<summary>, <example>, and <remarks>

Each of these three elements provides general information about the target. You've already seen `<summary>`, which you can use to provide basic information about a target. Since this information will appear in tooltips it can be a good idea to keep this information short and put additional information in `<example>` and `<remarks>`.

Often when you are introducing a class, it can be helpful to give an example of how that class should be used. The same applies to methods, properties, and so on. Rather than include this information in `<summary>` it can make sense to separate it into a new section, `<example>`:

```
/// <summary>
/// <para>
/// This summary is about a <c>class</c> that does interesting things.
/// </para>
/// </summary>
/// <example>
/// <para>
/// Try this:
/// </para>
/// <code>
/// MyPoet poet = new MyPoet("Homer");
/// poet.AddMuse("Thalia");
/// poet.WriteMeAnEpic();
/// </code>
/// </example>
```

Similarly, `<remarks>` is often used to provide a longer description of a target, and it may include more `<see>` and `<seealso>` elements for cross-referencing.

<param> and <typeparam>

These elements describe a parameter, either a standard method parameter or a type parameter, for generic targets. The parameter being referenced is set using a `name` attribute. These elements may occur several times if several parameters are used, for example:

```
/// <summary>
/// Method to add a muse.
/// </summary>
/// <param name="museName">
/// A <see langword="string" /> parameter specifying the name of a muse.
/// </param>
/// <param name="museMood">
/// A <see cref="MuseMood" /> enumeration value specifying the mood of a muse.
/// </param>
```

The `name` attribute of a `<param>` or `<typeparam>` element not only specifies the name of the parameter, but also will match the `name` attribute of any `<paramref>` or `<typeparamref>` elements that reference the parameter.

<returns> and <value>

These two elements are similar in that they both refer to a return value, where `<returns>` is used for the return value for methods, and `<value>` the value of a property, which can also be thought of as a return value. Neither of these elements uses any attributes.

For methods, you might use `<returns>` as follows:

```
/// <summary>
/// Method to add a muse.
/// </summary>
/// <param name="museName">
/// A <see langword="string" /> parameter specifying the name of a muse.
/// </param>
/// <param name="museMood">
/// A <see cref="MuseMood" /> enumeration value specifying the mood of a muse.
/// </param>
/// <returns>
/// The return value of this method is <see langword="void" />.
/// </returns>
```

And for properties:

```
/// <summary>
/// Property for getting / setting a muse.
/// </summary>
/// <value>
/// The type of this property is <see langword="string" />.
/// </value>
```

<permission>

This element is used to describe the permissions associated with a target. Actually setting the permissions is performed by other means, such as applying a `PermissionSetAttribute` attribute to a method; the `<permission>` element merely allows you to inform others about these permissions.

The `<permission>` element includes a `cref` attribute, so that you can if you wish reference a class that includes additional information, such as `System.Security.PermissionSet`.

For example:

```
/// <permission cref="System.Security.PermissionSet">
/// Only administrators can use this method.
/// </permission>
```

<exception>

This element is used to describe any exceptions that might be thrown during the use of the target. It has a `cref` attribute that you can use to cross-reference an exception type. You might, for example, use this element to state the range of allowed values for a property, and what would happen if someone attempted to set the property to a value that isn't allowed:

```
/// <exception cref="System.ArgumentException">
/// This exception will be thrown if you set <paramref name="Width" /> to a
/// negative value.
/// </exception>
```

<seealso>

As previously mentioned, the `<seealso>` element can be used as a top-level element. You can use several of these, which, depending on the tool you use, may be formatted as a list of references at the end of an entry for a target. For example:

```
/// <summary>
/// This is a summary for the MyPoet class.
/// </summary>
/// <seealso cref="MyParchment />
/// <seealso cref="MyTheme />
/// <seealso cref="MyToenails />
```

<include>

Including a lot of XML documentation in your source files can get a little messy, and you might like to consider placing it in completely separate files. This can also be desirable, for example, if someone else is providing the documentation for your code, since you don't have to give that person access to the source files themselves.

The `<include>` element allows you to do this, via its two attributes, `file` and `path`. `file` specifies the external XML file that contains the XML documentation you want to include, and `path` is used to locate the specific section of XML within the document using XPath syntax.

For example, you could reference some external XML as follows:

```
/// <include file="ExternalDoc.xml" path="documentation/classes/MyClass/*" />
public class MyClass
```

Here a file called `ExternalDoc.xml` is referenced. This may contain code such as:

```xml
<?xml version="1.0" encoding="utf-8" ?>
<documentation>
  <classes>
    <MyClass>
      <summary>
         Summary in an external file.
      </summary>
      <remarks>
         Nice, eh?
      </remarks>
    </MyClass>
  </classes>
</documentation>
```

This could then be equivalent to the following:

```
/// <summary>
/// Summary in an external file.
/// </summary>
/// <remarks>
/// Nice, eh?
/// </remarks>
public class MyClass
```

Adding XML Documentation Using a Class Diagram

Back in Chapter 9, you were introduced to class diagrams in VS, and since then you've seen how you can use class diagrams to create classes diagrammatically, with changes being reflected in your code in real time. You've seen how to add classes, add members, modify the signatures of methods, and so on. It should, therefore, come as no surprise to you that you can use class diagrams to add XML documentation to your classes, without having to get bogged down in source code.

Unfortunately, as you will see, adding XML documentation in this way isn't as flexible as adding it manually, but you do get the advantage of being able to do things very quickly, without having to remember any XML syntax.

You'll see the capabilities in the following Try It Out.

Try It Out   **Adding XML Documentation in a Class Diagram**

1. Create a new class library application called `DiagrammaticDocumentation` in the directory `C:\BegVCSharp\Chapter28`.

2. When the project has loaded, click on the `View in Diagram` button in the Solution Explorer window. You should see a diagram containing just the `Class1` class that is generated for you when you create a class library application.

3. Add a class called `DocumentedClass`, and modify its members as shown in Figure 28-3.

4. Click in the `Summary` box for the `GetFactors()` method, and then click on the ▢ button. Modify the text in the `Description` dialog as shown in Figure 28-4.

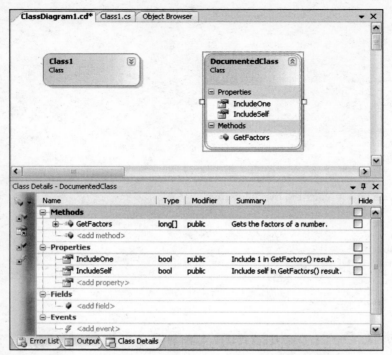

Figure 28-3

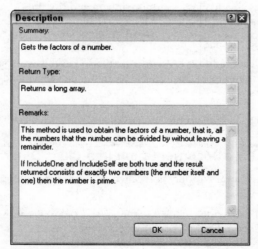

Figure 28-4

5. Similarly, modify the Value and Remarks text for the `IncludeOne` and `IncludeSelf` properties as shown in the following table.

Property	Value Text	Remarks Text
IncludeOne	A bool value.	If this property is set to true, then GetFactors() will include 1 in its long[] result.
IncludeSelf	A bool value.	If this property is set to true then GetFactors() will include its numberToFactor parameter in its long[] result.

6. Click on the class in the class diagram, and in the properties for the class, modify the Summary and Remarks for the class as shown in the next table.

Summary Text	Remarks Text
This class allows you to factorize a number according to certain rules.	Use GetFactor() to factorize a number according to the rules defined by the IncludeOne and IncludeSelf properties.

7. Examine the code for `DocumentedClass`. You should see the XML comments you have added in place, for example:

```
/// <summary>
/// Gets the factors of a number.
/// </summary>
/// <remarks>This method is used to obtain the factors of a number, that is, all
/// the numbers that the number can be divided by without leaving a remainder.
/// If IncludeOne and IncludeSelf are both true and the result returned consists of
/// exactly two numbers (the number itself and one) then the number is
/// prime.</remarks>
/// <param name="numberToFactor">The number to factor.</param>
/// <returns>Returns a long array.</returns>
public long[] GetFactors(long numberToFactor)
{
    throw new System.NotImplementedException();
}
```

How It Works

This example demonstrates how you can use a class diagram to set the XML documentation for a project. After reading the preceding section, you may be wondering why you haven't included cross-references between methods and like. For example, why wasn't the Remarks text for `GetFactors()` set as follows:

```
This method is used to obtain the factors of a number, that is, all the numbers
that the number can be divided by without leaving a remainder.

If <see cref="IncludeOne" /> and <see cref="IncludeSelf" /> are both <see
langword="true" /> and the result returned consists of exactly two numbers (the
number itself and one) then the number is prime.
```

The reason for this is that the text editor in the class diagram automatically escapes text that is entered into the Description dialog so that the result of entering the above is actually:

```
/// <summary>
/// Gets the factors of a number.
/// </summary>
/// <remarks>This method is used to obtain the factors of a number, that is, all
/// the numbers that the number can be divided by without leaving a remainder.
/// If &lt;see cref="IncludeOne" /&gt; and &lt;see cref="IncludeSelf" /&gt; are
/// both &lt;see langword="true" /&gt; and the result returned consists of exactly
/// two numbers (the number itself and one) then the number is prime.</remarks>
/// <param name="numberToFactor">The number to factor.</param>
/// <returns>Returns a long array.</returns>
public long[] GetFactors(long numberToFactor)
{
    throw new System.NotImplementedException();
}
```

This is unfortunately one of the inconveniences you have to cope with if you add XML documentation using a class diagram. It's great for adding text, but to embed XML documentation markup, you will have to modify the code manually.

Generating XML Documentation Files

So far, all the XML documentation you have added has been confined to the development environment while you are working with a project. If you want to actually do anything with the documentation you add, you have to set the project to output the documentation as an XML file.

To do this, you need to modify the build settings for your project as shown in Figure 28-5.

The only change is to check the XML Documentation File box. The output filename is then filled in for you, although you can modify this if you wish. It is generally a good idea to leave things as they are, since VS searches for the XML documentation file for an assembly in the same directory as the assembly. If you have a client application in a different solution to a documented assembly, you will only get the benefits of IntelliSense and help in the Object Browser if VS can find the XML documentation file.

Once the build setting for XML documentation is turned on, the compiler will be configured to actively search for XML documentation in your classes. While it isn't necessarily an error to omit XML documentation for a given class or method, VS makes a point of alerting you to anything missing, in the form of warnings in the Error List window. An example of this is shown in Figure 28-6.

These warnings are obtained from the previous example, and you can see that documentation is missing for the Class1 class (which you left unchanged) and for Properties.Settings and Properties .Settings.Value. These last two are from auto-generated code, so you don't have to worry about them.

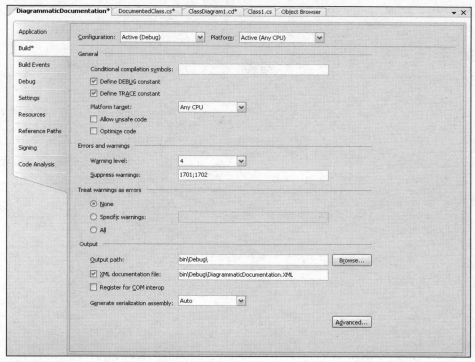

Figure 28-5

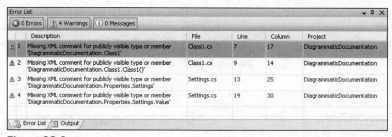

Figure 28-6

The XML documentation file created for the previous example is:

```xml
<?xml version="1.0"?>
<doc>
  <assembly>
    <name>DiagrammaticDocumentation</name>
  </assembly>
  <members>
    <member name="T:DiagrammaticDocumentation.Properties.Resources">
      <summary>
        A strongly-typed resource class, for looking up localized strings, etc.
      </summary>
    </member>
    <member
      name="P:DiagrammaticDocumentation.Properties.Resources.ResourceManager">
      <summary>
        Returns the cached ResourceManager instance used by this class.
      </summary>
    </member>
    <member name="P:DiagrammaticDocumentation.Properties.Resources.Culture">
      <summary>
        Overrides the current thread's CurrentUICulture property for all
        resource lookups using this strongly typed resource class.
      </summary>
    </member>
    <member name="T:DiagrammaticDocumentation.DocumentedClass">
      <summary>
        This class allows you to factorize a number according to certain rules.
      </summary>
      <remarks>Use GetFactor() to factorize a number according to the rules defined
        by the IncludeOne and IncludeSelf properties.</remarks>
    </member>
    <member
      name="M:DiagrammaticDocumentation.DocumentedClass.GetFactors(System.Int64)">
      <summary>
        Gets the factors of a number.
      </summary>
      <remarks>This method is used to obtain the factors of a number, that is, all
        the numbers that the number can be divided by without leaving a remainder.
        If IncludeOne and IncludeSelf are both true and the result returned
        consists of exactly two numbers (the number itself and one) then the number
        is prime.</remarks>
      <param name="numberToFactor">The number to factor.</param>
      <returns>Returns a long array.</returns>
    </member>
    <member name="P:DiagrammaticDocumentation.DocumentedClass.IncludeOne">
      <summary>
        Include 1 in GetFactors() result.
      </summary>
      <remarks>If this property is set to true then GetFactors() will include 1
        in its long[] result.</remarks>
      <value>A bool value.</value>
    </member>
```

```
      <member name="P:DiagrammaticDocumentation.DocumentedClass.IncludeSelf">
        <summary>
          Include self in GetFactors() result.
        </summary>
        <remarks>If this property is set to true then GetFactors() will include its
          numberToFactor parameter in its long[] result.</remarks>
        <value>A bool value.</value>
      </member>
    </members>
  </doc>
```

This document contains the following:

❑ A root level `<doc>` element containing all other information

❑ An `<assembly>` element containing a `<name>` element containing the name of the assembly to which the XML documentation applies

❑ A `<members>` element containing the XML documentation for each member in the assembly

❑ Several `<member>` elements, each with a name attribute stating what type or member the XML documentation contained by the `<member>` element applies to

The name attributes of the `<member>` elements follow a consistent naming scheme. They are all names belonging to one of the following namespaces, that is, they all start with one of the following letters:

❑ T: specifying that the member is a type (class, interface, strut, enumeration, or delegate)

❑ M: specifying that the member is a method

❑ P: specifying that the member is a property or indexer

❑ F: specifying that the type is a field or enumeration member (not shown in the example)

❑ E: specifying that the member is an event (not shown in the example)

Any errors in the XML documentation for a type will be shown in the generated file as a commented out `<member>` element, for example:

```
<!-- Badly formed XML comment ignored for member
   "T:DiagrammaticDocumentation.DocumentedClass" -->
```

Within a `<member>` element the XML documentation for a target is inserted exactly as is (unless there is a problem with the XML as shown).

Example of an Application with XML Documentation

For the remainder of this chapter you'll look at ways to use XML documentation files, and to make this easier you'll be using a fully functional example class library called DocumentedClasses, which comes packed with XML documentation of almost all types.

The classes in the DocumentedClasses library are shown in Figure 28-7.

Chapter 28

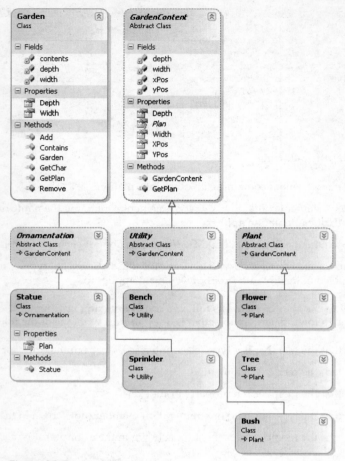

Figure 28-7

The idea behind this class library is that a client application can create an instance of a `Garden` class then add instances of classes derived from `GardenContent` to the garden. This can then be used to obtain a simple graphical representation of the garden. The classes effectively form a very basic garden design tool.

The downloadable code for this chapter includes this class library, should you wish to investigate the code for yourself, but there is no real need to present it all here.

Also included in the downloadable code is a simple client application called `DocumentedClassesClient`, with code as follows:

```
static void Main(string[] args)
{
    int gardenWidth = 40;
    int gardenDepth = 20;

    Garden myGarden = new Garden(gardenWidth, gardenDepth);
    myGarden.Add(new Bench(4, 2));
    myGarden.Add(new Bench(10, 2));
    myGarden.Add(new Sprinkler(20, 10));
    myGarden.Add(new Tree(3, 13));
    myGarden.Add(new Tree(25, 7));
    myGarden.Add(new Tree(35, 15));
    myGarden.Add(new Flower(36, 0));
    myGarden.Add(new Flower(37, 0));
    myGarden.Add(new Flower(38, 0));
    myGarden.Add(new Flower(39, 0));
    myGarden.Add(new Flower(37, 1));
    myGarden.Add(new Flower(38, 1));
    myGarden.Add(new Flower(39, 1));
    myGarden.Add(new Flower(37, 2));
    myGarden.Add(new Flower(38, 2));
    myGarden.Add(new Flower(39, 2));
    myGarden.Add(new Statue(16, 3));
    myGarden.Add(new Bush(20, 17));

    char[,] plan = myGarden.GetPlan();

    for (int y = 0; y < gardenDepth; y++)
    {
        for (int x = 0; x < gardenWidth; x++)
        {
            Console.Write(plan[x, y]);
        }
        Console.WriteLine();
    }
    Console.ReadKey();
}
```

This illustrates how to use the classes in DocumentedClasses, and results in the output shown in Figure 28-8.

As you can see, very basic indeed!

Luckily, if you are a garden designer there are better tools available. All you are interested in here is the XML documentation contained in DocumentedClasses.

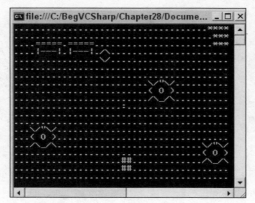

Figure 28-8

Making Use of XML Documentation

This chapter has mentioned in several places that there is much more that you can do with XML documentation than simply using it to supply IntelliSense information to VS—although this isn't to say that customized IntelliSense isn't an extremely useful feature.

Perhaps the simplest thing you can do with XML documentation is to ship it with your assemblies and leave it up to other people to make use of it, but this is far from ideal. In this section, you'll look at some of the possibilities for getting the most out of your documentation.

Programmatically Processing XML Documentation

The most obvious thing to do with XML documentation is to make use of the wealth of XML tools in the .NET namespaces. Using the techniques and classes you saw in Chapter 23, it is possible to load XML documentation into an XmlDocument object. The following Try It Out is a simple console application that does just this.

Try It Out   **Processing XML Documentation**

1. Create a new console application called XMLDocViewer in the directory C:\BegVCSharp\ Chapter28.

2. Add a using statement for the System.Xml namespace to Program.cs:

```
using System;
using System.Collections.Generic;
using System.Text;
using System.Xml;
```

3. Modify the code in Main() as follows:

```
static void Main(string[] args)
{
```

```
         // Load XML documentation file
         XmlDocument documentation = new XmlDocument();
         documentation.Load(@"..\..\..\..\DocumentedClasses"
            + @"\DocumentedClasses\bin\debug\DocumentedClasses.xml");

         // Get <member> elements.
         XmlNodeList memberNodes = documentation.SelectNodes("//member");

         // Extract <member> elements for types.
         List<XmlNode> typeNodes = new List<XmlNode>();
         foreach (XmlNode node in memberNodes)
         {
            if (node.Attributes["name"].Value.StartsWith("T"))
            {
               typeNodes.Add(node);
            }
         }
         // Write types to the console.
         Console.WriteLine("Types:");
         foreach (XmlNode node in typeNodes)
         {
            Console.WriteLine("- {0}", node.Attributes["name"].Value.Substring(2));
         }

         Console.ReadKey();
      }
```

4. Execute the application. The result is shown in Figure 28-9.

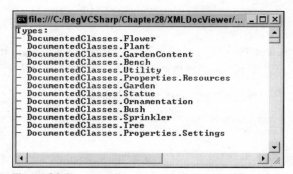

Figure 28-9

How It Works

This example demonstrates the basics of loading and processing an XML documentation file in
C# code. You start by loading in a documentation file, which in this case is the one generated by the
DocumentedClasses type library:

```
XmlDocument documentation = new XmlDocument();
documentation.Load(@"..\..\..\..\DocumentedClasses"
   + @"\DocumentedClasses\bin\debug\DocumentedClasses.xml");
```

Note that the string concatenation used here isn't necessary, but is done purely to make the code easier to read on a narrow page!

Next, you get a list of all the `<member>` elements using the simple XPath expression `//member`:

```
XmlNodeList memberNodes = documentation.SelectNodes("//member");
```

Once you have a list of `<member>` elements, you can search through them, looking for those that start with a `T` to get the elements that refer to types, and placing them into a `List<XmlNode>` collection:

```
List<XmlNode> typeNodes = new List<XmlNode>();
foreach (XmlNode node in memberNodes)
{
    if (node.Attributes["name"].Value.StartsWith("T"))
    {
        typeNodes.Add(node);
    }
}
```

You could of course achieve this in a single step, using a more advanced XPath expression that included an attribute check, but why overcomplicate things?

Finally, you output the names of the types found to the console:

```
Console.WriteLine("Types:");
foreach (XmlNode node in typeNodes)
{
    Console.WriteLine("- {0}", node.Attributes["name"].Value.Substring(2));
}
```

There's a lot more that you could do here, since navigating and processing XML files in .NET isn't a complicated process. However, since there are better ways of handling XML documentation, as you'll see in the next two sections, there is no real need to take this example further.

Styling XML Documentation with XSLT

Since XML documentation is, by definition, XML, there is plenty of scope for using XSLT transformations to convert your XML into HTML, or even to use XSLT formatting objects to create printable documentation.

At this point, we'd like to defer to the true master of (and driving force behind) C# — Anders Hejlsberg. He has published an XSLT document and associated CSS stylesheet to turn XML documentation files into stylish HTML. These two files, `doc.xsl` and `doc.css`, can be found in the downloadable code for this chapter in the directory `XSLTStyledXMLDocumentation`. All that is required to use these files is to add a processing directive to your XML documentation files as follows:

```
<?xml version="1.0"?>
<?xml:stylesheet href="doc.xsl" type="text/xsl"?>
<doc>
    ...
</doc>
```

You'll also find a version of `DocumentedClasses.xml` in the `XSLTStyledXMLDocumentation` directory that includes this directive. A sample of the result is shown in Figure 28-10.

The styling isn't perfect — `<seealso>` elements in particular don't come out right, and you can see in the screenshot that there are problems with `<code>` formatting — but overall it's pretty impressive. The files make an excellent starting point should you wish to make a Web page of your documentation. The way that the `<see>` elements link to anchors on the page is particularly good.

Perhaps the biggest problem with doing things this way is that everything appears in a single HTML page, which could get very large indeed.

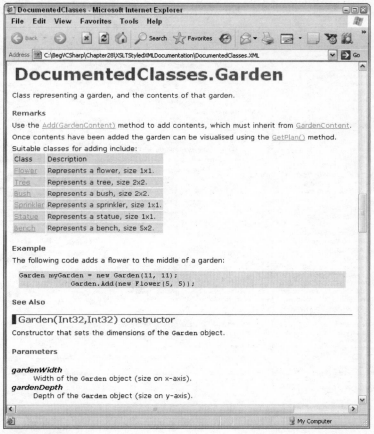

Figure 28-10

NDoc

The last way of processing XML documentation is the most powerful of the lot. NDoc is a third-party tool that is capable of converting your documentation into a number of formats, including MSDN-style help files.

To obtain NDoc (for free!), head to `http://ndoc.sourceforge.net`. At the time of writing, the current version is 1.3, and even though it hasn't yet been upgraded for VS2005, it's still functional (as long as you use the .NET Framework 1.0 version). The authors of NDoc (Don Kackman et al.) are currently working on a new version, which may well be released by the time you read this.

So, why all this fuss about something that we've just said is an old piece of software? The simplest way to answer this is to look at the results. Included in the `DocumentedClasses` class library project is a help file that was generated using this tool, called `Documentation.chm`. A sample screenshot of this help file is shown in Figure 28-11.

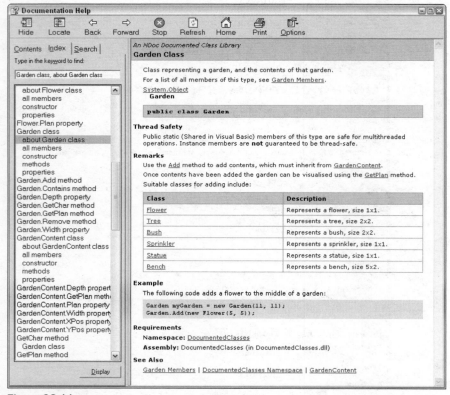

Figure 28-11

As you can see, the result pretty much justifies XML documentation in itself. Everything you expect is there, including quite a bit more than is in the source XML file. A lot of information, such as the namespace hierarchy for your namespaces and so on, is inferred from what is there.

We won't go into details about how to use NDoc here, partly because it's so simple to use that it hardly merits a discussion, and partly because the interface and capabilities may change with a VS2005 release. But we would strongly urge you to download it and find out for yourself just how useful this tool is.

Summary

In this chapter, you have looked at all aspects of XML documentation, from how to create it to what you can do with it. Specifically, you have seen:

- ❏ XML documentation syntax
- ❏ How to include external XML documentation
- ❏ How XML documentation is used in VS IntelliSense and the Object Browser
- ❏ How to use class diagrams to add XML documentation
- ❏ How to generate XML documentation files
- ❏ How to process XML documentation files in C#
- ❏ How to style XML documentation with XSLT
- ❏ How to use NDoc to compile help files from XML documentation

Admittedly, adding XML documentation to your projects can be a time-consuming process, and it can make your source code look a bit messy. But in large-scale projects, it is an essential part of development, and the end result is well worth the effort—especially when you use a tool like NDoc to finish things off.

Exercises

1. Which of the following elements can you use in XML documentation:

    a. `<summary>`

    b. `<usage>`

    c. `<member>`

    d. `<seealso>`

    e. `<typeparamref>`

2. Which top-level XML documentation tags would you use to document a property?

3. XML documentation is contained in C# source files. True or false?

4. What is the major disadvantage of adding XML documentation using a class diagram?

5. What do you need to do to ensure that other projects can make use of XML documentation in your class libraries?

Networking

Chapter 20 dealt with Web services, describing how to send messages from the client to the server in a platform-independent way with the SOAP protocol. In this chapter, you step into lower networking layers, programming with classes from the namespace System.Net. Web services itself uses this technology.

This chapter begins with an overview of programming client and server applications with classes from the namespaces System.Net and System.Net.Sockets, which make use of protocols such as HTTP, TCP, and UDP. You will cover both connection-oriented applications with TCP and connection-less applications with the UDP protocol.

In this chapter, you learn about:

- ❑   An overview of networking
- ❑   Networking programming options
- ❑   Using WebRequest
- ❑   TcpListener and TcpClient
- ❑   Socket programming

Networking Overview

Networking is about communicating with applications on other systems. The communication happens by sending messages. Messages can be sent to a single system where a connection is initiated before the message, as shown in Figure 29-1, or messages can be sent to multiple systems by a *broadcast*, as shown in Figure 29-2. With a broadcast, connections are not initiated, the messages are just sent to the network instead.

Networking can be best illustrated by showing the seven OSI layers. Figure 29-3 shows the stack of the OSI layers with their corresponding TCP/IP layers. Often the layers are also defined by numbers that are simply increments of the layers from bottom, where the physical layer is number 1, to the top, where the application layer is number 7.

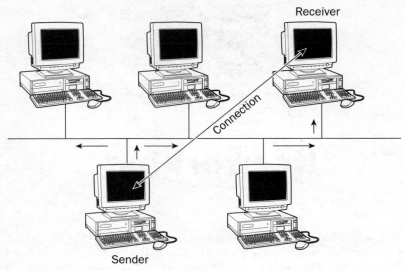

Figure 29-1

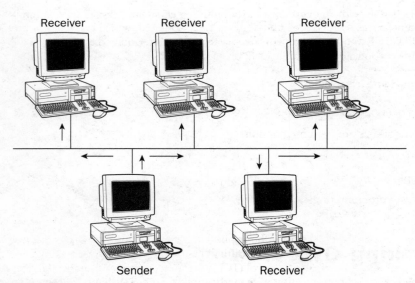

Figure 29-2

The lowest OSI layer is the physical layer. At the physical layer, physical devices (such as networking cards and cables) are defined. The data link layer accesses the physical network with physical addresses. The data link layer performs error correction, flow control, and hardware addressing. The address of your Ethernet network card shows up when you use the `ipconfig /all` command, as shown in Figure 29-4. The system shown here has the MAC address 00-04-23-83-D1-BB.

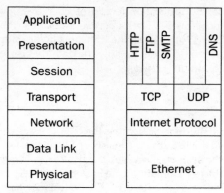

Figure 29-3

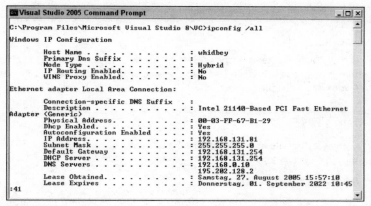

Figure 29-4

The network layer uses a logical address to address systems in a WAN. The Internet Protocol (IP) is a layer 3 protocol; at layer 3, an IP address is used to address other systems. In IPv4, the IP address consists of 4 bytes, for example 192.14.5.12.

The transport layer is used to identify the applications that communicate. The applications can be identified by endpoints. The server application waiting for clients to connect has a known endpoint to connect to. Both the Transmission Control Protocol (TCP) and User Datagram Protocol (UDP) are layer 4 protocols that use a port number (the endpoint) to identify an application. The TCP protocol is used for reliable communication, in which a connection is set up before data is sent, while with the UDP protocol communication is unreliable, because data is sent without a guarantee that it will be received.

Above layer 4, the OSI layers define a session, presentation, and application layer. The session layer defines services for an application, such as logging in to and out of an application. The session layer enables a virtual connection between applications. You can compare this with ASP.NET sessions discussed in Chapter 18. The presentation layer is about data formatting — within this layer encryption, decryption, and compression can happen. Finally, the application layer is the highest layer to offer networking features to applications, such as file transfers, e-mail, Web browsing, and so on.

With the TCP/IP protocol suite, the application-level protocols cover layers 4 to 7 of the OSI layer model. A few examples of these protocols are HTTP (Hypertext Transfer Protocol), FTP (File Transfer Protocol), and SMTP (Simple Mail Transfer Protocol). At the transport layer, endpoints are used to reach other applications; these application protocols define how the data that is sent to the other system looks. You will see later on what data is sent with HTTP.

Name Resolution

The Internet protocol requires IP addresses. Because the IP addresses aren't easy to remember (this is even more difficult with IPv6, where the IP address consists of 128 bits instead of 32 bits), a hostname is used. For communication between the systems, however, the IP address is required, as was discussed earlier. To map the hostname to the IP address, Domain Name System (DNS) servers are used. Figure 29-4 shows that the DNS servers with the IP addresses 192.168.0.10 and 195.202.128.2 are used by this system.

Windows has a command-line tool, nslookup, that can do name lookups (resolve IP addresses from hostnames), or reverse lookups (resolve hostnames from IP addresses). Reverse lookups are interesting because by analyzing the log files where the IP address of client systems can be found, you can determine the origin of the client system.

With .NET, you can perform name lookups with the Dns class in the System.Net namespace. With the Dns class, a hostname can be resolved to its IP addresses, or an IP address can be resolved to its hostname. Let's try it out with a simple project.

Try It Out   Using DNS

1. Create a new C# console application project named DnsLookup in the directory C:\BegVCSharp\Chapter29.

2. Import the namespace System.Net.

3. Invoke the GetHostEntry() method of the Dns class, as shown here, after checking the arguments from the Main() method.

```
static void Main(string[] args)
{
    if (args.Length != 1)
    {
        Console.WriteLine("Usage: DnsLookup hostname/IP Adddress");
        Console.ReadLine();
        return;
    }

    IPHostEntry ipHostEntry = Dns.GetHostEntry(args[0]);
```

4. Add the following code to the Main() method that follows the call to the GetHostEntry() method to write information about the resolved host to the console.

```
Console.WriteLine("Host: {0}", ipHostEntry.HostName);

if (ipHostEntry.Aliases.Length > 0)
{
    Console.WriteLine("\nAliases:");
    foreach (string alias in ipHostEntry.Aliases)
```

```
        {
            Console.WriteLine(alias);
        }
    }

    Console.WriteLine("\nAddress(es):");
    foreach (IPAddress address in ipHostEntry.AddressList)
    {
        Console.WriteLine("Address: {0}", address.ToString());
    }
}
```

5. Compile the application and start the program. Pass a hostname as command-line argument, for
    example `www.microsoft.com`. To start it from Visual Studio you can set the command-line argu-
    ments with the Debug configuration, as shown in Figure 29-5. You can also start a command
    prompt, change to the directory of the executable, and start the application with `dnslookup`
    `www.microsoft.com`. You should get output that looks similar to that shown in Figure 29-6.

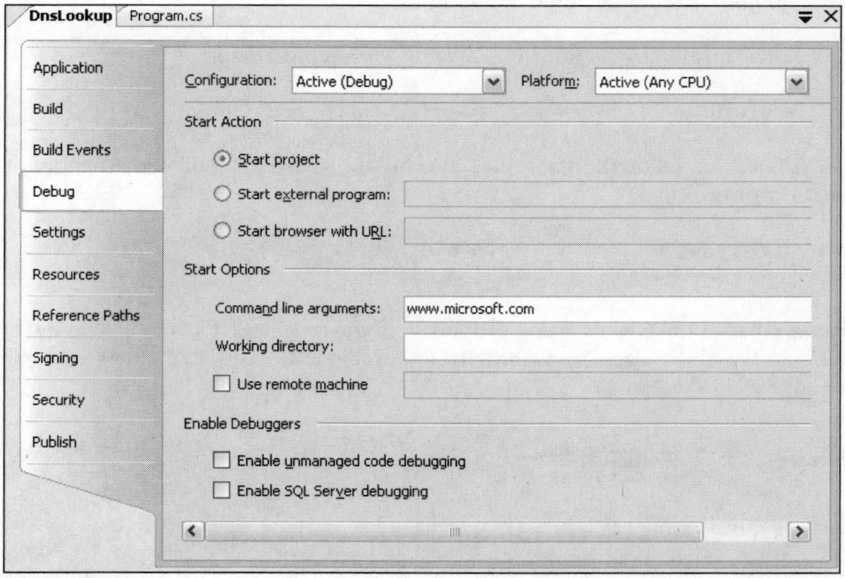

Figure 29-5

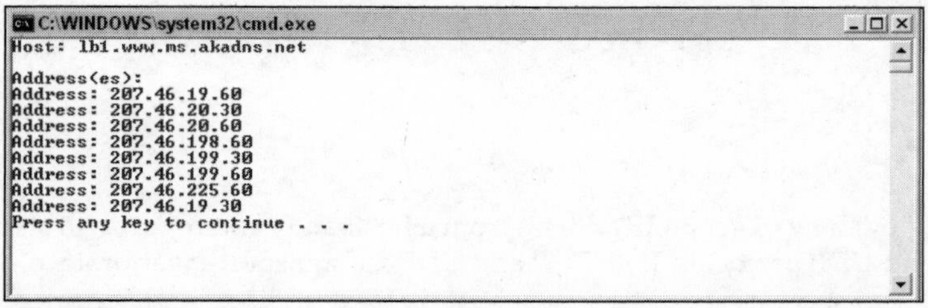

Figure 29-6

How It Works

The Dns class queries the DNS server to resolve hostnames to IP addresses and to do reverse lookups to get a hostname from an IP address. To do this, the Dns class uses the GetHostEntry() method, with which you can pass a hostname and an IPHostEntry will be returned. For reverse lookups, the GetHostByAddress() method can be called.

In all cases the Dns class returns an IPHostEntry. This class wraps information about a host. The IPHostEntry class has three properties: HostName returns the name of the host, Aliases returns a list of all alias names, and AddressList returns an array of IPAddress elements. The ToString() method of the IPAddress class returns the Internet address in a standard notation.

Uniform Resource Identifier

The resources that can be accessed across the network are described by a URI (Uniform Resource Identifier). You are using URIs every day when you enter Web addresses, such as http://www .thinktecture.com, in your Web browser. The class Uri encapsulates a URI and has properties and methods for parsing, comparing, and combining URIs.

A Uri object can be created by passing a URI string to the constructor:

```
Uri uri = new Uri("http://www.wrox.com/go/p2p");
```

If you go to different pages on the same site, you can use a base URI and construct out of it URIs that contain the directories:

```
Uri baseUri = new Uri("http://msdn.microsoft.com");
Uri uri = new Uri(baseUri, "downloads");
```

You can access parts of the URI by using properties of the Uri class. Let's look at a few examples of what you can get out of an Uri object that is initialized with the URI http://www.wrox.com/marketbasket .cgi?isbn=0764557599.

Uri Property	Result
Scheme	http
Host	www.wrox.com
Port	80
LocalPath	/marketbasket.cgi
Query	?isbn=0764557599

TCP and UDP

Now that you know how to get an IP address from a hostname, you're ready to step into the functionality of the TCP and UDP protocols. Both TCP and UDP are transport-layer protocols, as you saw in

Figure 29-3. Both of these protocols use a port number to identify the application that's to receive the data. The TCP protocol is connection-oriented, while the UDP protocol is connectionless.

The TCP protocol requires the server application to create a socket with a well-known port number, so that the client application can connect to the server. The client creates a socket with a freely available port number. When the client connects to the server, the client passes its port number to the server so that the server knows the path to the client. After the connection is established, the client can send data that is received by the server, and then the server can send some data that is received by the client. Of course, sending and receiving can also happen the other way around. With the QOTD (quote of the day) protocol (a QOTD server is part of the Windows component Simple TCP/IP Services) the server just sends some data after the client connects, and closes the connection.

The UDP protocol is similar in so far as the server must create a socket with a well-known port number, and the client uses a freely available port number. The difference is that the client doesn't initiate a connection. Instead, the client can send the data without doing a connection first. Without a connection there's no guarantee that the data is received at all, but the overall transfer is faster. The UDP protocol has the big advantage that broadcasts can be done with it — sending information to all systems in the LAN by using a broadcast address.

> Broadcast addresses are IP addresses where all bits of the host part of the IP address are set to 1.

Application Protocols

Let's look at application protocols that make use of TCP or UDP. HTTP is an application protocol that is layered on top of TCP. The HTTP protocol defines the message that is sent across the network. Using the HTTP protocol to request data from a Web server, a TCP connection is opened, and then an HTTP request is sent. An example of an HTTP request initiated by a browser looks like this:

```
GET /default.aspx HTTP/1.1
Accept: image/gif, image/x-xbitmap, image/jpeg, image/pjpeg,
application/vnd.ms-excel, application/vnd.ms-powerpoint, application/msword,
application/x-shockwave-flash, */*
Accept-Language: de-at,en-us;q=0.7
Accept-Encoding: gzip, deflate
User-Agent: Mozilla/4.0 (compatible; MSIE 6.0; Windows NT 5.1; .NET CLR 1.1.4322;
.NET CLR 2.0.50110)
Host: localhost:80
Connection: Keep-Alive
```

This sample request shows a GET command. Some of the mostly frequently used HTTP commands are GET, POST and HEAD. GET is used to request a file from the server. With the POST command a file is requested from the server, too. However, unlike the GET command, with the POST command additional data is sent after the HTTP header. With the HEAD command the server only returns the file's header information, so that the client can determine whether the file is different from data that is already in the cache.

The GET command requests the file on the server. Here, the server should return the file /default.aspx. The last section of the first line defines the HTTP version. If both the client and server support version 1.1, this version will be used for the communication. Otherwise, HTTP 1.0 is used. With HTTP 1.1 it is possible to keep the same connection (see the HTTP header information Connection: Keep-Alive).

After the first line of the request with the GET command, HTTP header information follows. The browser sends information about the browser with the request. In the example, you can see the Accept information where mime types of supported programs are sent. The Accept-Language header defines the languages that are configured on the browser. The server can use this information to return different information to the client, depending on the supported files and languages. With the User-Agent header the browser sends information about the client application used to request the page from the server. Here, Internet Explorer 6.0 is used with Windows XP. Windows XP has the identifier Windows NT 5.1. The server can also read if the .NET runtime is installed on the client system. Here, both .NET 1.1 and .NET 2.0 show up as supported .NET versions.

After the server receives a GET request, a response message is returned. An example of a response message is shown here. If the request is successful, the first line of the response shows an OK status and the HTTP version used. Then HTTP header information follows, which includes the Server, the Date, and the Content-Type and the length that follows the header. The header and the content are separated by two lines.

```
HTTP/1.1 200 OK
Server: Microsoft-IIS/5.1
Date: Sun, 12 Sep 2004 20:14:59 GMT
X-Powered-By: ASP.NET
X-AspNet-Version: 1.1.4322
Cache-Control: private
Content-Type: text/html; charset=utf-8
Content-Length: 991


<!DOCTYPE HTML PUBLIC "-//W3C//DTD HTML 4.0 Transitional//EN" >
<HTML>
 <HEAD>
  <title>Demo</title>
```

You can easily simulate an HTTP request by using the Telnet utility that you will do with the next Try It Out.

Try It Out   Simulate a HTTP Request

1. Start the telnet client by typing **telnet.exe** at a command prompt. The prompt Microsoft Telnet> appears.

2. To see the commands you type and send to the server, enter **set localecho** in the Telnet session.

3. Create a connection to the Web server in your LAN. If you have a Web server on the local system, enter **open localhost 80**. 80 is the default port number used with the Web server.

4. Send a request to the Web server by typing the command **GET / HTTP/1.1,** then press the Return key twice. With the / the default page from the server is returned, for example default.htm. Instead of using the /, you can also request specific filenames. Sending two newline characters marks the end of the transmission. Now, you get a response from the server that looks similar to the response shown earlier.

Networking Programming Options

The System.Net and System.Net.Sockets namespaces offer several options for networking programming. Figure 29-7 shows those options. The easiest way to do network programming is by using the WebClient class. Just a single method of this class is needed to get files from a Web server or to transfer files to an FTP server. However, the functionality of this class is limited. With .NET 2.0, you can use it only with the HTTP and the FTP protocols, and to access files.

The WebClient class itself makes use of the WebRequest and WebResponse classes. These classes have more functionality but are more complex to use.

If you need to create a server you can't use WebClient or WebRequest; you have to use the TcpListener class from the namespace System.Net.Sockets. The TcpListener class can be used to create a server for the TCP protocol, while the TcpClient class is used for writing client applications. With these classes, you are not bound to the HTTP and TCP protocols; you can use any TCP-based protocol.

If you have to use the UDP protocol, you use the UdpListener and UdpClient classes (which are similar to the TcpListener and the TcpClient classes) to write UDP servers and clients.

If you want to be independent of the protocol or require more control of the TCP and UDP protocols, you can do socket programming with .NET. Classes for socket programming are located in the System.Net.Sockets namespace.

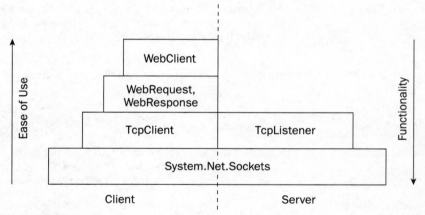

Figure 29-7

WebClient

Let's start with the class that is easiest to use: the WebClient class. This class is a component that can be dragged and dropped from the Toolbox to a Windows Forms application. You can use it with client applications to access HTTP or FTP servers or use it to access files in the file system.

The following table shows the major properties and methods of the WebClient class.

WebClient Properties	Description
BaseAddress	The property BaseAddress defines the base address of for a request that is made by the WebClient.
Credentials	With the Credentials property you can pass authentication information, for example by using the NetworkCredential class.
UseDefaultCredentials	If the credentials of the currently logged on user should be used, set the property UseDefaultCredentials to true.
Encoding	The Encoding property can be used to set the encoding of strings to upload and download.
Headers	With the Headers property you can define a WebHeaderCollection that can contain header information specifically for the protocol that is used.
Proxy	By default the proxy that is configured with Internet Explorer is used to access the Internet. If a different proxy is needed, you can define a WebProxy object with the Proxy property.
QueryString	If a query string needs to be sent to the Web server, you can do this by setting a NameValueCollection with the QueryString property.
ResponseHeaders	After sending the request, you can read the header information of the response within the WebHeaderCollection class that is associated with the ResponseHeaders class.

The WebClient class has simple methods to upload and download files, which are listed in the following table.

WebClient Methods	Description
DownloadData()	With the DownloadData() method, you can pass a string for the Web address that is appended to the BaseAddress, and a byte array containing the data from the server is returned.
DownloadString()	DownloadString() is similar to DownloadData(); the only difference is that the returned data is stored inside a string.
DownloadFile()	If the data that is returned from the server should be stored inside a file, the method DownloadFile() does all the work for you. The arguments to set with this method are the Web address and the filename.
OpenRead()	With the OpenRead() file you also download data from the server, but the data downloaded can be read from a stream returned by this method.
UploadFile()	To upload files to an FTP or Web server, the method UploadFile() can be used. This method also allows passing the HTTP method that should be used with the upload.

WebClient Methods	Description
UploadData()	While UploadFile() allows uploading files from the local file system, UploadData() sends a byte array to the server.
UploadString()	With UploadString(), you can upload a string to the server.
UploadValues()	With UploadValues(), you can upload a NameValueCollection to the server.
OpenWrite()	The method OpenWrite() sends content to a server by using a stream.

In the following Try It Out, you download a file from the Web with the WebClient class.

Try It Out — Using the WebClient Class

1. Create a new Console Application Project named WebClientDemo in the directory C:\BegVCSharp\Chapter29.

2. Import the namespace System.Net.

3. Add the following code to the Main() method.

```
static void Main(string[] args)
{
    WebClient client = new WebClient();
    client.BaseAddress = "http://www.microsoft.com";
    string data = client.DownloadString("Office");
    Console.WriteLine(data);
}
```

4. Compile and run the application.

How It Works

After instantiating the WebClient class, the property BaseAddress is set to http://www.microsoft.com. This is the left part of the address that is used with all the following requests. The method DownloadString("Office") requests the page http://www.microsoft.com/Office. All the returned data is stored in the variable data and written to the console.

WebRequest and WebResponse

Instead of using the WebClient class, you can use the WebRequest class to communicate with a Web or a FTP server, and it is also possible to read files. Behind the scenes, the WebClient class itself makes use of WebRequest.

The WebRequest class is always used in combination with the WebResponse class. First, you have to define the request that will be sent to the server by configuring a WebRequest object. Next, you can invoke the method GetResponse, which sends the request to the server and returns the response from the server in the WebResponse class.

The WebRequest and WebResponse classes are abstract classes, and thus not directly used. These classes are base classes as shown in Figure 29-8, and .NET 2.0 offers concrete implementations for the HTTP, FTP, and file protocols. Concrete implementations of these base classes are HttpWebRequest, FtpWebRequest, FileWebRequest, HttpWebResponse, FtpWebResponse, and FileWebResponse. The HTTP protocol is used by the HttpWebXXX classes, the FtpWebXXX classes make use of the FTP protocol, and the FileWebXXX classes allow you to access the file system.

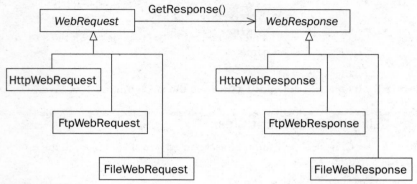

Figure 29-8

Writing an FTP client is a simple task with help of the FtpWebRequest class. In the next Try It Out, you create a Windows application that downloads files from an FTP server.

Try It Out   Get a File from an FTP server

1. Create a new Windows application named FtpClient in the directory C:\BegVCSharp\Chapter29.

2. Rename the file Form1.cs to FtpClientForm.cs. This also renames the class Form1 to FtpClientForm.

3. Add controls to the main dialog, as shown in Figure 29-9.

    The controls from this form and their property settings are shown in the following table.

Control Type	Name	Text Property
FtpClientForm	FtpClientForm	FTP Client
ListBox	listFiles	
Label	labelServer	Server:
Label	labelUsername	Username:
Label	labelPassword	Password:
TextBox	textServer	ftp://
TextBox	textUsername	Anonymous

Control Type	Name	Text Property
TextBox	textPassword	
Button	buttonOpen	Open
Button	buttonOpenDirectory	Open Directory
Button	buttonGetFile	Get File
CheckBox	checkBoxBinary	Binary Mode

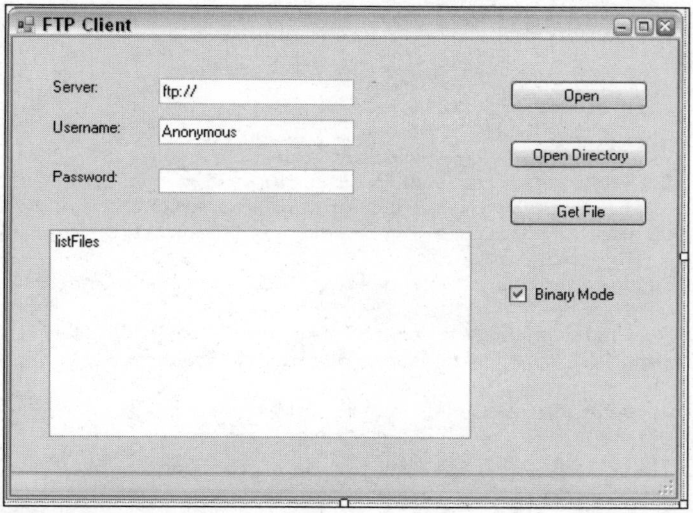

Figure 29-9

4. Using the Property Editor set the Enabled property of the buttons buttonGetFile and buttonOpenDirectory to false. These buttons will only be active when a file is selected.

5. Add a SaveFileDialog control to the form. This dialog will be used to ask the user where to store the file that is downloaded from the server.

6. Import the System.Net and System.IO namespaces.

7. Add the variable serverDirectory as a private member to the class FtpClientForm:

```
public partial class FtpClientForm : Form
{
    private string serverDirectory;
```

8. Add the helper method FillDirectoryList to the class FtpClientForm. This method fills the listbox with all the data that is inside the stream argument.

```
    private void FillDirectoryList(Stream stream)
    {
        StreamReader reader = new StreamReader(stream);
        string content = reader.ReadToEnd();
```

```
        string[] files = content.Split('\n');
        listFiles.DataSource = files;
        reader.Close();
    }
```

9. To make an initial connection to the server, using the Properties dialog, add a `Click` event handler to the button `buttonOpen` with the name `OnOpen`. Add the implementation to this handler as shown here:

```
private void OnOpen(object sender, EventArgs e)
{
    Cursor currentCursor = this.Cursor;
    FtpWebResponse response = null;
    Stream stream = null;
    try
    {
        this.Cursor = Cursors.WaitCursor;

        // Create the FtpWebRequest object.
        FtpWebRequest request =
                (FtpWebRequest)WebRequest.Create(textServer.Text);
        request.Credentials = new NetworkCredential(textUsername.Text,
            textPassword.Text);
        request.Method = WebRequestMethods.Ftp.ListDirectory;

        // Send the request to the server.
        response = (FtpWebResponse)request.GetResponse();

        // Read the response and fill the list box.
        stream = response.GetResponseStream();
        FillDirectoryList(stream);

        serverDirectory = null;
        buttonOpenDirectory.Enabled = false;
        buttonGetFile.Enabled = false;
    }
    catch (Exception ex)
    {
        MessageBox.Show(ex.Message, "Error FTP Client",
            MessageBoxButtons.OK, MessageBoxIcon.Error);
    }
    finally
    {
        if (response != null)
            response.Close();
        if (stream != null)
            stream.Close();
        this.Cursor = currentCursor;
    }
}
```

10. To open specific directory on the server add a `Click` event handler to the button `buttonOpenDirectory` with the name `OnOpenDirectory`. Add the code to this handler as shown here:

```
private void OnOpenDirectory(object sender, EventArgs e)
{
    FtpWebResponse response = null;
    Stream stream = null;
    try
    {
        string subDirectory = listFiles.SelectedValue.ToString().Trim();
        serverDirectory += "/" + subDirectory;
        Uri baseUri = new Uri(textServer.Text);
        Uri uri = new Uri(baseUri, serverDirectory);

        FtpWebRequest request = (FtpWebRequest)WebRequest.Create(uri);
        request.Credentials = new NetworkCredential(textUsername.Text,
                textPassword.Text);

        request.Method = WebRequestMethods.Ftp.ListDirectory;
        response = (FtpWebResponse)request.GetResponse();

        stream = response.GetResponseStream();
        FillDirectoryList(stream);
    }
    catch (Exception ex)
    {
        MessageBox.Show(ex.Message, "Error FTP Client",
                MessageBoxButtons.OK, MessageBoxIcon.Error);
    }
    finally
    {
        if (response != null)
            response.Close();
        if (stream != null)
            stream.Close();
    }
}
```

11. For downloading a file from the server, add a `Click` event handler named `OnDownloadFile` to the `buttonGetFile` button. Add the following code to this event handler method:

```
private void OnDownloadFile(object sender, EventArgs e)
{
    FtpWebResponse response = null;
    Stream inStream = null;
    Stream outStream = null;
    try
    {
        Uri baseUri = new Uri(textServer.Text);

        string filename = listFiles.SelectedValue.ToString().Trim();
        string fullFilename = serverDirectory + @"/" + filename;

        Uri uri = new Uri(baseUri, fullFilename);

        FtpWebRequest request = (FtpWebRequest)WebRequest.Create(uri);
        request.Credentials = new NetworkCredential(textUsername.Text,
                textPassword.Text);
        request.Method = WebRequestMethods.Ftp.DownloadFile;
```

```
            request.UseBinary = checkBoxBinary.Checked;

            response = (FtpWebResponse)request.GetResponse();

            inStream = response.GetResponseStream();

            saveFileDialog1.FileName = filename;

            if (saveFileDialog1.ShowDialog() == DialogResult.OK)
            {
                outStream = File.OpenWrite(saveFileDialog1.FileName);
                byte[] buffer = new byte[4096];
                int size = 0;
                while ((size = inStream.Read(buffer, 0, 4096)) > 0)
                {
                    outStream.Write(buffer, 0, size);
                }
            }
        }
        catch (Exception ex)
        {
            MessageBox.Show(ex.Message, "Error FTP Client",
                MessageBoxButtons.OK, MessageBoxIcon.Error);
        }
        finally
        {
            if (inStream != null)
                inStream.Close();
            if (outStream != null)
                outStream.Close();
            if (response != null)
                response.Close();
        }
    }
```

12. To enable the Open Directory and Get File buttons, you must add an event handler for the `SelectedIndexChanged` event of the `listFiles` list box. Name the event handler `OnFileSelection`.

```
    private void OnFileSelection(object sender, EventArgs e)
    {
        buttonGetFile.Enabled = true;
        buttonOpenDirectory.Enabled = true;
    }
```

13. After compiling the application, you can try it out. Start the application, which presents a screen like that shown in Figure 29-10. Enter an FTP server to connect to (for example, ftp://ftp.microsoft.com), and click the Open button. FTP servers that support anonymous users accept the username Anonymous. Some FTP servers that allow anonymous users check for a password that is in valid e-mail address format. This behavior is not used for security reasons but to write the file requests to a log file.

After a successful connection, the server's files and directories appear in the list box, as shown in Figure 29-11. Now, you can open other directories by clicking the Open Directory button, or download files by clicking the Get File button.

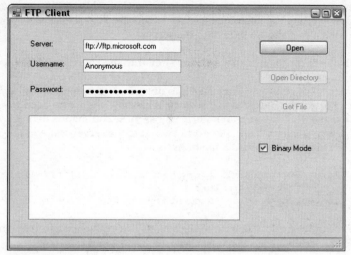

Figure 29-10

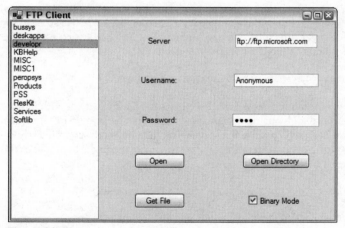

Figure 29-11

How It Works

When you send a request to an FTP server, an `FtpWebRequest` object must be created. The `FtpWebRequest` object is created by the factory method `WebRequest.Create()`. This method creates either an `FtpWebRequest`, an `HttpWebRequest`, or a `FileWebRequest` object, depending on the URL string that is passed to the method.

```
FtpWebRequest request =
    (FtpWebRequest)WebRequest.Create(textServer.Text);
```

After the `FtpWebRequest` object is created, it must be configured by setting its properties. The property `Credentials` allows setting the username and password used to access the server. The `Method` property defines the FTP request that should be sent to the server.

The FTP protocol allows commands that are very similar to the HTTP protocol's commands. The HTTP protocol uses commands like GET, HEAD and POST. The FTP protocol's commands are defined in RFC 959 (`www.ietf.org/rfc/rfc0959.txt`): RETR to download files, STOR to upload files, MKD to create a directory, and LIST to get the files from a directory. With .NET there's no need to know all these FTP commands, because the `WebRequestMethods` class has these commands defined. `WebRequestMethods` `.Ftp.ListDirectory` creates a LIST request to be sent to the server, `WebRequestMethods.Ftp` `.DownloadFiles` is used to download a file from the server.

```
request.Credentials = new NetworkCredential(textUsername.Text,
    textPassword.Text);
request.Method = WebRequestMethods.Ftp.ListDirectory;
```

When the request is defined, it can be sent to the server. The `GetResponse()` method sends the request to the server and waits until a response is received.

```
response = (FtpWebResponse)request.GetResponse();
```

To access the data from the response, the `GetResponseStream()` method returns a stream. In response to the `WebRequestMethods.Ftp.ListDirectory` request, the response stream contains all the filenames from the requested server directory. After an `WebRequestMethods.Ftp.DownladFile` request, the response stream contains the content of the requested file.

```
stream = response.GetResponseStream();
```

The returned stream containing the server directory's file listing is dealt with in the `FillDirectoryList()` method. The stream is read by using a `StreamReader`. The method `ReadToEnd()` returns a string of all the filenames that have been returned by the server. The filenames are separated by the newline character that is used to create a string array containing all filenames. This string array is set as the data source of the `ListBox` to display it in the form as follows:

```
private void FillDirectoryList(Stream stream)
{
    StreamReader reader = new StreamReader(stream);
    string content = reader.ReadToEnd();
    string[] files = content.Split('\n');
    listFiles.DataSource = files;
    reader.Close();
}
```

The stream that is received from the download file request is dealt with in the `OnDownloadFile()` method. A `SaveFileDialog` is opened so that the user can specify in which directory to store the file. The `saveFileDialog1 FileName` property returns the directory and filename selected by the user. The `File` class `OpenWrite()` method returns the stream indicating where the file from the server can be stored. The stream returned from the FTP server is read in a `while` loop and written into the stream of the local file.

You can read more about dialogs in Chapter 16.

```
inStream = response.GetResponseStream();

saveFileDialog1.FileName = filename;

if (saveFileDialog1.ShowDialog() == DialogResult.OK)
{
    outStream = File.OpenWrite(saveFileDialog1.FileName);
    byte[] buffer = new byte[4096];
    int size = 0;
    while ((size = inStream.Read(buffer, 0, 4096)) > 0)
    {
        outStream.Write(buffer, 0, size);
    }
}
```

Now you have seen how .NET classes can be used with well-known application protocols. If you want to create your own application protocol that is based on TCP, you can use the TcpListener and TcpClient classes, which are covered in the next section.

TcpListener and TcpClient

Classes from the System.Net.Sockets namespace provide much more control for network programming. Classes from these namespaces enable you to write your own server and define a custom protocol to transfer information from the client to the server and from the server to the client.

The TcpListener class can be used with the server. You can define a port number that the server should listen to with the constructor of the class. With the Start() method the listening begins. However, to communicate with a client the server must invoke the method AcceptTcpClient(). This method blocks until a client connects. The return value of this method is a TcpClient object that contains information about the connection to the client. Using this TcpClient object the server can receive data that is sent from the client, and send data back to the client.

The client itself makes use of the TcpClient class. The client can initiate the connection to the server with the Connect() method , and afterward it can send and receive data by using a stream associated with the TcpClient object.

In the following two Try It Outs, you create a simple server and a client application with the TcpListener and TcpClient classes. The server sends a list of picture files to the client, so the client can choose a file from this list to request that file from the server. With this application the client can make two requests: the LIST request returns the file list, while the PICTURE:filename request returns the picture in a byte stream.

Try It Out   **Create a TCP server**

Let's start by creating the server application.

1.   Create a new console application project in the directory C:\BegVCSharp\Chapter29 with Visual Studio. Give the application the name PictureServer.

2.   Open the Properties in the Solution Explorer. Double-click the item Settings.settings to open the Properties Editor. Add a property named PictureDirectory of type string and a property

971

named `Port` of type `int`, as shown in Figure 29-12. Set the value of the `PictureDirectory` to a directory of your system where you have pictures, for example `c:\pictures`. Set the value of the `Port` property to `8888` to define the server's port number.

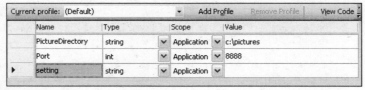

Name	Type	Scope	Value
PictureDirectory	string	Application	c:\pictures
Port	int	Application	8888
setting	string	Application	

Current profile: (Default)   Add Profile   Remove Profile   View Code

Figure 29-12

3. Add the helper class `PictureHelper` to the console application using Add ➪ Class in the Solution Explorer. The static methods offered by this class return a list of all files (`GetFileList()` method), return the file list in a byte array (`GetFileListBytes()` method), and return a byte array of a picture file (`GetPictureBytes()` method). This class uses file I/O to get filenames and to read a file.

You can read more about file I/O in Chapter 22.

```
using System;
using System.IO;
using System.Text;

namespace PictureServer
{
    public static class PictureHelper
    {
        public static string[] GetFileList()
        {
            string[] files = Directory.GetFiles(
                Properties.Settings.Default.PictureDirectory);

            // Remove the directory path from the filename.
            for (int i = 0; i < files.Length; i++)
            {
                files[i] = Path.GetFileName(files[i]);
            }
            return files;
        }

        public static byte[] GetPictureBytes(string filename)
        {
            FileInfo fileInfo = new FileInfo(filename);
            byte[] buffer = new byte[fileInfo.Length];
            using (FileStream stream = fileInfo.OpenRead())
            {
                stream.Read(buffer, 0, buffer.Length);
            }
            return buffer;
        }
    }
}
```

```
        public static byte[] GetFileListBytes()
        {
            // LIST request - return list
            string[] files = PictureHelper.GetFileList();
            StringBuilder responseMessage = new StringBuilder();
            foreach (string s in files)
            {
                responseMessage.Append(s);
                responseMessage.Append(":");
            }
            byte[] responseBuffer = Encoding.ASCII.GetBytes(
                    responseMessage.ToString());
            return responseBuffer;
        }
    }
}
```

4. Import the namespaces `System.Net` and `System.Net.Sockets` in the file `Program.cs`.

5. In the `Main()` method of the server application, add the code shown here:

```
class Program
{
    static void Main(string[] args)
    {
        TcpListener listener = new TcpListener(IPAddress.Any,
                Properties.Settings.Default.Port);
        listener.Start();

        while (true)
        {
            const int bufferSize = 256;

            TcpClient client = listener.AcceptTcpClient();
            NetworkStream clientStream = client.GetStream();

            byte[] buffer = new byte[bufferSize];
            int readBytes = 0;
            readBytes = clientStream.Read(buffer, 0, bufferSize);

            string request = Encoding.ASCII.GetString(buffer).Substring(
                    0, readBytes);

            if (request.StartsWith("LIST"))
            {
                // LIST request - return list
                byte[] responseBuffer = PictureHelper.GetFileListBytes();

                clientStream.Write(responseBuffer, 0, responseBuffer.Length);
            }
            else if (request.StartsWith("FILE"))
            {
                // FILE request - return file

                // get the filename
```

```
                string[] requestMessage = request.Split(':');
                string filename = requestMessage[1];

                byte[] data = File.ReadAllBytes(Path.Combine(
                        Properties.Settings.Default.PictureDirectory, filename));

                // Send the picture to the client.
                clientStream.Write(data, 0, data.Length);
            }
            clientStream.Close();
        }
    }
}
```

How It Works

To create a server application that waits for connecting clients using the TCP protocol, you can use the TcpListener class. To create a TcpListener object, you must define a port number for the server. Here, the port number is read from the configuration file with Properties.Settings.Default.Port. Then the Start() method is invoked to start listening for incoming requests.

```
        TcpListener listener = new TcpListener(IPAddress.Any,
                Properties.Settings.Default.Port);
        listener.Start();
```

After starting the listener, the server waits in the AcceptTcpClient() method until a client connects. The connection to the client is defined in the TcpClient object returned by AcceptTcpClient().

```
        TcpClient client = listener.AcceptTcpClient();
```

After the connection is initiated, the client sends a request to the server. The request is read in the stream. client.GetStream() returns a NetworkStream object. The data from this network stream is read into the byte array buffer and then converted to a string that is stored in the variable request.

```
        NetworkStream clientStream = client.GetStream();

        byte[] buffer = new byte[bufferSize];
        int readBytes = 0;
        readBytes = clientStream.Read(buffer, 0, bufferSize);

        string request = Encoding.ASCII.GetString(buffer).Substring(
                0, readBytes);
```

Depending on the request string, either a list of picture files or the bytes of a picture are returned to the client. The request string is checked with the String method StartsWith.

```
        if (request.StartsWith("LIST"))
```

The server sends data back to the client by writing the return data to the network stream:

```
        byte[] responseBuffer = PictureHelper.GetFileListBytes();
        clientStream.Write(responseBuffer, 0, responseBuffer.Length);
```

Try It Out   Create a TCP Client

The client application is a Windows forms application that shows the picture files available on the server. When the user selects a picture file, the picture is shown in the client application.

1. Create a new Windows Forms project in the directory `C:\BegVCSharp\Chapter29`, with the name `PictureClient`.

2. Rename the file `Form1.cs` to `PictureClientForm.cs`.

3. Add the server name and port number of the server to the application's property settings as you did with the server application. The server name has the property name `Server`, and the port number has the property name `ServerPort`. Set the value of the server to the name of your server and the port number to the port number of the server. In the example, server port number 8888 has been used.

4. Add controls to the main dialog as shown in Figure 29-13.

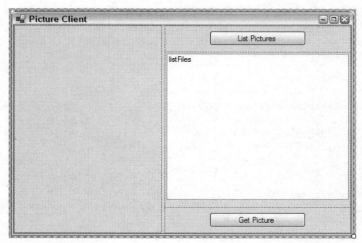

Figure 29-13

The main controls of this dialog are shown in the following table.

Control Type	Name	Text Property
PictureBox	pictureBox	
Button	buttonListPictures	List Pictures
ListBox	listFiles	
Button	buttonGetPicture	Get Picture

5. Import the namespaces `System.Net`, `System.Net.Sockets`, and `System.IO` in the file `PictureClientForm.cs`.

6. Add a `Click` event handler to the button `buttonListPictures` to include this code:

```
private void OnGetFiles(object sender, EventArgs e)
{
    const int bufferSize = 4096;

    // Connect to the server.
    TcpClient client = new TcpClient();
    IPHostEntry host = Dns.GetHostEntry(
        Properties.Settings.Default.Server);
    client.Connect(host.AddressList[0],
        Properties.Settings.Default.ServerPort);

    // Send a request to the server.
    NetworkStream clientStream = client.GetStream();
    string request = "LIST";
    byte[] requestBuffer = Encoding.ASCII.GetBytes(request);
    clientStream.Write(requestBuffer, 0, requestBuffer.Length);

    // Read the response from the server.
    byte[] responseBuffer = new byte[bufferSize];
    MemoryStream memStream = new MemoryStream();
    int bytesRead = 0;
    do
    {
        bytesRead = clientStream.Read(responseBuffer, 0, bufferSize);
        memStream.Write(responseBuffer, 0, bytesRead);
    } while (bytesRead > 0);
    clientStream.Close();
    client.Close();

    byte[] buffer = memStream.GetBuffer();
    string response = Encoding.ASCII.GetString(buffer);
    string[] fileNames = response.Split(':');
    this.listFiles.DataSource = fileNames;
}
```

7. Add a `Click` event handler to the `buttonGetPicture` button, and add this code:

```
private void OnGetPicture(object sender, EventArgs e)
{
    const int bufferSize = 4096;

    TcpClient client = new TcpClient();
    IPHostEntry host = Dns.GetHostEntry(
        Properties.Settings.Default.Server);
    client.Connect(host.AddressList[0],
        Properties.Settings.Default.ServerPort);

    NetworkStream clientStream = client.GetStream();

    string request = "FILE:" + this.listFiles.SelectedItem.ToString();
    byte[] requestBuffer = Encoding.ASCII.GetBytes(request);
    clientStream.Write(requestBuffer, 0, requestBuffer.Length);
```

```
      byte[] responseBuffer = new byte[bufferSize];
      MemoryStream memStream = new MemoryStream();
      int bytesRead = 0;
      do
      {
         bytesRead = clientStream.Read(responseBuffer, 0, bufferSize);
         memStream.Write(responseBuffer, 0, bytesRead);
      } while (bytesRead > 0);
      clientStream.Close();
      client.Close();

      pictureBox.Image = Image.FromStream(memStream);
   }
```

8. Now, you can start the server application and afterward the client application (see Figure 29-14). When you click the first button (List Pictures), a list of all pictures in the pictures directory (which has been configured on the server) shows up. Selecting a picture and clicking the Get Picture button transfers the picture to the client, and the picture is displayed in the picture box.

If you have the Windows XP firewall enabled, you are asked to unblock the program. For the server to listen on a specific port, you have to allow this. With the firewall settings you can also configure an exception for specific port numbers used during development.

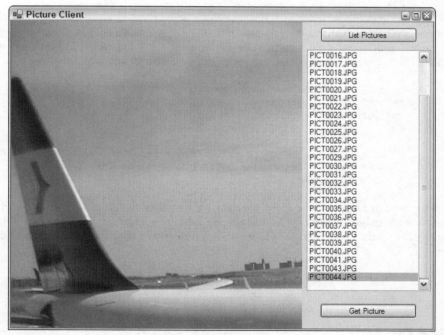

Figure 29-14

How It Works

The `TcpClient` class is used with the client to connect to the server. After creating the `TcpClient` object, the `Connect()` method initiates a connection to the server. The `Connect()` method requires an IP address and a port number. The IP address is read from the `IPHostEntry` variable `host`. The `IPHostEntry` that contains all IP addresses of the server is returned from the `Dns` class `GetHostEntry()` method. The server's name is read from the application configuration file with `Properties.Settings.Default.Server`.

```
TcpClient client = new TcpClient();
IPHostEntry host = Dns.GetHostEntry(
        Properties.Settings.Default.Server);
client.Connect(host.AddressList[0],
        Properties.Settings.Default.ServerPort);
```

Using a `NetworkStream`, data can now be sent to the server. The `NetworkStream` object can be accessed using the `GetStream()` method of the `TcpClient` object. Data to be written can now be sent to the server with the `NetworkStream` method. Because the `Write()` method requires a byte array, the string `"LIST"` is converted to a byte array with the `Encoding` class. `Encoding.ASCII` returns an ASCII `Encoding` object. With this object the `GetBytes()` method is used to convert the string to a byte array.

```
NetworkStream clientStream = client.GetStream();
string request = "LIST";
byte[] requestBuffer = Encoding.ASCII.GetBytes(request);
clientStream.Write(requestBuffer, 0, requestBuffer.Length);
```

The data that is returned from the server is read with the `clientStream` object's `Read()` method. Because it's not sure how much data is received from the server, a `do while` loop is used to read data as long as there is some. The data read is appended to a `MemoryStream`, which automatically resizes.

```
byte[] responseBuffer = new byte[bufferSize];
MemoryStream memStream = new MemoryStream();
int bytesRead = 0;
do
{
    bytesRead = clientStream.Read(responseBuffer, 0, bufferSize);
    memStream.Write(responseBuffer, 0, bytesRead);
} while (bytesRead > 0);
```

The picture is read in a similar way as the file data. The memory stream that contains the picture data is converted to an Image with the method `Image.FromStream`. (You can read more about images in Chapter 30.) The image is then assigned to the `Image` property of the `PictureBox`, so it is displayed in the form:

```
pictureBox.Image = Image.FromStream(memStream);
```

Summary

In this chapter, you learned how to use classes from the `System.Net` and `System.Net.Sockets` namespaces to create networking applications. You read how the `WebClient` class can be used to access Web servers. The simple FTP client you created illustrated how to use the `FtpWebRequest` and `FtpWebResponse` classes, which provide more control than the `WebClient` class. You also saw that, in addition to the `FtpWebRequest` class, the `HttpWebRequest` and `FileWebRequest` classes can be used.

This chapter showed that, because writing a server is not possible with the `FtpWebRequest` and `FtpWebResponse` classes, you need classes from the `System.Net.Sockets` namespace instead. You also learned how to create a TCP server with the `TcpListener` class and a client application with the `TcpClient` class.

In this chapter, you learned:

- ❑   How to use the `Dns` class for name lookups

- ❑   What the client sends with a HTTP request

- ❑   How to do HTTP requests with the `WebClient` class

- ❑   How to work with the `WebRequest` class, particularly how to get files from an FTP server with the `FtpWebRequest` class

- ❑   How to use a custom protocol with classes from the namespace `System.Net.Sockets`

Exercises

1.   Extend the FTP client application that makes use of the `FtpWebRequest` and `FtpWebResponse` classes so that it not only downloads files from the FTP server but also allows uploading files to the server. Add one more button to the form with the `Text` property set to Upload File, use the `OpenFileDialog` to ask the user for a file to upload, and then send a request to the server. For uploading files the `WebRequestMethods` class offers the `Ftp.UploadFile` member.

2.   Modify the Picture server and client applications that use the `TcpListener` and `TcpClient` classes, so that it is possible to upload picture files from the client to the server.

Introduction to GDI+

In the previous chapter, the term GDI+ was briefly introduced when you looked at printing in the .NET Framework. In this chapter, you have a real introduction to programming using the Graphics Device Interface classes (GDI+), the drawing technology of the .NET Framework. Mapping applications, games, computer-aided design/computer-aided manufacturing (CAD/CAM), drawing programs, charting programs, and many other types of applications require developers to write graphics code for their Windows Forms applications. Writing custom controls can also require graphics code. With this latest class library, Microsoft has made writing graphics code easier than ever.

Writing graphics code is one of the most enjoyable programming tasks. It is very rewarding to change your code and immediately see the results in a visible form. Whether you are writing a custom graphics window that presents something in your application in a new and different way or writing a custom control that makes your application more stylish and more usable, your application will be well received by the general public.

First, this chapter explains the mechanics of drawing using GDI+, and you write a few simple graphical example programs. Then you take a high-level look at some of the extensive capabilities of GDI+ such as clipping.

After the overview of each of these topics, you look at the classes you can use to implement the features. Knowing what you can do and understanding the class hierarchy is half the battle.

In this chapter, you learn about:

- ❑ Drawing surfaces as encapsulated by the Graphics class
- ❑ Colors as defined by the Color structure
- ❑ Drawing lines
- ❑ Drawing shapes
- ❑ Drawing text
- ❑ Drawing images
- ❑ Drawing into images (double-buffering)

Overview of Graphical Drawing

The first thing to learn about writing graphics code is that Windows does not remember what an open window looks like if that window is obscured by other windows. When a covered-up window becomes visible, Windows will tell your application, "Your window (or some portion of it) has now become visible. Will you please draw it?" You only need draw the contents of your window. Windows itself takes care of the border of the window, the title bar, and all the other window features.

When you create a window into which you want to draw, you typically declare a class that derives from `System.Windows.Forms.Form`. If you are writing a custom control, you declare a class that derives from `System.Windows.Forms.UserControl`. In either case, you override the virtual function `OnPaint()`. Windows will call this function whenever any portion of your window needs to be repainted.

With this event, a `PaintEventArgs` class is passed as an argument. There are two pertinent pieces of information in `PaintEventArgs`: a `Graphics` object, and a `ClipRectangle`. You explore the `Graphics` class first and touch on clipping near the end of the chapter.

The Graphics Class

The `Graphics` class encapsulates a GDI+ drawing surface. There are three basic types of drawing surfaces:

- ❑ Windows and controls on the screen
- ❑ Pages being sent to a printer
- ❑ Bitmaps and images in memory

The `Graphics` class provides functions to draw on any of these drawing surfaces. Among other capabilities, you can use it to draw arcs, curves, Bezier curves, ellipses, images, lines, rectangles, and text.

You can get a `Graphics` object for the window in two different ways. The first is to override the `OnPaint()` method. The `Form` class inherits the `OnPaint()` method from `Control`, and this method is the event handler for the `Paint` event that is raised whenever the control is redrawn. You can get the `Graphics` object from the `PaintEventArgs` that is passed in with the event:

```
protected override void OnPaint(PaintEventArgs e)
{
    Graphics g = e.Graphics;

    // Do our drawing here.

}
```

At other times, you might want to draw directly into your window without waiting for the `Paint` event to be raised. This would be the case if you were writing code for selecting some graphical object on the window (similar to selecting icons in Windows Explorer) or dragging some object with the mouse. You can get a `Graphics` object by calling the `CreateGraphics()` method on the form, which is another method that `Form` inherits from `Control`:

```
protected void Form1_Click (object sender, System.EventArgs e)
{
    Graphics g = this.CreateGraphics();

    // Do our drawing here.

    g.Dispose();    // this is important
}
```

Building an application that handles dragging and dropping is a somewhat involved affair and is beyond the scope of this chapter. In any case, this is a less common technique. You will do almost all of your drawing in response to an OnPaint() method.

Disposing of Objects

Everybody is familiar with the behavior of Windows when it runs out of resources. It starts to run very slowly, and sometimes applications will not be drawn correctly. Well-behaved applications free up their resources after they are done with them. When developing applications using the .NET Framework, there are several data types on which it is important to call the Dispose() method or else some resources will not be freed. These classes implement the IDisposable interface, and Graphics is one of these classes.

When you get a Graphics object from the OnPaint() method, it was not created by you, so it is not your responsibility to call Dispose(), but if you call CreateGraphics(), this is your responsibility.

> It is important to call the Dispose() method if you get a Graphics object by calling CreateGraphics().

The Dispose() method is automatically called in the destructor for the various classes that implement IDisposable. You might think that this removes your responsibility to call Dispose(), but it does not. The reason is that only the garbage collector (GC) ever calls the destructor, and you cannot guarantee when the GC will run. In particular, on a Windows 9*X* operating system with lots of memory, the GC may run very infrequently, and all resources may very well be used up before the GC runs. Although running out of memory triggers the GC to run, running out of resources does not. However, Windows 2000 and Windows XP are much less sensitive to running out of resources. According to the specifications, these two operating systems do not have any finite limits on these types of resources; however, I have seen Windows 2000 misbehave when too many applications were open, and closing some applications quickly restored correct behavior. In any case, it is better coding practice to manually dispose of any resource-hungry objects correctly and in a timely fashion.

There is another, easier way to deal with objects that need to be disposed of properly. You can use the using construct, which automatically calls Dispose() when an object goes out of scope. The following code shows the correct use of the using keyword in this context:

```
using (Graphics g = this.CreateGraphics())
{
    g.DrawLine(Pens.Black, new Point(0, 0), new Point(3, 5));
}
```

According to the documentation, the preceding code is precisely equivalent to:

```
Graphics g = this.CreateGraphics();
try
{
   g.DrawLine(Pens.Black, new Point(0, 0), new Point(3, 5));
}
finally
{
   if (g != null)
       ((IDisposable)g).Dispose();
}
```

Don't confuse this use of the using keyword with the using directive that creates an alias for a namespace or that permits the use of types in a namespace such that you do not need to fully qualify the use of the type. This is an entirely separate use of the using keyword — if you like, the block of code enclosed by the using keyword can be referred to as a using block.

Examples in this chapter handle calls to Dispose() using both styles. Sometimes, you call Dispose() directly, and other times you use the using block. The latter is a much cleaner solution, as you can see from the preceding code snippets, but there is no preferred method.

Before jumping into the first example, there are two other aspects of drawing graphics to examine — the coordinate system and colors.

Coordinate System

When designing a program that draws a complicated, intricate graphic, it is very important that your code draws exactly what you intend, and nothing but what you intend. It is possible for a single misplaced pixel to have a negative influence on the visual impact of a graphic, so it is important to understand exactly what pixels are drawn when invoking drawing operations. This is most important when creating custom controls, where you would draw lots of rectangles, horizontal lines, and vertical lines. Having a line run 1 pixel too long or fall 1 pixel short is very noticeable. However, this is somewhat less important with curves, diagonal lines, and other graphical operations.

GDI+ has a coordinate system based on imaginary grid lines that run through the center of the pixels. These lines are numbered starting at zero — the intersection of these grid lines in the upper-left pixel in any coordinate space is point X = 0, Y = 0. As a shorter notation, we can say point 1, 2, which is shorthand for saying X = 1, Y = 2. Each window into which you draw has its own coordinate space. If you create a custom control that can be used in other windows, this custom control itself has its own coordinate space. In other words, the upper-left pixel of the custom control is point 0, 0 when drawing in that custom control. You don't need to worry about where the custom control is placed on its containing window.

When drawing lines, GDI+ centers the pixels drawn on the grid line that you specify. When drawing a horizontal line with integer coordinates, it can be thought of that half of each pixel falls above the imaginary grid line, and half of each pixel falls below it. When you draw a horizontal line that is 1 pixel wide from point 1, 1 to point 5, 1, the pixels shown in Figure 30-1 will be drawn:

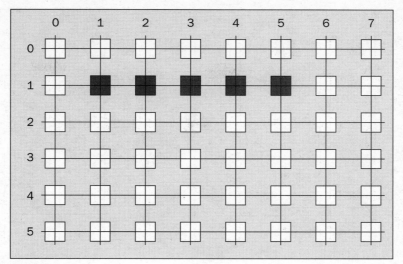

Figure 30-1

When you draw a vertical line that is 1 pixel wide and 4 pixels long, from point 2, 1 to point 2, 4, the pixels shown in Figure 30-2 are be colored in.

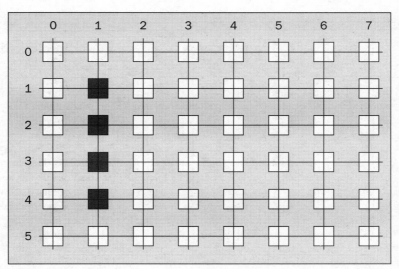

Figure 30-2

When you draw a diagonal line from point 1, 0 to point 4, 3, the pixels shown in Figure 30-3 are to be drawn.

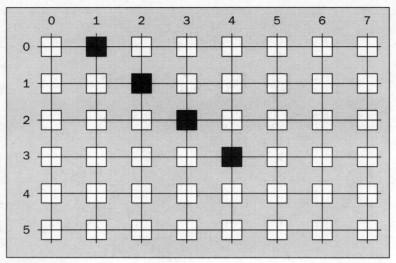

Figure 30-3

When you draw a rectangle with the upper-left corner at 1, 0 and a size of 5, 4, the rectangle drawn is shown in Figure 30-4.

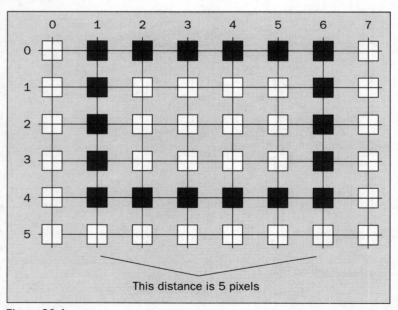

This distance is 5 pixels

Figure 30-4

There is something interesting to note here. A width of 5 was specified, and there are 6 pixels drawn in the horizontal direction. However, if you consider the grid lines running through the pixels, this rectangle is only 5 pixels wide, and the line drawn falls half a pixel outside and half a pixel inside of the grid line that you specified.

There is more to the story than this. If you draw with anti-aliasing, other pixels will be *half* colored in, creating the appearance of a smooth line, and partially avoiding having a *stair step* appearance on diagonal lines.

Figure 30-5 shows a line drawn without anti-aliasing.

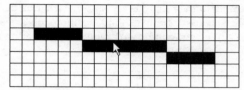

Figure 30-5

Figure 30-6 shows the same line drawn with anti-aliasing.

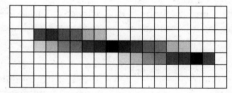

Figure 30-6

When viewed at a high resolution, this line will appear much smoother, without a stair step effect.

Understanding the relationship between the coordinates passed to drawing functions, and the resulting effect on the drawing surface makes it easy to visualize exactly which pixels will be affected by a given call to a drawing function.

There are three structs that you will use often to specify coordinates when drawing: Point, Size, and Rectangle.

Point

GDI+ uses Point to represent a single point with integer coordinates. This is a point in a two dimensional plane—a specification of a single pixel. Many GDI+ functions, such as DrawLine(), take a Point as an argument. You declare and construct a Point struct as follows:

```
Point p = new Point(1, 1);
```

There are public properties, X and Y, to get and set the X and Y coordinates of a Point.

Size

GDI+ uses `Size` to represent a size in pixels. A `Size` struct contains both width and height. You declare and construct a `Size` as follows:

```
Size s = new Size(5, 5);
```

There are public properties, `Height` and `Width`, to get and set the height and width of a `Size`.

Rectangle

GDI+ uses this structure in many different places to specify the coordinates of a rectangle. A `Point` structure defines the upper-left corner of the rectangle and a `Size` structure defines its size. There are two constructors for `Rectangle`. One takes as arguments the X position, the Y position, the width, and the height. The other takes a `Point` and a `Size` structure. Two examples of declaring and constructing a `Rectangle` are as follows:

```
Rectangle r1 = new Rectangle(1, 2, 5, 6);

Point p = new Point(1, 2);
Size s = new Size(5, 6);
Rectangle r2 = new Rectangle(p, s);
```

There are public properties to get and set all aspects of the location and size of a `Rectangle`. In addition, there are other useful properties and methods to do such activities as determining if the rectangle intersects with another rectangle, taking the intersection of two rectangles, and taking the union of two rectangles.

GraphicsPaths

There are two more important data types that you can use as arguments to various drawing functions in GDI+. The `GraphicsPath` class represents a series of connected lines and curves. When constructing a path, you can add lines, Bezier curves, arcs, pie shapes, polygons, rectangles, and more. After constructing a complex path, you can draw the path with one operation: a call to `DrawPath()`. You can fill the path with a call to `FillPath()`.

You construct a `GraphicsPath` using an array of points and `PathTypes`. `PathTypes` is a byte array, where each element in the array corresponds to an element in the array of points and gives additional information about how the path is to be constructed through each particular point. The information about the path through a point can be gleaned by using the `PathPointType` enumeration. For instance, if the point is the beginning of the path, the path type for that point is `PathPointType.Start`. If the point is a junction between two lines, the path type for that point is `PathPointType.Line`. If the point is used to construct a Bezier curve from the point before and after, the path type is `PathPointType.Bezier`.

In the following Try It Out, you will create a `GraphicsPath` object, and draw it to a window.

Try It Out   Creating a Graphics Path

Follow these steps to create and draw a `GraphicsPath` object:

1. Create a new Windows application called `DrawingPaths` in the directory `C:\BegVCSharp\Chapter30`.

2. Add the following using directive for `System.Drawing.Drawing2D` to the top of the code:

```
using System;
using System.Collections.Generic;
using System.ComponentModel;
using System.Data;
using System.Drawing;
using System.Text;
using System.Windows.Forms;
using System.Drawing.Drawing2D;
```

3.　Enter the following code into the body of `Form1`:

```
protected override void OnPaint (PaintEventArgs e)
{
    GraphicsPath path;
    path = new GraphicsPath(new Point[]{ new Point(10, 10),
                                        new Point(150, 10),
                                        new Point(200, 150),
                                        new Point(10, 150),
                                        new Point(200, 160)},
                            new byte[] {(byte)PathPointType.Start,
                                        (byte)PathPointType.Line,
                                        (byte)PathPointType.Line,
                                        (byte)PathPointType.Line,
                                        (byte)PathPointType.Line });
    e.Graphics.DrawPath(Pens.Black, path);
}
```

4.　Run the application, and you should see drawn the path shown in Figure 30-7.

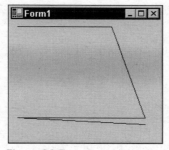

Figure 30-7

How It Works

The code to construct this path is a quite complex. The constructor for `GraphicsPath` takes two arguments. The first argument is a `Point` array; here, you use the C# syntax for declaring and initializing the array in the same place, and create each new `Point` object as you go:

```
new Point[]{
    new Point(10, 10),
    new Point(150, 10),
    new Point(200, 150),
    new Point(10, 150),
    new Point(200, 160)
}
```

The second argument is an array of bytes that you also construct right in place:

```
new byte[] {
    (byte)PathPointType.Start,
    (byte)PathPointType.Line,
    (byte)PathPointType.Line,
    (byte)PathPointType.Line,
    (byte)PathPointType.Line
}
```

Finally, you call the `DrawPath()` method:

```
e.Graphics.DrawPath(Pens.Black, path);
```

Regions

The `Region` class is a complex graphical shape comprising rectangles and paths. After constructing a `Region`, you can draw that region using the method `FillRegion()`. In the following Try It Out, you will create a `Region` object, and draw it to a window.

Try It Out   Creating a Region

The following code creates a region and adds a `Rectangle` and a `GraphicsPath` to it, and then fills that region with the color blue.

1. Create a new Windows application called `DrawingRegions` in the directory `C:\BegVCSharp\Chapter30`.

2. Add a using directive for `System.Drawing.Drawing2D` to the top of the code:

```
using System;
using System.Collections.Generic;
using System.ComponentModel;
using System.Data;
using System.Drawing;
using System.Text;
using System.Windows.Forms;
using System.Drawing.Drawing2D;
```

3. Enter the following code into the body of `Form1`:

```
protected override void OnPaint ( PaintEventArgs e)
{
    Rectangle r1 = new Rectangle(10, 10, 50, 50);
    Rectangle r2 = new Rectangle(40, 40, 50, 50);
    Region r = new Region(r1);
    r.Union(r2);

    GraphicsPath path = new GraphicsPath(new Point[] {
                                new Point(45, 45),
                                new Point(145, 55),
                                new Point(200, 150),
                                new Point(75, 150),
                                new Point(45, 45)
                                }, new byte[] {
```

```
                                    (byte)PathPointType.Start,
                                    (byte)PathPointType.Bezier,
                                    (byte)PathPointType.Bezier,
                                    (byte)PathPointType.Bezier,
                                    (byte)PathPointType.Line
                               });
    r.Union(path);
    e.Graphics.FillRegion(Brushes.Blue, r);
}
```

4. When you run this code, it will display as shown in Figure 30-8.

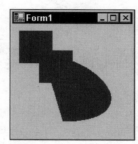

Figure 30-8

How It Works

The code to construct a region is also quite complex, though the most complex part of the example is constructing any paths that will go into the region, and you have already seen how to construct these from the previous example.

Constructing regions consists of constructing rectangles and paths, before calling the `Union()` method. If you desired the intersection of a rectangle and a path, you could have used the `Intersection()` method instead of the `Union()` method.

Further information on paths and regions is not particularly needed for an introduction to GDI+, so you will not explore them in any more depth in this chapter.

Colors

Many of the drawing operations in GDI+ involve a color. When drawing a line or rectangle, you need to specify what color it should be.

In GDI+, colors are encapsulated in the `Color` structure. You can create a color by passing red, green, and blue values to a function of the `Color` structure, but this is almost never necessary. The `Color` structure contains approximately 150 properties that get a large variety of preset colors. Forget about red, green, blue, yellow, and black—if you need to do some drawing in the color of `LightGoldenrodYellow` or `LavenderBlush`, there is a predefined color made just for you! You declare a variable of type `Color` and initialize it with a color from the `Color` structure as follows:

```
Color redColor = Color.Red;
Color anotherColor = Color.LightGoldenrodYellow;
```

991

You're almost ready to do some drawing, but here are a couple of notes before going on.

Another way to represent a color is to break it into three components: Hue, Saturation, and Brightness. The `Color` structure contains utility methods to do this, namely `GetHue()`, `GetSaturation()`, and `GetBrightness()`.

You can use the `ColorDialog` that you met in Chapter 29 to experiment with colors.

In the following Try It Out, you will create a color selection dialog and use it to see the relationship between colors defined using red, green, and blue, and colors defined using hue, saturation, and brightness.

Try It Out   Creating a Region

In a new Windows application, drag a `ColorDialog` control onto your form, and add a call to `this.colorDialog1.ShowDialog()`, after the `InitializeComponent()` call:

```
public Form1()
{
  InitializeComponent();
  this.colorDialog1.ShowDialog();
}
```

When you put up the form, the color selection dialog will also be put up.

Run the application, and click the Define Custom Colors button. You will see a dialog box that allows you to pick a color using the mouse and see the RGB values for the color. You can also get the hue, saturation, and luminosity values for the color (where luminosity corresponds to brightness). You can also directly enter the RGB values and see the resulting color.

Colors in GDI+ have a fourth component, the alpha component. Using this component, you can set the opacity of the color, which allows you to create fade in/fade out effects such as the menu effects in Windows 2000 and Windows XP. Explaining how to use the alpha component is beyond the scope of this chapter.

Drawing Lines Using the Pen Class

The first example here draws lines. In the following Try It Out, you draw lines using the `Pen` class, which allows you to define the color, width, and pattern of the line that your code is drawing. The color and width properties are obvious. However, the pattern of a line indicates whether the line is a solid line, or is composed of dashes and dots. The `Pen` class is in the `System.Drawing` namespace.

Try It Out   Pen Example

Follow these steps to draw some lines in a window using the `Pen` class.

1.   Create a new Windows application called `DrawingLines` in the directory `C:\BegVCSharp\Chapter30`.

2. Enter the following code into the body of `Form1`.

```
protected override void OnPaint(PaintEventArgs e)
{
    Graphics g = e.Graphics;

    using (Pen blackPen = new Pen(Color.Black, 1))
    {
        if (ClientRectangle.Height/10>0)
        {
            for (int y = 0; y < ClientRectangle.Height;
                y += ClientRectangle.Height / 10)
            {
                g.DrawLine(blackPen, new Point(0, 0),
                        new Point(ClientRectangle.Width, y));
            }
        }
    }
}
```

3. Now press F5 to compile and run the code. When you run it, it will create the window shown in Figure 30-9.

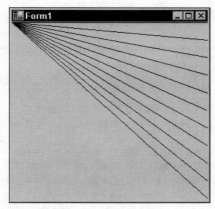

Figure 30-9

How It Works

Earlier in the chapter, I introduced the `Graphics` class. The first thing that you do in the `OnPaint()` method is to get the `Graphics` object from the `PaintEventArgs` parameter:

```
Graphics g = e.Graphics;
```

Note that because you are passed the reference to the `Graphics` object, and you did not create it, you do not need to (and should not) manually call `Dispose()` on it. However, since you are using a potentially resource-hungry `Pen` object for this example, I have wrapped the rest of the code in a `using` block, as described earlier, which will ensure that the object is destroyed as soon as possible.

Chapter 30

When you construct the pen, you pass as parameters to the constructor a color and a width of the pen. In this example, the color is black, and the width is one. This is the line of code to construct the pen:

```
using (Pen blackPen = new Pen(Color.Black, 1))
```

Every window into which you can draw has a client area, which is a rectangle that exists within the border and defines the exact area into which you can draw. You can get the client area from `ClientRectangle`, which is a public, read-only property of the form (inherited from `Control`). It contains the size (that is, the width and height) of the client area of the window into which you are drawing. The following code starts a loop that goes from zero up to the height of the client area (given by `ClientRectangle.Height`) in steps of 10. Note that you first check that `ClientRectangle.Height/10` is bigger than zero—without this, the loop will run indefinitely if the form is resized below a certain height. (Because `ClientRectangle.Height/10` is the loop increment, if this is zero, you'll loop forever.)

```
if (ClientRectangle.Height/10>0)
{
    for (int y = 0; y < ClientRectangle.Height;
        y += ClientRectangle.Height / 10)
```

Now you can draw the lines—when you draw each line, you pass the `Pen` that you just created, along with the starting point and ending point of the line:

```
g.DrawLine(blackPen, new Point(0, 0),
            new Point(ClientRectangle.Width, y));
```

> **Always call** `Dispose()` **on** `Pen` **objects.**

Just as for `Graphics` objects, it is important to either call `Dispose()` on `Pen` objects when you are finished with them, or use the `using` block, otherwise your application can deplete the Windows resources.

In this example, you constructed a `Pen`. However, there is an easier way to get a `Pen`. The `Pens` class contains properties for getting approximately 150 pens, one for each of the predefined colors that you learned about previously. The following version of the example works identically to the previous one, but instead of constructing a `Pen`, you get it from the `Pens` class:

```
protected override void OnPaint(PaintEventArgs e)
{
    if (ClientRectangle.Height/10>0)
    {
        for (int y = 0; y < ClientRectangle.Height;
            y += ClientRectangle.Height / 10)
        {
            e.Graphics.DrawLine(Pens.Black, new Point(0, 0),
                            new Point(ClientRectangle.Width, y));
        }
    }
}
```

994

In this case, you did not create the `Pen`, so it is not necessary to call `Dispose()`.

There are many more features of the `Pen` class. You could create a pen to draw a dashed line, or you could create a pen with a width thicker than 1 pixel. There is an `Alignment` property of the `Pen` class that allows you to define whether the pen is drawn to the left or right (or above or below) of the line that you specify. By setting the `StartCap` and `EndCap` properties, you can specify that your lines are ended with an arrow, a diamond, a square, or are rounded off. You can even program a custom start cap and end cap using the `CustomStartCap` and `CustomEndCap` properties. After learning about images, you will see how to specify a `Brush` with a `Pen` so that you can draw the line using a bitmap instead of a solid color.

Drawing Shapes Using the Brush Class

The next example uses the `Brush` class to draw shapes such as rectangles, ellipses, pie charts, and polygons. The `Brush` class is an abstract base class. To instantiate a `Brush` object, you use classes derived from `Brush` such as `SolidBrush`, `TextureBrush`, and `LinearGradientBrush`.

The `Brush` and `SolidBrush` classes are in the System.Drawing namespace. However, the `TextureBrush` and `LinearGradientBrush` are in the `System.Drawing.Drawing2D` namespace. This is what each brush class achieves:

- ❑ `SolidBrush` fills a shape with a solid color.

- ❑ `TextureBrush` fills a shape with a bitmap. When constructing this brush, you also specify a bounding rectangle and a wrap mode. The bounding rectangle specifies what portion of the bitmap to use for the brush—you don't need to use the entire bitmap if you don't want to. The wrap mode has a number of options, including `Tile`, which tiles the texture, `TileFlipX`, `TileFlipY`, and `TileFlipXY`, which tile while flipping the image for successive tiles. You can create very interesting and imaginative effects using the `TextureBrush`.

- ❑ `LinearGradientBrush` encapsulates a brush that draws a gradient of two colors, where the first color transitions to the second color at a specified angle. You specify angles in terms of degrees. An angle of zero specifies that the colors will transition from left to right. An angle of 90 degrees means that the colors will transition from top to bottom.

One more brush that I will mention is the `PathGradientBrush`, which creates an elaborate shading effect, where the shading runs from the center of the path to the edge of the path. This brush reminds me of when I was a child, and I would shade maps with colored pencils, making the color darker at the boundary between different states or countries.

> **Always call** `Dispose()` **on** `Brush` **objects.**

Just as for `Graphics` objects and `Pen` objects, it is important to call `Dispose()` on `Brush` objects that you create, or use the `using` block; otherwise, your application may deplete the Windows resources. In the following Try It Out, you will fill some shapes using some brushes.

Try It Out   Brush Example

Follow these steps to see brushes in action:

1. Create a new Windows application called `UsingBrushes` in the directory `C:\BegVCSharp\Chapter30`.

2. Add a `using` directive for `System.Drawing.Drawing2D` for the `LinearGradientBrush` to the top of the code:

```
using System;
using System.Collections.Generic;
using System.ComponentModel;
using System.Data;
using System.Drawing;
using System.Text;
using System.Windows.Forms;
using System.Drawing.Drawing2D;
```

3. In the constructor of the `Form1` class, add a call to `SetStyle()` after the call to `InitializeComponent()`:

```
public Form1()
{
    InitializeComponent();
    SetStyle(ControlStyles.Opaque, true);

}
```

4. Now, add an `OnPaint()` method to your class:

```
protected override void OnPaint(PaintEventArgs e)
{
    Graphics g = e.Graphics;
    g.FillRectangle(Brushes.White, ClientRectangle);
    g.FillRectangle(Brushes.Red, new Rectangle(10, 10, 50, 50));

    Brush linearGradientBrush = new LinearGradientBrush(
            new Rectangle(10, 60, 50, 50), Color.Blue, Color.White, 45);
    g.FillRectangle(linearGradientBrush, new Rectangle(10, 60, 50, 50));

    // Manually call Dispose().
    linearGradientBrush.Dispose();

    g.FillEllipse(Brushes.Aquamarine, new Rectangle(60, 20, 50, 30));
    g.FillPie(Brushes.Chartreuse, new Rectangle(60, 60, 50, 50), 90, 210);
    g.FillPolygon(Brushes.BlueViolet, new Point[] {
                            new Point(110, 10),
                            new Point(150, 10),
                            new Point(160, 40),
                            new Point(120, 20),
                            new Point(120, 60),
                            });
}
```

5. When you compile and run this program, it will display as shown in Figure 30-10.

Figure 30-10

How It Works

The first thing to remark about is the call to SetStyle() in the form's constructor. SetStyle() is a method of the Form class:

```
SetStyle(ControlStyles.Opaque, true);
```

This method changes the behavior of the Form class so that it will not automatically draw the background of the window. If you include this line, but don't draw the background of the window yourself, then anything underneath the window at the time of creation shows through, which is not what you want. Thus your next activity is to draw your own background onto the client area of the window.

Just as with the Pens class, there is a Brushes class that contains properties for getting approximately 150 brushes, one for each predefined color. You use this class to get most of the brushes in this example, with the exception of the LinearGradientBrush, which you create yourself.

The first call to FillRectangle() draws the background of the client area of your window:

```
g.FillRectangle(Brushes.White, ClientRectangle);
```

The creation of the LinearGradientBrush takes a rectangle, specifying its size, the two colors to be used for the gradient, and the angle (in this case 45):

```
Brush linearGradientBrush = new LinearGradientBrush(
        new Rectangle(10, 60, 50, 50), Color.Blue, Color.White, 45);
g.FillRectangle(linearGradientBrush, new Rectangle(10, 60, 50, 50));
linearGradientBrush.Dispose();
```

When you specified the rectangle for the brush, you used a rectangle of width 50 and height 50, which is the same size as the rectangle used when you defined the brush. The result is that the brush area just fits the rectangle. Try changing the rectangle defined in the creation of the brush so that the width and height are 10 and see what happens. Also, try changing the angle to different values to see the change in effect.

Drawing Text Using the Font Class

The next example uses the Font class to draw text. The Font class encapsulates the three main characteristics of a font, which are the font family, the font size, and the font style. The Font class is in the System.Drawing namespace.

According to the .NET documentation, a font family "abstracts a group of type faces having a similar basic design." This is a fancy way of saying that font families are things like Courier, Arial, or Times New Roman.

The font `Size` property represents the size of the font type. However, in the .NET Framework, this size is not strictly the point size. It can be the point size, but you can change a property called the `GraphicsUnit` via the `Unit` property, which defines the unit of measure for the font. To refresh your memory, one point is equal to 1/72 of an inch, so a 10-point font is 10/72 of an inch high. Based on the `GraphicsUnit` enumeration, you can specify the unit for the font as one of the following:

- point (1/72 of an inch)
- display (1/75 of an inch)
- document (1/300 of an inch)
- inch
- millimeter
- pixel

This means that you have an unprecedented flexibility in specifying the desired size of your font. One possible use for this might be if you are writing a text drawing routine that needs to work in an acceptable way on very high-resolution displays, low-resolution displays, and printers.

When drawing text, given a specific font, and given a specific drawing surface, you often need to know the width in pixels of a specified string of text. It is pretty clear why different fonts will have an effect on the width in pixels of a string—a smaller font will result in a width of fewer pixels. However, it is equally as important to know the drawing surface, because the pixel resolutions of different drawing surfaces are different. Typically, the screen has 72 pixels per inch. Printers can be 300 pixels per inch, 600 pixels per inch, and sometimes even more. Use the `MeasureString()` method of the `Graphics` object to calculate the width of a string for a given font.

The font `Style` property refers to whether the type is italicized, emboldened, struck-through, or underlined.

> **Always call** `Dispose()` **on** `Font` **objects.**

It is important to call `Dispose()` on `Font` objects that you create, or use the `using` block: otherwise, your application may deplete Windows resources.

When drawing text, you use a `Rectangle` to specify the bounding coordinates of the text to be drawn. Typically, the height of this rectangle should be the height of the font or a multiple of the height of the font. This would only be different when drawing some special effect using clipped text.

The `StringFormat` class encapsulates text layout information, including alignment and line spacing. The following example shows right and centered text justification using the `StringFormat` class. In the following Try It Out, you will create a `Font` object, and draw some text with it.

Try It Out   **Font Example**

Follow these steps to practice drawing text in a variety of ways:

1. Create a new Windows application called DrawText in the directory C:\BegVCSharp\Chapter30.

2. In the constructor of the Form1 class, add a call to SetStyle() after the call to InitializeComponent(). You also change the bounds of the window to give enough room to display the text that you want to display. The modified constructor is as follows:

```
public Form1()
{
    InitializeComponent();
    SetStyle(ControlStyles.Opaque, true);
    Bounds = new Rectangle(0, 0, 500, 300);

}
```

3. Now, add an OnPaint() method to your class:

```
protected override void OnPaint(PaintEventArgs e)
{
    Graphics g = e.Graphics;
    int y = 0;

    g.FillRectangle(Brushes.White, ClientRectangle);

    // Draw left-justified text.
    Rectangle rect = new Rectangle(0, y, 400, Font.Height);
    g.DrawRectangle(Pens.Blue, rect);
    g.DrawString("This text is left justified.", Font,
                 Brushes.Black, rect);
    y += Font.Height + 20;

    // Draw right-justified text.
    Font aFont = new Font("Arial", 16, FontStyle.Bold | FontStyle.Italic);
    rect = new Rectangle(0, y, 400, aFont.Height);
    g.DrawRectangle(Pens.Blue, rect);

    StringFormat sf = new StringFormat();
    sf.Alignment = StringAlignment.Far;
    g.DrawString("This text is right justified.", aFont, Brushes.Blue,
                 rect, sf);
    y += aFont.Height + 20;
    // Manually call Dispose().
    aFont.Dispose();

    // Draw centered text.
    Font cFont = new Font("Courier New", 12, FontStyle.Underline);
    rect = new Rectangle(0, y, 400, cFont.Height);
    g.DrawRectangle(Pens.Blue, rect);
    sf = new StringFormat();
    sf.Alignment = StringAlignment.Center;
    g.DrawString("This text is centered  and underlined.", cFont,
                 Brushes.Red, rect, sf);
```

```
        y += cFont.Height + 20;

        // Manually call Dispose().
        cFont.Dispose();

        // Draw multiline text.
        Font trFont = new Font("Times New Roman", 12);
        rect = new Rectangle(0, y, 400, trFont.Height * 3);
        g.DrawRectangle(Pens.Blue, rect);
        String longString = "This text is much longer, and drawn ";
        longString += "into a rectangle that is higher than ";
        longString += "one line, so that it will wrap.  It is ";
        longString += "very easy to wrap text using GDI+.";
        g.DrawString(longString, trFont, Brushes.Black, rect);

        // Manually call Dispose().
        trFont.Dispose();
    }
```

4. When you compile and run the code, it will create the window shown in Figure 30-11.

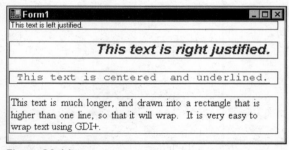

Figure 30-11

How It Works

This example contains a few of the most common text drawing operations.

As usual, you assign a reference to the Graphics object to a local variable, for your convenience. You also paint the background of the window white.

When drawing the text, you calculate the bounding rectangle for your text. You get the height of the font using the Height property. For illustrative purposes, you draw this rectangle in blue so that the bounding rectangle of your text is very clear. When you draw the text, you pass the text, the font, a brush, and a bounding rectangle:

```
        // Draw left-justified text.
        Rectangle rect = new Rectangle(0, y, 400, Font.Height);
        g.DrawRectangle(Pens.Blue, rect);
        g.DrawString("This text is left justified.", Font,
                Brushes.Black, rect);
```

You specify only the rectangle in which the text will go. The baseline of a font is the imaginary line that most of the characters of the font "sit" on. GDI+ and the font itself determine where the actual baseline will go — you have no control over that.

When you draw the text, you pass a brush to the `DrawString()` function. In this example, you pass only brushes that have a solid color. You could just as easily have passed other types of brushes, such as a gradient brush. After you have introduced images in the next section, I will demonstrate drawing text using a `TextureBrush`.

The first time that you draw text in this example, you use the default font for the form. This font is referenced in the `Font` property, which is inherited from `Control`.

```
g.DrawString("This is a left justified string.", Font,
             Brushes.Black, rect);
```

The next time you draw text in this example, you create a new instance of a `Font`:

```
Font aFont = new Font("Arial", 16, FontStyle.Bold | FontStyle.Italic);
```

This example shows not only how to create a new instance of a font, but how to give it a style. In this case, the style is bold and italic.

The example also shows creating a `StringFormat` object, so that you can draw right-justified and centered text. In GDI+, right-justified text alignment is referred to as `Far` alignment. Left-justified text is `Near` alignment.

```
StringFormat sf = new StringFormat();
sf.Alignment = StringAlignment.Far;
```

Finally, you draw some multiline text. Using GDI+, it could not be easier. All you need to do is to specify a rectangle where the width is less than the length of the string (in pixels), and the height is sufficient to draw multiple lines. In this case, you made the height equal to three times the font height.

Drawing Using Images

Images have many uses in GDI+. Of course, you can draw images into your windows, but you can also create a brush (`TextureBrush`) with an image and draw shapes that are then filled in with the image. You can create a pen from the `TextureBrush` and draw lines using the image. You can supply a `TextureBrush` when drawing text, and the text will then be drawn using the image. The `Image` class is in the `System .Drawing` namespace.

Another very important use of images is the graphics programming technique of *double-buffering*. Sometimes the drawing you wish to create is very elaborate and intricate and takes quite a bit of time to draw, even with today's fast machines. It is not a pleasing effect to see the graphic "creep" onto the screen as it is being drawn. Examples of these types of applications are mapping applications and complex CAD/CAM applications. In this technique, instead of drawing into a window, you draw into an image, and after drawing into the image is completed, you draw the image to the window. This is the technique known as double-buffering. Certain other graphics techniques involve drawing in layers, where first you draw the background, then you draw objects on top of the background, and finally you draw some text on top of the objects. If this drawing is done directly to the screen, the user will see a flickering effect. Double-buffering eliminates this flickering effect. You look at a double-buffering example a bit later.

`Image` itself is an abstract class. There are two descendants of `Image`: `Bitmap`, and `Metafile`.

The `Bitmap` class is a general-purpose image, with height and width properties. The examples in this section will use the `Bitmap` class. You will load a `Bitmap` image from a file and draw it. You will also create a brush from it and use that brush to create a pen to draw lines, and also use that brush to draw some text.

You look at the `Metafile` class near the end of this chapter, when you see an overview of the advanced capabilities of GDI+.

> **Always call** `Dispose()` **on** `Image` **objects.**

It is important to call `Dispose()` on `Image` objects that you create, or use the `using` blocks, otherwise your application may deplete the Windows resources.

There are several possible sources for a bitmap. You can load the bitmap from a file or create the bitmap from another existing image, or it can be created as an empty image, onto which you can draw. When you read the image from a file, it can be in the JPEG, GIF, or BMP format. In the following Try It Out, you will be able to see how to read an image from a file, and draw it in a window.

Try It Out   Image Example

The following is a very simple example to read an image from a file and draw it in a window.

1. Create a new Windows application called `DrawImage` in the directory `C:\BegVCSharp\Chapter30`.

2. First, you need to declare a private variable in your `Form1` class to hold the image after you read it from a file. After the declaration of the components variable, add the declaration of `theImage` as follows:

```
partial class Form1 : Form
{
    private Image theImage;
```

3. Modify the constructor so that it appears as follows:

```
public Form1()
{
    InitializeComponent();
    SetStyle(ControlStyles.Opaque, true);
    theImage = new Bitmap("Person.bmp");
}
```

4. Now, add an `OnPaintEvent()` method to your class:

```
protected override void OnPaint(PaintEventArgs e)
{
    Graphics g = e.Graphics;

    g.DrawImage(theImage, ClientRectangle);
}
```

5. Finally, you need to dispose of the `Image` that is stored in a member variable of your class. Modify the `Dispose()` method of the form class. Note that with Visual Studio 2005, the `Dispose()` method is in the file `Form1.Designer.cs`. The easiest way to open the file is to click the Show All Files button on the toolbar at the top of the Solution Explorer window. Here is the function:

```
protected override void Dispose( bool disposing )
{
    if (disposing)
    {
        theImage.Dispose();
    }
    if (disposing && (components != null))
    {
        components.Dispose();
    }
    base.Dispose(disposing);
}
```

Before running this example, you must get the BMP file called `Person.bmp` and place it in the `DrawImage\bin\Debug` directory. The `Person.bmp` file can be found in the code download, or you can use another bitmap you have, but remember to change the line

```
theImage = new Bitmap("Person.bmp");
```

that you added in step 3 to hold the filename of your own bitmap.

When you compile and run this code, you should see the display shown in Figure 30-12.

Figure 30-12

How It Works

In the constructor, you instantiate a `Bitmap` object and assign it to the `Image` variable you declared.

Then, in the `OnPaint()` method, you draw the image. When you draw the image, you pass a `Rectangle` as one of the arguments to the `DrawImage()` method. If the image is not the same size as the rectangle that you pass to `DrawImage()`, GDI+ automatically resizes the image to fit in the specified rectangle. One way to enforce that GDI+ will not resize the image is to pass the size of the image, retrieved from the `Width` and `Height` properties, to the `DrawImage()` method.

Drawing with a Texture Brush

You will now create a `TextureBrush` from the image you have just used, and look at the following three different examples of its use:

❑ Drawing an ellipse

❑ Creating a `Pen`

❑ Drawing text

In the following Try It Out, you start with the previous code example and make a few modifications to it.

Try It Out   Drawing an Ellipse with an Image

Follow these steps to see drawing some text using a `TextureBrush`:

1. Starting with the code in the previous `DrawImage` example, add another `Image` variable declaration to the `Form1` class:

```
partial class Form1 : Form
{
    private Image theImage;
    private Image smallImage;
```

2. In the form's constructor, create `smallImage` from `theImage`. When you create it, you specify a rectangle that is half the height and half the width of `theImage`. This creates a smaller version of the original image:

```
public Form1()
{
    InitializeComponent();
    SetStyle(ControlStyles.Opaque, true);
    theImage = new Bitmap("Person.bmp");
    smallImage = new Bitmap(theImage,
                 new Size(theImage.Width / 2, theImage.Height / 2));

}
```

3. Replace the `OnPaint()` method with this one:

```
protected override void OnPaint(PaintEventArgs e)
{
    Graphics g = e.Graphics;

    g.FillRectangle(Brushes.White, ClientRectangle);

    Brush tBrush = new TextureBrush(smallImage, new Rectangle(0, 0,
                    smallImage.Width, smallImage.Height));
    g.FillEllipse(tBrush, ClientRectangle);
    tBrush.Dispose();
}
```

4. Finally, you need to dispose of the two images that are stored in member variables of your class. Modify the `Dispose()` method of the class (in `Form1.Designer.cs`) as follows:

```
protected override void Dispose( bool disposing )
{
    if (disposing)
    {
      theImage.Dispose();
      smallImage.Dispose();
    }
    if (disposing && (components != null))
    {
      components.Dispose();
    }
    base.Dispose(disposing);
}
```

5. When you run this application, the window looks like Figure 30-13.

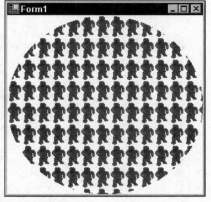

Figure 30-13

How It Works

When you create the `TextureBrush`, you pass a rectangle to the constructor to specify what part of the image will be used for the brush. In this case, you specify that you will use the entire image. Whatever is drawn using the `TextureBrush` uses the bitmap instead of a solid color.

Most of the code for this example has already been explained in this chapter. The difference is that you call the `FillEllipse()` method of the `Graphics` class, passing your newly created texture brush, and the `ClientRectangle` draws the ellipse in the window:

```
g.FillEllipse(tBrush, ClientRectangle);
```

In the following Try It Out, you will create a `TextureBrush`, then create a pen from the `TextureBrush`.

Try It Out — Creating a Pen from an Image

Now that you have created a `TextureBrush`, you can create a pen using that brush.

1. Starting with the code in the `DrawImage` example that you modified in the previous Try It Out, change the `OnPaint()` method so that it looks like this:

```
protected override void OnPaint(PaintEventArgs e)
{
    Graphics g = e.Graphics;

    g.FillRectangle(Brushes.White, ClientRectangle);

    Brush tBrush = new TextureBrush(smallImage, new Rectangle(0, 0,
                        smallImage.Width, smallImage.Height));
    Pen tPen = new Pen(tBrush, 40);
    g.DrawRectangle(tPen, 0, 0,
                        ClientRectangle.Width, ClientRectangle.Height);
    tPen.Dispose();
    tBrush.Dispose();
}
```

2. When you run this code, it looks like Figure 30-14.

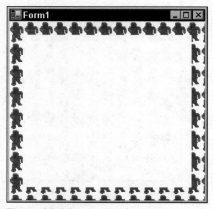

Figure 30-14

In the following Try It Out, having created a `TextureBrush`, you will draw some text with it.

Try It Out   Drawing Text with an Image

You can draw text using the `TextureBrush` also.

1.   Continuing with the code from the previous Try It Out, modify the `OnPaint` method as follows:

```
protected override void OnPaint(PaintEventArgs e)
{
    Graphics g = e.Graphics;
    g.FillRectangle(Brushes.White, ClientRectangle);

    Brush tBrush = new TextureBrush(smallImage, new Rectangle(0, 0,
                   smallImage.Width, smallImage.Height));
    Font trFont = new Font("Times New Roman", 32,
                   FontStyle.Bold | FontStyle.Italic);
    g.DrawString("Hello from Beginning Visual C#",
                   trFont, tBrush, ClientRectangle);
    tBrush.Dispose();
    trFont.Dispose();
}
```

2.   For this example, you'll actually use a different bitmap — change the line in the form constructor that sets the source for `theImage` to:

```
theImage = new Bitmap("Tile.bmp");
```

The `Tile.bmp` file can also be found in the download code.

3.   When you run this code, it appears as shown in Figure 30-15.

Figure 30-15

The call to the `DrawString()` method is similar to previous uses of that method. It takes as arguments the text, the font, your texture brush, and a bounding rectangle:

```
g.DrawString("Hello from Beginning Visual C#",
             trFont, tBrush, ClientRectangle);
```

Double-Buffering

I previously touched on the problems when drawing takes too long and the user has to wait a long time to see the graphics drawn. As I explained before, the solution is to draw into an image, and when you have completed all drawing operations, draw the complete image to the window.

In the following Try It Out, you can see the performance benefits of double-buffering. By not drawing to the screen until fully ready, you can improve the performance profile of your application.

Try It Out   Double-Buffering Example

Follow these steps to create an application that has performance issues:

1. Create a new Windows application called `DoubleBuffer`, and add the following `OnPaint()` method, which a draws large number of lines in random colors.

```
protected override void OnPaint(PaintEventArgs e)
{
    Graphics g = e.Graphics;
    Random r = new Random();

    g.FillRectangle(Brushes.White, ClientRectangle);

    for (int x = 0; x < ClientRectangle.Width; x++)
    {
        for (int y = 0; y < ClientRectangle.Height; y += 10)
        {
            Color c = Color.FromArgb(r.Next(255), r.Next(255), r.Next(255));
            using (Pen p = new Pen(c, 1))
            {
                g.DrawLine(p, new Point(0, 0), new Point(x, y));
            }
        }
    }
}
```

2. When you run this, you can see the drawing take place before your eyes (that is, if your machine is not *too* fast). After all the drawing is completed, the window looks like Figure 30-16.

Figure 30-16

3. Now you add the double-buffering — if you replace the `OnPaint()` method with this version, the graphics are drawn all at once, after a second or two:

```
protected override void OnPaint(PaintEventArgs e)
{
    Graphics displayGraphics = e.Graphics;
    Random r = new Random();
    Image i = new Bitmap(ClientRectangle.Width, ClientRectangle.Height);
    Graphics g = Graphics.FromImage(i);

    g.FillRectangle(Brushes.White, ClientRectangle);

    for (int x = 0; x < ClientRectangle.Width; x++)
    {
        for (int y = 0; y < ClientRectangle.Height; y += 10)
        {
            Color c = Color.FromArgb (r.Next(255), r.Next(255), r.Next(255));
            Pen p = new Pen(c, 1);
            g.DrawLine(p, new Point(0, 0), new Point(x, y));
            p.Dispose();
        }
    }
    displayGraphics.DrawImage(i, ClientRectangle);
    i.Dispose();
}
```

How It Works

The part of the code responsible for drawing the lines is straightforward — you saw the `DrawLine()` method earlier in the chapter. The only real thing of note in this part of the code is the `FromArgb()` static `Color` method, which creates a `Color` struct from the three supplied integer values, corresponding to the red, green, and blue parts of the color.

In the double-buffering code, (step 3), you create a new image that has the same height and width of the `ClientRectangle` with the following line:

```
Image i = new Bitmap(ClientRectangle.Width, ClientRectangle.Height);
```

You then get a `Graphics` object from the image using the following line:

```
Graphics g = Graphics.FromImage(i);
```

All of the drawing operations are the same as the previous code, except that they now draw into the image instead of directly onto the window.

Finally, at the end of the function, you draw the image to the window:

```
displayGraphics.DrawImage(i, ClientRectangle);
```

Because the lines are drawn first to an invisible image, you do have to wait a short while before you see anything.

Advanced Capabilities of GDI+

I have only just touched on the many capabilities of GDI+. There is much more that you can do with it — far more than can be achieved in a single chapter. However, to round off this chapter, I will introduce several areas of these advanced capabilities.

Clipping

There are three contexts where clipping is important.

First, when the OnPaint() method is called, in addition to the Graphics object, the event is passed a clipping rectangle. For simple drawing routines, you don't need to pay much attention to this clipping rectangle, but if you have a very elaborate drawing routine that takes a lot of time, you can reduce this drawing time by testing against this clipping rectangle before you draw. You know the bounding rectangle of whatever graphic or figure that you need to draw. If this bounding rectangle does not intersect with the clipping rectangle, then you can skip the drawing operation.

Figure 30-17 shows one window containing a bar chart that is partially obscured by another window.

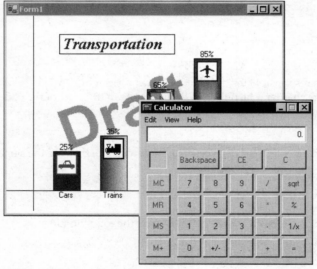

Figure 30-17

After the calculator has been closed, and after the Windows operating system has drawn the border of the window, the bar chart window looks like the one in Figure 30-18.

At this point, the OnPaint() method for the bar chart window would be called, with the clipping rectangle set to the area exposed by the closed window, shown in black in Figure 30-18. The bar chart would now need to draw the portions of its window that were previously underneath the overlying window. It would not need to redraw the car or trains bars, and in fact, even if the OnPaint() method tried to draw into the window in an area other than the exposed area, it could not. Any drawing that it did would be ignored. The bar chart window knows the bounding rectangle for the cars bar, and can determine if this rectangle intersects with the exposed portion of the window. Having determined that it does not intersect, the drawing routine will not redraw the part of the display covering the cars bar.

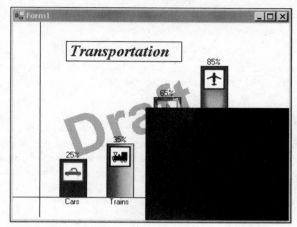

Figure 30-18

Sometimes when you need to draw only part of a figure or graphic, it is more convenient to draw the entire figure and clip the drawing to just what you want to see. You might have an image and want to draw just a portion of it. Rather than create a new image that is just a portion of the original image, you can set the clipping rectangle and then draw the image such that just the portion that you want to see shows through the clipping area. When creating a marquee, this is the technique you would use. By successively changing where you draw the text, and at the same time setting a clipping region, you can create the effect of horizontally moving text.

Finally, there is a technique where you can create a *view port* into a larger graphic. The user can move this view port around, by dragging the mouse on the graphic or by manipulating scroll bars. The view port also can be moved programmatically based on other actions that the user takes. In this case, setting a clipping region and drawing so that only what you want to see shows through is a good technique.

See the `Clip` property of the `Graphics` class in the .NET documentation for more information.

System.Drawing.Drawing2D

The classes in this namespace provide advanced two-dimensional and vector graphics functionality. You could use these classes to build a sophisticated drawing and image-processing application.

> *Vector graphics are a technique where the programmer doesn't address pixels at all. Rather, the programmer records multiple vectors, indicating such operations as "draw from one point to another," "draw a rectangle at a certain location," and so on. Then the developer can apply scaling, rotation, and other transformations. Having applied the transformations, all the operations are rendered at once to the window.*

This namespace includes:

❑   Advanced brushes. You have already seen the `LinearGradientBrush`, and I touched on the `PathGradientBrush`. There is also a `HatchBrush`, which draws using a hatch style, a foreground color, and a background color.

❑   The `Matrix` class, which defines geometric transforms. Using this class, you can do transforms on the drawing operations. For instance, using the `Matrix` class, you can draw an oval that is at a slant.

❑   The `GraphicsPath` class, which was already touched on. Using this class, you can define a complex path and draw the entire path at once.

System.Drawing.Imaging

The classes in this namespace provide advanced imaging support, such as support for metafiles. A *metafile* describes a sequence of graphics operations that can be recorded and later played back, and there are classes within the `System.Drawing.Imaging` namespace that allow you to extend GDI+ to support other image formats.

Summary

This chapter covered some of the classes in the `System.Drawing` namespace. You saw how the `Graphics` class encapsulates a drawing surface. You reviewed the mechanics of drawing, in which the `OnPaint` event is called whenever your window needs to be redrawn.

You explored colors and coordinate systems. You covered the `Point`, `Size`, and `Rectangle` structures used to specify positions and sizes on your drawing surface. Next, you saw some examples of drawing lines, shapes, text, and images.

In this chapter, you learned about:

❑   The `Graphics` class
❑   The `Color` structure
❑   Drawing lines using the `Pen` class
❑   Drawing shapes using the `Brush` class
❑   Drawing text using the `Font` class
❑   Drawing images using the `Bitmap` class
❑   Drawing into images (double-buffering)

You also learned that it is very important to call `Dispose()` on certain classes when you are done with them. Those classes are:

- ❏ Graphics
- ❏ Pen
- ❏ Brush
- ❏ Font
- ❏ Image

Finally, you had an overview of additional graphical capabilities in the .NET Framework.

Exercises

1. Write a small application that attempts to inappropriately dispose of a Pen object that was obtained from the Pens class. Note the error message that results.

2. Create an application that displays a three-color traffic light. Have the traffic light change color when the user clicks on it.

3. Write an application that inputs RGB values. Display the color in a rectangle. Display the HSB values of the color.

Index

attributes, 743
declaration, 744
documentation
  application example, 943–945
  basic documentation example, 928–929
  `<c>` element, 930, 932
  class diagrams, 937–939
  `<code>` element, 930, 932
  `<description>` element, 931
  element descriptions, 930–931
  `<example>` element, 931, 934
  `<exception>` element, 931, 936
  file generation, 940–943
  `<include>` element, 931, 936
  `<item>` element, 931
  `<list>` element, 931, 933
  `<listheader>` element, 931
  NDoc third-party tool, 949
  `<para>` element, 931–932
  `<param>` element, 931, 934
  `<paramref>` element, 931–932
  `<permission>` element, 931, 935
  processing, 946–948
  `<remarks>` element, 931, 934
  `<returns>` element, 931, 935
  `<see>` element, 931–932
  `<seealso>` element, 931–932, 936
  structural elements, 934–937
  style sheets, 948
  `<summary>` element, 931, 934
  `<term>` element, 931
  text formatting elements, 931–934
  `<typeparam>` element, 931, 934
  `<typeparamref>` element, 931–932
  `<value>` element, 931, 935
DOM (Document Object Model), 751–752
elements, 742–743
namespaces, 745–746
nodes
  creating, 759–760
  deleting, 761–762
  inserting new, 758
  overview, 744
  selecting, 762–765
  value changes, 756–757
parsers, 742
`ReadXml()` method, 813–814
root elements, 744

structure of, 744–745
`System.Xml` namespace, 751
validation, 746
well-formed documents, 746
`WriteXml()` method, 811, 813
XDR schemas, 748–749
XML documents, 741–742
XPath query language, 763
XSD schemas, 747–748
Extension property, 706
Extensions property, 562
extern keyword, 239
external assemblies, 862

F

f (form feed) escape sequence, 41
Field icon, Class View window, 220
Field value, attribute targets, 905
fields
  adding to classes, 248
  class member definition example, 243–244
  defining, 238
  objects and, 184–185
  `readonly` keyword, 238
  `static` keyword, 238
File class, 704
file dialogs, 492
file extensions
  dialogs, 505
  master pages, 625
file filters, dialogs, 494–495
file generation, XML documentation, 940–943
File Launch Condition option, Launch Conditions Editor, 563
file properties, File System Editor, 559
file system data
  `Directory` class, 704
  `DirectoryInfo` class, 706–707
  `File` class, 704
  `FileInfo` class, 704–706
  `FileStream` class
    file position, 709
    `FileAccess` enumeration, 708
    `FileMode` enumeration, 708–709
    overview, 707
    reading data using, 710
    writing data using, 712–713

G

GAC (Global Assembly Cache), 6, 874
GC (garbage collector), 6, 983
GDI+ (Graphics Device Interface)
Bitmap class, 1002
Brush class, 995–997
clipping, 1010–1011
Color structure, 991–992
coordinate system, 984–987
double-buffering, 1001, 1008–1009
Font class, 997–1001
Graphics class, 982–983
GraphicsPath class, 988
metafiles, 1012
object disposal, 983–984
Pen class, 992–995
Point struct, 987
Rectangle struct, 987
Region class, 988
Size struct, 987
SolidBrush class, 995
System.Drawing.Drawing2D namespace, 1011–1012
general-purpose functions, 137
generated files, Web services, 667–668
generic classes. *See also* **templates**
CollectionBase class, 337
constraining types, 348
creating, 345–347
default keyword, 347–348
defined, 325
defining, 350–352
delegates, 360
Dictionary<K, V> object, 343–344
flexible type creation, 327
generic lists, searching and sorting, 337–340
generic structs, 357
inheriting from, 354–355
interfaces, 358
List<T> object, 335–336
methods, 358–360
naked type constraint, 349
naming, 345
nullable types, 327–331
?? operator, 329–330
operators, 356–357
read-only access, 346
reflection, 346

System.Collection.Generic namespace, 326, 334–335
System.Text namespace, 334
unbounded types, 348
vector representation, 333–334
generic types, 198
GenericRow class, 915
GET function, 666, 959
get keyword, 240
GetBrightness() method, 992
GetBytes() method, 713
GetChildRows() method, 804, 806
GetCopy() method, 292
GetCustomAttributes() method, 888
GetData() method, 721
GetDeleteCommand() method, 816
GetDirectories() method, 439, 704
GetEnumerator() method, 277
GetExecutingAssembly() method, 903
GetExportedTypes() method, 903
GetFileList() method, 972
GetFileListBytes() method, 972
GetFiles() method, 439, 704
GetFileSystemEntries() method, 704
GetFolderPath() method, 494
GetHashCode() method, 213, 307
GetHostByAddress() method, 958
GetHostEntry() method, 956
GetHue() method, 992
GetInsertCommand() method, 816
GetItemAt() method, 433
GetItemChecked() method, 427
GetItemCheckState() method, 427
GetProfile() method, 639
GetResponseStream() method, 970
GetRowType() method, 923
GetSaturation() method, 992
GetSelected() method, 427
GetStream() method, 978
GetString() function, 124
GetType() method, 213
GetUpdateCommand() method, 816
GetVal() function, 124
GetWord() function, 129
Global Assembly Cache (GAC), 6, 874
global data versus parameters and return values, 138–140
global keyword, 364–365

Load event, 482
Load() method, 424–425
local variables, 135
LocalPath property, 958
Locals tab, 167
Location property, 666
logging files, debugging, 153
Login security control, 608
LoginName security control, 609
LoginStatus security control, 608
LoginView security control, 609
LogVisits property, 693
lollipop indication, classes, 225
long type, 35, 41
looping
  arrays and, 106
  do loops, 76–79
  for loops, 81–83
  foreach, 109–110, 287
  infinite loops, 87
  interrupts, 86–87
  variable scope, 137–138
  while loops, 79–81
LostFocus event, 396
lowest operator precedence, 50, 66

M

Main() function
  args parameter, 141–143
  command-line parameters, 141–143
  signatures, 140
managed code, .NET Framework platform, 6
managed providers, ADO.NET, 773
manifest files
  assemblies, 862–864
  ClickOnce deployment, 537–539
manipulation techniques, strings, 113–116
margins, print page setup, 520
markers, in comments, 31
master pages
  Content control, 629–631
  ContentPlaceHolder control, 625
  creation example, 627–628
  default, 626
  file extensions, 625
MasterPageFile property, 626

mathematical operators
  addition (+), 44
  decrement (–), 45
  division (/), 44
  explicit conversion, 45
  implicit conversion, 45
  increment (++), 45
  multiplication (*), 44
  remainder (%), 44
  subtraction (-), 44
  type conversion, 48
  variable manipulation, 46–48
Maxima() function, 157
MaximizeBox property, 733
MaxLength property, 403
MaxSize property, 529
MaxValue() function, 127–128, 133, 144
McAmis, David (*Professional Crystal Reports for Visual Studio .NET,* second edition), 555
MDAC (Microsoft Data Access Components), 555
MDI (Multiple Document Interfaces)
  application creation, 468–469
  defined, 466
  isMdiContainer property, 469
  MDI child, 468
  MDI containers, 468
  text editor creation, 471–472
MeasureString() method, 998
membership providers, authentication, 603
MemberwiseClone() method, 212, 234, 292
Menu navigation control, 632
menus
  Class View, Solution Explorer window, 21–22
  controls, 450
  creating manually, 451–453
  discussed, 450
  dividing into groups, 452
  events, 455
  MenuStrip control, 451
  merging, 473–474
  ToolStripMenuItem control, 454–455
Merge Module Project template, 548
MergeAction property, 473
MergeIndex property, 473
merging menus, 473–474
Message property, 366
MessageName property, 665

S